To
Dwell
Among
Friends

The University of Chicago Press
Chicago and London

Claude S. Fischer

To Dwell Among Friends

Personal Networks in Town and City

The University of Chicago Press, Chicago 60637
The University of Chicago Press, Ltd., London

©1982 by The University of Chicago
All rights reserved. Published 1982
Printed in the United States of America
89 88 87   5 4 3

Library of Congress Cataloging in Publication Data

Fischer, Claude S., 1948–
   To dwell among friends.

   Includes bibliographical references and index.
   1. Sociology, Urban.   2. Social structure.
3. Quality of life.   I. Title.   II. Title:
Personal networks in town and city.
HT111.F56   307   81–11505
ISBN 0–226–25137–3   AACR2
ISBN 0–226–25138–1 (pbk.)

To my parents, Ralph and Rosette Fischer,
and to my grandmother, Esther Cygelfarb

Contents

Preface ix

Acknowledgments xi

1 Personal Community 1

I   The Setting

2 The Communities, the Residents, and Why They
   Were There 17
3 Personal Networks: *An Overview* 33

II   First Issues

4 Urbanism and Psychological Strain 45

5 Urbanism and Social Involvement 54

6 Urbanism and Traditional Values 63

III The Social Contexts of Personal Relations

7 Kin 79

8 Nonkin 89

9 Varieties of Nonkin:
   Neighbors and Co-workers 97
10 Varieties of Nonkin:
   Organization Members and Just Friends 108

IV   Dimensions of Personal Networks

11 Personal Networks as Social Support 125

12 The Structure of Relations and Networks 139

13   The Spatial Dimension of Personal Relations 158

14   Homogeneity in Personal Relations:
     Stage in the Life Cycle 179

V   Subcultures

15   Urbanism and the Development of Subcultures 193

16   Involvement in Subcultures:
     Ethnicity and Religion 202
17   Involvement in Subcultures:
     Occupation and Pastime 216
18   Subcultures: *Alienation in Urban Public Life* 233

19   Conclusion 251

Appendixes

A   Methodological Appendix 267

B   Respondent Interview 315

C   Informant Questionnaire 346

     Notes 351

     References 431

     Index 441

Preface

This book is about how urban life changes personal relations and the ways people think and act socially: such matters as friendship, intimacy, involvement in the community, and life-style. I hope that it will, by extension, also inform our understanding of how modern society may have altered social patterns. It reports findings from a large survey especially designed to map the form and content of people's personal relations and to contrast social life in large cities to that in small towns. In the course of examining the urban issue, it also treats several general topics in the study of social networks.

After presenting the theoretical arguments and the setting of the research in part 1, the book answers in part 2 three common questions about urban life: Does it cause psychological distress? Does it cause social isolation? And does it cause a falling away from traditional mores? Part 3 examines the composition of personal networks—the role of kin, neighbors, co-workers, and the like. Part 4 deals with other properties of networks: the support they provide, their internal structure, their spatial distribution, and their homogeneity. And part 5 explores urban life's influence on people's social involvement in *subcultures* of various types, depicting at the end the clash of subcultures in, and individuals' consequent alienation from, urban public life.

I have written this book with the general reader in mind. There are typically, therefore, graphs rather than tables and relatively few numbers in the text. It is a summary of results and should be accessible to readers with only a modest grasp of statistics.

For the professional social scientist, I have placed the technical material in the back matter: appendixes discussing methodology and reprinting the survey instruments, and extensive footnotes describing the statistical analyses. Social scientists should also note that the data reported here are in the public domain, available from the Inter-University Consortium for Political and Social Research, Institute for Social Research, Ann Arbor, Michigan, and that other reports from this project can be obtained from the Institute of Urban and Regional Development, University of California, Berkeley.

Acknowledgments

The network of people and institutions that has supported this project, financially, intellectually, and socially, is vast. I cannot acknowledge all its members. First and foremost, however, are the more than 1,250 persons who, somewhere in the course of this project, willingly revealed their personal lives to us.

The major financial angel for the research behind this book was the Center for Studies of Metropolitan Problems, National Institute of Mental Health (grant number MH-26802, 1976–79). Its director, Elliot Liebow, was always a friendly ally to this project. At a few critical moments, small grants kept the study going through dry spells: from the Russell Sage Foundation through its then-director, Hugh F. Kline; from an Institutional Biomedical Sciences Support Grant (number RR07006-10); and from the Institute of Urban and Regional Development, Berkeley.

This institute, IURD, was the home of the project; it has been the home of all my research before and since. I am extremely grateful for the sizable and steadfast support that its director, Melvin M. Webber, has always provided; he is a great facilitator of many scholars' work. And the staff of IURD has been genially, often eagerly, helpful over the years.

The writing of the book was made possible by a John Simon Guggenheim Memorial Fellowship for the 1978–79 academic year. During that period of data analysis and writing, I was a visitor at the Center for Population Studies at Harvard University. I am thankful to William Alonso and Nathan Keyfitz, its directors, for making the center's space and services so generously available.

Many Berkeley doctoral students worked at times on the project, and, though their names are linked in the following pages to specific accomplishments, their general contribution of ideas and intellectual challenge ought to be noted. These people are: Daniel Finnegan, Robert Fitzgerald, Linda Fuller, Kathleen Gerson, Robert Max Jackson, Lynne McCallister, Susan L. Phillips, Carol J. Silverman, Ann Stueve, and Alison Woodward. M. Sue Gerson was my research associate and did yeoman work as project manager, liaison to the outside world, and all-purpose problem-solver. (All these people are innocent with regard to the statistical analyses in this book. Except where noted, that work is, for better or worse, my own.)

The Berkeley Survey Research Center was the subcontractor on this study, and many of its personnel contributed in diverse ways. Charlotte Coleman not only trained and supervised the interviewers but also gave many hours and creative ideas to the formulation of a novel survey instrument. Susan R. Koenig and Cynthia Ashley were hardworking field supervisors and two of the interviewers. William Nicholls provided the technical guidance needed to conduct the survey.

The completion of this book was assisted by yet more people. Paul Burstein, Norvall Glenn, and Benjamin Zablocki, as well as anonymous readers, commented helpfully on the manuscript. Gayla Trevino drew the figures. Dorothy Heydt, at IURD, computer-typset the tables. Alex Lapidus compiled the index.

Last on this list but first in the heart of its author: Ann Swidler. My wife contributed to this book by her typing not at all, by her editing just some, by her insights a good deal. But what the star of my personal network contributed most to this book was eight years of enthusiastic encouragement, understanding, and love.

1 Personal Community

In Manhattan's West Eighties where I
live, there is nothing to write about
but people.

Alfred Kazin, *New York Jew*

Few ideas saturate Western thought as does the conviction that modern life has destroyed "community." Virtually taken for granted by philosophers and citizens alike is the belief that modern society has disrupted people's natural relations to one another, loosened individuals' commitments to kin and neighbors, and substituted shallow encounters with passing acquaintances. Whereas, in traditional society, shared lives bred commonality and concord, in modern circumstances, expediential arrangements sow differences and discord. Community has disintegrated into a mass of atomistic and alienated individuals. The moral order, once undergirded by strong links among people, is now precariously maintained by institutions of mass control, by false community.[1]

The city plays a key role in this drama. Cities exemplify all that seems modern: industry and commerce, technology and mechanization, complexity and commotion, and especially scale—large buildings, large institutions, large numbers of everything. Also, urbanization is in fact a central process in economic modernization. Most important, there is a fundamental and useful, if not completely accurate, analogy: city is to small town as modern society is to traditional society, in all the respects just mentioned. That urban life vitiates community is a major subtheme in the idea of loss of community.[2]

This book empirically tests that subtheme. We asked 1,050 men and women living in fifty localities of varying urbanism to tell us about the people who were important in their lives. Detailed analyses of their answers fill the chapters to follow. This chapter argues that we can evaluate the loss of community thesis only by closely studying people's personal relations, the social worlds in which those relations are embedded, and the ways urbanism affects the choices and constraints people face in building their relations.

Although such thorough understanding of personal relations is crucial for evaluating the loss of community thesis, it is largely absent from most contemporary discussions of that idea. It seems that the mass society image of modern life is now so taken for granted that observers attend largely to the mass instruments of social integration—mass production, mass consumption, mass communications, and the like. How people deal with one another, the central stuff of the classic theories, is often ignored.[3]

Individuals' bonds to one another are the essence of society. Our day-to-day lives are preoccupied with people, with seeking approval, providing affection, exchanging gossip, falling in love, soliciting advice, giving opinions, soothing anger, teaching manners, providing aid, making impressions, keeping in touch—or worrying about why we are not doing these things. By doing all these things we create community. And people continue to do them, today, in modern society. The relations these interactions define in turn define society, and changes in those relations mark historical changes in community life.

Consequently, the essential concern for students of community is this: What shapes relations, and what consequences do different relations produce? For example, what types of people, living where, living when, turn to kin or to friends or to professional associates for various kinds of aid, or advice, or companionship? What difference does it make to individuals, or their families, or their society if their relations involve largely kin or largely nonkin, people nearby or people far way, culturally similar or culturally dissimilar associates? Did modern society, or does urbanism, alter the quantity of individuals' important relations, the communal quality of those relations, or the kinds of people with whom the individuals are involved?

Certainly, social science has moved beyond the issue of whether people in modern societies—or people in cities—have any personal relations at all. In the late 1950s and early 1960s, the literature was replete with the rediscovery of family and friendship in the large metropolis. We have moved beyond to consider exactly what kinds of social relations people have, with what consequences. This is the focus of the present work: describing the kinds of personal networks people have and linking those types to the kinds of places in which they live; or put another way, linking the character of individuals' personal communities to the characteristics of their residential communities.

Personal Networks

When I first began this study, the term "network," referring to an individual's relatives, friends, and associates, the set of people with whom an individual is directly involved, was rather esoteric.[4] It has since rapidly joined the lexicon of popular discourse, even attaining that dubious distinction of being turned into a verb (as in "networking" or being "networked"). This popularity has arisen in part because personal relations are inherently fascinating—is not gossip about people the staple of conversations? And perhaps the network idea has become popular in policy circles because networks have been discovered to be "social support systems."[5] Whom we know and whom we can depend on influences our success in life, our security and sense of well-being, and even our health.

In the excitement of discovery, enthusiasts have overstated the supportiveness of networks. We read the following claim, for example: "Considerable evidence now suggests that the vitality of family and friendship networks has a dramatic effect on health."[6] The evidence is not that strong (what does have a dramatic effect on health is income). More important, the consequences of relations are double-edged. Although they help sustain people's lives, both materially and morally, relations often cause loss and anguish, too. The child who spends long hours caring for an aged parent may also make no effort to hide anger and resentment toward the older person. The friend who holds your hand in times of crisis may also make burdensome requests for financial help. The neighbor who is eager to baby-sit and cook for the young mother may also be a pest. Many of the people we interviewed were, sad to say, far more socially burdened than socially supported—burdened by alcoholic husbands, delinquent children, senile parents, and the like. The sum of all these pluses and minuses is usually, for most people, positive, but we must not exaggerate the supportiveness of personal networks.

We cannot exaggerate, however, the overall importance of networks. It is through personal connections that society is structured and the individual integrated into society. Although modern nations have elaborate arrays of institutions and organizations, daily life proceeds through personal ties: workers recruit in-laws and cousins for jobs on a new construction site; parents choose their children's pediatricians on the basis of personal recommendation; and investors get tips from their tennis partners. The examples can be multiplied endlessly, but the point is the same: The interactions among the abstract parts of society—"the family," "the economy," and so on—usually turn out to be personal dealings between real individuals who know one another, turn out to be operations of personal networks.

Similarly, it is through personal ties that society makes its mark on us, and vice versa. Parents teach children society's rules, and schoolmates teach them society's tacit standards for bending those rules. All through life, the facts, fictions, and arguments we hear from kin and friends are the ones that influence our actions most. Reciprocally, most people affect their society only through personal influences on those around them. Those personal ties are also our greatest motives for action: to protect relatives, impress friends, gain the respect of colleagues, and simply enjoy companionship.

In general, we each construct our own networks. The initial relations are given us—parents and close kin—and often other relations are imposed upon us—workmates, in-laws, and so on. But over time we become responsible; we decide whose company to pursue, whom to ignore or to leave as casual acquaintances, whom to neglect or break away from. Even relations with kin become a matter of choice; some people are intimate with and some people are estranged from their parents or siblings. By adulthood, people have *chosen* their networks.

This idea of choice is an important matter. It often seems in sociology and social commentary that individual agency does not exist. Mass society theory is taken as fact; the source of people's actions is assumed to be social institutions and forces. Media manipulate, culture instructs, child-rearing molds, politics alienate, occupations regiment, organizations mobilize, change disorients, and so forth. At most, individual choices are the programmed responses of automatons—like Pavlov's dogs, we salivate when the latest product or toothsome starlet is flashed before us. Or we respond with blind, helpless reactions—"I'm mad as hell and I'm not going to take it anymore!" But, fundamentally, we are jetsam tossed about by tides and currents beyond our ken.

Against this pessimistic and elitist perspective (the authors of these statements usually do not place themselves among the sheep), network analysis stresses individual agency. Every day, we decide to see people or avoid them, to help or not, to ask or not; we modulate the nuances of our relations; we plan, anticipate, and worry about the future of those relations. We each *build a network*—which is one part of *building a life*. And in all this activity, we make choices as best we can to attain the values we hold dear.

Of course these are hardly free choices; they are constrained. In building networks, we are constrained by the pool of people available to us. We are also constrained by the available information; if a colleague never reveals his or her wit, we may lose the chance for a warm friendship. We are constrained by our own personalities; shyness or an explosive temper may cause us to forfeit close relations. We are constrained by society's rules and by social pressure; fraternization between subordinates and superiors is generally discouraged, for example. But the most severe constraints—sociologically if not psychologically—are posed by the *social contexts* in which we normally participate.

Most adults encounter people through their families, at work, in the neighborhood, in organizations, or through introduction by friends or relatives; they continue to know some people met in earlier settings, such as school or the army; only rarely do chance meetings, in a bar, at an auction, or such, become anything more than brief encounters. (Even such fleeting contacts are circumscribed in that the places we go are usually a small and very select sample of all the possible places we could go.) So, although Scarlett O'Hara's passion for Ashley Wilkes over Rhett Butler turned on fascinating differences in the two men's personalities, the important sociological fact is that they were remarkably similar men (in race, age, status, culture, and so on) compared with the millions of men in the world, or even in Georgia. All but a relative few out of those millions had been ruled out of Scarlett's fancies long before the fateful events at Tara.[7]

Once we have initiated a relation in a social context, we face the task of maintaining it. Here too we are constrained, albeit more subtly. Both people must continue to feel that the bond is worth the time, cost, and attention it requires; otherwise the tie is sundered or allowed to wither. Many circumstances can impede a relationship: clashing work schedules may sharply restrict opportunities to get together; the birth of a child may deplete the energy a parent can devote to friends; moving to a new city can make contact difficult and expensive; or changes in values can make conversation with old associates awkward. Such difficulties arise all the time; relations fade away all the time; ultimately, some bonds are no longer "worth it," whether "it" is time, money, energy, social pressure, or any of a number of costs.

The range of choice people have in both establishing and sustaining relations varies. The woman who works usually meets more people than the one who is at home all day; the elderly person who is still agile can keep in contact with more friends than the infirm one; an affluent individual can travel more, meet more pepole, and maintain contact more than the poor person can. In these ways, circumstances—jobs, family commitments, incomes, and similar conditions—influence, but do not determine, the relations we make and maintain. Most of these circumstances are socially patterned: work schedules are usually nine-to-five or conform to other shifts of particular industries; familial obligations are patterned by the needs of children, the school system, and persisting social mores; contact across distance is affected by transportation and communication systems and by individuals' access to them.

These patterns of circumstances might loosely be called a society's *social structure*. And, in ways illustrated here, aspects of the social structure limit individuals' discretion to form and maintain personal networks; they bound what would otherwise be the free expression of personality, taste, and will. The dimension of social structure that is of particular interest here is residential community. Where people live can, to varying degrees, mold their networks, by shaping the pool from which they draw, and the ease with which they can sustain, their relations.

Social Worlds

Within their constraints and their preferences, people tend to build networks composed of others very similar to themselves in background, position, personality, and way of life. Kin, of course, tend to be of the same race, religion, and national origin, and co-workers usually hold the same occupations. Other social processes indirectly encourage homogeneity by channeling people into specific structural locations. For example, residential differentiation in America makes it likely that potential associates in a neighborhood will be similar in income, race, and age; and entry requirements into occupations virtually guarantee that co-workers will have similar educations, while promotion systems tend to produce similarity in age as well. Thus individuals tend to choose associates from among people who are similar to them to begin with. From such pools of similars, people choose yet more similar friends on the basis of compatible tastes and values. And even these choices have been partly determined; people's interests, for example, are influenced by their genders, jobs, educations, and so on.

Given these circumstances, people tend to associate with people like themselves. In that sense, networks are "inbred." As a consequence of—and as a further cause of—this inwardly turned interaction, people come to share many experiences, attitudes, beliefs, and values; they tend to adopt similar styles of speech, dress, and appearance; they frequent the same places and engage in the same activities; in short, they develop a common culture.

A set of people having overlapping personal networks and sharing a common culture is a *subculture*. Most Americans recognize many distinct subcultures. The subculture of long-haul truck drivers, for example, has recently been celebrated in popular song and cinema. Truckers share a specialized occupation and, with it, fellowship and common interests and experiences. And they share a culture—language, self-presentation, ideals, and so on. Chicanos in urban barrios are another example: kinship, language, appearance, work, and residential segregation concentrate and isolate them. Their social ties are predominantly, often exclusively, with one another. And there is a distinctive culture, in part adapted and in part altered from Mexican culture—dialect, code of behavior, artistic sensibilities, cuisine, and so on—that marks San Francisco's Mission District and East Los Angeles as different milieus from other parts of those cities. Similar observations can be made of many other groups: steelworkers, health-food enthusiasts, artists, Italian-Americans, ghetto blacks, police, lumbermen, and, to be sure, college professors.

(Lest these examples imply that every member of a subculture is a living stereotype, I hasten to add that there is, of course, a great deal of individual variation. Some truck drivers prefer Cabernet Sauvignon to Coors, and Beethoven to Willie Nelson, just as some academics prefer baseball to the *New York Review of Books.* The point is that, despite individual variation, there is a common culture that is more often apropos than not, and, in actuarial terms at least, the shared cultural items tend to indicate group membership.)

This shared culture reinforces people's tendency to associate with others similar to themselves. Once having entered a structural position— say, by being hired for a job—and having come in the course of social interaction to adopt the group culture, an individual finds the company of fellow group members more comfortable and enjoyable than that of outsiders. There are shared references in jokes, efficient communications, and common preferences with fellow group members. Often, even subtle behavior—voice tone, eye contact, posture, and the like—can unconsciously make people more comfortable with "their own kind" than with "outsiders." Thus the cultural differences that emerge from social separation reinforce that separation.

Individuals' personal networks are sometimes embedded within a single subculture—as might be the case with an actor whose entire social life revolves around the theater—or sometimes bridge two or three subcultures—as might be the case with a second-generation immigrant, half of whose ties are with professional colleagues and half with people in her old ethnic community. In either instance, the relations within any individual's personal networks are part of larger social networks— subcultures—that, linked together, define the society. It is through these ramified interconnections (as well as through more bureaucratic institutions such as unions and courts) that any individual is integrated into society, first by bonds with individuals in his or her personal network, through them to a particular subculture, and through that to society as a whole.

The ideas I have just presented, although phrased in the comtemporary language of networks and subcultures, have a significant intellectual heritage drawn from the "Chicago school" of sociology. From the 1910s through the 1930s, sociologists at the University of Chicago closely examined the changing social character of that rapidly expanding metropolis. Their accounts depicted distinct groups of people coexisting in the city, each set off from the others—physically, socially, and morally. For example, the taxi-dance hall, with its workers and its clientele, was described as

a distinct social world, with its own ways of acting, talking, and thinking. It has its own vocabulary, its own activities and interests, its own conception of what is significant in life, and—to a certain extent—its own scheme of life.[8]

Today the taxi-dance hall is a quaint memory, but the quotation fits no less well the disco, the ballet studio, the private clubs of corporate executives, the union hall, the halls of academe, and other social worlds. The city is, in Robert Park's classic phrase, "a mosaic of little worlds that touch but do not interpenetrate."[9]

Also a heritage of the Chicago school is a concern with how these social worlds affect and are affected by human geography:

Ultimately the society in which we live turns out to be a moral order in which the individual's position, as well as his conception of himself—which is the core of his personality—is determined by the attitudes of other individuals and by the standards which the group uphold[s] . . . . It is because geography, occupation, and all other factors which determine so irresistibly and fatally the place, the group, and the associates with whom each one of us is bound to live that spatial relations come to have, for the study of society and human nature, the importance which they do.[10]

Urbanism

Personal networks are not inherently bound to a particular area. Some people are deeply involved with their neighbors, some with friends a continent away, and others with both near and distant associates, each in different ways. Nevertheless, personal communities are linked to residential communities. The technological changes of the last few generations notwithstanding, most of us still find the schools we attend, the jobs we hold, the places we go for entertainment, and the organizations we join within or near our towns. Most of our realistically possible associates reside within the local community or not far from it. The nature of that community—its layout, housing, history, businesses, services, institutions, jobs, transportation system, weather, traffic, crime rate, the people who live there and their ways of life—partly determines the choices and constraints we face in building our lives and personal networks.[11]

However, people and their networks are not passively molded by their communities. Indeed, people build their lives and their networks in part by their choice of where to live. Different kinds of people, with different social preferences, tend to prefer different kinds of places. People with the opportunity and resources to do so will sort themselves out according to those preferences. As a consequence of this *self-selection*, residents of one kind of neighborhood or town will tend to have different networks than residents of another type. For example, young single adults often prefer to live in urban centers, and retired men often prefer rural places where they can hunt and fish. Many in each category can and do move to the places they desire, and once there they build networks typical of their group—widely dispersed friendships for the singles, kin and neighbors for the elderly. Consequently, we find differences between the networks of city-dwellers and rural residents. The communities have influenced this process of self-selection, but this is a special kind of causal effect. Communities differ in the attractions they offer people and consequently attract selected types of people, and those people in turn bring with them dispositions to certain kinds of lives and networks. While I will closely chart this process of self-selection, most of the focus will be on how communities shape people once they have arrived.

Another way people use, rather than simply respond to, the community (or any social "force") is that they *anticipate* and *adjust to* structural constraints. People may anticipate, for example, that moving to a distant neighborhood will strain their friendships and may therefore decide not to move; or, having already moved, they may make extraordinary efforts to see their old friends. Therefore, though community features may shape network formation, we may not be able to see this causal influence in any straightforward way. By their knowledge of and strategies toward different communities, people may be able to keep the characteristics of their networks (for example, the number of friends they have) fairly constant from place to place. We may then be decieved into believing that aspects of community make no difference, when, in fact, they have serious though subtle effects.

Thesis

The key aspect of community—with respect to consequences for personal relations, according to both popular opinion and scholarly theory—is *urbanism*, loosely, the concentration of population in and around a community. Americans generally believe that urban life destroys, or at least distorts, personal relations; that urbanites, as a consequence of where they live, are estranged from kin, friendless, and lonely, at best moving restlessly from one expedient and shallow association to another. This interpersonal estrangement is one reason why, according to the popular view, cities also produce psychological distress and deviant behavior. Urban life, in sum, is socially, mentally, and morally unhealthy.[12]

This view is no surprise; the popular image of the city fits well with the image of modern society discussed earlier. It is also compatible with the standard scholarly view. According to long-dominant theory, the complexity of cities weakens social ties. The differentiated urban landscape, composed of many distinct districts and neighborhoods, fragments individuals' lives—work in one place, home in another, leisure in a third. Institutional complexity does the same—clubs, businesses, stores, restaurants, agencies, services, and the like pull people in various directions. In each of these different, nonoverlapping contexts, individuals know other individuals only in superficial and impersonal ways. In addition, the tumult of city life makes residents shrink from social involvement so as to protect their jangled nerves. This environment is contrasted with that of the small community, where there are only a few social settings and where relations overlap and reinforce one another in a tight local world. In the end, urbanites are less likely than small-town residents to have supportive social relations; their networks are sparse, composed of "impersonal, transitory, and segmental" bonds. And they are more likely, therefore, to suffer psychologically and to behave antisocially.[13]

The Chicago school presented this thesis most directly. Park wrote, for example, in 1925:

In a great city, where the population is unstable, where parents and children are employed out of the house and often in distant parts of the city, where thousands of people live side by side for years without so much as a bowing acquaintance, these intimate relationships of the primary group are weakened and the moral order which rested upon them is gradually dissolved. . . .

It is probably the breaking down of local attachments and the weakening of the restraints and inhibitions of the primary group, under the influence of the urban environment, which are largely responsible for the increase of vice and crime in the great cities.[14]

Ironically, Park and his colleagues often discovered cohesive urban subcultures, particularly among recent immigrants to the city. But they generally considered these as temporary exceptions to the continuing process of social disintegration. For them, this disintegration was the inevitable price paid for the city's liberation of individualism.

In fact, considerable research has cast doubt on the idea that urbanism promotes isolation, psychological distress, or deviance. Some of that research will be discussed in part 2; most of it I have reviewed elsewhere.[15] But the belief that city life creates social disintegration and alienation is still very much alive. First, the general public and opinion leaders remain convinced that the urban alienation thesis is entirely correct—as well they might, given how it seems to fit common experience.[16] Second, many in the scholarly community endorse the thesis, at least in part: essayists such as Robert Nisbet, Richard Sennett, and Peter Berger assert it; researchers in the burgeoning field of environmental psychology virtually accept it as canon; and some urban sociologists support it. For example, one sociologist writes that "modern urban existence does give rise to impersonality, expediential relationships, social distance, opportunism, and personal isolation. . . . Modern man does not feel more lonely, more anomic, more unsure."[17] Third, the Chicago school argument is clearly correct on some important points: for example, that rates of vice are greater in cities; that city people more often live alone than do rural people; that traditional values are less often endorsed; and that social conflict tends to increase with community size.

What kind of evidence would it take to convince us that urbanism did or did not impair personal relations and personality? Many sociologists are ready to dismiss the thesis of urban alienation on the basis of evidence that is, in fact, not sufficient. Most studies cited by critics discovered that urbanites see some relatives, have some friends, are mostly sane, and so on. Relatively few studies have compared people in cities with those in villages; fewer still have tried to isolate the effect of the community from the effects of other factors; and very few have addressed the core concern: systematic comparisons of the personal relations of people living in large communities to those of people living in small ones. The study reported in this book was explicitly designed to investigate this issue.

Counterthesis

Urbanism *does* have consequences for personal life, but not quite in the way postulated by the standard theories. The "subcultural theory of urbanism"[18] holds that community size leads to a variety of distinct and intense social worlds. How is this so?

First, cities, by their very nature, are more socially heterogeneous than small communities. Because they attract migrants from a wider hinterland, cities have a relatively varied racial, religious, and national composition. Also, the complex differentiation of urban society, especially in division of labor, means that there are more distinct social contexts—in jobs, organizations, locales, and so forth—that people occupy. Given the way people build personal ties, this means that urbanites will have more varied and distinct social networks than residents of small communities—Filipino-Americans associating with other Filipino-Americans, restaurant glassware supply salesmen with other restaurant glassware supply salesmen, and so on. Robert Park himself put it this way:

Certainly one of the attractions of a city is that somewhere every type of individual—the criminal and beggar, as well as man of genius—may find congenial company and the vice or the talent which was suppressed in the . . . narrow limits of a small community discovers here a moral climate in which it flourishes.[19]

And cities do more: they *intensify* the distinctiveness of their sub-cultures. The very numbers of people in any social location means that they are more likely to reach the "critical mass" it takes to become worlds unto themselves: to support institutions such as clubs, stores, and newspapers; to provide the entirety of an individual's social needs so that relations with outsiders are unnecessary; to enforce cultural norms; and to provide a clear identity. Moreover, so many distinct subcultures com-pressed into a small geographical area inevitably means contact, con-frontation, and conflict between people with differing styles of behavior and belief. (Think, for instance, of a conventional middle-class matron passing on the street a velvet-coated and bejeweled pimp; or of a balding, leisure-suited, cigar-smoking businessman entering a health-food restau-rant full of blue-jeaned, down-jacketed and hirsute college students.) In these encounters, fealty to one's own way of life is usually reaffirmed and subcultural boundaries are buttressed. Thus cities, as cities, make them-selves into those pluralistic mosaics of "little worlds."

If this theory is correct, city-dwellers should *not* generally suffer in personal relations, or by extension, in psychological health. Some, those who often have trouble finding one another, such as members of ethnic minorities and people with rarefied tastes, may actually be advantaged. In cities they can form social circles of their own. Furthermore, the forma-tion of such social worlds implies that the general *quality* of personal life in cities and small towns may be similar, but the typical *style* of life differs. That is, residents of small and large communities alike generally manage to sustain helpful and meaningful relations, but the kinds of people they know, what they do together, and the subcultures they repre-sent differ. It is on those variations in the content of relations—more than simply their existence—that this book concentrates.

This argument should not imply that urbanism, or residential commu-nity in general, dramatically affects people's personal networks. Other structural circumstances—age, marital status, job, income, health—and individuals' personalities much more strongly influence the kinds of net-works they have. Nevertheless, urbanism does affect personal relations, indirectly by affecting the economic, housing, and other social structures the individual confronts, thereby influencing self-selection, and directly by concentrating potential associates. The effects we find will be small and subtle, but nonetheless real and meaningful.

This discussion only previews the arguments and analyses that follow. Subsequent chapters will elaborate the issues, treating, first, the relatively

simple initial questions of whether urban life promotes psychological distress, social isolation, and deviation from traditional beliefs (part 2); second, how urbanism affects the contexts from which people draw their
relations (part 3); third, how it influences other dimensions of personal
networks—supportiveness, structure, spatial expanse, and homogeneity
(part 4); and, fourth, the ways urbanism affects membership in specific
subcultures and contact among subcultures (part 5). In each analysis we
will consider how the respondents to our survey varied, what affected this
variation, and specifically how living in more or less urban communities
contributed to the variation.

Before turning to these analyses, we must establish the context for
them. Chapter 2 describes the communities in the study, how and why we
chose them, the people we interviewed in those communities, and how
and why they came to live there. Chapter 3 describes how we found out
about the respondents' personal networks and the basic contours of that
networks.

I   The Setting

2

The Communities, the Residents, and Why They Were There

To answer the questions raised in chapter 1, we interviewed, from mid-1977 through early 1978, 1,050 adults living in fifty northern California communities. The communities varied in type from high-rise neighborhoods in central San Francisco to quiet small towns almost two hundred miles away. We asked respondents about their social relations, their communities, their personal backgrounds, and their feelings.

A mass survey like this is the only practical way to resolve the critical issues raised in the previous chapter. We must compare residents of large cities with those of small towns, people who have many relations with people who have few. Only by comparing people who differ can we tell whether that difference affects their lives. Furthermore, given all the idiosyncratic traits—personality, appearance, experience, and so on—that shape networks, we need a variety of people in each category, small town to large city, to be confident that there are meaningful differences between categories. All this requires studying *many* people. That in turn requires, first, a brief interview, because few people will sit still for long ones and few funding agencies will pay for them; and, second, standardized questions, so that all the interviewers are asking the same things from all the respondents. These needs call for a mass survey.

Surveys, to be sure, have their pitfalls. Ultimately, an interview consists of one person, usually a woman, asking another person a set of questions. The answers only partly reflect reality. They also reflect how clear the questions are, how much effort the respondent makes, how much rapport the interviewer develops, whether the television is on during the interview, and many other aspects of the questionnaire, interviewee, interviewer, and situation. These circumstances can confuse and cloud our analysis, but they usually do not hide the general tendencies. It is those general tendencies emerging from the individual detail and the "noise" of our research procedure upon which I will focus.

This chapter describes the communities in our study—where they were, how we chose them, and what they were like—and the range of people we interviewed. (The procedure is discussed at length in the Methodological Appendix.) The last section of the chapter deals with an important matter of substance rather than with method: where different types of people

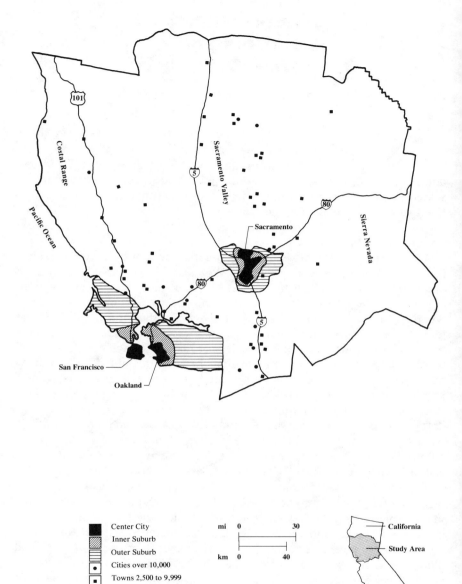

Map 1.   **Area of community sample, by sampling strata.**

tended to live, why they chose to live there, and what their tendencies and motivations imply for our understanding of urbanism.

Where and When
The Region and Time

We interviewed in a region shaped roughly like the upper-right quadrant of a circle, its center at San Francisco and its arc running from a point two hundred miles north to one two hundred miles due east (see map 1). This area includes more than twenty counties; cities such as Oakland, Sacramento, Stockton, Santa Rosa, Vallejo, and Chico, as well as San Francisco; the verdant agricultural regions of the North Central Valley and the Sacramento Delta; the rugged lumber territory of the North Coast; a few state and national parks; and the booming resort areas of the Sierras.

In contrast to many popular stereotypes, northern California is a relatively average region of the United States. And in contrast to various media images of San Francisco—whether the "beatnik" image of the 1950s, the "hippie" image of the 1960s, or the "gay" image of the 1970s—the Bay Area is relatively similar to others of the dozen largest metropolitan areas with respect to most characteristics of its communities and residents, such as type of housing, affluence, and age. People in and near the city of San Francisco, however, do tend to be somewhat more liberal than are people in other major metropolises ("Baghdad-by-the-Bay," a hometown columnist calls it).

The important issue for us in regard to life-style—or number of friends, or any other characteristics of community residents—is whether the kinds of differences among communities in northern California are roughly typical of community differences within other regions. Specifically, do large-city people differ from small-town people in northern California in the same way they differ elsewhere? They do. For example, in the late 1970s San Francisco had a very high crime rate, much higher than those of towns in its hinterland—but Los Angeles's rate was higher than those of towns in its hinterland, New York's was higher than those of towns in its hinterland, and so on. The same parallel contrasts between large and small places hold for liberalism, proportion of the population that is foreign-born, and most other traits. By extension, the differences—or lack of differences—we find among northern California communities in social networks should be applicable to differences among communities in other regions.[1] We will not be certain of this parallelism until comparable studies are conducted elsewhere, but it is a fair assumption. (A full account of the rationale for using northern California is provided in Methodological Apppendix sections 1.1 and 1.2.)

In 1977 northern California was struck by the second year of a major drought. The rains returned in full force by November, and, despite apocalyptic forecasts, neither the state's agriculture nor its general economy was seriously hurt. Throughout the region, housing prices soared, communities battled over building policies, and a property tax revolt brewed that would later culminate in California's Proposition 13 (the voter initiative that cut property taxes in half). On the edges of the major cities and beyond, the issue was growth: How many new subdivisions should be built to meet the insatiable demand for housing (often people lined up at construction sites hours before still-vacant plots were auctioned off), and who should pay for new schools and public services. Inside the major cities, the issue was orderly turnover: Which schools to close as families left the city and how to control the speculative fever and protect the casualties of "gentrification" (the process in which middle-class people purchase and restore homes in deteriorated inner-city neighborhoods, thereby displacing low-income families). Although seemingly more acute in northern California than elsewhere, these events of 1977, except the drought, were fairly common in many parts of the country.

The important historical consideration is not the specific year of our study, but its epoch. The last third of the twentieth century is a time when virtually all American communities are linked by highways, telephone lines, and television. Urban centers and their rural peripheries are socially much nearer to one another than even fifty years ago. People are moving beyond cities, into former agricultural land twenty to fifty or more miles away. The inner cities have been in "crisis" for perhaps twenty years: disadvantaged, decayed, disordered, nearly bankrupt, and wracked by unusually high rates of crime. These and similar features of our period should caution us about too hastily extrapolating our results backward or forward to other historical eras.

The Communities

To study how types of communities affected their residents' private lives, we needed a range of communities large enough to represent most of the variety that exists among places, but small enough so that we could learn in detail about each one. We randomly sampled fifty localities—small towns or census tracts in cities—spread across the region shown in map 1. (The actual sampling, as well as most technical steps involved in conducting the survey, was done by the Survey Research Center, University of California, Berkeley.) To make sure we would have enough respondents in small places, we drew more people from small communities and fewer from the big cities than a strictly representative survey would have done. Also, to simplify our analysis, we did not include any communities where more than 40 percent of the residents were black, or towns under 2,500 in population. These exclusions, I will point out later, tend to artificially weaken our findings. Within each community, we randomly selected two small neighborhoods, each containing from fifty to two hundred households living on two or three adjacent streets. (For a full description and explanation of the community sample, see Methodological Appendix sections 1.3 to 1.5.)

There are very many different types of communities and neighborhoods in the more than 30,000 square miles of our study area: high-rent apartment districts in San Francisco just a few blocks from high-crime public housing; wooded hillsides in suburban Contra Costa County, where children of downtown executives ride their horses bareback on windy roads; arid and still flatlands in the Sacramento Delta where new tract houses on raw lots stretch to the horizon; trailer parks in the Central Valley, surrounded by groves of small fruit trees and bearing names such as "Woodhaven" and "Quiet Oaks."

These communities and neighborhoods vary in many ways: topography, housing, population composition, income level, public services, and life-style, for example. While we consider many of the variations in our analysis, the focus is on urbanism.

Urbanism

The United States Bureau of the Census defines the urbanism of a community in terms of political boundaries, and that is the definition we used to draw the sample of communities. There were five strata, as shown on map 1: (1) census tracts in the center cities of the two largest "standard metropolitan statistical areas," San Francisco–Oakland and Sacramento ("SMSAs" include the counties of and around cities of over 50,000); (2) census tracts in those two SMSAs near the center cities—inner suburbs; (3) tracts in those two SMSAs distant from the center cities—outer suburbs; (4) large towns, outside those two SMSAs, over 10,000 in population; and (5) small towns, outside those two SMSAs, between 2,500 and 10,000 population. We randomly selected ten communities in each category.

Although this definition of urbanism is administratively useful, it is not always clear just what "urban" or "urbanism" means socially. Certainly it refers to population concentration. Some scholars define it as also meaning much more: nonagricultural economic activity, a certain type of housing, particular ways of acting, and so on. These other characteristics, however, are possible causes, consequences, or correlates of urbanism,

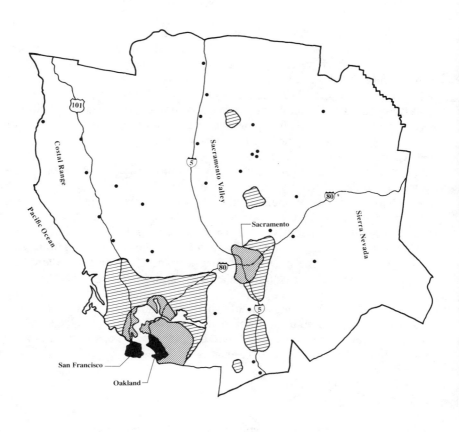

Pacific Ocean

Costal Range

Sacramento Valley

Sierra Nevada

Sacramento

San Francisco

Oakland

101

5

80

80

5

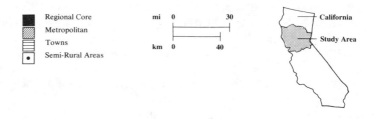

	Regional Core
	Metropolitan
	Towns
•	Semi-Rural Areas

mi   0   30

km   0   40

California

Study Area

Map 2.   **Area of community sample, by urbanism measure.**

but not urbanism itself. I prefer an elementary understanding of urbanism as the *number of people living in and near a community*. The words "and near" in the definition note the importance of the surrounding population; it too contributes to the urbanism of a place. For example, there are many municipalities with small populations, say 2,000, that are adjacent to large cities, whereas others are in the middle of open land, miles from any other settlement. We generally recognize the first as being more urban than the second. In this sense, people surrounding a community contribute to its urbanism along with the people living within it.

To capture this fuller sense of urbanism, we developed an urbanism score for each community that combines the population of its city with its proximity to other cities. Least urban on this scale is an agricultural center of about 3,000 residents, situated more than three hours' drive from San Francisco and a half-hour from the nearest larger town. Halfway up the scale is a community in a distant suburb of San Francisco, more than an hour's drive away during peak traffic hours, and in a city with a rapidly growing population of 50,000. Two adjacent San Francisco tracts share the top score; they were about fifteen minutes by trolley car from downtown (see Methodological Appendix section 4.3.1).

For ease of presentation and analysis, this urbanism scale can be divided into four relatively distinct categories, as shown in map 2. These are, from most to least urban:

The regional core: Twelve of our communities lie in the core of the San Francisco–Oakland metropolitan area, itself the hub of northern California. The twelve include six communities in San Francisco, two in Oakland, and four in the suburbs adjacent to Oakland. Each of the East Bay communities is within eight miles of the toll plaza to the San Francisco–Oakland Bay Bridge.

Metropolitan: Twelve communities fall into this group. Two places are in the city of Sacramento and most of the others are suburbs of San Francisco–Oakland (no closer than about thirteen miles from approaches to either bridge into San Francisco).

Town: The fifteen communities in this group include most of the large cities that are outside the two major metropolitan areas, cities ranging in size from Stockton (110,000) to Tracy (15,000). The category also includes distant suburbs of San Francisco–Oakland and suburbs of Sacramento or Stockton. These places might be thought of as urban, but not metropolitan communities.

Semirural: Most of the eleven places in this category are small towns of under 10,000 and are far from other communities; the remainder are distant, rustic suburbs of Sacramento.

Although we did not include villages or truly rural countryside in our sample (for reasons discussed in Methodological Appendix section 1.4), the semirural category does include places people clearly think of as small, or country, towns. One chamber of commerce claims that within its town "are all the factors needed for wholesome, quality living for those who enjoy the quiet, friendly pace of a smaller community. . . . [It] has maintained its valuable country living." Another of our semirural towns was featured in a San Francisco newspaper as a typical "booming" small town, with no violent crime, traffic, or housing problems. And generally respondents living in these semirural places described them as being small towns or rural.[2]

A few examples of the neighborhoods in the study (mid-1977) may make these categories less abstract:

Semirural. The illustrative neighborhood lies in a town of about 7,000 residents, in turn surrounded by heavily worked agricultural land. It is three hours' drive from San Francisco, considerably less from Sacramento, and only several minutes' drive on the state highway from a larger community. The center of town has a gas station, a liquor store, two convenience shops, a small restaurant—all somewhat dusty and aging—and a few abandoned stores. The neighborhood, a few blocks from "downtown" and near the interstate, includes four streets of one-story, 1950s stucco houses. Each house has small but well-kept front and back lawns. There would perhaps be a stereotypically suburban air to the place were it not for the vast expanses of agricultural land visible from the neighborhood's edge. The residents are overwhelmingly, but not exclusively, native-born whites and mostly working class, but they vary greatly in age, from retirees to young children of young couples. The vehicles parked in their driveways—modest campers and, more often, pickup trucks with gun racks—are visible signs of the residents' favorite pursuits.

Town. This neigborhood is in a Sacramento suburb of somewhat ambiguous identity and political status. The town could easily typify the recent wave of urbanization in the Sacramento Delta: a nearby neighborhood tripled in housing units between 1970 and 1977; other nearby streets have just been bulldozed from open land, and scores of duplexes and small single-family homes have been planted along them. The residents of this "older" neighborhood—late 1960s or early 1970s housing—are white, non-Hispanic, middle-class families. Many windows bear "block parent" signs, and many cars display stickers with the current evangelical slogan, "I found it." Major highways border the community, and shopping centers and franchise outlets provide most of the commerce. Community informants praise the area's schools and services but complain about its traffic and the lack of entertainment for young people. (A local shopping mall has become a site of "cruising," drinking, and gang fighting over the previous two years.) Residents boast of its convenience while criticizing the area's growth, housing density, and traffic.

Metropolitan.   The community in which this illustrative neighborhood lies might well serve as an archetypal East Bay suburb. Less than twenty years ago it was on the suburban "frontier," and now it seems to have aged gracefully as construction has swept miles beyond it. Building has not stopped, however, though now the construction is of townhouses, condominium apartment complexes, and quadraplexes, all of which have helped make the community more heterogeneous. The neighborhood in question comprises a few streets of quadraplexes, and its residents—young white adults, some with small children—contrast with the older, more affluent, empty-nest couples who live in the next neighborhood's large single-family houses. And, with age, the neighborhood has also become more central to the San Francisco region: a few major highways pass nearby; a line of the Bay Area Rapid Transit commuter railway borders the community; and the municipality now has about 100,000 residents. There is little consensus among the people interviewed here about the area's virtues or faults, but weather, shopping, and schools ranked among the former, while growth, traffic, and the "kinds of people" in the community were among the latter.

Regional core.   This neighborhood comprises two relatively modern apartment buildings set on a heavily trafficked residential street in central San Francisco. Two streets away is a secondary tourist attraction, near which sight-seeing buses often park. The neighborhood borders on a district whose population is changing from low-income minority families to middle-income white, childless couples (both hetero- and homosexual). The change has not quite arrived here, but its portents—brightly colored Victorian facades, yogurt stands, plant stores, and the like—can be spied a few blocks away. Immediately adjacent to the apartment buildings are largely deteriorated older houses, each still subdivided into a few cramped and dark flats. Aside from one or two mom-and-pop groceries, there is little commercial activity, but there is a good deal of trolley, bus, and car traffic, with accompanying noise and dirt. The apartment residents are middle-class, security-conscious residents of an area still dominated by poor Latino families. Despite the promise of an urban renaissance, there are still reminders of the urban crisis, such as the fatal shooting of a boy in the nearby high school in 1978.

Who

We sought to interview about a thousand people—English-speaking, eighteen years old or older, and permanent residents. We randomly selected households in each neighborhood and sent their residents letters telling them they would be approached and requesting their cooperation. Once an interviewer reached someone in a household, she randomly selected which adult to interview. In all, we approached 1,550 households. Of these, 185 were inappropriate (for example, no adult spoke English); in 67 no one ever seemed to be home, and members of 248 households refused to participate. But 1,050 people did complete the interview, a respectable 76 percent of all eligible households. Completion rates tended to be slightly lower in affluent big-city neighborhoods, but that does not seem to have affected our results. In general, there was little difference between the social characteristics of the people we sought to interview and those we succeeded in interviewing (see Methodological Appendix sections 1.6 to 1.8).

There are some differences between our respondents and northern Californians as a whole: fewer blacks, fewer males, fewer foreign-born, slightly more adults under forty and slightly fewer between forty and sixty. But the overall characteristics are not far off. This is a cross-sectional sample, and, though it is not strictly representative—it was drawn for theoretical, not descriptive, purposes—it is sufficiently so to justify inferring general trends and patterns from it to the general population.

Even with a perfect sample, interviews can never be neutral scientific instruments. As I noted earlier, the answers people give are influenced by the interviewer and by the immediate situation. To estimate such "artifacts," we analyzed several possible contaminants, including the month of the interview, the day of the week, and whether a third party was present. We concluded that few of these factors had noteworthy consequences and that none altered our basic conclusions (see Methodological Appendix section 4.2).

Who Lived Where—and Why

We found different kinds of people in different kinds of places:[3] young singles in certain neighborhoods, poor mothers in others, and so on. This residential differentiation is a familiar aspect of American communities; it is partly the outcome of the self-selection discussed in the previous chapter. Childless professional couples tend to prefer central locations with access to entertainment; parents on limited incomes look for single-family houses with backyards, usually finding them in distant suburbs; and elderly pensioners are so constrained by their poverty that they must often settle for small apartments in dangerous neighborhoods. As people sort themselves out, they also sort out types of social networks, because each kind of person tends to have somewhat different personal relations.

This type of self-selection, operating along the rural/urban continuum, means that urbanism will be *indirectly* associated with aspects of social networks. This indirect association is part of neither urban alienation theories nor subcultural theory. Both views expect community characteristics to operate on residents' networks *after* their arrival and to have measurable effects on those networks beyond any self-sorting by age, marital status, income, or other individual traits. Therefore, throughout this book I statistically adjust (or "partial") the results to remove the effects of this self-selection, to isolate the contribution of community characteristics beyond self-selection. For example, young adults named more friends than did older people, and, as we shall see below, young adults tend to concentrate in urban places. This self-selection helps create an association between urbanism and number of friends. We can statistically adjust the data to remove the contribution of age to this association, simulating a condition in which everyone everywhere was of average age. The remaining association between urbanism and friends cannot be explained by age—and may be a direct consequence of urbanism itself. In most analyses I correct for several self-selection factors simultaneously. (See Methodological Appendix section 4.4.)

Another type of self-selection may also help create an association between urbanism and social networks: choosing a place precisely because of personal relations. If some people move to, or stay in, small towns because they want more family life, and other people move to, or stay in, cities because they want less family life, we would observe an association between urbanism and family involvement: city residents would report fewer family ties than small-town residents.

The urban theories are less clear on what to do about this kind of self-selection. Although loss-of-community theorists sometimes describe freedom from social restraint as a lure of city life, their arguments suggest that the disintegrative effects of urbanism are largely involuntary; they are unintended consequences of individualism and should appear above and beyond even this kind of self-selection. Subcultural theory does expect some significant selective migration for network reasons. In particular, individuals who desire relations with people who are hard to find—members of minorities, groups with unusual life-styles—will often come to the city, where those people are more easily found. Yet subcultural theory also expects community differences that cannot be accounted for by such selective migration. The attainment of critical mass independently fosters homogeneous relations and distinctive social worlds. Therefore, throughout the book I pay special attention to self-selection for networks, but I usually adjust for it as well, trying thereby to isolate the unique contribution of the community to personal networks.

These considerations of selective migration make it imperative that we understand what kinds of people lived in communities of varying urbanism and why they lived there.

Who Lived Where

There were indeed strong connections between the urbanism of a community and the types of respondents who lived there. One critical difference was stage in the life cycle. The youngest in our sample, those under twenty-two and typically living with their parents, tended to live in less urban places, particularly in Town communities. Unmarried respondents between twenty-two and thirty-five concentrated disproportionately in the Regional Core. Married respondents, especially those with children, tended to live in moderately urban places, Metropolitan and Town communities. And the elderly concentrated most heavily in the Semirural places.

The second major dimension is social class, defined here simply as education and income. The more the respondent had of either, the more urban his or her community tended to be. For example, 43 percent of the college graduates in our sample lived in the Regional Core, and only 9 percent lived in Semirural places. Also, respondents tended to concentrate by ethnicity. The thirty-five blacks in our survey lived predominantly in Core communities, and most of the thirty-eight Mexican-Americans lived in Town communities (a distinctive pattern that will become important in subsequent analyses; see chap. 16).

Each of the major characteristics mentioned here—age, education, income, marriage, and children—was "independently associated" with how urban a respondent's community was. That is, among respondents of equal income, the more educated ones lived in the more urban places; among married respondents of equal age, those with children lived in less urban places; and so forth. These differences are a result of continuous sorting: even if we look only at respondents who moved in the previous five or ten years, we see the same patterns. Educated people, for example, were still moving toward the urban centers, and married people were moving away from them.[4]

This self-selection is not unique to our sample or to northern California. Generally in the United States, unmarried, well-educated, young adults congregate in the urban centers; low-income persons are disproportionately found in rural places; families are common in most areas outside the urban center, especially in suburban communities, and the elderly tend to live in small towns. This sorting process accelerated in the 1970s, as older people increasingly moved to rural areas, while the well-educated young moved from rural to urban places.[5] (Again, not all this "self-selection" is free and willing. Many parents, for example, find that landlords in San Francisco refuse to rent to people with children.)[6]

Reasons for Moving

We asked all our respondents, except the few who had lived their entire lives in the same places, the following question:
Here are some reasons people give for picking a particular area to live in. Which of these reasons were important to you (and/or your family) in deciding to live in the (NAME OF CITY) area?
Being near relatives or friends
The kind of people here
It's a good place for children to grow up or go to school
It's near job or school (yours or your husband's or wife's)
It's a beautiful area
It's a safe area
The things to do here
It's the right-sized town[7]
(Interviewers encouraged respondents to cite as many of the answers as applied to them and to volunteer any additional reasons.)
Respondents gave somewhat different reasons depending on where they lived. I will discuss only people who had moved to their communities in the previous ten years (earlier migrants' reasons for coming may no longer be relevant to the current character of the community) and who had participated in the decision (this excludes, for example, children who accompanied their parents). Although the most common answers were job or school (44 percent) and beautiful area (32 percent), there were major variations between more and less urban respondents: almost a third of Regional Core respondents said "the kind of people here." Fewer than 10 percent in any other place-type picked that answer. The most dramatic instances were people such as the two-year resident who said, "There are a lot of gays here; I'm comfortable and I don't have to worry about hang-ups." (Over half the apparent homosexuals[8] in our sample cited "kind of people," compared with 14 percent of everyone else.) But many other residents of the Regional Core besides avowed homosexuals thought of the kinds of people who lived in the Bay Area as a motivation for coming. In addition, about a third of Core respondents, far more than in any other type of community, cited "things to do here." Often, these

people would later rhapsodize about the area's theaters, restaurants, museums, and outdoor attractions.

Over half the Metropolitan residents cited job or school as a reason—somewhat more than Core or Town residents. They were also the most likely, at 18 percent, to volunteer that "the house" was the reason. This may reflect not only that many Metropolitan respondents had recently married or had young children, but also the state of the Bay Area housing market in 1977. Prices had become so high so quickly that people were moving twenty to fifty miles to find a house they felt was both appropriate and affordable.

Respondents living in Town communities were slightly likelier than others to give "being near relatives or friends" as a reason, and from other comments they made we can assume that this answer typically meant relatives. Semirural respondents were least likely to cite job or school as an answer (28 percent versus 48 percent of all other respondents), and their favorite answer was "it's a beautiful area."

To help understand how such motivations contribute to the process of sorting out types of people across types of places, table 1 combines categories of residents and communities (those kinds of people disproportionately found in those kinds of places) with the reasons they most and least frequently gave for moving to their communities.

The contrasts are striking: while young singles in highly urban communities most often cited what might be called discretionary life-style motives, notably types of people and things to do, young parents in moderately urban places rarely gave those reasons. Instead, the parents cited family commitments for living in Metropolitan and Town communities. The elderly in Towns and Semirural places present a mixed picture (caution: the recently arrived numbered only twenty-nine). Things to do were important—although not as important as those activities were to young people in the Core. And, to be sure, they were interested in quite different things—on the order of hunting instead of dating—but more important still for the elderly were family ties.[9]

We have already learned something important about urbanism and social life from these answers. The most urban places disproportionately attracted respondents because of social opportunities—people to know and things to do. And this attraction was felt particularly by unmarried, mobile, and well-educated young people. In contrast, any distinctive attraction of less urban places largely involved already existing social relations—kin—and practical considerations. To the extent that the reasons for moving to less urban places indicate life-style choices, they are choices of family and home.

This sort of selective migration toward cities by people seeking to form social relations (recall the particular example of homosexuals) suggests,

Table 1 **Most and Least Common Reasons Given for Moving to Current Community, for Selected Lifestyle Groups in Selected Places[a]**

	Young Singles Living in Regional Core	
Most Common Reasons	Beautiful Area	(48%)
	Kinds of People	(43%)
	Things to Do	(38%)
Least Common Reasons	Good for Children	(3%)
	Safety	(18%)
(N=)		(65)
	Young Marrieds with a Child Living in Metro or Town	
Most Common Reasons	Job or School	(55%)
	Kin (or Friends)	(32%)
	Good for Children	(22%)
Least Common Reasons	Things to Do	(3%)
	Type of People	(4%)
(N=)		(71)
	Elderly Living in Town or Semi-Rural	
Most Common Reasons	Kin (or Friends)	(55%)
	Beautiful Area	(31%)
	Things to Do	(28%)
Least Common Reasons	Good for Children	(0%)
	Job or School	(3%)
(N=)		(29)

[a]Includes only respondents living less than ten years in their current towns.

first, that there is indeed some self-selection on the basis of the desired way of life that contributes to city/small-town differences, and second, that the form of that self-selection is consistent with subcultural theory's description of how urban social worlds develop. This process was not, of course, invisible to Chicago school sociologists. Robert Park, for example, described such selective migration this way:

The attraction of the metropolis is due in part ... to the fact that in the long run every individual finds somewhere among the varied manifestations of city life the sort of environment in which he expands and feels at ease; finds, in short, the moral climate in which his peculiar nature obtains the stimulations that bring his innate dispositions to full and free expression. It is, I suspect, motives of this kind which have their basis, not in interest nor even in sentiment, but in something more fundamental and primitive which draws many, if not most, of the young men and young women from the security of their homes in the country into the big, booming confusion and excitement of city life.[10]

3 Personal Networks: An Overview

Personal networks differ greatly from one person to another. Part of this book's task is to describe and explain some of the general patterns in that variation. Educated people tend to have larger networks than less educated people do; urban residents average fewer relatives than small-town residents do. But beneath gross trends such as these lies a great deal of individual and idiosyncratic variation. A few cases will illustrate the point. (Descriptions of people are altered slightly to prevent identification.)

Among respondents with small networks are these:

Mrs. A, a widow for twenty-five years, named only seven people in her network (far fewer than the overall average of 18.5) of whom five were relatives and one was a live-in "boyfriend." She was, nevertheless, a happy woman by her own report and that of the interviewer: "Mrs. A is a pink-cheeked, white-haired woman with bright blue eyes who was wearing a very hip T-shirt that said, 'Where the hell is Vacaville?' She spent fifteen or twenty minutes explaining in humorous detail how she and her companion came to live together. I think she was trying to tell me it's a platonic relationship. She feels she needs someone since she's had several small strokes and she likes her own home and independence." This woman seems much like another widow we interviewed who was described as "a lady who had been widowed for three years after an apparently congenial and happy marriage. Her boyfriend is a platonic convenience. His wife died at the same time as her husband and, rather than be lonely, they spend much time together. She feels that this and her daughter are her main lifelines. She tends to live in the past a great deal. She feels her friends and her daughter are constantly after her to do more or to get involved more. She resents this because she feels her relative inactivity is by choice, not by fear of being involved. She feels her getting involved days are behind her and she has a right to be 'lazy.'"

In contrast to these cheerful women is Mrs. B, a middle-aged, married Hispanic woman who named only eight people including her husband, two adult daughters, three grandchildren, and two friends. Mrs. B. said she was "pretty unhappy," which was understandable given her circumstances. To help support her daughter's illegitimate child, she commuted a long distance for seasonal work in the canning factories of the Central Valley. Anxious and insecure, she barely knew anyone outside her family and worried that she was being interviewed because her neighbors had complained about her.

Another person with a small network was Mr. C. He had retired four years earlier from his job as a Long Beach city fireman to a modest mountain town, where his most important interest was bicycling. He discussed only seven people in the interview, and all but two were relatives. The interviewer found him pleasant but commented later that he "seemed pretty unhappy and has an almost deprived social situation. It's awfully hard to say if that's from choice or if the people there have been such creeps as he says."

There was also great variety among the respondents with large networks. For example:

Mr. D. was a twenty-eight-year-old "technocrat" for a state agency. Together with his professional wife and his young child, he had lived for two years in a suburb of Sacramento. The interviewer described him as a "warm, friendly young man," and his network seemed to match the personality: In addition to more than fifteen blood kin and in-laws, he listed a dozen co-workers, a half-dozen neighbors, and others totaling forty-five people. Although socially very active, he felt that he was most involved in work and with his co-workers.

Ms. E was a young nurse practitioner who had lived for a few years with her boyfriend on the outskirts of the Bay Area. Ms. E was active in professional organizations and public-interest lobbies, and her greatest interest was buying and restoring old Victorian houses. She listed twenty-nine people, including five who shared this interest, thirteen other friends, co-workers, or neighbors, and eleven relatives.

Mrs. F, homemaker, also named twenty-nine people, sixteen of whom were relatives. She belonged to no organizations, but she attended church weekly. She was described as an "attractive young mother of teenage children who lived in a modern ranch home with modern furniture" and as "very close to her family." At the time of the interview, two elderly relatives had dropped by and there were several telephone conversations concerning an upcoming family dinner. "She said she had an easy life. She really hasn't worked, was well-supported financially, and had good children."

Many factors contribute, in complex ways, to the size, composition, and character of individuals' networks: psychological traits, such as extraversion and self-confidence; personal background, including how many siblings they had, how often and far they have moved, how long and where they went to school; and current circumstances, such as whether they are employed and with how many co-workers, their health and ability to get around, their income, and the character of their neighbors. We can map only some of these factors and only some dimensions of people's networks. Yet, out of the great individuality and variety of social ties, some patterns nevertheless emerge. To understand how we discerned these patterns, it is necessary to understand how we measured respondents' social networks.

Measuring Networks

The people we are directly involved with constitute our personal social networks.[1] But involved in what way? There is the daily, active involvement of the hospital administrator in San Francisco who reported spending hours in conference with co-workers and all her spare time in sports, travel, and social events. And there is the passive, largely emotional involvement of a widow, living in a public housing project in Santa Rosa, who was described by the interviewer as follows:

This respondent is an elderly woman, lonely, suffering from very poor health, who has had a hard life . . . . She has several great-grandchildren and there were many photographs of them about the apartment, and certificates on the wall "awarded" to her by her great-grandchildren for being "grandmother of the year."

Generally, we can interpret involvement, or *relation,* in one of three ways. First, it can be formal, in the sense that there are socially recognized roles with reciprocal rights and duties, for example, mother/daughter, employer/employee, and neighbor/neighbor. Second, it can be sentimental: a person is involved with others in the sense that he or she cares about them and feels close to them. In one of our preliminary surveys we asked, "When you think about the people [you are involved with], which of the things we have talked about are most important to you?" Some expressed opinions like that of an insurance adjuster, father of two: "Caring about each other is more than anything else; if you care the rest comes along." Third, a relation can be defined as interaction and exchange: a person is involved with people with whom he or she shares activities, who provide material and emotional assistance, or both, and who receives the same in return. An example of such a perspective came from a twenty-five-year-old working mother: "Being able to talk about good times and bad times, and going out and having a good time." These three forms of involvement overlap a great deal; the people we are involved with in one of these ways tend to be involved with us in the other ways. But there is a distinction.

Our study defined "relation" specifically in the third sense: *People are related one to the other to the extent that they interact or exchange with one another,* whether that interaction is material, as in lending tools, sociable, as in partying together, or emotional, as in providing consolation. This is our theoretical definition of relation. In practice, we learned about most of the important people to whom the 1,050 respondents were formally and sentimentally attached, as well. (For more on the logic of our procedure, see Methodological Appendix section 2.0.)

Technique

Our goal was to have respondents describe their personal networks—the kinds of people they were involved with and the nature of those involvements—as completely and efficiently as possible. (We had only twenty to thirty minutes of each interview for this task.) The basic procedure was to get respondents to name the key people and then to ask them about each named person. We elicited those names by asking respondents to name the people who did, would, or could provide them with various kinds of support. We assumed that people who aided the respondents were usually assisted by them in return and were generally core members of their networks. Of the thousands of kinds of support we might have asked about and of the dozens we pretested, we finally settled on asking respondents to name the people:

1) who would care for their home if they went out of town—water plants, pick up mail, etc. (question 30);

2) (if respondents worked) whom they talked with about decisions at work (q. 46);

3) who had helped with household tasks in the past three months (q. 73);

4) with whom they had recently engaged in social activities (such as having over for dinner, or going to a movie—q. 74);

5) with whom they discussed common spare-time interests (q. 75);

6) (if respondents were unmarried) who were their fiancées or "best friends" they were dating (q. 76);

7) with whom they discussed personal worries (q. 77);

8) whose advise they considered in making important decisions (q. 78);

9) from whom they would or could borrow a large sum of money (q. 79); and

10) who over fifteen years old lived in same household (obtained from the enumeration of the household).

In answer to each question, respondents named as many people as they wished, but interviewers generally recorded only the first eight names (ten for the question on social activities). At the end of the series, the interviewers compiled lists of all the names mentioned (the average number was 12.8). They gave copies of these lists to the respondents and asked: "Is there anyone who is important to you who doesn't show up on this list?" (q. 81). Any additional names (an average of 5.7) were added to both copies of the lists. In some of the discussions I will distinguish between these two sets of names, because the first includes people we know provided support for respondents, while the second includes people who may or may not have done so.[2] In the end, most respondents named between twelve and twenty-four associates (with an average of 18.5).

With the list of names in each respondent's hand, the interviewer then asked:

1) the sex of every named person (q. 80);

2) all the "ways" the respondent "knew" the person, for example, as cousin, co-worker, fellow union member, friend (q. 80);

3) which persons respondents felt "especially close to" (q. 82);

4) which persons lived within five-minutes' drive (q. 83);

5) which lived more than an hour's drive away (q. 84);

6) which they saw at a favorite "hangout" (q. 85)'

7) (for homemakers) which were also full-time homemakers (q. 86);

8) (for workers) which were in the same line of work (q. 87);

9) (for respondents with an avowed ethnic identity) which were of the same ethnicity (q. 90);

10) (for respondents with a religious affiliation) which shared the same religion (q. 94); and

11) (for respondents with a favorite pastime) which shared the favorite pastime (q. 97).

(In addition, for all names, we know which kinds of exchanges the respondents claimed to receive from them, because we know which questions elicited the names.)

We obtained yet more information about a subsample of the names, up to five and usually no less than three per respondent, by having the interviewees fill out a questionnaire on each one. (The procedure for selecting which names is described on page 30 of the questionnaire, which appears in Appendix B.)

The questions asked:

1) how the respondent and the named person had met;

2) how many years they had known each other;

3) what city the person lived in;

4) how often they "got together";

5) the person's age;

6) the person's employment status;

7) the person's marital status; and

8) whether the person had children and how old they were.

This procedure yields two kinds of descriptions: First, for virtually all of the 19,417 people named by the 1,050 interviewees, we know certain characteristics of that person and his or her relation with the respondent. For the 4,179 "subsample" names, we know still more.[3] Second, by aggregating this information for each respondent, we can describe his or her network as a whole: the proportion of kin, number of co-workers, number of neighbors they feel close to, and so forth. These summaries might be thought of as pictures of each respondent's prviate "social world."

Description of the Networks
Size

A basic characteristic of respondents' networks is simply their size—how many people they named. This raw number can be misleading in some ways. For one, the number of names given was affected by the attitude of the respondent toward the interview. Reluctant respondents named fewer people than did cooperative ones.[4] They also volunteered less information throughout the interview. To take this bias into account, I constructed a measure of cooperativeness and used it to "correct" the results in various analyses (see Methodological Appendix section 4.2.3). Even if the number of names respondents gave was an accurate reflection of their entire personal networks, size does not necessarily indicate support, emotional depth, or other qualities of relations. Nonetheless, size is a place to begin and, within limits, an important attribute of an individual's personal community. For example, the larger respondents' networks were, the happier they reported feeling.

The heavy solid line of figure 1 indicates the percentage of our respondents who gave us lists of various sizes: 1 percent gave one to four names; 12 percent gave five to nine; and so forth. The most common list includes between fifteen and nineteen names. Figure 1 also breaks down the networks into two basic components: relatives and nonrelatives. On average, respondents named fewer kin than nonkin: means of 7.8 versus 10.7. Also, respondents tended to be roughly similar in how many kin they named (41 percent named between five and nine kin) but differed more in how many nonrelatives they listed. Finally, I should note that almost half the relatives listed, 46 percent, were named in answer to the question, "Is there anyone not on the list?" In contrast, only 19 percent of the nonkin were added at that point.

In most of the analyses that follow, we will be able to look only at summary statistics for the distributions—at differences in means. We should recall, nevertheless, the variation that underlies these summaries. The average network size is 18.5, but one person named only two and

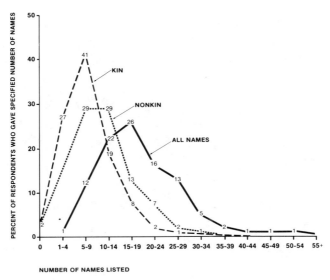

Fig. 1.   **Distribution of network sizes.**

another named sixty-seven; the person at the eightieth percentile reported twice as many as the respondent ranked at the twentieth percentile.

Social Contexts

Besides kinship, associates can be differentiated in various ways on the basis of the social situation, role, or context in which the respondent knows them. To provide such classification, interviewers asked respondents, after having compiled names, the following question:

This is a list of some of the ways people are connected with each other. Some people will be related in more than one way. So, when I read you a name, please tell me *all* the ways that person is connected with you right now. How is (NAME OF PERSON) connected with you now? Any other ways?

Relative (how are you related?)
Co-worker (someone you work with or see regularly at work)
Neighbor
Member of same organization
Friend
Acquaintance
Other (for example: spouse of friend, client, customer, former spouse)

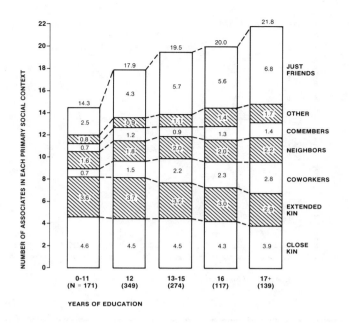

Fig. 2.   Social context composition of respondents' networks,
by respondents' education.

I used these descriptions to classify each named person by *social
context*—the social setting in which his or her relation with the respondent
existed at the time of the interview. Contexts are, except for two residual
categories, culturally and structurally circumscribed spheres of activity
(which may, but need not, be associated with specific physical settings) in
which social worlds can develop: family, work, neighborhood, and club.
The residual categories are friendship and "other." Of the 19,417 names
provided by our respondents, 42 percent were relatives, 10 percent co-
workers, 12 percent neighbors, 10 percent fellow organization members,
58 percent friends, 4 percent acquaintances, and 6 percent "other." This,
of course, adds up to more than 100 percent because many relations were
labeled in more than one way.

I assigned each relation to a single *primary social context* by applying a
hierarchical rule. This rule places a relation into one of seven categories
on the basis of the category's importance and the relation's probable
origin. The groupings and their ordering are: close kin (spouses, parents,
children, and siblings), extended kin, co-workers, neighbors, fellow
members of organizations, "other," and "just friends." The last category

includes people whom respondents only called "friends." (The rule works this way: If a named person was a relative, he or she was categorized as close or extended kin; if not a relative but a co-worker, he or she was categorized as a co-worker; if neither kin nor co-worker, but a neighbor, categorized as neighbor, and so on.) The result is that the 19,417 relations fall into the following groups:

23 percent are classified as close kin (an average of 4.3 per respondent);

19 percent as other kin (3.4 per respondent);

10 percent as co-workers (1.8 per respondent);

10 percent as neighbors (1.9 per respondent);

6 percent as organization members (1.1 per respondent);

6 percent as "other" (1.1 per respondent; these were commonly friends of friends or relatives, acquaintances, former co-workers or neighbors, fellow students, professional consultants, such as doctors or ministers, and so on); and

23 percent "just friends" (4.9 per respondent).[5]

The averages hide much variation. To illustrate the variations in the social context compositions of respondents' networks, figure 2 displays primary social contexts by respondents' education. The more education respondents had, the larger their overall networks, from an average of 14.3 for those who never graduated from high school to 21.8 for people who went beyond a four-year college degree. Perhaps more interesting yet is how the composition of the networks varies from one educational extreme to the other: 8.2 kin for the least educated down to 6.8 kin for the most, for 0.7 up to 2.8 co-workers, and from 2.5 up to 6.8 "just friends." The contrasts not only are sharp between the extremes, they are also relatively regular as one scans from least to most educated. These educational differences in networks are among the greatest in our results and, because of residential sorting, underlie some of the city/small-town differences in networks that I will focus on.

We know, of course, an immense variety of other facts about the networks respondents listed for us, based either on the entire sample of 19,417 relations or on the 4,179 subsample names. For example, on the average, respondents and their associates had known each other sixteen years; 10 percent of the associates lived in San Francisco; 61 percent were married; a bit more than half of the people named were women; respondents who were homemakers named an average of 5.7 other homemakers; and men named an average of 2.3 people as persons with whom they discussed personal matters, while women named 2.7. The details of these numerous measurements will be presented and explained as each topical discussion warrants.

A final observation about these networks: It is somewhat disconcerting and even threatening to systematically review and discuss with a stranger one's friends and family. It is not surprising, therefore, that some respondents were reluctant and even hostile; yet perhaps more surprising was the fact that most, by far, were generally forthcoming. How did people feel about this intrusion into their private social worlds?

Many potential respondents refused to be interviewed, of course, though these refusals were not a result of the network questions themselves. A relative handful of the actual respondents were extremely reticent and gave information about their relations only grudgingly. Yet, though respondents were told they could stop at any point, only nine broke off an interview. Other people found the experience saddening, reminding them of their isolation or their losses. A few widows, for example, could not help crying by the end of the hour. Also, a few of the depressed respondents turned to the interviewers for aid, asking for advice on seeking psychiatric help or finding companionship. In several strained and isolated families, our interviewers provided rare openings into the wider world.

At the other extreme, some respondents found the interview fun and stimulating, a pleasure rather than a burden. Most people, however, seemed to find being questioned about their social lives a basically neutral experience, or one that was occasionally thought-provoking, as in the instance of the maintenance man who said, as paraphrased by the interviewer, that "the interview had really made him think a lot about his life and he was surprised at how 'stay-at-home' he had become in recent years." This seemed the most common sort of reaction.

II   First Issues

4   Urbanism and Psychological Strain

Americans have long believed that city life is unnatural and unhealthy[1]—physically, socially, morally, and psychologically. From the founding fathers on, most respected thinkers have expressed this popular opinion in denunciations of urban perversity.[2] Journalist Kirkpatrick Sale was only carrying on a long tradition when he wrote, in 1978:

For some years now sociologists have compiled evidence that life in the larger American cities is—I can think of no better phrase for it—solitary, poor, nasty, brutish, and short . . . . the studies leave no doubt that as cities get bigger they are characterized by more deviance, criminality, social stress, anomie, loneliness, selfishness, alcoholism, mental illness, and racial and ethnic segregation.[3]

In spite of Sale's forcefulness, both the role of sociologists and the nature of evidence in support of this view are much more complex than his assertions suggest. Early sociologists, notably members of the Chicago school, certainly contributed much to the image of urban disintegration. Although they would hardly have used Hobbes's description of the state of nature and would have noted many positive features of city life, Park, Wirth, and their colleagues did claim that "personal disorganization, mental breakdown, suicide, delinquency, crime, corruption, and disorder might be expected . . . to be more prevalent in the urban than in the rural community."[4] Some sociologists today also endorse these or similar statements.

Yet most urban sociologists do not. They do not subscribe to this view because, first, research in the intervening forty years has cast severe doubt on it. Two or more of the ills Sales and Wirth list are probably characteristic of city life in general, and one or two others may be characteristic of city life only in America or only in American cities in the late twentieth century, but most indictments on lists such as these cannot be proved.[5] Many urban sociologists also reject this view because they believe that modern society has assimilated all places into economically, organizationally, and culturally uniform regional communities. Accordingly, "urban-nonurban differences are differences that have ceased to make a difference."[6]

In this chapter and the next two I will address, largely with the results of our survey, three of the most important questions concerning urban/ nonurban differences: whether urban residence undermines mental well-being, whether it tends to isolate people socially, and whether it encourages deviation from traditional social morality. Urban alienation theory answers yes to all three questions; its critics typically answer no to all three. As these chapters show, the facts are more complex than that.

Psychological Mood

Observers claiming that urbanism creates psychological distress have usually pointed to certain indirect indicators of a community's collective mental health, such as rates of admission to mental institutions or rates of suicide (nineteenth-century suicides, that is, since there is little urban/rural difference today).[7] These statistics can easily mislead, because they typically refer only to the behavior of highly unusual groups in the population and because differences in such rates can reflect many factors besides actual psychological conditions. A community may have a high rate of admission to mental hospitals, for instance, because its residents are prone to mental illness or because it has larger, better, less restrictive, more available, or more confidential psychological services than do neighboring communities; its facilities may even attract clients from other towns. Some social workers in San Francisco claim, for example, that its charities, soup kitchens, and cheap hotels attract disturbed people from around the state.[8]

Investigators interested in the psychological conditions of the general population have therefore turned to using mass surveys posing questions whose answers presumably measure mental stress. This approach has its own difficulties; but it has proved useful in comparing large groups of people.[9] Our interviewers asked a set of such questions (questions 106 to 116; see Methodological Appendix section 4.3.3).

We combined respondents' answers to these questions into scales indicating how *upset* (nervous, worried) they felt, how *angry* they felt, and how *pleased* with life they felt. We also combined these three into an overall "mood" scale indicating how pleased versus angry and upset respondents felt. While by no means measures of sanity or insanity, these scales do allow us to rank respondents on how anxious versus enthusiastic they reported feeling. Urban alienation theory—and popular opinion, too—predicts that as urbanism increases, morale decreases.

This is not what we found. Figure 3 displays the results for the overall mood scale. Across the bottom of the figure are the four community categories, ordered from least to most urban. The vertical axis represents

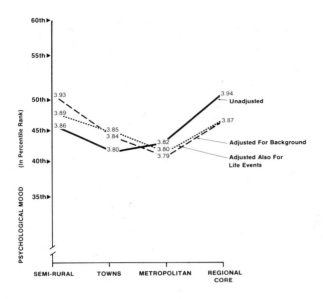

Fig. 3.   **Mean respondents' psychological mood, by urbanism.**

scores on the scale. Since the numbers have no inherent meaning, the figure translates them into percentile rank: scores that fell at the thirty-fifth percentile of all respondents, the fortieth percentile, and so forth. The solid line in the figure shows the actual mean scores of respondents according to the urbanism of their communities, not adjusted for self-selection. The 3.86 mean score of Semirural respondents indicates that the average for that group was just slightly above the forty-fifth percentile for all respondents; the 3.94 mean score for Core respondents places them just above the fiftieth percentile. (For a discussion of how the statistical associations in this study were calculated and how to evaluate them, see Methodological Appendix section 4.4.)

The solid line indicates that residents in different types of communities did not differ substantially in overall mood. There certainly was no linear connection between urbanism and mood, since Town and Metropolitan residents reported the lowest average mood. Examination of the separate subscales shows that respondents of varying residence differed hardly at all in how *pleased* they felt, that respondents varied in how *upset* they were roughly in the same way they did for overall mood—Town and Metropolitan people just slightly more upset that Semirural or Core people—and that Core respondents were substantially less *angry* than Town and Metropolitan respondents. There is no support in these raw

figures for the idea that urban residents are psychologically distressed.
The analysis does not end here; further questions must be raised. On
question concerns how truthful people were when they answered probe
such as "How often do you feel nervous, fidgety, or tense these days?"
Although generalizations from these kinds of data have usually bee
found reliable, we nevertheless built a check into the survey. After eac
interview, the interviewer was asked, "How open and forthcoming d
you think the respondent was about (his/her) problems and feelings: open
a little guarded, basically not frank?" Seventy-two percent (753) of th
respondents were judged to have been "open." When I redid the analysi
for these frank respondents only, the patterns just described emerge
even more strongly: Regional Core respondents were notably less angr
and more positive on overall mood than were frank respondents living i
Towns or Metropolitan places.[11] The conclusion stands.

A more far-reaching issue is whether self-selection is masking th
stressful consequences of urbanism. That is, urban life may still caus
psychological problems, but we may not see a correlation between th
two because urban residents possess certain characteristics that compen
sate for the mental damage of city life. For example, people in large
communities tend to be more affluent and to be childless—both person
characteristics that tend to improve morale. It is possible to adjust th
data statistically as if to hold constant these characteristics—to simulate
situation in which everyone is equal in all important respects other tha
place of residence.

The personal characteristics strongly associated with a better moo
were being childless, educated, affluent, employed, and male. All excep
the last also distinguished the more urban from the less urban re
spondents. Adjusting for these variables—that is, simulating a situation i
which all respondents were average in these characteristics—yields th
dashed line in figure 3. That line indicates that, were it not for life cycl
education, and so forth, Semirural respondents would be slightly higher i
mood and Metropolitan residents slightly lower in mood than the res
Two different types of respondents in those largely suburban Metropol
tan communities seemed to be particularly upset—the elderly and th
college-educated. For others, Metropolitan residence was not distinctiv
Nevertheless, the overall pattern is still not substantial (it is not significa
in the statistical sense) and does not warrant any conclusion about u
banism and psychological states.[12]

Psychologists have found that certain personal events, as well as pe
sonal characteristics, affect psychological well-being. Illness in the fam
ily, job changes, marital disputes, and other critical events, especial
when cumulative, have definite effects on mental and physical health. W
developed a scale of negative life events and added it to the statistic

controls.[13] The dash-dot line in figure 3 shows what the community means would be were everyone also equal on life events. In such circumstances there would be essentially no differences worth pursuing in overall mood.[14]

The evidence, in general, does not support the contention that urban life either causes or is associated with psychological distress. There is one interesting wrinkle in these findings, however. Low-income respondents living in Semirural places reported slightly higher overall mood than did low-income respondents with comparable backgrounds living elsewhere. (It is the low-income respondents who account for the uptick at the left side of the dashed line in figure 3.) This can be explained by life events; when those are held constant, the advantage of the Semirural people drops. More powerful as explanation, however, seems to be fear of crime. Low-income respondents who were worried about their safety scored considerably lower on overall mood than did those who were not, and low-income respondents in Semirural communities were less worried about crime than were those living elsewhere. If worry about crime is held constant, the advantage in mood of the Semirural respondents disappears.[15] The implication is that crime and the fear of it in urban places (Town through Core) contribute directly to demoralization. One interviewer reported that a homemaker in San Francisco, for example, "seemed very nervous throughout the interview. She was very upset when she talked about crime, having been burglarized three times." A further implication is that American cities would have absolutely no effect, or even positive effects, on psychological well being if they had—as they did in the 1950s—rates or crime more similar to those in the countryside.

Other Studies

The finding that there is no direct connection between urbanism and psychological well-being is not peculiar to our respondents or our technique. Various large- and small-scale studies of mental health also suggest that there is no urban/rural difference. One certainly cannot conclude that city life causes psychological distress. The following studies illustrate the extant research.

In 1960–62, the United States National Center for Health Statistics conducted a national survey in which 6,700 white adults were asked how many of eleven symptoms of psychological distress they felt. The results, adjusted for age and sex, showed that respondents in metropolitan areas reported, on the average, fewer symptoms than did respondents in non-metropolitan communities. (Within the metropolitan category, there was almost no difference by size of metropolitan area. Within the non-metropolitan category, residents of small urban places reported fractionally more symptoms than did rural people.)[16]

In 1972, the Louis Harris polling organization asked a national sample questions such as, "Do you ever take any pills or medicine to calm yourself down, or not?" (14 percent said yes); "Do you have anyone close to you who is or has been mentally disturbed?" (16 percent said yes); and "Has anyone in your family ever visited a psychiatrist or another doctor for help about a mental problem?" (21 percent said yes). There were essentially no differences in affirmative answers among residents of cities over 50,000 in population, suburbs, towns over 2,500, and rural places.[17]

In 1973, two sociologists in New Zealand surveyed pharmacists, asking how many prescriptions for tranquilizers they filled on an average Wednesday. Presumably, a relatively high rate of prescription in a community indicates a relatively high rate of tension. They found essentially no connection between community size and per capita prescription rate.[18]

None of these studies alone is conclusive, but, together and with others, they underline the moral of the present research: City life is neither associated with nor causes psychological distress. This not only gives us confidence in the findings with regard to people's subjective feelings, but also affirms the assumption behind this study that differences within northern California parallel differences within other regions.

Happiness

But there is one difficulty worth noting. In a few recent surveys asking people how happy or satisfied they are, or questions to that effect, residents of large cities have tended to say less often that they were happy. For example, a 1977 Gallup poll asked, "Generally speaking, how happy would you say you are—very happy, fairly happy, or not too happy?" In places under 50,000, 45 percent of respondents said "very"; in cities of one million and their suburbs, 36 percent said "very"; in between, the proportion was 40 percent.[19] Two questions arise: How does this square with our findings? And what does it say about the general conclusion that urbanism does not impair psychological well-being?

We asked respondents, "Thinking about your life as a whole, how happy would you say you are these days—very happy, pretty happy, pretty unhappy, or very unhappy?" (q. 116; this item was part of the "pleased" index). On average, respondents in the more urban communities answered the same way as those in the less urban places, before or after adjustment.[20] The reason for our finding of no association, in contrast to the national surveys, may be chance, peculiarities of northern California, or the absence of black ghetto neighborhoods in our sample. Some evidence suggests, however, that the difference results from either the absence in our sample of any of the very large central cities, such as New York or Chicago, or the greater frankness of big-city residents, or both.[21]

Setting aside comparisons with our own survey, the results reported by Gallup and others may have general implications. In 1972, I reanalyzed a few happiness and satisfaction polls that had been taken in the 1950s and 1960s.[22] Three salient points emerged. First, after adjusting the data for self-selection factors, more urban and less urban respondents did not differ in satisfaction, except at the extreme: residents of the three largest metropolitan areas (New York, Los Angeles, and Chicago) reported relatively low levels of happiness.[23] Perhaps fashionable cynicism in urban centers explains this remaining difference—a possibility, given that New Yorkers contributed most to this drop. Or perhaps residents of such cosmopolitan centers have especially high standards of comparison. In that regard, it is worth noting that young people and educated people tend to be relatively dissatisfied, presumably because of their high aspirations.[24] Second, residents of the major cities have not always reported less happiness; that difference appeared in the 1960s and widened in the 1970s.[25] The change suggests that the happiness dip reflects the particular "urban crisis" of the past fifteen to twenty years—the complex of escalating crime, racial strife, factory closings, housing crunches, school difficulties, and so on. Polls show that big-city residents are much more likely, and became increasingly more likely over those years, than small-town residents to be dissatisfied with their safety, housing, children's education, and similar community features.[26] Alternatively, the increase in metropolitan discontent may reflect the general decline in American's morale since 1960, a shift in attitude being led, as most shifts in attitude are, by big-city residents.[27] Third, there was some sign in my study that the community difference was due to the happiness of people who had moved from cities to suburbs or small towns. My report concluded with an explanation based on the Americans' belief in the small-town ideal: "this small metropolitan effect might be more economically explained by the contemporary state of [American] cities, and by the ability of affluent persons to leave those areas in pursuit of the ideal home in the ideal smaller community—and by the inability of others to do so."[28] On the other hand, a simpler explanation may be that extremely large cities have some inherent dissatisfying effect on their residents.

Conclusion

Whatever the explanation for the national surveys' findings on reported happiness, there still remains very little support for the proposition that urban residence generates "personal disorganization and mental breakdown," as Louis Wirth claimed and as most people believe. (Expression of happiness, though associated with the absence of psychic stress, is, it should be noted, quite distinct.[29]). Among our respondents, there was no uniform association between how urban their communities were and their expressions of being upset, being angry, being pleased with life, or their overall mood. Metropolitan residents tended to be slightly more upset and Core residents tended to be slightly less angry than other respondents, but these differences essentially washed out once the personal characteristics and the life events of the respondents were held constant. The results imply that, were all our respondents average in income, education, probability of being married, number of life changes, and so on, there would have been no observable difference in the psychological states we measured—and thus that there is no causal effect of urbanism.

This conclusion is a bit surprising, and not only because it challenges conventional wisdom. American cities' objective circumstances, compared with those of their hinterlands, have deteriorated to a historical low. With respect to physical condition, economic growth, public services, personal security, cost of living, and so on, urban centers have lost much of their edge or fallen behind small towns. To the extent that people's feelings of well-being respond to these conditions—and we saw that they respond to anxiety about crime—the 1970s were the years in which to witness any psychological damage of city life. We did not see any.

Although any single study such as this can be questioned (how valid are these psychological measures? Was some important dimension missed? What if we had interviewed the people who refused?), it fits well with other research pointing to the same conclusion: The charge that urbanism impairs mental well-being is unfounded. The study supports instead the position of sociologists who argue that such urban/rural differences no longer exist, or never did. Given that conclusion, it is worth speculating about why people so firmly believe that mental health is better in smaller communities.

One possibility is that seemingly deranged behavior is more visible in urban centers. Seriously troubled people often drift to cities, where there are more social services and perhaps fewer social pressures. Within cities, they tend to concentrate in certain low-rent districts, usually near downtown, and their public behavior is witnessed by far more people: outrageous carryings-on in midtown Manhattan are far more public than similar actions on isolated farms or in small towns.

A related possibility is that much of what people witness in cities is aberrant not in any clinical sense, but in a normative sense. The great social heterogeneity of cities provides many public situations in which people from one group are exposed to the incomprehensible, outrageous, or even offensive behavior of other groups. The observers often label that behavior as mentally "sick" (or morally sick, or both), when it is usually simply different or just socially deviant. (For more on this, see chap. 18.)

In spite of public perceptions—or journalists' assertions—there is little substance to this one of the three major beliefs about urbanism, that it is psychologically damaging. When we turn to the second belief, that urbanism is socially isolating, the verdict is a little more complex.

5   Urbanism and
        Social Involvement

According to the "Lonely Crowd" image of urban life that Americans widely accept, something about cities attracts or produces "solitary" individuals. Scholars depict a particular form of solitude: city-dwellers are socially active, perhaps frenetically so, but they have only fleeting and superficial social contacts; they lack the multifaceted and emotionally engaging relations necessary for true community.[1] This plaint is, of course, said as often about modern society as about the urban sectors of that society, for example: "The awful fact is that modern urban society, as a whole, has found no way of sustaining intimate contacts."[2]

Our respondents quickly confirm the first part of the image, that concerning social activity. The more urban their communities the more likely respondents were to have recently engaged in a variety of activities with other people, such as having someone over for lunch, or visiting someone, or meeting someone in a public place. The youth, education, income, and unmarried status of urbanites accounts for most of this difference, but not for all of it. Other traits equal, Core residents reported a slightly wider and Semirural residents a slightly narrower variety of social activities than did other respondents. Urbanism does contribute to activity.[3] But does this urban sociability just while away the hours for people lacking "true" friends?

This chapter addresses the question in four parts, examining, first, where the very isolated respondents lived; second, the correlation between urbanism and how many friends and relatives respondents named; third, the quality of respondents' relations with those people; and fourth, the findings of other studies.

The Isolates

Where did the solitary respondents live? I distinguished two overlapping groups of respondents: the 10 percent who named eight or fewer people, and the 5 percent who talked to no one about personal matters (see q. 77).

Sixteen people were both isolated and lacked a confidant. A few among these, whether actually friendless or not, may have simply been un-cooperative in the interview. In one such case, an affluent, self-described playboy in Oakland was anxious to usher the interviewer out. She noted, "the man was obviously entertaining his girl friend and really didn't want to bother with me." Others were alone because of acute disabilities or because of ethnic or class disadvantages. One woman, living in a small town, had suffered a stroke, was unemployed, and had to support two sons by herself. Most of her friends had left the area, and the remaining people she named were all fellow church members. One man, Mexican-born, had to support a wife and three children though unemployed and unskilled. "He said his family is very important to him and he doesn't like to socialize with other people." Another isolate was an alcoholic widower.

A few respondents among the sixteen seem to fit the image of the busy-but-lonely urbanite. Two lived in the same suburban community. One was a family man—long married, two children, a longtime resident—who was totally absorbed in the company he owned. "He was in a rush—said he brought work home ... glanced at his watch frequently, and gave short, quick answers.... He was cooperative and apologized at the end for being so rushed.... It seems his business is his main interest, with tennis second." This man belonged to no organizations, read no magazines, namedly only five people besides his family, and expressed no desire to know more people. The other was a woman, a divorced parent for many years, poorly educated, who managed real estate. Described as "hostile" by the interviewer, "she seemed embarrassed by the lack of names and took pains to explain how she likes to walk alone, to play music, to go swimming, and likes people but doesn't like to get too involved with them—a little defensive, I felt."

Overall, the isolated respondents—those who named eight or fewer people—tended to be older, poorer, formerly married (separated, divorced, or widowed), and uncooperative in the interview.[4] They were *not*, however, any more likely to live in urban than nonurban communities. The respondents without a confidant tended to be male, older, less educated, never married, and uncooperative. They too were evenly distributed across the urban spectrum. Adjusting the data to take into account that the small-town respondents were older, less affluent, and less educated but more often married than big-city residents does not noticeably alter the findings.[5]

Seriously, perhaps pathologically, isolated respondents were just as likely to reside in less urban as in more urban places. This challenges at least part of the lonely urbanite image, the part that symbolizes city life by the friendless rooming-house tenant.

Total Social Involvement

Another approach is to consider how residents of small and large communities differed in the total size of their networks. Care must be taken, however, in interpreting this measure. Groups might differ in average network size because they differ in the proportion of people who have small networks (i.e., solitary people) or because they differ in the proportion of people who have particularly large networks. In the latter case we are measuring not isolation, but gregariousness. Also, in some versions of the solitary urbanite thesis, the city-dweller has many contacts but few that are meaningful. Quality, not quantity, matters. Nevertheless, examining total numbers of associates is a necessary part of determining whether urban life is solitary.

Figure 4 presents the basic findings: the average number (logarithmic means)[6] of people respondents named, by each urban category. The solid line at the top of the figure indicates that Town and Metropolitan respondents named more people, overall, than did Semirural and Core respondents.[7] This association between moderate levels of urbanism and large networks might be explained by self-selection factors. That Semirural respondents were older than average and that Core respondents were often unmarried, for example, might account for the differences. Adjusting the numbers to take several such factors into account yields the dashed line at the top of figure 4. Other things equal, Core respondents named about two fewer associates, on the average, than did respondents living elsewhere.[8]

Something, then, about living in, or being attracted to live in, the urban hub of northern California reduced the size of respondents' personal networks. We begin to understand what that might be by breaking down those networks. The bottom of figure 4 presents one fundamental partitioning, separating relatives from other associates, and shows quite different patterns for the two sets. (Do not expect the averages for kin and nonkin to add up to the overall averages; these are logarithmic means.) The more urban the community, the more *nonkin* respondents named; Core respondents named about half again as many as did Semirural respondents.[9] This strong connection between urbanism and nonkin involvement can, however, be fully explained by the kinds of people who live in more urban and less urban places. The dashed line indicates that, had our respondents been otherwise similar to one another, where they lived would have made *no difference* in the number of nonkin they named.[10] But the more urban the respondents' communities, the fewer *kin* they named; or, more precisely, respondents in the Regional Core averaged fewer kin than did other respondents—40 percent fewer than Semirural respondents.[11] Adjusting the results for marital status and the like attenuates the pattern

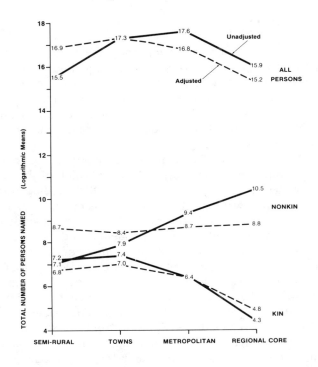

Fig. 4.   **Number of persons named, by urbanism.**

only slightly.[12] Had they been otherwise similar to other respondents, Core residents would still have named fewer relatives.

We have narrowed in on the community differences in total social involvement. Taking our respondents as a whole and adjusting for self-selection, Core residents were involved with unusually few relatives; residents in other types of places were equally involved with relatives; and residents in all types of communities, Semirural to Core, were equally involved with nonrelatives. The difference in kin ties will be pursued in part 3, as will finer distinctions among kin and nonkin and also among types of respondents. Suffice it to say here that there is no straightforward connection between urbanism and total social involvement. Even the Core respondents, with fewer kin, had at least as many nonkin associates and can hardly be considered friendless. In fact, Core respondents averaged, even after adjustment, just slightly more "friends" than other respondents did.[13] There is tantalizing evidence here about urbanism and the family, but little so far to sustain the charge that urbanism produces social isolation.

Quality of Relations

But do these numbers really speak to the concern with *community*? Are relations in town and city of equal depth, commitment, and intimacy? One author claims: "People who live in cities may think they have lots of friends; but the word friend has changed its meaning. Compared with friendships of the past, most of these new friendships are trivial."[14] (Note the familiar blending of urban/rural and modern/traditional distinctions.)

There are various ways of indicating the quality of respondents' relations. For example, we asked respondents, "Which of the people you named do you feel especially close to?" (q. 82). Adding up only the number of people who were called "close" yields much the same findings as adding up all people: other factors controlled, Core respondents named fewer "close" kin than did other respondents, and there was no difference among communities in the average number of "close" nonkin.[15]

This still refers to quantity of relations, however. We can focus on their quality by examining the characteristics of the specific relations themselves (rather than the characteristics of respondents' networks of relations; cf. Methodological Appendix section 2.5), asking whether ties described by urban respondents differed from those small-town respondents described. We can divide almost all of the 19,000-plus relations into those involving people to whom respondents reported feeling "especially close" (38 percent) versus those to whom they did not; people whom respondents called "friends" (59 percent) versus those whom they did not; and people whom respondents reported confiding in or seeking advice from (17 percent) versus those whom they did not. Also, we know how many total exchanges respondents reported having with each named person (an average of 1.1). On all these indicators, more urban respondents' relations were, on average, as intimate as, or more intimate than, less urban respondents' relations. This remains so even after adjusting for characteristics of the respondents, the associates, and the contexts of the relations.[16]

For more than 4,000 of the relations, we can specify two other characteristics: how many years the respondent and the person he or she named had known each other, and how often they "usually got together." As the hypothesis of "transitory" urban relations suggests, the larger the respondents' communities, the fewer years they had known their associates, an average of 14.2 years for Core respondents and 17.8 for Semirural ones. This difference, however, is fully explained by the fact that small-town respondents were older. Age and the like held constant, the relations of more urban and less urban respondents averaged the same number of years—except that Semirural respondents knew their *nonkin* associates for a slightly shorter time than did respondents living elsewhere (6.8 versus 8.3 years). City ties seem no more transitory than country ties.[17]

But finally, in frequency of getting together, decline of community theory predicts correctly: the more urban the place they lived in, the less often respondents met their associates. Semirural residents reported getting together with 61 percent of their associates once a week or more; Core respondents reported meeting only 47 percent of their associates that frequently. The difference is not great, but it is consistent and stable. After adjusting for respondent traits (educated people and older people got together with their associates relatively infrequently), characteristics of the relations (co-workers and close kin were seen more often; longtime associates *less* often), and, most important, distance between respondent and associates, Semirural respondents still tended to get together with their associates just slightly more often than did respondents living elsewhere.[18] A closer look reveals that Semirural respondents, all else equal, got together relatively often with nonkin who lived in their local community; they did not differ from other respondents in their frequency of getting together with other types of associates.[19] Ironically, Semirural respondents also knew this same group of local nonkin a relatively short time; that is, these tended to be *new* often-seen associates, not old often-seen ones.[20]

In total, there is faint evidence here for any claim that the quality of urban relations is inferior to those of small-town relations. The one item in favor—Semirural respondents' seeing their local associates a bit more often—is counterweighed by at least one item—that those associates were relatively new ones. We will look more closely at issues of relational quality when we examine specific social contexts (part 3) and other dimensions of networks (part 4). But with respect to personal ties as a whole, the kinds of measures used, and the range of places we have here, relations are generally of equal quality in small town and big city.

Other Studies

As with psychological well-being, we need to ask whether this verdict of no difference in amount or quality of social involvement is peculiar to the northern California study. Unlike the case of psychological well-being, prior studies have been few and only suggestive, at best. Nevertheless, they point to the same conclusion, that urbanism is neither associated with nor causes social isolation.[21] Two studies illustrate.

Albert Reiss, Jr., interviewed men in the Nashville area in the mid-

1950s and asked them to provide detailed "time-budget" accounts of how they had spent the previous working day. In terms of sheer hours and minutes in someone's company, the rural and urban men were equally involved with family. And the urban men had spent more time with friends than the rural men, especially more than the farm men.[22] In the 1970s, Patricia Crowe interviewed one hundred people, twenty in each of five different occupations, living in Innsbruck, Austria, and its surrounding towns and villages. Her Innsbruck respondents reported as many or more close friends, and as much contact with kin, as respondents in the smaller places.[23] These and similar studies, though not as comprehensive as our own, present the same conclusion: Urban life is not particularly solitary.

Why Not?

As with psychological well-being, we confront the contradiction between these findings and common experience. If urbanites are not in fact more socially isolated than small-town residents, why do most people think they are?[24] Several possibilities come to mind, including the greater visibility in cities of "pathological" isolates, the concentration of migrants whose origins are far away, and the substitution of geographically dispersed relations for neighborhood ties (see chap. 13). But I will focus on one specific explanation: the contrast between visible public behavior and invisible private relations.

In the public places—stores, post offices, street corners—of small communities, residents tend to encounter people they know. There are few such places and everyone uses them. These chance meetings are less common in large communities, where residents have many such public places even within walking distance. We asked our respondents, "When you are not at home [or at work/school], about how often do you run into someone you know?" (q.67). More than half the Semirural respondents answered "almost every day" compared with less than one-third of Metropolitan and Core respondents.[25] Conversely, in small communities there are relatively few strange or strange-looking people in public places, while there are many such in urban public places. As a result, public familiarity—saying hello to acquaintances, asking after the families of store clerks,[26] bantering with "friendly looking" strangers—is more common in smaller communities, while public impersonality and even suspicion are more common in larger communities (on the latter point, see chap. 18).

This public familiarity is commonly taken, I suggest, for private intimacy, and public impersonality for private estrangement. Indeed, public familiarity is all tied up with the very idea of small-town America. A woman in one of our Semirural communities said of it: "We know everybody. It's a friendly town. When you know everybody, you can say 'Hi,' like at the post office and bank. It's a small town and I like small towns and the friendliness." On the other hand, she also said, "I don't like Mexicans and there are a lot of Mexicans moving in. Pretty soon it won't be a small town anymore."[27]

But such public familiarity need have nothing to do with people's private lives. The friendly greeter on the streets may have few friends, while the reserved subway rider may have a thriving social life. A small-town resident explained to David Hummon, "I love the town because I am acquainted with so many people, not really on a social scale, but it's nice to walk down the street and see people you went to school with, even though you don't anymore say anything but 'hello.' You don't associate with them socially, but it's nice to know everyone and to know their relatives."[28] Usually, however, we as observers know only the public signs of people's private lives, and therefore we interpret rural familiarity as intimacy, urban reserve as alienation.

This gap between public and private is sharper in non-English-speaking countries where the very terms of address distinguish the two realms, but where it is also true that the former is not necessarily a good indicator of the latter. Crowe illustrates the point in the Austrian case:

From what informants said to me, it seems that people from all levels of urbanization misinterpret the public behavior of those living at different levels of urbanization. Villagers usually know each other, if not always by name, at least by sight. They often grow up together; their relationships, though seldom intimate, are personal. Villagers address each other familiarly using "*du*" instead of "*Sie*" and their manners are quite informal. Many do not know how to behave formally even where it would be appropriate; hence, they may avoid strangers. Urban strangers passing through and noting both the reticence toward outsiders and the great informality between fellow villagers conclude erroneously that the villagers have intimate relationships with each other . . . . Rural persons going to the city find that everyone behaves formally, for urbanites have impersonal relationships with most persons who they see during the day. They use "*Sie*" and act reserved . . . . there seems to be an assumption that because personal relationships predominate in villages, the likelihood of intimacy is greater. Villagers, of course, know that villagers often fail to have friends, but they assume that the impersonality of the city will make the likelihood of friendship even smaller.[29]

The contrasts may not be as dramatic in the United States, but the principle may be the same: We mistake public familiarity for private intimacy.

Conclusion

The second broadside against urban life is the charge that it is "solitary." Unlike the charge that large cities foster mental illness, this one cannot be quickly dismissed. Our survey, and others as well, contradicts the claim in most respects. Urbanites were no more likely than small-town residents to report especially small networks. There was no simple connection between how urban respondents' communities were and how many associates they named. As a descriptive matter, respondents in urban places named fewer kin but more nonkin than respondents in small communities. Holding constant self-selection, however, the only difference is the tendency for Core residents to have named fewer relatives than other respondents. Finally, our measures of intimacy and depth indicate that the urbanism did not impair the quality of respondents' relations.

Yet respondents did differ in two respects. As noted, residents in the Regional Core named fewer relatives, and residents of Semirural communities reported getting together more often with local nonkin than other respondents did. These two differences foretell important topics of parts 3 and 4, where we focus on community differences in people's styles of social life. But they are weak reeds of support for the claim of urban isolation. That claim must be rejected. What cannot be rejected is the third basic charge—that urbanism weakens traditional values.

6 Urbanism and Traditional Values

In America's community ideology, the small town is the repository for the traditional way of life and the large city is the showcase for deviant ways of life. To move from countryside to metropolis is to be exposed to and perhaps lured into abnormal, immoral, and possibly criminal behavior.

Unlike the belief that urbanites tend to be psychologically disturbed and socially isolated, there is a good deal of truth in the belief that urbanites tend to be morally deviant. Among our respondents, for example, residents of the Regional Core were over one and a half times as likely as others to be living with someone out of wedlock, two and a half times as likely to disclaim any religious identity, and a dozen times as likely to be openly "gay." These contrasts appear to be typical across America, and elsewhere too.[1]

This chapter demonstrates that, among the 1,050 people we interviewed, urban residence was associated with rejection of traditional values and was a significant cause of that rejection. The chapter also tries to explain how such an effect could exist when other postulated urban/rural differences do not.

Issues and Arguments

Both inchoate popular notions and elaborate academic theories assume that urbanites tend to believe and behave in nontraditional ways. (That this tendency can be valued as innovativeness or devalued as deviance is immaterial.) Both explain this unconventionality by attenuated social bonds and explain those, in turn, by the very nature of urban life. I have already sketched key parts of the argument as the "decline of community" thesis. Here I lay out its denouement, its account of how urbanism weakens the traditional way of life. The argument has critics who deny that urbanism has any such consequences. And there is also the subcultural argument that urbanism does weaken tradition not by attenuating social ties, but by creating them.

Breakdown and Release

"The main external check upon a man's conduct, the opinion of his neighbors, which has such a powerful influence in the country or small town, tends to disappear. In a great city one has no neighbors. No one knows the doings of his even his close friends; few men care what the secret life of their friends may be. Thus, with his moral sensibilities blunted, the young man is left free to follow his inclinations." This analysis, proffered by a New York City antiprostitution group in 1902, crudely summarizes the theory.[2] In the village, individuals tend to be bound by many strong, multifaceted, and interwoven relations founded on kinship, locality, and church. In the metropolis, individuals tend to be loosely connected to others by a few tenuous, specialized, and disjointed associations founded on self-interest. The strength of social ties determine the extent to which individuals are under *social control*.

Personal relations usually regulate individual behavior gently and non-consciously: family and friends teach us, by word and action, ways of understanding the world; they censure, punish, abandon us for deviation; and our loyalty to them commits us to conventional behavior—to work to feed the children, to be well dressed and gracious in public with our friends, to avoid shaming our colleagues, and so on. When personal ties unravel, social control weakens and individuals are "released" to act aberrantly.

By the lights of decline of community theory, and of the Chicago school,[3] this explains much about urban life: its vice, crime, radicalism, avant-garde life-styles, and the like. Urban communities are relatively disorganized, lacking effective local and church institutions and, most important, lacking effective family, neighbor, and other personal networks. Social control fails; deviations occur.

Critique

Few social scientists would challenge this argument's minor premise, that personal networks make individuals conform to group norms. They usually challenge the major premise, that city life debilitates personal networks. Citing ethnographies or the few surveys of family life and friendship in big cities, they claim that there are no urban/rural differences, or that any differences can be explained by coincidental facts, such as the selective migration of young people to cities or the character of specific urban economies. Cities, as cities, do not shape networks.[4]

But what then of the unconventional urban way of life? One response is to claim that cities are not, in general, prone to unconventionality: the crime, heresies, and other behavior taken as evidence of social disintegration are peculiar to American cities or to this historical period.[5] What Americans take to be inherent in city life is actually due to the specific character of our cities, particularly to their rapid growth two or three generations ago. Even now, these city/country differences are narrowing under "massification." There is some truth to this view; for example, cities have sometimes been less crime-ridden than their hinterlands. However, in most societies and most times, urbanites have been especially prone to deviate from tradition, in a wide variety of ways.[6]

Another response accepts some claim of urban unconventionality but explains it in terms of selective migration instead of social breakdown. The kinds of people drawn to cities attract deviants—unmarried men, for example, attract prostitutes—and nonconformists gravitate to cities, as in the case of homosexuals moving to San Francisco. Selective migration does explain much of urban deviance, but probably not all of it. Some evidence suggests that urban/rural differences in social orientation are simply too great to be accounted for only by self-selection, that urbanism itself generates nonconformity to mainstream values.[7]

Subcultural Theory

Then how do cities produce this outcome, if not by social breakdown? By buildup. My argument[8] is that cities generate alternative subcultures that promote nontraditional values. Urban subcultures give birth (or rebirth) to new ideas and styles, nurture them, and send them out into the rest of the urban world. It was largely in urban subcultures[9] that people recently began to endorse premarital cohabitation, long hair and beards, and skepticism about my country right or wrong patriotism. Views such as these were gently enforced on members and transmitted to the surrounding urban world. (Similar examples, with different "new" ideas, such as kings do not rule by divine right, or people should choose whom they marry, could be cited for other times and places.) Even extremely deviant behavior, crime, is largely generated in underworld subcultures. In sum, rather than breaking down social ties and releasing people's deviant instincts, urbanism encourages social ties in the small sectors of society and thereby breeds styles of life that mainstream society considers aberrant.

Both the classic argument and the thesis I have suggested predict that we will find urbanites to be less traditional than residents of smaller places, and that this difference cannot be fully explained by self-selection. Urbanism itself is a cause. Then the two arguments diverge. The breakdown thesis suggests that urbanism operates through the vitiation of social ties; therefore the relatively nontraditional are also the relatively isolated. Subcultural theory suggests that the nontraditional are as socially integrated as the traditional, only into different milieus, and that people are nontraditional to the extent that they are personally connected to innovative subcultures.[10]

Social Attitudes

In mid-1977, shortly before we began interviewing, a movie-house owner in Susanville, California—7,000 population, two hundred miles northeast of San Francisco—was forced by the police chief, an Episcopalian minister, a local judge, and others to cancel a showing of the X-rated film *Behind the Green Door*. About the same time, not only was the Bay Area chockablock with X-rated movies, but the Berkeley and San Francisco city councils passed ordinances protecting homosexuals, San Franciscans approved a resolution to stop enforcing antimarijuana laws, and the city's police chief paid a friendly visit to the annual Hookers' Ball, a lewd benefit for . . . hookers.

One could endlessly list examples of such cultural differences between small towns and large cities. With few exceptions, they show the nontraditionalism of urban life. The task here is to examine the differences at the individual level, among our respondents. Ideally, we should study respondents' actual behavior—attendance at X-rated movies, smoking marijuana and such—but asking people about slightly tainted actions is difficult; their answers may be evasive, and many specific actions are too rare to measure reliably. (We do, however, have a few quasi-behavioral indicators, such as whether respondents said they were cohabiting.)

Basically, we rely on a scale measuring respondents' opinions on social issues. This scale allows us to finely rank respondents from highly critical of nontraditional moral behavior to very accepting of it. Our confidence in the scale as an indicator of traditionalism is buttressed by the fact that people who acted nontraditionally scored as nontraditional on the scale, and also that our findings with it are consistent with research by others. Four items make up the scale: questions asking about sex before marriage, abortion, legalization of marijuana, and allowing homosexuals to teach in public schools. (Two other questions, whether mothers should seek employment and whether spouses should share housework, did not fit well into the scale, but respondents' answers to them followed much the same pattern.)

The questions were (qs. 32–37):

How do you feel about people who not married having sex relations— would you say that it is generally OK or generally wrong? (65 percent said "OK").[11]

Would you say that abortions should be legal whenever a woman wants one; legal only under certain circumstances; or always be illegal? (55 percent said "legal whenever"; 6 percent said "always illegal").

Do you think marijuana should be made legal or not?" (49 percent, yes; 45 percent, no).

Do you think homosexuals should or should not be permitted to teach in the public schools?" (52 percent, should; 34 percent, not).

Although answers to these questions are only verbal behavior, we have indications that respondents' actual life-styles were consistent with their statements. Respondents who claimed no religion, who lived with someone out of wedlock, who manifestly or apparently were homosexual, or who regularly read a "countercultural" magazine or newspaper (e.g., *High Times, Bay Guardian, Advocate*) were more likely than other respondents to give nontraditional answers to these questions.

Similarly, people who answered one of these items in a traditional way tended also to answer the other items that way. This provides some confidence that answers to the questions are largely expressions of a basic traditionalism, and that those answers can be combined into a single scale of traditionalism. (The items, more exactly, tap attitudes on individual liberty—or individual license—versus society's restraints. This represents only part of traditionalism. But, as just noted, pro-restraint answers to these items go together with other expressions of traditionalism.)

The more urban their communities, the less likely respondents were to endorse traditional opinions in answer to each of these questions. For example, while 52 percent of Semirural respondents said that sex before marriage is wrong, only 18 percent of Core respondents did; while 69 percent of Semirural respondents said marijuana should not be legalized, only 23 percent Core respondents did.[12] National surveys have also found that urban people are more liberal on these matters than are small-town or rural people.[13] And there is some evidence among the general public that action is consistent with attitude. In November 1978 Californians voted on an initiative that would permit school districts to refuse to hire people who had engaged in "public homosexual conduct." The initiative lost, statewide, 58 to 42 percent out of 6,680,000 votes. In the northern California region of our survey, the farther a county is from San Francisco, the higher the proportion of yes votes, votes to restrict homosexual teachers. For example, San Francisco County, at one extreme, voted only 25 percent yes; suburban Contra Costa County voted 39 percent yes; distant, agricultural Tehema County voted 52 percent yes.[14] That pattern is similar to one that appears on other liberal versus conservative tests, such as the vote on an initiative to support the farm workers' union.[15]

We can be confident, in sum, that the basic community differences in answers to the four questions we use are consistent with behavior and consistent with national patterns. Two divergences are worth noting:

One, the respondents to our survey, as a whole, were less traditional, as are northern Californians in general, than most of the nation. Two, the community differences reported here appear to be somewhat sharper than those reported nationally. I suggest two reasons the latter is true. Our urbanism scale captures the urban dimension better than those used in most research (and, since it is different, strict comparisons cannot be made). More important, by focusing on a single region we can highlight city/small town contrasts that often get clouded by regional differences in national studies.[16]

The traditionalism scale we used basically adds up respondents' answers to the four questions. It runs from 1.24, perfectly nontraditional, where 26 percent of our respondents scored, to almost 4.0, with only a scattering of perfectly traditional respondents; the average is 2.11.[17]

Urbanism and Traditionalism

The solid line in figure 5 shows that the more urban their communities, the lower respondents' traditionalism scores. The correlation is a strong one; the average Semirural respondent was at almost the seventieth percentile, while the average Core respondent was at the fortieth percentile in traditionalism.[18] What explains the association?

The breakdown thesis suggests that urbanism weakens social integration and that unintegrated individuals lose hold on traditional values. In the words of a nineteenth-century reformer, far from "mothers' watchful eyes, fathers' warning voices, and neighbors' tell-tale tongues," newcomers to the city are tempted into "every degree of wickedness, from the slightest excesses to the foulest villainies."[19] There is some evidence for this view. Family people are less common in urban centers, and family people tended to give more traditional answers. The more children respondents had at home, the more conservative their answers; the higher the proportion of kin in their network, also the more conservative. And the higher the proportion of local people in respondents' networks, the more conservative their answers.[20]

But this explanation is both incorrect and incomplete. Although conservatism accompanies family life, it is not evident that conservatism accompanies social integration in the more general sense; if anything, the opposite is true. The larger respondents' networks, especially the more nonkin they named and the more support they received from their associates, the *less* traditional they were.[21] These results do not mean that social integration promotes liberal attitudes—respondents with large networks tended to be liberal because they tended to be young and well-educated—but they do suggest that there is no direct connection

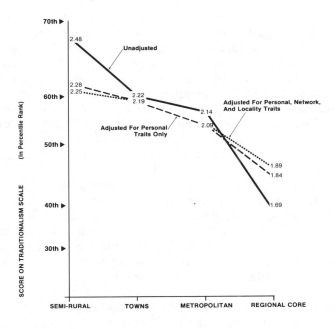

Fig. 5.   Traditionalism, by urbanism.

between greater social involvement and greater traditionalism. (There is an indirect connection, which I will discuss below.)

Self-selection partly explains why urbanites were less traditional than residents of smaller communities. Age was strongly associated with traditionalism. The least traditional were respondents in their twenties (less traditional than the teenagers in the survey), and beyond those years traditionalism increased to a peak among the elderly. The less education respondents had, the more traditional they were. The more children they had at home, the more traditional they were. Also, respondents who had been raised as Protestant fundamentalists were considerably more traditional than those raised in other faiths. These are the basic characteristics of respondents who gave traditional answers.[22]

Adjusting the scores for these personal differences—that is, assuming that everyone was similar in these respects—yields the dashed line in figure 5. Self-selection accounts for much of the community differences, but a strong contrast remains. Semirural respondents, on average, fall at the sixty-second percentile, and Core respondents at the forty-seventh.[23] Something aside from self-selection accounts for urban nontraditionalism.

The explanation may lie in the *kind* of social integration respondents in more urban or less urban places typically had (rather than the amount of social integration). As just noted, respondents who named a high proportion of local nonrelatives tended to give traditional answers.[24] (Except that among respondents in the Regional Core, those with a high proportion of local associates were less traditional, a point that will be important later.) Urban respondents tended to name relatively small proportions of kin or neighbors (see part 3). Consequently, network characteristics might account for the nontraditionalism of urbanites. This is evidence for a revised breakdown theory: Urbanism weakens attachment to kin and local community (in favor of other social ties); that, in turn, weakens attachment to traditional values.

It is weak evidence, however, largely because holding constant network composition hardly alters the association between urbanism and traditionalism. Even among respondents with similar proportions of relatives and of local associates, urbanites were considerably less traditional than small-town residents. The dashed line in figure 5 is hardly moved by also adjusting for network composition.[25] Something else about urbanism other than either self-selection or networks explains its connection with nontraditionalism.

One possibility is that the explanation is the San Francisco Bay Area; it is particularly liberal and nonconformist (see Methodological Appendix section 1.2). But this explanation does not suffice. Even if we remove the Bay Area respondents from the analysis, there remains a significant difference between Semirural and Metropolitan respondents, with Town respondents falling in between. More important, other studies with other surveys on social attitudes show that differences by size of community remain after adjustment—smaller differences, but of the same kind.[26]

Another explanation, closer to but not quite the subcultural model, focuses on the social composition, or "climate," of different communities. Even had our respondents been assigned to communities at random, their neighbors would not have been a random assortment. In urban places, they would have been relatively young and educated; in rural places, older and uneducated. Whatever influence members of a community have on one another would push the urban respondents in a nontraditional direction and small-town respondents the opposite way. In fact, respondents who lived in localities with high proportions of young adults and with higher than average educational levels tended to give less traditional responses than otherwise similar interviewees, suggesting that there was such a local climate of opinion effect.[27] However, that composition explains only a small part of urbanism's connection to nontraditional attitudes. The dotted line in figure 5, which shows the data adjusted also for local composition, is virtually unchanged from the dashed line. Semirural respondents rank, on average, at the sixty-first percentile, Core respondents at the forty-eight.[28]

To explain the remaining connection shown by the dotted line, we turn finally to subcultural theory, two propositions in particular. One is that absolute mass—not just proportion—is critical to a social climate effect. The other is that networks mediate such a climate effect; people pick up the ambient opinions largely through personal contacts.

I used two measures of "mass": the proximity of each locality to relatively high concentrations of college-educated people and of young people. (These measures differ notably from the two just discussed. Those locality measures indicate the proportion of young and educated people in the immediate area, irrespective of where in the region the place is situated. These measures are much less sensitive to the composition of the locality and much more sensitive to its proximity to relatively large concentrations of educated and young people.) Since young and educated people tend to be concentrated in urban areas, the measures are strongly associated with urbanism, and it is difficult to disentangle them from urbanism. Nevertheless, adjusting the data for concentrations of the young and educated reduces the remaining community differences to insubstantial magnitudes. Because it is difficult to separate urbanism per se, the general concentration of people, from the relative concentration of young and educated people, this demonstration does not prove—but does support—the contention that the absolute mass of nontraditional people in urban areas creates a general climate of opinion that in turn influences other people to be less traditional.[29]

Urbanism, Networks, and Traditionalism

If the subcultural analysis of nontraditionalism is correct, we should find that people's personal networks influence their attitudes both directly—the kinds of people they know affect what they believe—and indirectly by selectively transmitting, interpreting, or blocking influences from the wider environment. Two quite different studies illustrate how networks can either filter or magnify climates of opinion. In a survey of attitudes toward school busing for integration, Stephen Weatherford found that people tended to believe as their neighbors believed—whether for or against busing—to the extent to which they talked to their neighbors; otherwise the neighborhood climate made little difference. Myra Ferree found that socially active women tended to be polarized on women's movement issues. Those whose friends were housewives were especially negative, and those whose friends were employed were especially positive.[30]

We have already seen in our data the direct effects of a major network characteristic: kin involvement. Personal traits held constant, the greater the proportion of relatives in respondents' networks, the more traditional their opinions. Attitudes toward the family are also associated with traditional values. For example, respondents who said that it was important to live near relatives (q. 8) were likely to be traditional in their answers to our traditionalism scale questions.

The indirect effects of networks are more subtle and more interesting. People whose networks are generally closed to outside influences tend to be less affected by local climates of opinion than are people with more open networks. We will indicate that openness as the proportion of the network composed of kin. Respondents who were largely involved with kin should have been less affected by climates of opinion than people with more nonkin involvement. Conversely, people whose networks engage them in the community should be most affected by the flux of opinion there. We will indicate this by the percentage of *nonkin* respondents named who lived within a five-minute drive. (Although both a high proportion of kin and a high proportion of local nonkin tended to characterize traditional respondents, their effects on how urbanism influenced opinions were, we shall see, totally different.)

Figure 6 presents the findings. It shows the average traditionalism scores, already adjusted for self-selection and network characteristics, as they vary from the least urban to the most urban respondents. (For ease of reading, the figure simply presents the urban scale rather than the four urban categories.) Respondents are divided into four groups based on whether or not they were heavily involved with kin (if more than 40 percent of the people they named were kin) and whether or not they were heavily involved with local nonkin (if 30 percent or more of the nonkin they named lived within five minutes' drive).

Note that all the lines slope downward; for all groups, the more urban respondents' communities, the less traditional their answers. But the degree to which that is so varies by group. Compare, first, those heavily involved with local nonkin versus those not—the two lines with circled figures versus the two lines without, as bracketed on the right-hand side. The drop in traditionalism is more acute among the former than the latter, among the locally-tied than among those not. In fact, the two pairs of lines clearly cross. In less urban places, locally involved residents were substantially *more* traditional than otherwise similar respondents who were not locally involved, but in the highly urban places the locally involved were *less* traditional. The locally-tied small-town residents were more traditional than they would otherwise be; the locally tied big-city residents were less traditional than they would otherwise be. This pattern is entirely consistent with the proposition that climates of opinion—rural traditionalism and urban liberalism—affect people to the extent to which they are socially tied to local people.

Compare, next, those heavily involved with kin and those not—the two

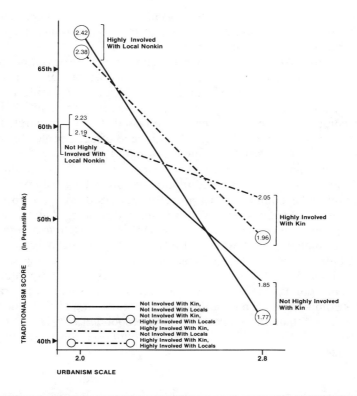

Fig. 6.   **Traditionalism, by urbanism scale, for subgroups based on kin and local involvement (adjusted).**

dash-dot lines to the two solid lines, as bracketed on the left. Although the contrasts are not as strong here and are a little more difficult to see, the drop in traditionalism is in fact less acute among the kin-involved than it is among those with small proportions of kin in their networks. In the least urban places, the kin-involved respondents were about as traditional as other respondents (of equal local ties, 2.19 to 2.23, and 2.38 to 2.42). But in the most urban places, the kin-involved were considerably less traditional than otherwise similar respondents who were not so heavily kin-involved (2.05 versus 1.85; 1.96 versus 1.77). Whatever had influenced the non-kin-involved respondents toward nontraditional attitudes had had much less influence on the kin-involved people.[31]

This complex interaction pattern makes sense if we understand both traditionalism and nontraditionalism as sets of values that we learn from other people—that we absorb from our social environment through the "pores" of our personal relations. It is more difficult to make sense of it if we view nontraditionalism as a release from personal relations, as resulting from a lack of social integration.

A final point. Among the assumptions underlying this explanation is the idea that social values, although always capable of being changed by personal influence, are deeply embedded. If so, they should reflect the opinion climates not only of respondents' current communities, but also of the communities in which they were raised. Earlier research suggests that size of community of origin does indeed affect people's current attitudes and values, sometimes more strongly than does the size of their current community.[32] We asked our respondents to estimate the size of "the kinds of places" they lived in most before the age of sixteen (q. 5). The smaller the community respondents reported growing up in,[33] the more traditional they were. This difference can be explained in part by what happened to people in their communities of origin and since: those raised in smaller places were more likely to have been reared as fundamentalists, received less education, and ended up living in smaller communities than those raised in larger places. All these intervening events and conditions held constant, respondents who were raised in smaller communities tended to answer questions in a slightly more traditional manner than did otherwise similar respondents.[34] This is the "cultural baggage" people bring from their childhood communities to their adult ones.

Conclusion

Of the three classic charges against urban life, that it is psychologically stressful, socially isolating, and morally aberrant, the first two gain little credence from this study. The third, however, is strongly affirmed. This is an especially striking finding, because critics of urban/rural theories are most certain that cultural differences among communities have disappeared or are just about to. Nevertheless, our respondents differed strongly in their social beliefs according to where they lived. The more urban their communities, the more willing they were to tolerate deviation from traditional strictures, such as those censuring premarital sex and homosexuality—and, it seems, the more likely they themselves were to deviate in these and other ways, such as irreligiosity.[35] (We probably underestimated the extent of the difference, since we had no truly rural respondents. National surveys show that rural people are notably more conservative even than residents of small towns.) Moreover, this strong cultural difference can be only partly explained by the personal characteristics of the respondents, the fact that the urbanites were relatively young, well-educated, and so forth. Urbanism itself contributes significantly to this cultural difference.

This finding might lend support to decline of community theory, particularly to the proposition that urbanization breaks down social relations, thereby releasing pepole from the moral inhibitions those relations had imparted and enforced. The questions in our traditionalism scale, all asking whether individuals should be allowed to do as they wish, underline the claim. Affirmative answers—urbanites' answers—seem to endorse normlessness, moral anarchy, and anomie.

There is a different interpretation of these items, however; what is important about them is not their permissiveness, but that each— abortion, sex, marijuana, homosexuality—taps elements of the "progressive" attitudes of our day. (Permissive individualism, in certain realms, is part of contemporary liberalism but is not inherent to it.) What urbanites disproportionately endorse are the newer ideas of the times, whether permissive or not; urbanism fosters novelty, not necessarily license.

There is evidence for the second interpretation. First, urbanites, are consistently more laissez-faire than small-town residents on some issues—abortion, alcohol, free speech for communists, censorship of pornography, and the like—but are less laissez-faire than small-town residents on other issues, such as enforcing civil rights laws, government regulation, and controlling guns. (In our study, for example, urbanites were considerably more willing to urge husbands to do housework than were respondents in smaller communities.)[36] Individual license is not the key; contemporary liberal ideology is.

Second, as the evidence here indicates, social integration does not necessarily promote traditional values. Being involved heavily with kin tends to go consistently with traditionalism. But, overall, social ties are not associated with traditionalism, suggesting that type, not amount, of integration is important. And even type does not account for much of urbanism's nontraditional effect. Moreover, social integration into the local community can—when that community's climate of opinion is nontraditional—weaken commitments to traditional values.

Third, historical evidence suggests that urban/rural cultural differences seem to conform to a value-diffusion model (rather than a value-breakdown model). Much as fashions in skirt length or hair length arise and become popular in cities and later diffuse to the countryside, new social ideas spread from metropolis to hinterland.[37] In some periods those new ideas may not be "liberating" at all. In the nineteenth century, for example, compulsory education, the prison, loyalty to the nation-state, and (according to Arthur Schlesinger, Sr.) the institution of the chaperone spread from urban to rural places. This evidence that new values arise and diffuse is inconsistent with the notion that one set of values exists and then breaks down.

All this is instead consistent with the theory that new ideas, behaviors, and values are created in urban centers, created in innovative sub-cultures. If so, they must necessarily be "nontraditional" and must be so all the time, because, even as this new idea becomes the tradition—over ten, fifty, or a hundred years—deviations from it, sometimes for better and sometimes for worse, are arising in the urban centers.

III   The Social Contexts of Personal Networks

7   Kin

The thrust of our findings in part 2 is that private lives in city and in small town differ not in quality but in style. Other characteristics being equal, residents of urban centers seem as psychologically well adjusted and as socially integrated as residents of the hinterland, but they are less likely to endorse and act in traditional ways. Similarly, and not by coincidence, city and small-town people differ also in the kinds—if not the amount—of personal relations they have and in the kinds of social worlds they inhabit. Part 3 begins exploration of how these social worlds vary by focusing on the *primary social contexts* of personal relations.

Primary social contexts are the major settings for personal relations—kinship, work, neighborhood, voluntary organization, or unstructured "friendship" (see chap. 3). Although context is typically the setting in which two people first meet,[1] it more importantly describes the terms under which they maintain their connection—where they see each other, the tasks they share, who else may be involved, the contingencies of their relation, and so on. Culture imposes additional conditions on the relation, conditions that vary according to context. There are expectations concerning how kin, neighbors, and so forth are supposed to behave toward one another. While people often ignore the rules of these "role relations," most often they conform, and in all cases they must consider the cultural prescriptions.

Structural opportunities and constraints, in addition to individual personality and preferences, determine with whom—that is, with people from what social context—individuals will associate. Workers, for example, quite obviously have a whole set of potential associates that nonworking people do not have. People still living in the communities in which they grew up typically have much easier access to relatives and to old school friends than do people who have moved on. The well-to-do can sustain social ties with associates from a wider spatial area than can people whose financial situations restrict their travel. Similarly, childless adults have more time to maintain friendships than do parents (especially, our data show, than do mothers of young children).[2] I will argue that community, notably urbanism, also affects the social contexts from which people draw their relations, albeit far more weakly than social class, life cycle, and other personal traits. Specifically, urbanism tends to expand people's opportunities for building social ties beyond the family and the neighborhood.

This chapter focuses on kinship ties: Who tends to be involved with kin, with what kinds of kin, and what do people receive from kin? Part of classic decline of community theory is the claim that urbanism weakens the family. Some aspects of that claim are supported by our findings.

Kinship

Kinship is, and has always been, the critical distinction people make among social relations. The differences between kin and nonkin are many and far-reaching. An accident of birth gives us a set of consanguine relations that can never, at least formally, be sundered. An accident of our spouses' births gives us affinal relations that are also difficult to break. While friends can be chosen and abandoned, relatives are imposed and presumably forever. What we owe to and what we can expect from relatives involves far more commitment, trust, and sacrifice than is the case with nonrelatives. We are even expected to assist kin whom we dislike or have never met.

To be sure, these rules are often breached. Many people in our sample were estranged from their relatives. For example, one woman claimed that none of her relatives was "important" to her because of a family feud over committing her grandmother to a sanitarium and disposing of the grandmother's tiny estate. Other respondents did not have to feud; they simply ignored their kin. Nevertheless, kinship is empirically critical. People largely maintain kin ties out of a sense of concern and obligation, whereas they maintain nonkin ties because of compatibility and enjoyment.[3] People usually turn to nonrelatives for sociability and casual assistance, but they commonly go to relatives for costly and critical help.[4] In our study, for example, kin constituted 26 percent of the people whom respondents saw socially, 48 percent of the people to whom respondents confided personal worries, but 67 percent of the people from whom respondents could borrow money.

Kin are treated differently from nonkin. And people who are heavily involved with kin are different from those who are heavily involved with nonkin. For most of our analysis here, we will measure kin involvement as the number of relatives respondents named who lived *outside* their households. (The basic findings are essentially the same if we include all kin.) Not surprisingly, married people named more kin than did the widowed or divorced, who in turn named more kin than the never married. Women named slightly more than men. Middle-income respondents named more than either low- or high-income respondents. And those who estimated that they had several relatives living in the general vicinity (q. 2) named more than those respondents who estimated only a few or none. (Having many relatives in the area was most common for respondents who had lived a long time in the same city and for less-educated respondents).[5]

It appears that kin were largely "given" to respondents rather than chosen by them. That is, number of kin in the vicinity and marital status largely determined how many kin people dealt with. (Perhaps more precisely, the fecundity of people's parents and parents-in-law determined the number of kin.) In contrast, the number of nonkin whom respondents named was determined by a variety of factors, some reflecting preference or cultural style (see next chapter).[6] Respondents who had left their communities of origin did thereby reduce their involvement with kin, but little else in the way of personal discretion made much difference.

Urbanism and Kinship

The "breakdown of the family" has long been a subplot of the decline of community drama. Portents of disintegration abound: rising divorce rates, special homes for the elderly, young adults living alone or out of wedlock, and many other modern developments mock our memories of warm and tightly knit families. Historians have been busy recently challenging those memories and reinterpreting those portents. But the proposition remains a powerful one: modernization and urbanization break down the family through strains that drive members apart and seductions that pull them apart. Breakdown means, ultimately, that kin care for one another less, share with one another less, and sacrifice for one another less. This study can speak only to the issue of urbanism, of course, and only to certain dimensions of family life.

The more urban respondents' communities (at least, beyond the Town level), the fewer kin they named; see the solid line at the top of figure 7.[7] Adjusting the data for personal traits (*not* including number of kin living in the area) yields the dashed line in the figure. Had respondents been similar in age, income, and so forth, residents of more urban places would still have averaged fewer relatives in their networks than residents of less urban places.[8] If we adjust for number kin estimated to live nearby, the conclusion remains the same:[9] living in especially urban communities apparently reduced involvement with kin.[10]

Why? A few explanations can be eliminated. One is that Town and Semirural respondents were more willing to list kin for propriety's sake but were not seriously involved with kin. This is partly true, but the

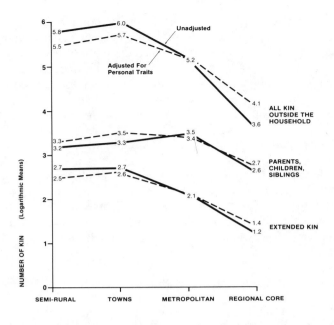

Fig. 7.   **Number of kin respondents named, by urbanism.**

community difference appears even if we count only relatives named in answer to specific exchange questions (rather than in answer to the catch-all question, "Is there anyone important to you...?").[11] Similarly, if we count only those kin whom respondents said they felt "especially close to" small-town respondents still named the most.[12] A second explanation is that family-oriented people choose to live in small communities and those who are not family oriented choose to live in cities. This is plausible; Semirural and Town respondents were especially likely and Core respondents were especially unlikely to agree that "it is important to live close to relatives and see a lot of them" (q. 8).[13] And the least urban respondents were the most likely to have moved to their communities because of kin (see chap. 2). Nevertheless, whatever respondents' views on this matter, the more urban respondents tended to name fewer kin than the less urban ones.[14] Also, if we exclude the 167 respondents who apparently moved for kinship reasons—having moved to their current cities in the previous ten years and given as one reason "being near relatives or friends"—the trend is still the same.[15] Self-selection by familism does not explain why urban residence went together with few kin ties. A third explanation is family size. Traditionally, urban-ites have had fewer children—and fewer siblings, in-laws, cousins—than

more rural people. Although we do not know the actual size of respondents' extended families, we do have their estimates of how many of
their relatives lived within an hour's drive. We also know which of the kin
they specifically named lived within an hour's drive. No matter the
number of kin in the vicinity, urban respondents named fewer of them
than did Semirural or Town respondents.[16] City people apparently associated with fewer relatives than they actually had available to them.

The explanation, in sum, seems to be that urban life encourages people
to "disregard" kin. (The reader may choose to label this "disregard"
either as liberation from constraining kinship obligations or as deser-
tion of loving kin.) Urban life, I suggest by way of explanation,
provides alternatives to relatives—personal alternatives, as in nonkin friends, and perhaps institutional alternatives, as in recreational
activies. Consequently, kin are less likely to appear in the daily lives
of urbanites and more likely to appear in those of rural people. This
explanation is similar to the thesis of family breakdown but differs in
subtle and important ways. For one, I am suggesting that kin ties are
replaced by nonkin ties. Most critically, I am arguing that kinship involvement becomes selective concerning with whom and when people
will be involved. Urban people, no less than rural people, *can* call upon
kin (setting aside the question of family size), but they have less occasion
to do so. They can be more selective in deciding when to mobilize which
specific kin relations for which specific purposes. As a rural sociologist
has put it, "The very structure of urban society permits the individual to
cultivate, with some impunity, the interpersonal relations he deems most
important, whether they be with kin or with friend."[17]

Most versions of the breakdown thesis seem to suggest that kinship ties
have unraveled all around the individual, almost indiscriminately, and
that they are unavailable precisely when the individual most needs them.
In contrast, I am suggesting that kinship ties continue unactivated until
needed; it is in crisis that they are especially active. Compared with rural
kinship, urban kinship is slightly more voluntary. In an important sense,
of course, voluntary kinship—for example, not feeling obliged to visit
one's uncle and aunt every week—is debilitated kinship. Certainly the
avant-garde urban ideology discussed in the last chapter endorses such
freedom from obligation. Also, kinship relations left dormant long enough
may wither away altogether. In these respects, my argument and the
breakdown argument are similar. But the subtle differences concerning
selectivity are critical.

One finding that testifies to this theoretical difference is shown in figure
7, where genealogically close relatives—parents, children, and siblings—
are distinguished from other kin. The more urban respondents named
notably fewer extended kin than did the less urban respondents—Core

people named 57 percent fewer, on average, than Semirural people—but the community differences were considerably smaller for nuclear kin. Only Core respondents differed, and they named only 21 percent fewer nuclear kin than did Semirural respondents. Furthermore, this difference in nuclear kin can probably be accounted for by the fact that Core respondents tended to live considerably farther from their nuclear kin than did other respondents.[18] The point seems to be that urbanites were more likely to "shed" extended rather than nuclear kin, indicating some degree of selectivity.

Urbanites also manifested such selectivity with respect to the specific situations in which they would turn to kin. Although city respondents named, on average, fewer relatives in answer to each question than small-town respondents did, the difference between them was narrower in answer to two specific questions: Whose opinion do you consider seriously in making important decisions? and Who could you ask to lend you money? These "crises" called forth almost as many kin in big as in small communities, unlike the everyday situations, such as social activities, in which small-town people were much more involved with kin that were big-city people.[19] This finding is consistent with those reported from urban surveys showing that people typically turn to relatives in crises or when requesting a major sacrifice, when, for instance, they need someone to nurse them through an illness.[20] (In one of our pilot surveys, we asked respondents whom they might ask to nurse them after an operation. The kinds of people named were much the same as those who could lend money; 62 percent, for example, were kin.)[21] I am suggesting here that this discrimination is slightly greater in urban places than in nonurban places where kin are active in more ways.

Finally, how much of a difference urbanism makes in respondents' involvements with kin depended on the specific type of kin. Urban respondents were less likely than small-town respondents to report feeling close to, relying greatly on, or getting together often with the *parents* they named. Put another way, urban respondents were more likely to name parents to whom they did not feel close, did not often turn to, or did not often see. But there was no consistent pattern with respect to other types of kin. For instance, city and small-town respondents did not differ in how involved they were with siblings they named.[22] (Perhaps this special estrangement from parents arose from clashes in traditional versus modern life-styles.)

These findings lend some weight to the claim that the decline in kin involvement with greater urbanism is less a sign of family disintegration and more a sign of selective family integration.

Aggregative Effects

To this point we have established that living in more urban communities tended to reduce the number of kin—especially extended kin—respondents named. The effect is substantial, in the sense that Core respondents named almost 40 percent fewer relatives than did Semirural respondents—25 percent fewer, adjusting for self-selection. Yet these findings may still underestimate the full implications of the difference. Those implications concern the cumulative, or aggregative, effects of the urban tendency to disregard kin.

One such effect concerns the tone of the respondents' entire networks, whether or not the social milieus in which they operated tended to be familistic. We can indicate whether respondents were immersed in such a familistic world by simply considering which respondents named more kin than nonkin; 34 percent did. (Whether respondents' networks were mostly kin was, of course, determined by both the extent of their involvement with kin and, even more, the extent of their involvement with nonkin, which will be discussed in the next chapter.) Those who did were typically married, often parents, living near many relatives, less educated, not currently employed, women, and middle-aged (if women) or elderly (if male). They were also typically residents of less urban places: 47 percent of Semirural, 42 percent of Town, 32 percent of Metropolitan, and only 13 percent of Core respondents had networks composed mostly of kin. That is, while one of every two Semirural respondents lived in a largely familistic personal world, only one of every eight Core respondents did. This difference can be largely accounted for by differences in marital status, education, and so forth. Nevertheless, even had our respondents been identical in all those respects, the most urban ones would still have been less likely to have majority kin networks.[23]

But in the real world (as opposed to the statistically adjusted world) the difference in kin involvement has another aggregative effect. Whatever the sources of kin involvement, the concentration in one place of people whose social lives focus on kin creates a special atmosphere and way of life that have consequences of their own. The community in our sample whose residents averaged the greatest number of relatives was an area of extremely rapid growth about fifty minutes' drive from San Francisco—an "exploding area on the urban frontier," in the words of one observer. It had, in 1977, acres of newly built and partly built moderately priced homes, busy shopping centers, overcrowded schools, children on tricycles all over the sidewalks, and a "kaffee-klatsch" atmosphere. One informant commented that "families in this area seem to be in the age range twenty-five to fifty and raising children. There are so many children that friendships are easy to make. Neighbors seem to help each other."

Another pointed out that "people have to travel too far to work, are too far in debt with house payments and over-buying." The second most kin-involved place was a similar community thirty minutes farther from San Francisco. The third typified a different kind of kin-oriented community, a small town. It was a literally dusty town on the edge of a slightly larger agricultural center, with virtually no stores or services of its own. Residents were exclusively white and almost exclusively low-income family members and retirees who lived in patched-up bungalows or in trailers. An interviewer noted: "Some people really enjoy the quiet, slow pace; others find it dead and boring.... There is an amazing stillness in the air. A police officer mentioned to me that it is an unforgiving community and that once a person does something wrong, it's not likely to be forgotten."

At the other extreme, the three communities whose residents named the lowest average number of relatives are true center-city neighborhoods, two in San Francisco and one in the East Bay. Their housing was dense—deteriorating or rehabilitated old houses or new apartment buildings. The residents were an urban mélange of low-income young whites, largely single or childless and quite often homosexual. The streets were lined with restaurants, coffee houses, record stores, and other services. The ambience of these places was radically different from that of the familistic neighborhoods.

The influences between a residential community and the personal lives of its residents run, of course, both ways. In one direction, residents shape a neighborhood. As unattached adults replace families in an area, for instance, they attract commercial services and reduce the number of children on the street. But communities also shape residents' personal lives. As childless people continue to move in, the earlier arrivals find more compatible neighbors, and yet more services spring up to cater to their needs. Meanwhile, the remaining families find that it is harder to meet people like themselves, that stores which had served them disappear, that it is too expensive for their relatives to live nearby, and that the ambience encourages public consumption over private familism. In ways such as these, by services, the example of neighbors, and "atmosphere," places encourage consistent ways of life. And even for the residents who maintain their own unique ways, life involves coping with the ways of others—children in the driveways of family neighborhoods, expensive boutiques in young single's neighborhoods; loud family arguments in the first, unconventional public behavior in the second. By such processes the aggregation of kin- or nonkin-oriented people affect the experiences of all people. The former tend to aggregate in less urban places, the latter in more urban places.

Conclusion

Among respondents to our study, stage in the life cycle and number of relatives in the vicinity basically determined the number of relatives they named. In other words, how many kin people were involved with largely depended on how many kin they had. Within these limits, other social characteristics made little difference. Men were slightly less involved with kin than were women; high-income people less than middle-income people; those who had moved away from their communities of origin—and thus from their kin of origin—than those who stayed. And urban residents were less involved with kin than were Town or Semirural residents.

Is this evidence of the breakdown of the family, itself part of the decline of community? Possibly. (This certainly contradicts one particular version of decline of community theory, the argument that modernization and urbanization have scared people into retreating from public life to private family life.)[24] But this could instead be evidence of increased kin selectivity. Urban residents, like men, the well-to-do, and the residentially mobile, have more social options outside the family than do small-town residents. They are also, given the evidence of the last chapter, less compelled by local values to embrace all kin. Urbanites can be more selective. In line with this claim, Core respondents were more likely to consider the kin they did name as "friends" than were Town or Semirural residents; that is, they were less likely to include kin who were only kin. In fact, in terms of the kin "friends" respondents named, there were barely any community differences.[25] Urban residents were also more likely, as we saw, to discriminate between nuclear and extended kin and to be selective with respect to which interaction they called upon kin for.

This disengagement from extended kin, according to most decline theorists, leaves a vacuum in people's social worlds. Robert Nisbet writes, for example, that, while kin and neighborhood groups have weakened, "their place has not been taken to any appreciable extent by new forms of association."[26] In our survey, at least, this vacuum does not appear. Respondents who reported few kin the vicinity tended to be heavily involved instead with nonkin (see next chapter). Also, the degree of social support respondents could expect from people outside their households (see chap. 11) depended more on how many nonkin they named than on how many kin. Nevertheless, the substitution of nonkin for kin may have deeper consequences. Nisbet writes that with "the failure of new social relationships to assume influences of equivalent evocative intensity, a profound change has occurred in the very psychological structure of society."[27] Although our survey hardly taps this psychological structure in depth, we can say that nonkin ties tend to accompany feelings of well-being at least as strongly as do kin ties.[28]

Although our individual respondents show no personal ill effects (and perhaps good effects) of substituting nonkin for some kin ties, the collective effects may be quite different. One such effect is to create local social climates. Some neighborhoods are familistic and others are nonfamilistic. The latter are especially likely to be urban places, in part because of selective migration and in part because of urbanism itself. And there is another potential consequence: kinship has always been the essential interpersonal glue of society; friendships can be seen as luxuries people develop in times of security, affluence, and freedom. One wonders about how strong unexercised kin ties will be in times of social trauma. If economic collapse, war, mass migration, or some other catastrophe struck northern California, could these people, particularly the city-dwellers, rely on their otherwise inactive kinship relations for survival? That our respondents did maintain ties with nuclear kin and that they felt they could call upon them in an emergency is reassuring. So are the findings from social histories that past generations have been able to activate latent kinship ties in crises. But the question lingers: Can families that do not play together survive together?

8   Nonkin

If people's involvement with relatives is largely ascribed by circumstances—albeit less so for urban people—the contrary seems true of involvement with nonkin. Individual taste, social skill, and character shape the number and the kinds of friends and acquaintances people have. Interviewers' descriptions of our most socially active respondents convey some sense of their especially affable personalities. There was, for example, the young middle-class "go-getter":

The respondent spends a lot of time jogging, swimming, and playing tennis, and he loves to ski. In addition, he enjoys wine-tasting and -collecting and is very knowledgeable about wines. He grew up in [this suburb of San Francisco] but says it is not at all important to him to have family near. He, in fact, would rather not, does not like to feel obligated to attend family dinners. He does have several friends whom he enjoys seeing often. His manner was friendly and open and he said he likes people, likes to work with people. He is currently working as a bond salesman while he finishes his master's degree in education.

Quite different in style was this young working-class man:

The respondents is a wavy-haired, bearded young man who apparently loves animals—befriends and feeds strays, has three cats I think, but never changes the kitty box. His ramshackle one-story tract house was truly a public health menace. Three bags of garbage sat in the kitchen, the kitty box was under the kitchen table, and sundry beer bottles and other debris were scattered about . . . . Two young girls were visiting when I arrived and talked to me while the respondent made a phone call. He has a passion for old cars. He has five, all in various stages of rebuilding and all modified. They are his chief worry and expense. His wife left him a few months ago, taking their child. He has an "open house" policy—people drifting in and out—sort of like the stray animals he befriends.

There are many other individual patterns: the successful professional with a long list of colleagues and contacts; the small-town storeowner whose shop was the local men's hangout and loan office; and the elderly churchgoer who named all the members of the choir.

Personality is important, but external circumstances also firmly shape individuals' social involvement. Current circumstances—working on an assembly line or in an office, being youthfully vigorous or agedly fragile, having children to put to bed or no one waiting at home, needing to ration each dollar or having plenty of play money, and so forth—as well as past circumstances, help determine how many and what types of people the individual can meet and how easily he or she can continue to see those people. Such circumstances structure the opportunities for and constraints on individual choice in making and maintaining social ties.

Such structural effects can be simply illustrated by the case of employment. Table 2 shows approximately how many associates respondents had met in each of a few different ways. It compares two groups of respondents, those fully employed at the time of the interview, and those who were keeping house.[1] (The results for retirees, by the way, look similar to those for homemakers.) Obviously, homemakers had met far fewer people at work than had respondents employed outside the home; an entire social context was closed to them. They were also less likely to have met people through a friend, perhaps because many of the friends who introduce people to one another are work friends. Instead, homemakers turned to kin and neighbors. And yet those alternatives did not fully compensate for their being homebound. In the eighteen months before the interview, homemakers had formed about one fewer social tie than had full-time workers (2.0 versus 2.7).

In other ways as well, meeting nonkin depended largely on access to social settings. For example, childhood friends were disproportionately likely to be named by young respondents and those who had not moved away from home since their youth; school friends by respondents who were currently in school or who had gone to several schools (i.e., respondents with advanced degrees); associates met as neighbors by veteran residents of the neighborhoods; and people met through spouses by married or widowed respondents. Young respondents were especially likely to have formed ties through common friends. Of 16- to 21-year-olds' nonkin associates, 26 percent were introduced by a friend, compared with 10 percent for respondents over 64. Probably the differences in time, energy, competing commitments, and disposable income available to people of different ages (as well as the reduction, with age, in friends who could serve as introducers; see p. 115) account for the contrast. These factors, too, free or constrain people in forming social networks.

Community of residence, I have been arguing, also molds the opportunities for and constraints on forming relations, though it is far weaker and more indirect than circumstances such as employment. Mostly, commu-

Table 2	Approximate Average Number of People Respondents Had Met by How They Had Met, for Full-Time Workers and Homemakers[a]		

		Full-Time Workers (N = 550)	Homemakers (N = 149)
How Met	At Work	3.4	0.3
	Through Friend	2.5	1.2
	As Neighbors	2.5	4.4
	Through Spouse or Child	0.8	1.4
	As Kin	6.2	7.8
	Other Ways	3.5	3.5
		The Only People Met in Previous Eighteen Months	
How Met	At Work	0.7	0.0
	Through Friend	0.7	0.2
	As Neighbors	0.7	1.2
	Through Spouse or Child	0.1	0.2
	Other	0.6	0.2

[a]See note 1 for explanation of how figures were calculated.

nity influences the kinds of nonkin that people become involved with rather than the total number of nonkin. This chapter, however, will focus on general nonkin involvement, serving thereby as an overview of the next two chapters' consideration of specific social contexts.

Total Nonkin Involvement

Who tended to be involved with many nonkin? Affluent people and educated respondents were much more heavily involved with nonkin that were otherwise similar respondents of lesser social standing; and both education and income independently contributed to knowing many nonkin. Other factors constant, young respondents named more nonkin than older ones did, though age and gender combined in a complex way: under forty, men named more than women; over forty, the opposite was true.[2] Employed respondents named more than did nonworking respondents; non-Hispanic whites named more than respondents of other groups; and respondents with few relatives living nearby named more friends and acquaintances than did those with many nearby kin. Finally, cooperative respondents named more nonkin than did uncooperative ones (which may be seen as an accident of our technique or as a reflection of respondents' personalities).[3]

Most of these differences can be interpreted as varying opportunities and constraints. That certainly seems to be the case with income and employment. Kin in the vicinity apparently limit individuals' opportunities—or needs—to have nonkin ties (recall the young man's comment on family dinners early in this chapter). Women were slightly more inhibited by relatives in the vicinity than men were, perhaps because the normative obligation to keep in touch with kin is stronger for women.[4] Other differences might be interpreted as reflecting personality or structure or both. Take education, for example. Other studies have also shown that educated people are involved with larger numbers and more diverse types of nonrelatives than are comparatively uneducated people. This difference is often attributed to the social skills educated people tend to have: self-confidence and grace in approaching strangers and expanding acquaintanceships, sensitivity in dealing with the psychological nuances of personal relations, cognitive flexibility in managing intersecting social commitments, and so forth.[5] But there are also structural advantages that accrue with education. One who has been through high school, through college, and through a postgraduate program has been exposed to at least one, two, or three more sets of potential friends and acquaintances than the person who finished only grade school (and has been exposed in the circumstances most favorable for cultivating friendships). Education, aside from what it may do to people psychologically, is a source of great social opportunity.[6]

Urbanism and Nonkin

The subcultural theory of urbanism I have proposed suggests that, because urban residence also provides access to potential associates, it should also increase people's involvement with nonkin. This turns out to be only conditionally correct—for certain types of people, for certain types of associates.

A reader who turns back to figure 4 (p. 57) will see the overall findings. The more urban their communities were, the more nonkin respondents named—an increase of about 50 percent from the average for Semirural respondents to the average for Core respondents. This pattern can be wholly explained, however, by the education, youth, and income of urban residents. Were respondents in all places equal in these respects, they would not have differed in nonkin involvement.[7] (Urbanism might still be an important indirect cause of nonkin involvement. If city life encourages

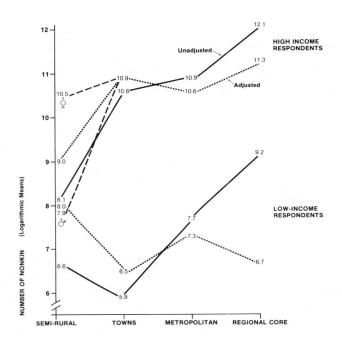

Fig. 8.   **Number of nonkin named, by urbanism, for high- and low-income respondents.**

residents to become educated, provides high-paying jobs, and attracts sociable young people, it can be said to cause increased social ties. But it would not do so directly, by providing access to potential associates.)[8]

A few of the complications are illustrated in figure 8, where the results are separately presented for low- and high-income respondents (divided at $15,000 of household income, 1977—roughly $22,000 in 1981 dollars). Among both groups, urban residents named more nonkin than did residents of smaller places (shown in the solid lines). When education, age, and the like are held constant, the greater involvement of urbanites disappears (broken lines). In fact, among low-income respondents, Semirural residents reported the highest (adjusted) average of nonkin. As we shall see in the next two chapters, this advantage of Semirural residents largely accrued because of their involvement with fellow church members and, to a lesser extent, neighbors. Among high-income respondents, Semirural residents named fewer (adjusted) nonkin than did others. (In fact, were high- and low-income respondents otherwise similar in age, education, and so forth, affluent Semirural respondents would have named *fewer* nonkin than nonaffluent ones.) Upon closer inspection, it turns out that affluent men in Semirural places named remarkably few nonkin (after adjustment; see male and female symbols in figure 8).[9] I have been unable to explain fully why this was so, but the fact that affluent small-town men were not involved with church associates was one likely contributor to their isolation.

Other variations appear when the respondents are divided by age. Among those under thirty-six, the more urban the respondents, the more nonkin they named. (This was especially true for young married people without children.) But residence made no difference in the involvement of respondents thirty-six to sixty-four years old. Holding constant education, income, and the like weakens but does not eliminate this contrast: for the middle-aged, living in the Core slightly depressed nonkin involvement; for the young, living in Semirural places depressed nonkin involvement.[10]

Some of these complexities become simplified when we break down the general category of nonkin into its primary social context components. (Other complexities will, of course, emerge.) Figure 9 does precisely that for respondents from each type of community. It is immediately apparent that residence is differentially associated with the various components. As urbanism goes up, the average number of neighbors drops (from 25 percent to 13 percent of all nonkin), organizational members are roughly constant, but co-workers increase, as do "others" and, especiallly, "just friends." The principles explaining the connections between urbanism and each type of involvement are probably different. Certainly the theoretical arguments involved in the controversy about urbanism and personal relations treat some of these contexts quite differently. The next two chapters are devoted to exploring those separate principles and arguments.

Aggregation

Before proceeding with those detailed examinations, we should pause to consider, as we did in the previous chapter, how the residential differences described here—whatever their causes—affect community life. Two of the places with the highest average number of nonkin were Core communities, one in San Francisco and the other in the East Bay.

The latter is on the verdant western slope of the hills that run north and south several miles east of the bay. It is populated by professionals of various ages who live in large and stately houses (though some of the older homes have been subdivided). The houses are laid out on winding,

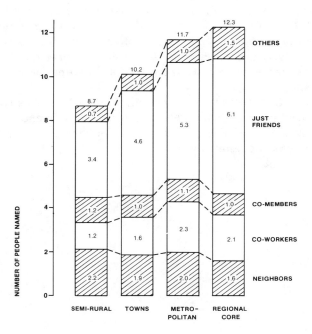

Fig. 9.   **Average composition of nonkin networks, by urbanism.**

leafy streets, from which at various turns picture-postcard views of the Golden Gate and "the city" can be glimpsed. The community exudes an atmosphere of cosmopolitanism and affluence. Typically—or perhaps stereotypically—residents of this community are the kind who shop at gourmet delicacy stores, attend the ballet, believe in "self-actualization," send their children to private schools, and engage in politics that have been labeled "limousine liberalism." The respondents here named considerably more nonkin, on average, than did respondents anywhere else.

The San Francisco example is a neighborhood close to the city's main tourist attractions. It is densely built with restored, repainted Victorians, graceful art deco apartment buildings (with twelve-foot ceilings), and a few less graceful modern buildings (with eight-foot ceilings). Although there are families and well-to-do senior citizens, young, childless adults, typically well-educated and somewhat affluent, dominate the area. The district is noted for the chic shopping, dating, and entertainment street that runs down its center and that is constantly jammed with cars and pedestrians. In 1977 I noted the following establishments, among others, in the space of three or four blocks: hair stylist, antique store, grocery store, fabric store, law offices, chair store, clothing store, stereo store, glass-blowing shop, furniture store, real estate office, optometrist, kitchenware store, bank, pie shop, picture-framing store, two movie houses, and a few coffee shops.[11]

Whatever the sources of these two communities' characters, the private lives of their residents are both the causes and the consequences of a distinct community life, one with a focus on the public, outside world rather than on the domestic family circle.

9   Varieties of Nonkin: Neighbors and Co-Workers

The structural circumstances that encourage people to build relations in one context sometimes impair their ability to build relations in another context. Full-time workers, for example, were especially likely to be involved with people they had met on the job, but especially unlikely to be involved with neighbors. Theoretical concerns also lead us to distinguish among contexts. Decline of community arguments typically stress modern urban individuals' loss of connection to "natural" and multifaceted groups, such as neighbors and friends, and their desperate substitution of functional and formal associations, such as co-workers and voluntary organizations. The subcultural theory I have argued suggests somewhat similar urban/rural differences, but it derives those predictions from a different principle: the expansion of individuals' range of choice in making and maintaining personal relations.

This chapter and the next explore the sources of people's involvements with different varieties of nonkin and, particularly, the role of urbanism in supporting those involvements. The varieties are discussed roughly in order of voluntarism, from the given set of neighbors to the chosen set of "just friends."

Neighbors

A 1976 letter to the editor of the *Los Angeles Times* touched a deeply felt concern among Americans: "There is a terrible sense of 'losing our roots' today. Could we not make once again neighborhoods into 'real' neighborhoods where people know each other and care about each other as our forefathers surely did. . . . Think what healing this would bring to the sickness of our times—loneliness, isolation, and lack of roots." Whether this statement is historically accurate or not, the absence of involvement with neighbors is a frequent complaint about city life.[1] A high-school teacher told one of our interviewers that the worst thing about living in San Francisco was "the fact that it is a city: I just don't know my neighbors. That's what appeals to me about a small town."

Classic theories of community echo these views. In the village of bygone days, people were deeply involved with neighbors. Functionally interdependent and familiar since childhood, neighbors knew each other well, saw each other often, and relied on one another greatly. In the modern city, neighbors are just vaguely familiar strangers. They scarcely know, hardly see, and rarely depend on one another. This leaves the modern urbanite bereft of important material, social, and emotional support. An alternative view, congruent with subcultural theory, agrees that modern and urban people are less involved with neighbors, but it interprets the differences in another way. The bygone village required involvements with neighbors; if not neighbors, who else? The modern city allows neighbor involvement, but it also allows involvement beyond the neighborhood, as people wish. And there is no reason to suppose that the freely chosen extraneighborhood ties are any less supportive than the neighborhood ties urbanites continue to have.[2] (Chap. 13 will explore in more depth these theoretical concerns about the local community as the "authentic" community.)

Despite popular ideas about natural or "real" neighborhoods, intense involvement with neighbors was far from typical, even in our small towns. Virtually all our respondents had chatted with a neighbor out of doors in the few months before the interview, and most had dropped in on, or been dropped in on by, a neighbor. But only half the respondents said they ever borrowed "something small, like a cup of sugar or a few nails" from their neighbors.[3] And many of the neighbors whom respondents named—about a third—were named in answer to only one specific question: who they would ask to care for their homes when away.

We skirted the problem of defining "neighbor" by letting respondents define it. Neighbors were people whom respondents called "neighbor" in answering the question, "How is (NAME) connected with you now?" (q. 80), and whom they did not also label a relative or co-worker. (As it turned out, respondents reported that 8 percent of their "neighbors" lived more than five minutes' drive away, so there is some error here.) We defined the "neighborhood" in the analysis more exactly, as a set of households (usually between fifty and two hundred) in a single, coherent, and relatively bounded area, ranging in size from a single apartment building to several intersecting streets. (For more detail, see Methodological Appendix sections 1.5 and 3.2.)

Explanations of involvement with neighbors focus (aside from personal sociability) on people's competing commitments to, and their experience in, the neighborhood versus the world outside. For example, longtime residents and parents with young children should be relatively more involved, because they are more tied to the place. Much of this thinking, in contrast to that of the decline school, treats neighbor relations as residual, relations people have in addition to, or instead of, more rewarding ties outside the neighborhood. Suzanne Keller has argued, for instance, that middle-class people tend to know more neighbors in a casual way than working-class people do, but that the latter are more likely to be dependent on one or two neighbors. There is evidence, from this study and others, to back that view.[4]

Respondents named 1.3 neighbors, on the average (logarithmic mean). Longtime residents of the neighborhood, new arrivals in the city, people not working full time, married respondents, educated respondents, and homeowners (essentially equivalent to residents of single-family houses) were especially likely, all else equal, to name neighbors. Purposeful self-selection also played a role: respondents who had given "the kind of people here" as a reason for moving into the neighborhood within the previous ten years named slightly more neighbors, on average, than did otherwise similar people.[5] (There is also self-selection by moving out, as in the case of the elderly woman who was going to leave her suburban neighborhood, in part, she said, because none of the neighbors had expressed any concern about her husband's heart attack.)

These differences affirm the competing commitments interpretation: full-time workers are drawn outside the neighborhood, while married people, homeowners, and old-timers tend to be committed to it. An intriguing complication underlines the point: respondents new to the neighborhood and new to the city reported more neighbors, on the average, than did respondents who had recently moved to the neighborhood from elsewhere in the same city.[6] This illustrates competing commitments: the local mover is still involved with the same kin, co-workers, and even ex-neighbors as before and tends to ignore the new neighbors. The long-distance mover is far from old ties and often looks to new neighbors for replacements.

Neighboring and Community

Neighborhoods also differ in the involvement residents have with one another. In two of our neighborhoods, for example, respondents named an average of more than four neighbors. One neighborhood was a relatively new development of modest single-family homes, inhabited by young families, and situated in one of the most distant communities in the sample. The town is part of the rapidly growing resort and retirement area of the Sierras. The other example is also a quiet, family neighborhood with somewhat more spacious and slightly older single-family homes. It lies near the downtown of an explosively growing city an hour from San Francisco. At the other extreme, for example, residents of one neighborhood averaged less than one neighbor apiece. This area is a block of large, moderate-rent apartment buildings near a freeway inter-

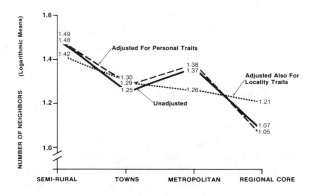

Fig. 10.   **Number of neighbors named, by urbanism.**

section and an industrial park in a close suburb of San Francisco. The residents of this noisy and somewhat dangerous block were childless adults of various ages. A divorcee who lived in this neighborhood told the interviewer "the neighborhood was fine for her because she was never at home. None of her friends live in the neighborhood and if she did spend much time at home, it would drive her crazy." Certain idiosyncrasies also affected neighborhood sociability. In one town, respondents complained of cold and clannish neighbors, characteristics they attributed to Scandinavian heritage. But generally the neighborly neighborhoods were homogeneous, not very dense, full of children, and growing rapidly.[7]

Neighborly neighborhoods tended also to be in the less urban communities. As the solid line in figure 10 shows, Semirural respondents named the most (1.5) and Core respondents named the fewest (1.1) neighbors.[8] Taking into account personal differences—length of residence, education, and so forth—does not change the pattern much. Taking account of homeownership does; one reason Core residents named few neighbors is that they tended to be renters. All things considered—the dashed line—however, had respondents everywhere been equal in background, homeownership, and motivation for moving, the Core residents would still have named slightly fewer neighbors than average.[9]

What about Core neighborhoods depressed involvement with neighbors? One factor seems to be heterogeneity. Homogeneity in style of life promoted neighborhood involvement, and Core neighborhoods were least likely to be homogeneous. More important was growth. Residents of rapidly growing neighborhoods were most involved with their neighbors, but Core neighborhoods were not growing. (Many were actually declining in total population.) When these local characteristics are taken into account, neighborhood involvement is roughly equal among the types of communities, as indicated by the dotted line in figure 10. (Although the figure shows a steady decline, the trend is not substantial.)[10]

But where does that leave the theoretical speculations that urbanism reduces neighborhood involvement, either because of social disintegration or because of wider choice? It leaves those theories searching for confirmation in more subtle aspects of the results. On the part of subcultural theory, three such subtleties will be considered: that urbanism reduces the proportional role of neighbors in people's social worlds, that it reduces neighbor involvement for certain groups of people, and that it leads to more selective involvement with neighbors.

About one-fourth of the respondents might be said to have had neighbor-centered networks, in that at least 30 percent of the nonkin each of them named were neighbors (over twice the proportion of most respondents).[11] These people were most likely to have lived in Semirural communities and least likely to have lived in Core communities. Forty percent of Semirural respondents, 26 percent of Town, 24 percent of Metropolitan, and 13 percent of Core respondents had neighbor-centered networks. Adjusting for self-selection factors and characteristics of the neighborhoods narrows this difference but does not eliminate it. (All else equal, 34 percent of Semirural respondents would have had neighbor-centered networks, compared with 19 percent of Core respondents.)[12] The implication is that urbanism alone may not reduce the absolute number of neighbors people deal with, but it does reduce the proportional role of neighbors. Put another way, urbanism adds social ties outside the neighborhood.

The thesis that urbanism provides options beyond the neighborhood suggests that its effect should be contingent on how mobile people are. People who are out of the house often and travel easily should be somewhat independent of the neighborhood, almost no matter where they live. But people who are tied to home and who cannot travel easily should show the effects of urbanism most—enmeshed with neighbors in small towns, ignoring neighbors in big cities. Trends in the data, albeit modest ones, support this contention. The extent to which small-town residents tended to be more involved with neighbors, either absolutely or proportionally, than big-city residents was greater, all else equal, among low-income respondents, among the elderly, among nonworking people, and among the generally more constrained than among other respondents.[13]

Finally, a variety of signs indicate that urbanites are more selective with respect to neighbors than are small-town residents. One kind of selectivity is obvious: urbanites, typically living among many neighbors in dense neighborhoods, included a smaller proportion of them in their networks.[14] Furthermore, as in the case of relatives, Core respondents were more likely to consider the neighbors they did name as "friends" than were other respondents.[15] The more urban the community, the closer respondents reported feeling toward listed neighbors. And the more urban, the greater the range and intimacy of activities respondents shared with those neighbors.[16] (Put another way, small-town respondents were more likely to cite neighbors only with respect to neighborly activities, especially looking after the house.) On only one indicator of intensity were urban respondents less involved with the neighbors they listed: the more urban the community, the *less* frequently respondents said they got together with those neighbors.[17] Most of these results suggest that urbanites, though naming slightly fewer neighbors, were slightly closer to those they did name, results supportive of the argument that urban residents are more selective in forming relations with neighbors.

Summary

Involvement with neighbors seems to have more of a "residual" than a "natural" quality. The most involved respondents tended to be those with few sources of extraneighborhood (nonkin) ties: those not working or working only part time, those who had not lived elsewhere in the city, and those committed to home by marriage or home-ownership. Differences between city and small town can be viewed in a similar way.

Urban residents are less involved with neighbors than are small-town residents. Other studies besides this one suggest as much.[18] This difference arises, I argue, because of the alternatives available just beyond the urban neighborhood. In our sample, urban residents were involved with relatively few neighbors—Core residents with roughly two-thirds as many, on average, as Semirural respondents. Age, education, and other personal characteristics do not explain the difference. Neighborhood characteristics do explain much of it. The homogeneity in life-styles and the rapid growth of less urban places account for most of the overall connection between urbanism and fewer neighborhood ties. Yet the theory that city life itself provides alternatives to the neighborhood gains some support from three findings: neighborhood characteristics notwithstanding, urban respondents were less likely to have neighbor-centered networks; neighborhood characteristics notwithstanding, relatively immobile respondents in small communities were involved with more neighbors than were relatively immobile respondents in large communities; and urban respondents were more deeply tied to the neighbors they did name than small-town respondents were to theirs—a sign, I suggest, that the former were more selective. All this modestly buttresses the argument that, because of urbanism—population concentration—itself, small-town residents, especially the less mobile ones, must turn to neighbors for lack of alternatives, but that city residents can turn to neighbors only if they find them compatible.

(Details of the findings indicate that these social alternatives lie just beyond the urban neighborhood, in the city itself. The population density of respondents' municipalities is more strongly associated with how few neighbors they named than is urbanism overall—that is, more strongly associated than is the location of the community within northern California.)[19]

The point about choice I am making has been, of course, put forward by others. Bertrand Russell, for instance, stated, or rather, overstated it fifty years ago:

The idea that one should know one's immediate neighbors has died out in large centers of population but still lingers in small towns and in the country. It has become a foolish idea, since there is no need to be dependent upon immediate neighbors for society. More and more it becomes possible to choose our companions on account of congeniality rather than on account of mere propinquity.[20]

Co-workers

Whether or not people are involved with their fellow workers varies in part by job or industry. Studs Terkel, in *Working*, quotes a construction machine operator about after-hours drinking:

You're tense and most everybody'd stop and have a beer or a shot. . . . They have a clique, like like everyone has. Your ironworkers, they go to one tavern. Maybe the operators go to another one. The carpenters go to another place. They build buildings and tear 'em down in the tavern (laughs). [p. 51]

On the other hand, a telephone operator complains:

I've worked here almost two years and how many girls' first names do I know? Just their last name is on the headset. You might see them every day and you won't know their names. [p. 67]

In this section we will explore what features of people's jobs, their off-the-job lives, and their communities encourage the formation of social ties with fellow workers. The formation of such a "workplace community" differs from, though it overlaps considerably with, the "occupational community," a network of people in the same line of endeavor, whether or not they actually work together. (The office staff in my department are my co-workers, but sociologists around the world are my occupational colleagues.) Chapter 17 will deal with the occupational community; here we will deal only with co-workers.

How do workplace relations fit into the theoretical schemes we have been considering? Awkwardly. Decline theory suggests that modernization and urbanization foster such kinds of instrumental ties—at the expense of "natural" ties with kin and neighbors. These relations are likely to be segmental, devoted solely to the business at hand. Subcultural theory yields contradictory predictions. On the one hand, large and specialized workplaces in cities should provide people with increased opportunity to form relations on the basis of common work interests, relations that can later expand to other interests. This argument predicts greater co-worker involvement for urban residents. On the other hand, the workplace, like the neighborhood, provides a predetermined set of potential associates. One is typically "given" one's co-workers, like it or not. Where alternatives are hard to find, in the small community, people will rely on that pool; where alternatives are easier to find, in the large community, people will more often look outside the workplace. This argument predicts less co-worker involvement on the part of urban residents.

An obvious but important point must be noted: you cannot associate with co-workers if you do not work. That entire set of potential acquaintances and friends does not exist, leaving the choice of associates to be made from among those in settings to which almost everyone has access, such as kin, neighbors, and past acquaintances. Consequently I will confine the analysis here to the 663 respondents who were working full time or part time when they were interviewed.

The basic measure of co-worker involvement is the number of people the respondent named whose "primary social context" was work. The (logarithmic) average is 2.0. We also consider the number of co-workers that respondents named some time in the interview besides (or instead of) in answer to the question, "Is there anyone you talk with about how to do your work?" These "off-the-job" co-workers presumably shared parts of respondents' lives having nothing to do with work. Their (logarithmic) average is 1.2. Although the two measures are similar, they differ subtly. For example, manager-administrators named relatively few co-workers overall, but relatively many off-the-job co-workers. Managers may not consult many co-workers, but those they do talk to about work appear elsewhere in their lives as well.

Students of worklife have suggested several features of jobs that encourage workers to be involved with one another, both at and away from the workplace.[21] Most of these features—physical isolation, unusual or long working periods, social stigma—make it difficult to see people outside the workplace. Other features—shared danger, common ethnic background, team organization, recruitment to the job through personal ties—stimulate comradeship among co-workers. Classic examples of tightly knit groups are underground coal miners, typographers, and police officers.

Few of our respondents were members of classic workplace communities (only four were policemen and none were coal miners, for example); instead, respondents were scattered among a wide variety of largely urban industries and occupations. Respondents working for local government or in professional services such as hospitals, schools, and law offices reported substantially more co-workers, on the average, than did other respondents (especially if they worked below the managerial or professional level). Although there were differences by occupation (professionals and craftsmen named many co-workers, while machine operatives, salespeople, and service workers named few), these differences are largely accounted for by industry. Most occupational differences were not significant in themselves.[22]

Full-time workers were consistently more involved with fellow workers than were part-timers, and longtime employees more than new ones. As in the case of neighborhoods, time in a specific location encouraged drawing social relations from it. Self-employed respondents, for evident reasons, named fewer co-workers than did employees.[23] Finally, respondents who worked unusual hours, early or late shifts, and *male* respondents who had moved to their current communities for job-related reasons named slightly more off-the-job co-workers than did other respondents. Respondents' personal characteristics only slightly influenced involvement with co-workers: more educated and more cooperative respondents named slightly more co-workers.[24]

Urbanism and Co-worker Involvement

No clear patterns appear when we consider community differences in worker involvement. All respondents lumped together, people in the large communities named more co-workers than did those in smaller communities. But this was largely because urbanites were more likely to be working. When only working respondents are considered, the differences virtually disappear. Semirural workers averaged fewer co-workers than did workers living elsewhere (1.5 versus 2.1), but this can be explained both by job characteristics—Semirural workers were more likely to be self-employed, for example—and by self-selection—Semirural workers were less educated and less likely to have moved to their communities for their jobs.[25] No clear patterns emerge, either, if we count only off-the-job co-workers,[26] or if we analyze the probability that respondents had networks that were co-worker-centered.[27] Overall, aside from self-selection—people who were likely to be employed and to be in industries conducive to forming social relations were more likely to live in large communities—urbanism had no consistent effect on involvement with co-workers.

One finding, however, does pique interest. High-salaried Core respondents named fewer off-the-job co-workers (those named elsewhere than in q. 46) than did comparable well-paid respondents living elsewhere. Put another way, whereas in most communities high-salaried respondents were more involved with co-workers off the job than were low-salaried workers, the reverse tended to be true in Core communities.[28] One is tempted to explain this finding in terms of the theoretical arguments presented earlier. Perhaps Core residence restricts the possibilities people have to widen the scope of their work ties, though why it should do so only for high-salaried workers is not obvious. Perhaps the combination of high income and Core residence allows people sufficient social opportunities outside the workplace so that they can "afford" not to cultivate co-workers. Or this result may be accounted for by some job characteristic we did not capture, perhaps the bureaucratic hierarchy of San Francisco firms.

The fundamental finding is that urbanism is only weakly and equivocally associated with co-worker involvement. This ambiguity also appears when we consider the particular co-worker relations themselves. Co-workers named by Core respondents were more likely than those named by Semirural ones to be drawn upon in various ways, such as for sociable activities, but this tendency is not significant. At the same time, Core respondents' associates were no more likely to be called "close" and were seen less often than were Semirural associates.[29] In sum, the conclusion must be: no evident effect.

Conclusion

While the co-worker data say little about urbanism, they do show again that commitment to, or restriction to, a social context promotes social relations in it, perhaps at the cost of relations outside of it. Years on the job, hours worked, working unusual hours, and moving for the job promote involvement with co-workers at and away from the workplace and, in most cases, also promote co-worker-centered networks. For example, full-time workers named almost twice as many co-workers as otherwise identical respondents who worked part time (2.2 versus 1.1), named two-thirds more off-the-job co-workers (1.3 versus 0.7), and were three times more likely to have a work-centered network (.21 versus .07). We already saw that they tended to name fewer neighbors.

The import of all this for our theoretical concerns is unclear. Perhaps the two urban effects discussed earlier cancel each other out: urbanism increases the attraction of co-workers by concentrating many people in those jobs and industries—for example, professional services—conducive to work-based relations and, at the same time, decreases people's dependence on those involuntary, given sets of co-workers.

10   Varieties of Nonkin: Organization Members and Just Friends

Almost everyone has neighbors, but virtually no one can determine who those neighbors will be. Most employed people have co-workers, but very few people can determine who those co-workers will be. In these two instances, only slightly less so than with relatives, we are given a small set of acquaintances from which we pick a few for intensive involvement. Organization members are different, however, because by and large we decide which organizations to join and how much to participate, thereby at least partly determining the pool of potential associates. Just friends—friends who are not kin, or neighbors, or co-workers, or fellow club members, or any other type of role-relation except friend—differ even more. Chosen or retained outside any specific social context, pure friendship ties are maintained by no structural or cultural supports, only by the voluntary choice of the two friends (and, perhaps, by the social pressure of common friends). Their voluntarism and seeming detachment from the "natural" contexts of family and place make relations with organization members and friends an important theoretical subject. Are these relations more common among urban than small-town residents? Are these the segmental and superficial acquaintanceships described in the classic portrait of urban alienation, or are they the personally fulfilling relations that city lovers claim are possible only in populous settings?

Fellow Members of Organizations

Social scientists are ambivalent about voluntary organizations. Following de Tocqueville, some have described clubs, professional associations, and volunteer groups as the skeletal structure of large democracies; without healthy organizations, mass society threatens to collapse into anomic totalitarianism. But the purposeful and formal quality of such groups has led others to compare them unfavorably with natural and informal groups, such as kin and neighbors. Some have suggested that estranged people try to replace intimate relations with the company of organization members. Historian Sam Bass Warner, for example, claims that Philadelphia's growth in the nineteenth century destroyed "the informal neighborhood street life which had characterized the small-scale community of the eighteenth-century town. In response to these new conditions all Philadelphians, of every class and background, reacted in the same way to the loss of old patterns of sociability and informal community. They rushed into clubs and associations."[1] Some individuals in our survey illustrate this view of organizations as refuges from urban alienation. An eighty-three-year-old woman in Oakland, for instance, focused her activities in a church senior citizen group, in part because she was frightened and distrustful of her black neighbors. This illustration is not indicative, however, of most organization members and their relations. In most instances, organizational relations form one facet of general social involvement.

There was in our survey, for example, a thirty-eight-year-old professional man who lived in Sonoma County and worked in Oakland. Despite the long commute, he belonged to ten organizations and was active in many, even leading the Boy Scouts and coaching Little League. He was also involved in his church and had developed strong friendships with fellow members. In another example, a suburban guidance counselor had met her husband in a remodeled-van club, and she belonged to professional, alumni, and homeowners groups. Yet, this active thirty-three-year-old was also involved with a variety of neighbors, co-workers, and friends. A final example is a young, poorly educated laborer who had lived in Stockton all his life. Uninterested in the interview until it turned to the topic of religion, he described himself as a dedicated member of a fundamentalist church and named many people who shared his commitment. Perhaps this person and the elderly lady in Oakland could be described as finding solace and companionship only in a formal organization. But for the other two people membership was just one aspect of their general social involvement. Their cases are the more common.

The more organizations respondents belonged to, not only the more fellow members they knew, the *more nonmembers* they also knew. Those who belonged to three or more organizations named 10.4 nonkin *non*members, compared with 8.1 for those who belonged to no organizations.[2] This finding is difficult to reconcile with the idea that organizations substitute for personal relations. Also, the nature of respondents' relations with fellow organization members is inconsistent with depicting them as one-dimensional. Associates whose primary social context was organizational (i.e., they were not also kin, neighbors, or co-workers) were more likely than any other category of associates to be called "friends" (except, of course, for "just friends"); they were more likely than co-workers or neighbors to be called "especially close," or to go out socially with respondents, or to discuss hobbies with respondents, and about as likely as other nonrelatives to discuss respondents' personal problems. These characteristics seem to describe good friends who happen also to be in the same organizations. The findings are, in general, consistent with claims other researchers have made that organizations complement, rather than substitute for, personal relations.[3]

Who Named Co-members?

In general, more educated, more affluent, and older respondents—especially older women—belonged to more organizations.[4] And respondents who belonged to more organizations tended to name more fellow members to their networks, an average of 0.4 names for each organization.[5] Beyond number of organizations, there is little to distinguish the respondents who named many co-members, except that they tended to have resided longer in their cities.[6]

But not all organizations and members are alike. Consider some of the organizations these respondents named: a San Franciscan listed the symphony, Marin County Club, the Bar Association, Republican party, and Golden Gate Tennis Club; a Sacramento suburbanite belonged to the Fair Oaks Swim Club, a college fraternity, the California Teachers' Association, and a touch football league; and a resident of a large town gave a Methodist women's group, the PTA, a bridge club, a softball league, and the Brownies. To these groups might be added the Sierra Club, Elks, Datsun-Z Drivers of California, Bible Study Circle, Teamsters, homeowners associations, United States Citizen Band Radio Association, Bill's Burgers softball team, Oakland Museum, Legion of the Purple Heart, Moose, Wednesday Night Dance Club, United Farm Workers, Sons of Italy, and all the rest of California's organizational variety.

It would have been preferable to analyze which associates respondents knew in which organizations. We did not record that information,[7] but we can estimate it by dividing the respondents according to the kinds or organizations to which they belonged. The most important division separates the 154 respondents who belonged to a church or another religious organization (and many belonged to secular groups, as well) from the 532 who belonged only to nonreligious organizations. The former were older, longer-term residents, a bit less educated than the latter, and two-thirds were women. Most important, respondents in the church or church-linked organizations named almost *three times* as many co-members—and twice as many proportionally—as respondents in nonchurch organizations.[8] Also, for the religious members, unlike secular group members, any organizational memberships beyond the church-based one were largely superfluous in introducing more associates into their networks.[9]

For most respondents, in sum, formal organizations supplement informal social activity instead of replacing it. Those who relied most on their organizational ties were members of religious organizations. They knew roughly a fifth of all their associates primarily in the context of an organization and about a third of all their associates at least shared membership with them (in contrast to one-tenth and one-sixth, respectively, for members of secular organizations). Strict application of the notion that organizational ties are superficial replacements for intimate ties would imply that these religionists—largely nonurban, as we shall see—were most needy of such replacements. Perhaps they were. But churches are special kinds of organizations tied to family, ethnicity, locality, and tradition. In that sense, religious organizational relations might be not alternatives to, but the very stuff of, primordial or "natural" social worlds.

Urbanism and Organizational Ties

The standard argument goes: Urbanism breeds isolation; isolated people join organizations; therefore, urbanism fosters organizational membership and relations. Chapter 5 disputed the first proposition; the last few pages disputed the second; therefore it is no surprise that the conclusion also fails—and churches are one reason it does.

Urban respondents, in fact, belonged to more organizations than did respondents in less urban places. From Semirural to Regional Core, the average number of organizations people listed was about 1.5, 1.5, 1.9, and 2.0.[10] City-dwellers were especially likely to belong to political lobbies, neighborhood organizations, cooperatives (notably, the Berkeley-based cooperative stores), professional associations, and ethnic associations. Small-town respondents were most notably members of farm organizations, such as the Grange (an organization to which no one in Metropolitan or Core communities belonged), and churches or church-linked groups such as sports teams.[11] The only reason urban residents belonged to more secular organizations is that they tended to be better educated and more affluent. As other American research has also shown, urban life itself did not apparently encourage people to join organizations.[12]

Despite their slightly more numerous organizational memberships, urbanites named no more co-members than did respondents in small communities; the average ranged from 0.5 in Semirural places to 0.4 in Regional Core places. Adjusting for self-selection makes little difference.[13] If we consider only the 686 respondents who belonged to at least one organization, the findings are much the same.[14] What makes a difference is whether the respondent belonged to a religious organization.

Figure 11 presents the basic comparisons. The top pair of lines refer to the 154 members of religious organizations, the bottom pair to the 532 members of solely secular organizations. Within each pair, the lower line

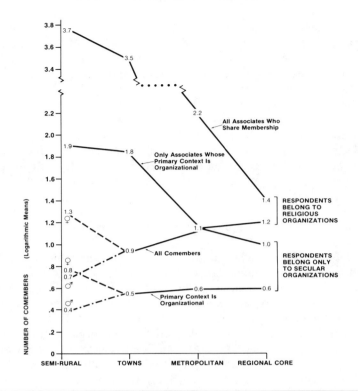

Fig. 11.   Organizational co-members, by urbanism, for religious and secular organization members.

concerns us first. It indicates the number of associates named whose primary social context was organizational.

The secular group evidences no connection between urbanism and number of co-members. Semirural men named relatively few (0.4) and Semirural women relatively many (0.8), but urnbanism seems irrelevant to the number of co-members. (Adjusting the means for self-selection changes this line, and the others, very little, so the adjusted data are not shown.)[15] For the religious group, however, urbanism makes at least a modest difference. Semirural and Town respondents named about 1.9 co-members, Metropolitan and Core respondents about 1.2, or two-thirds as many.[16] This pattern must be interpreted cautiously, because relatively few respondents belonged to religious groups. Nevertheless, it suggests that churches are more significant sources of social ties for their members in small communities than for their members in large ones, perhaps in part because urban members have more nonkin involvements outside the organization.[17]

The contrast between religious and secular organizational ties is underlined by considering *all* the associates with whom respondents shared organizational memberships, whether or not those associates were also relatives, neighbors, or co-workers. The upper lines of each pair in figure 11 show the community differences on that count. Again, respondents belonging only to secular organizations differed little according to where they lived.[18] But members of religious organizations differed greatly, ranging from a mean of 3.7 for Semirural respondents to 1.4 for Core respondents.[19] Small-town life, although it did not affect involvement with fellow members of secular organizations, markedly increased involvement with fellow members of religious organizations—both by increasing involvement with people solely in that context and by increasing the likelihood that people known in other contexts would also be members.

Conclusion

We cannot resolve the issue of the voluntary organization's role in American democracy. But our survey does suggest that formal organizations are more often supplements to already active social lives than they are ersatz replacements for lost community. Our findings also fail to support the contention that urbanites seek emotional shelter in formal organizations. If any of our respondents sought refuge in organizations, it was small-town respondents, who were especially likely to form or expand their relations within a church or church-based setting. They were involved in more relations of this sort than comparable church members living in urban places.

We can interpret this small-town involvement in churches in one or both of two ways. First, we can reverse urban alienation theory and argue that people cultivate acquaintances met in religious or other small-town organizations for lack of alternative relations. Some evidence suggests that these small-town organizational ties were, in fact, relatively superficial. Respondents in small communities were less likely than urbanites to consider co-members "friends."[20] They were also slightly less likely than otherwise similar urbanites to feel "close" to co-members and to draw upon co-members for a variety of activities—although they reported getting together with co-members more frequently than urban residents did.[21] Other than meeting often, small-town residents appeared less involved with each co-member. (Put another way, urban respondents tended to be more selective, as they seemed to be with kin and neighbors, only being involved with—or only naming—co-members who were important to them.) In this view, church fellowship is the formal substitute for informal ties.

A second interpretation is that being involved with many fellow members of a religious group is part of the family-neighborhood-church complex that lies at the heart of the traditional way of life. The data in figure 11 indicate that Town and Semirural respondents were involved both with relatively many co-members and with relatively many kin and neighbors who also shared membership in religious groups. Moreover, fellowship in a church organization may, in itself and without other activities, form the basis of deep and fulfilling relations. In this view, the involvement of small-town residents described here are part of a cohesive, traditional social world.

Just Friends

"Just friends" includes a variety of associates who have known each other only informally or who once shared a formal social context but no longer do. What these diverse relations have in common is the willingness (not necessarily reciprocated) of the respondent to call the other person a "friend." Whatever their origins, these relations are relatively independent of institutional support. (Unlike co-workers, just friends need not meet every weekday, and, unlike kin, just friends do not have clear rules about mutual responsibilities, such as seeing one another on holidays.) These are essentially voluntary relations, the content and future of the bond being always at the discretion of each party. Gerald Suttles makes the point this way:

Friendships are subject to private negotiations to an extent unparalleled in most other social relations. Persons may break their friendship, revise it, or simply drift away from one another without notifying anyone else. Losing a friend may be painful but it is an option that can be taken without consultation or an official change in status.[22]

One implication of this free-floating nature is that friendships, more than other kinds of relations, reflect personal taste. Just friends are therefore more likely than most other associates to be similar to one another (see chap. 14), to spend free time together, and to feel close to one another.[23] Just friends should also reveal more unambiguously the personal opportunities and constraints individuals face in building networks—their access to potential friends and their financial resources for keeping in contact, for example.

This free-floating nature is also a key to the theoretical significance of just friends. According to both decline and subcultural theories, urbanism increases residents' opportunities for making acquaintanceships outside of family, neighborhood, and church. But for most theorists of the first school, such urban ties, disconnected from basic social settings (and from one another—see chap. 12) and grasped at amid the urban hurly-burly, typically cannot reach the depth of "true friendship" found in small towns. The city-dweller's friendships are relatively superficial and evanescent. For subcultural theory, these friendships, because they are selected from a slightly greater range of possibilities, should be at least as fulfilling as rural ones, and probably more, and should also provide more possibilities for forming communities of interest.

Who Had Many Friends?

Personable people tend to name many friends. Although we did not assess respondent personality, there are indications that it was related to the number of just friends people named: respondents whom the interviewers thought were busy and active named roughly twice as many just friends as those whom interviewers thought did not have much to do (see q. I-22). And respondents judged to be cooperative named many more than those judged recalcitrant. Our analysis focuses, however, on the social characteristics, constraints, and opportunities that affected how few or many just friends respondents named.[24]

Respondents who named many just friends tended to be young (although elderly women named more friends than did middle-aged women); educated; affluent; never married (especially important for women); childless; non-Hispanic white; and without many relatives in the area (especially important for affluent respondents).[25] These characteristics tend to describe people with relatively few restrictive commitments on the one hand and many resources on the other—both enabling one to tend one's garden of friendships.

Urbanism

If young, unmarried, educated, and affluent people have more just friends, then on that basis alone we would expect urbanites, who are especially likely to be in these categories, to have more just friends than residents of smaller communities. In our survey they did. Semirural respondents named an average (logarithmic mean) of 2.3 just friends, Town respondents 3.1, Metropolitan respondents 3.6, and Core respondents 4.5. The average number more than doubled from one end of the town-metropolis continuum to the other.[26] An important implication is that, as one moves from rural to urban, the social worlds of typical residents and of their neighbors are composed of relatively loose and voluntary relations based on a variety of informal commitments. (Perhaps it is this characteristic of urban bonds that gives the impression that they are adventitious and transitory.)

The key question is whether urbanism itself—by increasing the pool of potentially intimate friends or by increasing the distractions of passing acquaintanceships—contributes to this greater number of just friends. The answer is, for our respondents as a whole, only slightly so. Adjusting the data to simulate a situation in which all respondents were similar in age, race, income, and so forth yields means of 3.0 for Semirural respondents, 3.2 for Town, 3.4 for Metropolitan, and 3.6 for Core respondents.[27] Although steadily increasing from least to most urban, these means differ only modestly (i.e., they are not statistically significant). For technical reasons, however, I probably underestimated this trend,[28] which leaves us with the rather insipid conclusion that urbanism probably, though slightly, added to residents' store of just friends.

The effects of urbanism are better defined for some particular types of people. I had thought that those would be relatively constrained or immobile people for whom population concentration would be critical. It appears that the opposite is true. Figure 12 shows the just friends results separately for low-income and high-income respondents. Among both groups, the urban respondents named considerably more just friends than did the small-town respondents. But, only among high-income respondents is there seemingly any independent contribution of urbanism. Among low-income respondents, the youth, education, and unmarried status of urbanites fully accounts for their more numerous friendships.[29] Similar contrasts can be shown for people with access to a car versus those without, for childless young adults versus parents, for men versus women, and for those generally unconstrained versus those with serious impediments to mobility. Among people in the first group of each pair, urbanism itself seems to contribute slightly to having more just friends, while among people in the second group urbanism is only incidental. In sum, it appears that urban life has its effect, however interpreted, only for people with the freedom and resources to take advantage of the social opportunities it provides.

Some evidence suggests that the opportunity these unconstrained people take advantage of is not simply the concentration of people, but specifically the concentration of people like themselves. Childless adults live disproportionately in urban centers, and their concentration in those centers seems to explain the slightly greater number of just friends that the urban respondents in this group had. Similarly, affluent people live disproportionately in urban areas, and their concentration there seems to

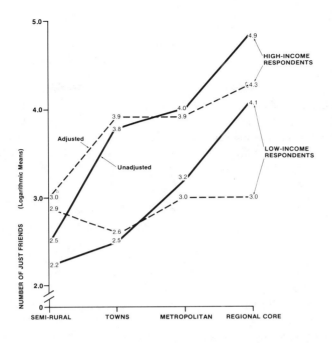

Fig. 12.   **Just friends, by urbanism, for low- and high-income respondents.**

explain why urbanism promoted just friends among the affluent respondents.[30]

Conclusion

The fewer commitments and the more resources people have, the more free-floating friendships they can make and, probably more important, the more they can maintain. These two sets of characteristics—appearing specifically in the form of youth, bachelorhood, childlessness, absence of nearby kin, education, and income—are more commonly found among urban residents. Consequently, urban people in our survey typically had more just friends than did small-town people. This, of course, strongly challenges received wisdom. If we ask, through statistical manipulation, whether urbanism itself boosts such friendships beyond the effects of self-selection (or whether urbanites had more friends only because they were young, educated, and so on), the answer is equivocal. Overall, urbanism at best slightly increases the number of just friends. For people with time, mobility, and resources, urbanism more clearly promoted friendships.

But what sorts of friendships are these? Are the urban ones more superficial and fleeting than the small-town friendships? Not by any indicator we have. Other than a barely perceptible tendency for urbanites to get together with their friends slightly less frequently, the relations of urban respondents with their just friends were as enduring, as likely to be perceived as close, and as likely to involve a variety of activities as the relations of small-town respondents with their just friends.[31] More urban and less urban respondents did not have friendships of any different quality. The difference is that the former had, all else equal, a slightly greater number of friendships.

Summary

One way of consolidating the detail of the last few chapters is to employ the traditional/modern distinction. This concept, hoary as it is, highlights the small town/big city differences we have found in social contexts. The set of relations generally considered traditional are relatives, neighbors, and fellow members of religious organizations; the rest—co-workers, fellow members of secular organizations, just friends, and others—are labeled modern. The solid lines in figure 13 show the community differences in how many people respondents were involved with in each type of social context. As urbanism increased, respondents named fewer associates from so-defined traditional contexts (10.0 to 6.7) but named many more associates from so-defined modern contexts (5.9 to 10.5).[32] Proportionally, about 63 percent of Semirural respondents' relations were traditional versus 39 percent of Core respondents' relations.

(A note on "others": this heterogeneous group includes some purely formal relations such as landlords, ministers, or doctors, but it also includes a greater number of informal relations, such as friend of a friend, schoolmate, and ex-neighbor. In fact, two-thirds of others were labeled "friend," and more so by urban residents. Overall, the more urban the community, the more others respondents named—with or without the adjustment.)[33]

The traditional/modern contrast is sharper yet if we classify each respondent according to kinds of relations he or she stressed. About a fourth of all respondents in each community category named an average proportion of associates in each type of relation; that is, their networks had roughly typical profiles. But 49 percent of Semirural respondents had networks with high proportions of kin, neighbors, or fellow members of

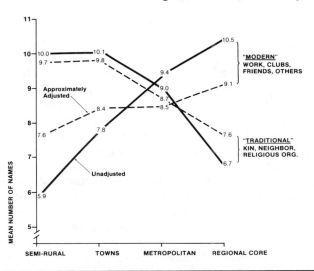

Fig. 13.   **Number of names given, by urbanism, according to a traditional/modern distinction among primary social contexts.**

religious organizations—of traditional relations. This figure drops steadily to 14 percent for Core respondents.[34]

These strong differences mean that urban and small-town people tend to experience quite different personal milieus. Moreover, the ambience of each person's community—irrespective of his or her own personal network—also varies systematically from less urban to more urban places. The city coffee shop stands instead of the community church; noisy parties shatter one's sleep rather than screeching children; newspapers cover leisure and "life-styles" in lieu of school plays and neighborhood bake-offs.

Town life and city life do not, in themselves, directly create most of these differences in personal networks. They are indirectly very important, because town and city tend to attract or repel, by their economic, social, and physical features, different kinds of people—the young, educated, and unattached toward cities, the old, less educated, and married toward towns. The congregation of these types of people, in turn, creates characteristic ways of life in each place. Still, above and beyond such self-selection, towns and cities themselves—that is, degrees of population concentration—add further to this difference in social worlds. The dashed lines in figure 13 suggest that, even were our respondents all similar in personal traits, the ones residing in small communities would have still had predominantly traditional networks, and the more urban respondents networks equally or predominantly modern.[35] Semirural respondents would have drawn roughly 56 percent of their relations from traditional contexts, compared with 54, 51, and 46 percent from otherwise similar respondents in Town, Metropolitan, or Core communities, respectively.

This traditional versus modern distinction in small-town and big-city people's social ties is probably not news; it fits some of our preconceptions about rural and urban life. What may be news are four findings.

First, city people are not isolated. Instead, they are more involved with friends, co-workers, co-members of secular organizations, or others than are residents of smaller places. People in both kinds of communities have personal relations, but personal relations of different kinds. Second, something about urbanism itself contributes at least modestly to this difference in social worlds. Certainly the differences are mostly a consequence of self-selection: some types of people move cityward and other types move countryward, and sometimes people move precisely because they seek particular social worlds. Nevertheless, even with these factors taken into account, urbanism still tends slightly to promote friendships and other relations at the expense of kinship, neighborhood, and church. Third, the something about urbanism that does this appears to be the concentration of people similar to the individual, whether it be childless adults, the elderly, or the affluent. Fourth, urban residents' relations with their associates in each context are (with the exception of parents and the exception of getting together often) at least as involving and intimate, if not more so, than small-town residents' relations with theirs.

Another scheme, connected to the traditional/modern distinction, can be used for synthesizing our findings on social contexts: to examine the causes of involvement in various contexts and interpret those causes in terms of the opportunities and constraints people encounter in making and maintaining social ties. This yields a particular view of town/city differences.

The causes of an individual's involvement with people in a specific social context are, in part, idiosyncratic to those contexts. Individuals tend to be more involved with neighbors if they are married, have lived most of their time in the city in that particular neighborhood, and do not hold a full-time job. Individuals tend to be more involved with co-workers if they work long or unusual hours and have been in the same job a long time. Nevertheless, there are underlying commonalities to these lists of traits, and to longer lists presented in the last few chapters. They involve commitments, voluntary or otherwise, to a particular context, often at the cost of relations in other contexts. The voluntary element appears, for example, in self-selection: men who moved to a city for a job were more involved with co-workers; women who picked a neighborhood for its residents knew more neighbors. The less-voluntary element appears, for example, in the many ways that aging leads to a kin- or neighbor-centered network.

Such commitments and constraints can be managed or overridden by plentiful resources—social, financial, and temporal. We can see this by looking at who gets involved with the virtually free-floating "just friends." Youth, absence of family commitments, education, and income provide enormous opportunities for forming and sustaining such friendships. In all, a lack of resources encourages involvement with kin, neighbors, and, for workers, co-workers, while a wealth of resources leads to secular organization members, just friends, others, and perhaps co-workers too.

The connection of constraint and opportunity to the traditional/modern distinction is this: Traditional contexts, particularly kin and neighborhood, are basically contexts to which people are constrained. (This is true, too, of the church contexts when we realize that churches are typically local institutions and membership is typically inherited.) In their ideal form, they approximate closed, corporate groups, outside of which interaction is difficult and, consequently, within which intense interaction is inevitable. Modern life provides people with resources—affluence, physical security, education, transportation, and so on—that allow them to sustain social ties outside those traditional contexts. The workplace separated from home is one modern and relatively voluntary context. Still, aside from his being able to quit a job, a person's workplace ties are somewhat constrained. The most voluntary and unconstrained ties are those with fellow members of secular organizations and especially with "just friends." It is their very voluntary nature—or call it disposable or evanescent nature—that makes them appear so modern.

The traditional/modern distinction, as used by the decline school in particular, also implies that relations within traditional contexts are more fulfilling and supportive than those in modern ones. The logic of that claim is based on constraint, too: The intensity of traditional relations derives in large part from their necessity, the lack of alternatives to them. Isolated villages, for example, breed functional interdependency, out of which personal sentiment may arise, precisely because of their isolation. This inherent logic of the decline argument implies that modern society has wrecked community and social relations precisely by providing individuals with personal resources they can use to seek relations where they will.[36]

Urbanism might be seen as just such a personal resource, albeit a marginal one, in that cities provide larger pools of potential associates than small towns do. Consequently, urban residents tend to associate with kin and neighbors less and just friends more. Also, they seem to become somewhat more selective as to which kin and neighbors they will associate with. Urbanites were closer to and more involved with the extended kin and neighbors they did name. These effects of urbanism are not large, nor would we expect them to be. The community is a very general backdrop to lives led most intensely in the very specific settings of home, block, workplace, and so on. Rarely if ever do people actually sift systematically through a community's residents in search of associates. They make contacts sporadically and sustain them idiosyncratically. Yet the influence of urbanism, while indirect, subtle, and marginal, is real.

As to the quality of relations, we have no evidence to support the contention that the relations urbanites choose are less fulfilling than the ones small-town residents choose. What we seem to see here is a difference not in quality of life, but in style of life.

IV   Dimensions of Personal Networks

11

Personal Networks as Social Support

As a by-product of meeting specific individuals and deciding which relations to pursue, each person builds a personal network that has several collective properties. The group of people with whom he or she is involved may be cohesive or fragmented, homogeneous or heterogeneous, spatially concentrated or dispersed, or may vary in a number of other ways—ways the individual usually did not plan in making or maintaining each particular bond.

Four such dimensions of personal networks are considered in this part of the book; how much total social support the network provides the individual, the formal structure of the network, the spatial dispersion of associates in the network, and the homogeneity (in age) of the network. These are only four of many possible network attributes we could have examined. They are raised together in connection with the issues of urbanism and the decline of community. Modern city life has been charged with weakening the supportiveness of people's networks, thereby leaving individuals in serious social and psychological jeopardy. Modern society and urbanism have, according to classic theory, reduced the interactional density of relations and networks; this structural change is given as one reason for the presumed drop in supportiveness. In modern societies and cities, according to both decline theory and subcultural theory, personal networks are less likely to be concentrated locally, to be communities of "place"; what this means for "true" community is a matter of debate. And in urban places, according to subcultural theory, it is easier to form relations on the basis of commonality. The resultant networks are likely to be homogeneous in various ways, which in turn promotes involvement in subcultures.

That topic will bring us to the consideration of subcultures proper in part 5.

Adequate Social Support

Evidence rapidly accumulating in the past several years indicates that personal networks generally protect individuals from many vicissitudes of life. People with spouses, friends, and helpful relatives

Table 3	Scheme for Coding Respondents on the Adequacy of

Type of Support	Questions Names Were Given On
Counseling	Discuss Personal Matters Seek Advice
	(Percent of Respondents)
Companionship	Social Activities Discuss Hobbies
	(Percent of Respondents)
Practical	Care for Home Discuss Work Help Around House Lend Money
	(Percent of Respondents)

[a]Number of names of people living *outside* the household.

tend to be physically and psychologically healthier than those without; they seem to come through crises such as unemployment and widowhood with less bodily and mental damage.[1] The case that networks are a miracle cure has, as is often so with new intellectual fads, been overstated. Few of the studies are free of methodological doubts, the direction of causality is almost always uncertain (Do people with friends become happy, or do happy people make friends?), and the aggravating aspects of personal relations have been largely ignored. Nevertheless, it is better to have than to have not.

That urbanites tend not to have much social support is, as I have mentioned at several points, part of the popular and scholarly charges against city life. Lack of support presumably results from certain features of urban networks—disconnection from kin and neighborhood, transience, little interconnection—and in turn presumably explains certain features of urban life—deviance, disorder, and so on. Although this study has challenged some elements of the claim, for example, that urbanites are psychologically disturbed or that their specific relations lack intimacy, we have not yet directly assessed the extent to which their networks provided respondents with various kinds of social support.

This chapter addresses several aspects of social support: who had a secure amount of social support versus who was at risk of going without; what sorts of relations provided what sorts of support; how respondents felt about the support they had; and how networks were also social bur-

Their Social Support

Number of Names[a] for Each Category of Adequacy		
Inadequate	**Marginal**	**Adequate**
0	1	2+
(15%)	(20%)	(65%)
0,1	2,3	4+
(03%)	(11%)	(86%)
0,1	2,3	4+
(06%)	(19%)	(75%)

dens. Although our focus throughout is on community differences, we will inevitably learn much about the general sources of social support as well.

The analysis focuses on three types of social support, defined a priori: *counseling*—advice on and discussion of personal matters; *companionship*—visiting socially, going out together, discussing a hobby; and *practical*—a variety of material assistance. Instead of examining how many people each respondent knew, we will see whether or not the respondent had "adequate" support of each kind. Since little basis exists for asserting exactly how many counselors, companions, or helpers is adequate, the standard is a relative one: I assumed that, at any given time, most people have adequate support. So I will focus on the minority of respondents who reported relatively few real or potential supporters in each category; everyone else, that is, respondents who had moderate networks and those who had extremely large ones, will be treated as indistinguishable. (In fact, some evidence suggests that the curative powers of personal relations appear once people have more than a minimum number of supporters—usually one.)[2] We are looking for the people "at risk" of weak support in particular domains. While respondents who lacked one kind of support tended also to lack another, there were many instances in which people lacked one but not the others.[3]

Table 3 shows how the "name-eliciting" exchange questions are used to code the adequacy of respondents' support.[4] For example, the counseling scale counts the number of people (living outside the household) whom respondents named either as people with whom they discuss personal matters (q. 77) or as those whose advice they seek (q. 78). Sixty-five percent of the respondents named two or more people outside the household as counselors; this is coded as "adequate." Twenty percent named only one person, which is coded as "marginal," because these respondents risked having this single counselor unavailable during a particular crisis. The remaining 15 percent named *no one* outside the household and are coded as having "inadequate" support. Thus, our measure of counseling support is a lopsided three-point scale, running from 1, inadequate (15 percent) to 2, marginal (20 percent), to 3, adequate (65 percent). The same logic applies to companionship and practical support.

I focus on associates *outside* the household primarily because the key theoretical issues involve the extent to which the *community* provides support. Also, in some cases, the listing of household members was either trivial—for example, saying that one went out with one's spouse—or overlooked—for example, some people simply forgot their spouse in listing counselors. Also, including or excluding household members made little empirical difference in assessing companionship or practical support. It made some difference in assessing counseling, because spouses and spouse-surrogates were important confidants, especially for men. Therefore I examined marital status closely in analyzing counseling support.

Who Had Adequate Support?
Counseling

Both men and women had weaker counseling support (from outside the household) if they were married than if they were not, but this was especially so for men. Men were more likely to turn only to their spouses, and they thereby more often risked having marginal support than did women, who typically had counselors besides their husbands. Aside from married men, other high-risk groups were older respondents; married women with children at home; non-Anglo women; and people living with other adults. Other adults, like spouses, substituted for extrahousehold confidants. Social class was not particularly important by itself. Educated respondents had slightly more adequate counseling support than less-educated respondents, but that can be explained by their youth and marital status. Various combinations of life-cycle stage—age, marriage, and children—together with gender largely account for who had adequate counseling.[5]

Overall, urbanites were a bit *more* likely than residents of smaller communities to have adequate counseling (see fig. 14, bottom set of lines).

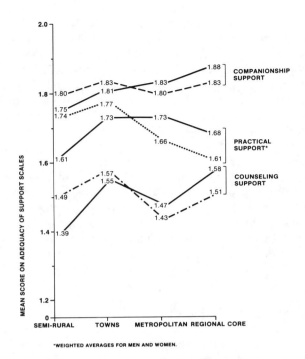

Fig. 14.   **Mean scores on three social support measures, by urbanism.**

That was largely because urbanites were younger, less likely to be married, and less likely to have children. If we take such self-selection factors into account, the remaining community differences—the dot-dash line—are no longer substantial.[6]

There is, however, a perturbation worth noting: women who lived in metropolitan places, especially if currently or formerly married, and particularly if college educated, were more likely than other women to lack counseling support. This finding and a similar one on respondents' psychological mood lend a bit of weight to the charge that suburban life has unique estranging effects on wives and ex-wives.[7]

Companionship

Not surprisingly, the more social activities—going out with someone, having visitors—that respondents claimed to have (q. 74), the more social companions they named. Respondents claiming more than the average number of activities were virtually certain to have "adequate" companionship.[8] Generally, unconstrained respondents cited more activities: younger, unmarried, childless, educated, and affluent respondents. As we have found with social networks, age restricted the social activities of men more than those of women, while marriage and children restricted the activities of women more than those of men. And, as noted in chapter 5, living in a more urban place itself contributed to the variety of activities people engaged in.[9]

No surprise, then, that these are the same types of people, with only slight differences, who were most likely to have adequate companionship: young, childless (especially if female), educated, affluent, and members of organizations. Urbanism was *not* an independent factor. Although Core residents were a bit more likely and Semirural residents a bit less likely to have adequate companionship, those differences are generally accounted for by youth, childlessness, income, and so on (see top lines of figure 14).[10] Aside from a few quirks in the data,[11] it appears that the same people living in big city or small town would have equally adequate sociability.

Practical Support

Working people were more likely to have adequate practical support than those not employed, of course, since discussing work was one such support. Also, younger people, whites, and organization members tended to have adequate support. Generally, the more children at home, the less likely respondents were to have adequate support from outside the household. In this case children may both inhibit formation of outside ties and also substitute for them—helping around the house, for example. Although one might think that income would also substitute for personal support, so that affluent people would name fewer helpers, affluent people in fact had more secure practical support than the poor. And elderly women had more adequate support than elderly men. Aside from the last point, these findings confirm the venerable philosophical verity that "them that's got, gets."[12]

Unlike the situation with counseling and companionship, big-city and small-town respondents had equally adequate practical support (see solid line in middle pair of figure 14). Semirural men were more likely than other men to be "at risk," but overall the community differences were weak. When we adjust the support scale for self-selection, a difference does emerge: urbanites were *less* likely to have adequate practical support than otherwise similar people in smaller places (broken line).[13]

Since practical support includes a grab-bag of unrelated items (see table

3), we must ask which specific kinds of material assistance urbanites were shy of. The missing supporters were people to care for their homes when they were away (pick up the mail, water plants, etc.) and people to help them around the house (painting, repairs, etc.).[14] Both are the kinds of "neighborly" assistance that neighbors and kin are most likely to provide. And it is neighbors and kin, we saw in part 3, whom small-town residents were more likely to name. Perhaps urbanites, being less often home-owners, had less call for such aid; or perhaps they just did without. (Also, small-town respondents almost always called on different people for the two tasks; city residents were more likely to call on the same people.) Work advice and financial aid do not require such proximity, and urban-ites had more supporters of those types than did residents of smaller communities.

As a simply descriptive matter, the average city respondent had practi-cal support equally secure as that of the average town respondent. But that description belies the fact that, had the average city respondent been of equal age, comparable employment status, and so forth with the aver-age town respondent, he or she would have had slightly less adequate practical—especially house-related—support.

Who Is at Risk?

Who, then, is "at risk" of having marginal or inadequate support?[15] Certain groups appeared repeatedly in our canvass: older re-spondents, especially older men lacking counselors; parents—that is, re-spondents with children at home—mothers and low-income parents most notably; non-Anglos, particularly black women; and respondents with less education and income, especially in companionship (but not in coun-seling).

Our findings on urbanism and social support are not especially dra-matic, except in an ironic sense. The conventional thesis is that urbanites are relatively rich in material help but poor in intimacy and fellowship. We found that the more urban respondents had more adequate counseling and companionship support, but no more practical assistance than other people. These differences were largely a result of self-selection—young, unmarried, childless, educated people disproportionately choosing to live in the urban places—and otherwise there was little if any difference by urbanism (except the city-dweller's relative lack of house helpers). From a diagnostic perspective, the small towns, not the large cities, are the places to find people without social support. From a theoretical perspec-tive, people are about equally likely to have social support (except in house-related matters), however big their communities.

Who Provides What Support?

Although small-town and big-city respondents differed little in how much they could count on social support, they differed considerably in the sources of their support, particularly, as we saw in part 3, in whether they turned to kin or nonkin. Moreover, respondents living in all sizes of communities selected certain kinds of associates for certain kinds of aid.

Different social contexts were drawn upon for different purposes: for counseling, respondents tended to ask spouses, other nuclear kin, and "just friends." For companionship, they spent time overwhelmingly with just friends. For practical support, it depended on the specific need: neighbors would look after the house; a variety of relatives and just friends helped with tasks around the house; co-workers discussed work problems; and older-generation relatives, notably parents, could supply a loan.[16]

(This substantive point has a methodological implication: if network researchers ask people about counseling support, they will hear about nuclear kin; if they ask about companionship, they will hear about just friends; and so on.)

Although respondents tended to nominate associates of their own gender for most support, they also disproportionately named women as counselors, especially women relatives. They also tended to prefer people of the same age and those they had known a long time for the role of confidant. In contrast, respondents tended to ask older men—especially, but not exclusively, fathers—for financial aid. For companionship, respondents tended to name people their age or younger, often unmarried, and also disproportionately female.[17]

The profiles of different types of supporters could be further detailed, but one point already emerges: support tends to come from specialized sectors of networks. We typically have a good time with friends but turn to relatives in a crisis. Older men provide money, women of the same age provide an intimate conversation. To be sure, these are not rules of any kind; respondents varied greatly in whom they chose for specific support. Some, for example, always named kin and some almost never did. What we cannot determine, but which further analysis may reveal, is the extent to which associates can be substituted satisfactorily. How satisfying are close relatives as companions? How secure are people who rely on friends for loans?

Who Provides What for Whom?

Different types of needs seem to call for different types of associates. And in part 3 we saw that different types of people tend to choose different types of associates. Here we combine these two considerations and ask whether respondents varied in which kinds of associates they used for which kinds of support. Since the possible permutations of this analysis are many,[18] we will focus on only a few comparisons, largely to illustrate the point that different combinations of needed support and needy person lead to calling on different supporters.

One such combination involves education and kinship. Generally, educated respondents relied less on kin than did uneducated respondents. But this varied by specific support. Other respondent characteristics held constant, a college graduate's confidant was about twenty percentage points less likely than a grade-school graduate's confidant to be a relative; the college graduate's social companion was about ten points less likely to be a relative; but the college graduate's source of a loan was just as likely to be a relative as was the source for the grade-school graduate.[19] Another variation involves age and fellow organization members. Older respondents were especially likely, compared with younger respondents, to have co-members as social companions, but not especially likely to have them as counselors or practical helpers. I suspect that this reflects the tendency of older people to be involved in church-based social activities but to otherwise rely on children and neighbors.

Similar, though slight, combinations appear with urbanism. As I noted briefly in chapter 7, urban residents' disposition to associate with nonkin was somewhat muted when it came to seeking advice on a serious decision or borrowing money.[20] In crises, small-town and big-city people turn equally to kin. Similarly, urbanites tended to prefer just friends to neighbors more than small-town residents did, but this urban preference for friends over neighbors was strongest with respect to companionship and weakest with respect to practical aid.[21]

These sorts of comparisons could be multiplied endlessly. The basic lesson is that not only do people vary in whom they generally turn to, they also vary in how they match particular needs with particular associates.

Evaluations and Reactions

So far, we have been imposing our own measurements, as outsiders, of respondents' social support. How did the respondents themselves evaluate and how did they subjectively react to the support their networks provided?

We approached this topic in two ways: asking respondents themselves to evaluate the adequacy of their social relations according to the three types used here, and seeing whether there was a connection between the support respondents had (as we measured it) and their general reports of well-being. Asking people to evaluate their personal relations is difficult; there is a natural tendency to be upset or defensive, or both, when asked, in essence, Does anyone care for you? After much experimentation, we finally asked these three questions (qs. 101–3) near the end of the interview:

Thinking about the people you know, do you sometimes wish you knew more people you could talk with about personal matters and problems, or do you feel you already know enough people to talk with right now? (q. 101)

Do you sometimes wish you knew more people you could get together with to have a good time, or do you feel you already know enough people like that? (q. 102)

What about having people you can rely on to help you with things when you need it, things like work around the home or lending money—do you sometimes wish you knew more people like that, or do you already know enough people to rely on for help? (q. 103)

The irony, however, is that respondents with adequate support on our scales were just as likely to say they wished they knew more people as were respondents who scored as marginal or inadequate. Indeed, respondents with more support tended slightly more often to say they wished they knew still more people. Even if we abandon our adequacy scales and just count the number of people named as supporters of each type, the respondents with many associates were as likely as, or more likely than, respondents with few to say they wanted more.[22] In part this results from the tendency of older people, who had smaller networks, to say they knew enough people. What they had was little; what they wanted—especially in the way of companions—was also little. But, even taking that and similar complications into account, we cannot assert any connection between lacking social support and expressing the need for it. Others have noted a similar effect: Campbell, Converse, and Rodgers found that respondents to a national survey who said that they had many "good friends" were more likely than those who said that they had "not many" to be interested in making new friends. The researchers suggest that there is a "very general trait of 'gregariousness' leading some people to make many friends and to be very receptive to still more."[23]

Although the connection between people's actual social support and their evaluation of it may be equivocal, there was a clear connection between social support, especially companionship, and general feelings of well-being. The more *companions* respondents named—particularly, the more they named *beyond* "adequacy," beyond four—the more likely they were to score high on our measure of psychological mood (see chap. 4). This was also the case, though less strongly so, for the number of practical supporters. Respondents with many outside-the-household counselors were neither more nor less likely to be content. When other factors— marital status, age, income, and so forth—are held constant, the critical factor is companionship. The more companions respondents had, the better they felt.[24]

These supporters, it should be recalled, are only people outside the household. Two kinds of associates inside the household also affected respondents' mood: spouses improved it; children depressed it.

Urbanism plays a minor role in all this. Urban respondents differed from otherwise similar small-town respondents only in having slightly less secure practical support, but the number of practical supporters made little difference in people's overall mood. Would urban and small-town respondents have differed in psychological mood if they had all had equal numbers of supporters of each kind? Only a little. If all respondents had been similar in social support as well as in age, income, and so on, Core and Semirural residents would have reported feeling slightly better in overall mood than residents of Town or Metropolitan communities.[25] This suggests that living in moderately urban places, holding constant self-selection and holding constant how urbanism might affect social support, is slightly more depressing than living in either smaller or larger places. But the difference is small, and the constructed comparison is so artificial that we should not place much emphasis upon it.

Networks as Burdens

Our friends and relatives not only support us, they also require us to support them. They can give pain as well as pleasure. Some of the most poignant illustrations of this in our survey were young or middle-aged women caring for disabled parents. Other instances included wives of alcoholics; an elderly couple, he with emphysema and she with a rheumatic heart, trying to sustain a daughter, son-in-law, and grand-daughter on their Social Security payments; the up-and-coming businessman in chapter 8 who complained about having to attend family dinners; the small-town widow who objected that her daughter insisted on doing *too* much for her and impaired her sense of independence; and the family an interviewer described this way:

There is a lot of tension in the respondent's household. He had a heart attack recently and is very dependent on his wife for help. He was probably domineering before, but his condition has put him in a situation where he is dependent upon someone he probably gave a lot of shit to at one time. His daughter recently tried to knife the father of her baby when she was drunk. The wife feels a lot of pressure, which she lays back on the respondent. Everything is just a bit out of control. The wife asked me what she should do, and she looked to me for consolation when we were alone.

(These cases are, of course, not typical. There is also the family of an interviewer described this way: "Respondent and his wife were a really adorable young couple who were enthusiastic, and articulate, and young, and in love [sigh].")

Although we could not fully explore who it was respondents supported,[26] we did ask two questions designed to identify those respondents who felt burdened:

About how often do you feel that the people you live with make too many demands on you these days—a lot of the time, some of the time, only once in a while, or never? (q. 104; scored from never to a lot)

About how often do you feel that your friends and [other] relatives make too many demands on you...? (q. 105)

Women with young children were far more likely than others to say that they felt too many demands from members of their households. In general women and parents, especially parents of infants and toddlers, were most likely to feel pressed by their households, but the combination of being a women and being a parent was especially deadly. Other things equal, a thirty-year-old woman with a five-year-old and a one-year-old child would have scored over half a step more "demanded" than her husband (i.e., from scoring about halfway between "some of the time" and "once in a while" to scoring at "some of the time"). Having a spouse, on the other hand, moderately reduces feelings of demand. In addition to these features of the household, part-time workers (who tended to be women), and respondents undergoing some stressful life events were more likely than others to feel harassed. The general point is clear: children demand and women respond to those demands, as well as to the demands of others. Those pressures, in turn, are felt and reported.[27] (Urbanism has no clear connection with these feelings of household demands.)

Just as having children leads to feelings of household demands, so having friends leads—though less strongly—to feelings of demands from outside the household. Respondents who named more companions—all else equal—complained a bit more about the demands of friends and relatives. Companions were therefore a source both of pleasant feelings (see above) and of harried feelings. Also contributing to expressions of too many demands from outside the household were being young, undergoing stressful life changes, and having children. The last two suggest that other strains may make the demands of friends feel even more onerous.[28] Urbanism is unrelated to this sense of demands.

Companions are the prime social source of pleasure,[29] but they are also (next to children) the prime source of felt harassment, albeit more the former than the latter. And by this harassment, companions slightly reduce people's feelings of total well-being.[30] This paradox only hints at an important area for future research: the double-edged nature of personal relations.[31]

Conclusion

The connection between objectively having social support and subjectively benefiting from it seems, in these data, weak. This weak connection might be explained in terms of the "buffering" effect of social networks, that they are important primarily in helping one to cope with crises.[32] Had we examined only people going through some trauma, perhaps counseling and practical support would have had more effect on their psychological reactions. Companionship, which is a daily rather than an episodic concern, *was* a source of felt well-being. An additional explanation of the weak connection between support and feeling might be that the psychological costs of personal relations subtract from many of their benefits.

Nevertheless, we have learned a few things about social support. The principles of opportunity and constraint that dictated the sheer number of associates respondents had also shaped whether they had even adequate social support. Those whose activities were circumscribed—parents, especially mothers of young children; the elderly, especially men; the poor; and minorities—tended to be "at risk" of lacking support. Those with wider opportunities—the young; the educated; and the affluent—were more often secure in their social support. In spite of the romantic notion that the underprivileged make up in human wealth what they lack in material wealth, the principle seems to be in matters social, too, that "Unto everyone that hath shall be given. . . . But from him that hath not shall be taken away."

The social support people receive tends to be, at least as we measured it, relatively specialized: companionship from friends, practical help from relatives or neighbors, and counseling from immediate relatives and friends. This specialization by function is overlaid by respondents' preferences—the educated for calling on friends, women for calling on kin, and so forth.

The thesis that urban residents lack adequate social support finds, as earlier chapters foreshadowed, little empirical support. As a diagnostic matter, if we were simply asking where among our respondents could we find those ''at risk'' of lacking social support, we would look in the small communities, at least with respect to counseling and companionship. As an analytic matter, if we ask what effect urbanism has on the adequacy of social support, we would say it had little. Otherwise similar respondents in small town and city would have averaged the same level of counseling and companionship. The more urban ones would have been at slightly greater risk with regard to practical aid, especially lacking people to look after their homes or to help around the house. (On the other hand, since they were less likely to live in detached dwellings and to be homeowners, urbanites may have needed less of this kind of help.) But the overall effects are small. Similarly, small-town and city respondents did not differ in their reactions to the flip side of social support; they felt about equally harassed by their associates.

It seems that, although small-town and city respondents drew on different types of people for support, they nevertheless generated—with the house-care exception—roughly equally supportive networks.

12   The Structure of Relations and Networks

A young secretary living with her parents in a small wine-country city said that her community felt safe because "everyone here knows you and knows what's going on. If you meet someone you can find out if they can be trusted. In San Francisco, you probably wouldn't know anyone who'd know them, so if something happened, it'd slide, I guess." At the same time, she was concerned that "you can't tell one person something without it getting to everyone else."

This woman is expressing her ambivalence about a structural property of networks, the extent to which their members are interconnected, or their *density*. The more of a person's associates who are associates of one another, the more dense his or her network. Network density is one of two dimensions of networks that have long concerned sociologists. The other might be called relational density. It is usually labeled *multistrandedness*—how many different ways an individual is involved with someone. If all I do with my colleague is discuss sociology, our relation is single-stranded, or specialized; if we also see each other socially, it is double-stranded; and if we also share a pastime; it is triple-stranded.

This chapter first discusses why many sociologists consider these two properties so important. Second, it examines who among our respondents had dense networks or multistranded relations, and why—in particular, whether these were more common in smaller communities. Third, it attempts to assess whether these structural properties had any social psychological consequences.

The Issues

Multistrandedness and density are, in most critiques of modern urban life, the key properties missing in people's networks. The specific terms themselves are rarely used, but they are implied by phrases such as "everyone knows everyone," "tightly knit communities," and "full and rich relations" that are used to describe traditional or rural life. By reducing network density and multistrandedness, modernization and urbanization have presumably alienated people from one another.

Argument

In the bygone village, people were involved with one another in many ways:[1] the shopkeeper you bought from in the day you drank with at night. Similarly, the people you were involved with were involved with one another: the person you lent five dollars lent his hammer to the person who lent you a hoe. This multistrandedness and density was a consequence of isolation; the handful of people around were the only people available, and so one got to know them all and know them well.

Modern technology and urbanization changed that. They allowed access to many more people. You could buy from someone who sold more cheaply and drink with someone else more witty. And people did. Relations became specialized, single-stranded. And the chances that any of these dispersed associates knew one another were less, so networks became less dense.

This change was ultimately for the worse. Single-purpose relations may be efficient, but they are superficial, fleeting, unreliable, and psychologically unfulfilling. Similarly, a loosely knit network cannot provide the collective fellowship, security, and—as the secretary complained—mutual supervision characteristic of a dense network.

Counterargument

Many criticisms have been made of this tale called the decline of community. One challenges the image of the cohesive village, arguing that it was instead a hostile and lonely place, where intimate relations, if any, existed only among kin.[2] More relevant here are two specific points: first, that people with social choices do not necessarily build low-density and single-stranded networks; and, second, that such networks are not necessarily less supportive than dense and multi-stranded ones.

First, individuals with access to many others may still develop multi-stranded and dense networks. The sports car enthusiast, for example, may choose all of his or her social ties from among fellow enthusiasts even though other relations are available. Although the constrained person must necessarily have dense and multistranded networks (if any social ties at all), the relatively unconstrained person may or may not. Consequently, the connection between having the opportunity for more ties and having loose, single-stranded networks is likely to be weak. The more important difference may be in the choice of which relations to be involved in.

Second, multistrandedness and density may not promote personal intimacy and security. There are two variations to this counterargument.

One is that multistrandedness and density are not the causes but the *consequences* of intense involvements. If you get along well with someone in one context, you will decide to do other things with them—not vice versa. And if you are heavily committed to a specific social world, many of the people you know will know each other—not vice versa. The other variation is the claim that multistrandedness and density actually *impede* intimacy. The old adages warning against doing business with a friend or dating someone in the office reflect a widespread belief that mixing types of interactions can damage relations. Similarly, intermeshed relations may mean that people are always on guard with one another for fear that a damaging revelation may circle back, or that closeness with one person may lead another to be jealous.

These arguments reduce, for us to two significant questions: Does urban life—and perhaps, by extension, modern life—promote single-stranded and low-density networks? Are such networks less intimate and supportive than multistranded and dense ones? I will describe who in our sample had multistranded and dense networks, considering both the types of people and the other characteristics of networks that were associated with these two features. Then I will turn to assessing the consequences, if any, of multistrandedness and density.

Multistrandedness

Our measure of multistrandedness counts the specific interactions respondents expected to have with their associates, using the name-eliciting exchange questions (for example, "Who would you ask to take care of your house...?"). This measure is meaningful for only 69 percent of all the relations that respondents listed. Excluded are the relations with people named in reply to the question, "Is there anyone else important to you who doesn't show up on this [preliminary] list?" (q. 81; unless we wanted to say that these relations had zero strands). Consequently, all the network characteristics used here refer to the initial set of 13,475 names; for example, number of kin refers to number of kin excluding those named on the "anyone else" question.[3]

The measure is a simple one: for each person named we counted the number of different questions in answer to which they were named: caring for the house, discussing work, helping around the house, visiting or going out together, discussing hobbies, being a "fiancee," discussing personal problems, advising on decisions, lending money, and sharing the household (the latter only if over fifteen years old).[4] For each respondent we have two scores: the absolute number of associates they mentioned three or more times (the average is 2.3, or eighteen percent of all the names elicited on any of the questions), and the average number of mentions per associate (the average of this average is 1.6).[5]

Who Has Multistranded Ties?

Ideas about who has multistranded relations—the same people who probably also have dense netwroks—can be expressed in terms of the opportunities and constraints people face. Generally, people with limited mobility, skills, and access to others should, by lack of alternatives, be involved in multiple ways with the same persons.[6] The underlying assumption is that when people can develop specialized relations they will (although that may be short-sighted on their part).

The description that emerges from our data is somewhat more complex; it suggests that amount of social activity is as important as the number of people available. Respondents with large networks actually had *more,* not fewer, multistranded relations (associates named three or more times) than respondents with small networks. Thus, respondents could be involved with many people but still rely on a few particular individuals in several ways.[7] Young singles, for example, averaged about two more multistranded relations than did the elderly, while also generally knowing more people. At the same time, it is true that respondents with large networks had a slightly lower *average* number of strands *per relation* than did those with smaller networks.[8] Networks of ten averaged about 1.6 strands per relation, while networks of twenty averaged about 1.4. This implies that, as people expand their networks, they include more multistranded ties, but at a decreasing rate.

Who tended to have many multistranded relations? The same people who tended to have large networks: the young, educated, employed, and members of organizations (and also relative newcomers to the neighborhood). Taking network size into account by looking at average multistrandedness, youth is the major distinguishing feature of people whose relations tended to be multistranded. Little else made much difference.[9]

These results suggest that we should change our ideas about multistrandedness. How many things a person does with another is a consequence not only of how many people the first knows but also of how many things he or she does. People who are not employed cannot talk with anyone about their jobs; people who are reticent about discussing personal difficulties cannot have others as counselors. The strong decline in multistrandedness with age reflects the lessened activity of older people; retirement and housekeeping operate similarly. Educational attainment does not reduce multistranded ties because the expanded activities of the educated almost keep pace with their expanded networks, resulting both in more specialized relations and in more diffuse ones. In sum, the more one does, the more multistranded one's ties can be.[10]

Urbanism

Network theorists have explicitly argued that urbanites have less stranded networks than residents of small communities. Jeremy Boissevain, for example, argues that, compared with the residents of a small community,

The size of the universe from which [the person who lives in a large city] can recruit social relations is much larger, as is the range of institutions and activities in which he can participate. He has, potentially, a different public for every role he plays. Moreover, . . . each member of his city network is in a similar position. . . . Neighbors often do not know one another, or if they do exchange only nods. They most probably do not go to the same clubs, church or family feasts. Nor do they work to- gether. In short, they tend to maintain single-stranded relationships with a large variety of persons.[11]

This is not what we found; big-city residents had networks of essentially the same level of strandedness as otherwise similar small-town residents (and to the extent that Boissevain's description is at all accurate, it should have read "she," not "he").

Semirural respondents listed notably *fewer* multistranded relations (ones where the other person was named three or more times) than did other respondents. This was to be expected, given that older respondents name fewer multistranded relations and Semirural respondents tended to be older. Standardized for such self-selection characteristics (and for size of the networks), respondents in different places differed little in their number of multistranded associates. There was only a slight tendency for women in Towns to report more multiple ties than women elsewhere.[12] The results using *average multistrandedness* point to the same conclu- sion: little difference in strandedness by urbanism, except that women in Towns (especially nonworking women) averaged slightly more strands per relation than did any other group.[13] We must conclude that, de- scriptively, urban residents have *more* multistranded networks, but living in urban places itself neither increases nor decreases strandedness.

People in the modern sectors of society—the young, educated, and urban—have, at least by this analysis, roughly as multistranded networks as their counterparts in the traditional sectors. This challenges the stan- dard formulas. Those models ought to be recast, I suggest, by realizing that, when individuals gain access to more people, rather than simply spreading their social life more thinly, they may actually enjoy richer social lives.

Consequences

By definition, associates whose relations with a respondent were multistranded provided that respondent with more social support than did those whose relations with him or her were single-stranded. But, in addition, those associates were also more likely to be thought of as "close" (if nonkin; among kin, except for siblings, the number of exchanges an associate provided made little difference in felt closeness).[14] Also, the more strands in a relation, the more often the participants "got together."[15] Empirically and on the face of it, people's multistranded relations are more intimate and functionally more important than their single-stranded ones. (Whether there is also a hidden social or psychological cost in mixing functions is not evident.)

But this connection between the strandedness of a *relation* and its intimacy does not necessarily mean that having *networks* high in average multistrandedness is similarly advantageous. By definition, the more times respondents named people, the more supporters of particular types they had (so our measures of strandedness and of adequate support must correlate). There is little evidence in terms of respondents' subjective feelings, however, that the averge multistrandedness of their networks made much difference. People with multistranded networks were a bit *more* likely to say they wished they knew more people to have fun with, but this and other slight correlations tend to dissipate when personal and network characteristics are held constant. Multistrandedness is basically the ratio of people's social activities to their social partners—"social" defined most broadly. Both activities and partners seem to increase together (and sense of well-being increases with them). No wonder, then, that the ratio of the one to the other makes little difference.

Network Density

Measuring density was more complicated than measuring multistrandedness. We wanted to know which of the people a respondent was involved with were, as far as the respondent knew, also involved with one another. We could not ask about every possible pair of names; for some respondents it would have been more than a thousand pairs. So we chose to ask about the special subsample of up to five people, the same people about whom we asked detailed questions such as "How did you

meet this person?'' The interviewer selected the five names by going back
to six key questions—caring for the home, visiting or going out socially,
discussing hobbies, discussing personal matters, giving advice, and lending money—and picking the first name given in answer to each one, excluding household members, until she had five. (See p. 30 of the questionnaire—preceding q. 80—for the specific procedure.) These associates
were much like the rest, differing noticeably only in including proportionally fewer extended kin, more people living nearby, and more people
respondents felt ''close'' to.[16] Since many respondents gave no names, or
only household names, or always the same names, we obtained a full list
of five for only 39 percent of the respondents; 32 percent had four; 19
percent had three; and 10 percent had two or less.

I excluded those respondents with two or fewer names from the subsequent analysis. Such respondents, basically those with generally small
networks, lived disproportionately in Semirural communities. Seventeen
percent of our respondents there are lost to this analysis, compared to 8 or
9 percent elsewhere, and they tended to be men, uneducated, and with
very few friends. I will return to these missing respondents when com-
menting on the results. In any event, we are left with 941 respondents for
whom we could analyze density.

The interviewer listed the three to five names on a matrix (reproduced
on p. 30-B of the questionnaire), which allowed her to ask, for each pair of
names ''Do _____ and _____ know each other well?'' (A sure yes answer was taken to mean a relation existed in the eyes of the respondent. If
the respondent did not know or was unsure, the answer was coded no.) It
would have been desirable but impractical to confirm these answers with
the named people or to go into the details of the relations. We necessarily
rely on the respondent's interpretations and perceptions of these relations.

This matrix generates two measures. For each named person, we know
how many, and what proportion, of the others the respondent thought he
or she knew well. And, for each respondent, we know how many relations
he or she thought existed among the associates. The standard way of
translating this latter number into a measure of density is to divide it by
the total number of relations there could have been—ten if the respondent
was asked about five names, six if asked about four, three if asked about
three. The average density ratio was .44 (44 percent of the possible ties
existed); 10 percent of the respondents had ratios of zero and 11 percent
had ratios of one.[17] Although this statistic was calculated for a small
portion of the network, we take it to be a good approximation of the
density of entire network. (Density and average multistrandedness correlated at $r = .21$.)

Who Has Dense Networks?

The extant theories answer this question much as they answer the same one concerning multistrandedness: people whose circle of acquaintances is and has been limited. Elizabeth Bott, for example, suggests that dense networks will be found among longtime residents of stable neighborhoods and those who have been confined by social or physical impediments to the company of kin and neighbors.[18] In these kinds of circumstances people whom people know, know one another.

Our data generally *confirm* these expectations. The more relatives and the fewer nonrelatives in a respondent's network, the denser it was. For example, networks composed more than one-half of kin averaged a density ratio of .59, compared with .41 for others. But this difference only illustrates a more general finding: networks tended to be dense when drawn heavily from any one or two social contexts. Networks drawn from a single context averaged a density ratio of .84, from two contexts .65, from three .49, and from four or more .38. (The notable exception that "proves" the point is the "other" context; networks largely composed of such heterogeneous others had very low density, .34.) The more diverse people's sphere of activity, the less dense their networks.[19] This finding implies, first, that density is at least in part a by-product of the contextual character of the network. If one's network is drawn heavily from one or two contexts, it will be dense. Second, it underlines the importance of opportunities to form ties outside the basic contexts; without such opportunities, people end up with dense ties.

Given this and what we learned earlier about networks, we would expect that dense netwroks would be more common among people from lower social strata. Less affluent and, especially, less educated respondents did have denser networks. In part this resulted from their involvement in fewer social contexts. But personal and network characteristics held constant, less educated respondents still had notably denser networks than educated ones. Length of residence in the city (not the neighborhood, as Bott predicted) was also a major factor; residents of eleven years or more had especially dense networks. That both class and residential stability remain important after taking into account the content of the network (e.g., number of kin; diversity of contexts) suggests, as one explanation, that education, affluence, and mobility allow individuals to make and maintain relations with people from various *specific* contexts, even when those associates are members of a common general category. For example, educated people may have complex work ties with co-workers who do not know one another well; highly mobile people may, in the course of their travels, pick up several "just friends" who are not friends of one another.[20, 21]

Concretely, the kinds of persons who reported high density in their networks were, for example, minority-group women with few associates, all of whom were kin; or retired people, all of whose friends were either neighbors or fellow church members; or nineteen-year-olds, just graduated from high school and still living at home, with a "crowd" of school friends whom their parents knew. Respondents with low-density networks varied in type, but many were like the young woman management trainee, who had lived in San Francisco for two years since moving from the suburbs and who had strong relations with five people: a brother in the hometown, an old school friend in Berkeley, a former co-worker in Oakland, a new "just friend" in the city, and a new neighbor. None of these people knew each other well, she said.

Dense networks arise not simply from one's own characteristics, but also from those of one's associates. Having highly educated friends or kin, whatever one's own education, will probably lead to low density because their style is not conducive to their knowing others of one's friends. Similarly, living in a community of people prone to high- or low-density networks will, if one is involved with those people, shape one's own network.

Urbanism

Standard theories and popular belief are correct in claiming that network density drops with increases in urbanism. As the solid line in the center of figure 15 shows, the more urban respondents' communities were, the less dense their networks tended to be.[22] Although the differences, from an average of .52 in Semirural places to .35 in Core communities, may not seem large, they are roughly as great as the differences between poor and rich respondents, or between old-timers in a city and newcomers. It tends to be, as most people believe, that in small towns "everybody knows everybody."[23]

Self-selection, different types of people coming to live in different types of places, does not fully account for this variation in density. Even had all respondents been roughly equal in education, length of residence, and so on, the urban ones would still have had less dense networks (with Semirural respondents averaging .49 and Core respondents .39).[24] Controlling also for the contextual characteristics of the networks—number of kin and the diversity of contexts from which nonkin were drawn—yields much the same findings, as shown by the dashed line in the center of figure 15.[25] The differences are noteworthy, if not dramatic; moving from Semirural to Core would alone reduce density by about the same amount as dropping five relatives from the network. In sum, urbanism reduces density in ways besides self-selection or altering network composition. (Had we not lost

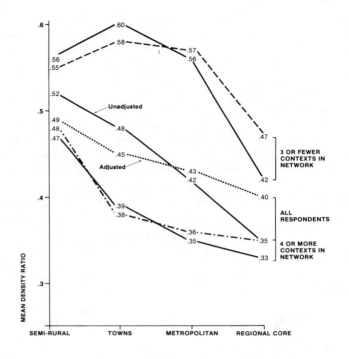

Fig. 15.   **Density ratio, by urbanism, by number of network contexts (only respondents with three or more associates in the special subsample).**

17 percent of the Semirural respondents whose networks were too small to yield density measures, the average density of the Semirural group would quite likely have been yet greater.)[26]

Some insight into how this urban effect happens can be gained by splitting the respondents into two groups—those who drew relations from relatively few different social contexts and those who drew from many— also shown in figure 15. Among those with few, the major difference in density is between Core respondents and others. Although these Core respondents had associates in only one or two settings—say, only kin and neighbors—their associates were less likely to know one another than were associates of comparable but less urban respondents. More striking, Semirural respondents who drew from several contexts nevertheless had relatively high density networks (even higher than Core respondents with few contexts).[27] An illustration brought to mind is a playground pick-up basketball game. In the city, the players probably have never met before;

in the small town, the players, even if they come from different social situations, will probably know one another. The young secretary was right: in San Francisco, people you know are less likely to know each other.

Subjective Effects of Density

That network density has consequences for groups seems clear. The more interconnected a set of people, the more easily they can communicate and act. Whether the interconnectedness of an individual's associates has consequence for him or her is not so clear. Although several studies have crudely estimated density, very few have done it well.[28] The limited evidence is mixed on whether dense networks actually provide more support to their members than do loosely knit networks.[29] But people in dense networks seem to feel closer to and to be more involved with their associates.[30] The sharpest evidence comes from a recent study of young men, half of them veterans, in three eastern communities. Among these men, the denser their networks (largely composed of friends), the better they scored on measures of mental health.[31] This is the kind of evidence needed to support the classic argument that intertwined networks better protect and regulate individuals than do loosely knit networks.

We cannot, with this survey, assess whether people in denser networks also received more actual support,[32] but we can see whether they felt differently about their support. They did. The denser respondents' networks—up to a point—the less likely they were to wish they knew more people to talk to or to have fun with, and the more likely some were to score high on our measure of "psychological mood." The results, however, are complex. Before casting off into these murky waters, I should note that three particularly difficult passages will be encountered: density's connections with these feelings are irregular, in that often high- and low-density respondents felt more like one another than they did like medium-density respondents; density went with a better mood among less affluent respondents but went along with a worse mood among affluent ones; and, most complex, network density must be broken down into separate relations before we can gain some grasp of the process. The last traverse will suggest that the critical aspect of density is not the overall knit of relations, but the existence of one or two particularly central associates.

Although, as the last chapter reported, having relatively many supporters did not reduce how likely respondents were to say they wanted more, having supporters who were interconnected did reduce the wish for more. Respondents with low network density were especially likely to say they wished they knew more people to "talk with about personal problems" and to "get together with to have a good time." Comparing respondents who were otherwise similar in personal characteristics, this wish for more people drops as density increases—until about .7 density. After that level, the wish to know more *increases* with increases in density.[33]

Figure 16 shows the other association between the density of respondents' networks and their feelings, this one with psychological mood. (Although the psychological mood scale includes three components— feeling upset, feeling angry, and feeling pleased, the results reported here are largely a result of density's association with being *pleased*.) In general, respondents with dense networks felt no differently than other respondents: the heavy solid line in the figure's center is virtually flat. However, as the broken line shows, if other characteristics of respondents and their networks are held constant—most important, number of nonkin, which also increases mood—then the denser respondents' networks, the higher their scores. In other words, had our respondents been similar in personal characteristics *and* other network characteristics, those with greater social density would have reported feeling better.[34]

Figure 16 also shows one of the complexities alluded to earlier: The denser the networks of low-income respondents (under $15,000 household income), the *better* they felt; the denser the networks of high-income respondents, the *worse* they felt![35] This is difficult to explain, but the following is one possibility.

Two contradictory aspects of networks affect feelings of well-being: size—especially number of nonkin—and network density. (Typically, the more nonkin in the network, the lower its density.[36] And respondents who named more nonkin generally reported feeling better.)[37] But large, low-density networks pose a management problem: one sees different people at different places at different times, often involving scheduling and logistical problems. Because of their material and social resources, affluent people may be best able to make good use of such networks, while they are problematic for low-income people. An alternative strategy for the latter is to rely on a small clique of people, perhaps specifically one or two key associates. For example, a working-class housewife may find it just too difficult to schedule lunches with several scattered friends, and may come to rely more on kaffeeklatsches with a group of neighborhood friends. For low-income people, the more their networks—or parts of their networks—approximate an easily managed clique, the better off they are. This suggests that classic ideas about density may be correct, but only for those who lack the resources to manage dispersed networks.

It is not obvious what the results would have looked like had we had the "lost" cases with too few subsample associates. Examination of the characteristics of these people suggests that the connection between den-

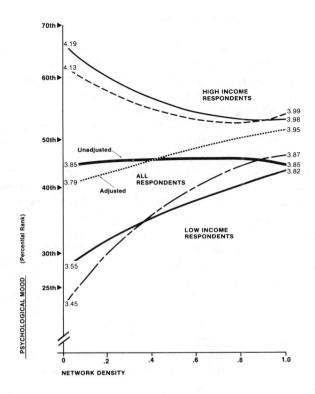

Fig. 16.   **Psychological mood, by network density, by household income (only respondents with three or more associates in the special subsample).**

sity and satisfaction with networks would have remained—they probably had dense networks, and they tended to be relatively satisfied. The connection between density and mood may have been slightly weakened—the lost respondents tended to score below average on mood.

Still, we need to understand why respondents with dense networks felt better about their relations than did respondents with loosely knit networks. One possibility is that we have the causality reversed: Perhaps people with satisfying relations generate density by bringing together their cherished associates. Or perhaps genial people attract a clique around them. Another possibility is that density is indeed the cause, that it improves the quality of the specific relations in the network. It is to those specific relations that we now turn.

Disaggregating Density

The classic models imply that dense networks, unlike loosely knit ones, are more than the sum of their constituent relations. One way of understanding this idea is to assume that each of one's associates is individually more supportive, intimate, and surveillant by virtue of being connected to one's other associates. He or she is probably better informed about, more often gets together with, and feels more responsible for one than would otherwise be the case. Another way to understand this idea is to assume that one's associates are, in dense networks, more likely to act collectively (for example, to console you in a group rather than one by one), and that collective action is especially powerful. Either way, respondents should report deeper involvement with each associate, the denser their networks of associates.[38]

When we turn to specific relations we need to separate two aspects of network density: the number of other associates that any single associate knows—*centrality*—and the interconnections among those other associates in the network—*others' density*. These two components can combine in various ways. Figure 17 illustrates some of these combinations for networks of five people, using the darkened circle to represent the specific associate of interest. (The illustrations take for granted that the respondent is connected to all five.)

While some combinations are rarer than others—especially in the top left or bottom right corner, suggesting that interconnections breed more interconnections—considerable variability is possible. The associate in the lower right knows as many of the others as does the one in the upper right, but only in the latter instance do they know one another.

Among the associates of our respondents, the more central they were, the more involved they were with the respondent, in a variety of ways. For example, the chances that an associate was named as a supporter two or more times—that is, had a multistranded relation—went up from .22 for associates who knew none of the others to .37 for those who knew a few of the others, to .47 for those who knew at least two-thirds of the others. Similarly, while 34 percent of the unconnected associates were labeled as "especially close," 50 percent of the moderately central and 65 percent of the highly central were so labeled. Central associates were indeed close associates.[39]

More difficult to determine than the correlation is the causal relationship: Do people who know others we know thereby become intimate and supportive, or do our intimate and supportive associates thereby come to know others in our networks? Probably both. Besides meeting and learning about someone through other people, we get to know them better in group settings. At the same time, people we have known over the

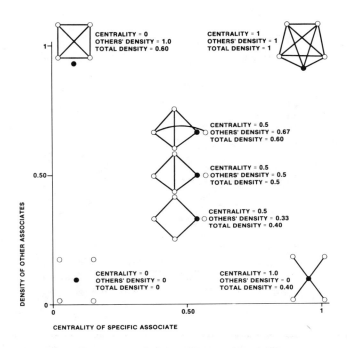

Fig. 17.   Illustrations of how centrality and others' density combine to form total density.

years—and central associates were known longer than noncentral ones[40]—come to know the other people in our lives.

In either case, these results may explain why respondents with dense networks were content with the social and confiding qualities of their ties: they had specific associates, central ones, who provided those supports. And this may in turn explain why these same respondents were slightly happier, too. (It may also explain why there was no connection between density and whether respondents felt they had adequate practical help: overall, central associates were *not* more likely, for example, to lend money than noncentral associates.)

In reaching for this explanation, however, a new puzzle emerges: whatever the centrality of the specific associate was, the greater the density among *the others* in the network, the *less* involved that specific associate was with the respondent. Figure 18 illustrates the finding for two kinds of involvement—whether the associate was a social partner of the respondent (i.e., elicited on q. 74; whether the associate was a confidant yields very similar results) and whether the associate was called "especially

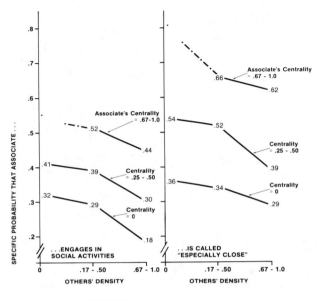

TOO FEW CASES TO PERCENTAGE

Fig. 18.   **Probability that associate engaged in social activities
with or was "close" to respondent, by others' density
or by associate's centrality (only associates in special
network subsamples of four and five associates).**

close" by the respondent. As the density of others in the network increased, the intensity of the associate's tie to the respondent decreased,
no matter whether the associate knew the others or not.[41]

Why would interconnections among others in the network reduce the
role of a particular associate? It may be easy understand why an associate
who knew none of the others (upper left of figure 17) would be relatively
unimportant. He or she would be an outsider to a clique—either not
valued enough by the respondent to be included or not valued because of
being excluded. That does not explain, however, why associates who
were central (right side of fig. 17) also became less significant as the others
became more interconnected.

One answer is that *relative* centrality is almost as important as absolute
centrality. The more of one's other associates a specific associate knows
(absolute centrality), the stronger one's relation to him or her—either
because the interconnections strengthen the tie, or because close as-

sociates come to know the others, or both. In addition, the more of one's associates a specific associate knows, *compared with the others* (relative centrality), the stronger the relation—either because that person had to have been a closer intimate than the others in order to be more central than they (for example, people's parents probably meet more of their children's friends than their children's co-workers do), or because relative centrality allows associates to become more important "brokers" in the network than the others (for example, the friend who knows more of the others—perhaps by virtue of having introduced the others—will be turned to first for news of the social circle or for mobilizing people), or both. An associate's role declines as the density of the others increases, because his or her position in the network hierarchy declines.

Another answer is that others' density actually weakens relations in people's networks. It may keep active relations with relatively unimportant associates who would otherwise be "let go." Distant cousins are seen when visiting parents, the guys at the bar are seen together, friends bring their spouses, and so on. In dense networks, these tag-alongs are central—they know the others—but are not critical to one's life. In low-density networks, where third parties do not sustain the ties, such people drift away and are replaced by somewhat more intimate associates.[42]

Whatever the explanation, the finding is that the more interconnected a network, the weaker the tie to any specific member. This is paradoxical, given that total network density tended to go with feeling content about one's relations.

That connection between overall density and saying one "knows enough people" apparently can be accounted for by the presence in dense networks of one, or two, or at most three very central, intimate, supportive associates. At least, it is the centrality of a particular associate, rather than the density of the overall network, that predicts the intensity of the respondent's relation with that associate. Put broadly, dense networks may be felt as supportive because they necessarily include a couple of particularly supportive individual relations. The availability of one or two crucial and central associates may also explain the greater overall sense of well-being that low-income respondents with dense networks had compared with those with low-density networks (see figure 16). It is the availability of a few strong ties, not the whole network, that makes the difference.[43]

Had we not "lost" 109 respondents because they gave us too few names, the connection between density and the closeness of the relations would have been weaker. The missing respondents were notably less likely to report feeling close to their associates or turning to them for discussion of personal issues.

Conclusion

Major theoretical statements about the effects of modernization and urbanization on personal relations argue, in essence, that, as individuals' opportunities for meeting and seeing other people widen, they dissipate their attention among more associates. This has, in turn, two unforeseen and ultimately unfortunate consequences. It reduces the ways individuals are involved with any associate—multistrandedness—thereby producing shallower relations. And it reduces the interconnections among their associates—network density—thereby producing less supportive personal communities.

Our findings render a mixed verdict on these ideas. Respondents with widened access to other people—the young, affluent, educated, and urban—did *not* have less stranded relations. I suggested that people sustain extensive involvements with each of their associates even as the total number of associates increases, because the total level of their activities tends to increase almost apace. The people with many friends tend also to be the people with many different things they do with friends (work, go to movies, share a hobby, talk, and so on). We also found that respondents' more multistranded relations were typically their most intensive ones, as well. But the overall level of strandedness of respondents' networks had no special consequences. On this network dimension, the major theories fail.

They do better on network density. The wider the pool of respondents' potential associates, particularly as indicated by their being educated and living in urban places, the substantially less dense their networks, even if size of the network and other factors are held constant. The small town versus big city differences in network density are substantial. (Here it is possible that our sample has affected our conclusion: in rural California, the white working class typically provides the kin-based, high-density networks. In urban California, the comparable working class may be black or non-English-speaking, and not sampled in this study. Our statistical adjustments should have corrected for such differences but may not have done so adequately. Only future research can resolve this possibility.)

There also appear to be some subjective consequences associated with network density: feeling satisfied with the number of people available to confide in or have a good time with, and, among low-income respondents, a general sense of well-being.

Closer examination of network density suggests that these reactions may be accounted for by the presence in dense networks of one or two particularly close and multistranded relations. The associates in these specific relations are important to the respondents and know the respon-

dents' other associates. Interrelations among the other associates, however, only detracts from the strength of that relation. These key allies,
rather than overall density, may account for feelings of satisfaction and
overall well-being.

Closer examination also reveals the possibility that the direction of
causality is reversed. Density, or centrality, may be not the cause of
personal support, but its by-product. When associates are active and
intimate, they become central, and that increases density. And, when
people have one or two such close associates, they feel they have enough.

The strongest case for the classical theories that can be built from this
data uses the evidence that, among low-income respondents, urbanism
decreases network density, and lowered density in turn decreases psychological mood. The net effect of urbanism on mood via reduced density
is slight, but nonetheless worth noting. Add to that the slight reduction
urbanism caused in the number of nonkin low-income respondents knew
(see figure 8)—and nonkin were important for mood—and it is possible to
make the case that, among low-income people, living in urban places
alters social networks so as to decrease felt quality of life (see also next
chapter).[44]

These effects are small and partly in doubt because of the missing
respondents—disproportionally Semirural men with few friends—but
they are intriguing. They do not, however, suggest that urbanism per se
reduces mood for low-income people. Although Semirural low-income
respondents tended to have relatively high morale, all else equal, the
overall trend is insubstantial (see chap. 4, note 15). They do suggest that
living in smaller communities—especially Semirural ones—might provide
low-income people with the kinds of social ties that boost morale. Why
this should be so for low- but not high-income people is curious. One
possibility is that the same level of income in small towns actually goes
further because of lower cost of living, so these small-town residents may
be less poor than they seem. Another is that the complex social opportunities of urban life are too difficult for such groups to handle. A third is
that low-income people in the typically high-income cities have fewer
opportunities to meet people like themselves. This last hypothesis brings
us to the topics of the next two chapters: the spatial locus of respondents'
ties and the extent of similarity between people in those relations.

13   The Spatial Dimension of Personal Relations

Intimately wound into the concern about the decline of community is the belief that the "authentic" personal community is the local one—that neighbors, nearby kinfolk, and the local church form the only truly supportive community. Daily, dense interaction and functional interdependence among a small group of people who share a commitment to a place are the bases for sustaining personal relations. But modern, urban people have become rootless and lost their connection to this local community as they have chased fleeting relations in the wider world. This view, that contiguity is critical for communal bonds, is strongly held by scholars and general public alike. Counter-arguments can be made, however: that modern life allows people to build more personally rewarding relations than are attainable in the local community and to create social worlds almost entirely free from the artificial limits of place, to create "community without propinquity," and this kind of community is ultimately the most personally fulfilling.[1]

In this chapter I join these arguments by examining whether urbanism encourages extralocal relations at the expense of local ones and what the consequences of that might be. In the course of that investigation, we will see who tends to have local and who tends to have cosmopolitan networks and will look at the characteristics of nearby versus distant ties.

An Overview of Spatial Dispersion

Throughout the discussion, we will consider relations at three distances: within five minutes' drive, between five minutes' and one hour's drive, and over one hour's drive away. We used five minutes because it approximates the local community—a small town or a section of a large city. We used one hour because it roughly delimits the outside commuting or casual visiting distance, and it covers approximately a metropolitan area or a rural county.[2]

Two sets of associates are excluded from most of the discussion: members of the respondents' households and nearby people who were named *only* in answer to the question, "Who would take care of your home if you were away?'' This question almost necessarily calls forth nearby associates (about 80 percent of the time), often associates who do nothing else with or for the respondent. These house caretakers constituted a large portion of the neighbors discussed in chapter 9. In this chapter, I shall focus instead on local associates who played wider, or at least different, roles in respondents' lives.

Overall, respondents named 4.8 local associates, 6.3 middle-distance (five to sixty minutes' drive) ones, and 5.4 distant ones. The role of relatives in this count—and in the overall analysis—varied greatly. While 30 percent of local and middle-distance associates were kin, 62 percent of the distant ones were kin. Also, the kinds of respondents we identify as being involved with local versus distant associates depends on whether we consider kin or nonkin. For instance, longtime residents of the city named more local kin but no more local nonkin than did newcomers.[3] These sorts of findings lead us to separate kin and nonkin. Most of our attention will be on nonkin; it is relations with nonkin that are crucial to theories about the local community; it is nonkin who are, in that sense, our neighbors and fellow citizens.

The single most powerful predictor of where respondents' associates lived was the respondents' education. The tendency reported in earlier chapters for respondents to name more nonkin the more education they had applied largely to middle-distance or distant nonkin. Those with postgraduate education named about one and a half times as many local nonkin, three times as many middle-distance nonkin, and more than four times as many distant nonkin as did respondents who failed to graduate from high school. The educated had more spatially dispersed networks of relatives, too. Postgraduates named about two-thirds fewer local relatives, but about one-third *more* distant relatives than did the least educated. Education—a mark of ''modernism''—strongly promotes the geographical dispersion of networks.

Urbanism is also associated with spatial dispersion, but not as strongly. Figure 19 shows the differences for nonkin and kin separately. Semirural respondents picked almost half their nonkin associates from the locality, compared with less than a third for Metropolitan and Core respondents. With kin there is also a general, albeit weak, trend toward greater spatial distribution among urbanites. The proportion of relatives who lived within five minutes' drive drops from 26 percent in Semirural places to 20 percent, to 18 percent, and finally to 15 percent in Core communities.

Figure 19 points out an important contrast in understanding kin ties versus nonkin ties. One can plausibly explain the community differences in where nonkin associates lived by people's choices of associates: the smaller the community, the more people pick and keep friends from

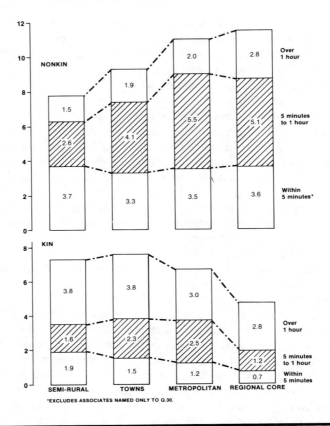

Fig. 19.   **Spatial distribution of networks, nonkin and kin, by urbanism.**

nearby. The community variations in where kin lived cannot be explained that way (a person cannot decide to pick a brother from the next town); it must involve, at least in part, people's choice of where to live: the smaller the community, the nearer to their relatives people decide to live. One reason for such a decision is probably the housing market. In small places one may have to live either very near or very far from one's kin; in metropolitan areas one can easily live almost any distance away. Another reason may be self-selection by taste: respondents in smaller places more typically felt it important to live near relatives than did respondents in larger places.[4] Finally, perhaps residents of smaller places are more likely to marry locals than are urbanites. In any case, this causal distinction between kin and nonkin, together with the rationale that the critical theoretical concern is nonkin, leads us to focus on nonkin in the next sections.

Ties to the Local Community

Of the 3.5 local nonkin the average respondent named, more than a third were labeled "neighbor." Respondents with long tenure in the neighborhood and relatively short tenure in the city, those who gave "kinds of people" as a reason for picking the neighborhood, and those who were living in rapidly growing neighborhoods were most likely to be involved with their neighbors (in ways *besides* as home caretakers; cf. chapter 9). Expanding the pool of associates threefold to include all those living in the general locality yields somewhat different results.

Younger, affluent, and more educated respondents typically named more local nonkin. But when various factors are considered simultaneously, the key characteristics that describe respondents with numerous local ties are being a longtime resident of the neighborhood; being a young male; and, only slightly, being educated and affluent.[5] (Although educated and affluent respondents named *absolutely* more people nearby, *proportionally* they named fewer, because they named many more distant people, as we shall see below.)

How involved people are with local residents also depends on the kind of community in which they live, how they fit into the community, and their activities there. The axial characteristic of communities is urbanism, and most Americans believe that local social ties are greater in small towns. In one national survey, for example, 39 percent of small-town and rural residents said that people in their community "got together quite a bit," but only 16 percent of city residents said that.[6] The research evidence, though not overwhelming, indicates that city-dwellers are, in fact, typically less involved with their fellow residents than are suburbanites or nonmetropolitan people.[7]

Our findings partly confirm those popular impressions. If kin and nonkin are combined in figure 19, we see that the more urban the community, the fewer associates within a five minutes' drive (exclusive of house caretaking specialists). The averages range from 5.6 for Semirural respondents to 4.9, 4.7, and to 4.3 for Core respondents (as a percentage of all associates: 37, 29, 27, and 27). And this pattern cannot be explained by length of residence or other personal traits.[8]

Residents of the different types of communities did *not*, however, differ in how many local *nonkin* they named. Semirural and Core respondents each averaged about 3.5 local associates. Still, there are proportional differences with respect to nonkin—proportional differences in two senses. Urban respondents chose a smaller proportion of their nonkin from the local area: 47 percent for Semirural respondents to 36, 32, and 31 percent for Core respondents. (The critical difference here, as controlling for other variables shows, is between Semirural and others.)[9] And urban respondents named a considerably smaller proportion of all the residents of their localities. Conservatively estimated, Semirural respondents chose, on average, one nonrelative from every 3,000 people within five minutes' drive, Town respondents one from every 4,300, Metropolitan respondents one from every 8,600, and Core respondents one from every 17,000. Obviously these estimates are purely heuristic,[10] but they do make two important points. First, in spite of having far more nearby people to choose from, urbanites associated with only about the same total number of local nonkin as did residents of smaller places. Second, since these ratios indicate the relative penetration of respondents' networks into the locality (i.e., the chances that any given resident was directly or indirectly tied to a respondent), urbanites were in that sense less involved locally than small-town residents.

Nevertheless, urban and small-town respondents named about the same absolute number of local nonkin. Was that because community size does not affect social ties to the locality, or was it in spite of its effects? Figure 20 addresses this question. It presents the same data as does figure 19, but in slightly altered form. For statistical reasons, it uses a logarithmic modification of the numbers of nonkin (so the numbers in figures 19 and 20 cannot be simply compared), and it uses the urbanism scale rather than the four urban categories.[11] Still, the same basic pattern appears: respondents in moderately urban places named insignificantly fewer local nonkin than did those at either extreme (solid line in fig. 20).[12]

The central dashed line, "adjusted for personal traits," indicates, however, that were it not for their personal characteristics—age, low education, and low income—respondents in our smallest communities would have named substantially more local nonkin than respondents living elsewhere. If one could have assigned people to communities randomly, those assigned to Semirural places would have averaged about 50 percent more local nonkin than people in Metropolitan places.[13] Living in a small town did, it seems, increase people's involvement with fellow residents. The effect is less powerful than that of tenure in the neighborhood but is about as great as that of education.

What *about* urbanism reduces local involvement? Before considering the global characteristics of communities that might explain the results—population composition, access to potential associates, and so on—we

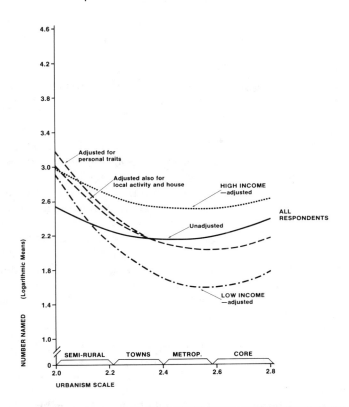

Fig. 20.   **Number of nonkin within five minutes' drive, by urbanism (associates named solely as house caretakers are excluded).**

will consider two specific aspects of respondents' places in their communities: their housing and their activity in the local area.

Being Active Locally and Living in a House

The more things people do in their communities, the greater their chances of meeting and keeping in touch with fellow residents. How much they do in the locality depends partly on what the community provides. Our measure of local activity gave respondents one point each if they:

Shopped (for things other than groceries) within five minutes' drive once every two weeks or more often (q. 61)—56 percent did;

Went out to enjoy themselves (other than visiting friends) within five minutes' drive once every two weeks or more often (q. 64)—46 percent did;

Had a favorite bar, restaurant, or coffee shop within five minutes' drive that they visited fairly often (q. 68)—14 percent did; or

Had a particular place, like a park or restaurant, within five minutes' drive where they could go to see their friends and actually saw at least one person on their list there—15 percent did.[14]

Respondents who scored high on this scale named substantially more local nonkin than those who scored low—about 0.6 more associates for each point on the scale.[15] Younger people, especially younger men, tended to be most active locally. But what the community was like also made a difference: the communities with the highest average scores were those in the Regional Core, especially in central San Francisco. These are the places with wide varieties of stores, bars, restaurants, and other services within a few blocks. The communities with the lowest scores tended to be poor or, even more often, suburban communities. The latter typically had few services within walking distance and were often near—but more than five minutes' drive from—large cities or regional shopping centers that drew residents away.[16]

Respondents who lived in single-family houses also named more nearby people on their lists. All else equal, living in a detached home added about half a name to the average respondent's list of local nonkin.[17] This is not surprising. The general impression is that people in houses know more neighbors than do people in apartments. Several explanations have been offered for this difference: that apartment dwellers consider their residences only temporary way stations; the architecture of multiple dwellings discourages contact; responsibilities of ownership encourage involvement; the neighborhood density associated with multiple units causes people to withdraw; people with particular social preferences choose to live in houses rather than apartments, and many others.[18] Whichever theory is valid, living in a detached house, like local activity, depends partly on the community. Respondents, even those of similar income and stage in the life cycle, were more likely to live in detached houses if they lived in less urban places. Semirural respondents were three times as likely as otherwise similar Core respondents to live in such homes.[19] In that sense, urbanism reduces local ties by reducing the kind of housing conducive to those ties.

Together, being active locally and living in a detached house explain only a small part of why urban residence depressed local social ties. The broken line "adjusted also..." in figure 20 shows the consequences of holding these and other factors constant. For the sample as a whole, the least urban respondents would still name slightly more local nonkin than would more urban respondents who were otherwise similar in personal traits, housing, and local activity.[20]

The other broken lines in the figure allow us to specify who was affected by urbanism this way: it was lower-income respondents. Urban respondents with above-average household incomes (upper, dotted line) differed little from comparable small-town respondents, but the urban respondents with below-average household incomes (lower dash-dot line) differed considerably from their small-town matches.[21] (A similar contrast appears if one compares relatively immobile respondents with mobile ones, and, to a lesser extent, women with men.)

Community Characteristics

What about urbanism reduces local ties in this irregular fashion? Many characteristics, including the nature of the local population, local services, neighborhood density, and the like, as well as population concentration itself, could be examined. They were. It is difficult to disentangle each of these from the others, however, because they tend to come in packages—urbanism, housing density, minorities, no growth, and so on, all together.[22] There are signs amid all the complexity that the greater the concentration of blacks in the area, the fewer local associates our (overwhelmingly white) respondents named. This was especially so for the less mobile respondents. And the more rapid the growth of housing, the more local associates respondents (especially women) named.[23] Since cities have both more black residents and less growth than do Semirural communities, these factors can explain part of the connection between urbanism and reduced local involvement. Still, some small connection remains, among low-income respondents at least, suggesting that some intrinsic quality distinguishing city from small town affects how many local ties residents have.

One theory is that this intrinsic quality is population density; it forces people apart. Residents of crowded communities withdraw from one another as a way of protecting themselves from stress.[24] My argument—presented earlier in chapter 9—resembles the decline theory: urban residents are pulled, not pushed, out of their localities. The social opportunities of the surrounding metropolitan region compete with potential local ties; in small towns there is far less competition because the surrounding area is sparsely settled. Consequently, urbanites can and do go away from home for social relations more often than do small-town people. One item of evidence in support of this pull rather than push thesis is that the density of the communities made less difference in local involvement than did overall urbanism of the communities—urbanism meaning not only the concentration of people locally but also the proximity of a place to other concentrations of people. If respondents were being pushed away from their communities by the stress of density, we would probably have found the opposite, that density accounted for the effects of urbanism.[25]

(This pull may also help explain the slightly greater local involvement of Core compared with Metropolitan respondents. Residents of the Core had only moderately more regional possibilities but had far more local social options than did Metropolitan residents.)[26]

The evidence that low-income respondents were much more affected by urban residence than were high-income respondents can be interpreted for either position. A density-push explanation would be that high-income city-dwellers can buffer themselves from the urban stress with homes on quiet side streets, security guards, soundproof walls, frequent vacations, and the like. Not needing to protect themselves from crowding stress, they can be as locally sociable as their country cousins are. An opportunities-pull explanation would be that higher-income people are generally able to overcome social and travel constraints, so that even in smaller communities they can go farther for associates, leaving local options behind. Also, in Metropolitan areas, residential differentiation allows the affluent to be more selective about who their fellow residents will be, thereby finding more congenial people nearby. The data do not allow me to choose among these possibilities.[27]

Contrary to both the density-push and the decline of community theses, my argument implies that urbanites substitute more distant relations for the foregone local ones. These should be relations at least as substantive as the ones left behind, not the superficial and transitory ones predicted by decline theory. The evidence presented in the next section suggest that this prediction is correct.

Ties to the Regional Community

The sixty-minute driving radius roughly outlines the metropolitan or, for rural areas, the regional community. Modern people most often work, shop, and interact socially in those thousands of square miles rather than the few square miles of their local communities. Eighty-four percent of our employed respondents commuted to a job five to sixty minutes from their homes; most respondents often shopped and entertained themselves in districts beyond their immediate localities; and 43 percent of respondents' nonkin associates lived five to sixty minutes away. These all indicate what Melvin M. Webber has called the "nonplace urban realm," a society that virtually transcends spatial limits.[28] According to his analysis, the citizens of this placeless realm should typically be those with the most access to space-transcending technology.

Our findings are consistent: educated and affluent people named considerably more middle-distance nonkin than did other respondents. But other factors count as well, factors reflecting opportunities to get out into that wider community and constraints against doing so. In the category of opportunities, working full time, and having lived many years in the city also contributed to naming more associates. In the category of constraints, being older, having children at home, and not having ready access to a car reduced the number (as we have come to expect, children were more constraining for women than for men). Having access to a car made a big difference only in Metropolitan and Town communities. Perhaps in the Core public transportation sufficed, and in Semirural places a car was not enough to provide middle-distance ties. Underlining the constraint side of the equation, these factors—especially full-time employment, age, and access to a car—were considerably more important in determining whether low-income respondents named many middle-distance associates than they were for high-income respondents.[29] Not all Americans have yet entered the placeless realm.

Community Differences

The communities whose residents named the most middle-distance associates tended to be in the suburban or peripheral areas of the San Francisco Bay Area. The residents were often young, childless, and employed in professional jobs. The communities whose residents named particularly few midrange associates were basically of two types: first, low-income, minority enclaves, one in Oakland and one public housing project in the Sacramento Valley, and, second, three "freestanding" small towns. Each of these small towns was under 5,000 population, surrounded by open countryside, and at least ten miles from the nearest other town of consequence. One could claim that there simply is no one with whom to associate within five to sixty minutes' drive of such isolated towns, but that is only partly true. In fact, within forty highway miles of each place there are urban areas totaling more than 40,000 people, and thousands more people live scattered around the countryside. In an absolute numerical sense, there certainly were enough people within this range. In a social sense, there were probably not enough people of the specific types needed to meet particular individual needs.

Figure 21 shows how involvement with middle-range associates varied with urbanism. The examples of the last paragraph manifest themselves: respondents in the very least urban places named far fewer than did other respondents, and respondents in Core but not absolutely central communities—for example, in the East Bay—named the most (see solid

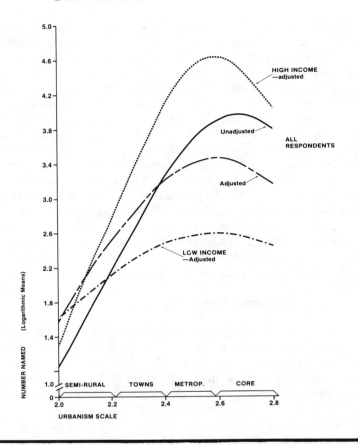

Fig. 21.   **Number of nonkin five to sixty minutes' drive away, by urbanism.**

line).[30] When the results are statistically adjusted for personal traits— Metropolitan respondents were, for example, most likely to be employed full time—the community differences follow the central broken line. Although somewhat attenuated, the differences are still substantial, with middle-distance ties least in the least urban places and most in the suburbs immediately adjacent to San Francisco.[31]

Figure 21 also shows that, after adjustments, high-income respondents evidenced stronger community differences than did low-income respondents. The general pattern was essentially the same for both groups—living in Metropolitan-Core communities went with many middle-distance ties and living in Semirural places went with few such ties—but it was much more so among the affluent.[32]

What it was about inner suburban communities that encouraged respondents to have social relations in the five-to-sixty-minute range is
unclear.[33] The dispersion of social ties is certainly consistent with our
image of suburbia as housing sprawl—fast highways, scattered services,
and the like. But most Town and Semirural places are also astride major
throughways. It is also difficult to square this simple sprawl explanation
with the fact that Metropolitan respondents named more *neighbors* than
did Town or Core respondents. I suggest that the immediate density or
sprawl of the community is not the critical factor—although it plays a
role—but that the location of the community is. The greater the population accessible in the one-hour range, the more social opportunities available, the more people will form relations at that distance.

Our San Francisco respondents, however, named slightly *fewer*
middle-distance associates than did the suburbanites. Here local density
may have had an effect. Perhaps the much greater density of San Francisco communities provided competitive social possibilities not present in
the suburban places and thereby encouraged residents to stay a little
closer to home. (Or perhaps an idiosyncrasy of this region explains the dip
at the end of the ascending line. San Francisco is bordered on the west by
ocean, and trips north or east must funnel through two bridges. As a
result, San Franciscans may actually have less access to the Bay Area's
population than do residents of the East Bay, whose one-hour radius
encompasses San Francisco, most of the metropolitan area, and, for
some, even parts of the Central Valley. (See the map on page 18.)

It is striking, and probably not coincidental, that the lines in figure 21
look like inversions of those in figure 20. It suggests, as I have argued, that
ties to the regional community compete with ties to the local community.
That competition is minimal in small towns and greatest in highly urban (if
not central city) areas. Moreover, the opportunity for regional associates
is one that more affluent people seem best able to take advantage of.
While low-income respondents added middle-distance associates roughly
in proportion to their loss of local ones, high-income respondents more
than compensated.[34] As to the decline of community debates, people do
seem able to form social ties beyond the "village walls."

Distant Associates

Many of the distant associates (those living more than an
hour's drive away) respondents named were not, it seems, involved in any
active relations, at least as we measured those relations. This was especially true of distant kin. Instead, the faraway people respondents named
often represented latent or sentimental relations: respondents recalled

whom they might turn to at some future time or whom they cared for. This distinction between active and latent will arise again when we consider the character of relations at various distances. Our first concern is simply to differentiate respondents who named many nonkin living more than an hour away from those respondents who named few.

The major difference between the two sets of respondents is length of residence in the city. All else equal, a newcomer named twice as many distant nonkin as did a resident of several years. (The difference was even more acute in number of distant relatives.) Almost as important was education. All else equal, a college graduate named about a third more distant nonkin than a high-school graduate did. The highly educated and the highly educated's friends are both likely to have been and to continue to be mobile. If they keep in touch, they keep many distant relations. In addition, being affluent, childless, and a young man increased a respondent's chances of naming distant nonkin.[35]

Figure 22 shows the community differences in the number of distant nonkin respondents named. The more urban their community, the greater the number of distant nonkin respondents named (solid line); the average almost doubles from Semirural to Core.[36] If farflung social ties are signs of cosmopolitanism, then cosmopolitanism is indeed more common in urban centers. Excluding newcomers from the analysis makes the urban advantage a bit stronger yet; even among longtime residents, city life involves distant associates.

This urban cosmopolitanism, however, can be explained, in large part by the greater education, affluence, and youth of urban respondents. Had all respondents been average on these counts, the community differences would have looked like the middle broken line in figure 22. People at either extreme—least urban or most urban—would have named slightly more distant nonkin than did those in the moderately urban places.[37] There appears to be some difference in what *sorts* of distant associates the most- and the least-urban named. Core respondents tended to more often name very distant nonkin, people living outside the state, while Semirural respondents were a bit more likely to name associates within the state. This in turn may be explainable by selective migration. Core residents were more likely to have moved long distances (for example, some were professionals with advanced degrees from East Coast schools), and Semirural residents were likely to have moved from elsewhere in California (many were retired men from southern California).[38] Still, we might speculate that something unique about each extreme of the urban continuum encourages distant ties—perhaps the paucity of potential relations available near small towns and the cosmopolitan connections of big-city life.

A detail of our results lends some credence to this speculation: in

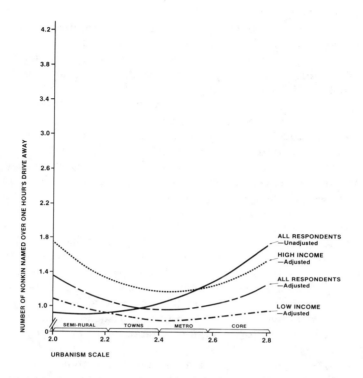

Fig. 22   **Number of distant nonkin, by urbanism.**

Semirural communities, the more distant nonkin respondents mentioned, the fewer local ones they named; in Core communities, it was strongly the reverse—having many local ties went together with many distant ones.[39] The suggestion is that some trade-off is required in small towns between near and far relations, while in big cities the two reinforce one another.

Implications

What difference do these differences in the spatial dimension of social networks—the tendency for urban people to have more geographically extended relations—make? This question is enmeshed in the debate over the "decline of the local community." Whereas some heralds of modern technology claim that spatial extension allows deep and fulfilling fellowship, more traditional commentators contend that such extended ties are shallower and more fleeting than local involvements.

One modern exponent of this latter view posits, in an assertion more extreme than most would make but in the general spirit nonetheless, that for psychological health people need daily intimate conversations with friends—outside of any formal context like work.[40] Modern man, according to this theory, has traded in such solid local attachments for cosmopolitan acquaintanceships and has thereby bought anxiety and alienation as well. (President Carter, in his "spiritual malaise" speech of July 1979, voiced the same idea when listing the decline in community involvement, together with selfishness and irreligiosity, as errors that have brought a moral crisis upon us.)

A different way to look at the issue is to demystify locality without claiming that it is irrelevant. How far away people are is one characteristic of theirs we consider when deciding whether to pursue or abandon a relation. Like quirks of their personalities or social handicaps they may have (say, an exasperating child), distance is a cost of the relation. Other factors being equal, we tend to lose touch, probably somewhat unconsciously, with people if we find equally or more companionable people closer by. Friendships turn over; that is part of life. But particularly rewarding, simpatico relations can survive life changes and difficulties. Residential mobility is just such a life change, and distance is just such a difficulty. People will hold on to a distant associate, if they can, to the extent to which the effort it requires is more than matched by its rewards. (The costliness of that effort will, of course, vary with the individual's personal resources and constraints.) This line of thought brings us to a nonintuitive conclusion: since local associates "cost" less and distant ones cost more, people find their distant associates *more* rewarding, on the average, than their nearer ones. The distant ones must be especially rewarding, according to this logic, or else they would be dropped. Put another way, the only distant friends we keep are our very best friends; nearby friends need not be so special. This, of course, contradicts the belief that local relations are most intimate.[41]

We use a similar calculus in managing each specific relation. We consider distance, among other factors, when we ask someone to help around the house or to come to dinner. Just as we may specialize our relations with respect to social context—confiding in friends and borrowing money from parents, for example—so we specialize with respect to distance. For example; about 80 percent of persons who would care for respondents' homes lived within five minutes' drive, while only 40 percent of money-lenders did. Local associates provide certain social interactions, distant ones others, as practicality dictates; there is nothing intrinsically superior about local ties. Indeed, to the extent that distance is not a barrier, farther associates are preferred (by the same logic that makes farther associates more intimate ones.)

This clash in views reduces to these questions: What is the relative quality of local versus extralocal relations? Who, local or extralocal associates, provides which kinds of support? What difference does the spatial distribution of ties make?

Perceived Intimacy

Are people emotionally "closer" to their nearer associates or their farther associates? Among our respondents, it is the farther ones. We asked people to tell us which of those on their lists they felt "especially close to" (q. 82). The percentages of associates who were cited, by how far away they lived, are shown below.

	Within Five Minutes' Drive	Five to Sixty Minutes' Drive	More Than Sixty Minutes' Drive
All associates	33%	31%	47%
Nonkin	25	21	38
Just friends	25	26	41

There is little difference between the nearby and the middle-distance associates. (But recall that associates who were named only as house caretakers are excluded. Were they included, a smaller proportion of people living within five minutes' drive would be classified as "close.") Distant associates, however, were notably more likely to be called "close" than were the others. Furthermore, these differences cannot be explained by which respondents named the distant associates, by the kinds of people they named at the various distances, or by other features of their relations. All those things held constant, associates—especially nonkin—who lived more than an hour away were more likely to be considered "close" than were nearer ones.[42] (Although this result may seem surprising, it replicates a finding from a survey of men's three best friends conducted in Detroit in 1965.)[43]

The problem with this analysis, one might rejoin, is that these distant ties are merely sentimental. People insist that their spatially extended friendships are alive when they have actually lost any real involvement with those distant friends. We turn, therefore, to considering specific exchanges.

Exchanges

We can examine exchanges ranging from casual sociability to emergency aid. Distance is more costly for the former and is less costly, though not negligible, for the latter. Figure 23 presents some relevant

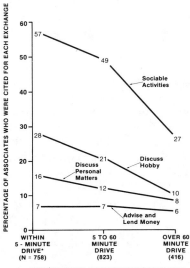

Fig. 23   **Percentage of nonkin named as providing specified exchanges, by distance (those named solely as house caretakers are excluded).**

data; it displays the percentage of nonkin at each distance who were named in answer to five specific exchange questions: engaging in social activities, such as visiting or going out to dinner together (q. 74); discussing a common hobby (q. 75); discussing personal matters (q. 77); receiving advice on important decisions (q. 78); and lending money (q. 79). (Note again that associates who were named *only* as house caretakers are not counted in the base figures; were they counted, all the percentages for the five-minute category would be substantially lower. For example, only about one-third of local nonkin, rather than 57 percent, would be social companions.)

The figure shows that as one moves from exchanges for which distance is crucial to ones for which it is a marginal cost, from contacts requiring frequent physical presence to ones calling for occasional interactions possible by telephone or mail, and from casual matters to critical matters, the advantage of close associates declines (the downward slope of the lines becomes less steep). For sociable interactions, distant associates were much less often cited than nearby ones. For discussion of hobbies, which often involves engaging in the hobby together, nearby associates were again more commonly cited, though not as much more. Physical presence promotes discussing personal matters, but it is not essential and the advantage of local associates is marginal. Giving advice on important decisions and lending money in an emergency can easily be done occasionally and at a distance, and there is no advantage to proximity.

As in the analysis of felt closeness, these patterns cannot be explained by who named distant associates, who those associates were, or the nature of those relations. Those factors taken into account, distant nonkin associates were notably less likely than nearby ones to be social companions, only slightly less likely to be confidants—either as advisors or as discussants—and *more* likely to be sources of emergency loans than nearer associates.[44]

The implication of these findings is that there is indeed nothing mystical about proximity. Nearby associates are preferred when nearness is critical. When proximity is less critical—and these are often situations involving the most intimacy, sacrifice, and faith—there is little or no preference for those nearby. These findings are consistent with those Barry Wellman has reported from his Toronto study: in matters of minor need, people turn to neighbors, and in matters of great need they turn to intimates wherever those people live. Indeed, where the need is very great, distance is no object, because people will come from far away.[45] They are similarly consistent with other findings on neighbors, that they largely provided house care and rarely provided "serious" assistance.[46] And these results also instill confidence in those just reported on felt closeness, because they suggest that in many subtle but important ways—for example, "just knowing that they are there if you need them"—distant friends do tend to be more rewarding.

All this suggests that distance be considered simply as another cost of social relations. If this view is valid, then resources, particularly financial ones, should cancel some of the effects of distance. More specifically, distance should make less difference for affluent respondents. That was in fact so. Affluent people had more spatially dispersed networks than less affluent ones. And the constraints placed on their interactions by distance were weaker. That is, the drop-offs in interaction with associates indicated by the slopes in figure 23 were slightly less acute among affluent respondents.[47]

This difference between moneyed and unmoneyed respondents is important because, though the arguments I have presented might be taken to imply that proximity makes no difference, that is incorrect. Proximity is important to the extent that distance is an insupportable cost, which it tends to be for the poor, the elderly, burdened mothers, and the like. We have already seen that for these groups local associates form a substantial portion of their networks (and whether there may be more rewarding associates for them over the horizon is moot). If local social ties were intrinsically superior ties, as decline theories often imply, they should be so for all respondents, not just for the constrained.

Subjective Evaluations

The contrast between the more and the less affluent appears in another form as well. We can ask what difference having near, middle-distance, or distant associates made to respondents' feelings about their relations and their overall sense of well-being (other things being equal). The answers are: (1) Among nonaffluent respondents, the more distant nonkin they named, the slightly *more* likely they were to say they wanted "more people to talk to" and "to have a good time with" (an increase of .02 in the chances of saying "want more" for each distant nonkin). My hunch is that the distant associates who made respondents feel lonely were left-behind friends not yet replaced. The spatial distribution of associates made *no* difference at all to affluent respondents.[48] (2) For everyone, the more nonkin respondents named, the more "pleased" they were on our psychological measures (see chap. 4). For the nonaffluent, naming many middle-distance, but especially many local nonkin, most strongly contributed to positive feelings. For the affluent, nonkin at whatever distance were equally associated with positive feelings.[49]

All these findings point to the same conclusion: respondents did not live in spaceless realms. For some, social life was quite constrained to nearby places. But neither did respondents seem to suffer from "decline of community" ills. They were attached to both near and distant associates, depending in part on how much distance each associate was "worth," what interactions they engaged in, and how easily the individual could pay the freight of distance. Consequently, local ties were not, as claims that local attachment is fundamental to psychological well-being would have it, more intimate or crucial than far ones. In fact, the opposite tended to be true. Respondents kept distant associates in their networks precisely because they were intimate or crucial associates, a qualification not as stringently applied to nearer associates.

In one respect distance is intrinsically and overwhelmingly important: frequency of face-to-face meetings. the farther away respondents lived from an associate, the less often they got together with him or her. How important frequency of contact is, in turn, as a *cause* of intimacy and support is not at all clear. The results presented here suggest that it is not critical; it may, in fact, be more a consequence than a cause of closeness.[50]

Conclusion

The motivating issue in this chapter has been whether urban life (and by extension modern life) weakens social ties to the locality in favor of more spatially extended ties, thereby undermining the "authentic" community. This in turn generated specific questions with respect to our survey: Did urban respondents have more spatially dispersed networks than small-town respondents? What consequence did place of residence itself have for spatial extension? What might explain urbanism's effect? What qualitative difference did the spatial extension of respondents' networks have?

The decline of community perspective on this issue is that local ties are distinctly superior to extended ones—that a local community is supportive in ways spatially dispersed networks cannot be. Modern, urban life encourages people to pursue distant ties, thereby vitiating the local community and ultimately redounding to urbanites' personal loss. The counterargument I have introduced at points contends that distance is a cost of social interaction like any other cost people consider when making and maintaining relations. Local ties are special only in the "cheapness." When alternative ties become competitively cheap—through rapid transportation or through population agglomeration—people will form relations over greater distances for the appropriate purposes. Since the logic is the same for the near and the far relations, no negative consequences should appear. Indeed, the more extended networks may be a greater resource.

As both decline theory and this counterargument predict, urbanites had more spatially extended networks than did small-town respondents. Looking at nonkin associates only, respondents at all levels of urbanism had about the same number of local ties, but the more urban respondents had many more associates who lived more than five minutes' or one hour's drive away. The contribution of urban residence itself—that is, the differences holding constant age, education, and the like—is less obvious, but it does seem to have encouraged spatial dispersion.

Living in Semirural places apparently encouraged having many local ties—at least among low-income respondents. The least encouraging places for local ties were not Core communities, but Metropolitan ones. The best explanation for this pattern seems to be that residents of small towns have few opportunities for forming satisfying social relations with people outside yet near their communities, while in highly urbanized areas residents can easily find many satisfying ties outside the locality. This interpretation is buttressed by the finding that living in Semirural places severely discouraged having relations with people living five to sixty minutes' drive away. And living in Metropolitan communities was most encouraging of such regional ties (especially for high-income respondents). Place of residence itself made only a small difference in how many relations people had beyond one hour's drive, though it seems that living in either the very least urban places or the very most urban ones may have encouraged such distant connections—the former perhaps for lack of adequate nearer ties, the latter perhaps because of San Franciscans' links into national social networks.

Urbanism, in sum, did encourage spatially extended relations. What consequences did those, in turn, have? Few, and these were largely for low-income respondents for whom distance is a relatively great cost. First, respondents actually felt "closer" to their distant associates than to their nearer ones. This is peculiar if one imagines that proximity and intimacy are mystically linked, but expectable if one sees distance as a cost in the rational calculus of social relations. Second, respondents were as likely to draw upon distant as near associates for those kinds of support for which distance is not a logistical problem (for example, providing advice). The more practical considerations demand proximity, the more likely respondents were to ask nearer associates. Third, the spatial distribution of respondents' networks had weak effects on their subjective feelings. But here was a possible case for decline theory: among low-income respondents only, and all else being equal, living in Semirural places encouraged local ties, and local ties increased feelings of being pleased with one's life.[51] (This is a particular advantage of Semirural communities rather than of low urbanism generally, since Town residence conferred no advantage over Core residence.) Other than this, however, little we have found suggests that the spatial extension of social relations fostered by urbanism—by modern life, generally—exacts any particular cost or confers any particular benefit. Perhaps once more we are dealing with style rather than quality of life.

Homogeneity in Personal Relations: Stage in the Life Cycle

The most striking fact about personal relations from an actuarial point of view is how similar people are to one another. Given the great variety of people we could know, we in fact do know people remarkably much like ourselves in race, age, background, values, and taste.[1] As I pointed out in chapter 1, two factors produce this homogeneity of social ties: personal preference and structural constraint. People usually are most comfortable with, and therefore choose, others who share their views and values—this pattern has been called "homophily"—and consequently the chosen typically resemble the choosers.[2] But people can select friends only from among other people available to them, and that pool is shrunken tremendously by the social contexts in which people participate. The pool is already composed of similar people even before the choice.

Standard sociological theories provide contradictory expectations about how modernization and urbanization alter the contextual sources of this homogeneity. On the one hand, both changes bring individuals into contact with far more diverse types of people than was possible in the traditional village. Some descriptions imply, therefore, that urbanites' private worlds reflect in microcosm the social heterogeneity of the city. Other arguments contend, however, that modern complexity and structural differentiation create more segregated social contexts and thus more segregated networks. With regard to age, for example, school classes, residential segregation, specialized services, and similar institutions separate people into age-graded social networks. The latter is the more sophisticated modernization thesis.

The subcultural theory I have presented also contends that access to many others, either through modern transportation or through population concentration, increases the homogeneity of networks—with or without structural changes—simply because individual preference is given wider scope. To the extent that personal compatibility and social similarity go together (and they do; see below), wider choice will yield greater homogeneity. This selectivity, in addition to structural changes accompanying the attainment of "critical mass," promotes urban subcultures based on shared personal traits or interests.

Part 5 of this book pursues the connection between urbanism and involvement in subcultures of various kinds—ethnicity, religion, occupation, and pastime. This chapter is a stepping-stone to that discussion. It deals solely with the similarity in the stage of the life cycle between respondents and their associates. It looks specifically at how close in age respondents were to their associates and whether they were similar in marital status.

In analyzing the effects of urbanism, we consider first how it affected the life-cycle positions of respondents' associates: Did the named people tend to be older or younger, married or not, as a consequence of where respondents lived? We consider, second, how urbanism affected *similarity* in age or marital status: Did respondents in more urban places end up with more life-cycle homogeneity in their networks? Third, we will briefly consider what difference homogeneity in life-cycle stage might make to a personal relation.

Throughout, we will be examining *relations,* not respondents or networks: 4,179 relations for which we know detailed characteristics of the respondents' associates.[3] Among those, I will focus most intensely on the 1,512 relations with *nonkin* whom respondents had met *since arriving* in their current cities of residence. These relations should reflect most clearly the effects of community on the types of associates respondents had.

Overview of Homogeneity

Respondents overwhelmingly named associates of the same age and marital status as themselves, but the degree of similarity varied considerably by the social context of the relation. The average difference in age between respondents and the relatives they named—siblings excepted—was twenty-four years (for siblings, five), but the difference in age between nonkin averaged eight years. Among nonkin relations, the age gap between neighbors was wider, at eleven, and among just friends was narrower, at six, than between associates in other contexts.

The similarity in age between respondents and the nonrelatives they named is dramatic: in more than half the instances (54 percent), the difference in age is five years or less. Young respondents tended to be closer in age to their nonkin associates than did older respondents, partly because they were near to, and often still in, age-segregated contexts (school, the military, entry-level jobs, etc.), and partly perhaps because each extra year means less socially and psychologically as people age. Almost as important as age in determining the difference in age was the social context in which the pair had originally *met*. Those who had met as children or in school were especially similar, an average of only two years apart.

People who had met at work or by the introduction of a third friend were also relatively close in age. Other factors such as sex or education made little difference in how close in age associates were.

Similarity in marital status follows roughly the same pattern. Married respondents named married associates, never marrieds named never marrieds, and divorced or widowed respondents disproportionately named divorced or widowed associates. Again, social context made a major difference. For example, a married respondent was only 1 percent more likely than an unmarried respondent to name a married associate if that associate was a cousin, nephew, or some other extended relative, but the married respondent was 30 percent more likely to do so if the associate was a neighbor and 42 percent more likely to name a married associate if that associate was just a friend. And, again, the context of meeting was also important. Nonkin met before adulthood tended to have never been married, while those met in an organization or in the neighborhood tended to be married (holding constant the respondent's marital status). Also, parents and middle-aged respondents tended to name married rather than never-married associates.

In sum, our survey shows—as did several before it and as common experience teaches us—that people associate with people like themselves. In part this reflects our preference for dealing with people who share our way of life. By way of life I mean a broad set of commonalities—including values, interests, conversational patterns, economic position, and historical or personal experiences—that make a relation more comfortable and rewarding. Evidence of such preferential selection includes the finding that age and marital similarity were much greater among nonkin than among kin, and greatest among "just friends"—the set of associates whom respondents had the most discretion in choosing and keeping.

In part this homogeneity also reflects the social contexts to which respondents had access. Their own stages in the life cycle held constant, respondents still in touch with preadult associates tended to know young and never-married people. Those working or who had formed associates at work knew relatively many married people of their own age; and those relying on neighborhood contacts tended also to associate with married people. In ways such as these, social contexts and their "inhabitants" shape individuals' personal worlds. To what extent is the community an important social context of this kind?

Urbanism and Age

The urbanism of a community can affect the age composition of people's networks, as the earlier discussion indicated, in two ways. First, if urbanism has the special qualities ascribed to it by various theories, it may promote age homogeneity. Second to the extent that urban populations typically differ in age from small-town populations—and they do, the adults being generally younger in cities—then people will meet and probably maintain younger associates in the large city than in the small town. And there is a third causal effect, one we have considered throughout the book: self-selection. If young people are drawn to cities, and if people pick age-similar associates, then the associates of typical city people will typically be young. In exploring all these possibilities, we will look at the nonkin whom respondents met since arriving in their current towns of residence. This is a conservative analytic procedure, since we discard in many cases associates respondents met when they lived in a *neighboring* town, but it provides a rigorous test of the idea that the community is the cause of the differences.[4]

The left-hand graph in figure 24 (heavy solid line) shows that the more urban the community, the younger respondents' associates tended to be, from an average of 41.8 years old to an average of 37.1.[5] This variation can, however, be fully explained by the fact that urban respondents tended themselves to be younger. Adjusted for such self-selection, there is no particular difference by community in the average age of associates (dotted line, from 39.1 to 38.2).[6] This suggests that urban residence itself did not increase or decrease the average age of respondents' associates. But there was a small effect of the *local* community nonetheless: respondents in specific communities with relatively many older residents tended to name slightly older associates (not shown on graph). For associates as a whole, however, this made only a minor difference.[7]

The older the respondents, the more difference the local community made to their networks. Among the youngest respondents (those under thirty), neither the urbanism of the community nor the age of their fellow residents affected the age of their own associates (see lowest pair of lines). Associates of middle-aged respondents reflect the overall pattern: they tended to be younger when respondents lived in more urban places (solid line, from 44.4 to 39.7), but had the respondents all been of equal age that would not have been so (dashed line, from 42.3 to 41.1). And for these respondents, living in communities of older people raised the average age of their associates mildly.[8] For associates of elderly respondents, our results are very tentative, because we have only 151 friends and acquaintances to work with. Urbanism makes no consistent difference, but the age composition of the local community does: the older the people living around them, the older the associates they named.[9] This is consistent with other studies of the elderly that show that they depend greatly on having other elderly people nearby in order to form social ties.[10]

In sum, urbanism itself did not affect the average age of respondents'

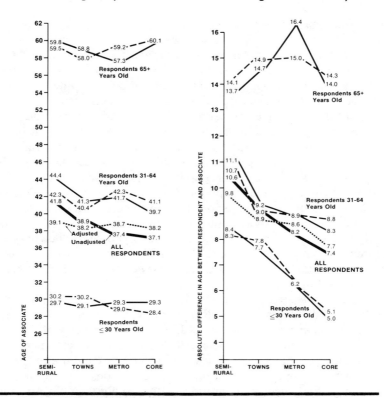

Fig. 24.   Age of associate and difference in ages, by urbanism (includes only nonkin members of special subsample whom respondents had met since moving to current city).

networks. But the age composition of the immediate locality did—for middle-aged and, especially, for elderly respondents.

Similarity in age is a different story. The right-hand side of figure 24 shows that the larger the community, the narrower the average span in years between a respondent and his or her associate, from 10.6 to 7.4 years; that is, the more similar they are in age.[11] This effect can be explained in part by the fact that younger people were typically closer in age to their associates and also tended to be urbanites. When such self-selection factors were taken into account, urbanism still apparently promoted age similarity, but barely so, narrowing the age gap to two years from Semirural to Core, 9.8 to 7.7.[12] Dividing the relations according to the ages of the respondents clarifies the pattern.

For the youngest respondents, urbanism substantially shrank the age gap, from an average of 8.3 years apart in Semirural places to 5.1 in Core communities. In fact, little else besides size of community made much difference in how similar in age young respondents were to their associates. For middle-age respondents, community of residence made only the slightest difference. Those in Semirural places tended, all else equal, to have a slightly wider difference in age from their associates, 10.7 years, than did those living elsewhere, 8.9 years.[13] Among the elderly, the pattern reverses: there is an irregular tendency for the more urban respondents to report *wider* differences in age than the Semirural ones. This reversal—a wider age gap in the more urban places—largely reflects the characteristics of the local population: elderly respondents in communities with many elderly people had associates who were closer in age to them than did elderly respondents elsewhere, and those sorts of communities were much more common in small towns.[14] (This finding dovetails with the earlier finding that the more elderly people in a neighborhood, the more neighbors elderly people knew.) That local composition taken into account, urbanism itself made no difference to the elderly, ranging from 14.1 to 14.3 in figure 24.

These results suggest that, for older respondents, the important context is the immediate community. If there are many older people nearby, they will tend to have older associates. Urbanism, a property of the wider area in which the community is situated, has little direct effect, probably because older people's social lives tend to be spatially circumscribed. (Urbanism has an indirect effect on the elderly's ties via the processes that encourage the selective migration of the young to cities and the old to small towns.) For young respondents, the urbanism of the wider context, rather than the composition of the immediate community, makes a difference, probably because their social lives are not so spatially circumscribed. That difference is not overwhelmingly large, but urban residence did seem to promote slightly more age similarity than did small-town life. (The difference appears also in comments such as that made by an engineering student living with his parents in Stockton who complained: "Most of my friends have moved. There is not too much socially and entertainment-wise going on here. The big city has more variety.") The middle-aged are distinct in that their social ties exhibited modest or negligible effects of both local population composition and of urbanism. Neither notably influenced the age similarity of their ties.

Urban life seems to promote age homogeneity basically for the young. If it does so through institutional changes, then those institutional changes must specifically affect the young. An easier explanation may be that urbanism expands the choices of both those who need wider choices and those who are able to take advantage of them. The elderly, a minority in our society, seek other older people as associates, but they can only effectively select nonkin from the immediate community. Therefore the locality is critical but urbanism is not. The middle-aged, the plurality in our society, are mobile and can easily find associates of the same age almost anywhere; neither the local community nor urbanism is important. The young adults, a minority like the elderly, need in some sense also to "search" for associates, but they can search over a wide range; for them urbanism is a significant aid.

Urbanism and Marital Status

Given the concentration in urban places of unmarried people, it is no surprise that the more urban respondents' communities were, the less likely it was that the associates they had developed since arriving there were married. Figure 25 shows that the chances that a given respondent's nonkin associate was married dropped from 63 percent to 62, 50, and 37 percent from Semirural to Core (solid line).[15] One component of the unmarried are the never married, and they increased as a proportion of respondents' associates from 14 percent to 19, 23, and 36 percent (lower solid line). The major reason for these community variations is, of course, self-selection, that urban respondents tended themselves to be unmarried, young, and childless. When these factors are held constant (center dotted and lower dashed lines), the community differences are attenuated.[16] Still, the associates of respondents living in Core communities were less likely to be married and more likely to have never been married than the associates of otherwise similar respondents living elsewhere. Core residence—more specifically, residence in San Francisco—encouraged knowing unmarried people.[17]

The issue of homogeneity is addressed in the separate graphs in figure 25 for associates of married and of never-married respondents. For the married (top pair of lines), community of residence made little difference, except that respondents living in Core communities were less likely to know similarly married associates. This is a little misleading, however, because married respondents in Core communities selected a considerably more married set of associates than their environment provided,[18] and they ended up with a majority of married associates (about 60 percent). Still, for married respondents, urbanism—at least high levels of it, San Francisco—introduced marital *heterogeneity*.

Analysis of the associates of never-married respondents is somewhat tentative for two reasons: first, there are few in this chapter's sample (329), especially in Semirural places (29); and, second, never-married respondents include two distinct groups—those living on their own and those very young adults, some still attending school, who lived with their parents (typically in smaller communities). While the first type of never

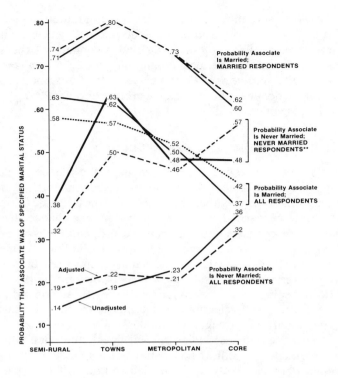

PROBABILITY THAT ASSOCIATE WAS OF SPECIFIED MARITAL STATUS

*NEITHER MARRIED NOR COHABITING.

Fig. 25.   **Marital status of associate, by urbanism, by marital status of respondent (includes only nonkin members of special subsample whom respondents had met since moving to current city).**

marrieds tend to be involved in the urban world of young singles, the latter tend to be involved in the suburban or small-town world of late adolescence.[19]

The unadjusted pattern reflects this complication (the solid line, .38 to .48). Town respondents' associates were especially likely to be never married; these respondents were clearly the youngest among the never marrieds. Adjusting the data for age and other personal traits corrects, though incompletely, for these characteristics of self-selection. The dashed line (.32 to .57) indicates that, were never-married respondents alike in most respects other than community, the associates of the more urban ones would have been more often never married—that is, the relations would have been homogeneous.[20] At the least, we can say that the handful of never-married respondents in Semirural places would have had networks composed of fewer than one-third never-married people, while the many in the Core would have had networks composed of a majority of never-married people.[21]

These findings, together with those on age, suggest the following reinterpretation of how urbanism affects network homogeneity: Urbanism generally increases people's access to people like themselves and to people unlike themselves—simply by increasing the sheer numbers of both. For people whose status is a majority or plurality (for example, married people), the increase in similars is of marginal importance; such people are available almost anywhere, and especially in small communities. The increase in dissimilars (e.g., never-married people) that urbanism brings may be of more consequence since they are now available in large numbers for the first time. The result: In cities majority people may know more minority people; they tend toward network *heterogeneity*, if in any direction at all. For people in minority statuses (e.g., the never married), the increase in dissimilar others (e.g., the married) is of little importance; such unlike people are all around them in most places and especially in small communities. The increase in people similar to themselves is more consequential since they now have a large pool of like people to choose from for the first time. The result: In cities minority people know more minority people like themselves; they tend toward network *homogeneity*.

This is quite an abstract model and must of course be modified. The qualifications include the fact that the composition of the local community also has an influence, depending on how mobile the individual is. In cases of relative immobility, local composition outweighs any effects of urbanism—as we saw with the elderly, where involvement with other elderly people depended on the number of elderly nearby, irrespective of urbanism. Another qualification is that these effects are contingent on the extent of group segregation. If, for example, blacks and whites, or Anglos and Hispanics, are thoroughly segregated in both small town and large city, an increase in absolute numbers may be irrelevant. Another qualification is that all these effects are modest in size. Nevertheless, the model is consistent with our findings on age and marital homogeneity. It is more consistent with the data than are theories that urbanism is irrelevant to network homogeneity or theories that urbanism promotes homogeneity through the rise of general segregative institutions. (If the latter were true, we would not find our results so conditional.) The model predicts, finally, that in other comparisons—say, Protestants and Catholics—it is the minority for whom urbanism promotes network homogeneity. That will be examined in part 5.

Consequences

Many people feel uncomfortable with the life-cycle segregation common in our society. It seems unwholesome that young adults may see largely young adults, that the elderly often live in old folks' ghettos, that children spend most of the day with children of exactly the same age. There are practical problems that arise: parents of infants may not know any teenagers who can baby-sit, and their own parents may be far away in a retirement town. More important may be the experiential losses—for example, the loss of guidance a young adult might have received from an elderly friend, the loss of joy an older person might have had from being around children. Still more, this separation may contribute to the disintegration of our society into small, age-pure islands. If urbanism promotes age segregation, it also promotes these ills.

We cannot assess, through our survey or most others, the deepest consequences of network homogeneity. We can, however, ask how relations that were homogeneous differed from those that were not. What went on in those relations and how did people feel about them?

Studies of the elderly suggest that older people actually benefit from being able to form ties with other elderly people and seem to do much better in age-segregated settings than in mixed settings.[22] Young people are noisy and frightening; other old people are quiet and empathic.

Ann Stueve and Kathleen Gerson found, in analyzing a survey on the best friends of Detroit-area men, that respondents tended to feel "closer" to friends nearer to them in age, though they actually saw those friends less often.[23]

The data from this study are moderately consistent. The nearer in age a respondent was to his or her nonkin associate, the more likely it was that the respondent felt especially close to that person, the longer that relation was likely to have existed, the greater the number of exchanges the named person was likely to provide (i.e., the more "stranded" the relation), the likelier it was that the respondent consulted the associate on personal matters, and (weak and inconsistent) the more often the two got together. These correlations persist even after taking into account characteristics of the respondents, characteristics of the named associates, other characteristics of their relations, and social context.[24] In sum, age-similar relations tended to be more lasting, intense, and intimate than otherwise identical age-dissimilar ones.

Whatever the long-term consequences of having age-similar relations, it seems clear that our respondents either slightly preferred their associates who were closest to them in age or experienced, perhaps unconsciously, that those associates were the more rewarding ones. Either would be understandable. People of the same age tend to have common personal experiences (for example, women in their fifties have typically seen their children leave home), have common historical experiences that shape values (for example, being unemployed in the Depression or being a college student in the late 1960s), experience certain transitions at about the same time (for example, having a first child), and tend to be roughly equal in sophistication, authority, and resources. All these similarities make people more compatible with, understanding of, and rewarding for one another. This is the positive side of the homogeneity coin.

Conclusion

Both general theories of modernization and subcultural theory lead us to expect that urban residents will tend to have more socially homogeneous networks than small-town residents, but the processes they invoke as explanations differ. Modernization theories, such as decline of community, essentially contend that urban structural and institutional changes create social contexts (such as bureaucracies) that constrain people's social choices to pools of similar people. Subcultural theory contends that population agglomeration widens the range of individual choice (and the ability of congenial groups to form), which, given the connection between similarity and compatibility, in turn leads to slightly more homogeneous networks in cities.

Looking specifically at life-cycle stage as a basis of similarity, our survey provides only mixed confirmation of the theoretical expectation, and it forces a reconstruction of the argument. The results indicate that, all else being equal, young respondents were more likely to associate with young people in large than in small communities; middle-aged respondents were barely affected one way or the other; and old respondents were more likely to associate with other elderly people if they lived in *neighborhoods* of elderly people, small town or large city notwithstanding. Never-married respondents named more never-married people if they lived in heavily urban places, but so did married respondents—the latter indicating increased heterogeneity, not homogeneity.

Although urbanism does affect network homogeneity (albeit modestly), its effect is selective. Such selectivity is difficult to fit into a general model that argues that urbanism generates systematic social differentiation and segregation. It is also difficult to fit into a simple subcultural model that argues that urbanism increases homophily for everybody. Instead it suggests a modification of the basic subcultural argument: for members of majority or plurality groups in the society, finding similar people is not a problem, for they are all around. Urban residence introduces the possibility of meeting many minority members (e.g., never-married adults), and thus the possibility of making *heterogeneous* relations. For minority members, finding like people is a problem, since only a relative few are around. Urban residence makes it possible to choose from among many fellow minority members and thus to increase the homogeneity of one's network. Thus urbanism can have an asymmetric effect—increasing heterogenerity with respect to those characteristics an individual shares with many people and increasing homogeneity with respect to those he or she shares with few. And in both processes, whether urbanism globally or the composition of local area specifically matters depends in turn on the mobility of the individual.

This post-hoc explanation of our results will bear reexamination in the next part of the book.

V Subcultures

15 Urbanism and the Development of Subcultures

One of the pleasures of the "city" that our San Francisco respondents often mentioned was its social diversity: the color, excitement, and cosmopolitanism, and the educational experience of living amid many distinct cultures. One of the vexations of San Francisco that our respondents often mentioned was also its social diversity: the chaos, odiousness, and prejudice, and the upsetting experience of living amid many distinct cultures. Usually, different illustrations were provided for each case—restaurants in Chinatown as a positive feature, for example, and racial violence as a negative feature. Nevertheless, the praises and the complaints both largely refer to the same thing, the many subcultures in the city.

This part of the book focuses on the fate of the individual and the individual's personal relations in this "mosaic of little worlds." Do cities give rise to subcultures? Does city life draw individuals, through their social relations, into these subcultures? How do individuals experience the diversity of people around them? How do communities fare as vessels—unmelting pots—of such bubbling subcultural stews?

This chapter presents an overview of the connection between cities and subcultures. It expands the theoretical argument first sketched in chapter 1, and it shows how larger communities typically have more numerous and more diverse subcultural institutions. Chapters 16 and 17 address the issue of whether urban residence itself encourages people to develop social ties within specific subcultures, to be "members" of social worlds. Four specific types of subcultures are considered: ethnic, religious, occupational, and pastime. Many more types could have been examined—age-based, sexual, and political subcultures, for example—and some will be discussed in passing, but practicality required focusing on only a few. Chapter 18 examines the personal reactions of individuals and the collective response of communities to the mélange of urban subcultures.

The Argument

Decline of community arguments, other than those that simply contend that urbanites are isolated and lonely, generally posit that rural and urban people have different systems of social bonds. Personal relations in the village setting, whether few or many, are embedded in a common culture. Built around kinship, locality, and church, this community has a firm core of beliefs, values and norms. Each individual is tied to it by family, neighbors, and religious leaders. In the urban setting, people's relations are dispersed in many directions, either linking them with no cultural community at all or linking them weakly with several disparate social worlds. In the first possibility, the relations are little more than isolated interactions; in the second, people, in Robert Park's words, "pass quickly and easily from one moral milieu to another," engaging in relations that are shallow and transitory.[1] In either instance these relations, no matter how many, fail to integrate people into a coherent culture, for they are connections to no moral milieus or to too many. The result of this modern condition is that people are left culturally and morally rudderless; that in turn creates social disorder, evidence of which is all around us.[2]

The counterargument I and others have made is that urban life is marked not by the breakdown of *community,* but by the build up of plural *communities:* a diversity of cultural groups, each its own variation of the national culture. My term is "subcultures." These subcultures are founded on many bases other than kin and locality—on ethnicity, occupation, life-style, and so on. Most notably, cities have subcultures formed of people who are minorities in the wider society (and, by extension, modern society is marked by small and unusual subcultures). And though these social worlds cannot be as all-encompassing as the total community of yore, people do find fellowship, guidance, and meaning in them.[3]

Argument and counterargument are somewhat similar in their analyses of urban/rural differences. In particular, both describe the city as consisting of many cultural elements. And both, though for different reasons (as discussed in chap. 5), expect social disorder. They clash on several points, the key one here being the nature of personal networks in such circumstances. The decline of community argument (complex version) implies that city residents have many social relations but have few and superficial ties to any one social world. The diversity of communities school (as we might call it) argues that urbanites are at least as involved in their social worlds as small-town residents are in theirs, but that their worlds are more specialized and uncommon. This disagreement forms the theoretical background for the rest of the book.[4]

Subcultures and Cities

What is a subculture? It is easier to recognize one than to define it. Among the subcultures that sociologists have carefully described are working-class Italian-Americans in eastern cities, "hippies," policemen, Slavic-American steelworkers in Chicago, welfare families in the black ghetto, the upper-class corporate elite, the Hasidic Jews of Williamsburg, and skid-row alcoholics. Most of us recognize these distinct groups as separable social and cultural entities, and we have handy labels, such as "hardhats" and "country-club set," for referring to them.

More exactly, I mean by "subculture" much the same as Park meant by "social world" when he wrote of the urban mosaic,[5] or what A. B. Hollingshead meant by "behavior system," which he described in 1939 this way:

Persons in more or less continuous association evolve behavior traits and cultural mechanisms which are unique to the group and differ in some way from those of other groups and from the larger socio-cultural complex. That is, every continuing social group develops a variant culture and a body of social relations peculiar and common to its members. This complex on the overt side may be characterized by discernible behavior of the group members in relation to each other, and to those who do not belong; and on the covert side, by an ethos or ideology which includes mores, codes, and other rules, which take the form of sanctions binding upon the membership in their relations to each other and to the external social world. Knowledge, techniques, attitudes, and behavior traits are all integrated into a more or less congruous system within which the participant members orient their lives and acquire status in the community and society. These constitute the criteria by which a specialized group is differentiated from other technical groups, and from the larger, incoherent "Great Society." Such a complex constitutes a behavior system.[6]

I suggest defining a subculture as a large set of people—thousands or more—who:
—share a common, defining trait, usually a nationality, religion, occupation, or specific stage in the life cycle, but also perhaps a hobby, disability, sexual preference, ideology, or other distinctive feature;
—tend to associate with others sharing that trait;
—adhere to a set of values and norms that are distinct from those of the larger society;
—patronize institutions (clubs, newspapers, stores, etc.) identified with their distinctive trait; and
—have a common way of life.
Subcultures and membership in them are matters of degree. Some subcultures have network "boundaries"—an absence or a sparsity of relations between members and nonmembers—that are very sharp, while others have fuzzy boundaries. Some subcultures have cultural features that distance them from the rest of the society; for others the differences

are subtle. We might say, based on research, journalistic accounts, and our own data, that Jews and Chicanos form more distinct subcultures in America than do Irish-Americans and German-Americans. And the professional worlds of dance, sports, and steelwork seem more distinct that those of file clerks, stationery suppliers, or housemaids.

Similarly, some people are more immersed in a subculture than are others. The extent to which individuals' personal relations are exclusively with other group members, their behavior is typical of the group, and their self-identity is in terms of the group varies greatly. Some people are partial members of more than one distinct subculture; they have been called "marginal men." Illustrations can be found among the antiheroes of Jewish-American fiction who are often trying to step into a professional world but still have one foot painfully caught in the immigrant ghetto. Many people cannot be located in any particularly distinct subculture at all. These may be people who are tenuously connected to several worlds—such as the urbanites of classic theory—but more commonly they are people whose personal networks basically reflect national culture: white, Protestant, middle-aged, middle-class people with middle-American friends, interests, and values. Bob Slocum, the anxious sales executive in Joseph Heller's *Something Happened,* is perhaps an archetypal member of the middle majority.

Urbanism promotes a diversity of subcultures and membership in them through three processes:

1. *Selective migration.* Large urban centers attract migrants from a wider range of regions and nations than do small communities, and they thereby accumulate a greater variety of ethnic, nationality, and religious groups. Initial migration of this sort spurs more of the same by network members. The more El Salvadorians come to San Francisco, the more want to come. Although a small town may occasionally have immigrants of one or two types, only large cities have immigrants of very many types.

2. *Critical mass.* The sheer agglomeration of people in any social category makes possible key elements of a vibrant subculture—enough associates to develop inbred social networks, enough clients to support institutions, and enough collective strength to protect the group from political or cultural incursions. Occasionally, one or two vibrant minority subcultures appear in a small community, but typically only large cities have a full range of them. Both of these two processes, selective migration and critical mass, are more important for small groups than for large ones, since affiliation is more problematic for their members and aggregation is likely to make a major difference in the small group's visibility and institutional supports.

3. *Intergroup friction.* Contact among subcultures usually leads to some contrast and conflict among them, which then reinforce individuals'

identification and involvement with their own groups. This is not to say that small-town residents are lacking in prejudice, only that they actually meet and react to outgroup people less often.[8]

This theory implies that we should find a greater variety of identifiable ethnic, religious, occupational, and hobby groups in the larger than in the smaller communities. We should also find that the larger communities have more institutions for specialized subcultures. And we should find that urban residence is associated with, and contributes to, *deeper*, not shallower, involvement in social worlds—at least for people with specialized backgrounds and interests. That is, members of small minorities or people with unusual concerns have greater difficulty than others do in finding like associates (see argument in previous chapter). They should therefore benefit most from the density of potential associates available in cities. And we should find that our urban respondents were more sensitive to group differences and tensions than small-town respondents were. The evidence from our study turns out to be mixed and certainly complex, but more often than not it confirms these expectations.

Subcultural Institutions

A glance at the newspaper easily illustrates the differences between large cities and small towns in the presence of subcultural variety. Compare, for example, the announcements of community activities and meetings in three of the towns in our study, as shown in table 4.

Granted, Berkeley may be a bit more exotic than other Core communities. Nevertheless, the more urban a place, the more numerous and more various its subcultural institutions. There were, in 1977: eight Irish organizations in San Francisco, none elsewhere in the region; twelve Italian newspapers in San Francisco, one elsewhere; thirty-one museums, no more than four elsewhere; twenty-one tennis clubs, no more than eight elsewhere; and thirteen singles' organizations versus no more than six elsewhere. San Francisco did not, however, have more of every institution; it had, for example, fewer rod-and-gun clubs than some other places. The point is that it is not simply size of population that matters, but size of the specific population—in this last instance, hunters and fishermen.

Figure 26 illustrates the connection between urbanism and the availability of subcultural institutions of various kinds in our communities. (An institution was considered "available" to a community if it was within the city limits of its town or the city limits of the largest other town within ten miles of the community; see Methodological Appendix section 3.7.) Generally, the more urban the community, the more of these specialized institutions are available to the residents. The differences are

**Table 4   A Sample of Community Activities Listed in the
                Newspapers of Three Towns**

Growing Mountain Town	Small Wine-Country City	Berkeley
2 swimming activities	2 bridge clubs	Cross-cultural couples meeting
	Model railroaders	
3 bus trips (to zoo, a fort, and Lake Tahoe)	5 branch meetings of Alcoholics Anonymous	Black women
		Black co-eds
Girls' club		Middle-years groups
Teenagers' dance	2 square dances	Lesbian parents
Request for people to show travel slides	Senior citizens' group	Transvestites/transsexuals rap
	The Grange	
A reflexology class	The Masons	Drop-in group for parents and children
		Round dancing
		And many more

greater than the figure implies because the scale is split. There were, for example, about sixteen times as many music stores in the Core places as in the Semirural places (39 versus 2.5). The figure also indicates important qualifications to the general pattern: ethnic institutions were less available to Metropolitan residents than to Town residents (and were Sacramento removed from the Metropolitan category, its average would be lower still). Also, the differences are less extreme for subcultures that draw great interest in small towns—notably rod-and-gun clubs. Both the ethnic and the rod-and-gun cases indicate that total population aggregation is less important than aggregation of the specific population concerned, be it Chinese-Americans or hunting and fishing enthusiasts. Finally, note that the rarer the institution—for example, theaters versus music stores—the stronger the effect of urbanism.[9]

These data and much research in social geography[10] show that the absolute size of a social group, even beyond its proportion in the popula-

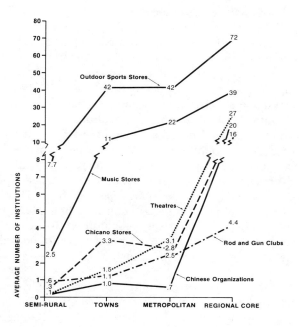

AVERAGE NUMBER OF INSTITUTIONS

Outdoor Sports Stores

Music Stores

Theatres

Chicano Stores

Rod and Gun Clubs

Chinese Organizations

SEMI-RURAL   TOWNS   METROPOLITAN   REGIONAL CORE

Fig. 26.   **Average number of illustrative subcultural institutions available per community, by urbanism.**

tion, has consequences. For the community, aggregation probably means that its different social groups are relatively cohesive, organized, visible, and even militant, which in turn increases the likelihood of conflict. For the individual, such institutions can provide means of maintaining identity, meeting people, and sustaining preferred activities. And, aside from the institutions, numbers—not proporiton of the population—provide individual members with a choice of compatible associates.[11]

A group's *proportion* in the population is often very important; if there is a much larger and competitive subculture in the community, the smaller can be overwhelmed no matter how numerous its members, and if a subculture is alone in a community it persists almost no matter how small. Nevertheless, the simple aggregation of group members increases the institutions available to them and, presumably, the viability, visibility, and vitality of their subculture. And that presumably goes together with more social relations among the members.

Individuals in Subcultures

The issue that occupies us most in part 5 is the degree of involvement individuals have in various subcultures: Who tends to be involved heavily, minimally, or not at all in subcultures of various kinds? More specifically, does urbanism lead to a diffusion of involvement, a variety of dispersed and shallow commitments? Or does urbanism lead to deeper and more intense involvement in subcultures?

Subcultures can be, and are, based on a variety of characteristics, from age, as in senior citizen communities, to many aspects of life-style. But for our brief, prestructured interviews we had to specify in advance a few types of subcultures about which to ask our respondents. These were *ethnicity, religion, occupation,* and *spare-time interest.* This selection meant forgoing analysis of many other subcultures: bohemian, homosexual, drug, "old money," and jet-set subcultures, for example. Our analysis necessarily focuses, therefore, on more conventional subcultures and unfortunately loses the more unusual—and presumably more urban—ones.[12]

Our procedure for each type of subculture was, with slight variation, to ask the respondents to name the appropriate subgroup to which they belonged, if any. Those who gave more than one—say, Italian and Irish, or golf and chess—were asked to pick a "most important" one. Interviewers then asked the respondents to examine the list of names they had given throughout the interview and to point out the people who were also members of the subgroup. Interviewers followed that with a few questions designed to assess how involved with the group the respondent was in other ways. In addition, we coded how many organizations respondents belonged to and how many magazines they read that were connected to their groups—for example, photography magazines for amateur photographers.

This method leads us to demarcate a theshold of subcultural involvement based on a minimum level of network involvement. All respondents were divided into members and nonmembers of each type of subculture. To be classified as a member, a respondent had to have specified a single identity for that type of subculture—for example, Polish for ethnicity, or playing the viola for pastime—and to name at least one *nonrelative* who shared that identity. This is minimal, or marginal, membership. Respondents who provided no self-identification, or two equally important identifications, or whose identity was not buttressed by any social relation were considered nonmembers. With pastime, for example, twenty-six respondents said they were interested in some form of horticulture; fourteen said it was their single or most important pastime; but only ten named a horticulturally inclined nonkin associate. Only the ten are considered members. Decline theories of urbanism would predict that proportionally more city-dwellers might belong to more subcultures, but these would be shallow involvements. Subcultural theory predicts that city-dwellers would more often be members and, among members, be more deeply involved than small-town residents—especially if their group or interest made involvement problematic.[13]

The dimension of involvement that will concern us most in the next two chapters is social involvement—personal relations with other subculture members. But we will also briefly consider other aspects of involvement, most especially whether the respondent identified that subcultural membership as his or her most important identity.[14] Chapter 16 assesses involvement in two types of subcultures to which one presumably inherits membership through kinship—ethnicity and religion. Chapter 17 examines involvement in two more voluntary types of subcultures—occupation and pastime.

Involvement in Subcultures: Ethnicity and Religion

Ethnicity and religion provide the closest thing to a "critical experiment" for choosing between decline of community theories and diversity of communities theories. Ethnic and religious groups are usually considered "primordial" affiliations, fundamental commitments in the way that family and home are, and the sources of intense personal ties. Urbanism, according to decline theory, weakens ethnic and religious bonds, disperses members' loyalties, activities, and involvements, and thereby dissipates ethnic culture and religious coherence. According to subcultural theory, urbanism *bolsters* ethnic and religious community, particularly if the group is small enough so that affiliation is difficult. The bolstering involves selective migration, the attainment of critical mass, and intergroup friction—all greater in cities. Urbanism may also change the subcultures, as the ethnic and religious groups selectively accept cultural items from each other, or as they reorganize to face the challenge of urban diversity. Yet groups' borders, identities, and internal personal networks are sustained, even strengthened.

For both ethnicity and religion, our analysis of these issues proceeds by first asking who among our respondents were "members" of particular groups—that is, who among them clearly identified with a specific group and named at least one nonkin or affinal relative who was also a member. Second, we measure how socially tied to their subcultures members were by counting how many of the nonkin they named were also members.[1] Third, we briefly review community differences on other dimensions of involvement, such as belonging to a formal ethnic organization. Some paradoxical results emerge in this respect, and throughout we will consider how the effects of urban residence may depend on characteristics of the individual, specifically on his or her ethnicity, religion, religious commitment, and religious behavior.

Ethnicity

Americans, except those caught up in the "new ethnicity," do not typically see themselves as ethnics. In her analysis of surveys in Boston and Kansas City, Diane Barthel found, as we also found, that many people insist they are "just Americans," even when they obviously have a foreign heritage. According to her study, most Americans deny that their national origin makes them unique, claim "no special comfort around their ethnic fellows," deny any ethnic pride, and apparently prefer that ethnicity "remain on a 'team sport' level of identification."[2] We are interested in, first, which northern Californians went beyond ethnic rooting to be at least marginal members of ethnic groups.

Membership

We asked our respondents this question (q. 89):
Some people describe themselves by their race, ethnicity, or national background. On page 7 of the [answer] booklet are some examples of those descriptions (Chinese, Italian, Black, Irish, Portuguese, Chicano/Mexican-American, Russian, Basque, Filipino, Arab, Greek, Japanese). How would you describe yourself?
Respondents who gave answers such as "American," "white," or "none" were not asked the subsequent questions. Respondents who gave more than one ethnicity were asked, "Is (either/any) of these more important to you (than the other/s)?" Of the 643 respondents who gave any appropriate ethnic identity, 491 named only one or picked a more important one. We asked these respondents, "Are any people on the list of names also [of that ethnicity]?" Of these, 287 respondents checked off at least one nonrelative or one affinal relative as a fellow ethnic. I classified these 287 as members of an ethnic group. The largest sets of respondents were Irish, Italian, black, Mexican, and German. In all, 27 percent of our sample is ethnic for this analysis.[3]

Respondents who had been raised abroad, and black, Mexican, Asian, Jewish, and Catholic respondents were especially likely to be part of this 27 percent. Little else distinguished the ethnics among our respondents[4]—except place of residence. Semirural respondents were notably less likely to be members of ethnic groups than were respondents in larger communities: 14 percent, compared with 29, 30, and 34 percent of Town, Metropolitan, and Core respondents, respectively.[5] These statistics probably *under*estimate the true difference in northern California, because our survey included neither blacks in predominantly black neighborhoods nor people who did not speak English—both prone to be ethnic group members and to live in Core communities.[6] The implication of this difference, whatever its cause may be, is that urban life and ethnicity tend to go together.

The explanation of the difference is largely self-selection; that is, the foreign-reared, nonwhites, Jews, and Catholics tend to live in and move to the most urban places. Nevertheless, when self-selection factors are taken into account, some difference remains: Semirural respondents were still slightly less likely to be ethnic group members than otherwise identical respondents living elsewhere.[7]

The community differences could be explained by the tendency of the most self-conscious and segregated ethnic groups to congregate in cities, though some social scientists argue persuasively that it is city residence *itself* that makes such groups cohesive.[8] Yet an additional aspect of urbanism besides selective attraction must account for the remaining contrast between Semirural and other respondents. It is probably the simple lack of numbers, of fellow ethnics, in small towns. The potential difficulties of minorities in small towns are illustrated by the Korean man in a Semirural community who drove with his family an hour and a half to attend a Korean church in Sacramento, and by a black man in a small town who, after having "passed" for many years, was uncovered, fired from his job, and ostracized.

Depth of Social Involvement

Among the 287 ethnic group members in our sample, the ones who named the most nonkin members of their own groups tended to be black, Jewish, Asian, or Mexican-American—and not to be Irish or Northern European. And the more urban the community, the *more* fellow ethnics they named, a threefold increase from 1.0 in Semirural to 3.0 in Core communities (see fig. 27);[9] in percentage terms, from 18 to 38 percent of all nonkin.[10] The urban population, these findings suggest, is distinct not only in its ethnic composition but also in the extent of involvement resident ethnics had with fellow members.

Other findings show that the urban ethnics were more likely to belong to ethnic organizations or read ethnic magazines and to express some ideological commitment to their group than were small-town ethnics.[11] (And, as in the case of membership, the findings here underestimate urban involvement; they do not reflect, for example, the thousands of recent, non–English-speaking immigrants from Hong Kong in Chinatown, or undocumented immigrants from Latin America in San Francisco's Mission District.) These results portray the city as a mosaic of intense ethnic worlds rather than as a landscape of ethnic disintegration.

Selective migration—blacks, the foreign-born, Jews, and Catholics tend to live in larger towns—accounts for most the differences in depth of involvement. Controlling for these and other types of self-selection—by education, age, and so forth—substantially reduces the effects of urbanism (see lower dashed line in figure 27). The trend, not statistically significant largely because we have only 287 ethnics, still indicates that

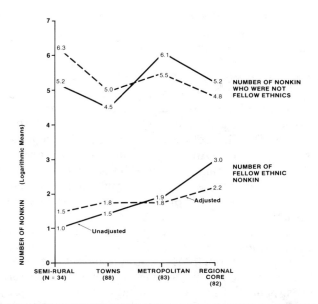

Fig. 27.   **Number of fellow ethnics and of other nonkin named by ethnics, by urbanism.**

ethnics in the urban places, especially in the Core, named about 45 percent more fellow ethnics than they would have if they had lived in small communities.[12] (They would not, however, have been more organizationally active or ideologically invested.)[13]

Another aspect of subcultural involvement is the extent to which members associate with people *outside* the group. The fewer outside ties, the more encapsulated the individual's network, and probably the more firmly bound he or she is to the group. Mexicans, blacks, and the foreign-reared were especially likely, and Western Europeans were especially unlikely, to be cut off from outsiders, other factors held constant. Figure 27—top, solid line—shows that there was no straightforward connection between living in urban places and how many out-group nonkin respondents named. But the *adjusted* figures indicate a slight decline as urbanism increases; respondents in urban places would have named slightly fewer out-group members than their counterparts in small communities.[14] If we combine the adjusted two trends shown in figure 27 and calculate the ratio of out- to in-group associates, the figures summarize a tendency that might well be labeled "ghettoization." Semirural ethnics named an adjusted 4.1 out-group associates for each in-group associate, Town ethnics named 2.7, Metropolitan named 3.0, and Core ethnics named 2.2 outsiders for each insider. Urban residents may not be isolated as individuals, but urban ethnics may be more *collectively* isolated from the wider society than otherwise comparable small-town ethnics.[15]

Specific Groups

The connection between where respondents lived and their ethnic involvement varied from one ethnic group to another. Since the number of respondents in each group is quite small—the largest set is composed of fifty-seven Irish-Americans—and group members are unevenly distributed—for example, only one Italian lived in a Semirural place and only two Germans lived in Core communities—we cannot say much about particular ethnicities.[16] But the case of Mexican-Americans is particularly instructive.

The urban Mexican-Americans tended to be relatively *un*involved with other Mexican-Americans; those living in Town communities were most heavily involved with one another. Mexicans are unique, however, in *not* being relatively concentrated in the large urban centers; for historical and economic reasons, people of Mexican descent form a greater proportion of the Central Valley population than of the Bay Area population. And, in our data, the greater the *relative* concentration of Mexican-Americans in and near a community, the higher the proportion of fellow Mexican-Americans our respondents named. That is, while urbanism went together with fewer Mexican-American friends, the concentration of Mexican-Americans went together with more in-group ties.[17] This particular case suggests that the massing of a specific group, particularly relative to other groups, is more important than urbanism per se.

Conclusion

If ethnicity poses a "critical experiment," then our results are not nearly as clear-cut as we would wish. Nevertheless, they indicate that urbanism—or at least the concentration of specific ethnic groups—more often bolsters than breaks down ethnicity. As the urbanism of the community increased, respondents were more likely to be "ethnics." Although much of that difference could be explained by self-selection, Semirural respondents were still less likely to be members of ethnic groups than were similar respondents living elsewhere. And the more urban the community, the more involved member respondents were with other members. Much of this, too, can be explained by self-selection. But remaining community differences point to urban bolstering of ethnicity (particularly if the Mexican case is set aside); certainly, little in the data suggests that city life weakens ethnicity.

Two aspects of the results call for caution: weak trends and inconsistency between social involvement and other forms. First, some of the adjusted results are modest and not statistically significant. In part this reflects the role of a group's relative population concentration in promoting ethnic involvement, as illustrated by the Mexican case. Such concentration is typically, but not universally, associated with total population concentration, or urbanism. (Italians, as another example, are concentrated both in San Francisco and in the wine-producing Napa Valley.) In part, also, our estimates of urbanism's correlation with ethnicity are *conservative,* for reasons mentioned earlier. Despite the modesty of the trends, other recent research supports some of the elements of the argument: that ethnic attachments persist in urban areas, and that group size is a critical contributor to ethnic persistence.[18]

Second, while urbanism was generally associated with more ethnic social involvement, even encapsulation, it was not associated in any straightforward way with other aspects of ethnic involvement—ideological commitment, organizational ties, and so on. I had imagined that all aspects of involvement would work together, but the empirical results force some rethinking. Although the inconsistencies between social and other types of involvement might be explained by technical problems in measuring involvement, a more interesting possibility is that they reflect *changes* in ethnicity resulting from urbanism.

There is evidence that city life alters ethnic groups and membership, that it modifies culture, language, and even specific identity (for example, changing self-definitions from "Neopolitan" to "Italian"), while still sustaining in-group ties and distinctive ethnic behavior. Peter Rose's study of Jews in small-town New York and their children illustrates the point. He found that the small-town Jews tended to be more conscious of their identity than Jews who lived in the city; they often saw themselves as representatives of the faith to a Gentile community. Their consciousness was also bound up with a desire to see their children live in a large city, where they felt that keeping the faith was more likely. The key difference between town and city was the lack of Jewish friends and a Jewish community in the small towns. The children who had moved to the city, ironically, felt that they had weaker Jewish identities, for many probably because they did live in Jewish milieus.[19] With a comfortable cultural environment, urban Jews may be less conscious of who they are and yet more involved with fellow Jews and perhaps more distinctively Jewish in their way of life.

Our data are mildly consistent with such a view of ethnicity, though we have no real indicators of ethnic life-style. As urbanism increases, ethnic involvement may be less conscious and purposeful, but more social and deeper.

These arguments should not imply that city life is always more ethnic than rural life or that a particular ethnicity will persist forever. Obviously, Irishness remains stronger in rural Ireland than in San Francisco, and San Francisco's Irish are probably becoming less distinctive with every passing generation. The real implication is that ethnic social networks, and whatever comes with them, such as distinctive life-styles, are likelier to persist in the urban centers than in the small towns of any given society.

Religion

The issues raised by religious involvement are much the same as those raised by ethnic involvement. In the classic theoretical view, the collapse of faith and of religious fellowship (the two are, we shall see, linked but far from identical) under the influence of urbanization is yet another way that community disintegrates.

In contemporary America, adherence to traditional articles of faith is less common in urban places than in small towns.[20] In our sample, residents of the Regional Core were much more likely than other respondents to say "none" in answer to the question, "What religion are you—Protestant, Roman Catholic, Jewish, or something else?" (q. 93): 39 percent of Core respondents said "none," compared with 20 percent of Metropolitan, 14 percent of Town, and 16 percent of Semirural respondents. (This, of course, is a test not of faith, but of allegiance.) Yet, among the 78 percent of respondents who did claim a religious identity, the differences by community in the extent of their religious fellowship were not as great, and in certain instances, were exactly the opposite—urbanites were more involved. As with ethnicity, there are hints that social involvement and self-consciousness may separate in urban communities.

Being a Religionist

I classified a respondent as a member of a religious group if he or she claimed a religious identity in the question just described and also named at least one person other than a blood relative who was of the same religion. For Protestants with a denominational allegiance, *same religion means same denomination:* 52 percent of the respondents were, by this definition, religionists.[21]

Respondents who had been raised as Catholics or as Jews were more likely to be religionists, while respondents who had been raised in liberal Protestant denominations were least likely to be members of a denominational subculture.[22] Middle-aged, but not elderly, respondents were likely to be religionists. And parents were especially likely to be religionists, lending weight to the stereotype that the church is sought out for children.[23]

The community differences in membership are irregular. Town and Metropolitan respondents were most likely to be religionists, at 61 and 53 percent respectively. Core and Semirural respondents were least likely, at 44 and 48 percent respectively.[24] This inverted-U pattern seems to reflect two trends: the tendency of Core respondents to profess no religion at all and the tendency of Semirural respondents to name no nonkin co-religionists at all. This latter trend is especially acute for Semirural respondents not raised as Protestants, suggesting that non-Protestants risked "falling away," or religious isolation, or both, by living in small towns.[25] In sum, living in *large* towns but away from the Bay Area encouraged being a member of a religious subculture.

Depth of Social Involvement

When we consider only the 550 religionists, this curvilinearity disappears: the more urban the community, the *more* nonkin co-religionists respondents named, from 1.8 for Semirural residents to 3.3 for Core residents (see Fig. 28).[26] Urban religionists tended to name more nonkin of their own faith or denomination than did small-town religionists largely because they tended more often to be unmarried and educated. Had all respondents been equal in these respects and in the specific religion they professed, the community differences would have appeared as the lower dashed line in figure 28. Core respondents would have named just slightly more and Semirural respondents just slightly fewer than an average number of co-religionists.[27]

Figure 28 also shows the association between urbanism and naming nonkin outside the faith. "Ghettoization" seems, all else equal, slightly greater in Town and Core than in Metropolitan and Semirural places.[28]

These findings provide little thrust for my theoretical argument, but they move us roughly in the direction of believing that urbanism more likely supports rather than weakens the subcultural involvement of religious people. That drive accelerates when we examine specific subgroups.

Urban residence tended especially to affect the social involvement of several kinds of respondents—women and affluent people, for example. Three such groups deserve special examination: Catholics, respondents who rarely if ever attended church services, and respondents who told us that religion was "most important" to them. For each of these three sets, the more urban the community, the more co-religionists they named. On the other hand, for Protestants, for regular churchgoers, and for those who did not identify most strongly with religion, urbanism was largely

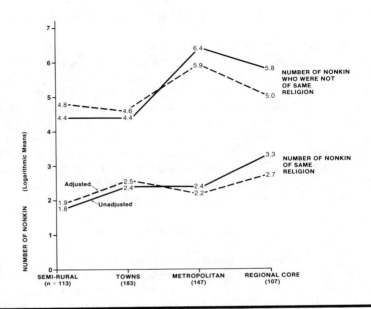

Fig. 28.   **Number of fellow religionists and of other nonkin named by religionists, by urbanism.**

irrelevant. Figure 29 provides an overview of the following discussion. In simplified form it shows how urban respondents in each of the three critical categories tended—other factors held constant—to name more co-religionists than their small-town counterparts, while in the residual category urban respondents named slightly fewer than did their small-town counterparts.[29]

Consider Catholics first. Core Catholics named considerably more Catholic nonkin (3.7) and the twenty-one Semirural Catholics named considerably fewer (1.3) than did otherwise similar Catholics living in between. For Protestants, urbanism made little difference. In terms of the *percentage* of nonkin who were co-religionists, urbanism actually tended to depress slightly the number of nonkin of the same denomination whom Protestants named.[30] My explanation is that urbanism largely expands the possibilities of subcultural involvement for members of minorities. In this instance the minority is Catholic; knowing other Catholics is difficult in small communities, but not in urban places. (Presumably, had our sample been large enough, we could have shown this to be true also of Jews, Christian Scientists, and so on.) For Protestants, however, finding other Protestants—either by meeting people of the same denomination or by switching denominations—is about equally easy almost anywhere.[31]

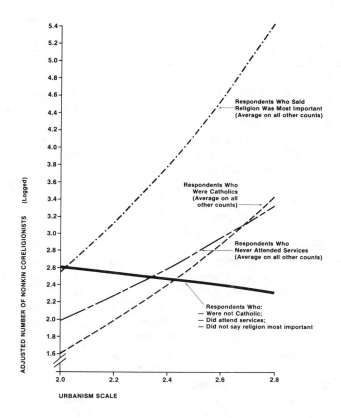

Fig. 29.   Number of nonkin co-religionists named, by urbanism, for subgroups of respondents (adjusted).

Second, Core respondents who never attended religious services named more than twice as many co-religionists as did otherwise similar church-shunners in Semirural communities.[32] Put another way, in the smallest places, nonattenders named far fewer co-religionists than did their neighbors who went to services regularly, but in the largest places the attenders and the nonattenders named almost equally many co-religionists. (*Note:* Urban religionists generally attended services less often than small-town ones.)

A guide to understanding this finding is Gerhard Lenski's distinction between *associational* religion, involvement in church and church-related groups, and *communal* religion, involvement with friends and relatives who are co-religionists. He argues that modern, urban life separates these two forms of religious involvement.[33] Churches are the associational institutions of religious subcultures. As such, I would argue, they are critical for forming social ties in small or dispersed communities that lack the communal institutions for religious fellowship that are available in large cities—informal social circles, clubs, neighborhood hangouts, lodges, newspapers, political leadership, and so on. In the small town, religious subcultures either exist around the local church or do not exist at all. A few points in our data support this interpretation: nonattenders in Semirural places were virtually shut out of social involvement with coreligionists; the co-religionists whom Semirural respondents named were most likely to be neighbors and townsmen (54 percent lived within five minutes, compared with 40 percent of Core respondents' co-religionists); and in chapter 10 we found that Semirural respondents were especially likely to name people from religious organizations. All these items suggest that the local church plays a greater and perhaps functionally necessary role in the religious subcultures of small but not of large communities.[34]

Third, among those respondents who said that religion was "most important" to them (choosing among work, ethnicity, pastime, and religion; q. 100)—forty-eight fundamentalist Protestants, sixteen other Protestants, eighteen Catholics, one Jew, and fifteen others (largely Mormons)—the urban ones named considerably more co-religionists than did their counterparts living in smaller communities.[35] The two groups—strong and weak identifiers—named about equally many co-religionists in small communities but differed greatly in urban places, where the strong identifiers named many more. Because of the relatively few respondents in this group—only eleven Core residents, for example were strong identifiers—the finding is not statistically reliable. But the differences are large, as the line in figure 29 shows, and thus worthy of attention.[36] Furthermore, strong and weak identifiers differed in the same way with respect to how near their co-religionists lived. Among those who said religion was not most important, urbanites were *less* likely to live in the same community as their co-religionists; but among those who said religion was most important, the more urban their community, the *more* likely they were to live near their co-religionists. That is, for respondents who cared most about their religious identity, urbanism meant *more* and *nearer* co-religionists; for those who did not stress religion, urbanism meant no more and somewhat more distant co-religionists.

We should pause in this headlong rush through the maze of findings to note the paradox of the last two sets of results. Seriously religious people are typically likely to attend services often.[37] Yet we found that urbanism encouraged social involvement for those strongly identified with their religion and also for *nonattenders*. This complex pattern can be described in another, perhaps more revealing way. Social involvement with co-religionists may be either the result of church attendance, with or without deep religiousness, or it can be the result of deep religiousness, with or without church membership. (Although very religious people typically attended services, some did not. A few, for example, watched television evangelists.) In Semirural places, social involvement was largely dependent on church attendance; strong or weak religious identification made little difference. In more urban places, the two—attendance and identification—were equally important sources of social involvement.[38] To use Lenski's concepts, the associational and communal aspects of the religious subculture seem more closely linked in small places; in particular, church attendance was required for social ties. In large communities the two separate; one can be tied to co-religionists without attending services, especially if one feels strongly about religion.

The main point, these complexities aside, is that urbanism apparently promoted social involvement with co-religionists among three particular groups: Catholics, nonattenders, and respondents who said that religion was most important to them. What these disparate categories have in common is the people they jointly exclude: modestly religious people with easy access to co-religionists, such as Protestants who attend their nearest church as a regular social activity. For the latter kind of people, the fellowship of co-religionists is neither pressing nor troublesome, and community of residence makes little difference. For those who did find religion a pressing concern, or meeting co-religionists a problem, or both, population concentration supported social involvement in a religious subculture.[39]

Other Aspects of Religious Involvement

Community differences in other aspects of religious involvement showed a similar but fainter pattern. Overall, urban respondents were slightly *less* involved than the small-town respondents, but there were countertrends among Catholics, nonattenders, and, especially, among those who said religion was most important.

Although there was a slight tendency for *formal* religious activity—belonging to a religious organization (other than a church), such as a choir or charity, or subscribing to religious periodicals—to decline as the urbanism of respondents' communities increased, this tended not to be true among nonattenders, and it was quite the reverse for respondents who said religion was most important. For the latter, the more urban, the more formally active they were. For those who cared much, urbanism apparently encouraged formal activity as well as social ties.[40]

Church attendance itself is a unique and complex indicator of subcultural involvement. Going to services combines devotion, the opportunity to associate with co-religionists, and formal organizational activity (but most strongly the latter, and attendance is *not* clearly linked to faith).[41] Churches and synagogues are organizations for community involvement and child-rearing, as well as places of prayer. We see signs of the nonreligious role among our own respondents. The more educated they were and the more children they had, the more regularly they attended—but only if they said religion was *not* most important to them. (Being educated and having children made no difference in whether serious religionists attended often.) That is, *associational* reasons seemingly impelled people who were casual about their religion to attend. In any event, urbanism tended to *depress* attendance at services among all our religionists (and especially among fundamentalist and "other" Protestants).[42, 43]

Conclusion

Summarizing in broad strokes, urban residence did *not* reduce the involvement of respondents in religious subcultures, and for some types of respondents living in urban places seemed to increase their involvement, particularly their social involvement. I can also offer a more fine-grained synthesis of the findings. Urbanism seemed to have three consequences, two of which in turn depressed involvement, and one strong but conditional one that in turn increased involvement.

First, people living in urban places tend to absorb nontraditional beliefs (see chap. 6). That means, in contemporary America, that they tend to be less orthodox and to have less faith in organized religion. Thus, in our study, urbanites were less willing to claim a religion at all and, among those who did, less likely to say religion was most important and less likely to attend services than were their small-town counterparts. Second, among religionists, those living in urban places were less likely to be involved in the *associational* dimension of their membership. In small towns, I suggest, the church is part of the neighborhood-kin-church complex of social relations and is an important context for knowing people.[44] Those who do not attend church typically do not know co-religionists. In cities, there are other contexts and other opportunities for social relations, so the church is less attractive in that way, and urbanites are therefore less likely to meet co-religionists there. (In fact, were it *not* for their more regular church attendance, small-town Protestants would have been *less* socially involved with members of their denominations than were urban Protestants.)[45]

But, third, the countervailing effect of urbanism is to increase people's access to the *communal* dimension of their membership. The aggregation, to a critical mass, of fellow religionists in and around the community increases the possibility of social ties and fosters institutions besides the church. This consequence of urbanism is especially likely to outweigh the first two among minorities, for whom finding associates is a problem; infrequent church attenders, who lack that organization as a regular setting for seeing people; and the deeply religious, who seek greater involvement than possible with conventional religious activity.[46]

The findings for those three groups depict, albeit faintly, the following picture. In the small town, there is typically one diffuse religious community, a Protestant one, also incorporating local neighborhood ties. For conventional Protestants, going to the nearby church regularly is a sure way of knowing co-religionists. They can do this anywhere, village or metropolis, but are a bit more likely to do so in small towns. In terms of making social ties, the town/city distinction means little to them. For other people, just any nearby church will not provide communal relations. These people may be non-Protestants, Protestants who care greatly about a specific denomination, or people who do not like church services. Whatever the reason, in small towns they are isolated from co-religionists; only the population concentration in large towns and cities allows them to find fellowship. For the seriously religious, the small-town church provides some but not enough involvement. In cities they are able to become more active and more deeply engrossed in a religious subculture.

In the city, the religious community is sharply differentiated; there are plural communities. One dimension of plurality, of course, is theological: Catholics, orthodox Jews, Zen Buddhists, and so on, have their own social worlds. More important theoretically is differentiation by type of involvement. Many urbanites do without religion altogether. Another set of people are involved communally but not associationally. Like the Catholic who swears to his Catholic friends that his wife will never drag him to Mass, or the backsliding Southern Baptist now living in the big city and hanging out with fellow ex-Southerners, these people have a religious community without explicit religion. And then there is the relative handful of very religious people who are more deeply involved socially and organizationally in a religious subculture than is usually possible in a small town.

These distinctions recall the arguments made earlier with respect to ethnicity, that urbanism may separate and alter elements of ethnic involvement. Urban ethnics may be less self-conscious and formal about their membership and yet seem to be more immersed in an ethnic social world than their small-town cousins. Urban religionists may be less devotional, and yet many seem to be more immersed to a religious community than their small-town fellows. Urbanism may provide multiple bases of subcultural involvement and perhaps multiple versions of such subcultures, or multiple communities, to join.

17   Involvement in Subcultures: Occupation and Pastime

In contrast to the descent-based and traditional ties of ethnicity and religion, relations based on occupation or a shared hobby typify more voluntary and modern kinds of associations. They—like relations founded on political alliance, cultural tastes, sexual proclivity, common handicap, and so on—are more constructed than they are given. And they are, both decline and diversity theorists would probably agree, more possible in modern, urban societies where people have the freedom and resources to form allegiances around such historically "new" interests. We saw in chapter 15 that the institutions for subcultures based on these interests were more evident in urban than in nonurban places. Here our question is whether individual members are personally more immersed in those subcultures if they live in urban places.

Line of Work

"People of the [horse-racing] world are a close fraternity," said jockey Eddie Arroyo. "We work together, we travel together. The whole shebang moves from one state to another. We automatically seek each other out. We're good friends."[1] The horse-racing world, as Arroyo describes it, illustrates a tight subculture based on people's line of work: a convergence in one setting of industry (entertainment) and specific occupations (athletes, managers, journalists, etc.); heavy commitments of time and energy; and personal relations that go beyond the hours and tasks of the job. Other kinds of jobs also typically harbor such social worlds, for example, dockwork, steel production, mining, police, journalism, and politics.[2] Still other lines of work seem not, at least to outside observers, to be so cohesive: odd-jobbing, insurance adjustment, stenography, retail appliance sales, and so on.[3] Our data shed some light on what determines the level of social involvement typical in a line of work. But our basic concern is whether urbanism stimulates such involvement. Our conclusion is, not in these data.

Earlier, in chapter 9, we investigated respondents' involvement with co-workers, involvement in a *workplace* network. Here we investigate respondents' involvements with people "doing the same kind of work," whether or not those people also worked at the same place. We asked all currently employed or laid-off respondents to tell us which of the people they had listed they "think of as doing the same kind of work you do?" (q. 87). We chose such a loose measure of occupation, respondents' own interpretations of "line of work," because we did not want to impose our perhaps inappropriate occupational categories. Do widget salesmen see themselves as being in sales or in widgets? Did Arroyo see himself as an athlete or as a horse-racing person? As it turns out, this choice of question was probably an error.

Membership

I counted a respondent as a member of an occupational subculture if he or she was working *full time*[4] and cited *anyone* on the list in answer to the question. In all, 448 respondents qualified. Besides being employed full time, these 448 tended to be relatively educated, young (but over twenty-one), male if in high-status occupations and female if in low-status occupations. Members named an average of 3.3 people who were in the same line of work, or 20 percent of all the people they named.

Metropolitan and Core respondents were considerably more likely than others to be members. Fifty-one percent of each group qualified, compared with 39 percent of Town and 30 percent of Semirural respondents. Urbanites were more often fully employed, better educated, and younger, all of which together fully account for the community differences.[5] Thus, urbanites were more often involved in occupational social worlds, but place of residence is not directly the reason why. (It might indirectly be the reason if urbanism generates full-time jobs that are unavailable in small towns, as is likely.)

Social Involvement

Our basic measure of how involved respondents were with fellow members of their occupational world is simply the number of such people they named, supplemented at points in our analysis by other indicators.

Differences in social involvement by type of job and workers' activities on the job were many and intricate. Suffice it to say that, all else equal, high-level professionals were heavily involved and laborers tended to be uninvolved with people in the same line of work. And respondents who worked unusual hours, or many hours a week, or both, typically named more colleagues.[6] Respondents also differed in social involvement according to their own personal characteristics, but how they differed was related to the kinds of jobs they had and other factors. Among the findings: The more children aged twelve and older respondents had at home, the less involved they were with colleagues—particularly if they did *not* say that work was "most important" to them.[7] Also, the longer less-educated respondents had lived in the city, the fewer fellow workers they associated with off the job. That is, *recent* uneducated migrants were especially likely to turn to work associates for a variety of interactions.[8]

I expected to find that the more urban the communities were, the more people from their own lines of work respondents would name. That was not the case; the results turned out to be more complex. For the 448 members of work subcultures as a whole, there were few community differences, and in those instances Town residents were slightly more involved and Core residents slightly less involved than respondents living elsewhere. Those community differences, however, were contingent on industry, occupation, and especially on whether or not respondents said that work was "most important" to them.

Overall, there was little variation by urbanism in how many colleagues members named, as the solid middle line in figure 30 indicates (from 3.2 to 3.1). The solid line at the bottom represents the number of people in the same line whom respondents named somewhere in the interview *besides* the question, "Who do you discuss work with?" That is, it subtracts from the total those co-workers with whom respondents' relations were purely work-related (just as we dropped neighbors who were named only in answer to the house-care question and thus subtracted those relations that were purely neighborly). Here, too, though the trend is downward, from 1.9 to 1.6, it is insubstantial.[9] Although there were strong trends one way or another among specific subgroups, there was *no general* association between urbanism and social involvement in a work subculture.

These findings suggest that the deduction derived from subcultural theory is wrong—or that there has been an error in our method. If the reader will excuse some special pleading, let me suggest what that error might be. (I am moved to make the plea because of other research suggesting that there are urban/rural differences in this regard.) Unlike our approach to analyzing other subcultures, we did not label the specific work group for the respondent; we simply asked, "Which of these people do you think of as doing the same kind of work?" It may well be, though I cannot demonstrate it here, that the subjective definition of "same line" widens as the number of people actually in the respondent's line of work, objectively defined, shrinks. For example, the city patrolman may define "same line" as "city patrolman," while the small-town officer might define it as "public safety official," or even "government employee." The city pediatrician may think of other pediatricians while the small-town one might think of other doctors. Such a definitional difference

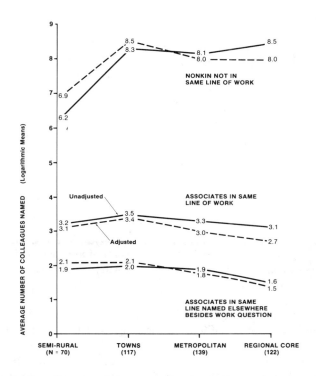

Fig. 30.   Number of associates in the same line of work and of other nonkin named by workers, by urbanism (includes only members of work subcultures—respondents working full time who named at least one person in the same line of work).

would mask a substantive difference in the specialization of occupational subcultures and of people's immersion in them.[10] Since I cannot remove this "mask" (if it exists), I will proceed with the manifest results.

When specific job characteristics and individual traits are held constant so that we can isolate the direct consequences of community, we find a tendency for workers in the smaller places, especially in Town communities, to be more socially involved with colleagues than were workers in larger, especially in Core, communities. As the dashed lines in figure 30 show, the Core residents would have, had they been the same kinds of people holding the same kinds of jobs, named slightly fewer colleagues than would have Town and Semirural residents.[11] Combined with the differences figure 30 shows in how many noncolleagues respondents

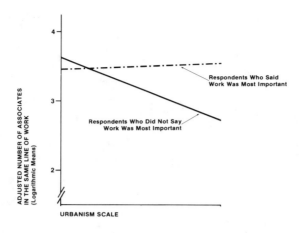

Fig. 31.   **Number of associates in the same line of work, by urbanism, by whether or not work was most important (adjusted).**

named,[12] our findings suggest that less urban respondents were slightly more involved in occupational worlds than highly urban respondents—at least as measured here.

There are notable variations in these patterns by subgroups. For example, all else equal, craftsmen and operatives living in Towns were considerably more involved with fellow workers than were craftsmen and operatives living elsewhere, but Town professionals were slightly less involved than were professionals living in more urban places. The most important subgroup variations in community effects, however, are revealed by distinguishing those respondents who said that work was most important to them (q. 100). As figure 31 indicates in a simplified way, the 271 work subculture members who did *not* identify strongly with their line of work typically named fewer colleagues—other characteristics held constant—the more urban their communties. But the 175 members who *did* say work was most important to them named about the same number of associates wherever they lived. Much the same pattern holds true for percentage of the network that is composed of colleagues, for the number of colleagues who were named elsewhere besides the work discussion question, and, less so, for how often the respondents said they got together socially with people in their line of work.[13]

Another, perhaps more useful, way of describing the pattern in figure 31 is to say that in less urban communities there was little difference in how much the strongly and weakly identified were socially involved with colleagues, while in more urban communities the strong and weak identifiers differed noticeably—mostly because weak identifiers in cities named considerably fewer colleagues.[14]

An explanation of these findings—admittedly post hoc—is that the urban environment allows workers more *choice* of social worlds than do the Town or Semirural environments, to increase social involvement with colleagues, or for those who do not care so much about their jobs, to withdraw in favor of other personal relations. This argument suggests a parallel between the workplace and the neighborhood. In chapter 13, I argued that urbanism provides options besides local involvement. Similarly, in small communities, full-time workers rely on co-workers as their basic pool of relations, whether or not the job is an important commitment to them. In larger communities, those workers whose attention is drawn elsewhere—to ethnicity, religion, leisure pursuits, friends—withdraw from the work setting without being isolated as a result. Meanwhile, those whose focus is on work sustain their involvement.

Some evidence supports this interpretation. First, the (adjusted) decline from Semirural to Core involves solely associates in the same line of work who were also co-workers—that is, who worked at the same shop or office. If we instead count only people in the same line who worked *elsewhere,* there are essentially no differences by community.[15] Thus the results indicate a connection between community and a *workplace,* rather than a general occupational, subculture. Second, in a pattern very similar to that which we found in looking at religious involvement, the relative importance of identification versus formal participation shifted from small town to large city. In Semirural and Town communities, naming co-workers went together with involvement in formal work organizations, whether or not the respondents said that work was most important; in Core communities, it was almost the opposite—saying work was most important counted.[16] It seems that involvement with co-workers becomes more a matter of taste and less a matter of circumstance as urbanism increases.

(This argument implies that, in urban but not in small-town places, identification causes social involvement with co-workers. It may be that, in urban but not in small-town places, social involvement causes identification with work. Either way, identification with work and relations with colleagues come as a package more often in urban places.)

This post hoc argument might help explain why there was a decline in social involvement from less to more urban communities among weak identifiers. It does not, however, provide support for subcultural theory's prediction that involvement in a work subculture should increase with urbanism for strong identifiers. There are insignificant trends indicating that urban strong identifiers had more occupational associates than small-town ones. But, the evidence in support of the prediction is, in total, very weak.

Other Dimensions of Involvement

All else equal, Town workers were more likely to express commitment to their jobs—either saying that their work was most important or impressing interviewers enough so that they were described as heavily involved in work—than were Core or Metropolitan workers.[17] (Consistent with this finding, Town workers were most likely and Core workers were least likely to say their jobs were interesting; see q. 44.) And there was a tendency for workers to be less formally involved in a work subculture—by belonging to a work organization, such as a union, professional association, or factory sports team, or by reading a work magazine—the more urban their communities.[18]

Conclusion

Subcultural theory argues that urbanism encourages individual involvement in social worlds based on occupation. There is little evidence here to support that claim, and some to suggest the opposite.

Urban respondents were more often members of occupational subcultures, simply because they were more often employed and worked at more involving jobs. As a purely descriptive matter, there were no community differences in how many social ties to colleagues members had; we were as likely to find heavily involved workers living anywhere. But that similarity partly resulted from the higher education and professional status of the more urban workers. Statistically adjusting the data so that all work subculture members were "equal" in these respects, we found that living in Towns encouraged and living in the Core discouraged involvement with co-workers—that is, with colleagues at the workplace. (Residence did not affect involvement with colleagues employed at other work sites.) Pursued still further, social involvement was contingent on the combination of respondents' communities and their identification with work: urbanism *reduced* involvement with co-workers for those who did not identify work as their most important identity. I suggested that urbanism provides additional sources of social ties for workers with other interests, and therefore that this finding does not necessarily contradict subcultural theory. Instead, it might support the argument that urbanism allows for more individual choice. And urbanism had virtually *no effect* on the social involvement of workers who did consider work most important.

On other dimensions, work identification itself and formal participation in an occupational world, urbanism tended to slightly depress involvement in work subcultures.

More occupational subcultures *exist* in urban than in nonurban areas, because more people work full time and more work at the kinds of jobs that generate subcultures. This fact has consequences, because these worlds—the professionals who work in the hospitals near San Francisco's black ghetto; the journalists who work out of downtown's collection of newspapers and television stations; the hawkers, bouncers, dancers, and entrepreneurs of the topless shows on Broadway; and so on—are part of the urban context. But we have no evidence here that urbanism per se spurs individual involvement in these worlds.

This failure contrasts with growing evidence from other research that urbanism does spur "class consciousness"—involvement in, attachment to, and activity in defense of, class groups (typically lower-status ones).[19] It is this evidence that led me to suggest that out measurements may have systematically underestimated the extent to which urbanites were more involved in occupational worlds that were small-town residents.

A Note on Homemakers

This discussion of work has referred to work for pay. Many Americans' work is never added into the gross national product, even though it also involves consultation and mutual support. We asked full-time homemakers in our sample: "Which of [the people on your list] are also full-time homemakers?" (q. 86; this group did not include retired workers currently acting as homemakers). The 149 homemakers (all but one female) cited an average of forty-five fellow homemakers, or an average of thirty percent of all the people they named—considerably more immersion in a homemaking "world," if such exists, than even highly educated professionals had in theirs.

The thirty-eight Semirural homemakers named an average of 5.2 homemakers each, followed by the twenty-five Core homemakers at 4.6; Town homemakers named the fewest, 4.0. But, if personal traits are held constant, it appears that urbanism tends to reduce homemakers' involvement with one another. Had they been otherwise similar, Semirural homemakers would have named the most, 5.5 homemakers or 39 percent of their network, and Core homemakers the least, 3.8 or 32 percent.[20] We have too few respondents in this group to say anything with certainty, but the trend is consistent with a hearth-and-home description of small-town life. It is also consistent with our findings on the occupational associates of workers who were not strongly identified with their work. Perhaps for homemakers and for such workers both, colleagues are a residual category.

Pastime

In modern society, it seems, people have founded personal relations on many new kinds of common interest. The label "lifestyle" is loosely applied to these interests, but it covers a wide compass. There are groups that follow professional sports, musical genres, art forms, and the like, and they often include a core of heavily committed members (for example, the people in fan clubs that travel to their teams' away games). Varieties of private conduct and morality become public commitments and also the bases for social ties—organic food, holistic health, evangelical beliefs, for example. Similarly, public issues generate social movements that are sometimes very involving, such as the women's movement, environmental lobbies, and the antiabortion campaign. Most commonly, avocations can become passions, and the passionate join together, whether it be around dirt-bike riding, woodcarving, softball, backpacking, CB radios, or a multitude of other hobbies. Between 1968 and 1977, the number of national hobby or sport organizations increased 61 percent, and the number of national public-interest associations virtually doubled.[21]

We explored various ways for finding out about all these groups, but practicality led us to focus on one specific life-style domain: leisure activity or hobby. For some people, their life-style *is* their pastime—for example, the woman we interviewed who was president of a singles' club and the gay activist—but a hobby is generally more restricted in scope than is a life-style. Thus our question is: Does urbanism encourage involvement in hobby-based subcultures?

One part of the answer is clear: urbanism, in northern California and no doubt elsewhere, supports formal institutions and services for the hobbyist. Cities have more art galleries, stores, instructional services, and museums for the artist; more tennis stores, clubs, and teachers for the tennis buff; and so on. As with other types of subcultures, the presence of such institutions in urban communities means more visibility and organization for their subcultures.

Membership

We asked respondents, "Is there any particular activity—like a sport, organization, or some spare-time interest—you devote a lot of time to or find especially interesting?" If they answered yes, we asked what it was, and if they gave more than one answer, we asked, "Which of these do you find most important or devote the most time to, or are they about the same?" (q. 96). We pursued the issue with those respondents who gave us a single major interest. In retrospect, the question probably elicited more sports and fewer other interests like politics or evangelism than other phrasing would have.[22]

Forty-seven percent of our respondents both specified a single avocation and listed at least one nonrelative who shared it; these I called members of a hobby subculture. Semirural respondents were slightly less likely to be members, but their greater age, lower income, and marital status fully account for that difference.[23]

The specific activities members cited did vary by urbanism: overall, 26 percent of the members named an individual outdoor sport such as fishing, hunting, or jogging. Semirural respondents were especially likely to name these activities. Thirteen percent of respondents named other kinds of sports, but Core residents were least likely to do so. (Virtually no Core residents named an indoor sport like bowling.) The other kinds of interests were scattered over fifty categories that I collapsed into four. Crafts and related pursuits, such as gardening, animal husbandry, carpentry, knitting, and stamp collecting were more often cited by Metropolitan and by Semirural respondents. Artistic performance, such as playing music and taking photographs, was mentioned by Core respondents and rarely by Semirural ones. Organizational activities—church auxiliaries, Red Cross, fraternal orders, and such—were about equally common across the board, except that the specifics varied: none of the sixteen participants in church clubs lived in the Core, but five of the six members of political groups did. The remaining activities were classified as "other." Town and Core respondents both tended to cite reading and following sports, but in addition the Town respondents also included a few recreational-vehicle enthusiasts and the Core respondents a few followers of the arts. Basically, sports involvement declined with urbanism; crafts were most common in Metropolitan and art in Core places.

Social Involvement

I expected that social involvement would increase with urbanism. That was *not* so for the 497 members of pastime subcultures *as a whole*. Metropolitan residents named slightly more fellow hobbyists than others did (especially among sports enthusiasts), but the community differences in social involvement are generally meager.

Since these differences are so meager—Semirural members named 3.1 (adjusted) fellow hobbyists and Core members 2.8—I have dispensed with the figure showing them. The lines are basically flat.[24]

As with religion and work, however, the answer respondents gave to the question, "Which [work, ethnicity, religion, or spare-time activities] is most important to you?" specified the community differences. Figure

32 shows, in simplified form, how urbanism differentially affected the total number of fellow hobbyists respondents named.[25]

The 334 members of pastime subcultures who did *not* say their activities were most important to them tended, albeit unevenly, to name fewer fellow hobbyists the more urban their communities (all else, including type of pastime, held equal). In fact, if we count only those fellow hobbyists who were named at least twice in the interview and were thus in some sense important associates, the decline in number that accompanied an increase in urbanism is roughly linear. But the 159 respondents who said that their activities *were* most important to them showed the opposite pattern: all else equal, the more urban the community, the more fellow hobbyists they named.[26]

Also as in our discussions of religion and work, these results can be stated in a different way: the more urban the community, the wider the gap in social involvement between strong and weak identifiers. (Compare the distances between the two lines in figure 32.) And, as before, Core and Semirural respondents differed in whether personal interest or formal involvement fostered social ties. Core respondents who felt that their pastime was most important named many sharers in it, irrespective of whether or not they were formally involved in the pastime (i.e., whether they belonged to a pastime organization or read a pastime magazine). Semirural respondents who were formally involved named many sharers in their pastime, irrespective of whether they said their pastime was most important. (Unlike the results with religion and work, however, Metropolitan respondents were more similar to Semirural than to Core respondents in this regard.)[27] In sum, urbanism again seems to encourage social involvement on the basis of interest, irrespective of institutions.

Other Indicators of Involvement

Respondents living in Town and Metropolitan communities were especially likely to be "committed" to their spare-time activity, saying it was most important or impressing the interviewer with their involvement; Town respondents were particularly committed to organizations and "other" hobbies, and Metropolitan respondents particularly to sports, arts, and crafts.[28] The connection between such ideological commitment and social involvement is, as we have seen, tenuous, particularly in smaller places. A most striking example is the three Semirural respondents who were interested in artistic activities. All three were committed to their art, in stressing its importance to them, but they named only the minimum number of fellow artists (two respondents named one nonkin, and one respondent named two).

Town and Metropolitan respondents were also a bit more likely to

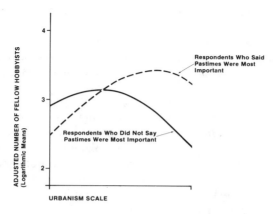

Fig. 32.   **Number of fellow hobbyists named, by urbanism, by whether or not respondent said spare-time activities were most important (adjusted).**

belong to formal hobby organizations or read hobby magazines than were other respondents; Core respondents were least likely to do either.[29] Respondents differed little by community in whether they said it was important to live near fellow hobbyists (q. 99).[30] The three Semirural artists who were "into" their art but knew few fellow artists said that living near other artists was especially important—perhaps a sign that affirmative answers to this question indicate a desire for involvement more than actual involvement.

Summary

Subcultural theory predicts that urbanism should increase individuals' involvement in leisure subcultures. The plethora of "life-style" and hobby-related institutions that accompany city life lend weight to the argument. But our survey provides a more complex answer. Urbanites were no likelier to be members of hobby subcultures than were residents of smaller places, though the urbanites' interests ran toward the less common hobbies—crafts in the Metropolitan communities, arts in the Core—rather than the more typical sports interests of Semirural and Town residents. Urban hobbyists were more involved with fellow members than were otherwise similar respondents in smaller communities—but only among those who said their spare-time activities were most important to them. Among those who did not say that, urbanism tended to slightly discourage social involvement. As we found with religious and occupational subcultures, urbanism seems to separate the committed from the casual subculture members, the former becoming more engaged and the latter less engaged with fellow members.

On other dimensions of involvement, however—ideological commitment, formal activity, desire to live near co-hobbyists—Town and Metropolitan hobbyists tended to be slightly more involved than either Semirural or Core ones. A major incongruity arises concerning Core members who said their pastime was most important: although they reported many, and a high proportion of, fellow hobbyists, these Core residents tended *not* to participate formally (by magazine or organization) in their pastime. Indeed, among Core hobbyists there was no connection between formal involvement and social involvement. This too is consistent with our findings on religion and work, that in larger communities formal involvement becomes disconnected from the number of personal relations.

At the beginning of this chapter I suggested that occupation and pastime were similar in being voluntary contexts for social ties, compared with ethnicity and religion. In the course of the analysis, however, I distinguished the two, arguing instead that the workplace may be a residual social context for full-time workers, much as the neighborhood is for residents. The fewer choices people have for making social ties, the likelier they are to rely on the workplace. Thus, among workers who did not care very much about their work, ties to co-workers were increased by living in smaller towns. Pastimes, on the other hand, are indeed voluntary activities. Thus, for those who cared much about their leisure activities, ties to fellow hobbyists were increased by living in larger cities.

Despite this distinction between work and leisure, there were parallels in our findings about urbanism's consequences for involvement in occupational and pastime subcultures. First, urbanism did not seem to directly affect whether respondents were minimal members of such subcultures (though cities may provide more and better jobs). Second, living in urban places may have slightly depressed members' ideological commitments to and formal participation in these subcultures. Third, casual members of these subcultures living in larger communities were involved with *fewer* fellow members than comparable casual members living in smaller places. These first three points cast doubt on the subculture thesis.

But, fourth, among members who thought that what they did was most important, urbanism did not reduce social involvement. For serious hobbyists, urban residence clearly *increased* social involvement. For these people, like members of small religious groups, finding associates is a problem, and urban residence helps. For serious workers, urbanism had no net effect on social involvement (but I suspect that better measures of work subculture and of work commitment would have yielded positive effects of urbanism for this group). Fifth, perhaps most striking, urbanism seemed to differentiate the ways people were involved. In urban places, the serious workers and hobbyists were clearly more involved socially than were the casual members; in small places they were not. And in large places formal involvement was differentiated from social involvement—members often had many associates who shared their membership without any formal participation; in small places members had both social *and* formal ties or had neither. Thus, as I suggested in the last chapter about ethnicity and religion, city life may offer the possibility of subcultural involvement for those seriously interested in it, independent of formal institutional supports.

Involvement in Subcultures: An Overview

As I said early in part 5, ethnicity, religion, occupation, and pastime do not exhaust the types of subcultures that might be affected by urbanism. Involvement in criminal subcultures, for example, is probably greatest in the largest communities, but our survey provides no evidence about it. (Our only admitted drug dealer, however, lived in central San Francisco.) Involvement in homosexual subcultures, to take an example pursued further in the next chapter, is no doubt greater in the Bay Area than in its hinterland. Another, and quite different, subculture we necessarily ignored is that of Anglo teenagers. These adolescents are concentrated not in the largest cities, but in the suburbs. And that is where their most visible collective activity occurs: cruising, loitering, clashing with police, and so on. The Anglo teenagers illustrate the point that the concentration of a particular group, not urbanism alone, contributes most to subcultural vitality.

We can only speculate about these three subcultures. For four types of subcultures, however, we now have some evidence on urbanism and individual involvement with which we can address the general theoretical debate. Subcultural theory contends that urban residents are more involved, socially and otherwise, in ethnic, religious, occupational, or leisure subcultures than are residents of smaller communities. This presumably comes about, first, because of selective migration—minorities prefer cities, employed people are especially likely to live in cities, and so on. Second, groups are typically better able to attain critical mass in urban centers, to reach numbers large enough to sustain social and organizational life. Since the important factor is the size of the specific group, the difference urbanism makes is conditional: urbanism gives little help to majority groups, such as Protestants, for whom adequate size is rarely difficult to attain; it helps small groups most, for example, opera fans. And for groups that are atypical by being concentrated in small communities—Mexican-Americans in northern California, for example, or Anglo teenagers—subcultural involvement will also be high in some less urban places. Third, the contact among groups in cities leads to some social and cultural estrangement among them, thereby strengthening in-group loyalty. This retreat from the storm of clashing cultures into the safe harbor of one's own social home is likely to be accentuated by urbanism largely for members of majority groups; minorities experience intergroup tension almost everywhere.

This claim of subcultural intensification resulting from urbanism contradicts the general predictions of decline theories, which imply that urbanization detaches people from social worlds, especially "primordial" worlds, or promotes only shallow involvement in several social worlds.

Without repeating the results of our analyses or the summaries of them provided in this and the previous chapter, it seems fair to say that subcultural theory more closely fits the data than does decline theory. Except with respect to occupation, urban life seemed to support in-group social ties more than it seemed to weaken them—especially in the cases of the two kinds of worlds that decline theory expects to wither in the urban setting—religion and ethnicity. More specifically, urban life seemed to encourage social ties in those groups for which social ties were *problematic*: ethnics, non-Protestants, the seriously religious, and those serious about their pastimes. It is still fairer to say that a modified version of subcultural theory fits best. (The size, cut, and style are fine, but the theoretical suit still needs some alterations.)

Urban residence per se tended to encourage social ties with fellow members, but by itself it was irrelevant to, or even discouraged, other modes of involvement—formal participation, expressions of commitment, and such. Perhaps the subcultural intensification of city life (insofar as urbanism directly affects individuals) involves only an intensification of social relations; formal institutions play a small role. Indeed, it seems that personal relations were less often bound up with formal participation—union membership or church attendance, for example—in the cities than in the towns. Instead, relations were more closely linked to a serious personal interest in that social world. And this point suggests another—that in urban centers social relations were more culturally specialized: urbanites were relatively involved with associates in the social world they considered most important and relatively uninvolved with associates, if any, in other worlds.[31] In smaller communities, involvement was moderate whether or not the individual was personally invested in that world. Urbanism, by this logic, fosters social involvement in the subculture(s) of *choice*, rather than the subculture(s) of circumstances. This altered explanation would also cover the contradictory results we obtained with occupational involvement: for most full-time workers, the workplace community is a social world of circumstance, not choice.

The reader may feel that subcultural theory has been so altered to fit the data that it is now more a custom-made product than a ready-to-wear garment off the theoretical rack. Yet the basic findings are still that urban respondents tended to be more, rather than less, socially immersed in social worlds (of choice) than small-town residents.

Another complication arises, however. According to at least one interpretation of decline theory, the problem of city life, and by extension, of modern life, is not that individuals lack involvement in any social world and drift about in an anomic limbo, but that individuals partake in *too many worlds*. Louis Wirth argued, for example, that "by virtue of his different interests arising our of different aspects of social life, the individual acquires membership in widely divergent groups, each of which functions only with reference to a certain segment of his personality." The ultimate consequence of having such diverse memberships is some kind of alienation and, perhaps, personality disorder.[32]

We can address the question to our data: Of how many of the four types of subcultures were respondents members—members in that they claimed an identity and named at least one nonkin fellow member? And did that number vary by urbanism? Overall, respondents belonged to an average of 1.7 subcultures. And there was a difference by urbanism: Semirural respondents averaged fewer subcultural memberships, 1.3, than did respondents living elsewhere; more of the Semirural respondents, 22 percent, belonged to none of the four subcultures. Respondents living in Town, Metropolitan, or Core communities did not, on average, differ much from one another. (Adjusting the averages for self-selection, for age and employment, for example, does not alter the conclusion.)[33]

This finding buttresses the claim that living in a small town leads to involvement in fewer social worlds than does life in more urban places. The finding might be methodologically qualified, however, by the fact that the contrast is due solely to the tendency of Semirural respondents to have no memberships at all (rather than of urbanites to have multiple memberships) and by the fact that Core respondents did not report any more memberships than did Town ones. A yet more substantive qualification may be that small-town residents were more often members of another type of subculture, not included among the four: the local culture of neighbors and nearby kin (see part 3).

Moreover, this analysis counted only minimal memberships in subcultures. What of deeper involvements, at levels that might be seriously shaped by urbanism and, in turn, might shape psyches? The average respondent was socially involved in 0.9 subcultures to the depth of naming three or more nonkin who were fellow members. That average varied considerably by urbanism; Semirural respondents averaged 0.6 deep involvements, Core respondents almost twice as many, 1.1. But urban residence did not directly *cause* these additional involvements; self-selection did. Because the more urban respondents were typically younger, better educated, more often employed full time, and so on, they tended to report a greater number of such intense connections to the four types of social worlds.[34]

As a descriptive matter, then, Park, Wirth, and others were correct about urbanites' "multiple worlds": the larger the community, the more people can "pass quickly and easily from one moral milieu to another"—if by moral milieus we mean the social worlds of ethnicity, religion, occupation, and pastime. A hypothetical average person who moves from small town to big city moves from an environment where the people about him or her have few if any subcultural involvements to one in which such involvements are a bit more common. By virtue of the move, the average person may go from having no involvements to having one, though that might just mean trading neighborhood and kin ties for relations based on some other commonality. He or she may join a nonlocal subculture. But this hypothetical mover is *not* apt to increase the number of deep subcultural involvements by virtue of the move alone; the number of such commitments is a product of employment, education, race, and other characteristics he or she usually brings along. What is apt to increase by virtue of the move alone, albeit slightly, is involvement with fellow ethnics, *if* the person is an ethnic; involvement with co-religionists, *if* the person is a Catholic or cares much about religion (church attendance and orthodoxy, however, are likely to drop); and involvement with co-hobbyists *if* the person cares strongly for that. Relations based on interests this experimental individual cares less about are likely to be fewer in the city.

Subcultural theory contends that urbanism increases subcultural involvement by three processes: self-selection, critical mass, and intergroup friction. We have evidence in these two chapters that the first process operates. Among the people who tend to live in urban places are blacks, foreign-born residents, and other ethnically conscious people; Catholics and Jews, who are especially involved in religious communities; and fully employed, educated, and professional workers, who are particularly involved in occupational communities. We have some evidence though it is inconsistent, supporting the critical mass idea. Urbanism, holding constant self-selection, tends to foster social relations in those subcultures for which social ties are difficult. But we have as yet not addressed the issue of intergroup contact. The next chapter does.

Alienation in Urban Public Life

We have focused, so far, on people's private lives within each of the "little worlds which touch but do not interpenetrate." It is in public, however, that these worlds not only touch, but also rub against and occasionally collide with each other. The frequency and intensity of meetings among diverse subcultures sharply distinguishes the public life of the big city from that of the small town. This contrast, I will argue, also leads observers of public life to believe that cities break down community and give rise to individual alienation. What cities really do is breed a plurality of communities that, through the public encounters of their members, become collectively estranged from one another.[1]

Public and Private Acts

Largely stimulated by well-publicized incidents that seemed to illustrate urbanites' indifference to people in need (the best known being the murder of Kitty Genovese in Kew Gardens, New York City), many psychologists have in the last decade or so been conducting research on how city life affects social interaction, especially encounters in public places.[2] Several investigators have performed field experiments in communities of varying sizes—seeing where "lost" letters are most likely to be forwarded by their finders, where people are most willing to take time to give directions to a stranger, and so on. In spite of methodological problems, the research suggests that American city-dwellers are, in fact, less forthcoming to strangers than are small-town Americans.[3]

This tentative conclusion can be combined with more certain findings —that intergroup conflicts, such as race riots and strikes, increase with urbanism,[4] that people generally believe that cities are impersonal,[5] and so on—to yield a description of urbanites as more estranged from, even aggressive toward, one another than are small-town people. Environmental psychologists typically argue, by way of explanation, that individuals' cognitive and social capacities are strained by the stimulation, complexity, demands, and sheer numbers of people encoun-

tered in the city. Chronic withdrawal becomes the urbanites' coping
mechanism and psychological style; indifference to, and isolation from,
other people protects the endangered psyche.[6]

Although this theory may be compatible with the research evidence on
public behavior, there is little evidence for the psychological *processes*
that it presumes explain the behavior. For example, city and small-town
people do not seem to differ in their personal dispositions to help; it is the
concrete situations they face that seem to differentiate their behavior.[7]
Also, city-dwellers are, on the average, no more psychologically distressed and have no fewer intimate friendships than do residents of
smaller places (see chaps. 4 and 5). Indeed, this contrast between signs of
public estrangement and signs of *private* integration in cities poses a
strong challenge to any sweeping theory of urban life. There are various
ways of integrating the positive and negative findings. Some are ad hoc.
The most important among these involve fear of crime. The reserve
American urbanites display may result not from any personality traits
such as alienation, but from a realistic fear of becoming a victim. Too
many stories have been published of Good Samaritans picking up hitch-
hikers or allowing people into their homes to use the telephone who have
died for their willingness to help. In fact, the police specifically discourage
Good Samaritanism: A syndicated article "Ways to Foil a Pickpocket"
says, "Always be on guard if a stranger approaches you for any
reason—to ask for a light, directions, the time, or the like."[8] A Berkeley
police film on rape says, "Women should never let a stranger use their
home phone, no matter what the emergency."[9] And some research evidence suggests that this anxiety, which is for good reason greater in more
urban places, may well account for the differences in helping behavior
between the American small town and big city.[10]

Although contemporary fear of crime may suffice as an explanation, a
more general interpretation is the analysis presented most fully by Lyn
Lofland in her book, aptly titled *A World of Strangers*.[11] She argues that
behavior in public settings where people do not know one another requires a special etiquette—careful, nonintrusive, reserved, *impersonal*.
This style is sometimes read as indifference and alienation, but it really
says little about personality. It is a situational, not a psychological style.
Lofland writes that the city-dweller "did not lose capacity for the deep,
long-lasting, multi-faceted relationship. But he gained the capacity for the
surface, fleeting, restricted relationship."[12] And, one may add, the ability
to recognize the proper occasions for each.

To this argument I would add another: that avoidance, or friction, or
both, among people in the public sphere—which are more common in city
than in countryside—result also from contacts among contrasting and
often competing subcultures. The subcultural heterogeneity and vitality of

urban centers leads to encounters between people who not only are personally strangers to one another but also are culturally strange, perhaps even threatening, to one another. This is a different sense in which the city is a "world of strangers." The less private and more public the sphere—for example, outside residential neighborhoods, in spaces such as train stations—the more common such cross-cultural encounters, be they physical, verbal, or just visual. Misunderstanding, distrust, reluctance to help (bystander assistance tends to be racially segregated, for example),[13] and conflict are occasionally going to follow. And they are more likely to occur in public urban places than in the typically more homogeneous public rural places. The subcultural argument implies that, as urbanism strengthens the little worlds of the urban mosaic, it also increases the strain between pieces of that mosaic.[14]

An important difference between this argument and Lofland's is that the strangers in the city, though not personally known to one another, *are* known categorically and stereotypically. Students of the Third World urbanization have described this kind of familiarity in various cultures. Gerald Berreman writes of India, for example:

> The *urbanite* is well-versed in the identification of a wide variety of strangers as representative of both corporate and noncorporate social categories. He knows superficial signs of their identity, their stereotypically defined attributes, the varieties of situations and social information necessary for interaction with them and methods of defining and delimiting interaction in the impersonal and instrumental world of urban interaction. He also knows when situations are not impersonal and instrumental, and how to act accordingly and appropriately.... [This] applies to the work-a-day world of the city—the bazaar and other public places. It is less applicable to interaction within residential neighborhoods and relatively "private" setting.[15]

An additional consequence of this public/private distinciton is that it distorts our understanding of community life. We see in cities the public interaction, whether it be reserved or hostile, and extrapolate it to private interaction and even to personality—seeing urbanites as dispositionally cold or rancorous—when there may be in fact little correspondence between public and private acts.

This chapter tries to account for our common perceptions. It describes findings from the survey suggesting that urbanism increases intergroup friction and suspicion, but indicating also that this distrust is not a projection of personality but reflects, instead, anxiety about distant and culturally different fellow urbanites.

The Visibility of Subcultures

I have argued at length that urbanism increases the chances for members of subcultures to meet and know one another; the increase is especially critical to members of small social groups. More central to the present topic, however, is the contention that *nonmembers'* chances to encounter members increase rapidly with urbanism. Indeed, here is a critical difference between people in large social groups and those in small ones—Protestants versus Catholics, whites versus blacks, middle-class versus rich people, and so on. Irrespective of their proportion of the population, members of minority groups in both small towns and large cities live amid and often meet people of the majority. (The urban members may, if they live in segregated areas, actually encounter fewer majority people than their small-town brethren do; Jewish children in New York may, for instance, rarely meet Gentiles.) The opposite is true for majority members. In small communities, they may be oblivious to the presence of a minority; in large communities, majority members must be more aware of and sensitive to the numerically, even if not proportionally, large minority groups. Add to this the fact that, typically, minority groups are also proportionally larger in urban places, and it is clear that public encounters with minorities are much more common for majority people in large than in small communities.

What an urban resident, whether a "typical American" or the member of a small subculture, sees when he or she walks through urban centers is the public display of a variety of social worlds, each appearing exotic, or distasteful, or even threatening. Take San Francisco's Mission District. At the corner of Twenty-fourth and Mission Streets, the crossroads of Latin San Francisco, teenage Hispanic boys rap after school. Dressed in variations of their basic uniform—black shoes, baggy black chinos, black windbreaker over a white T-shirt, slicked hair topped by a baseball cap, the brim pushed back to reveal a stylized signature on the underside—they whistle at the brightly repainted 1950s automobiles, the low-riders, which blare "golden oldies" from their radios as they cruise the strip. Nearby, in coffee houses decorated with Art Nouveau posters and announcements of "self-awareness" classes, young, affluent white couples—or singles who want to be coupled—sip costly coffee concoctions. Dressed in variations of their basic uniform—shaggy hair and beard for males, long straight hair for females; goose-down vest or jacket over flannel shirt; loose, worn-out denim jeans; and expensive running shoes—these members of the "hipoisie" listen to classical music while reading underground newspapers or plotting real-estate deals that may ultimately dispossess the Hispanic teenagers. A short walk farther is Castro Street, where homosexual men are shopping or just strolling about to watch the action. Dressed in variations of their basic uniform—construction boots, clean skintight blue jeans, tank tops over bare muscled shoulders, brush moustache, and short, recently cut hair, sometimes topped by a Stetson or a motorcycle cap—they pass stores exhibiting male erotica and pick-up bars projecting onto the sidewalk a steady jukebox, disco beat.

The walker in the city is likely to find members of these groups both interesting and disturbing—as they find one another. Not only do they encounter one another where their neighborhoods overlap, but they often pass in major public places—the boulevards, large stores, buses, and so on. They know one another—categorically. And each sees the others as somewhat foreign, somewhat lesser, and a source of unease in the city.

The Mission District's subcultural display is atypical in its vividness and apposition. After all, surrounding these scenes are the homes of thousands of white working-class families, most leading quiet "middle American" lives. (Also, few if any places in San Francisco can match this cultural juxtaposition.) But the basic observation remains valid: cities tend to have many more of these kinds of displays than small towns do. And the public manifestation of "foreign" subcultures is part of the urban experience for all groups—gays, "hip" couples, Latinos, or middle Americans.

Examples: Blacks and Gays

The effects of urbanism on subcultures—both bolstering them and setting them into tension with one another—can be better understood by looking closely at two specific cases in the Bay Area: blacks briefly, and homosexuals more extensively.

Black/white relations dominate contemporary America's ideas about intergroup contact. Although the racial situation emerged from the rural South, it is a particularly urban issue. Especially in 1960s and 1970s, busing, institutional racism, street crime, community control, law-and-order, block-busting, and white flight were battle cries shouted over urban combat fields. The San Francisco Bay Area is one of those battlefields, though the race issue has not been as overwhelmingly dominant here as in other major metropolises. Blacks came relatively late to the Bay Area—largely during World War II to work in the shipbuilding industries—and they have been scattered in separate pockets around the Bay. Although they were a majority in the city of Oakland, in 1977 blacks were little more than 10 percent of San Francisco's population, and they concentrated in two dwindling ghettos. Nevertheless, there is a strong black institutional and public presence on both sides of the Bay. There are black business elites and newspapers in each place; two of San Francisco's supervisors are, at this time, black women; one of California's most powerful politicians is a black representative from San Francisco; the mayors of both Oakland and Berkeley are black; blacks are on both city councils; and the Black Panthers have virtually joined the Oakland establishment. This black presence is, as we shall see, reflected in the perceptions and reactions of nonblacks, too.

Perhaps even more useful as an illustration, because they are not entangled with the complex history of blacks and whites in America, are the homosexuals of San Francisco. The "gay" community is large, concentrated, very visible, and essentially a community of choice. In these ways it allows us to bring into sharp relief subtle processes common to more typical subcultures. A notable homosexual presence in San Francisco can be traced back to the Gold Rush days; in 1853, 20 percent of the prostitutes arrested in the city were male. In the 1930s, specific bars served predominantly homosexual clienteles, but no residential concentration accompanied them. The key changes occurred in the 1960s with the founding of activist organizations and three "gay" newspapers. By one account, the advertising pages of those newspapers were of vital importance: Businesses expressed interest in homosexual customers, and the enthusiastic response led to special shopping streets. These streets, in what had been deteriorating white districts, became places of congregation and then centers of distinct homosexual neighborhoods. The advantage of homosexual renters and buyers—two or three incomes, no children—allowed the intensive housing rehabilitation that has made some streets showplaces of "gentrification." With the establishment of definite homosexual neighborhoods, the growth and intensification of the subculture accelerated.[16]

Today the number of homosexuals and the size of the "gay" community (not, of course, the same thing) are a matter of controversy. Estimates of the homosexual population in the city range as high as 200,000, or over 30 percent of all men, women, and children in San Francisco. A more accurate estimate is that perhaps 12 to 15 percent of all voting-age adults are homosexual.[17] Nevertheless, the visibility and power of homosexuals exceeds this deflated figure. They probably represent 20 percent or more of the Anglo population, and perhaps 25 percent of all Anglo men living in the city. Having relatively high disposable incomes, they are important consumers of goods, services, and housing. Having relatively more free time as well and often dressing in distinctive fashion, male homosexuals visually dominate certain public places. Specialized institutions—taverns, newspapers, a legal defense group, a medical association, a business association, a softball league, bookstores, and the like—flourish. And the wider community has recognized the power of organized homosexuals: Seats on the city boards are de facto reserved for homosexuals; the Board of Education takes steps to treat "gay life-style" as a legitimate alternative in school courses on family life;[18] the police actively recruit homosexuals for the force; and politicians—state and national, as well as local—openly campaign for "gay" endorsements and votes.

The power of the homosexual community, however, has been exaggerated, by friend and foe alike, most notoriously in a nationally televised documentary shown in 1980. The program pointed out that the 1979 mayoral candidates courted the "gay" vote, which they certainly did. But it ignored the facts that both candidates were Jewish, that black politicians were important power-brokers, that the endorsement by the widow of the prior Italian mayor was critical, and that all the voting blocs were courted. In other words, the homosexual vote, while large, is far from dominant.

The size and vitality of subcultures such as the black and homosexual ones help distinguish public city life from public small-town life. These subcultures provide variety, stimulation, and entertainment. They are also sources of new customs, fashions, and ideas for nonmembers. But just as often, and probably more, these subcultures represent a threat, an irritation, and even an enemy to nonmembers.

Intergroup conflict tends, as I noted above, to increase as urbanism increases. Racial tension was quite evident in the Bay Area in the late 1970s: police officers shooting black suspects, with resulting protests by blacks; black youths attacking white bus passengers; political battles over urban renewal (and its accompanying "Negro removal"), and so on.

Tension between homosexuals and others was also evident: A mayoral candidate steadfastly refused to retract his comment about a lesbian couple: "Tolerance, yes; glorification, no"; when the slayer of Mayor Moscone and homosexual supervisor Harvey Milk was convicted of manslaughter rather than homicide, homosexuals rioted against city hall and the police rioted against homosexual bars on Castro Street; black tenants heatedly objected to being displaced by homosexual "gentrifiers"— "'The gay community has taken houses of one black family after another,' shouted Idaree Westbrook, fifty-three, a black educational consultant, at a recent community meeting between blacks and gays. 'You've taken the Haight-Ashbury, don't deny it, and now you're moving in on the Western Addition'";[19] and letters to the city newspapers occasionally complain of distasteful public behavior by homosexuals.

Such tensions are, of course, not exclusive to large cities. There were, for example, cross-burning incidents in an outer suburb of San Francisco;[20] a bar owned by homosexuals was burned down in rural northern California;[21] and the agricultural towns of the San Joaquin Valley have chronic clashes between Anglos and Mexican-Americans. Nevertheless, large and small communities differ significantly in three important respects: (1) On average, urban instances of intergroup conflict are more frequent, more extensive, and more serious. For example, racial violence in 1960s America and violent strikes in nineteenth-century France were disproportionately common in large cities.[22] (2) Urban communities tend to have conflict on all fronts—black/white, Spanish/Anglo, homosexual/ heterosexual, young/old, rich/poor, and so on—where small ones tend to have conflict on only one or two. And (3) much urban conflict revolves around the subcultures themselves—their ways of life, organization, and rights—rather than around neutral or universal topics.

This last point is drawn from my reading of several northern California newspapers during late 1977 and early 1978. There was plenty of controversy everywhere. In the Town and Semirural areas, that controversy focused largely on problems of growth: how much growth will there be, where, and who will pay the taxes; to which school will new students go; what is the status of mobile homes; where will sewer lines be put; how will traffic be controlled; will sidewalks be built; and so on. Occasionally an issue of culture and values might emerge, over closing a "dirty" movie house or opening a bar. And the city of Stockton had some racial strife, partly related to busing. But in the Core communities, the general issues (or their reverse, such as which schools to close in response to declining enrollments) were supplemented by many involving group relations—for example, over what level of recognition or of repression homosexuals should face; the number of women, blacks, Hispanics, or homosexuals who should be on the police force; the rights of low-income and minority tenants to stay in housing desired by affluent whites; "invasions" by one group into another's territory (e.g., the Chinese into San Francisco's Italian North Beach); preservation of neighborhood businesses against conversion to upper-middle-class boutiques; students' rights to political expression; and a host of additional intergroup problems signaled by the rhetoric of "law and order" and "community control." In sum, intergroup conflict in small places seems to arise largely over straightforward conflicts of material interest ("Don't put the sewage treatment plant on *my* road!"). In large places it tends to arise as well over subcultural relations themselves. This, together with their greater intensity and diversity, distinguishes urban conflicts. And such conflicts, together with positive cultural exchanges between diverse groups, distinguish urban public life.

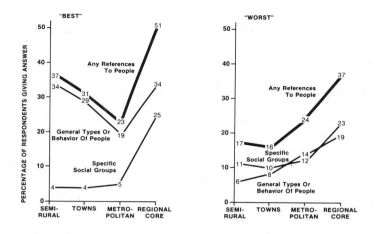

Fig. 33.   **Percentage of respondents giving people as "best"**
or "worst" features of their towns, by urbanism.

Subjective Reflections

These kinds of city/town differences in contacts between subcultures are reflected in the perceptions of residents. We asked respondents, "What would you say are the best things about living in [name of city] these days?" And the same question concerning the "worst things" (q. 19, 20). We coded the answers into many categories, including six types of references to the other people who lived in the respondents' towns. Four categories covered references to specific social groups: to class or income groups; race or ethnicity; religion; or life-style groups (e.g., "hippies," "gay," "intellectuals"). Two categories were more general: references to behavior (e.g., "helpful," "cliquish," "civic-minded"); or general social allusions (e.g., "nice," "friendly," "my kind"). In all, 35 percent of the respondents referred at least once to people in answer to the "best things" question. As figure 33 shows, Core respondents were most likely and Metropolitan respondents least likely to cite people as a positive feature of their towns or cities. The pattern in figure 33 cannot be explained by self-selection factors (the adjusted figures are so similar, they are not shown); it indicates differential reactions to the community.[23]

There is something misleading about the line for "general types or behavior of people" in the graph for "best": The comments of Core residents had a quite different tenor than did those of Semirural and Town residents. The latter more commonly mentioned general amiability or homogeneity as the "best" features of their communities; the Core residents tended instead to speak of social variety as a positive feature. Small-town residents often mentioned best things such as:

Friendly people.

Oh, people are friendly and neighborly. We sort of watch out for each other.

The community itself: A lot of people who belong to things.

In contrast, the best things in this category that Core residents named tended more often to be:

The variety of people... the people are young...a mixture of classes and ethnic groups.

The various ethnic groups are not separated: you can mingle and learn as much as you want to.

Different types of communities like Chinatown and Japantown.

All the various cultures are important; I don't want to be in a waspy neighborhood.

Thus not only were Core respondents most likely to perceive people generally as a community virtue, they tended to view the social heterogeneity of these people as the specific advantage, in contrast to Semirural respondents' stress on homogeneity and compatibility. And, as the lowest line in the "best" graph shows, Core respondents were much more likely to mention specific social groups as advantages (e.g., "young people"; "educated types"; "other Chinese"). Moreover, when Semirural respondents did make specific references, they again tended to praise homogeneity—to say, for example, "It's an all-white area," or "It's out of the nigger district."

The mosaic of social worlds typical of cities is even more strongly reflected in the differential perceptions respondents had of their communities' disadvantages, the "worst things." The comments about specific ethnic and racial groups, especially by urbanites who had never learned the appropriate euphemisms, are stark:

A white divorcee on welfare in San Francisco: "So many Asian people....I feel I'm in Asia now.... There are no white people anymore...they buy up everything. They bought up the Sunset District."

A recent Asian immigrant: "I think the worst thing is you have so many black people.... As I live here for two years, I find that black people, some of them, have not a very good life.... The black people do so many bad things like grab ladies' pocketbooks, and pick the pocket, and get drunk on the street."

A very elderly widow in Oakland: "Colored people on the buses.

They can call you 'white bitch' and ask you for a fix. . . . [They] won't let you off the bus. They stand in front of the door—not to me, but to my friend."

And there were complaints about life-style groups, about "street people" in Berkeley, for example:

A bank management trainee: "Burned-out people. People can get by living on the street. That's OK, but they need help. There are some wasted people around here."

And there were many complaints about homosexuals in San Francisco:

An unemployed professional man: "Actually, there are too many gays. After a while it bothers me. You can feel like a minority."

A young single woman: "The gays are taking away from families coming to the city. It's degenerate. You question whether if you had a family you wanted to raise them here—the bars, the rowdiness, the gay men kissing. If straight people did it it would bother me, too. My boyfriend and I were on Castro Street Monday night and we got the feeling from gay couples walking down the street that we were intruding. . . . It's so cliquey and they behave so outrageously in public, it's like they have no use for straight people."

These urbanites' comments also reflect the disparate experiences of the majority and the minority, because the people criticized in these ways tended to extol the *tolerance* of the city. This was true of black respondents and especially true of homosexuals. For example:

A homosexual paraprofessional in San Francisco: "[Best?] Freedom. It's really OK to be who you are. . . . It's a very enlightened area. Sexuality is really OK."

A "gay activist": "[Best?] It's a concentration of some of the most liberated life-styles in the world. It can be at times such a one continual high that it goes on for weeks and weeks at a time."

But that is not how many heterosexuals saw their city; it was not totally "O.K." And the difference in perspective is, I contend, intrinsic to urbanism. While the minority enjoys autonomy and fellowship not available in small towns, the majority is exposed to ways of life it would neither see nor tolerate in a small town.

Core respondents were not the only ones, of course, to complain about the character and behavior of other subcultures in their communities.

Some residents of small towns complained about "bikers," "low-class people," or transients, and many complained about Mexican-Americans. Nevertheless, urban respondents were generally the most likely to complain about other types of people (see fig. 33).

There was another, and very important, complaint that urbanites volunteered more often than small-town respondents: *crime*. One of every ten Semirural respondents, one of every five Town respondents, one of every four Metropolitan respondents, and one of every two Core respondents said that crime was a worst feature of their communities.[24] Some of those complaints about the lack of "law and order" were indirect complaints about the types of people who were presumably most lawless— that is, code words for race and ethnicity. Most complaints probably just reflected realistic anxiety about the experience of crime.

It would *not* be correct to interpret the differences in complaints about people as the product of differences in *personality* between more urban and less urban residents, to wit, as the result of prejudice. Urbanites are *not* more prejudiced, in the sense of harshly prejudging individuals on the basis of race, creed, or color, than are nonurban people; indeed, they tend to be less prejudiced against minorities.[25] They also tend to be less prejudiced against homosexuals, as evidenced both in nationwide surveys[26] and in our own data (see chap. 6). Urbanites complain more about other types of people *in spite of* being less prejudiced.

The differential complaints (and boasts) of large-city and small-town respondents are products of their *situations:* the greater size, visibility, and power of small subcultures and the more frequent intergroup contacts that accompany city life. This urban experience increases both the positive and the negative aspects of subcultural variety, and these are in turn reflected in the perceptions and feelings of the residents.

Feelings of Distrust

The same phenomenon is also reflected in feelings of suspicion and distrust. There is evidence that American urbanites are, all else equal, slightly more likely than residents of small communities to express feelings of distrust toward other people—for example, to answer no to the question, "Do you think most other people can be trusted?" The differences are small, but, when educational and other factors are held constant, urbanites are a bit more suspicious than otherwise similar people living elsewhere.[27] Add this to the findings discussed earlier of less helpfulness in cities, and one can claim that urbanites are indeed less trusting of others.

Again, it would be incorrect to infer personality differences, to conclude that urbanites are characterologically more estranged from people than are small-town residents. Instead, this too reflects the urban situation: the "world of strangers" and the subcultural variety that leads people to distrust those unknown and culturally different "others." It is an anxiety about values, life-styles, and the unpredictability of others' behavior, including their possible criminal behavior.

This interpretation is supported in our survey by an "experiment." We divided the typical trust question into two parts (q. 17 and q. 18):

Thinking of the neighborhood as a whole, would you say that most people who live here *can* be trusted or *cannot* be trusted? (Can, cannot, or can't say.)

What about most of the people who live in [name of city]—would you say that most of them *can* or *cannot* be trusted?

There were essentially *no* community differences in how respondents answered the neighborhood question: 89 percent of Semirural, 85 percent of Town, 86 percent of Metropolitan, and 85 percent of Core respondents trusted their neighbors. There *were* noticeable community differences in how residents answered the city question: 76 percent of Semirural, 68 percent of Town, and 60 percent of Metropolitan and Core respondents said "can trust." The point is this: If expressions of distrust were only projections of personality, they should be projected equally onto both questions. But if expressions of distrust were also reflections of the situation, specifically of anxieties about dissimilar strangers, their connection with urbanism should be differentiated by question in just this way. Urbanites were as likely to trust those familiar to them, their neighbors, as were small-town people. But urbanites were much more likely to face, especially outside their neighborhoods, unfamiliar, dissimilar, and potentially threatening others. And their distrust of those others is understandable.

Expressions of distrust are greatly influenced by education and income (educated and affluent people tend to trust more) and other self-selection factors. Figure 34 allows us to take those into account. The answers to the trust questions are presented in the form of a three-point scale: 1, trust; 2, can't say; and 3, can't trust. The solid lines indicate the findings I have just reported: no community differences on the neighbor item, differences on the city item.[28] The dashed lines indicate the differences, adjusted for several personal characteristics, most notably social rank. The contrast between the questions is at least as sharp. A significant community difference, albeit a weak one, emerges on the neighborhood item; were it not for urbanites' higher education and other trust-building traits, they would have expressed slightly more distrust of their neighbors than small-town respondents. But on the city item the statistical controls reveal that the personal characteristics of the respondents had masked yet a stronger community difference.[29]

Some aspect of urban residence, it appears, actually caused residents to feel distrustful; that is, just slightly distrustful of neighbors and substantially distrustful of those elsewhere in the town. That aspect may be the fear of being victimized. This possibility is suggested not only by our earlier finding that urbanites were much more likely to complain about crime and my argument that self-protection rationally calls for suspicion, but also by the behavior and comments of our respondents. On several occasions in the larger cities, interviewers found that respondents were very anxious about letting them into their homes and would explain their hesitation by recounting recent burglaries and muggings they or their neighbors had experienced. Many respondents directly linked the crime problem to estrangement among people. A woman reared in the South and living in San Francisco for less than two years said, for example: "I think it is an unfriendly city. It's hard to make friends. And there is so much fear of crime, to a large extent, no one trusts anyone else."

We have a measure of crime anxiety. We asked respondents: "Generallly speaking, do you think of this neighborhood as a very safe place, a somewhat safe place, or not a safe place to live?" (q. 14; although the question does not specifically refer to safety from crime, the reference is clear in context, because the question follows one about homes being broken into). Respondents who felt unsafe tended also to distrust their neighbors and to distrust others in the city.[30] If we statistically adjust respondents' answers to the distrust questions for their anxiety about safety, the community differences are as shown by the dot-dash lines in figure 34. Feeling unsafe fully explains the connection between urbanism and distrust of neighbors. That is, had respondents in the various communities been similar in personal traits and feared crime equally, they would have trusted their neighbors equally. But, because of greater fear in urban places, there was slightly greater distrust there.[31] However, feeling unsafe explains only a small part of urbanites' greater distrust of people elsewhere in the city. Had respondents in various communities been similar in personal traits and in fear, it would still have been the case that the more urban the community, the greater the distrust of others in the city.[32] (Ideally, I should have adjusted the answers to the city item for fear of city crime, not of neighborhood crime, but we did not ask the right question. Other evidence indicates that the conclusion would have been the same anyway.)[33] Something about urban life generated suspicion of distant strangers in the community but not of proximate neighbors.

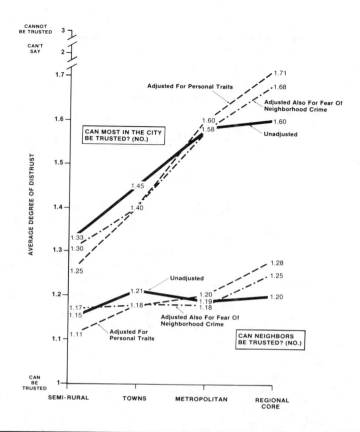

Fig. 34. **Degree to which respondents distrust neighbors and others in city, by urbanism.**

The Familiar and the Unfamiliar

  I suggest that we can best understand our and others' results through an extrapolation of subcultural theory, distinguishing the consequences of urbanism for private social worlds from those for the public world. Urbanism does not create interpersonal estrangement within subcultures; if anything, it tends to promote social involvement. Even the neighborhood, though diminished in importance by urbanism, remains a setting of familiar people. Urbanites were as likely to neighbor casually, to borrow from neighbors, and to trust their neighbors as were small-town residents. But beyond the immediate physical or social arena, the city is, more than the small town, a "world of strangers." It is a world of strangers in two senses: the people encountered in public are *unknown*, and they are *dissimilar*. The unknown aspect is clearly reflected in respondents' answers to our questions. As I reported in chapter 5, we asked people, "When you're not at home [or at work/school], about how often do you run into someone you know—almost every day, at least once a week, about once a month, or less often than that?" (q. 67). Urban residents typically said they ran into someone less often than Town or Semirural respondents.[34] Also, urban respondents were less likely to answer that "people knowing each other here" was one of the best or worst things about the city, and they were more likely to answer that "people not knowing each other here" was a worst feature.[35] People do see cities as populated by personally unfamiliar others. And that may be the main source of urban anxiety.

But another source is that individuals see the city as a world of dissimilar others: people of various races, nationalities, classes, and ways of life. These dissimilar people are familiar, not personally, but as categories with certain traits, often negative traits—avaricious, noisy, lazy, violent, irresponsible, and so on. The evidence shows the greater propensity of respondents in large communities to specifically cite such categories of people as the best and worst things about their cities (fig. 33). This tension between subcultures is also a source of what James Q. Wilson has called "urban unease"—a pervasive anxiety about the behavior of strangers.

Both sources of anxiety also lead to a public style that seems, and is, impersonal. A San Franciscan put it this way to David Hummon:

> I'm a city person. I've had exposure to city life, I feel comfortable in the city, I can get around. I know how to deal with people on a very informal basis. There are certain rules: how to get along in a city, what to expect from people that you don't know. In a small town, I think there is much more of a personal level of what's expected. While in the city, you don't have the opportunity to get to know people that well. I think a lot of small town people—that really throws them for a loop. They can't understand how everybody's just getting along.[36]

This urban public style of just getting along is, however, just that—public. It is segregated from a private style that, as far as we can tell, is as personal and intimate as that of nonurban places. This contrast between the two realms of people's lives also lies behind the comment a recently arrived New Yorker made in another study. After describing his satisfaction with his new friendships in the city, he complained:

> The difference is "out there" in the city, not "in here" with the people who live in the city. It's peculiar, but I haven't met anyone yet

who admits to living "out there"—all say they live "in here" with us humans. Where are all the bastards from?[37]

This public/private distinction also explains, in part, why many astute observers, as well as most of the general public, believe that city life alienates people and drives them to aberrant behavior. We see strangers behave impersonally in public and believe they are impersonal people, when in their own private communities they are as personal as we are in ours. We see members of "foreign" groups look or act oddly and believe they are odd people, when in their own social worlds they are no odder than we are in ours. (See also the discussions at the end of chaps. 4 and 5, on why we believe that city life deranges and isolates people.)

Conclusion

In presenting subcultural theory at the beginning of chapter 15, I extracted three key predictions for empirical examination: that urbanites were more deeply involved in subcultures than were residents of smaller communities because of selective migration; that they were more involved because of critical mass; and that urbanism generates differentiation and tension among subcultures. The first prediction was borne out fairly well and the second with only mixed success in the two preceding chapters. In this chapter we found both in the qualitative and in the quantitative material, at the level of group action and in individual responses, that urbanism did indeed generate intergroup tension. And all three conclusions would have in all probability been stronger had we interviewed in rural places, in black ghettos, and with foreign-speaking people. City life seems, for various reasons, to promote vibrant social worlds. One consequence is cultural borrowing between these worlds— the spice in the city's cultural ragout. Another is tension among these worlds—bitterness in the ragout.

19   Conclusion

Last chapters can be misleading. Like medieval maps whose terrae incognitae are filled with fanciful creatures, summaries cannot hide the fact that some of the landmarks were misdescribed or misplaced, many trails were not pursued, and much terrain was left unexplored. Authors may amend their charts with legends calling on heartier adventurers to take the untrod paths. This concluding chapter is such a sketch. It is divided into three discussions. First, it reviews our findings on how people generally differed in the characteristics of their personal networks. Second, it reviews specifically how the networks of urban and small-town people differed. (Since this book has continually moved to the rhythm of the decline of community controversy, I will refrain from beating that drum too often here.) And, third, it tries to place the findings in context: What does this study say of city life today? Of city life in general? What might that mean for policy?

Personal Background and Personal Networks

Because this book has concentrated on how people's residential communities affect their personal communities, it has skimmed over the many other and typically more important factors that shape people's social networks. Only a diligent reader of the notes could have gotten the full story of how age, or gender, or income influenced personal relations. This section gathers together some of the findings from our survey, indicating which characteristics of the respondents tended to affect their networks most, and discusses how and why such traits may have had those effects.

The personal characteristic that seemed most consistently to affect respondents' networks is *education*. Other things equal, the more educational credentials respondents had, the more socially active they were, the larger their networks, the more companionship they reported, the more intimate their relations, and the wider the geographic range of their ties. In general, education by itself meant broader, deeper, and richer networks.[1] The possible exception involves network density. Educated respondents had notably less interconnected relations than did otherwise similar but

251

less educated respondents. Whether density is indeed an attribute of "richer" networks is, however, not clear.

The composition of respondents' networks also differed according to their education. In particular, the more education respondents had, the more they drew upon nonkin rather than kin, and the more they drew especially upon that informal category, "just friends." The highly educated respondents did not lack kin ties, however; they simply seemed to be more selective in relying on kin. Compared with less educated respondents, they were as likely to borrow money from, less likely to spend leisure time with, and much less likely to confide in relatives than in nonrelatives.

These educational differences, which resemble those described by other researchers,[2] might be explained in various ways. Perhaps they result from personality differences that precede education; the cognitive sophistication that leads some people to succeed in school may also contribute to social skills useful for making and maintaining friendships. Or schooling itself, which implicitly teaches skills such as punctuality, empathy, and reasoning, may teach social skills too—skills such as the ability to present oneself favorably to others, perceive emotional nuances, negotiate resolutions of conflicts, and so on. Or schooling may operate in a straightforward structural manner: schools, from kindergarten to doctoral programs, are ideal places to meet and make friends with people of similar ages, backgrounds, and interests. Consequently, the more schooling, the more friends. Whether these explanations, singly or together, account for the phenomenon or not, education was the most critical source of differences in the structure and content of respondents' networks.

Income, measured as household income, also made a sizable difference, even with education and other factors held constant. The more income, the more nonkin respondents named, and the more secure the practical and companionable support they received. These findings challenge the romantic notion of working-class or lower-class sociality. The poor people we interviewed not only lacked friends, they also tended to be involved with fewer relatives than were the middle-income respondents.[3]

We might also explain income's effects in terms of personality; successful types of people are successful both materially and socially. More likely, however, income is important because it provides concrete resources that aid in building and keeping a wide network—resources that allow people to telephone and travel easily, to entertain guests, to go out socially, to free time for themselves from household tasks, and so on.[4] In line with this interpretation was the finding that income often conditioned the effects of other background traits. For example, children hindered social activity (and psychological well-being) less, spatial separation from associates seemed to matter less, and community characteristics typically had less effect on networks for the affluent than for the nonaffluent. In general, affluent respondents seemed less hampered by constraints and better able to take advantage of far-flung social opportunities than were the less affluent respondents.

The *stage in the life cycle* that respondents were in had complex consequences, differing for men and women. The older the respondents were, all else equal, the less social activity they engaged in, the smaller their networks (in particular, the fewer nonkin they named), the less reliable their social support, the more spatially circumscribed their ties, and the less intense their relations. All this was generally more strongly so for men than for women. In fact, middle-aged women tended to be unusually sociable, and old men were the most isolated.[5]

Marriage tended to expand possibilities for social ties around the home—married respondents named more kin and neighbors than did comparable unmarried respondents—and to restrict possibilities elsewhere, notably for women.[6] Being married, as opposed to never having been married, was associated with, for example, naming fewer co-religionists and co-hobbyists, naming fewer "just friends," and having less intense relations with those friends. In one important respect, however, men were more affected by marriage than women: married men reported fewer confidants than did never-married men, which was not so for women. It appears that men tended to fully satisfy their needs for a confidant by turning to their wives, while wives drew on intimates besides their husbands.

Children clearly restricted the social involvement of their parents, especially of their mothers. Women with children at home had fewer friends and associates, engaged in fewer social activities, had less reliable social support, and had more localized networks than did otherwise similar women without children. This was true to a lesser extent of fathers as well. And, as other research has shown, children take a psychological toll, too. Mothers reported feeling more harassed and generally felt worse than did other respondents.

As these comments indicate, *gender* had important, if largely indirect, effects on social networks. Women tended to be involved with more relatives and to have more intimate ties than did otherwise similar men. Young women, particularly mothers, were more constricted in various ways, such as in the number of "just friends" they had, than were young men, but older women reported more expansive social networks than did older men. Elsewhere, Stacey Oliker and I have suggested a twofold explanation for these findings: that women are, by virtue of biology, socialization, cultural expectations, structural position, or all four, more disposed to be sociable and personally sensitive than are men,[7] but that their material situations, over the life cycle, at first constrain their ability to establish friendship networks (because they are typically occupied with home care and child-rearing) and then later allow them to express their disposition (notably when children leave home).[8]

Other personal characteristics besides gender, life cycle, income, and education also affect the form and content of people's networks—ethnicity, for example. It appears that blacks and Chicanos had smaller, less supportive, and more culturally encapsulated networks than did comparable Anglos. But our sample precludes drawing any conclusions about racial and ethnic differences (we did not interview in black neighborhoods and we interviewed only English-speakers). We are also limited in what we can say about other factors such as employment history and family size, because interview time limited our focus. These and many other possible correlates of network characteristics await further analyses of the data. (This last sentence falls into the category of exhortations to bold adventurers.)

The various correlations between respondents' backgrounds and their networks that we did uncover can be understood in terms of two organizing constructs: first, personality and, second, the structure of opportunities and constraints. We have not really examined personality in this study. Had we been able to measure dimensions such as introversion/extraversion, fatalism/mastery, cognitive dogmatism/complexity, and the like, we would have no doubt been better able to explain the differences in networks among our respondents.

The second organizing theme was addressed in our sociological analyses. People's positions in the social structure—their educational and financial resources, status in the labor force, ethnic memberships, family commitments, residential locations, and so on—expose them to varying opportunities for forming personal relations and provide them with varying means for taking advantage of those opportunities. The woman who works outside the home, for example, meets an entire set of people, some of whom might become her friends, that is unavailable to the woman who does not work. (The latter has a somewhat easier time, however, getting to know her neighbors.) The working woman who has two children to care for has more difficulty making and keeping such potential friends than does the childless working woman. The man who has lived in several communities has had the chance to meet many more possible friends than one who has lived in one place all his life, but whether the roamer holds on to his far-flung ties or is alone in his new community depends, in part, on his income, family burdens, vacation schedule, and so on. Personality dispositions toward smaller or larger networks operate within such structures of opportunity and constraint.

These considerations lead to many new questions about personal backgrounds and personal networks, some answerable from the northern California data, some requiring additional surveys. The network researcher might ask, for example: How do specific job schedules, training, hierarchies, and responsibilities affect people's abilities to construct relations on and off the job? How do networks change during expected transitions, such as marriage and retirement, or unexpected ones, such as divorce or death of a parent? When relations end in these or similar circumstances, who breaks off—the person in transit or the other—and when does it happen? What kinds of people integrate their associates from more than one social world, say, kin with co-workers? What distinguishes people who sustain atypical networks, say, young people with older friends, or whites with black associates? What are the functional and temporal links between formal involvements, as in organizations, and informal social ties? This list of questions can, of course, go on endlessly. It is meant only to confess that, as far as the general study of networks is concerned, this books has barely outlined the territory, and to encourage other explorers.

Urbanism and Networks

Three basic questions summarize the central issues of this book: Do people residing in more and in less urban places differ systematically in their personal networks and social worlds? Does urbanism itself affect those networks and worlds, or do any differences between city and small-town residents reflect only self-selection, the tendency for people to sort themselves out among communities according to personal background and taste? And if urbanism does contribute to differences in networks and worlds, what about urbanism explains the contribution it makes—population concentration itself, or corollary factors such as population composition and housing stock?

Many experts discount any contemporary differences in ways of life between metropolis and village. Perhaps there were once particular urban and rural ways of life, but now there is only a national way of life. John Palen writes, for example:

The urban versus nonurban characteristics that played such a powerful role in the sociology of an earlier era have for decades been bereft of explanatory power. As we enter an era of national metropolitan society, the metropolitan-versus-nonmetropolitan dichotomy loses is empirical and explanatory utility....
Urban-nonurban differences are differences that have ceased to make a difference.[9]

How much of a difference makes a difference depends, of course, on the observer's standards. Still, our findings appear to me to challenge such claims. For example, the more urban respondents in the sample (who were far from the most urban in the nation) included 40 percent fewer relatives and almost 50 percent more nonrelatives in their networks than did the least urban respondents (none of whom were actually rural). The former tended to have considerably less dense networks than the latter. The most urban young or Catholic respondents averaged considerably more young or Catholic friends than did their least urban counterparts. The highly urban respondents were considerably less traditional in their opinions than the least urban ones. And so forth. As a purely actuarial matter, this study suggests that the average urbanite leads a notably different way of life than the average small-town person. And it seems to be a difference that continues to matter. (Indeed, in some aspects of social values, the differences may actually be widening.)[10]

Many of these differences, and much of the magnitude of others, can be explained by self-selection. Young people prefer cities, the elderly prefer small towns; affluent people tend to live in more urban places, poor people in less urban places; most foreign-born people immigrate to cities, while rural residents tend to be natives; people who seek good jobs and good times tend to move cityward, people who prefer being near relatives and open space move countryward. Because of these and many other processes of selective migration, urban residents tend to be quite different, in personal characteristics, from residents of small towns. And those personal characteristics, in turn, lead to different typical ways of life in town and city.

To say that self-selection explains some of the differences between town and city is not to say that urbanism is irrelevant to those very same differences. It remains an indirect cause by stimulating selective migration. Although part of urban/nonurban self-selection is coincidental, most of it results from processes originating in the nature of urbanism itself. A few of those processes are peculiar to contemporary America. For example, the greater dilapidation and physical danger in our center cities, compared with their peripheries, encourages more people with children and more people who are affluent to move away than is common elsewhere in the world or was true in earlier times. (More on this below.) Consequently, the contrast between the urban center and suburb in residents' incomes and stages in the life cycle is sharpened. Other self-selection processes seem to be consistently and historically linked to urbanism. In most times and societies, for example, young adults have moved from country to city; the highly skilled have done the same, leaving the less skilled behind; metropolitan residents have been more affluent than people in the hinterland; and minority ethnic groups have congregated in the large centers.[11] Through these processes of self-selection, urbanism is indirectly the cause of some differences in way of life. To the extent, for instance, that cities, by their very nature, attract the highly educated and provide well-paying jobs, and to the extent that education and wealth promote friendship, then cities can be said to indirectly promote friendship.

The selective sorting of people along the rural/urban continuum has important implications for forecasts of cultural differences between big city and small town. There are many signs today of national homogenization; in particular, many people and industries are moving from metropolitan to nonmetropolitan areas. These signs point to further narrowing of town/city differences. But selective migration is, at the same time, widening those differences. While many older people are retiring from the city to the country, college-educated young adults are still moving from country to city. Consequently, the age and educational differences between residents of urban centers and their hinterlands are actually getting sharper.[12] And from that it follows that the social and behavioral contrasts between city and country are probably also getting sharper, for this reason alone. It may well be, ironically, that as modern technology and institutions (like Social Security) increasingly free people from being tied to a place, they may accentuate cultural differences among places.

Aside from its possible consequences through self-selection, urbanism may also have direct consequences on people's networks and behaviors. We can never know what the personal relations of our city and our town respondents would have been like had they all been of average age, education, tenure in the neighborhood, and so forth. But statistical adjustments based on social science conventions allow us to simulate such an "all else equal" situation and to estimate the unique, direct contribution of urbanism to residents' ways of life. Our use of these procedures—in a conservative manner—suggests that in many ways urbanism did affect networks and attitudes, that city residents' private lives would have differed from those of small-town residents even had the two groups been otherwise similar.

The third question raised—What about urbanism accounts for its effects?—has been even harder to answer, largely because many community characteristics are tightly wound together around urbanism, characteristics like housing density, population composition, and the availability of specialized services. Nevertheless, at a few points I have been able to make the case that population concentration itself—particularly the aggregation of specific populations in support of subcultural involvement—accounts for community differences. Where that is true, it is possible to say that the general theoretical proposition that urbanism alters social life has been supported.

Keeping in mind the analytical framework of these three questions—Do more urban people differ socially from less urban ones? Is urbanism a direct cause of this difference? What about urbanism is responsible?—we can review the basic results of the northern California survey.

Capsule Summary

More urban and less urban respondents listed roughly the same amount of social ties; neither group was more likely than the other to be isolated. Nor did the quality of their relations differ (though the least urban respondents tended to see their associates a bit more often). But the composition of the two groups' networks differed markedly. Small-town respondents tended to be more involved with relatives, city respondents with nonkin.

Holding constant self-selection, urban residence apparently discouraged involvement with kin, especially with extended kin, and encouraged respondents to be more selective concerning which relatives they called upon. Urbanism seemed to similarly discourage involvement and encourage selectivity with neighbors. And urbanism appeared to discourage involvement with church members; it did not, however, much affect involvement with fellow members of secular organizations. Although urban respondents included more co-workers in their networks than small-town respondents did, that was due solely to the urbanites' youth and greater education. Urban respondents were definitely involved with more "just friends"—the large category of associates called "friends" who shared no other social context with the respondents—than were small-town respondents, though urban residence itself contributed to this number only among the affluent. I concluded part 3 by suggesting that urbanism clearly reduced respondents' involvements with people drawn from the "traditional" complex of kin, neighborhood, and church and slightly increased their involvements with people drawn from more modern and more voluntary contexts of work, secular associations, and footloose friendship. And I argued, with rather limited evidence, that whatever direct causal force urbanism had could be attributed to population concentration itself.

Some structural features of personal networks also differed between city and town. City respondents typically had more "stranded" relations—relations involving multiple kinds of exchanges, which can be seen as indicative of interpersonal intensity—than did small-town respondents. But this difference can be explained by self-selection. The urban respondents also had less "dense" networks—networks in which one's associates know one another—than did respondents in smaller places. In this case community of residence itself apparently made a difference.

What such density meant turned out to be a complex question. Having one or two special associates (who also knew all the others) seemed to go together with respondents' feeling more satisfied with their relations, at least among the less affluent. And urbanism itself apparently tended to encourage respondents to draw their friends from a wider geographical range. That did not, in turn, weaken those relations; geographically distant associates tended to be at least as personally close to respondents as geographically nearer ones.

In part 4 we examined the connection between urbanism and respondents' personal ties to specific subcultures. The preceding chapter's findings had suggested that for respondents with "atypical" traits—in that case the young and the never married—urban residence promoted ties to people similar to themselves. Our results with regard to subcultural involvements tended to be consistent: living in urban areas itself, apparently increased ethnic group members' ties to fellow members. (The key community attribute was the concentration of the specific ethnic group.) Urban life seemed to increase the involvement of respondents with people of the same religion—*if* the respondents were Catholics, attended church rarely, or felt strongly about their religion. (This effect appeared in spite of greater urban secularism.) And living in cities seemed to increase the number of people respondents knew who shared their pastimes—*if* the respondents were especially attached to those pastimes. Urbanism did not, however, increase respondents' ties to people in their own "line of work"; indeed, among those who felt that their work was *not* most important to them, it may have weakened involvement. There was a tendency, overall, for urban residence to help encapsulate respondents in specific subcultures.

But the findings also suggested that this encapsulation is contingent and complex. City versus small-town residence makes little difference in how involved respondents were with fellow members of subcultures when knowing fellow members is seemingly easy, if the subculture is large and omnipresent (white Protestants, for example). And the effect of urbanism was also contingent on the respondents' interests in the specific subcultures. City life seems to aid people in finding other people who share their "most important" interest, but not in finding those who share lesser interests. It may, in fact, help them avoid the latter. These contingencies suggest that city life supports subcultural involvement when it is a problem. The complexities of our findings also include the separation of social involvement from formal involvement. While urban residence tended to increase the social, it did not promote the formal and may actually have discouraged it. Indeed, it appears that, as urbanism increases, personal relations within a subculture become increasingly detached from formal ties to it (via church attendance, unions, clubs, and so on).

Among all these various aspects of personal networks, there are many in which city and town respondents differed, and some in which urbanism itself made a difference. What consequences did these differences have? The urban respondents could generally count on support from their associates more than the small-town respondents could. But that was largely a result of self-selection. Urban residence did not directly alter respondents' social support, except perhaps to reduce the amount of practical neighborly assistance they received.

City and town respondents did not differ psychologically, and we could not find much evidence here (or in other research) that urban life directly, or through its effects on networks, seriously affected anxiety or mental health. There was some evidence, however, that fear of crime, which was more common in cities, reduced people's sense of well-being. And there was clear evidence that urban life, both because of crime and because of its subcultural variety, led to feeling more distrustful of people in the wider community. This finding suggests that urbanism may engender public estrangement but not private estrangement.

City and town respondents, finally, differed sharply in their social behavior and in their attitudes about social behavior. The small-town people were considerably more traditional than the big-city people. Self-selection explained much of the difference, but urbanism explained much of it, too. I argued that urbanites are first to learn the novel values that emerge in cities and only later diffuse to the hinterlands. The new values are taught, in part, by people's associates (and in part also by public experiences with strangers—the very experiences that reinforce intergroup tensions). We found that respondents' networks did influence this process of learning: those who were heavily involved with relatives tended to remain more traditional even when living in urban areas than those who were not much involved with kin. And respondents who were heavily involved with local friends and acquaintances were more extreme, either for or against traditional views, depending on whether they lived in town or in city, than were those not so tied to nearby people.

When I look over the entire complex set of findings, the basic capsule description that emerges is that urbanism tends to produce a different *style* of life, but not a different *quality* of life. That is a brute simplification, of course, in many ways. For example, urbanites have more supportive networks than small-town people, and cities may be the *in*direct cause of the support if urban economies selectively attract residents with great personal resources. Also, there are some specific groups—say, ethnics or classical music aficionados—who may benefit socially from moving to cities. Yet there are others—say, elderly white Protestant widows—who may benefit from the opposite move.

In fact, there is one strong thread in this empirical tapestry that, if followed all the way, might lead to the conclusion that urbanism impairs quality of life. All else held constant, respondents with below-average household incomes who lived in Semirural communities tended to have more local nonkin associates, bound up in denser networks, than did low-income respondents residing in other places. The Semirural people tended also to report a slightly more positive sense of well-being than their counterparts elsewhere. For substantive and methodological reasons, I have not focused on this finding,[13] but it is a thread that ought to be followed in future research. The overall picture remains that the town/city contrasts involve the ways people lead their lives more than the aggregate quality of those lives.

All these claims must, of course, be qualified. Much of the analysis involved new survey techniques and measures, the basic validities of which are not secure. At a few points I have noted difficulties with the procedures we used. Any theoretical conclusions are also contingent upon the nature of the sample. The exclusion of rural people, of black neighborhoods, of foreign-language-speakers, and of adolescents may have led us to underestimate city/country differences on some issues— say, subcultural involvement—and to overestimate them on others—say, ties with kin. The location of the study, northern California, may raise questions about generalizability. I am sanguine on this score, in part because of occasional parallel findings from other studies, but the question will not be resolved until the research is replicated elsewhere (see Methodological Appendix section 1.2). Finally, many of these findings make only weak statements about the causes of individual differences in personal relations; that is, urbanism does not explain very much of the variation in social networks among individuals. I did not expect it would, since the community is only a very general background for social behavior. People's more immediate circumstances—their tastes, habits, jobs, resources, family commitments, and so on—definitely alter their opportunities, constraints, and choices more than do variations in community. Nevertheless, the effects of urbanism we observed were often substantively (if not statistically) large, and even small effects often made major contributions to our *theoretical* understanding of the link between the residential community and private life (see Methodological Appendix section 4.4.4).

Theory and Practice

The global theoretical concerns sketched in chapter 1 and reiterated throughout the book stem from efforts to understand the personal consequences of urban life and, by extension, of modern life. The decline of community perspective leads to arguments that urbanism weakens social bonds and thereby produces psychological and social disorganization. What I have labeled the diversity of communities perspective (within which I include subcultural theory) leads to arguments that urbanism helps generate varieties of social worlds within which people build communal and supportive networks. These diverse worlds may give rise to seeming deviance, and they may clash with one another, but they are internally integrated.

If we accept, at least for discussion, that this conclusion is valid, what might it imply for the sociology of community? It suggests that the discipline should leave behind the simple question whether urban life is disintegrative to pursue how rural and urban life are differently integrated. We might ask, for example, how people learn about, choose among, and build relations in the social worlds that are available in their communities, be those worlds the kin-neighborhood-church complex of small towns or the variegated subcultures of the large cities. What consequences do various aspects of residential communities have in establishing the trade-offs people must make in selecting places to reside and worlds in which to live? Do some people fall into isolation through the cracks of the urban mosaic who might not have done so in a rural monochrome? Questions such as these stem from an assumption that people's residential communities are composed of one or more social worlds rather than of the atomistic mass described by most decline theories.

At the group level, the sociology of community would focus on how the "moral order" is maintained in communities of cultural complexity. Often it is barely maintained, if at all (as in Belfast, Northern Ireland). Studies could examine cultural domination and assimilation, physical coercion, residential segregation, formal negotiation, the construction of crosscutting personal ties, redefinitions of cultural codes, and other processes of accommodation. They could examine the rules and habits individuals learn for managing their private networks and their public behavior in such settings: avoidance, adoption of a public etiquette (which may include modes of impersonality), learning the signals and vocabularies of "foreign" groups, and so on. These are the sorts of topics—some of which are already being studied—that arise if we think about the diversity of communities rather than the decline of a community. And, perhaps ironically, it returns us to the empirical work, if not the theory, of the Chicago school.

In assessing this study's contribution to what Barry Wellman has termed "the community question," we must consider not only the technical limits of the research that I have just noted, but, more important, its historical period as well. While the theoretical aspiration is to develop general and universal statements about urbanism's consequences for human behavior, there are many particularities of any specific era that bridle a rush to generalization.

The relationship between city and countryside in the United States in 1977 differed in several ways from that relationship elsewhere in the world or in earlier times. I mentioned a few ways in chapter 2, such as most people's access to rapid communication and transportation and the unprecedented reversal of migration back to rural areas. Most important, I believe, is the relative slippage of the city in the material conditions of life. The American city of this generation has quickly become a relatively more miserable place to live, *compared with the countryside,* than was true in recent generations. I stress the comparative statement. The city of the 1970s was far less dirty, dissolute, and dangerous than the city of the 1870s, and the city of the 1970s was in several respects (quality of jobs and of housing, for example) on average a better environment than the countryside of the 1970s. But the relative advantage of the city has declined precipitously. Since roughly 1960 in the United States, the urban centers have decayed considerably, as contrasted to suburb and small town, in physical condition, quality of public schools, availability of housing, number of businesses and jobs, and residents' safety. Why this is so is the subject of many other books. The point for us is that, in comparing urban and nonurban in 1977, we have picked a historical low point for the American city.

I would stress, among the material conditions, the danger posed by crime. It is commonplace today for Americans to say that being robbed or attacked is a "cost" of living in the city. But this was not—and is not elsewhere—always so. It seems that property crime, such as burglary, and vice crimes, such as gambling and prostitution, generally accompany urbanism in most societies and times. But violent crime has typically been at least as great in rural areas as in cities.[14] This was true, too, in the United States as recently as the 1940s and 1950s. It was only since the early 1960s that cities attained such vastly greater rates of crimes against persons (and fear of it) than smaller communities.[15] In 1948, only 3 percent of American city-dwellers said that crime was their cities' worst problem; by 1972, 21 percent said it.[16] It is now the most common reason city residents give for wanting to move away.[17] The tight embrace that predatory crime has on our cities is not "natural," but a product of our times.

That embrace has palpable consequences for the relationship between metropolis and hinterland. Our survey has shown, for example, that fear of crime is one reason people move from city to country; weighs particularly on urban residents' minds as a disadvantage of their communities; impairs urbanites' feelings of well-being; and increases urbanites' distrust of their neighbors. It probably also injures people socially and psychologically in ways we did not investigate. (Moreover, these effects have, for technical reasons, probably been underestimated.)[18]

I am arguing, then, that we have contrasted city and countryside at a historical moment especially unfavorable to the city. A study such as this done just twenty-five years ago (and, perhaps, twenty-five years hence) would probably have shown stronger psychological, and even social, advantages to the city than shown here.[19] This study may represent the worst case.

But my claim is only speculative. We remain with the real findings of our 1977 survey, as summarized in the previous section. Even those challenge the decline of community thesis, at least as applied to urban/ rural contrasts. City people seem basically as socially and psychologically integrated as small-town people. Urbanism does not seem to weaken community, but it does seem to help sustain a plurality of communities.

What might all this mean for policy? Our findings—and their historical context—certainly suggest that efforts to reduce the size of our cities, as recommended by some (including journalist Kirkpatrick Sale, quoted in chap. 4), are misspent. If our goal is to increase individual well-being, changing the size of our cities will do little and do it at great cost. It is far better to focus on increasing income, health, safety, and other immediate conditions of life. If our goal is to improve people's personal networks, razing cities will, again, not do. Some types of people would improve their networks by moving from city to country, and some would accomplish it by doing the reverse. The sum—the "gross national personal support system"—would probably be maximized by having increased mobility among a range of places, not by squashing down the high end of the urban scale (even if it could be done). Anyway, some of that redistribution is happening already, as selective migration accentuates the residential segregation of types of people between city and countryside. All an antiurban policy—or, more accurately, an accentuation of this nation's long-standing antiurban policy—would do is weaken the networks of people in small minorities and interest groups.

If our goal is to affect the collective good (as opposed to the sum of individual good)—for example, to reduce deviance, social change, intergroup tension, and crime—then an antiurban policy is more plausible. (In theory; in practice, it would be ridiculously inefficient.) If we could miraculously disperse much of the population of our largest metropolises, we might reduce conflict among ethnic and class groups, reduce the propagation of disruptive life-styles, reduce some of our public estrangement and callousness, and perhaps reduce crime and vice.

But to choose this policy means to choose one set of values over another. It means to promote traditional middle-American culture over variant American subcultures. Cities generate these collective problems because (subcultural theory contends) they allow subcultures to emerge and grow around a variety of identities and interests. Among the consequences are pluralism, innovation, and creative change. And another consequence is that these groups demand their rights and express their values. That outspokenness, in turn, leads to tension and unease. A less urban society would be more comfortable for the "typical" American, less comfortable for the "atypical" American. If we attempt to make this change, we should know the moral choice we make.

These comments make clear my skepticism about policies that mean to alter the urbanism of our society as a way of attaining social ends. I am interested in urbanism not as a device for policy, but as a tool for understanding the links between social structure and the individual and for understanding the nature of personal life in modern society. But I have opinions—informed ones, I trust—on policy matters. On the current condition of our large cities, the solutions lie not in eliminating the cities, but in improving them. (Look around the world: you *can* have metropolises without murder.) I would point policy in the direction of economic aid to the hard-core poor; reducing "street crime" and related disorders in the schools;[20] aiding in the industrial transformation of center cities from blue-collar to white-collar work; and physical rehabilitation of the infrastructure of streets, utilities, and the like. (Where the money for this will come from is another matter.)

There are some hints in this study concerning how public policy might help improve the quality of people's personal networks. Helpful policies would attempt to expand opportunities for and reduce constraints on people's meeting people of like interests. And they would improve people's access to their relatives and past friends. Concretely, such policies might, for example, make it easier for young women to enter various work contexts, by improving child-care arrangements and reducing sex discrimination; increase the access of the elderly to one another, by making it financially easier for them to move from changing neighborhoods, providing neighborhood centers—preferably linked to religious institutions—increasing the elderly's mobility, and safeguarding them on the streets; direct workers in the social services to help people "at risk" in forming supportive social relations—and perhaps help them to remove burdensome social relations; and guarantee all people some minimal "lifeline" access to inexpensive, flexible, and efficient transportation and communication.

The community side of such policies might simply be to facilitate people's selective migration to places where there are people like themselves. Some kinds of people flourish in towns and some kinds flourish in cities. And people generally do better in communities with others of their kind. Such a policy, of course, might well accentuate the city/town differences described in this book. Indeed, all the policies I have just mentioned work to accelerate modern trends toward the formation of a culturally pluralist society. And that has the kinds of public costs I described a few paragraphs back. We thus return to a moral and political choice between competing values.

A   Methodological Appendix

This appendix discusses in detail several procedural matters described only briefly in the text, specifies characteristics of the data set and its development, and explains some of the decisions that lay behind the analyses of this study.

Outline of Appendix

1.0	The Sample
1.1	Choosing Northern California
1.2	But How Weird Is San Francisco?
1.3	The Area of the Study
1.4	The Sample of Communities
1.4.1	Defining "Communities"
1.4.2	The Stratified Sample of Localities
1.4.3	Excluded Localities
1.5	The Sample of Neighborhoods and Microneighborhoods
1.6	The Sample of Respondents
1.7	The Sampling and Interview Procedures
1.7.1	Overview
1.7.2	Selection of Communities and Neighborhoods
1.7.3	Selection of Housing Units
1.7.4	Fieldwork Strategy
1.7.5	Field Staff, Training, and Supervision
1.7.6	Fieldwork Methods
1.8	Evaluation and Use of the Sample
1.8.1	Field Outcomes
1.8.2	Biases and Omissions
1.8.3	Analysis of Response Rate
1.8.4	Weighting
1.8.5	Basic Description of the Sample
2.0	Measuring Social Networks
2.1	Methods Used in Previous Mass Surveys
2.2	Defining a Network
2.2.1	Goals
2.2.2	Defining a Relation
2.2.3	Selecting a Subset of the Network to Study
2.2.4	Limitations of the Approach

2.3	Describing the Network
2.3.1	Descriptive Techniques
2.3.2	Asking Detailed Questions about a Subsample of Names
2.3.3	Potential Sources of Error
2.4	Evaluation of the Technique
2.5	Using the Network Data
2.6	Potential Bias
2.7	Summary
3.0	Community Data
3.1	Goals
3.2	Levels of Aggregation
3.3	Census Data
3.4	The Informant Questionnaire
3.4.1	Selecting Informants
3.4.2	Splitting Communities
3.4.3	The Questionnaire
3.4.4	Coding Questionnaires
3.4.5	Reported Changes
3.5	On-Site Observations
3.6	Newspapers
3.7	Telephone Directories
4.0	Data Analysis
4.1	Organization of the Data
4.2	Possible Methodological Artifacts
4.2.1	Weighting for Sampling
4.2.2	Interviewer Differences
4.2.3	Respondents' Cooperativeness
4.2.4	Gender Distribution
4.3	Measuring Critical Variables
4.3.1	Measuring Urbanism
4.3.2	Network Measures
4.3.3	Other Often-Used Measures
4.4	Statistical Analysis
4.4.1	General Approach
4.4.2	Clustering and Standard Errors
4.4.3	Standard Procedures and Methods
4.4.4	Small Statistical Associations

1.0 The Sample
1.1 Choosing Northern California as the Sample Area

Analytical simplicity called for studying a single region, because differences among regions are likely to mask differences among types of communities. Pooling metropolitan areas into one analysis, as is typically done in national surveys, often confounds type of community with type of region. Ideally, one would compare places within several regions. But to do that well would require unavailable bountiful resources. I decided, therefore, to study a single region, the findings from which could reasonably be generalized to other areas.

Northern California was convenient and well known. The question therefore was not whether it was the best region for study, but whether there was some rationale for *not* choosing it. Since any single region will always be atypical in some respects, the issue becomes, Just *how* atypical is northern California? Is it too atypical to generalize from?

The core of the region is the San Francisco–Oakland "standard metropolitan statistical area" (SMSA). Twenty-three of our fifty communities are in this SMSA. In population size, San Francisco–Oakland ranks about midway among the dozen largest SMSAs in the United States. On most social indicators—population composition, economic traits, housing stock—it is *not* exceptional. Its crime rate and cost of living tend to be relatively high (as is its amount of sunshine), but there is little to suggest that it is particularly unusual among the top dozen areas.

Nine other of our fifty communities fall inside the Sacramento SMSA, which ranked forty-first in population in 1970. The Sacramento area is also relatively typical of similar-sized SMSAs on most indicators, standing out largely in its low level of manufacturing employment (it is the state capital) and high crime rate. By and large, there is little reason to consider northern California particularly unusual among urbanized regions in the United States.[1]

More important for this study is whether the region is atypical in its *internal variation*. That is, do differences among communities *within* northern California parallel those within other regions? They tend to. For example, the San Francisco–Oakland and Sacramento SMSAs tend to differ from SMSAs in their size classes in parallel ways: relatively high growth from 1960 to 1970, low rates of manufacturing employment, and high rates of crime. As long as we can assume that the way communities differ from one another (or types of people differ from one another) in northern California is no different from the way they vary elsewhere, generalizations about such differences are legitimate.

1.2 But How Weird Is San Francisco?

One challenge to this assumption is the belief that the city-county of San Francisco, usually together with the city of Berkeley and Marin County, is especially atypical in its deviant life-styles. Eastern journalists commonly refer to it as a "notoriously open city" (Tom Wicker); "a city that has always valued wide-open life-styles" (*Newsweek*); a "home for a plethora of cults" (*New York Times*), and so on.

Much of this is simply a popular stereotype founded on a colorful historical pageant. Contemporary events, such as a crime wave in 1976, the People's Temple mass suicide in Guyana in 1977, followed quickly by the assassination of the mayor and a city councilman, and extravagant claims of residents and outsiders alike—as for example, in hyperbolic estimates of the homosexual population—seem to confirm the stereotype.

There is some truth to the deviant or avant-garde image of San Francisco. It and the metropolitan area tend to rank high, if not first, among American metropolises in rates of crime, heroin addiction,[2] premarital sexual activity,[3] and suicide.[4] Some survey data suggest that residents are less traditional and conservative than those in other metropolises.[5] A California poll found, for example, that 60 percent of Bay Area residents said they knew someone who was homosexual, compared with 52 percent of Los Angeles metropolitan area respondents.[6] Still, the picture is not uniform: for example, the rate of divorce in San Francisco was, in 1970, no higher than elsewhere in California or in the West,[7] and people were about as residentially stable as most Americans.[8]

Even if San Francisco were somewhat more "deviant" than other major cities, the question remains whether it is more deviant compared with its hinterland than are other major cities compared with theirs. That is more difficult to answer, but there is reason to believe not. At least San Francisco's contrast to its hinterland on this dimension is much the same as Los Angeles'.

This last statement is based on general knowledge of the state and in part on some rough examination of data. I selected four measures—vote for Carter in the 1976 election; vote for Proposition 14 (an initiative sponsored by the United Farm Workers and generally interpreted as an acid test of "left" allegiance); vote on a 1978 proposition to restrict homosexuals from being schoolteachers; and total crime rate for 1974–75. I compared San Francisco County with other northern California counties (roughly all those above the thirty-seventh parallel) and Los Angeles County with the remainder of the state. The data indicate that San Francisco County indeed differs from its hinterland in the same direction and to about the same degree that Los Angeles County differs from its hinterland.

Ultimately, the question of how much one can generalize from northern California to the rest of the nation will be answered by comparing the findings of our study with those of others'. Some comparisons are provided in the text. For example, the differences between large-city northern Californians and small-town ones on issues of social morality are much the same as those found between large-city Americans and small-town Americans in national surveys (chap. 6).

1.3 The Area of the Study

The geographical area of the study is outlined in maps 1 and 2 (pp. 18 and 22). It was defined as San Francisco and northern California counties within two hundred miles north and east of the city. The two hundred mile range is a compromise between the desire to include remote communities and the high cost of doing so. Although we lost truly rural places in the far north, we did include small communities that, though in the San Francisco "sphere of influence," are on a daily basis quite independent of it. Still, this is a study not of rural versus urban, but of small town versus large city.

The area of the study is only the northern half of northern California. The southern half of the region is cut off by a line running along the San Francisco–San Mateo border, highway 580 as it bisects Alameda County, and the southern borders of San Joaquin, Calaveras, and Alpine counties. The reason for this decision was, again, to simplify the analysis of urbanism. South of the Bay is San José, one of the fastest-growing cities in the nation. (At the time of the study, the city had about 560,000 people, compared with San Francisco's 650,000.) This creates a bipolar metropolitan structure, with many communities in the southern portions of both the West and East Bay areas being suburbs of San José rather than of San Francisco–Oakland. By dealing only with the northern half of the region, we more closely approximate the ideal-typical metropolis and simplify measures of urbanism. The sample therefore does not reflect with complete accuracy the social profile of the region, but it still preserves the cross-sectional quality of our sample. There are many communities of various classes, racial compositions, and ages in both the North and the South Bay.

1.4 The Sample of Communities

1.4.1 *Defining "communities."* The first problem is deciding how to delimit the basic ecological unit, the locality. This is a persistent problem in the sociology of community. A locality, in theory, has some social and symbolic, as well as physical, coherence. Its borders should enclose an economic, behavioral, institutional, and cultural unit. In reality they rarely do—usually only when there are major barriers to social interaction, such as open farmland, freeways, streets dividing different racial groups, and so on. Most often, one locality shades imperceptibly into another. Thus the *locality is egocentric;* for most purposes (the major exceptions being administrative), each person's true locality is roughly a circle around his or her home, modified by barriers of varying intensity that deflect attention, activity, and loyalty to a noncircular zone. The locality is essentially egocentric, and that is how it is conceived in our analysis of spatial behavior, as in chapter 13.

Such theoretical concerns notwithstanding, practical considerations dictate the use, at least for sampling, of administrative units. But what size units? A block, set of blocks, census tract, set of tracts, city, county? For sampling and statistical purposes, the *locality* was operationally defined as a *census tract* in the two largest metropolitan areas—the San Francisco–Oakland SMSA and the Sacramento SMSA—and in cities over 10,000, but as the *municipality* for nonmetropolitan towns under 10,000. The census tract is convenient and apropos in various ways. Typically its population is a few thousand, as is that of our small towns; its geographical area is usually easily walkable, making it a local unit; and census lines are usually drawn along geographically and socially meaningful boundaries (though we did have to redraw boundaries for a few localities during the data analysis; see section 3.4.2).

These units—metropolitan and city tracts, small towns—are the "communities" of the sample. The project design required a variety of communities, but no more than we could gather detailed quantitative and qualitative data on and could visit personally. I estimated the appropriate practical number at fifty. I preferred to expend resources on developing the survey instrument rather than on expanding the sample size. A reasonable compromise appeared to be a target of one thousand respondents over fifty communities.

1.4.2 *The stratified sample of localities.* The theoretical issues call for comparing a wide range of communities, from center city to small town. However, Californians are not distributed evenly across these categories. Had we selected the fifty localities proportional to population, the sample would have yielded too few small towns. Consequently, we set up five *strata* to guarantee that each analytical category would be fully represented. And we selected ten localities within each stratum to guarantee internal variety. The strata were:

1. *Major center cities:* census tracts in the cities of San Francisco, Oakland, or Sacramento.

2. *Inner Suburbs:* Census tracts in the San Francisco–Oakland SMSA, outside the center cities but within fifteen miles of downtown San Francisco or ten miles of downtown Oakland; and census tracts in Sacramento, but within ten miles of its downtown.

3. *Outer suburbs:* All other tracts in the San Francisco–Oakland SMSA, and most other tracts in Sacramento County (some particularly distant parts of Sacramento County and all of Yolo, Sutter, and Plumas counties were excluded).

4. *Large cities:* Census tracts in all other cities and towns in the area with ten thousand or more inhabitants (as of 1970)—the largest are Stockton (108,000), Vallejo (67,000), and Santa Rosa (50,000).

5. *Small towns:* Towns and unincorporated places with 2,500 to 9,999 inhabitants in 1970 that were not in categories 2 or 3. (Urbanized places in the Napa-Vallejo, Santa Rosa, and Stockton SMSAs, and in parts of the Sacramento SMSA were excluded from the study if they were under 2,500 in population.)

One cost of this stratification was to sacrifice representativeness. That could be partly overcome by weighting the cases (see discussion of weighting below, sections 1.8.4 and 4.2.1). Our experiments with the data suggested that weighting made little difference to the measures of association among the variables. Another and irretrievable cost is the lessened ability to make comparisons among localities within the most urban areas. We had, for example, only six San Francisco tracts.

1.4.3 *Excluded localities.* A few types of places had to be excluded:

Places under 2,500. We excluded census "places" with under 2,500 population in 1970 (unless they were in the San Francisco–Oakland SMSA or the Sacramento urbanized area). This eliminated the rural end of the continuum and about 13 percent of the region's population. Some reasons for this exclusion were: (*a*) *Practical*—Interviewing in nonmetropolitan places under 2,500 can be difficult and costly. Since few census data are available, all housing units must be completely enumerated. Also, interviewing along country roads is time-consuming. (*b*) *Theoretical*—Such communities are often quite different ecologically from places over 2.500. Many are wide expanses of farmlands or wilderness in which "neighborhood" has a far different meaning than elsewhere. Many of the topics, survey questions, and analyses of the study would then become inappropriate. (*c*) *Analytical*—The most important reason was that few published data are available for nonmetropolitan places under 2,500. Our plan was to use social, economic, and ecological attributes of communities to help explain the variations among them. We would then have been unable to complete our analyses of critical issues.

The cost of this decision was, of course, to hinder our ability to generalize about the rural/urban continuum. There is reason to believe that, had we included places under 2,500, the community differences we did find would have appeared still sharper. Gallup polls, for example, show that, while residents of small towns are relatively traditional compared with city people, residents of places under 2,500 are even more traditional. Thus the place differences in social opinions or kinship involvement we found are conservative estimates of rural/urban contrasts. Where we found no differences, say in psychological states, we have no guide for projecting our data below the 2,500 line.

Predominantly black localities: Localities 40 percent or more black in 1970 or found to be mostly black in 1977 were excluded from the sample. Research suggests that the power of residential discrimination to confine blacks, and the concentration of desperate circumstances in ghetto areas, makes community life there quite different from elsewhere. Although such neighborhoods form a crucial part of the contemporary urban scene, their distinctiveness becomes a major source of "noise" for studying the specific topics of this book. Had we included them, in the end we would probably have had to separate the black neighborhoods for analysis. And we would have had too few of them to draw any conclusions about black areas. At the same time, our sample of predominantly white localities would have been reduced. Personal networks and community life in black neighborhoods should be studied well—in other words, with a large sample—or not at all.

The cost of this decision is not only to limit the generalizability of our findings largely to people (black or not) living in nonblack areas, but possibly also to distort our *description* of small-town versus large-city differences. Had ghetto areas been included, we might have found, for example, more psychological problems and social isolation in large communities, and perhaps also more kinship, neighborhood, and ethnic involvement. (On the other hand, we also excluded, in various ways, the camps of migrant farm laborers, which artificially reduced the distress level of smaller places.) Analytically, however—that is, in terms of understanding the actual *consequences* of small-town versus large-city life—we probably would have reached essentially the same conclusions, because we controlled for racial and income differences in our analysis of causal effects. To the extent that the personal situations of black ghetto residents are products of being black, poor, unemployed, divorced, and such— rather than being urban—such controls lead us to much the same conclusions as does our sampling strategy.

Had our basic goal been to *describe* accurately the social lives of Californians in small and large towns, the exclusion of the black areas would have been fatal. Since our basic goal was *test theories* about urbanism and social life, the exclusion means only that our conclusions are limited to predominantly white communities. (Note, however, that individual blacks were interviewed.)

Group quarters areas: We also excluded areas with large institutional populations—military bases, hospitals, college dormitories,—because they are "unusual" residential communities. With only ten localities per stratum, it was important to include only "normal" places. By a similar logic, we excluded the city of South Lake Tahoe, a hotel-motel service area for the gambling center of Stateline, Nevada. These decisions probably do not affect our theoretical analyses.

Two "lost" counties: By simple error, two predominantly rural counties in the region were overlooked in the sampling. (This was our error, not that of the Survey Research Center.) These counties account for about 15 percent of stratum 4's population and 2 percent of stratum 5's. Weights were constructed to help correct for this oversight but did not noticeably affect the basic findings (see section 1.8.2). We will never know what the statistics would have been with those counties included, but the analytical findings were probably affected little.

1.5 The Sample of Neighborhoods and Microneighborhoods

The same logic that led us to cluster our interviews into fifty communities led us to cluster them into two neighborhoods per community: to link features of people's social lives to features of their immediate residential environments. That required collecting data on a manageable number of neighborhoods, which, in turn, required clustering the interviews.

Moreover, these neighborhoods should be coherent social units, not arbitrary spatial zones. And this raised a problem. The standard sampling unit is the census *block,* typically a unit bounded by four streets. (In low-density areas a "block" can ramble over a few square miles.) But the block is often not a coherent social unit. Intersecting streets can have quite different traffic patterns, housing types, and residents. Also, social interaction is most commonly across the street—which would be into a different block—rather than around the corner or to the back of the block. We decided, therefore, to define neighborhoods rather than blocks as the basic sampling subunit.

Neighborhoods were typically formed in two steps. First, using the 1970 census, M. Sue Gerson and I divided each locality—that is, census tract or small town—into two or more neighborhoods, or block sets: sets of one or more contiguous blocks, consisting of 150 or more households (and averaging about 200 households). We used geographical features— major roads, creeks, and such—and social characteristics—type and age of housing, racial and class composition—to delimit block sets that were as coherent and homogeneous as possible. (In places without block data, enumeration districts were used instead of block sets.) The Berkeley Survey Research Center (SRC) staff then randomly selected two block sets from each locality (without replacement and with probability proportional to housing units).

Second, I visited the one hundred block sets and further subdivided

each into one or more microneighborhoods, or face blocks, of about fifty
or more households, on the basis of housing style and condition, traffic
patterns and access, types of residents, and similar criteria. (This task
frequently requiring remapping areas where new building had occurred
since 1970.) Occasionally the resultant microneighborhood was a single
block; more often it was part of one block plus the face of the block across
the street. Or it might be both sides of a street for several blocks. Quite
often, I split a single block-long street into two different microneighborhoods, as in cases where part of a street was single-family homes and the
rest apartment buildings. In a few cases a large apartment building was a
microneighborhood by itself. The microneighborhoods I mapped varied
greatly in form and shape, but they were all as ecologically and socially
homogeneous as I could make them, given the constraints of minimum
size, contiguity, and my limited acquaintance with them. Where more
than one microneighborhood was noted in each neighborhood, the SRC
staff randomly selected one for the survey. The net result was one
hundred microneighborhoods (one each in a hundred neighborhoods), two
in each of fifty communities. (One microneighborhood was later dropped
because it was mostly black.)

I.6 The Sample of Respondents

Our target sample consisted of adult, competent, nonin-
stitutionalized, English-speaking, permanent residents of the one hundred
neighborhoods. Of these traits, a few deserve discussion:
Adults: The strongest effects of community probably are on minors,
because they are least able to avoid or adjust to the consequences of
place. But two sets of considerations restricted this study to adults. One is
practical: federal rules are much more restrictive for studying minors. The
second is the inappropriateness for minors of some of our concerns and
questions: issues of residential choice, work life, and community groups
often do not apply. (Several of our network questions were routinely
answered "my parents" by minors.) The consequence of our exclusion
of minors is probably to *underestimate* community differences, particularly with respect to individuals' access to associates and services.
English-speaking: Practical considerations also dictated that we interview only English-speaking respondents. In northern California, there are
a few substantial foreign-speaking populations—Spanish, most notably,
and also Chinese, Japanese, Filipino, Portuguese, and others. *Accurate*
interviewing in a foreign language requires a complex process of translating questions, in addition to using foreign-speaking interviewers. I again
preferred to expend resources on development of our network methodology. As it turns out, only about 2 percent of the potential respondents we

approached were ineligible for the study on the basis of language. Those people lived disproportionately in the more urban places, so the probable consequence of this exclusion was to *underestimate* the extent to which urbanism is associated with involvement in ethnic subcultures.

Permanent: We excluded people in the community who were there only on weekends or for a month or two each year. Also, we occasionally encountered people in the process of moving away. Fourteen had left after we initially approached them, and we made no effort to track them down to complete the interviews. The substantive consequences are unclear but probably are minor.

1.7 The Sampling and Interview Procedures

This section describes the specific technical steps involved in drawing the samples of communities and respondents. It is abbreviated from a report by William L. Nicholls, II, "Sampling and Fieldwork Methods of the Northern California Communities Study" (Survey Research Center, University of California, Berkeley, October 1979).

1.7.1 *Overview.* A disproportionately stratified, multistage cluster sample was employed. Ten communities were selected in each of the five master strata. To ensure adequate socioeconomic diversity among the sampled communities, the population of communities in each master stratum was further divided, when feasible, into five strata by mean family income. Then two communities were chosen from each stratum, and two neighborhoods from each community, with probability proportional to size. The number of housing units selected per neighborhood was chosen to maintain equal probability of selection (and self-weighting) within each master stratum.

1.7.2 *Selection of communities and neighborhoods.* In central-city, large-city, and suburban areas (strata 1–4), communities were defined as census tracts of the 1970 United States Census; the small towns (stratum 5) were communities in their own right. The methods of community selection for strata 1–3 will be described first. A description of the somewhat differing community selection procedures for the small-town (5) and large-city (4) master strata follows.

Sampling frames were constructed for the metropolitan strata from the Fourth Count Summary Tapes of the 1970 United States Census. Census tracts consisting entirely of group quarters were removed from the population. When only part of a tract was devoted to such purposes, only that part was excluded, and the population and housing unit counts were revised accordingly. Census tracts with a black population of 40 percent or more of the total also were deleted. Most were at least 60 percent black, and the few with 40 to 60 percent black were assumed to have increased their black populations in the seven years between census and time of survey. Within each master stratum, the tracts were then arranged in sequence by mean family income and divided into five strata of approximately equal numbers of household residents. Since we reserved the option of rejecting individual communities selected by probability methods, three tracts were selected from each income stratum, two primary selections and an alternate. The two primary selections were chosen with replacement and with probability proportional to their number of household residents in 1970.

The selection of small towns followed essentially the same procedures, sampling from a list of incorporated and unincorporated places reported by the 1970 census with total populations between 2,500 and 9,999.

Somewhat different procedures were necessary for the large cities (stratum 4), since they varied greatly in size and sometimes contained as few as three tracts each. Two stages of sampling were used to reach the tract level. First, ten selections were made at the city level without replacement and with probability proportional to their numbers of household residents by systematic random sampling from a cumulative list of city sizes. Because of its large size, Stockton was selected twice, while eight other cities were each selected once. The latter were poststratified into four pairs of two cities each to preserve the paired primaries selection design. Small tracts and enumeration districts were combined with others in the same town, and military bases and other inappropriate tracts were removed by the same criteria employed in previous master strata. Stockton tracts were divided into two strata by mean family income, and one tract was selected from each stratum. One tract was selected from each of the remaining sampled cities.

Although we reserved the option of rejecting the primary probability selections, we employed it infrequently, largely to ensure a variety of places within each income-by-stratum cell. Replacements or reselections were employed in four of the sample's cells.

The ethnic composition of sampled neighborhoods generally was not known until interviewers began calling at the homes. One central-city neighborhood had become almost totally black and Hispanic since 1970, and another had become almost evenly divided between minority and nonminority residents. No interviews were completed in the first, and only nonminority respondents were interviewed in the second. These neighborhoods were not replaced, since they were assumed to reflect ethnic transitions occurring in many central-city areas. Instead, the overall sampling fraction of the central-city master stratum was increased to complete additional interviews in nonblack neighborhoods of central-city areas.

I.7.3 *Selection of housing units.* All the housing units in each neighborhood were listed in advance of interviewing, either by the SRC staff or by me (if more than two hours' drive from Berkeley). Housing units were then chosen from the listing sheets by systematic random sampling. No substitutions of alternate housing units were permitted.

The number of housing units sampled for each neighborhood was chosen to maintain equal probability of housing unit selection (and self-weighting) within each master stratum and to allow for differing rates of ineligible and nonresponding units anticipated by master stratum. In two master strata, it was necessary to augment the initial samples to reach the goal of at least two hundred completed interviews in each. In the central cities, both the portion of ineligible households and the proportion of nonresponding eligible households proved higher than anticipated. In the small towns, insufficient allowances had been made for vacation and summer homes that were not the usual residence of their owners.

I.7.4 *Fieldwork strategy.* The fieldwork on a geographically dispersed sample survey of one thousand hour-long interviews may be organized in a variety of ways. One may employ a large field staff to complete the work in a short period of time or use a smaller staff and spread the work over a longer fieldwork period. One also may recruit interviewers at many locations to interview in their local areas or utilize a central staff who travel across the study area interviewing in many different communities. We elected to employ a relatively small, centrally trained and supervised staff traveling throughout the study area, for two primary reasons:

First, the interview was an unusually demanding one for the interviewers, both in its need for establishing and maintaining rapport and in its complexity. By selecting and training relatively few interviewers, only the most capable ones would be required, training and briefing costs could be minimized, and the staff could be more closely supervised.

Second, by rotating this small staff across the range of communities sampled, observed variations by community and degree of urbanism would be less likely to be contaminated by differences among the interviewers. To reduce the contribution of interviewer differences to the results, we tried to assign all interviewers to each of the five urbanism master strata. In addition, at least two interviewers were assigned to each community, and results from a community frequently represent the work of three or more interviewers. As a consequence, interviewers spent more than the usual numbers of hours traveling, and the fieldwork extended over a five-month period.

I.7.5 *Field staff, training, and supervision.* The field staff consisted of sixteen interviewers, one of whom withdrew early in the fieldwork. Most had extensive experience in previous surveys. The interviewers were selected to represent a variety of personality types and backgrounds, ranging from a young woman in her early twenties to a retired man in his sixties. None were full-time students. The interviewing staff was closely supervised by SRC, and indirectly by us, throughout the course of fieldwork. (On interviewer differences, see section 4.2.2.)

I.7.6 *Fieldwork methods.* The following advance letter was mailed to each sample housing unit approximately four days before the interviewer first called at the home. The text, appearing on Survey Research Center letterhead, read:

12 August 1977

Dear Northern Californian:

I am writing to ask one member of your household for an hour's time to help with an important study. Many of us are concerned about the quality of life in different kinds of communities. For this reason, we at the Survey Research Center of the University of California are studying the main reasons why some neighborhoods and towns are more pleasant to live in than others.

How do the places in which people live affect the kinds of friendships they form and the kind of relationships that develop? What types of neighborhoods are more satisfying? To be able to answer questions like these, we want to ask you about the kinds of people you know, how you use your neighborhood and your larger community, and how you feel about such things.

Your address was chosen for this survey as part of a scientifically selected sample of communities in Northern California. To obtain a true picture of the many kinds of communities in our part of the state, we need the cooperation of every household. We will select a member of your household to interview when we come to the door and learn how many people live there. I want to assure you that everything our interviewers are told will be held in strictest confidence. The results will be summarized and presented in statistical form, so that no individual, family, or neighborhood can be identified.

Within a few days, an interviewer will call to arrange to talk with one member of your household. He or she will carry proper identification and will be happy to answer any questions you have about the survey. Participation is, of course, voluntary.

I hope you will welcome our representative when he or she calls, for I am confident that you will enjoy the interview. The more we learn about communities, the more that can be done to make them better places to live.

Thank you in advance for your cooperation.

Sincerely,

Claude S. Fischer, Ph.D.
Project Director

Interviewers were instructed to make at least four initial calls at each sample housing unit to find someone at home, including at least one evening and one weekend call. Once an adult household member was found at home, at least three additional calls were made, when necessary, to locate and interview the appropriate respondent. Two broken appointments were generally considered tantamount to a refusal. At most households where the person answering the door or the intended respondent decline to participate in the survey, another interviewer, experienced in refusal conversion, was assigned for a second attempt. Special efforts were made in central-city neighborhoods where resistance is typically greatest, while the standard numbers of callbacks often were unnecessary in some suburban and small-town communities to reach acceptable response rates.

Respondents were chosen within households by probability methods recommended by Leslie Kish[9] that attempt to counteract the tendency for males to be home less often than females. Substitution of another household member for the randomly selected respondent ($n = 26$) was permitted only when the designated respondent was mentally incompetent, institutionalized or too ill to be interviewed for a month or more, or continuously away from home for at least a month.

Interviewing began in the last week of August 1977 and continued through the second week of February 1978. No interviews were conducted during the Thanksgiving weekend or between 20 December and 1 January, because we felt that these would be socially unusual periods. The few interviews in February were restricted to cases with unresolved field outcomes as of 31 January.

I.8 Evaluation and Use of the Sample

I.8.1 *Field outcomes.* The results of the fieldwork are shown by detailed outcome codes in table A1. Interviews were completed at 1,050 households, or 75.8 percent of those apparently eligible.

As shown in table A1, field losses were greater in central-city areas than in the rest of the sample. These included the losses of ineligible minority neighborhoods and disproportionate numbers of households otherwise classified ineligible. However, even among eligible households, the central-city response rate was only 63.9 percent compared with response

Table A1	Summary Field Outcomes by Strata		
Outcomes	**Central City**	**Inner City**	
Completed Interviews	53.5%	74.7%	
Direct Refusal	18.9	12.0	
Indirect Refusal	5.6	3.4	
Too Ill, Senile	1.8	1.4	
Never Home, Couldn't Reach	3.8	2.1	
Ineligible Household	10.5	3.1	
Not a Household	5.9	3.4	
Total Tries	391	292	
Percent Eligible of Total Tries	83.6	93.5	
Percent Complete of Eligibles	63.5	79.8	

rates of 69 to 80 percent in each of the remaining urbanism master strata. This pattern parallels the experiences of many other sample surveys.

1.8.2 *Biases and omissions.* Selecting one adult respondent from each sample household, as is commonly done, involves two related biases: it slightly oversamples persons living alone, and it slightly oversamples women. This familiar sex bias of surveys is further increased because women are somewhat more willing than men to be interviewed. The part of the bias deriving from the respondent selection procedures may be compensated for by weighting procedures, but such weighting is rarely applied, since the biases typically are small and rarely affect the conclusions of the study. We did, however, face a small problem in that sex ratios within specific communities were heavily skewed in several cases, creating some instability in estimates of gender differences (see section 4.2.4).

More serious was the inadvertent omission of two counties within the study area from the sampling process. The two omitted counties contained two of the study area's forty-five small towns and five of its twenty

Outer Suburb	Large Cities	Small Towns	Total
75.8%	68.7%	71.4%	67.7%
12.8	12.4	12.5	14.1
5.1	5.0	2.4	4.4
0.7	0.3	1.0	1.0
1.5	1.0	1.7	2.1
1.1	2.0	1.0	4.0
2.9	10.7	9.8	6.6
273	307	287	1,550
96.0	87.3	89.2	89.4
79.0	78.7	80.0	75.8

large cities. The omissions obviously detract from the accuracy of estimates to describe the study area. However, when the sample is employed to draw general sociological conclusions about the effects of urbanism, the omissions should be less important. Since the area was arbitrarily chosen to include a range of communities, the omission of part of it further restricts the variety of communities. But it should not substantially alter the pattern of associations among communities. Moreover, weighting the data to compensate for the underrepresentation of certain strata (income substrata within urban strata) barely affects the results.

I.8.3 *Analysis of response rate.* Linda Fuller, of our research team, analyzed the correlates of response rates. The key predictor was community: middle-income tracts in center cities had the lowest completion rates. Weights were calculated for six categories of community: center city versus other by low, middle, or high tract income. Distributions of test variables were not significantly changed by this weighting, nor were the associations among test variables. More complete analyses of response rates by Robert Fitzgeral and Linda Fuller[10] later indicated subtle distortions and in partial effects estimates resulting from the social and geographical distribution of refusals. However, these were not likely to have notably altered our conclusions.

I.8.4 *Weighting.* SRC calculated four weighting procedures that adjust the data for the sampling process. First, each case was weighted by the reciprocal of the probability of the selection of its housing unit, taking all prior stages of selection into account and also correcting minor arithmetic errors. Second, the initial weights were adjusted for varying rates of nonresponse at the strata level. Third, the large-city and small-town master strata were adjusted for omissions from the two overlooked counties. Fourth, each record was further weighted by the reciprocal of the number of eligible adults in its household to compensate for the minor bias of the respondent selection procedures. Weights resulting from the above steps were multiplied by a constant to provide a weighted total of 1,050 cases.

The cumulative weight adjusted simultaneously for the sampling strata, differential response rates, omitted counties, and distribution of single-person households. Several key analyses were rerun with this weight. It made little difference (see section 4.2.1).

I.8.5 *Basic description of the sample.* Table A2 describes the basic (*un*weighted) demographic and social characteristics of the 1,050 respondents.

2.0 Measuring Social Networks

(Most of this section is abstracted from a paper by Lynne McCallister and myself.)[11] Most successful studies of egocentric social networks (the associates of, and their relations to, particular individuals) have relied on in-depth interviews with a limited number of respondents. We could not use this method. The necessity of a mass survey forced us to develop a standardized interview that could elicit accurate descriptions of networks, could be administered by professional interviewers as twenty to thirty minutes of an hour-long interview, and could be easily translated into machine-readable data.

We developed this procedure by extensive informal interviewing (conducted largely by Lynne McCallister), and by the use of two pilot surveys of about eighty respondents apiece, each pilot also preceded by a "minipilot" survey of about fifteen people.

Table A2   Respondent Characteristics (Unweighted)

		Percent of Sample
Gender	Male	45.5
	Female	55.5
Age	16-20	5.3
	21-30	29.8
	31-40	21.7
	41-50	10.8
	51-60	14.3
	61 +	18.1
Education	2-8 Years	6.4
	9-11	9.9
	12	33.2
	13-15	26.1
	16	11.1
	Over 16 (including technical education)	13.2
Marital Status	Never married	20.9
	Living together, opposite sex	5.2
	Living together, same sex	0.8
	Married	52.8
	Separated	4.8
	Divorced	13.6
	Widowed	7.8
Employment Status	Full-time	52.4
	Part-time	10.8
	Looking, laid-off	4.8
	Retired	13.1
	Not working	18.9
Race (Interviewer code)	White Anglo	84.5
	Mexican-American	4.2
	Other Spanish	2.5
	Black	3.7
	Chinese, Japanese, Korean	1.8
	Other Asian	1.6
	Other	1.7

2.1 Methods Used in Previous Mass Surveys

Most often, the strategy of previous researchers was to gather the names of a small number of individuals who were related in some manner to the respondent and then to obtain detailed information about the characteristics of those persons, the nature of the respondent's relations with them, and their relations with each other. For example, the respondent might be asked to name his or her best friends, or the people he or she "feels closest to," or to generally describe a category of people, as for example, "Do most of your friends know each other?"[12]

We rejected these strategies for two basic reasons: First, the definitions of personal networks were too narrow and imprecise for our purposes. In particular, the sets of names obtained in this way seemed likely to exclude one or another of whole categories of important individuals such as kin, co-workers, or co-members of organizations. Second, they seemed to invite systematic errors of interpretation. People interpret terms such as "best friend" and "feeling close" in a variety of ways. For example, some define "closeness" in terms of categories of relations ("She is my sister, therefore we must be close"), while others reserve the term for people they trust with confidences or like to spend leisure time with.

In addition, previous strategies seemed vulnerable to errors in reporting. We found, in pretesting, that interviewees had surprisingly poor recall of the people they knew, and in the absence of extensive probing they were likely to forget important persons. Also, the sensitivity of this topic (evoking a fear of appearing unpopular or unloved) may invite respondents to pad their list of relations with people who are relatively inconsequential in their lives.

Such measurement errors are likely to be systematically related to characteristics of the respondents. For example, isolated and lonely respondents are probably more likely to exaggerate, and well-educated people are less likely to confuse "closeness" with role expectations.

2.2 Defining a Network

2.2.1 *Goals.* The criteria used to select which part of the social network to ask about, given that time constraints allow us to learn about only a part, will strongly influence descriptions of respondents' social worlds. For this study we wanted to consider those members of respondents' networks who most affected them by shaping their attitudes and behavior and by influencing their well-being. In addition, we wanted to use criteria for inclusion that could be interpreted consistently by respondents, so that the networks would be comparable across them. The first step was to define "network."

2.2.2 *Defining a relation.* The definition of "relation" bounds the network; it determines which people are to be included and which are to be excluded. We can identify three general analytic approaches to defining a relation.

Affective: A relation is an orientation—love, hate, respect, or such—of two actors toward one another, a feeling about one another and/or about the pair as an entity.

Normative: A relation is a specific, culturally defined set of expectations, obligations, and rights between incumbents of two social positions—in other words, a "role relation" (for example, father/son; teacher/student; neighbor/neighbor).

Interdependence or exchange: A relation is an interdependence between two actors, such that the actions of one affect the outcomes (rewards, punishments) of the other. The relation can be indirect, but of most interest are direct relations, or exchanges, so that a relation is an exchange or set of exchanges between two actors.

We adopted the last definition because it was most concrete and most comparable across respondents, and because it permitted us to use our implicit exchange theory of behavior to identify the people who shape individuals' attitudes, behaviors, and well-being.[13] Our decision was reinforced by success in early pretests with questions that referred to exchanges; people could reliably answer them.

An exchange approach would include among the members of the social network anyone whose behavior rewards or punishes ego or who is directly rewarded or punished by ego. Such exchanges include a broad range of positively and negatively valued interactions such as providing advice or information, going out together, borrowing a cup of sugar, verbal abuse, or caresses. For present purposes, however, we excluded purely impersonal interactions, those dictated by specific social positions and not individual characteristics (for example, a sales transaction).

One difficulty is identifying an appropriate time frame for such interactions; this is the problem of dormant, or latent, exchanges. If there are two actors who are not at this moment exchanging anything, yet they *did* exchange in the past, or there is an expectation that they will (or might) exchange, should we or should we not call this a relation?

Our solution to the problem was both theoretical and practical. We redefined a direct "relation" as the probability of exchange between two actors (as perceived by the respondent). Any two people in the world have some, usually infinitesimal, probability of exchanging; it is the pairs with relatively high probabilities of exchanging who interest us, whom we say have a "relation." In this view, past exchanges, probable exchanges, feelings, and roles all provide indicators of the subjective expected probability of exchange. It was therefore possible for us to exercise the practical expedient of asking about these nonexchange topics, as well as about on-going exchanges, in order to identify relations.

2.2.3 *Selecting a subset of the network to study.* We had respondents identify the members of their core networks by using four kinds of name-eliciting questions. These questions ask respondents to name:

The people they usually go to for some kind of regular exchange (for example, "Sometimes people get together with others to talk about hobbies or spare-time interests they have in common. Do you ever do this? IF YES: Who do you usually do this with?").

The people they would be likely to go to if they needed a rare but important exchange (for example, "If you needed to get a large sum of money together, what would you do—would you ask someone you know to lend it to you; go to a bank, savings and loan, or credit union; or do something else?" [IF R WOULD ASK SOMEONE] "Who would that be?").

The people who were recently sources of a valued exchange (for example, "In the past three months, have any friends or relatives helped with any tasks around the home, such as painting, moving furniture, cooking, cleaning, or major or minor repairs? Who helped you?").

The people who are likely to be sources of various exchanges we do not ask about (for example, adult members of the respondents household). See chapter 3 and Appendix B for the full list of questions.

We chose to study networks this way because it comes closest to meeting the criteria for a network definition that we outlined: including people who most affected respondents' beliefs, actions, and well-being, and providing reliable and valid samples of the core network. The claim of reliability and validity is based, in part, on our extensive informal pretesting. When we compared the initial answers people gave us with their elaborations after further probing, we found that questions about likely sources of rewarding exchanges elicited more complete and consistent answers than did questions about roles or feelings, probably because exchange questions ask people to either describe or imagine a concrete situation, rather than to associate names to vague labels. We discovered that respondents had more consistent interpretations of the behaviors described in exchange questions than they did of terms such as "best friend," "coworker," or "feel close." And the results of our first pilot survey showed that we could use a small set of questions about general exchanges to identify most of the people respondents relied on for other, undiscussed, interactions as well.

2.2.4 *Limitations of the approach.* Not all important network associates are identified by such questions. In asking about general exchanges, we inevitably miss respondents' associates who are sources of unidentified, *specialized* exchanges.

There are other potentially important network members the method also tends to systematically miss, including: sources of negative exchanges—people who have the power to punish the respondent (for example, employers or cantankerous relatives); recipients of exchanges—people who currently receive aid or support from the respondent; and weak ties—those acquaintances who, as Mark Granovetter has argued, sometimes provide key assistance in a rare life-changing event, such as finding a job.[14]

We experimented with questions designed to identify important specialists, recipients, and weak ties, and we concluded that the costs (in interview time) of these questions exceeded the benefits. They typically identified few significant associates, many of whom were also identified by other questions.

In theory, we also excluded relations with exclusively affective or normative content, such as role models and unrequited loves, though in practice some associates with such relations to respondents were included in the lists.

In addition to these potential limitations, there are errors in measurement. The set of people identified by our questions may not accurately represent the core network when respondents either failed to name all likely sources of rewarding exchanges or mistakenly named people who were actually not sources of these exchanges. These errors will arise when respondents misinterpret a question, fail to recall the right people, or abbreviate their answer to speed up the interview.[15] An example of a consistent problem is the taken-for-granted associate. Some people were so constantly involved in respondents' lives that they often were not mentioned in answer to specific questions. This is particularly true of spouses. And in a later study Ann Stueve and Laura Lein found this to be a consistent problem with regard to elderly parents as well; they were so often present that they tended to be overlooked in answer to specific exchange questions.[16]

We handled this partly by sensitizing interviewers to the problem. Nevertheless, the problem alerts us to the difference between the method's accuracy with regard to the names given in answer to specific items and its accuracy with regard to the names as a whole. Our analyses of the pilot surveys shows that there were notable reliability problems in clearly specifying who provided what. (On average, about a third of the appropriate names seem to be forgotten in answer to specific questions.) But the reliability of the whole list was greater (with roughly 10 percent missed—and these 10 percent tended to be specialists, not omnipresent associates). Associates missed by the specific question tended to be picked up somewhere else in the interviews—at least in the household enumeration or the "is there anyone else important" question. The implication is that our findings with respect to specific exchanges are to be trusted less than those with respect to whole networks.

2.3 Describing the Network

After eliciting the core network, we had respondents describe its members in three ways: (1) *personal characteristics,* such as sex, location of residence, and subcultural memberships, (2) *the contents of relations with the respondent,* such as whether they were neighbors and whether the respondent felt close to the person; and (3) *the extent of the interconnections among network members,* that is, the "density" of the network.

2.3.1 *Descriptive techniques.* The "name-eliciting" questions used to obtain the list of associates also provided our first description of the network by indicating some of the contents of the respondents' relations with the people named. (For example, if the name was mentioned in response to "Who do you talk with about your work?" we can assume that work discussions formed one relation binding the two people.)

After asking the name-eliciting questions, the interviewer compiled a list of all the names the respondents had given. With a copy of this list in the respondent's hand, the interviewer then asked two types of questions about the names: (1) *questions referring to each name separately:* for particularly important characteristics, the respondent was asked to describe each person on the list (for example, "How is Mary related to you?"); and (2) *questions referring to the list as a whole:* for dichotomous items (e.g., yes/no; same/different), the respondent was asked to chose those names that fit a particular description—for example, "Which of these are also [SAME OCCUPATION]?" or "Which live within a five-minute drive?"

Asking the respondent to select which names on a list fit a description allowed us to rapidly characterize the associates in many ways. The cost is that those descriptions are largely simple dichotomies—same occupation (or religion, etc.) as respondent or not, in the neighborhood or not. As a partial remedy, we did seek fuller descriptions of a few names.

2.3.2 *Asking detailed questions about a subsample of names.* There were other descriptions of the network members that we wanted but that were either not of sufficient priority or that would have been too time-consuming to ask about all the names. We decided to ask these questions about a subset of the list (five names or less), a subset intended to be representative of the core network and yet variable in the specific relations members had with the respondent. The subset was chosen by a special procedure: selecting the first name the respondents gave to each of the six key name-eliciting questions: (1) who would take care of the respondent's home when he or she is away; (2) with whom the respondent spends leisure time; (3) with whom the respondent discusses a hobby; (4) with whom the respondent discusses personal problems; (5) to whom the respondent turns for advice; and (6) from whom the respondent can borrow money. Household members were excluded.

The respondent answered detailed questions about these people—for example, their age and how they had met—by filling out a self-administered questionnaire included in Appendix B. We also wanted to estimate the extent of the "network density" (the interconnections among members of the network), and we did this by having the interviewer ask the respondent whether each pair of the up-to-five selected persons "know each other well." The ratio of affirmative answers to the total possible is the usual measure of density. At the same time this gave us, for each of the up-to-five names, a measure of "centrality"—the number of other network subset members each one knew well.

2.3.3 *Potential sources of error.* In general we expected that errors in identifying *who* was in the network would be much more serious than errors in describing their characteristics. However, three types of errors of the latter kind should be noted.

Errors in describing the characteristics of network members: Previous work suggested that at the level of description we sought—for example, same ethnicity or not, resides nearby or not—the descriptions should be fairly accurate.

Errors in describing relations: Respondents may give inaccurate descriptions of relations by either failing to mention one of the sources of a specific exchange or by mentioning people who were not really sources of the exchange.

Subset sampling error: The accuracy of descriptions based on the subsample of five names depends on the representativeness of this sample. This is a particular problem because the subsample is not random.

2.4 Evaluation of the Technique

Besides intensive debriefing of the interviewers who conducted our two pilot surveys, we performed relatively complex statistical analyses of those surveys. (The full report appears in the Jones and Fischer paper.) The results suggest that this network methodology identified most of the people respondents relied on for important personal exchanges such as borrowing money, discussing personal problems, and social entertainment. The people who were identified came from a wide range of the social contexts within which respondents participated—family, work, and so on. In addition, the networks appeared to be comparable across different kinds of respondents.

The goal of efficiently identifying broad and comparable networks, being thereby able to describe respondents' social worlds, was attained at the cost of some measurable loss of accuracy, particularly with regard to specific questions. Time constraints precluded questions that identify relations such as weak ties, specialists, and recipients of exchanges. And included questions sometimes picked up people who were less important than those we missed. By using general questions referring to whole lists of names and detailed questions referring to only a subsample of names, we accepted some error in describing each associate and relation. Because we lack measures of external validity, we cannot provide a definitive assessment of this method. However, detailed examination of two pilot surveys led us to conclude that it succeeded reasonably well in describing the personal networks of many individuals. Other researchers who are interested in using this method in longer interviews may wish to expand the number of questions and apply various techniques for double-checking the accuracy of the lists.

2.5 Using the Network Data

This procedure produced a set of names for each respondent—from 2 to 65, an average of 18.5—with descriptions of each named person and his or her relation to the respondent. In all, we had basic information on 19,417 relations and supplementary information on 4,179 of those.

We analyzed these data in two ways. One way was to ask questions about relations per se, to treat the relations as units of analysis (e.g., What is the correlation between how long respondents knew people and how likely they were to confide in those persons?). More commonly, we were interested in respondents' networks as wholes (e.g., the correlation between the age of respondents and the proportions of their networks that were kin). Characteristics of entire networks spoke more directly to the theoretical issues, were for reasons just discussed more reliable, and posed fewer statistical difficulties.

To measure networks, we *aggregated* the relational data. (Robert Fitzgerald performed the technical steps using the SPSS [Statistical Package for the Social Sciences] "Aggregate" program.) This involved, in essence, counting up several dozen categories of relations for each respondent. With respect to kinship, for example, we aggregated total number of kin named; total number exclusive of those living in the household; total exclusive of those cited only in answer to the question, "Is there anyone else important to you?"; and so forth. (The permutations are virtually inexhaustible. One could correlate, for example, the number of female in-laws living within five minutes' drive who recently helped around the house with the number of male friends living over an hour away who were of the same religion.) These counts were easily turned into percentages and ratios.

The analysis we conducted largely employed these counts and percentages, supplemented in several places with consideration of data at the relational level.

2.6 Potential Bias

Size of network, and especially number of nonkin, correlates most strongly with age (inversely) and education. Is that an artifact, perhaps a consequence of the researchers' themselves being young and highly educated? Possibly, but probably not. We were concerned about this problem from the beginning, and we consciously tried to include questions that would tap important social exchanges for young and old, rich and poor. For example, we asked about "help around the house," an exchange particularly important for the elderly, and we listed bars and parks as well as restaurants as places where respondents might meet friends. We also dropped questions from our pretests when interviewers reported difficulties in comprehension.

Beyond that, we took two steps to further minimize bias. We included the question, "Is there anyone who is important to you who doesn't show up on this list?" precisely because it compensated for possible biases in the choice of exchange questions. Indeed, without the names added at that point—an average of 5.7—the connection of age and education with network size would have been yet stronger. (The number of names added was considerably more variable than the number of names given in answer to the exchange questions, and it correlated less highly with respondent traits.) Also, in virtually all our analyses, we adjusted the network data for the extent to which the respondent was cooperative (see section 4.2.3 below). Since educated people tended to be more cooperative, this correlation worked to slightly deflate the effect of education.

It remains possible, of course, that class or age biases still distort our results, despite our best efforts.

2.7 Summary

The mass survey often forces researchers to make trade-offs between breadth and precision. It also forces them to develop exact operational definitions of their theoretical concepts so that the large quantity of information they obtain will be comparable across respondents.

Our goal was to identify members of respondents' networks who significantly affected their attitudes, behavior, and well-being, using as few questions as possible. For theoretical reasons, we defined relations as valued interactions. For practical reasons, we eliminated from the networks types of ties that could not be identified efficiently, while allowing back in important ties that may not have been exchange-based through use of the "is there anyone else" question. We decided to use "name-eliciting" questions to define the networks. And, finally, we chose to describe most of the network members by a checklist procedure, reserving detailed descriptive questions for a subsample of names.

How successful this method is depends on its substantive uses. But it is evident that this technique is a major advance over most previous network surveys. As an illustration, if we had used only the question, "Who are the people you think of as your closest friends?"—an item typical of earlier studies—we would have (in our second pilot survey) identified an average of four network members per respondent, instead of seventeen; thought that the average network was composed of only 14 percent kin, instead of 41 percent kin; and missed 72 percent of the people whose advice respondents sought.

3.0 Community Data
3.1 Goals

We sought to code a wide variety of information about the communities and neighborhoods in which the respondents lived so that we could explain variations in respondents' networks and attitudes by ecological factors other than simply urbanism. We also wanted such information during the sampling process to help eliminate any particularly unusual places. And we wanted to understand each of our fifty places as unique entities, to generally "flesh out" our picture of respondents' environments.

3.2 Levels of Aggregation

Information was collected for various levels of community. There were:

County: Basic census data, typically for 1970; on some measures, such as population, for 1977.

Municipality: Census data, 1970, were also collected for the municipality, but much of that information was incomplete because certain statistics were not available for places under ten thousand in population. For our small-town stratum, informant questionnaires also applied to the municipality.

Census tract: This was the "community" for all places in metropolitan areas and large cities. In certain cases discussed below (section 3.4.2), the community was less than the whole tract. We collected 1970 census data on this unit and also asked our informants to describe the unit. Observational and documentary data were also collected for the tract.

Block clusters ("neighborhoods"): These sets of blocks in cities, or enumeration districts in small towns, were largely used for sampling (see section 1.5). But they also provided the key measure of growth: the total number of housing units in April 1970 and in summer 1977.

Face block ("microneighborhood"): This was the ultimate sampling unit, but because it was a unit we defined (see section 1.5), no published data were available on it. I coded descriptions of the microneighborhood on several dimensions (see section 3.5 below) for eventual statistical use.

3.3 Census Data

M. Sue Gerson organized the collection of census data and other comparable statistical material for each of the levels of aggregation for which they were available. These data covered population characteristics, housing, and similar topics. Unfortunately, the census material had three serious problems. First, almost all were seven eventful years out of date. Although a few counties had conducted censuses for 1975, these were spotty. (For what we found out about changes since 1970, see section 3.4.5.) Second, census data at our community level were often incomplete for small towns and parts of small cities outside metropolitan areas, Third, the census lines often combined areas that were physically, socially, and culturally distinctive, averaging together their disparate traits. For these reasons we developed, used, and placed considerable emphasis on our mail questionnaires.

3.4 Informant Questionnaire

We wanted to bound our localities in a meaningful way—to encompass all of one "community," but only one; update the 1970 census data on critical variables; and add information that is not collected in the census—neighborhood activism, descriptions of local life-styles, listing of critical community issues, and such. The idea of asking informants was taken from a National Opinion Research Center Study,[17] but we did not have the resources to conduct in-person interviews. Consequently, C. Ann Stueve led our effort to develop a mail questionnaire and a sampling of informants; Alison Woodward and Susan Phillips organized the actual survey and coding of questionnaires.

3.4.1 *Selecting informants.* We tried to survey a range of people who would be knowledgeable about the communities and who came from different areas of community life. The appropriate names were culled from telephone directories, newspapers, names encountered during on-site visits, and names recommended by other informants. Some communities ended up with a few informants in several sectors; others had no informants in certain sectors.

We kept mailing out questionnaires, trying to attain at least five informants in each locality. Ultimately, we received 332 responses, an average of 6.6 for each of the original fifty places, from 3 to 8 for each one. The informants included people from the following categories:

Real estate	21%
School officials	18
Churches	12
City planners	10
Banks, business, chamber of commerce	9
Police and fire	8
Post office	7
Community groups	4
Others (elected officials, librarians, private citizens)	10

3.4.2 *Splitting communities.* One of the questions we asked informants read, "We can't tell for certain where a neighborhood begins and ends. Does the area outlined on the map [each questionnaire was accompanied by a map of the census tract or small town] accurately describe a local community of [sic] neighborhood, or are our boundaries misplaced?" Informants often disagreed with the census (and each other) about community boundaries, but in eight cases there was enough consensus that the map included more than one meaningful community to lead us to subdivide them and to redo the mail survey. In a single instance, both sampled neighborhoods fell within only one of the newly defined communities, and we simply sent óut questionnaires with a corrected map. In seven cases, each sampled neighborhood fell into a separate community, and we replicated the process for both parts. For all eight redefined communities, the area referred to in the census data is larger than the informants' community. And in seven cases we actually have two sociologically meaningful communities in place of one—for a grand total of fifty-seven informant-described communities in our sample, rather than fifty.

3.4.3 *The questionnaire.* The eight-page mail questionnaire is reproduced in Appendix C. The topics it covers are, in brief: housing and business changes since 1970; ethnic, life-cycle, and income characteristics of the residents, and changes since 1970; life-styles; fear of crime; commercial facilities; best and worst features of the community; ratings of local services; and confirmation of boundaries.

3.4.4 *Coding questionnaires.* Daniel Finnegan developed a coding procedure for converting the individual responses of our informants into aggregate scores for each community. This procedure involved weighting the response categories to the various questions according to how consistently they were used and how well they discriminated among places. Each community was assigned a score based on the percentage of informants there who selected an answer category times the weight of that answer.

3.4.5 *Reported changes.* We coded, for each of the one hundred *neighborhoods,* the modal responses by our informants to the question, ''Has there been any major change in the ethnic, racial, age or income characteristics of this area [the community—tract or small town—as shown on an accompanying map] since 1970?'' The modal responses, by neighborhood, showed some systematic differences by urban category:

Ethnic: Most Semirural, Town and Metropolitan places were unchanged since 1970 (64 percent of each), but those reported to have changed tended to have more blacks. Almost all Core communities were reported as changed, but in various directions, with the plurality having more *whites* (evidence of San Francisco's ''gentrification'').

Age: Semirural places were about evenly split between having more older and having more younger residents. Both Metropolitan and Core places tended to be described as becoming younger.

Income: About half of Semirural, Town, and Metropolitan places changed, most but not all to richer residents. Most Core neighborhoods were reported to be in communities that had become richer.

In sum, there was considerable perceived change; that change was not uniform within urban categories; and it differed systematically across categories of urbanism.

3.5 On-Site Observations

Before the microneighborhoods were drawn, I personally visited each neighborhood (block cluster) in each community. While driving and walking around, I dictated notes on what I saw, and then turned them into a few-hundred-word report on the neighborhood, distinguishing among the microneighborhoods where relevant. These descriptions covered types of people in the area; housing stock; stores and services; schools and churches; transportation; industries and offices; open spaces; ambience; detectable life-styles; and visible signs of change since 1970. Much later I used these reports to numerically code information on the *microneighborhoods* (face blocks) on several of these dimensions. I make no claim that these ratings are very reliable, but they are the only data we have on microneighborhoods (aside from the residents' interviews).

3.6 Newspapers

To fill in the background of each community, I regularly perused several newspapers for at least several months. This allowed us to set community concerns in perspective, to learn of local informants, and to understand references respondents made, and it also had incidental returns. (As an example of the latter, we learned about a widely publicized rape and the panic it caused in one of our communities just in time to postpone our interviewing there.)

3.7 Telephone Directories

One category of data was obtained from the classified pages of the local telephone directories: the number of institutions of various types available in or near the community—art galleries, Italian newspapers, Chinese stores, and such. The classified pages were scanned for institutions in the same *municipality* as the given locality, or in the *nearest larger municipality* if within ten miles of the sample locality (e.g., Oakland for Berkeley). This means that a community was credited with institutions in its own city and, if its city is a suburb, with institutions in its central city. Obviously the telephone directory method has its drawbacks: it misses informal institutions, counts institutions of various sizes equally, and is not sensitive to exact distances between specific communities and specific institutions (which would have required mapping each one). Nevertheless, it serves as a crude measurement device for data that are otherwise unavailable.[18]

4.0 Data Analysis
4.1 Organization of the Data

The quantitative data we produced yielded three basic files (and a few supplementary ones):

The respondent file: This file contained the survey responses of the 1,050 respondents—their opinions, reported behavior, background characteristics, and so on. The only network data, as such, in this file were simple counts of how many names were given in answer to each name-eliciting question.

The name file: This file contained records for the 19,417 names respondents provided—basic characteristics of each named person, the questions that elicited that name—and some characteristics of the respondents who named them. A subset of this file, the SAQ (self-administered questionnaire) file, contained only the records for 4,179 subsample names, the ones on whom respondents filled out SAQs and answered questions about network density.

The community file: This file contained one hundred records of community data—from the county to the face-block level—for each of the microneighborhoods in the sample (although one case was irrelevant since we did not ultimately interview there—see section 1.7.2).

These files were combined through two major procedures: first, aggregating information about the names from the name file into 1,050 records, one for each respondent, and attaching those counts to the respondent file; and, second, disaggregating the community file into 1,050 records and also merging that with the respondent file. (Robert Fitzgerald did the technical work on the first, Carol Silverman that on the second.) Although some of the analyses reported here are on the one hundred communities, the 19,417 relations (actually on a 20 percent random subsample of the full name file), and on the 4,179 SAQ relations, the vast majority of our analysis was conducted on the merged, composite file of respondent records.

4.2 Possible Methodological Artifacts

Survey data are never to be taken at face value; they are constructed by an interviewer and an interviewee during a particular hour—a different questioner, a different time may yield different answers.

Table A3   **Selected Results Under Four Correcting Procedures: Uncorrected; Weights; Without Unusual Interviewer;**

	Mean Values by Urbanism (Adjusted for Covariates[a])	
		Semi-Rural
Overall Mood	Uncorrected	3.91
	Weighted[b]	3.93
	Without Interviewer	3.91
	Without Gender Skew	3.92
Number of Kin Outside Household	Uncorrected	7.15
	Weighted[b]	6.74
	Without Interviewer	7.24
	Without Gender Skew	7.33
Number of Nonkin	Uncorrected	10.28
	Weighted[b]	11.31
	Without Interviewer	10.37
	Without Gender Skew	10.08

[a]Covariates: Age, married, number of children, education, household income; gender as crossed factor.

We were concerned about possible systematic biases that may have significantly altered the findings. Before we began substantive analysis, Carol Silverman explored and was able to dismiss several possible artifacts: date of the interview, day of the week, number of calls necessary to attain the interview, whether someone else was present, and how well the respondent understood the questions. Four other issues seemed worth pursuing: sampling procedure and response rate, interviewer differences, respondents' cooperativeness in the interview, and gender distribution in specific communities.

4.2.1 *Weighting for sampling.* Our sampling procedure introduced several potential problems (see section 1.8, above). To the extent that these were associated with urbanism, and a few were, they could seriously alter our basic conclusions about the correlates of urbanism. There is no way of capturing interviews that were never conducted, but by assuming some within-community homogeneity (which is the assumption behind the concern itself) and testing various strategies for weighting respondents by community, we can produce results that are partly "corrected" for sampling procedure. William Nicholls, of the Berkeley Survey Research Center, constructed a few such weights, and I tested two. One weight corrects for sampling stratification (i.e., it weights

Without Gender-Skewed Localities

Town	Metropolitan	Core	beta
3.84	3.80	3.86	.06
3.86	3.82	3.87	.05
3.83	3.80	3.88	.07
3.83	3.80	3.87	.07
7.46	6.77	5.06	.18***
7.36	6.69	5.03	.19***
7.53	6.81	5.33	.15***
7.63	6.75	5.07	.18***
10.65	11.28	10.60	.05
10.92	11.51	10.91	.04
10.73	11.27	11.05	.05
10.97	11.36	11.10	.07

[b]Weighted for *all* possible distortions.
*** p < .001

each case in each stratum in proportion to the stratum's true proportion of the population) and response rates (which were lower in the central cities). The second weight incorporates the first but also corrects for the two "lost" counties, the differences between strata in household size, and some slight arithmetic errors in the sampling calculations (see section 1.8.4).

Although means and standard deviations are altered by the weights, the key interest is whether correlations are altered. I ran a correlation matrix of eight assorted variables against another eight unweighted, with weight 1, and with weight 2. In only 17 of the 64 correlation trios did any two of the three differ by more than .02. In only 3 out of 192 comparisons were the correlations significantly different, fewer than would be expected by chance.

I also replicated many of the basic analyses reported in the text with full weighting (weight number 2). The differences are quite small, especially in the adjusted figures. A small sample of those is shown in table A3. The adjusted mean number of kin for the Semirural category drops 6 percent, and the adjusted mean of nonkin for the Semirural category increases 10 percent, but no real substantive difference emerges. That is the general conclusion from our trials with weighting.

4.2.2 *Interviewer differences.* There is no doubt that differences among interviewers account for some of the differences in respondents' answers. Our sensitivity to this problem led us to use only sixteen interviewers (seven of whom did at least 55 percent of the interviews); to try to have interviewers circulate among all five sampling strata; and to have each community canvassed by at least two interviewers (see section 1.6.4 above). Still, interviewer effects inevitably emerge, and they cannot be easily separated from community effects.

Carol Silverman, in comparing interviewers with multiple discriminant analysis, found that one interviewer, with more than fifty interviews, tended to obtain consistently different answers than did other interviewers. (Two other interviewers also appeared distinctive, but they completed less than half as many interviews.) This particular interviewer reported fewer names than any other, as well as differing in other ways. Our impression, from personal acquaintance, was that she was more nonchalant about probing for names and also more successful in extracting confessions of psychological problems, especially from men. She also interviewed disproportionately in the highly urban communities.

Consequently, we replicated some analyses (unweighted), eliminating her interviews. A small sample of these appears in table A3. The difference this correction makes is also slight. Removing her interviews largely affects the Core category; the major change is to raise the adjusted mean number of Core nonkin from below the grand mean (10.60 versus 10.72) to above the grand mean (11.05 versus 10.86). In sum, this interviewer probably introduced a slight bias toward underestimating Core respondent's networks, but too small a bias to alter any substantive conclusions.

4.2.3 *Respondents' cooperativeness.* Interviewees who were more reluctant to do the interview, as judged by the interviewer afterward, gave fewer names in answer to the network questions, reported fewer magazines that they read, had fewer complaints about their community, reported less tension, and so on; they made less effort. We combined three interviewer ratings into one scale: "What was the respondent's *initial* attitude about being interviewed?" (q. I-5); "What was the respondent's attitude *during* the interview?" (q. I-6; both collapsed into three categories); and "How forthcoming do you think the respondent was about (his/her) personal problems and feelings?" (q. I-13). Respondents who scored as cooperative on this scale were significantly more forthcoming on many items, even holding constant background factors. They tended, for example, to add more names to the "anyone else" question. (Differences among interviewers, a recent study suggests, can be captured by such a measure of cooperativeness.)[19]

Background factors do not explain very well who was more or less cooperative (a sixteen-variable regression equation explains only 7 percent of the variance). All else constant, education was most conducive to cooperation, followed by being female, a long-time resident of the city, and not very worried about neighborhood crime. Also, Metropolitan and Town residents were rated significantly more cooperative than either Core or Semirural respondents, all else equal. It is likely that the respondent's personality, the particular circumstances of the interview (for example, if the respondent has a pressing appointment), and the specific interviewer accounted for much more of the variance in cooperativeness.

In much of our analysis, we corrected the data by adjusting for respondents' cooperativeness, assuming that it was an exogenous cause of responses. (We did not adjust for it in analysis of psychological variables because, to the extent that cooperation reflected respondents' mental states, correcting for it would be circular.) There is a potential problem: since the interviewers supplied these ratings *after* the interview, the causality may be the reverse. Perhaps interviewers decided how cooperative respondents were on the basis of how many names they provided. No doubt some reciprocal causation is involved, but I chose to emphasize the priority of cooperation on two grounds: it led to conservative hypothesis-testing, and interviewers' reports from the field clearly showed that a dimension ranging from hostile to enthusiastic did, in fact, capture a real difference among respondents. Adjusting for cooperativeness tends to alter most estimates of the effects of education, gender, and Semirural residence, though each change is rather small. In correlations with number of nonkin, for example, partialing for cooperativeness reduces the .38 correlation with education to .35, increases the $-.09$ correlation with being female to $-.12$, and decreases the $-.16$ correlation with Semirural residence to $-.14$.

4.2.4 *Gender distribution.* One accident of the sampling procedure was that it yielded heavily skewed gender ratios in some localities. Some had female-to-male ratios of 16:4, 12:3, and the like, and a few had ratios of 2:15, 6:11, and the like. These skewed sampling clusters produced a higher standard error for gender than for most other variables (see section 4.4.2). The skews are potentially even more important because, in several places in the analysis, there appeared to be significant interaction effects between urbanism and gender. To determine the possible effects of the sampling on our substantive conclusions, I divided the respondents into two groups—those in "normal" localities and those in skewed ones (where the proportion female was twenty points higher or lower than in the whole sample, 55.5 percent)—and replicated a few key analyses in each group. Ten places, with 17 percent of the sample, fell into the skewed category.

Indeed, the interaction effect of gender by urbanism on number of nonkin, which is described in chapter 8, is largely due to respondents in the "imbalance" subset; it is not significant in the "normal" subset. Also, the adjusted main effect for urbanism is negative in the imbalance group (beta = .13) and roughly positive in the "normal" group (beta = .07). Table A3 shows the results for three measures of dropping the skewed sampling clusters. Mood is hardly affected; kin differences become a bit more negatively linear; and, most noticeably, nonkin becomes slightly more positively associated with urbanism. (The Core mean is 110 percent of the Semirural one, rather than 103 percent.) The changes, however, are not sufficient to alter our substantive conclusions. And, of course, one cannot simply eliminate clusters the way this exercise does. (How do we tell which of the interviews represent sampling accidents?) But it alerts us to the tentative nature of the gender-urbanism interactions.

4.3 Measuring Critical Variables

4.3.1 *Measuring Urbanism.* In chapter 2, "urbanism" was defined as the number of people in and near a community. While most ways to measure population concentration tend to rank communities in roughly the same order, the standard ones typically are flawed because they are based on administrative boundaries. City—that is, municipal—population does not distinguish municipalities in a congested area from those of equal size in open countryside. The standard metropolitan statistical area (SMSA) classification, which groups entire counties into metropolitan or nonmetropolitan categories and is the basis of the strata used for sampling (see section 1.4.2), also relies on administrative boundaries. Anomalies occur, for example, when a small suburb at the edge of a metropolitan county is ranked as more urban than a larger town just across the county line.

Population potential: "Population potential" most closely approximates our definition of "urban." It refers to the extent to which population is concentrated at a single point: the nearer people are to this point, and the more people there are, the higher the possible social interaction, or population potential, of the point. More precisely: The potential social interaction with respect to an individual at point i generated by the population of area j will increase as the population of area j increases and the distance between point i and the people in area j decreases. The equation that shows the population potential at i of the population of area j is: $V_{ij} = P_j^\alpha \cdot \kappa/D_{ij}^\beta$, where V is potential, P is the population of area j, D is the distance between point i and area j, and α, β, and κ are constants. These terms are summed over all areas, j, to equal total population potential for point i.[20]

Imagine a huge translucent map. We place light bulbs under the map, one below each community. The wattage of each bulb is proportional to the number of people in the community—say one hundred watts for the bulb beneath San Francisco and five watts for the one under the least populated place. When all the bulbs are turned on, the total pattern of light will show, by its brightest and darkest areas, the relative population potential of each point.[21]

Population potential can also be weighted to represent specific aspects of the population—for example, mean income of the population—thereby providing a measure of personal income potential (which might be used to predict demand for consumer goods). We calculated a set of such potentials, as well as population potential itself. Our procedure, developed and carried out largely by Daniel Finnegan, was as follows.

We calculated straight-line distances from each community in our sample to the approximate population center of every county in the sampling area and additional counties bordering the area to the north and south. Where a sample community fell within such a population center—all San Francisco localities, for instance—we calculated distances to its own county in a way designed to reflect the relative centrality of the community in the city.[22] As a result, each city district has a unique score. (We used 1977 estimates of county populations published by the State Department of Finance.) For each of the fifty communities, we summed over thirty-eight terms—the population of each county divided by its distance from the community—to obtain population potential. By modifying the population estimate with weights representing racial, age, income, or other characteristics (often necessarily based on 1970 statistics), we also obtained variations on population potential.

An urbanism scale: Population potential, by itself, was not an adequate indicator of "urban," largely because of certain anomalies unique to this sample. The metropolitan center of northern California is in the southeastern corner of the area, at the periphery of the geographical area. The population potential measure gives great weight to centrality and thereby yielded several unusual rankings. Most notably, the San Francisco communities ranked lower than a few of the East Bay communities. By any sociological or commonsense interpretation of "urban," the reverse should be true. It appears that, at least in this case, population potential underestimates the contribution the immediate vicinity makes to urbanism. Therefore I sought to combine a few measures into one urban scale.

Four measure were considered: the five-category stratification variable used for sampling (and based on SMSAs); population potential; municipal population; and an urban scale often used in survey research. (The latter has seven equally spaced categories ranging from non-SMSA places to center cities of metropolitan areas of 500,000 or more.) The correlations, across the fifty communities, of these measures are:

	Metropolitan	Potential	Municipal	Final Scale
Sampling strata (1970 data)	.86	.80	.70	.85
Metropolitan scale (1970)		.85	.58	.81
Population potential (1977)			.55	.88
Municipal population (1970)				.88

These figures suggest, first, that the measures are strongly similar; second, that municipal population represents an attribute somewhat distinct from the other three; and, third, that a combination of one of the first three—preferably population potential—and municipal population would best capture urbanism. The last conclusion is also based on the assumption that population potential needs to be complemented by a distinct measure of *local* population, rather than by a similar, global measure of population distribution. Another analysis lends some weight to that assumption: respondents' perceptions of their towns as "large city, small city, suburb, small town, or wilderness" (q. 4) tended to reflect both city population and population potential. Both were significant predictors.

The scale we finally used is composed equally of population potential and municipal population. (Specifically, Z-scores were added together, multiplied by 100, and added to 300.) Because the distribution of that scale is skewed (skewness = 1.07; the median was .40 standard deviations below the mean), we logged it to the base 10. The distribution of scores is:

≤ 2.03	3	
2.04–2.12	4	Semirural
2.13–2.21	4	
2.22–2.30	8	
2.31–2.39	7	Town
2.40–2.48	6	
2.49–2.57	6	Metropolitan
2.58–2.66	4	
2.67–2.75	0	Regional Core
2.76+	8	
	50	

Mean =	2.41	Median =	2.36
SD =	0.24	Skewness =	0.24
Minimum =	1.97	Maximum =	2.82

Four categories: For a few reasons, I wanted to categorize the fifty communities into three to five groups of roughly equal size: as a heuristic device for both reading and presenting the data; to reflect distinctively meaningful types of places; to allow us to see nonlinear trends; and to permit us to look for interaction effects between urbanism and other variables with analyses of variance. (Multiplicative interaction terms with the ratio scale, which could be used in regression analyses, are typically difficult and time-consuming to interpret. For most of the many analyses conducted here such effort was, I felt, misplaced.)

The four crude categories, as indicated above, involved some compromise between the desire for equal numbers in each category and the distribution of urbanism scores. This compromise is acceptable; the underlying urbanism scale ought not to be reified. Although better than earlier scales, it is still arbitrary in its use of county and city boundaries (for example, Oakland community A ranked only .04 above Oakland community B, which was three miles away, yet ranked .18 above suburban community C, which was only two-and-a-half miles away but over the city line). Moreover a clustering based solely on the original scale would yield eight distinct categories. Nevertheless, the sacrifice of precision warrants attention, and, accordingly, correlations of the dependent variables with the original scale were examined as part of virtually all analyses.

Finally, Table A4 compares the categorization of the fifty communities according to this fourfold typology to the five strata from which they were drawn. Although the scale correlates .84 with the strata variable, there are a few notable differences in communities' rankings: (1) Instead of ranking equally with San Francisco, Sacramento ranks with Bay Area suburbs. Similarly, Sacramento suburbs are ranked as less urban in the new scale than in the stratification variable. (2) Small communities near large ones (e.g., small towns near San Rafael) are ranked as more urban than are similar-sized towns in the sparsely populated hinterland. These changes seem consistent with our conception of urbanism.

This measure captures urbanism at the global level. Each community is ranked largely in terms of its location in the general population distribution of northern California, which is consistent with most of the theoretical concerns in the study of urbanism. On some points, however, local population concentration is the key. On issues of neighboring, for example, neighborhood density may be most important. In those sorts of analyses, I introduced such local measures in addition to the urbanism scale.

4.3.2 *Network measures.* As described above, our basic measures of respondents' networks come in the form of counts (or percentages formed from those counts). The distributions of these sums tend

Table A4	Distribution of Communities by Sampling Strata		
Strata		**Small Town**	**Small City**
Urban	Semi-Rural	8	1
Categories	Town	2	8
	Metropolitan	0	1
	Regional Core	0	0
Mean Urbanism Scale (Logged) Score		2.12	2.28

[a]Sacramento.

to be skewed, piled up at the lower numbers. I experimented with various transformations designed to correct for the skew: square root, log to base 10, and bringing in the top 5 percent of outliers. Generally, any transformation, especially logging, tended to increase correlations very slightly, with gains of about .01 to .03 (though somewhat more with the spatial network variables). In most preliminary analyses, I used raw counts, but for the final analyses I most often employed logarithms. Little of substance changed.

A different problem arises when we consider relations as the units of analysis. Since respondents contributed differentially to those units (from one to five names apiece in the subsample set of 4,179, and from two to sixty-five in the entire set of 19,417 names), various relations are interdependent. Correlations between characteristics of relations might, in those circumstances, actually be correlations between characteristics of respondents who provided many names. To assess the possible distortion introduced, I ran some parallel analyses with relations treated, on the one hand, as independent units with unit weight, and on the other, weighted by the reciprocal of the number of names the respondent contributed. (E.g., if the respondent named twelve people, each one he or she named was weighted .083.) This produces a set of approximately 1,050 whole units, to which each respondent contributed equally. Exploratory analyses (conducted on a 20 percent random sample of the name file and on the SAQ file) indicated negligible differences between the two procedures both in central tendencies and in associations between variables, altering test correlations by less than .03. (An unresolved problem is the appropriate N for significance tests; earlier researchers faced with this question, such as Edward O. Laumann and Barry Wellman, opted to use the total number of relations.)

and Urban Categories

Outer Suburb	Inner Suburb	Center City
2	0	0
3	2	0
5	4	2[a]
0	4[b]	8
2.37	2.53	2.75

[b]East Bay cities adjacent to Oakland and San Francisco Bay.

4.3.3 Other often-used measures

Education: Although we obtained years of education from each respondent, I decided that years are not the appropriate interval; indicators of credentials are. Consequently, the measure of education used virtually throughout the analysis has five categories: did not graduate high school (0 to 11 years education); graduated high school; some college (13 to 15 years education); college graduate (or 16 years education); and beyond (17 years education, including technical schools).

Household income: Income is a difficult problem, because some respondents refuse to answer and others lie. In regard to the latter problem, Robert Fitzgerald calculated respondent's *expected* incomes based on education, number of earners in the family, number of cars, and so forth. He examined the interviews of those who reported incomes two standard deviations above or below those predicted and determined that six people were almost certainly lying. In most of the analysis reported here on the respondent data, estimated household incomes were calculated for both the missing and the misleading respondents based solely on the educations. Although this correction applied to only a couple of dozen cases, it allowed us to avoid calculation errors owing to missing data. (We did not use measures of occupational status, except specifically in analysis of co-worker ties, for two reasons. First, the theoretical rationale linking occupational prestige per se and most effect variables is opaque. Second, given the complex and multidimensional nature of the occupational structure, I am not—as many others are not—persuaded that a unidimensional prestige scale is helpful.)

Psychological well-being: Kathleen Gerson was in charge of developing the psychological items we used, which involved: first, canvassing the survey questions that had been used by others to measure "mental

health," feelings, life stressors, and the like (we drew heavily from Norman Bradburn's well-being items);[23] second, selecting and adapting a
short set of items from the list, supplemented by ones we generated in
conjunction with Charlotte Coleman of SRC; third, preliminary screening
of many potential items in the pretest for Pilot Survey II; and, fourth,
statistical analysis of twenty items used in Pilot II, eliminating difficult,
redundant, and unreliable items, and those that seemed most biased or
affected by social desirability.

After the main survey data were in, Susan Phillips analyzed the remaining items and developed the basic scales we used: feeling upset
(qs.106, 112, 115), feeling angry (qs. 109 and 114), and feeling pleased (qs.
108, 111, 113, 116). These can all be interpreted as various manifestations
of individuals' personal morale. Reliability was tested (using the SPSS
reliability program) for males and females; low, medium, and high education respondents; and for each sampling stratum. For feeling upset, re-
liabilities ranged from .72 to .77, with .75 overall; for feeling angry, from
.63 to .75, and .68 overall; and for feeling pleased, from .67 to .77 overall.

4.4 Statistical Analysis

4.4.1 *General approach.* The past two decades have seen
tremendous advancement in the precision of sociologists' statistical tools.
In this book, I have neither sought nor pretended to such exactitude. The
statistics here are much more heuristic, perhaps for some even "loose."
This is so for two major reasons: the thoretical focus of my analysis, and a
desire to avoid misplaced concreteness.

First, my interest was not to specify models that explain a specific
phenomenon, but instead to test hypotheses. In the former case, the
researcher has a single effect that he or she wishes to account for most
fully and exactly. If this is carried off well, it becomes possible to make
statements such as, 22 percent of the effect of X on Y is mediated by Z.
Ultimately, all empirical social scientists would like to make such precise
statements. But there is a necessary prior stage of work, devoted to
determining what are the key variables, both causes and effects, and
whether and how and under what conditions they are linked to one
another.

Specific hypotheses answering such questions are tested by exploring
many dimensions on each side of the causal chain, including several versions of several dependent variables, careful derivation and testing of
corollary and particular propositions from more general ones, and track-
ing down the reasons for unexpected, anomalous, or inconsistent findings.
Put simply, my goal was not to explain all the reasons why, for example,
some people had more friends than others. My goal was to test theories

linking characteristics of people's communities to characteristics of their private worlds. While the first goal would have led us toward precise modeling, the latter led us to more general hypothesis testing.

Second, even in hypothesis-testing there is a place for statistical precision, to determine, for example, whether two means differ at exactly $p < .05$. Such precision with the kind of data we have here is, I believe, misplaced concreteness. The numbers to be manipulated are ultimately and unalterably "soft": the network measures are new, somewhat arbitrary, clearly subject to known and unknown biases, yet to be refined by social scientists in the way other measures have been; the sample is analytic, not exactly random or representative; 24 percent of the would-be sample was not interviewed; and so on.

These limitations undermine pretensions to exactness. Consequently, I used standard formulas for estimating statistical significance, despite our cluster sampling (see next section), and was relatively relaxed about probability levels. Alpha equals 5 percent was my rule of thumb, but theoretical interest was a more important criterion, so that a pivotal finding on a subsample significant at $p = .11$ was worthy of more attention than an offhand finding at $p < .001$.

4.4.2 Clustering and standard errors. Our sampling procedure involved drawing a disproportionately stratified, multistage cluster sample. For these kinds of samples, standard errors are typically larger than those of simple random samples of the same number of respondents. William Nicholls of the Berkeley Survey Research Center calculated appropriate compensatory adjustments. For estimating most *percentages* within strata, inflation factors of 1.2 (strata 1, 3, 5), 1.4 (stratum 2), and 1.5 (stratum 4) should be applied to standard errors; 1.5 for weighted total sample percentages. For variables strongly homogeneous within clusters —for example, housing type—the inflation factors should be doubled.

There is, however, another procedure for estimating the confidence researchers should have in their sample statistics: random subsample replication. This procedure involves assessing the internal stability of sample statistics. It is especially appropriate to samples purposely drawn by other than simple random sampling and to projects seeking to make theoretical statements within theoretically defined domains rather than descriptive statements about a general population.[24] It would have been nearly impossible to calculate the thousands of significance tests examined in this study by such techniques. But I did compare the confidence intervals generated by the SPSS program (on the assumption of simple random sampling) with those produced by the "Jackknife" technique[25] for several correlation coefficients and partial regression coefficients. In a few instances, the jackknife estimates yield *greater* confidence than do the standard estimates (most notably, with regard to the correlation coefficient of number of nonkin with urbanism). In a few cases, typically with gender as one variable, the Jackknife estimates are less reliable than the SPSS ones. On average, among the illustrative statistics I calculated, the Jackknife standard errors are about 110 percent of the SPSS estimates. A *conservative* conclusion would be that the significance levels reported in the text should be, if one wishes to be very exact (far more so than most researchers), demoted about a peg each: $p < .05$ is $p < .10$; $.01$ is $.05$; and $.001$ is $.01$. Basically though, most important correlations in the study are about as stable as reported in the text, despite our clustering.

4.4.3 Standard procedures and methods. My typical analysis involved the following steps: cross-tabulation or one-way analyses of variance to establish the correlates of given dependent variables and to examine associations for nonlinearity; multiple regression analyses to reduce control variables to a few major and significant variables (coincidentally calculating partial correlations for urbanism); several two-, three-, or four-way analyses of variance, crossing urbanism (four categories) by other major or theoretically critical variables—gender, marital status, and so on—to test for interaction effects; N-way analyses of covariance, using the selected control variables for the whole sample, and one-way analyses of covariance *within levels of the important crossed variables.* In many analyses with too many covariates, dummy variables for the urban categories were entered into regression equations. By testing the increment in R^2, I obtained a test of significance equivalent to that of hierarchical analysis of covariance with the urban factor entering last. The effects estimates are not identical but are very close to those produced by the multiple classification analysis table in the SPSS ANOVA program.

The available SPSS MANOVA package—which would have been most appropriate for the last step—had serious "bugs." This left the ANOVA package, which does not calculate means adjustments for interaction effects. To estimate adjusted interactions, it was necessary to run separate analyses of covariance within levels of the crossed factor. That procedure, however, does not yield cell means adjusted for differences between levels in the means of the covariates. I made the adjustment in several cases that warranted the effort. But most often the effort was not warranted. Thus, in reading some of the figures displaying interaction effects—for example, figure 12—it is reasonable to compare all the unadjusted means to one another, and all the adjusted means on a single line with one another, but it is *not* reasonable—except where specifically stated—to compare a mean on the adjusted line with a mean on another one.

Another possible difficulty arises with regard to dichotomous variables, which appear in several analyses as dependent variables in regression equations. The problem of violating assumptions of normality, however, seems not to be particularly serious when the total proportions of cases range between 25:75 and 75:25, and when there are many cases. Typically, our analyses satisfy those criteria. In a few cases, I used dichotomies as skewed as 5:95, and no doubt there is some error in those estimates. Even with such a split, however, more than fifty cases fall into the lesser category. Moreover, the general drift of the results—for example, the direction of the correlations—appears to be robust. Significance levels and variance explained are both, of course, quite probably underestimated in these cases.[26]

4.4.4. Small statistical associations.

In much of the analysis, the statistical associations are relatively small, especially those we focus on so closely, correlations with urbanism. The size of the correlations can, however, be misleading, because they often cover significant substantive differences. For example, even though the correlation between urbanism and number of nonkin (logged) is only .176, the average for Core respondents, 10.5, is 48 percent greater than the average for Semirural respondents, 7.1. Although the partial correlation between urbanism and number of nonkin fellow ethnics explains less than 1 percent of the variance, Core respondents' adjusted average, 2.2, was 43 percent greater than that of Semirural respondents, 1.5. The small correlations result not from the absence of substantive effects of urbanism, but from the great number of other effects—both technical effects, such as unreliability, skewness, interviewer techniques, and so on, and substantive effects, of personality and many other unmeasured variables—that increase the variance. Urbanism may be important (in ceteris paribus conditions) and yet not explain much of the variance.

Another point to keep in mind is that the tests for effects of urbanism are all conservative. Not only do they assume that personal characteristics precede community variables—for example, that education causes urbanism and that urbanism does not at all cause education—they also assign all jointly explained variance to the control variables. For example, in the equation of number of just friends regressed on education and urbanism, I reported the unique effect of urbanism, $\Delta R^2 = .014$. In fact, education and urbanism share an additional explained variance of .029. But the analyses reported in this book assign such explanatory power totally to the control variables.

There is yet a more profound reason why structural variables—of which urbanism is one—are not likely to correlate strongly with network variables, even if there are actually strong effects. As I argued elsewhere:

Even if sociologists had perfect measures, they might still typically discover small associations between structural factors and network characteristics, because people anticipate and adjust. . . . People are active constructors and protectors of their social networks. Individuals probably try to maintain networks with certain characteristics suited to each one's preferences—in number of friends, style of interaction, time spent with kin, and so on. Using roughly accurate popular understandings of the world, people can anticipate the effects of certain changes and act accordingly to protect their networks (for example, refusing a job promotion that might estrange them from coworker friends). And, once some effect has occurred, they can adjust so as to restore the network structure (for example, letting some prior friendships lapse after having made some new friends). To the extent to which people can anticipate, adjust, decide, and act in these protective ways, their networks are resilient to outside forces and will "bounce back" to their original shapes. (The ability to do this depends, of course, on the opportunities and constraints each individual faces.) And to the extent that people in a society share common preferences for social relations, personal networks will therefore tend to vary within a much narrower range than is theoretically possible.

For the empirical study of networks, these anticipations and adjustments mean that, although it may be in principle true that structural factors have great effects on networks (hypothetically, it could be demonstrated by experiment), those effects would not be seen in a cross-sectional study of the general population, because, at any given moment, most people are maintaining networks within the narrow, common range. For example, if we could move people randomly to city or suburb and prevent their adjustments, such as purchases of new cars, we might well see strong differences in the networks of the two groups, differences that we cannot see in a real population. One way around this problem is to study people's networks extensively over time, watching the adjustments they make to changes in their lives. Even this technique fails to indicate their anticipations and changes they *avoid* making. Another technique, which we have used on occasion in this book, is to look at groups of people who are limited in their ability to anticipate, choose, or adjust for strong effects of structure on networks. Nevertheless, the problem—if we have indeed touched on a real phenomenon—is a significant and difficult one. Not only might it explain low correlations here, it raises a major issue in the study of the individual and social structure generally: There may be real effects of social structure on individual lives—real in that we could create them experimentally, real in that people must adapt in order to neutralize them—but that we can observe only dimly with our usual techniques.[27]

B

Respondent Interview

Interviewer _____ Date Assigned _____

Date Letter Sent _____

LABEL
Address _____
Tract-Block-Line _____

RECORD OF CALLS

Call #	Date	Hour	Result of Call	Int. #
1				
2				
3				
4				
5				
6				

Respondent's Name _____ Phone # _____ None ☐

By Observation: 1. W 2. B 3. Ch 4. Or 5. Other _____

Comments:

315

-a-

INTRODUCTION

Hello--I'm working for the Survey Research Center on a study of the quality of people's lives and the quality of life in their communities. This is part of a large study being done all over Northern California. I'll be asking you about the kinds of people you know; how you're feeling about things; and what you think of life in this neighborhood. You may recall that you or someone in your household received a letter from the Survey Research Center describing this study. As that letter explained, I would like to ask a number of questions of a member of your household. (May I come in?)

I. First, in order to figure out who is eligible for this interview, I need to get an idea of who lives in this household. *(RECORD IN TABLE 1)*

1. What is the name of the head of the house?

2. What are the names of all the other adults who live here?

3. Now how about the children? I'd like their names in order of age, beginning with the oldest. (Any others?)

4. Is there anyone else who usually lives here, like a roomer or boarder?

5. Have I missed anyone who is away temporarily? Any babies?

II. *FOR EACH PERSON LISTED, ASK AS NECESSARY AND RECORD IN TABLE 1.*

E1a. How is PERSON related to the head of this household?

E2. Is that a (man) (woman) (boy) (girl)?

E3. How old was PERSON on (his/her) birthday?

E4. Is PERSON now married, widowed, divorced, separated, or has (he/she) never been married?

E5. Is PERSON now employed full-time or part-time? *(COUNT 30 HOURS OR MORE PER WEEK AS FULL-TIME.) IF NOT EMPLOYED: Is PERSON looking for work or on layoff from a job?*

Include in Enumeration

a. *Everyone who usually lives here whether related or not.*

b. *All persons staying or visiting here who have no other home.*

c. *Persons who have a home elsewhere but are staying here most of the week while working or attending college.*

Do Not Include in Enumeration

a. *College students away at school or here only on vacation and weekends.*

b. *Persons away in the Armed Forces.*

c. *Persons away in an institution such as a nursing home, mental hospital, or sanitarium.*

d. *Persons visiting here with usual home elsewhere.*

Office Removal SRC#: [T-Z] ____ Pers. #: ____ TABLE 1 Adults: 1 2 3
After Coding 7/2 Place: ____ N: (10) ____ (5-6) Resp.#: ____ 1 2 3 4 5 6+ ****
(8-9)

E1

Pers Num 11-12	Name	E1a Relation to: HH Head (13)	E1b R (14)	E2 Sex 15	E3 age 16-17	RES SEL NUM 18	E4 Marital Status 19	E5 Labor Force Status 20	21
01		1. Head 2. Spouse 3. Parent 4. Child 5. Ot Rel 6. Nonrel	2 3 4 5 6	1. M 2. F			1. Mar 2. Sep 3. Wid 4. Div 5. NvM	1. Emp full 2. Emp part 3. Lkg/lyf 4. Retired 5. None	
02		2. Spouse 3. Parent 4. Child 5. Ot Rel 6. Nonrel	2 3 4 5 6	1. M 2. F			1. Mar 2. Sep 3. Wid 4. Div 5. NvM	1. Emp full 2. Emp part 3. Lkg/lyf 4. Retired 5. None	
03		2. Spouse 3. Parent 4. Child 5. Ot Rel 6. Nonrel	2 3 4 5 6	1. M 2. F			1. Mar 2. Sep 3. Wid 4. Div 5. NvM	1. Emp full 2. Emp part 3. Lkg/lyf 4. Retired 5. None	
04		2. Spouse 3. Parent 4. Child 5. Ot Rel 6. Nonrel	2 3 4 5 6	1. M 2. F			1. Mar 2. Sep 3. Wid 4. Div 5. NvM	1. Emp full 2. Emp part 3. Lkg/lyf 4. Retired 5. None	
05		2. Spouse 3. Parent 4. Child 5. Ot Rel 6. Nonrel	2 3 4 5 6	1. M 2. F			1. Mar 2. Sep 3. Wid 4. Div 5. NvM	1. Emp full 2. Emp part 3. Lkg/lyf 4. Retired 5. None	
06		2. Spouse 3. Parent 4. Child 5. Ot Rel 6. Nonrel	2 3 4 5 6	1. M 2. F			1. Mar 2. Sep 3. Wid 4. Div 5. NvM	1. Emp full 2. Emp part 3. Lkg/lyf 4. Retired 5. None	
07		2. Spouse 3. Parent 4. Child 5. Ot Rel 6. Nonrel	2 3 4 5 6	1. M 2. F			1. Mar 2. Sep 3. Wid 4. Div 5. NvM	1. Emp full 2. Emp part 3. Lkg/lyf 4. Retired 5. None	
08		2. Spouse 3. Parent 4. Child 5. Ot Rel 6. Nonrel	2 3 4 5 6	1. M 2. F			1. Mar 2. Sep 3. Wid 4. Div 5. NvM	1. Emp full 2. Emp part 3. Lkg/lyf 4. Retired 5. None	
09		2. Spouse 3. Parent 4. Child 5. Ot Rel 6. Nonrel	2 3 4 5 6	1. M 2. F			1. Mar 2. Sep 3. Wid 4. Div 5. NvM	1. Emp full 2. Emp part 3. Lkg/lyf 4. Retired 5. None	
10		2. Spouse 3. Parent 4. Child 5. Ot Rel 6. Nonrel	2 3 4 5 6	1. M 2. F			1. Mar 2. Sep 3. Wid 4. Div 5. NvM	1. Emp full 2. Emp part 3. Lkg/lyf 4. Retired 5. None	

-1-

SRC: ___ ___ ___ ___   5-6/01
     (1-4)
                    7/1
          Place ___ ___ ___ ___   N
                 (8-9)   (10)

                    Time: _____

My first questions are about where you have lived and where you'd like to live.

1a. How long have you lived in (NAME OF CITY)?
    IF NECESSARY: Is that all your life?   11/

              Less than 6 months. 1
              6 to 11 months. 2
              1 or 2 years. 3
              3 to 5 years. 4
              6 to 10 years 5
              11 to 20 years. 6
              More than 20 years. 7
              All my life (SKIP TO NEXT PAGE) 8

b. | Booklet | Here are some reasons people give for picking a particular area
   | Page 1 | to live in. Which of these reasons were important to you (and/or
   your family) in deciding to live in the (NAME OF CITY) area? (CODE AS
   MANY AS APPLY)

    Being near relatives or friends. 1   12/
    The kind of people here. 1   13/
    It's a good place for children to grow up (including
    children's schools). 1   14/
    Near my (or my husband's/wife's) job or school . . . 1   15/
    It's a beautiful area. 1   16/
    It's a safe area 1   17/
    The things I (we) can do here. 1   18/
    It's the right sized town for me (us). 1   19/
    Other (SPECIFY: _____
    _____) 1   20/
    R was dependent child. 1   21/

                                                                  22-23/

                                                                  01

-b-

-2-

2a. Do you have any immediate family--such as parents, children, brothers or sisters, or in-laws--living in this area, that is, within about an hour's drive of here?

Yes...1
No (SKIP TO 3)...2   24/

b. Counting adults only, about how many of your (and your SPOUSE'S) relatives live in this area--just one or two, 3 to 6, or more than that? I mean individuals, not couples.

One or two...1
3 to 6...2
More than that...3   25/

3. | Booklet Page 2 | If you could live anywhere you liked (and didn't have to worry about the needs of (your family)/(the people you live with), which one of the types of places listed on this page would you say best describes the kind of place that you personally would like to live in? (RECORD BELOW)

4. Which of those do you think best describes the place you live in now? (RECORD BELOW)

5. Which of these kinds of places did you live in most before you were 16 years old? (RECORD BELOW)

	26/	27/	28/
	R3	R4	R5
Large city	1	1	1
Small city	2	2	2
Suburb	3	3	3
Small town	4	4	4
Farm, rural area, or wilderness	5	5	5
Other (SPECIFY:	6	6	6
Don't know; can't say	9	9	9

29/

10

-3-

6a. What state (country) did you live in most before you were 16?   30-31/

b. What city, place, or part of the country do you think of as home: (NAME OF CITY), Northern California, the West Coast, the Midwest, or what?   32-34/
_____   35/

7a. How long have you lived in this neighborhood? IF NECESSARY: Whatever you think of as your neighborhood.

Less than 6 months...1
6 to 11 months...2
1 to 2 years...3
3 to 5 years...4
6 to 10 years...5
11 to 20 years...6
More than 20 years...7
All my life (SKIP TO NEXT PAGE)...8   36/

b. | Booklet Page 3 | On this page are some reasons people give for picking a particular neighborhood. Which of these reasons were important to you (and/or your spouse/family) in deciding to live in this neighborhood? (CODE AS MANY AS APPLY)

Being near relatives or friends...1   37/
The kind of people here...1   38/
The recreational facilities here...1   39/
Good schools for children...1   40/
Being close to (my/spouse's) work or school...1   41/
The stores and services here...1   42/
The appearance of the neighborhood...1   43/
This (house/apartment) was right...1   44/
Other (SPECIFY:)1   45/
R was dependent child...1   46/

47-48/

11

-4-

8. Some people feel it's very important to live close to their relatives and see a lot of them; for others, it's not that important. How important is it to you--very important, somewhat important, or not too important?

       Very important 1
       Somewhat important. 2
       Not too important 3   49/

9. Which kind of neighborhood do you prefer--one where people drop in on each other, where they visit only when invited, where they just chat outside their homes, or where people pretty much go their own way?

       Drop in 1
       Visit when invited. 2
       Just chat outside 3
       Go their own way. 4
       No difference 5   50/

10. During the past few months, have you dropped in on any of your neighbors or had any of your neighbors drop in on you just for a casual visit?

       Yes 1
       No. 2   51/

11. During the past few months, have you invited any (other) neighbors over to your home, or have any of your (other) neighbors invited you over to their home?

       Yes 1
       No. 2   52/

12. During the past few months, have you stopped and talked with any of your neighbors outside your home?

       Yes 1
       No. 2   53/

-5-

13. Do you think most people in this neighborhood worry about their homes being broken into, or don't they worry about that kind of thing?

       Yes, worry 1
       No, don't worry 2
       Don't worry because of precautions. 3   54/

14. Generally speaking, do you think of this neighborhood as a very safe place, a somewhat safe place, or not a very safe place to live?

       Very safe 1
       Somewhat safe 2
       Not very safe 3   55/

15a. In this area, is there any kind of local group, such as a homeowners' association, a block club, or other sort of neighborhood organization?

       Yes 1
       No *(SKIP TO 16)* 2
       Don't know *(SKIP TO 16)* . . . 3   56/

b. Do you happen to belong to (this/any of these) group(s)?

       Yes 1
       No. 2   57/

16. In terms of general lifestyle, do you think that most of your neighbors are pretty much like you, or are they quite different from you?

       Pretty much like me 1
       Some like, some different . . . 2
       Quite different from me 3
       Can't say 4   58/

-7-   SRC# ___ 5-6/02

(1-4)

7/1

21a. Since you've lived in this neighborhood, have you always lived in this (house/apartment)?

Yes (SKIP TO 22)............1
No............2   11/

b. How long have you lived in this (house/apartment)?   12/

Less than 6 months............1
6 to 11 months............2
1 to 2 years............3
3 to 5 years............4
6 to 10 years............5
11 to 20 years............6
More than 20 years............7

22. Do you own or rent this (house/apartment)?   13/

Own............1
Rent............2
Other (SPECIFY): _____ 3

23. How many rooms are there in this (house/apartment), counting the kitchen but not counting the bathroom(s)?   14-15/

One............01
Two............02
Three............03
Four............04
Five............05
Six............06
Seven............07
Eight............08
Nine............09
Ten or more............10

24. Do you have enough space in your (house/apartment) for (your needs/the needs of your household)?   16/

Too much space............1
Yes............2
No............3

-6-

17. Thinking of the neighborhood as a whole, would you say that most of the people who live here can be trusted or cannot be trusted?   59/

Can be trusted............1
Can't say............2
Cannot be trusted............3

18. What about most of the people who live in (NAME OF CITY)—would you say that most of them can be trusted or cannot be trusted?   60/

Can be trusted............1
Can't say............2
Cannot be trusted............3

19. What would you say are the best things about living in (NAME OF CITY) these days?

61-62/
63-64/
65-66/
67-68/
69-70/

20. What would you say are the worst things about living in this (city/town)?

71-72/
73-74/
75-76/
77-78/
79-80/

10

-8-

25. When you are inside your home, how often do you hear noise from outside your (house/apartment)—often, sometimes, very seldom, or never?

Often. 1
Sometimes. 2
Very seldom. 3
Never. 4   17/

26. About how often do you feel that the work you do around the house puts too many demands on you—much of the time, pretty often, occasionally, or almost never?

Much of the time 1
Pretty often 2
Occasionally 3
Almost never 4
R does no work around house. . . . 5   18/

27. If you could live anywhere you liked [and didn't have to worry about (your family/the people you live with)], would you personally rather live in a house or an apartment?

House. 1
Apartment. 2
Other (SPECIFY): _____ 3
Doesn't matter 4   19/

28. If you could afford to spend twice as much money on housing, would you move to another neighborhood, move to another home in this neighborhood, or stay in this (house/apartment)?

New neighborhood 1
Same neighborhood, new place . . . 2
Same house/apartment 3
Don't know 4   20/

29a. Do you by any chance have a second home or some other place where you live or visit for at least 30 days during the year?
IF NECESSARY: The 30 days can be spread out during the year.

Yes. 1
No (SKIP TO NEXT PAGE) . . . 2   21/

b. Where is that? _____ (City) _____ (State)   22-24/
25-26/

02

-9-

As I mentioned earlier, one of the things we are studying is people's social relationships. I'll be asking you for the first names of people you know. Later, I'll ask you more about these people.
IF NECESSARY: I'm just asking for names to keep things straight.

30a. When people go out of town for a while, they sometimes ask someone to take care of their home for them—for example, to water the plants, pick up the mail, feed a pet, or just check on things. If you went out of town, would you ask someone to take care of your home in any of these ways while you were gone?

Yes 1
No (SKIP TO 31) 2   27/

b. IF YES: Could you give me the first names of the people you would ask?
IF SOMEONE IN HOUSEHOLD NAMED, PROBE: Suppose (everyone who lives here/both of you) were away at the same time, who would you ask?

_____ 28-29/
_____ 30-31/
_____ 32-33/
_____ 34-35/
_____ 36-37/
_____ 38-39/
_____ 40-41/
_____ 42-43/
_____ 44-45/

31. When you watch the news or read the papers, do you prefer to learn about national and international events, or do you prefer to find out about things that happen in your local community?

Prefer national and international events. 1
Prefer local events. 2
Equally interested in both. . . . 3
Not interested in either. . . . 4   46/

And now I'd like to ask your opinions about some of the things that people talk about these days.

32. Would you say that abortions should be legal whenever a woman wants one; legal only under certain circumstances; or always be illegal?

Always legal. 1
Legal under certain circumstances . . 2
Always illegal. 3   47/

02

-10-

33. How do you feel about people who are not married having sex relations—would you say it is generally o.k., or generally wrong?

Generally o.k. 1
It depends. 2
Generally wrong 3

48/

34. How do you feel about husbands and wives splitting the housework—things such as cooking, cleaning, and so forth? Do you think that they should each do about half the work that has to be done around the house, or do you think the wife should do most of it?

Each should do about half . . . 1
It depends. 2
Wife should do most 3
Wife should do all 4

49/

35. How do you feel about a woman with young children working even if her family doesn't need the money? Would you say that it is generally o.k., or generally not a good idea?
IF NECESSARY: Before the children start school.

Generally o.k. 1
It depends. 2
Generally not a good idea 3

50/

36. Do you think the use of marijuana should be made legal or not?

Yes 1
It depends. 2
No. 3

51/

37. Do you think that homosexuals should or should not be permitted to teach in the public schools?

Yes, should 1
It depends. 2
No, should not. 3

52/

-11-

38a. (CHECK ENUMERATION) You are (working full-time/working part-time/not working)--is that right?

Yes, full-time. 1
Part-time 2
Not working (SKIP TO 40). 3

53/

b. Do you have more than one job?

Yes, more than one job. 1
No, only one job. 2

54/

c. About how many hours a week do you work on the average?

Number of hours
[ ] 55-56/

d. Are your working hours usually from around 8 or 9 in the morning to around 5 or 6 in the afternoon, or do you have a different working schedule?

Yes, 9 to 5 (SKIP TO f) 1
No, different 2

57/

e. IF DIFFERENT: What is your usual schedule?

58/

IF R WORKS AT MORE THAN ONE JOB, ASK FOLLOWING
QUESTIONS ABOUT JOB R SPENDS MOST TIME IN

f. Do you work for someone else (on your main job) or are you self-employed?

Employed by someone else. 1
Self-employed 2

59/

g. How long have you been (working for your present employer/self-employed in that line of work)?

Less than 6 months (SKIP TO 43) . 1
6 to 23 months. 2
2 to 3 years. 3
4 to 5 years. 4
More than 5 years 5

60/

61/

02

-12-

39a. In the last year have there been any major changes or difficulties in your job situation--something like a promotion, a transfer, new responsibilities, or a major disagreement with someone at work?

Yes 1   62/
No (SKIP TO 43) 2

b. IF YES: What was that?

63-64/
65-66/

SKIP TO 43

40. IF NOT WORKING: What do you spend most of your time doing--are you looking for work, on layoff from a job, (retired), (going to school), (unable to work), (keeping house), or doing something else?
(CODE LOWEST NUMBER IF MORE THAN ONE ANSWER)

Looking for work. 1   67/
On layoff from a job. 2
Retired 3
Going to school 4
Unable to work. 5
Keeping house 6
Something else (SPECIFY: _____) . 7

41. If you could arrange your life just the way you wanted, would you prefer to have some kind of paying job, or would you rather not have a job?

Prefer job. 1   68/
Prefer no job 2
Other (SPECIFY: _____) . . . 3

02

-13-

42. When did you last work at all, even for a few days?

Within past 4 weeks 1   69/
1 to 11 months ago. 2
1 to 5 years ago. 3
6 to 10 years ago 4
More than 10 years ago. 5
Never worked (SKIP TO 47) . . . 6

43a. What kind of business or industry (do/did) you work for?   70-72/
PROBE: What (do/did) they do or make at the place where you work(ed)?

b. What kind of work (do/did) you do?   73-75/
PROBE: What (is/was) your job title?

IF R NOT CURRENTLY WORKING, SKIP TO 47

44. On the whole, would you say your job is really interesting, or would you say that it's o.k., or would you say that it's boring?   76/

Interesting 1
O.k.. 2
Boring. 3

45. About how often do you feel that your work puts too many demands on you-- much of the time, pretty often, occasionally, or almost never?   77/

Much of the time. 1
Pretty often. 2
Occasionally. 3
Almost never. 4

78-80/

02

-14-

SRC# (1-4) —— 5-6/03

7/1

46a. Some people never talk with anyone, either on or off the job, about how to do their work. Other people do discuss things like decisions they have to make, work problems they have to solve, and ways to do their work better. Is there anyone you talk with about how to do your work?

Yes 1
No (SKIP TO NEXT PAGE). 2   11/

b. IF YES: Who do you talk with about how you do your work?

_____ 12-13/
_____ 14-15/
_____ 16-17/
_____ 18-19/
_____ 20-21/
_____ 22-23/
_____ 24-25/
_____ 26-27/
_____ 28-29/

[SKIP TO NEXT PAGE]

47. IF R NOT WORKING: On the whole, about how much of the work around the house--such as cleaning, cooking, and small repairs--do you yourself do-- all of it, most of it, some of it, or none of it?

All of it yourself. 1
Most of it. 2
Half and half. 3
Some of it. 4
None of it (SKIP TO NEXT PAGE). . 5   30/

48. On the whole, would you say the work you do around the house is really interesting, or would you say that it's o.k., or would you say that it's boring?

Really interesting. 1
O.k.. 2
Boring. 3   31/

03

-15-

[IF R HAS NO SPOUSE, SKIP TO NEXT PAGE]

49a. (CHECK ENUMERATION) Your (SPOUSE) is (working full-time/working part-time/ not working)--is that right?

Yes, full-time. 1
Yes, part-time. 2
Not working now (SKIP TO c). . . 3   32/

b. Does (he/she) have more than one job?

Yes (SKIP TO 50). 1
No (SKIP TO 50). 2   33/

c. IF NOT WORKING NOW: What does (he/she) spend most of (his/her) time doing--looking for work, on layoff from a job, (retired), (going to school), (unable to work), (keeping house), or doing something else? (CODE LOWEST NUMBER IF MORE THAN ONE ANSWER)

Looking for work. 1
On layoff from a job. 2
Retired. 3
Going to school. 4
Unable to work. 5
Keeping house. 6
Something else (SPECIFY: _____/. 7   34/

d. When did (he/she) last work at all, even for a few days?

Within past 4 weeks 1
1 to 11 months ago. 2
1 to 5 years ago. 3
6 to 10 years ago. 4
More than 10 years ago. 5
Never worked (SKIP TO NEXT PAGE). 6   35/

50a. What kind of business or industry (does/did) (he/she) work for? PROBE: What (do/did) they do or make at the place (he/she) work(ed)? (IF MORE THAN ONE JOB, PICK JOB SPOUSE SPENDS MOST TIME ON)   36-38/

b. What kind of work (does/did) (he/she) do? PROBE: What (is/was) (his/her) job title?   39-41/

03

-16-

Now I'd like to ask you about some of the places you go and how you get around in the area.

51a. Do you drive, at least occasionally?

Yes 1
No (SKIP TO 53) 2   42/

b. Do you (or anyone else living here) own or have regular use of a car, truck, or motorcycle?

Yes 1
No (SKIP TO 53) 2   43/

c. IF YES: How many vehicles do you (or anyone else living here) own or have regular use of?

Number of vehicles [   ]   44-45/

52a. IF ONLY ONE VEHICLE: Who has that vehicle most of the time--is it mainly yours, do you share it, or does someone else have it most of the time?

Mainly respondent's (SKIP TO NEXT PAGE) 1
Shared (SKIP TO 53) 2
Mostly someone else's (SKIP TO 53) . . . 3   46/

b. IF MORE THAN ONE VEHICLE: Is there some vehicle for you to use whenever you want to?

Yes (SKIP TO NEXT PAGE) . . . 1
No 2   47/

53a. IF NO DIRECT ACCESS TO VEHICLE: Do you ever find you want to go someplace in the local area, but don't go because you have trouble getting there?

Yes 1
No (SKIP TO NEXT PAGE) 2   48/

b. IF YES: Does this happen a lot of the time, some of the time, or just every once in a while?

A lot of the time 1
Some of the time 2
Every once in a while 3   49/

03

-17-

IF R IS NOT CURRENTLY EMPLOYED, SKIP TO NEXT PAGE

54. How do you usually get to work--do you (drive), get a ride, take the bus, car pool, walk, or something else?
IF NECESSARY: How do you go most often?

Drive. 1
Get a ride/car pool. 2
Ride to bus/BART/ferry . . . 3
Bus/BART/ferry 4
Walk only. 5
Other (SPECIFY: ____) . . . 6
Work at home (SKIP TO NEXT PAGE) . 7   50/

55a. Do you work in (NAME OF CITY), or somewhere else?

(NAME OF CITY) (SKIP TO 56). . . . 1
Somewhere else 2   51/

b. What city do you work in?   52-54/

56. About how long does it usually take you to get to work?
IF NECESSARY: To the job you spend the most time on.

1 to 4 minutes. 1
5 to 14 minutes. 2
15 to 29 minutes 3
30 minutes to 59 minutes . . 4
60 minutes to 89 minutes . . 5
Between 90 minutes and 2 hours . 6
Over 2 hours 7
It varies too much to say. . 8   55/

03

-18-

IF R DOES NOT HAVE AN EMPLOYED SPOUSE, SKIP TO NEXT PAGE

57. How does (SPOUSE) usually get to work--does (he/she) (drive), get a ride, take the bus, car pool, walk, or something else?
IF NECESSARY: How (he/she) goes most often.

56/
Drive 1
Get a ride/carpool 2
Ride to bus/BART/ferry 3
Bus/BART/ferry 4
Walk only 5
Other (SPECIFY: _____) . . 6
Works at home (SKIP TO NEXT PAGE) . . 7

58a. Does (he/she) work in (NAME OF CITY), or somewhere else?

57/
(NAME OF CITY) (SKIP TO 59) . . 1
Somewhere else 2

b. What city does (he/she) work in? _____

58-60/

59. About how long does it take (her/him) to get to work?
IF NECESSARY: To the job (he/she) spends most time on.

61/
1 to 4 minutes 1
5 to 14 minutes 2
15 to 29 minutes 3
30 minutes to 59 minutes . . . 4
60 minutes to 89 minutes . . . 5
Between 90 minutes and 2 hours . 6
Over 2 hours 7
It varies too much to say . . . 8

03

-19-

60a. When you need something small, like a cup of sugar or a few nails, do you usually borrow from someone, do you go to the store, or do you do one or the other depending on the situation?

62/
Usually borrow (SKIP TO c) . . . 1
Usually go to the store 2
One or the other depending
(SKIP TO c) 3

b. IF GOES TO STORE: When the stores are closed, do you borrow what you need from someone, or do you go without?

63/
Borrow 1
Go without (SKIP TO 61) 2
Has never happened (SKIP TO 61) . 3

c. When you do borrow, do you borrow from your neighbors?

64/
Yes 1
Sometimes 2
No 3

61a. Is there an area within a 5 minute drive of here where people can shop for things other than groceries?

65/
Yes 1
No (SKIP TO NEXT PAGE) 2

b. IF YES: How often do you shop (there/at any of these places) for things other than groceries--at least once a week, at least every couple of weeks, at least once a month, or less often than that?

66/
At least once a week 1
Once every couple of weeks . . 2
Once a month 3
Less often 4
Never shop in local area . . . 5
Never shop at all (SKIP TO 64) . 6

IF R DOES NOT LIVE IN SMALL TOWN, SKIP TO NEXT PAGE

c. IF R LIVES IN SMALL TOWN: Are there any other areas in (NAME OF CITY) where people can shop for things other than groceries?

67/
Yes 1
No (SKIP TO 63) 2

68-80/

03

-21-

64a. Is there an area within a five minute drive of here where people can go out to enjoy themselves, not counting visiting friends in their homes?   37/

    Yes. 1
    No *(SKIP TO NEXT PAGE)*. 2

b. *IF YES:* How often do you go out to enjoy yourself (there/at any of these places)--at least once a week, at least every couple of weeks, at least once a month, or less often than that?   38/

    At least once a week. 1
    Once every couple of weeks. . . . 2
    Once a month. 3
    Less often. 4
    Never--in local area. 5
    Never go out to relax *(SKIP TO 67)*. 6

> IF R DOES NOT LIVE IN SMALL TOWN,
> SKIP TO NEXT PAGE

c. *IF R LIVES IN SMALL TOWN:* Are there any other areas in *(NAME OF CITY)* where people can go out to enjoy themselves?   39/

    Yes. 1
    No *(SKIP TO 66)*. 2

04

-20-   SRC# $\overline{(1-4)}$ ——   5-6/04
                           7/1

62. How often do you shop for things other than groceries in other areas of *(NAME OF CITY)*--at least once a week, at least every couple of weeks, at least once a month, or less often than that?   11/

    Once a week. 1
    Once every couple of weeks. . . . 2
    Once a month. 3
    Less often. 4
    Never shop elsewhere in city. . . 5
    There is no other place 6

63a. In what other cities or towns do you shop for things other than groceries at least 3 or 4 times a year?

    None [ ] *(SKIP TO NEXT PAGE)*   12/

b. *FOR EACH:* About how far away from your home is *(CITY OR TOWN)*--less than 10 miles, between 10 and 30 miles, or more than 30 miles?

CITY OR TOWN WHERE SHOP AT LEAST 3 or 4 TIMES A YEAR	Less than 10	10 to 30	Over 30	
_____	 1	2	3	13/ (14-16)
_____	 1	2	3	17/ (18-20)
_____	 1	2	3	21/ (22-24)
_____	 1	2	3	25/ (26-28)
_____	 1	2	3	29/ (30-32)
_____	 1	2	3	33/ (34-36)

MILES FROM HOME

04

Page -22-

65. Not counting visiting friends in their homes, how often do you go out to other parts of (NAME OF CITY) to enjoy yourself--once every couple of days, at least once a week, at least every couple of weeks, at least once a month, or less often than that?

Every couple of days..........1
Every week....................2
Every couple of weeks.........3
Once a month..................4
Less often....................5
Never go out, elsewhere in (NAME OF CITY).......6
There is no other place to go...7   40/

66a. To what other cities or places, if any, do you go out to enjoy yourself, at least 3 or 4 times a year? (LIST EACH ON SEPARATE LINE UNDER b)

None [ ] SKIP TO 67   41/

b. ASK FOR EACH: About how far away from your home is (CITY OR TOWN)-- less than 10 miles, between 10 and 30 miles, or more than 30 miles?

CITY OR TOWN WHERE RELAX AT LEAST 3 OR 4 TIMES A YEAR	MILES FROM HOME			
	Less than 10	10 to 30	Over 30	
	1	2	3	42/ (43-45)
	1	2	3	46/ (47-49)
	1	2	3	50/ (51-53)
	1	2	3	54/ (55-57)
	1	2	3	58/ (59-61)
	1	2	3	62/ (63-65)
				66-80/

04

Page -23-

SRC# (1-4) ——— 5-6/05
7/1

67. When you're not at home [or at (work/school)], about how often do you run into someone you know--almost every day, at least once a week, about once a month, or less often than that?
IF NECESSARY: Well, I mean someone you're not expecting to see.

Almost every day........1
Once a week.............2
Once a month............3
Less often..............4
Never...................5   11/

66a. Do you stop in at any restaurant, bar, or coffee shop fairly often, say once a week or more?

Yes.....................1
No (SKIP TO NEXT PAGE)..2   12/

b. IF YES: Is that within about 5 minutes' drive of here?

Yes.....................1
No......................2   13/

c. Do you know anyone who works there by name?

Yes.....................1
No (SKIP TO NEXT PAGE)..2   14/

d. IF YES: How many people who work there do you know by name?

Number of people [ ]   15-16/

e. Do you know anyone in (that person's family/any of those people's families) by name?

Yes.....................1
No......................2   17/

05

-24-

69a. | Booklet Page 4 | Please turn to page 4 in the booklet and read through the list of types of organizations people can belong to. (PAUSE) Do you presently belong to any of those types of organizations?

18/

Yes 1
No (SKIP TO 70) 2

b. IF YES: Which of those do you belong to? (CIRCLE ALL THAT APPLY)

01 Business or civic groups 1   19-20
02 Church connected groups 1   21-22
03 Charity or welfare organizations 1   23-24
04 Cooperatives (farming, consumer, child-care, etc.) .. 1   25-26
05 Country clubs 1   27-28
06 Ethnic, racial, or national organizations 1   29-30
07 Farm organizations 1   31-32
08 Fraternal lodges or veterans' organizations 1   33-34
09 Special interest groups (issue-oriented groups or lobbies) 1   35-36
10 Labor unions 1   37-38
11 Neighborhood associations 1   39-40
12 PTA or other school related groups 1   41-42
13 Political clubs or organizations 1   43-44
14 Professional organizations or groups 1   45-46
15 Social clubs, card playing, music, or hobby groups .. 1   47-48
16 Sports teams or clubs 1   49-50
17 Youth groups (Scout leader, Little League manager, etc.) . 1   51-52
                                                                53-54
                                                                55-56

70a. Do you belong to any (other) type of organization not listed on the card?

57/

Yes 1
No (SKIP TO INSTRUCTION) ... 2

b. IF YES: What would that be? (RECORD ON CHART)

IF NO ORGANIZATIONS IN 69 OR 70, SKIP TO 72

W ☐ 58
E ☐ 59
R ☐ 60
A ☐ 61

62-80/

-25-

SRC# (1-4) — — 5-6/06

7/1

71. ASK FOR EACH ORGANIZATION # LISTED BELOW: What is the name of the (TYPE) organization you belong to? (PROBE FOR EXACT TITLE AND DESCRIPTION)

RECORD TYPE #
FROM 69a, 70b   NAME OF ORGANIZATION

11-12/
13-14/
15-16/
17-18/
19-20/
21-22/
23-24/
25-26/
27-28/
29-30/
31-32/
33-34/

72. What newspapers or magazines, if any, do you read regularly? (PROBE FOR EXACT TITLES)   None ☐

-27-

SRC# (1-4) --- 5-6/07
7/1

* b. *IF YES:* May I have the first names of the people you do these things with?

11-1'/
13-14/
15-16/
17-18/
19-20/
21-22/
23-24/
25-26/
27-28/
29-30/
31-32/

75a. Sometimes people get together with others to talk about hobbies or spare-time interests they have in common. Do you ever do this?

33/

Yes 1
No *(SKIP TO 76)* 2

* b. *IF YES:* Who do you usually do this with?

34-35/
36-37/
38-39/
40-41/
42-43/
44-45/
46-47/
48-49/
50-51/

> *IF R HAS SPOUSE OR SURROGATE, SKIP TO NEXT PAGE*

76a. Do you have a fiancé(e) or one best friend you are dating or seeing a lot of?

52/

Yes 1
No *(SKIP TO 77)* 2

b. *IF YES:* What is (his/her) first name?

53-54/

55-80/

07

-26-

EXPLANATION

Now, some of the next questions might apply to people you know who live out of town, so I want to remind you that we are interested in them, as well as people who live nearby (and the people who live with you).

73a. In the past three months, have any friends or relatives helped with any tasks around the home, such as painting, moving furniture, cooking, cleaning, or major or minor repairs?

35/

Yes 1
No *(SKIP TO 74)* 2

b. *IF YES:* Who helped you?

36-37/
38-39/
40-41/
42-43/
44-45/
46-47/
48-49/
50-51/
52-53/

74a. [Booklet Page 5] Please read through the list of activities on page 5 of the booklet. Which, if any, of these have you done in the last three months?

Had someone to your home for lunch or dinner. 1   54/
Went to someone's home for lunch or dinner. 1   55/
Someone came by your home to visit. 1   56/
Went over to someone's home for a visit. 1   57/
Went out with someone (e.g., a restaurant, bar, movie, park). 1   58/
Met someone you know outside your home (e.g., a restaurant, bar, park, club). 1   59/
(R volunteers other activity) 1   60/
None *(SKIP TO 75)* 1   61/

62-80/

06

-28-

SRC# (1-4) ___ ___   5-6/08

7/1

77a. When you are concerned about a personal matter--for example, about someone you are close to or something you are worried about--how often do you talk about it with someone--usually, sometimes, or hardly ever?

Usually 1   11/
Sometimes 2
Hardly ever 3

★ b. When you do talk with someone about personal matters, who do you talk with?
PROBE: Anyone else?

Never talk [ ]   12/

_____ 13-14/
_____ 15-16/
_____ 17-18/
_____ 19-20/
_____ 21-22/
_____ 23-24/
_____ 25-26/
_____ 27-28/

78a. Often people rely on the judgment of someone they know in making important decisions about their lives--for example, decisions about their family or their work. Is there anyone whose opinion you consider seriously in making important decisions?

Yes 1   29-30/
No (SKIP TO 79) 2

★ b. IF YES: Whose opinion do you consider?
PROBE: Is there anyone else?   31/

_____ 32-33/
_____ 34-35/
_____ 36-37/
_____ 38-39/
_____ 40-41/
_____ 42-43/
_____ 44-45/
_____ 46-47/
_____ 48-49/

08

-29-

50/

79a. If you needed to get a large sum of money together, what would you do-- would you ask someone you know to lend it to you; go to a bank, savings and loan, or credit union, or do something else?

Ask someone you know 1
Bank, savings and loan, or credit union (SKIP TO c) 2
Both 3
Something else (SPECIFY) _____

AND SKIP TO c) 4

★ b. Who would that be? (RECORD BELOW UNDER [b])

[b]

          b
        51-52/
_____ 53-54/
_____ 55-56/
_____ 57-58/

[d]

          d
        59-60/
_____ 61-62/
_____ 63-64/
_____ 65-66/

c. What about in an emergency situation--is there anyone (else) you could probably ask to lend you some or all of the money?

Yes 1   67-68/
No (SKIP TO NEXT PAGE) 2

d. IF YES: Who would that be? (RECORD UNDER [d] ABOVE)   69/

08

-30-

LIST SELECTION PROCEDURE

In answer to the last set of questions, you've given me the names of some of the people you know. Now, I'm going to pick out the names of a few of those people and ask you to give me a little more information about them.

* 1. SELECT NAMES. TAKE FIRST NAME GIVEN IN RESPONSE TO EACH STARRED QUESTION ON THE YELLOW PAGES, STARTING WITH PAGE 9, AND ENTER ON MATRIX FORM. IF PERSON HAS ALREADY BEEN SELECTED, OR PERSON IS IN R'S HOUSEHOLD, GO ON TO NEXT PERSON ON THE LIST UNTIL YOU GET A NAME FOR THAT QUESTION. TAKE A TOTAL OF FIVE NAMES IF POSSIBLE. SOME RESPONDENTS WILL HAVE NAMES ON EACH OF THE SIX STARRED QUESTIONS; USE ONLY THE FIRST FIVE STARRED QUESTIONS FOR THOSE RESPONDENTS.

2. ASK R QUESTIONS ABOUT NAMES ON MATRIX FORM.

3. ENTER NAMES ON SELF-ADMINISTERED QUESTIONNAIRES.

To find out a little bit more about these people I'd like you to complete these forms for me. While you're doing that, I'll be organizing a list of all the names you've mentioned so I can ask a few more questions about them as well. Please circle only one answer for each question except question 8.

4. TURN BACK TO THE ENUMERATION AND LIST HOUSEHOLD MEMBERS 16 AND OVER IN ORDER, EXCLUDING R. THEN TURN TO COLORED (YELLOW AND IVORY) PAGES STARTING AT PAGE 9 AND CONTINUE COMPILING A LIST OF NAMES. CHECK FOR ACCURACY OF NAMING AND CORRECT MISTAKES. IS THE SAME NAME USED FOR A PERSON EACH TIME? IF NOT, MAKE NAMES CONSISTENT. IS THE SAME NAME USED FOR TWO PEOPLE? IF SO, USE INITIALS TO DIFFERENTIATE. IF GIVEN LAST NAME ONLY, USE INITIALS. (BE SURE TO CHECK 7Bb, PAGE 27, AND LAST NAME, IF GIVEN.)

* STARRED QUESTIONS ARE: TAKE CARE OF HOME (p. 9), SOCIALIZE (p. 27), LEISURE ACTIVITY (p. 27), PERSONAL MATTER (p. 28), JUDGMENT (p. 28), AND BORROW MONEY (p. 29).

N ☐ 70/

Y ☐☐ 71-72/

73-80/

SRC# (1-4) —— 5-6/09

7/1

-31-

80. [Booklet Page 6] Please turn to page 6 of the booklet. This is a list of some of the ways people are connected with each other. Some people will be related in more than one way. So, when I read you a name, please tell me all the ways that person is connected with you right now.

How is (NAME) connected with you now?
PROBE: Any other ways?
(WRITE RELATIONSHIP NEXT TO NAME ON LIST FORM)

> Relative (PROBE: How are you related?)
>
> Co-worker (someone you work with or see regularly at work)
>
> Neighbor
>
> Member of same organization (PROBE: What organization is that?)
>
> Friend
>
> Acquaintance
>
> Other (FOR EXAMPLE: spouse of friend, client, customer, former spouse)

CODE SEX.
IF NECESSARY: Is that a man or a woman?

[TEAR OFF LIST AND HAND TO RESPONDENT]

81a. Is there anyone who is important to you who doesn't show up on this list?

Yes 1
No (SKIP TO 82) 2   11/

b. IF YES: Who is that? ADD NAME. GET RELATIONSHIP AND SEX. CODE 1 IN COLUMN 81 OF LIST FORM.

82. Which of the people on this list do you feel especially close to?

No one 0
Any names (CODE 1 IN COLUMN 82) . . 1   12/

09

-32-

83. Which of the people on this list (other than the people who live here with you) live within about a five-minute drive from here?
IF NECESSARY: Within a mile.

No one............. 0
Any names (CODE 1 IN COLUMN 83) .. 1
13/

84. Which of the people on this list live outside this area, that is, more than an hour's drive from here?
IF NECESSARY: 30 to 40 miles.

No one............. 0
Any names (CODE 1 IN COLUMN 84) .. 1
14/

85a. Some people have a particular place they know they can go to and find their friends when they want to--it might be a park, club, coffee shop, a restaurant, or some other kind of place. Do you have any place like that where you and your friends tend to see each other?

Yes............. 1
No (SKIP TO NEXT PAGE)...... 2
15/

b. IF YES: Is that place within about a five-minute drive of here?

Yes............. 1
No............. 2
16/

c. Which of the people on this list do you usually see there?

No one............. 0
Any names (CODE 1 IN COLUMN 85) .. 1
17/

09

-33-

1. IF R FULL-TIME HOUSEWIFE, GO TO 86;
2. IF R EMPLOYED, LAID-OFF, LOOKING FOR WORK, OR RETIRED, SKIP TO 87;
3. IF R NEVER EMPLOYED, STUDENT, OR UNABLE TO WORK, SKIP TO NEXT PAGE.

86. IF R IS FULL-TIME HOUSEWIFE: Please look at the list of names again. Which of those people are also full-time homemakers?

No one (SKIP TO NEXT PAGE)..... 0
Any names (CODE 1 IN COLUMN 86) .. 1
18/

87a. IF R EMPLOYED, LAID-OFF, LOOKING FOR WORK, OR RETIRED: Please look at the list of names again. Which of those people do you think of as doing the same kind of work you (do/did)?

No one (SKIP TO NEXT PAGE)..... 0
Any names (CODE 1 IN COLUMN 87) .. 1
19/

b. How would you describe this kind of work?
20-21/

88a. Do you ever get together with a group of (TYPE OF WORKERS LISTED IN 87b) to socialize outside of work hours? (DO NOT INCLUDE LUNCH HOUR)

Yes............. 1
No (SKIP TO NEXT PAGE)...... 2
22/

b. IF YES: How often would you say that you get together--at least once a week, a few times a month, once a month, every few months, once or twice a year, or less often than that?

At least once a week....... 1
A few times a month....... 2
Once a month......... 3
Every few months........ 4
Once or twice a year....... 5
Less often than that....... 6
23/

09

-14-

89a. | Booklet Page 7 | Some people describe themselves by their race, ethnicity, or national background. On page 7 of the booklet are some examples of those descriptions. How would you describe yourself?
(RECORD RESPONSE)
IF NECESSARY: These are just examples.
IF ASKED WHY YOU WANT TO KNOW: We would like to know whether any of the people you know are of the same race, ethnicity, or national background as you.

_____   24-25/
_____   26-27/

    ┌───┐
    │ IF SINGLE DESCRIPTION GIVEN, SKIP TO 90;   │
    │ IF "NONE," "JUST AMERICAN," "DON'T KNOW," SKIP TO 92 │
    └───┘

b. IF MIXTURE: Is (either/any) of these more important to you (than the other/s)?

        Yes (SPECIFY: _____) . . . 1   28/
        No (SKIP TO 92) 2

                                                  29-30/

90a. Are any of the people on the list of names also (ETHNICITY IN 89a or b)?
        Yes 1   31/
        No (SKIP TO 91) 2

b. IF YES: Which ones are they? (RECORD 1 IN COLUMN 90 ON LIST)

91. Is it important to you to live in a place where there are other (ETHNICITY) people?
        Yes 1   32/
        No 2

92a. Did members of your family regularly speak a language other than English in your home when you were growing up?
        Yes 1   33/
        No (SKIP TO NEXT PAGE) 2

b. Do you ever speak it with your family or friends these days?
        Yes 1   34/
        No 2

09

-35-

93a. Now I'd like to ask you a little bit about your religion. What religion are you--Protestant, Roman Catholic, Jewish, or something else?
        Protestant 1   35/
        Catholic (SKIP TO 94) 2
        Jewish (SKIP TO 94) 3
        Something else (SPECIFY: _____
        AND SKIP TO 94) 4
        None (SKIP TO c) 5
                                (SKIP TO 94)

b. IF PROTESTANT: What denomination is that?
        _____   36-37/

c. IF NONE: What religion were you brought up in?   38/
        Protestant 1
        Catholic (SKIP TO 96) 2
        Jewish (SKIP TO 96) 3
        Something else (SPECIFY: _____
        AND SKIP TO 96) 4
        None (SKIP TO 96) 5
                                (SKIP TO 96)

d. IF PROTESTANT: What denomination were you raised in?
        _____   39-40/

94a. Are any of the people on the list of names (also) (RELIGION/DENOMINATION)?   41/
        Yes 1
        No (SKIP TO NEXT PAGE) 2
        Don't know (SKIP TO NEXT PAGE) . . 3

b. Which ones are they? (RECORD 1 IN COLUMN 94)

09

-36-

95a. Do you attend or take part in the religious activities of any (church/synagogue/spiritual group)?

Yes 1
No (SKIP TO c) 2   42/

b. IF YES: About how often do you attend (church/synagogue)--almost every week, about once a month, once or twice a year, or less often than that?   43/

Almost every week 1
About once a month 2
Once or twice a year 3
Less often than that 4

c. How important is it to you to live in an area where there is a (DENOMINATION church/synagogue/temple)--very important, somewhat important, or not too important?   44/

Very important 1
Somewhat important 2
Not too important 3

96a. Is there any particular activity--like a sport, organization, or some spare time interest--you devote a lot of time to or find especially interesting?   45/

Yes 1
No (SKIP TO 100) 2

b. IF YES: What is that?   46-47/

_____   48-49/

| IF ONLY ONE ACTIVITY, SKIP TO NEXT PAGE |

c. IF MORE THAN ONE ACTIVITY: Which of these do you find most important or devote the most time to, or are they (all) about the same?   50-51/

No single activity ☐ SKIP TO 100

09

-37-

...also (ACTIVITIES)?

Yes 1
No (SKIP TO 98) 2   52/

97a. Are any of the people on this list also (ACTIVITIES)?

b. IF YES: Which people are they? (CODE 1 IN COLUMN 97)

98a. Do you ever get together with a group of [ACTIVITIES] to have a good time other than when [ACTIVITING]?   53/

Yes 1
No (SKIP TO 99) 2

b. IF YES: How often would you say you get together other than (ACTIVITING)--about once a week or more, about once or twice a month, or less often than once a month?   54/

Once a week or more 1
Once or twice a month 2
Less often than once a month . . . 3

99. How important is it to you to live in a place where you can be around other people who (ACTIVITY)--very important, somewhat important, or not very important?   55/

Very important 1
Somewhat important 2
Not very important 3

09

-38-

100a. In the last few minutes I've asked you questions about work, ethnicity or national background, religion, and spare time activities. Sometimes people feel that one aspect of their lives is particularly important to them. Is one of the descriptions I just mentioned especially important to you?

Yes 1   56/
No (SKIP TO 101) 2

b. IF YES: Which description is that?   57/

Work 1
Ethnicity or national background . . . 2
Religion 3
Spare time activities 4

101. Thinking about the people you know, do you sometimes wish you knew more people you could talk with about personal matters and problems, or do you feel you already know enough people to talk with right now?

Wish knew more 1   58/
Already know enough people 2

102. Do you sometimes wish you knew more people you could get together with to have a good time, or do you feel you already know enough people like that?

Wish knew more 1   59/
Already know enough people 2

103. What about having people you can rely on to help you with things when you need it, things like work around the home or lending money—do you sometimes wish you knew more people like that, or do you already know enough people to rely on for help?

Wish knew more 1   60/
Already know enough people 2

09

-39-

Booklet Page 8: Please look at page 8 of the booklet.

[IF R LIVES ALONE, SKIP TO 106]

	A LOT OF THE TIME	SOME OF THE TIME	ONLY ONCE IN A WHILE	NEVER	
104. About how often do you feel that the people you live with make too many demands on you these days? (READ ALTERNATIVES).	1	2	3	4	61/
105. About how often do you feel that your friends and (other) relatives make too many demands on you?	1	2	3	4	62/
106. How often do you feel unhappy or a bit depressed these days?	1	2	3	4	63/
107. How often do you feel overwhelmed—that is, there is too much going on in your life for you to handle?	1	2	3	4	64/
108. How often do you feel particularly excited about or interested in something these days?	1	2	3	4	65/
109. How often do things get on your nerves so much that you feel like losing your temper?	1	2	3	4	66/
110. How often do you find that you have time on your hands with little to do?	1	2	3	4	67/
111. How often do you feel that things are going the way you want them to?.	1	2	3	4	68/
112. How often do you feel nervous, fidgety, or tense these days?	1	2	3	4	69/
113. How often do you feel pleased with what you're doing these days?.	1	2	3	4	70/
114. How often do you feel you are boiling inside with anger because of others these days?	1	2	3	4	71/
115. How often do you feel worried or upset?	1	2	3	4	72/

73-80/

09

-40-

116. Thinking about your life as a whole, how happy would you say you are these days—very happy, pretty happy, pretty unhappy, or very unhappy?

Very happy. 1
Pretty happy. 2
Pretty unhappy. 3
Very unhappy. 4

11/

Sometimes major events in people's lives affect their activities and relationships. I'd like to ask you whether any of these things have happened to you in the last year or so.

117a. Has a close relative or friend of yours died in the last year?

Yes 1
No (SKIP TO 118). 2

12/

b. IF YES: How was that person related to you? (CODE ALL THAT APPLY)

Spouse. 1   13/
Parent. 1   14/
Brother/sister. 1   15/
Child 1   16/
Other relative. 1   17/
Close friend. 1   18/
Other (SPECIFY): ___ / 1   19/

118a. In the last year, have you or anyone close to you had a serious illness or injury?

Yes 1   20/
No (SKIP TO 119). 2

-41-

b. IF YES: Who was that? (CODE ALL THAT APPLY)

Respondent. 1   21/
Spouse. 1   22/
Brother/sister. 1   23/
Parent. 1   24/
Child 1   25/
Another relative. 1   26/
Friend. 1   27/
Other (SPECIFY): ___ / 1   28/

c. Did that affect your daily activities much?

Yes 1   29/
No. 2

IF R DOES NOT HAVE SPOUSE, SKIP TO 120

119a. Have you and [(your) (SPOUSE)] been having any trouble getting along in the last year?

Yes 1   30/
No (SKIP TO 120). 2

b. IF YES: How serious would you say these difficulties are—very serious, somewhat serious, or not too serious?

Very serious. 1   31/
Somewhat serious. 2
Not too serious 3

120a. Have you had any financial problems?

Yes 1   32/
No (SKIP TO NEXT PAGE). . . 2

b. IF YES: How serious would you say they are—very serious, somewhat serious, or not too serious?

Very serious. 1   33/
Somewhat serious. 2
Not too serious 3

-42-

121a. Do you have any chronic illness or disability?

    Yes 1   34/
    No *(SKIP TO INSTRUCTION)*. . . . 2

b. *IF YES:* In general, how much does this limit your ability to get around-- a lot, some, or not at all?

    A lot 1   35/
    Some 2
    Not at all 3

Now, just a few background questions and then we'll be done.

> *IF R NEVER MARRIED, SKIP TO INSTRUCTION*

122. You said you were (married/divorced/separated/widowed). How long have you been _____?

    Number of years   36-37/
    If less than one year, number of months   38-39/

123. Do you have any children who do not live here with you?
IF NECESSARY: Of any age.

    Yes 1   40/
    No *(SKIP TO INSTRUCTION)*. . . . 2

b. *IF YES:* How many?

    Number of children not in household   41-42/

> *IF R NOT "LIVING TOGETHER," SKIP TO NEXT PAGE*

124. *IF R "LIVING TOGETHER":* You said that you're living with (SPOUSE). How long have you been living together?

    Number of years   43-44/
    If less than one year, number of months   45-46/

-43-

125a. What was the highest grade or year you completed in school?

    Grade school: 0 1 2 3 4 5 6 7 8 *(SKIP TO 126)*   47-48/
    High school: 1 2 3 4 (9 10 11 12)*(SKIP TO 126)*
    College: 1 2 3 4 5 plus (13 14 15 16 17)
    Technical/ trade/business: 1 2 3 4 5 plus *(SKIP TO 126)*

49/

b. *IF COLLEGE 5+:* What was the highest degree you received?   50/

    B.A., B.S. 1
    B.A., M.S. 2
    Ph.D. 3
    L.L.D. 4
    D.D. 5
    M.D. 6
    D.D.S. 7
    Other *(SPECIFY:_____)* 8

126a. Are you attending any school or taking any classes this fall?

    Yes 1   51/
    No *(SKIP TO NEXT PAGE)* 2

b. *IF YES:* Are you working toward a diploma or degree?

    Yes 1   52/
    No *(SKIP TO NEXT PAGE)* 2

c. *IF YES:* What diploma or degree do you expect to receive next?   53/

    High school diploma 1
    Junior college degree (AA) . . . 2
    Four year college degree (BA, BS) . 3
    Master's 4
    Ph.D., M.D., L.L.D., D.D.S. . . . 5
    Technical/professional 6
    Other *(SPECIFY:_____)* 7

d. About how often do you feel that your school work puts too many demands on you--much of the time, pretty often, occasionally, or almost never?   54/

    Much of the time 1
    Pretty often 2
    Occasionally 3
    Almost never 4

-44-

IF R DOES NOT HAVE A SPOUSE, SKIP TO INSTRUCTION

127a. What was the highest grade or year your (SPOUSE) completed in school?

Grade school: 0 1 2 3 4 5 6 7 8 (SKIP TO 128)

High school: 1 2 3 4 (9 10 11 12) (SKIP TO 128)

College: 1 2 3 4 5 plus (13 14 15 16 17)   55-56/

Technical/
trade/business: 1 2 3 4 5 plus (SKIP TO 128)   57/

b. IF COLLEGE 5+: What was the highest degree (he/she) received?   58/

B.A., B.S. 1
M.A., M.S. 2
Ph.D. 3
L.L.D. 4
D.D. 5
M.D. 6
D.D.S. 7
Other (SPECIFY): _____ 8

IF HOUSEHOLD HEAD IS R OR R'S SPOUSE, SKIP TO NEXT PAGE

128a. What kind of business or industry does (HOUSEHOLD HEAD) work for?
    PROBE: What do they do or make at the place where (he/she) works?   59-61/

b. What kind of work does (he/she) do?
    PROBE: What is (his/her) job title?   62-64/

10

-45-

129. | Booklet
Page 9 | Please look at page 9 of the booklet and give me the letter of the income group that includes your personal income before taxes. This figure should include all of your income--wages, salaries, interest, dividends, (child support), and all other incomes. |
|---|---|

IF UNCERTAIN: What would be your best guess?
(CIRCLE THE NUMBER AND ENTER IN "INCOME CODE" BELOW)

A. None or loss. 00   J. $15,000 to $19,999. 09
B. Less than $3,000. 01   K. $20,000 to $24,999. 10
C. $3,000 to $3,999. 02   L. $25,000 to $29,999. 11
D. $4,000 to $4,999. 03   M. $30,000 to $34,999. 12
E. $5,000 to $5,999. 04   N. $35,000 to $39,999. 13
F. $6,000 to $7,999. 05   O. $40,000 to $49,999. 14
G. $8,000 to $9,999. 06   P. $50,000 to $74,999. 15
H. $10,000 to $11,999. 07   Q. $75,000 and over. 16
I. $12,000 to $14,999. 08

Income code [ ]   65-66/

IF R IS ONLY ADULT IN HOUSEHOLD, SKIP TO NEXT PAGE

130. Please give me the letter of the income group that includes your (family/household) income before taxes. This figure should include all of the (family/household) income--wages, salaries, interest, dividends, child support, and all other incomes.

IF UNCERTAIN: What would be your best guess?
(CIRCLE THE NUMBER AND ENTER IN "INCOME CODE" BELOW)

A. None or loss. 00   J. $15,000 to $19,999. 09
B. Less than $3,000. 01   K. $20,000 to $24,999. 10
C. $3,000 to $3,999. 02   L. $25,000 to $29,999. 11
D. $4,000 to $4,999. 03   M. $30,000 to $34,999. 12
E. $5,000 to $5,999. 04   N. $35,000 to $39,999. 13
F. $6,000 to $7,999. 05   O. $40,000 to $49,999. 14
G. $8,000 to $9,999. 06   P. $50,000 to $74,999. 15
H. $10,000 to $11,999. 07   Q. $75,000 and over. 16
I. $12,000 to $14,999. 08   R. Income not shared 17

Income code [ ]   67-68/

10

-48-　　　SRC# (1-4)　　5-6/11

7/1

DO NOT ASK--INTERVIEWER OBSERVATIONS

1. Respondent's ethnicity:　11/

   White or Anglo. 1
   Mexican American. 2
   Other Spanish-American. 3
   Black. 4
   Chinese, Japanese, Korean . . . 5
   Other (SPECIFY: _____)　6

2. Did the respondent have any difficulty hearing the questions?　12/

   Yes, great difficulty. 1
   Yes, some difficulty. 2
   No, none at all 3

3. Did the respondent have any difficulty reading the answer booklet?　13/

   Yes, could or did not read at all. 1
   Yes, read with great difficulty. . 2
   Yes, read with some difficulty. . . 3
   No, none at all 4

4. Did the respondent have any difficulty understanding the questions?　14/

   Yes, great difficulty. 1
   Yes, some difficulty. 2
   No, none at all 3

5. What was the respondent's initial attitude about being interviewed?　15/

   Very interested or enthusiastic . . 1
   Somewhat interested 2
   Indifferent 3
   Somewhat reluctant. 4
   Very reluctant. 5
   Hard to tell. 6

11

-46-

131a. Is there a telephone in this (house/apartment)?　69/

   Yes (SKIP TO c). 1
   No 2

b. IF NO PHONE IN (HOUSE/APARTMENT): Is there a telephone (in this building) on which you can be called?　70/

   Yes. 1
   No (SKIP TO END) 2

c. IF CAN BE REACHED ON ANY PHONE: May I have the number? RECORD ON FRONT COVER.

71-80/

Thank you very much for your time and cooperation.

Time: _____

-49-

6. What was the respondent's attitude during the interview?

Friendly, eager, volunteered information 1
Cooperative, but not particularly enthusiastic 2
Indifferent or bored 3
Often irritated or hostile--seemed anxious to get it over with 4
Hard to tell 5
16/

7a. Was anyone else present during the interview?

Yes, for most of the interview . . 1
Yes, for some of the interview . . 2
Yes, but only for a minute or two (SKIP TO 8) 3
No, not at any time (SKIP TO 8) . . 4
17/

b. IF OTHER PRESENT FOR MORE THAN A MINUTE OR TWO: Who else was present?

           YES
Husband or wife 1 18/
Other adult household member (18 or over) 1 19/
Teenager (13 to 18) 1 20/
Child or infant (under 13) 1 21/
Friend, visitor, other (SPECIFY: _____) 1 22/

8. Did the respondent speak with a foreign or regional accent?

Yes, a heavy accent 1
Yes, a slight accent 2
No 3
23/

9. Did the respondent have any obvious physical disabilities or impairments, such as loss of limb, paralysis, facial disfigurement, serious speech problems, palsy, or the like?

No, none of these 0
Yes (SPECIFY: _____) 1
24/

-50-

10a. In giving you names of people, did you get the impression that the respondent was exaggerating by giving you extra names?

Yes 1
No (SKIP TO 11) 2
25/

b. IF YES: On what questions did that happen?

11a. Did you get the impression that the respondent was trying to limit the number of names (he/she) gave you?

Yes 1
No (SKIP TO 12) 2
26/

b. IF YES: On what questions did that happen?

12. Aside from what (he/she) said in answer to the specific questions, is it your impression that the respondent leads a very busy and active life; that (he/she) doesn't really have much to do; or that (he/she) is about average?

Very busy and active 1
Doesn't have much to do 2
About average 3
27/

13. How open and forthcoming do you think the respondent was about (his/her) personal problems and feelings?

Open 1
A little guarded 2
Was basically not frank 3
28/

14. Did you observe any signs of tension or stress in the respondent's behavior?

No 1
Yes, some 2
Yes, a lot 3
29/

-51-

Comments

Please give a brief report of your contact with the respondent, including any information or impressions that you think might help us understand the respondent's household structure, sexual orientation, situation in the neighborhood, social relations, and personal feelings. Also, please note anything particular about the appearance of the respondent and (his/her) home that would help us understand the type of person (he/she) is.

30-31/
32-33/
34-35/

15. What kind of building does the respondent live in?   36/

Single family detached. 1
Duplex, town house, row house . . . 2
Low-rise apartment (2 stories or less). 3
High-rise apartment (3 stories or more). 4
Trailer 5
Other (SPECIFY: _____) 6

11

-52-

16. What types of buildings are on the respondent's street (both sides of street on same block): (CODE ALL THAT APPLY)

Single family detached homes. . . 1   37/
Duplexes, town houses, or row houses 1   38/
Low-rise apartments (2 stories or less) 1   39/
High-rise apartments (3 or more stories). 1   40/
Trailers. 1   41/
Commercial facilities 1   42/
Industry. 1   43/
Institutional structures (schools, churches, hospitals, etc.). . . 1   44/
Other (SPECIFY: _____) 1   45/

17. How far is the respondent's building from the nearest adjacent building-- a few feet, no more than the width of a driveway, or more than that?

A few feet or less. 1   46/
No more than the width of a driveway. 2
More than that. 3

18. What does the front door of the respondent's (house/apartment) face?

Corridor. 1   47/
Inner court. 2
Another building. 3
Front lawn. 4
Sidewalk. 5
Other (SPECIFY: _____) 6

19. Did you see any of the following in the respondent's home or on its grounds? (CODE ALL THAT APPLY)

Burglar protection signs. 1   48/
Alarms. 1   49/
Barking dogs. 1   50/
Many locks on door. 1   51/
Chain-link fence. 1   52/
Grills on doors, windows. 1   53/
None of these or not ascertainable. 1   54/

NON-INTERVIEW INFORMATION

SRC# (1-4) _____ 5-6/B 7/5
Place (8=9) N (ID)

N1. Was this dwelling unit occupied or vacant?
1. Occupied 1   11/
2. Vacant (COMPLETE BOX BELOW) . . . 2

CHECK ONE:

□ Structure demolished, in process of demolition, or obviously not inhabitable. . . . 1   12/

□ Confirmed vacancy of inhabitable structure (LIST NAME AND ADDRESS OF NEIGHBOR CONFIRMING VACANCY) . . . 2

□ Unconfirmed vacancy. EXPLAIN WHY VACANCY COULD NOT BE CONFIRMED: _____ . . . 3

□ Temporary residence of person with usual residence elsewhere . . . 4   13/

N2. Reason for non-interview in occupied dwelling unit (CHECK ONE):
□ No one ever at home in four calls 1
□ Someone seems to be home, but no one answers the door . . . 2
□ Respondent never at home in four calls, other household member. . . . 3
□ Direct refusal. (Respondent or other household member said (he/she) would not cooperate.) INDICATE REASON IF GIVEN: _____ . . . 4
□ Indirect refusal. Always "too busy," two or more broken appointments, etc. EXPLAIN: _____ . . . 5
□ R does not speak English. 6
□ Other. EXPLAIN: _____ . . . 7

N3. IF YOU DID TALK TO SOMEONE: Did you talk to the designated R or not?
Yes, spoke to R. 1   14/
No, spoke only to someone else . . 2

N4. PLEASE ANSWER THE FOLLOWING QUESTIONS FOR THE RESPONDENT, IF POSSIBLE, IF NOT FOR WHOEVER YOU TALKED TO:

a. Sex : Male 1   15/
         Female 2

b. Ethnicity : White 1   16/
               Black 2
               Chicano 3
               Asian 4
               Other 5

c. What kind of building does R live in?
   Single family detached 1   17/
   Duplex, town house, row house, ... 2
   Low-rise apt. (2 stories or less), . . 3
   High-rise apt. (3 and over stories) . . 4
   Trailer. 5
   Other (SPECIFY: _____ . . 6

-53-

20. How well kept up is the outside of the respondent's house and yard/ apartment building?

Very attractive 1   55/
Well kept up. 2
A bit worn down 3
Very poorly kept up 4

21. How well kept up are the outsides of the few buildings near the respondent's dwelling?

Very attractive 1   56/
Well kept up. 2
A bit worn down. 3
Very poorly kept up. 4
A mixture of well kept up and poorly kept up. 5

22. How much activity--cars and/or people--was there on the street?

A great deal. 1   57/
Some. 2
Almost none. 3

PLEASE CHECK TO BE SURE THAT YOU'VE SPECIFIED THE RELATIONSHIP OF OTHER HOUSEHOLD MEMBERS TO THE RESPONDENT ON THE ENUMERATION PAGE, COLUMN E1b. INCLUDE AS "CHILD" ANY MINOR FOR WHOM R (OR SPOUSE) IS PRIMARILY RESPONSIBLE.

11

SRC# _____
(1-4)
Pers. # _____
(5-6)
7/3
Place: _____
N: _____
(10)

_____
(NAME)

1. How did you first meet this person? 11-12/
01. We're in the same family
02. Grew up together
03. In school
04. At work
05. As neighbors
06. In a group or organization
07. Through a friend
08. Through my (husband/wife)
09. Through my child
10. Other (HOW: _____)

2. About how many years have you 13-14/
known this person?
_____ years

3. What city does this person live in? 15-17/

_____
(CITY)

_____
(STATE)

4. How often do you usually get together 18/
with this person?
1. More than once a week
2. About once a week
3. Two or three times a month
4. About once a month
5. Several times a year
6. About once a year
7. Less often than that

5. What is this person's age? 19-20/
_____ years

6. Is this person currently 21/
employed either full-time or
part-time?
1. Employed full-time
2. Employed part-time
3. Not currently employed

7. Is this person presently 22/
1. Married
2. Widowed
3. Divorced
4. Separated
5. Never married
6. I don't know

8. Does this person have children? 23/
(CIRCLE ALL THAT APPLY)
1. No--no children 24/
2. Yes--pre-school children 25/
3. Yes--school-age children 26/
4. Yes--children over 18 27/
5. I don't know

MATRIX FORM

NAMES FROM STARRED ✳ QUESTIONS

LIST THE 5 SELECTED NAMES DOWN THE COLUMN: LIST THE FIRST 4 OF THEM ACROSS
THE TOP, IN THE SAME ORDER. IN THE SPACES PROVIDED. ASK ABOUT ALL RELATIONSHIPS
IN COLUMN 1; THEN ABOUT ALL RELATIONSHIPS IN COLUMN 2, ETC.

	Do 1, and (2,3,4,5) know each other well?	Do 2, and (3,4,5) know each other well?	Do 3, and (4,5) know each other well?	Do 4, and (5) know each other well?
1. _____				
2. _____	Yes.....1 No.....2			
3. _____	Yes.....1 No.....2	Yes.....1 No.....2		
4. _____	Yes.....1 No.....2	Yes.....1 No.....2	Yes.....1 No.....2	
5. _____	Yes.....1 No.....2	Yes.....1 No.....2	Yes.....1 No.....2	Yes.....1 No.....2

✳ STARRED QUESTIONS ARE:

TAKE CARE OF HOME	p. 9
SOCIALIZE	p. 27
LEISURE ACTIVITY	p. 27
PERSONAL MATTER	p. 28
JUDGMENT	p. 28
BORROW MONEY	p. 29

SRC# ____ (1-4)

QUESTION	NAME	SEX	RELATIONSHIP	R1	R2	R3	R4	R5	R6	R7	PLACE N
81 82 83 84 85 86 87 90 94 97		M F	Relative: NON RELATED Friend: F Acquaintance: A Co-worker: W Co-member of Org: NAME OF ORG. Neighbor: N Other: SPECIFY								
(5-7/ (8) (9)(10)(11)(12)(13)(14)(15)(16)(17)		(18)		(19-20)(21)(22)(23)(24)(25)(26) (27-28)(29)							

SPOUSE

#	Name	M	F
00		1	2
01		1	2
02		1	2
03		1	2
04		1	2
05		1	2
06		1	2
07		1	2
08		1	2
09		1	2
10		1	2
11		1	2
12		1	2
13		1	2
14		1	2
15		1	2
16		1	2
17		1	2
18		1	2
19		1	2
20		1	2
21		1	2
22		1	2
23		1	2
24		1	2
25		1	2
26		1	2
27		1	2

C   Informant Questionnaire

UNIVERSITY OF CALIFORNIA, BERKELEY

BERKELEY · DAVIS · IRVINE · LOS ANGELES · RIVERSIDE · SAN DIEGO · SAN FRANCISCO   SANTA BARBARA · SANTA CRUZ

INSTITUTE OF URBAN AND REGIONAL DEVELOPMENT   BERKELEY, CALIFORNIA 94720
642-4874

My colleagues and I at the University of California are engaged in a study of how different features of local communities affect the people who live in them. To do this, we are collecting information about fifty neighborhoods and towns in Northern California, including the area outlined on the enclosed map. We understand that you are in a position to be particularly knowledgeable about this area, and we would greatly appreciate your answering a few questions about it. Would you please take a few minutes to fill out this brief questionnaire and return it to us in the enclosed self-addressed, stamped envelope?

Your advice on these matters is very important to our understanding of the quality of life in local areas. The information you provide will be held in strictest confidence. It will be published only in the form of statistical summaries or descriptive profiles in which no individual, agency, or neighborhood can be identified.

We hope you will agree to participate in the study. The more we learn about people and their communities, the more that can be done to make them better places to live. Let me thank you in advance for your time and cooperation. I think you will find the questionnaire an interesting one.

Sincerely,

Claude S. Fischer, Ph.D
Project Director

COMMUNITIES IN NORTHERN CALIFORNIA

INSTRUCTIONS

Please help us by answering the following questionnaire about the area outlined on the map above. Try to answer all the questions, even if you feel unsure about some of your responses; your estimates and best guesses will provide us with valuable information. Skip questions only if you are totally unfamiliar with the topic.

1. Looking at the map, how much new construction and/or demolition has there been since 1970? PLEASE CHECK ONE ANSWER FOR EACH OF THE FOLLOWING.

	A lot	Some	A few	None
a) How many new homes and/or apartments have been built since 1970?	☐	☐	☐	☐
b) How many housing units have been torn down since 1970?	☐	☐	☐	☐
c) How many houses and/or apartments have been renovated or restored since 1970?	☐	☐	☐	☐

2a. How much commercial or industrial building has there been in this area or nearby (i.e., within a five minute drive) since 1970? PLEASE CHECK ONE BOX.

☐ A lot	☐ Some	☐ A little
☐ No recent building		☐ Not applicable -- no businesses or industry nearby.

2b. How many large plants or businesses in or near this area have shut down and not been replaced since 1970?

☐ A lot	☐ Some	☐ A few
☐ No recent shut downs		☐ Not applicable -- no plants or businesses nearby

-3-

3. How many people living in this area belong to each of the following racial or ethnic groups? PLEASE CHECK ONE BOX FOR EACH GROUP.

	Almost Nobody	A Few	Less Than Half	About Half	More Than Half	Almost Everyone
a) White	☐	☐	☐	☐	☐	☐
b) Black	☐	☐	☐	☐	☐	☐
c) Asian	☐	☐	☐	☐	☐	☐
d) Mexican-American or other Spanish speaking group	☐	☐			☐	☐
e) Other (Please specify) ___	☐	☐			☐	☐

4. How many families or households in this area belong to each of the following household types? PLEASE CHECK ONE BOX FOR EACH TYPE.

	Almost None	A Few	Less Than Half	About Half	More Than Half	Almost All
a) Young singles or young couples without children	☐	☐	☐	☐	☐	☐
b) Households with children under eighteen	☐	☐	☐	☐	☐	☐
c) Older people without children at home	☐	☐	☐	☐	☐	☐

5. Would you say that most households in this area have fairly low annual incomes (under $8000), fairly high annual incomes (over $20,000), mostly in between ($8000 to $20,000), or is there a real mix of incomes in this area?

☐ Most have fairly low incomes
☐ Most have fairly high incomes
☐ Most have something in between
☐ Real mix of incomes in the area

348 Appendix C

-4-

6. Has there been any major change in the ethnic, racial, age, or income characteristics of this area since 1970? Any other major changes?

[ ] Yes →   [ ] No → PLEASE SKIP TO QUESTION 7.

6a. PLEASE CHECK ALL MAJOR CHANGES THAT APPLY AND BRIEFLY DESCRIBE THEM.

[ ] Ethnic/racial? _____

[ ] Age? _____

[ ] Income? _____

[ ] Other? _____

7. Would you say that people here are pretty similar to each other in their lifestyles (e.g., leisure time activities, appearance, and the like), or is there a lot of variety?

[ ] Everyone is pretty similar   [ ] There is a lot of variety   [ ] There are one or two distinct groups

8. Have most people in this area lived here for a long time (over 15 years), for a moderate amount of time (5 to 15 years), for a short time (less than 5 years), or does it vary a lot?

[ ] Long time   [ ] Moderate amount of time   [ ] Short time   [ ] Varies a lot

9a. How worried would you say that people here are about crime in this area?

[ ] Very worried   [ ] Somewhat worried   [ ] A little worried   [ ] Not at all worried

9b. What kind of crime are they most worried about? _____

-5-

10. How active would you say most residents are in community affairs?

[ ] Very active   [ ] Moderately active   [ ] Not too active

11. Is there any street or center in this area or nearby (i.e., within a five minute drive) where residents can either shop or go for entertainment?

[ ] Yes →   [ ] No → PLEASE SKIP TO QUESTION 12.

11a. Where is the nearest one(s) located? _____

11b. What is its name, if any? _____

12. What would you say are the best things about living in the area outlined on the map?

13. What would you say are the worst things about living in this area?

-6-

14. In the next set of questions, we'd like your estimates of how well various services are meeting the needs of the people who live in the area.

a) Thinking about the number of roads and highways, their upkeep, and the amount of traffic, how easy is it for residents (who drive) to get where they want to go?

☐ Very easy   ☐ Pretty easy   ☐ Not too easy   ☐ Difficult

b) Thinking about the availability of public transportation and its routes, schedules, and crowding, how easy is it for residents to get where they want to go on public transportation?

☐ Very easy   ☐ Pretty easy   ☐ Not too easy   ☐ Difficult

c) How would you rate the quality of the public schools that most children in this area attend?

☐ Very good   ☐ Good   ☐ Fair   ☐ Poor

d) Thinking about the amount of crime in this area and about the size and responsiveness of the police force, how would you rate the quality of police protection in this area?

☐ Very good   ☐ Good   ☐ Fair   ☐ Poor

e) Thinking about the availability and quality of other public services (e.g., fire protection, garbage collection, sewage disposal), how well do these services meet the needs of the residents in this area?

☐ Very well   ☐ Pretty well   ☐ Not too well   ☐ Poorly

f) How wide a range of stores and commercial services (e.g., hardware stores, department stores, laundromats) is there in this area or nearby?

☐ Wide range   ☐ Fair range   ☐ Limited range   ☐ No stores or services conveniently available

g) How wide a range of outdoor recreational facilities (e.g., parks, lakes, golf courses, tennis courts) is there in this area or nearby?

☐ Wide range   ☐ Fair range   ☐ Limited range   ☐ No facilities conveniently available

h) How wide a range of indoor entertainment facilities (e.g., movies, bars, bowling alleys) is there in this area or nearby?

☐ Wide range   ☐ Fair range   ☐ Limited range   ☐ No facilities conveniently available

-7-

15. How seriously has the water shortage affected the income and jobs of people in this area?

☐ Very seriously   ☐ Somewhat seriously   ☐ Not seriously   ☐ No effect at all

16. We can't tell for certain where a neighborhood begins and ends. Does the area outlined on the map accurately describe a single local community of neighborhood, or are our boundaries misplaced?

☐ Boundaries OK → PLEASE SKIP TO QUESTION 17.
☐ Boundaries misplaced

16a. PLEASE CORRECT OUR BOUNDARIES ON THE MAP, AND DESCRIBE BELOW WHY YOU MADE THE CHANGES YOU DID. FEEL FREE TO WRITE ON THE MAP.

_____

_____

_____

17. Does the area on the map have a name? (Use the boundaries you have drawn if ours are misplaced.)

☐ Yes →   ☐ No → PLEASE SKIP TO QUESTION 18.

17a. What is its name? _____

18. How familiar are you with the area outlined on the map?

☐ Very familiar   ☐ Somewhat familiar   ☐ Not too familiar

19. Are there any other people or agencies that might be able to give us more information about this area -- for example, local shop-keepers, ministers, people active in local civic affairs, real estate agencies, or the like? If so, where might we contact them?

Name _____

Address _____   Phone Number _____

-8-

20. If we need further information, may we call you?

☐ Yes →   ☐ No

20a. Where can we reach you and when is the best time to call?

Name: _____

Phone Number: _____

When available: _____

Thank you for your help. If there is anything else that is special about this area, we would greatly appreciate your comments.

Comments:

Serial Number _____

Notes

Chapter 1

1. This thesis is omnipresent. It appears, albeit with notable variations, in the work of social philosophers as different as de Tocqueville, Marx, Durkheim, Tönnies, Simmel, and Fromm. Among the notable variations is the extent to which this breakdown in community also brings with it individual freedom (cf. Simmel, Parsons, Shils) or totalitarianism (cf. Fromm, Marcuse, C. W. Mills). Among the contemporary statements are those of Maurice Stein, *Eclipse of Community* (New York: Harper and Row, 1960), and Robert Nisbet, *Community and Power* (New York: Oxford University Press, 1969). Treatments of the theme include Thomas Bender, *Community and Social Change in America* (New Brunswick: Rutgers University Press, 1978); J. Gusfield, *Community* (Oxford: Basil Blackwell, 1975); Raymond Williams, *The Country and the City* (New York: Oxford University Press, 1973); and Leo Marx, *The Machine in the Garden* (New York: Oxford University Press, 1964). I present my own interpretation, in detail, in chapters 1 and 10 of C. S. Fischer et al., *Networks and Places* (New York: Free Press, 1977).

2. This link is clear in the major theoretical statements (e.g., Emile Durkheim's *Division of Labor in Society* [1893] New York: Free Press, 1933); in literary expression (see Raymond Williams's *Country and the City*), and in social science analyses—for example, anthropologists at a recent symposium interchangeably used the modern/traditional and the urban/rural distinctions (*Scale and Social Organization,* ed. F. Barth [Oslo: Universitetsforlaget, 1978]). There are, of course, problems with this analogy, particularly the vivid existence of large cities in traditional societies. Nevertheless, it is important and fruitful (cf. my discussion of urbanism in the context of the classical theories of the "great transformation" in C. S. Fischer, "The Study of Urban Community and Personality," *Annual Review of Sociology* 1 [1975]:67–89).

3. Stephen Lukes points out, for example, that Durkheim's main concern was to answer the question, "What are the bonds which unite men with one another?" (S. Lukes, *Emile Durkheim* [Baltimore: Penguin, 1973], p. 139).

4. A few of the initial formulations of "network analysis" as used here are: E. Bott, *Family and Social Network,* 2d ed. (New York: Free Press, 1971); J. A. Barnes, "Class and Committee in a Norwegian Island Parish," *Human Relations* 7 (1954):39–58; J. Henry, "The Personal Community and Its Invariant Properties," *American Anthropologist* 60 (October 1958):827–31; F. E. Katz, "Social Participation and Social Structure," *Social Forces* 45 (December 1966):199–210. Among the basic references are J. C. Mitchell, ed., *Social Networks in Urban Situations* (Manchester: University of Manchester Press, 1969), and J. Boissevain, *Friends of Friends* (London: Basil Blackwell, 1974).

5. Research on "social support" for physical and mental health has burgeoned in recent years. See, for example, L. F. Berkman and S. L. Syme, "Social Networks, Host Resistance, and Mortality," *American Journal of Epidemiology* 109 (1979):186–204; S. Cobb, "Social Support as a Moderator of Life Stress," *Psychosomatic Medicine* 38 (1976):300–314; A. Dean and N. Lin, "The Stress-Buffering Role of Social Support," *Journal of Nervous and Mental Diseases* 164 (1977):7–15.

6. P. Starr, "Impersonal Caretakers," *New York Times Book Review* 6 April 1980, p. 30.

7. On the formation of relations, see L. M. Verbrugge, "The Structure of Adult Friendship Choices," *Social Forces* 56 (December 1977):576–97, and R. M. Jackson, "Social Structure and Process in Friendship Choice" in Fischer et al., *Networks and Places*.

8. P. G. Cressy, "The Taxi-Dance Hall as a Social World" (1932), in *The Social Fabric of the Metropolis*, ed. J. F. Short, Jr., pp. 193–209 (Chicago: University of Chicago Press, 1971).

9. R. E. Park, "The City: Suggestions for the Investigation of Human Behavior in the Urban Environment," in *The City*, ed. R. E. Park and E. W. Burgess (Chicago: University of Chicago Press, 1967), p. 40 (originally published 1925).

10. R. E. Park, "The Urban Community as a Spatial Pattern and a Moral Order" (1926), in *Robert Park on Social Control and Collective Behavior*, ed. R. H. Turner (Chicago: University of Chicago Press, 1971), pp. 67–86.

11. For a detailed discussion of the role of the local community, see P. Rossi, "Community Social Indicators," in *The Human Meaning of Social Change,* ed. A. Campbell and P. E. Converse, pp. 87–126 (New York: Russell Sage, 1972).

12. This stream of thought in America has been documented by M. White and L. White, *The Intellectual versus the City* (New York: Mentor, 1962), among others. David Hummon presents the "folk" understandings of the general population in "Community Ideology" (Ph.D. diss., Department of Sociology, University of California, Berkeley, 1980). And a survey conducted in urban Arizona shows the pervasiveness of these beliefs: 92 percent said that people were friendlier in nonmetropolitan than in metropolitan communities; 83 percent said mental health was better, and 78 percent said it was better to raise children in less urban places (table 6 in E. H. Carpenter, "Residential Preference and Community Size," report no. 7, Department of Agricultural Economics, University of Arizona, 1975). A national survey showed similar patterns (Louis Harris Associates, *A Survey of Citizen Views and Concerns about Urban Life* [Washington, D.C.: Department of Housing and Urban Development, 1978]).

13. The major source works are: G. Simmel, "The Metropolis and Mental Life" (1905), in *Classic Essays on the Culture of Cities*, ed. R. Sennett, pp. 47–60 (New York: Appleton-Century-Crofts, 1969); R. Park, "The City: Suggestions for Investigation of Human Behavior in the Urban Environment" (1916), in R. Sennett, *Classic Essays*, pp. 91–130; L. Wirth, "Urbanism as a Way of Life," *American Journal of Sociology* 44 (July 1938):3–24; R. Redfield, "The Folk Society," *American Journal of Sociology* 52, no. 4 (1947):293–308; and S. Milgram, "The Experience of Living in Cities," *Science* 167 (March 1970):1461–68. Similar points are found in the work of Tönnies, Durkheim, and others. For a summary of the argument, see C. S. Fischer, *The Urban Experience* (New York: Harcourt Brace Jovanovich, 1976), chap. 2.

14. Park, "The City," pp. 24–25.

15. Fischer, *Urban Experience*.

16. On the public's views, see note 12. On opinion leaders, see virtually any article or political speech—liberal or conservative—concerned with alienation, family, stress, moral decay, or "quality of life." Consult almost any document drafted from an environmentalist-organie-holistic perspective.

17. F. Davis, quoted by G. Berreman, "Scale and Social Relations," in Barth, *Scale and Social Organization*, p. 73.

18. C. S. Fischer, "Toward a Subcultural Theory of Urbanism," *American Journal of Sociology* 80 (May 1975):1319–41; see also Fischer, *Urban Experience*.

19. Park, "The City as a Social Laboratory" (1929), in *Robert Park on Social Control and Collective Behavior*, ed. R. H. Turner (Chicago: University of Chicago Press, 1971), p. 18.

Chapter 2

1. That is, I am assuming, in the absence of any reasons not to, that there is no interaction effect between urbanism and region.

2. Of the residents of Semirural places, 79 percent picked the term "small towns" or "farm, rural, wilderness" when asked to describe their towns (q. 4). The major exceptions were residents of two distant suburbs of Sacramento—ranking at the top of the Semirural category—most of whom preferred the term "suburb."

3. The analysis in this section was prepared in part by Robert Fitzgerald.

4. These comments are based on several analyses of the associations between urbanism and individual characteristics. Table N1 summarizes one of those analyses. Cross-tabulations using smaller periods generally confirm the same point: differentiation along the urbanism continuum is as great among recent movers as among longtime residents, or greater. (Treating urbanism as a dependent variable in a casual model is problematic, since there are certainly feedback loops. For example, urban jobs often pay more than equivalent rural ones, cities provide more community colleges, and so forth. My point is not, however, to present a true causal model, but simply to demonstrate the independent association of each trait with urbanism. It remains plausible that most of each association can be explained with urbanism as the dependent variable. The strength of the associations among newcomers supports that claim.)

5. It is difficult to match our correlations between individual characteristics and urbanism with those from census data. One reason is that our categories are quite different from those of the census, and another is that our interviews were done seven years after the most complete census estimates. My impression is that a thorough comparison would show that the associations of education and life cycle with urbanism among our respondents are stronger than those in the 1970 census. This may not be sampling error, however, but instead may be an accurate reflection of a rapidly changing situation. According to census estimates, while there has been an overall net migration, especially of retirees, from metropolitan to nonmetropolitan areas, young and well-educated adults have shown a net migration in the other direction, toward central cities. (See, for example, B. J. L. Berry and D. C. Dahman, *Population Redistribution in the United States in the 1970s* [Washington, D.C.: National Academy of Sciences, 1977].)

6. *San Francisco Examiner*, 28 October 1979.

7. We developed the list of responses from those that eighty respondents in one of our pilot surveys gave in answer to an open-ended question on the topic.

8. Our coding of who was a homosexual is based on the interviewers' impressions. Often, those impressions were in turn based on straightforward statements by respondents, but there no doubt is some error here. See chapter 18 for more on homosexuals in our study.

9. These claims would be unwarranted if the table merely reflected life-cycle differences and not place differences—if, for example, young singles everywhere cited people and things to do. In fact, the reasons result from both person and place: (1) While 43 percent of young singles in the Core cited "people," only 24 percent of others in the Core did, *and only 12 percent of young singles elsewhere* did. Similar differences emerge with respect to "things to do." (2) While 55 percent of young parents in Town or Metropolitan places cited job or school, 48 percent of others in those communities did, and only 38 percent of young parents elsewhere did. (3) While 55 percent of elderly respondents in Town or Semirural places cited kin (or friends), only 29 percent of others in those places did so (and three of seven elderly living elsewhere did). In sum, both place and life-cycle stage contribute to the answers people gave.

10. R. E. Park, "The City: Suggestions for the Investigation of Human Behavior in the Urban Environment" (1916), in *The City*, ed. R. E. Park and E. W. Burgess, pp. 1–46 (Chicago: University of Chicago Press, 1967, esp. p. 40.)

Table N1	Regression of Urbanism Scale on Respondents'

Characteristics	
Lifecycle Stage	
Married	
Separated/Divorced	
Widowed	
Under 22 Years Old	
Age (16 to 81)	
Over 64 Years Old	
No. Children 0-12	
No. Children 13+	
Education	
Household Income	
Labor Force Status	
Employed	
Retired	
R^2	

[a]Respondents who had lived in their communities less than ten years (N = 592).

Chapter 3

1. Lynne McCallister was responsible for elaborating and testing this methodology, with advice and assistance from other staff members, notably Robert Max Jackson in its early stages. Methodological Appendix section 2.0 describes the logic and development of the methodology.

2. The names given in answer to the "is there anyone else" question pose a methodological problem. We assumed that many of the people listed this way do, in fact, provide important material, social, or emotional services to respondents, but that we simply did not ask the right questions. On the other hand, this group is disproportionately composed of what might be called "sentimental" ties—old friends not seen for many years, grandchildren who call on Mother's Day, and others we feel fond of but who play virtually no role in our current lives. One elderly woman, for instance, included her "other great-grandchild" but could not remember the child's name, since they had never met. Statistical examination suggests that respondents who named many people in answer to the specific exchange questions also named many here, but that the number added was considerably more idiosyncratic or random. The coefficient of variation for number of added names is 1.04 compared with .41 for number of names listed before the "anyone else" question, and the correlations between background variables and the number listed are lower for the added than for the early names. Also, these names are disproportionately kin, 63 percent compared with 16 percent of the early names. In most of the analyses, I have included these added names,

Characteristics

All Respondents		Recent Movers[a]	
Partial beta	**Zero-order r**	**Partial beta**	**Zero-order r**
−.28**	−.20	−.30**	−.26
−.06*	.08	−.06	.05
−.12**	−.13	−.05	−.11
−.11**	−.04	−.12**	−.03
−.09	−.18	−.22**	−.26
−.01	−.17	.01	−.18
−.11**	−.11	−.11**	−.15
−.08**	−.12	−.09*	−.19
.22**	.34	.19**	.33
.13**	.16	.12**	.11
−.04	.18	−.02	.19
−.06	−.15	−.05	−.17
.213		.253	

* p < .05
** p < .01. See Methodological Appendix, Section 4.4.2, for discussion of significance testing in these data.

since many of those people provided unmeasured exchanges and the inclusion usually does not distort the results. In other parts of our analysis, I will make the distinction. Exclusion of the "added" names tends to *sharpen* differences in sex, age, education, and marital status and to alter them slightly.

3. This subsample of 4,179 names is basically representative of the entire set of 19,417, with a few noteworthy exceptions. Respondents were somewhat likelier to call people in the subsample "friends" and to say they "feel close" to those people. The subsample includes a higher portion of people who live nearby and a smaller portion of extended kin.

4. A scale measuring respondents' cooperativeness in the interview accounted for 8 percent of the variance in total network size.

5. The hierarchical rule is based on two associated principles: functional priority and probable origin. First, the continuum from close kin to just friends ranges from relatively nonvoluntaristic relations in contexts with important functional requirements to relatively voluntaristic relations in contexts with no necessary functional purpose. Second, in various combinations of role relations, the ones given priority by this rule are more likely to describe the origin of the relation (e.g., co-workers probably more often become fellow club members than vice-versa). As it turns out, this hierarchical rule makes little difference except to the category of "friends." It distributes 55 percent of the 11,317 "friends" into other categories. I was able to examine the empirical association between "primary social context" and how the relation was actually formed for the subsample of names about whom respondents answered the question, "How did you meet this person?" Of the names classified as kin, 95

Psychological Scales	Semi-Rural (N = 236)	Town (300)	Metropolitan (272)
Table N2	**Mean Scores on Psychological Scales, by Urbanism,**		
	Unadjusted		
Not Upset	3.34	3.21	3.20
Not Angry	3.41	3.28	3.30
Pleased	4.35	4.35	4.40
Total Mood	3.86	3.80	3.82
	Adjusted for Background		
Not Upset	3.39	3.24	3.16
Not Angry	3.45	3.32	3.27
Pleased	4.44	4.39	4.36
Total Mood	3.93	3.84	3.79
	Adjusted Also for Life Events		
Not Upset	3.33	3.26	3.18
Not Angry	3.41	3.33	3.29
Pleased	4.42	4.40	4.37
Total Mood	3.89	3.85	3.80

percent were in fact reported to have been met "in the same family," "through my spouse," or "through my child." Of those classified as co-workers, 72 percent had been "met at work" (the next largest group, 8 percent, had been met "through a friend"). Of neighbors, 74 percent had been met "in the neighborhood" (8 percent had met "in a group or organization"). Of fellow organization members, 51 percent had met "in a group or organization" (14 percent "through a friend"). Thus, for each of these primary social contexts, the majority of associates had met in that same "primary context" (more accurately, same type of context—co-workers could have met on a different job, neighbors in a previous neighborhood). The "other" category was, of course, heterogeneous, and "just friends" also came from a variety of original contexts: 29 percent had met through another friend, 14 percent at work, 11 percent in school, and so on.

Chapter 4

1. Susan Phillips conducted the preliminary data analysis for this chapter.

2. A major source on American attitudes toward city life is M. White and L. White, *The Intellectual versus the City* (New York: Mentor, 1962). See also I. Howe, "The City in Literature," *Commentary* (May 1971); C. E. Schorske, "The Idea of the City in European Thought: Voltaire to Spengler," in *The Historian and the City*, ed. O. Handlin and J. Borchard, pp. 95–115 (Cambridge: M.I.T. Press, 1963). Paul Boyer catalogs the stern opinions of nineteenth-century American reformers in *Urban Masses and Moral Order in America, 1820–1920* (Cambridge: Harvard University Press, 1978). For a sampling of average contemporary Americans' views, see David Hummon, "Community Ideology" (Ph.D. diss., Department of Sociology, University of California, Berkeley, 1980).

Before and After Adjustment

Regional Core (242)	eta/beta	p <	Linear r with Urbanism
3.34	.08	.10	−.01
3.53	.12	.01	.04
4.45	.06	N.S.	.04
3.94	.09	.10	.03
3.29	.10	.05	−.06
3.48	.10	.05	−.00
4.35	.05	N.S.	−.05
3.87	.08	.10	−.05
3.29	.05	N.S.	−.04
3.48	.09	.10	.01
4.35	.03	N.S.	−.04
3.87	.06	N.S.	−.03

3. K. Sale, "The Polis Perplexity: An Inquiry into the Size of Cities," *Working Papers for a New Society*, January–February 1978, p. 67.

4. L. Wirth, "Urbanism as a Way of Life" (1938), reprinted in *Classic Essays on the Culture of Cities*, ed. R. Sennett, pp. 143–64 (New York: Appleton-Century-Crofts, 1969), esp. p. 162.

5. For a review of the literature and a bibliography on the social and psychological correlates of city size, see C. S. Fischer, *The Urban Experience* (New York: Harcourt Brace Jovanovich, 1976). For an extensive discussion of economic factors, see H. L. Richardson, *The Economics of City Size* (London: Saxon House, 1973).

6. J. J. Palen, "The Urban Nexus: Toward the Year 2000," in *Societal Growth*, ed. A. Hawley, pp. 141–56 (New York: Free Press, 1979), esp. p. 155.

7. J. P. Gibbs, "Suicide," in *Contemporary Social Problems*, 3d ed., ed. R. K. Merton and R. A. Nisbet, pp. 271–312 (New York: Harcourt Brace Jovanovich, 1971).

8. "The Bay Area Is a Rest Stop for the Mentally Ill in Flight," *San Francisco Examiner*, 6 July 1980.

9. A major concern is whether answers to brief multiple/choice questions can be trusted and whether they really indicate psychological health. An extensive literature exists suggesting that the items we used do differentiate between the psychologically better-off and worse-off. These studies give us confidence that, in spite of "noise," surveys can reliably compare the average psychological well-being of different groups. For a recent study, see W. R. Gove and M. R. Geerken, "Response Bias in Surveys of Mental Health: An Empirical Investigation," *American Journal of Sociology* 82 (May 1977):1289–1317.

10. The zero-order differences in psychological scores are presented in the top panel of table N2.

11. "Frank" respondents, as judged by the interviewers, lived disproportionately in

Metropolitan and Town communities (79 percent of the first and 74 percent of the second group were frank, compared with 66 percent of both Semirural and Core respondents). Among these, the unadjusted means for overall mood are, from Semirural to Core: 3.88, 3.78, 3.82, 3.98 (eta = .12, $p < .02$; $r = .05$). Adjustments made to this or other scales yield much the same findings as for the total sample, with a tendency for Core respondents to remain somewhat more positive than they are in the total sample. The major differences between the sample of frank respondents and that of all respondents are that, after complete statistical controls are applied, Core respondents remain significantly less angry than other respondents, and that Town respondents are as low as Metropolitan respondents on overall mood.

12. All the scales were regressed on the following variables (figures in parentheses indicate the significant betas for predicting overall mood): being never married, being married (.11), number of children under thirteen (−.12), number of children thirteen and over (−.08), being employed, education (.12), income, income squared (.19), and being female (−.06); $R^2 = .12$. (Among frank respondents, the results were similar except that women were not lower.) The adjusted means, calculated after adding three dummy variables—being a Core, a Metropolitan, or a Town resident—to the equation, are shown in the second panel of table N2. The beta and significance tests indicate the added explanatory variance.

13. The negative life events scale counted the number of events or conditions that the respondent (or the interviewer) reported as having occurred in the previous year and that our analysis showed to noticeably impair morale—marriage, separation or divorce, leaving a job, moving, an illness or another person's illness that restricted the respondents' activities, a disability that was restrictive, some negative change at work, anticipating a residential move, "very" or "somewhat serious" marital problems, and "very" or "somewhat serious" financial problems (qs. 119 and 120). The average was 1.25 events, with a standard deviation of 1.20. This scale was consistently and strongly associated with being upset and angry and with being less pleased. Controlling for the negative events scale may be questioned, particularly because it includes two subjective items—marital problems and financial problems—that are similar in form to, and strongly associated with, the psychological measures (gamma = .67, .57, respectively, with overall mood). The scale without those two items, however, tends to behave similarly, though it is not as strongly correlated with overall mood ($r = −.21$ without, versus −.32 with). The negative events scale tended to be lowest for Semirural and Core respondents (means of 1.10, 1.39, 1.31, and 1.16, from Semirural to Core; eta = .10, $p < .05$), but did not differ significantly by urbanism after controls for social class, children, being married, age, and gender (1.11, 1.31, 1.31, and 1.24; beta = 07, n.s.; it was not at all significant for "frank" respondents). Ultimately, I decided to include this scale as a control because it does capture personal traits not otherwise tapped—for example, the intermittent employment of cannery workers in Town communities.

14. See bottom panel of table N2. Among "frank" respondents, Core residents were significantly less angry than others, all else equal.

15. The measure of fear of crime is the answer to the question, "Generally speaking, do you think of this neighborhood as a very safe place, a somewhat safe place, or not a very safe place?" (q. 14), asked just after one concerning burglaries. Among low-income respondents (household incomes less than $15,000), the answers, scored 1 to 3, correlate −.30 with the mood scale; the partial, controlling for personal background, is also −.30. At the same time, feeling unsafe correlates .20 with urbanism and −.26 with Semirural. The means for mood, adjusted for only personal traits, are: 3.80, 3.66, 3.71, and 3.71 (beta = .028, n.s.; partial $r = .02$). Overall, the interaction effect of income × urbanism was *not* significant.

16. L. Srole, "Urbanization and Mental Health: Some Reformulations," *American Scientist* 60 (September/October 1972):576–83. A comparable result is reported for New Zealand in S. D. Webb, "Mental Health in Rural and Urban Environments," *Ekistics* 266 (January 1978):37–42.

17. While no controls were imposed, it is unlikely that a partial correlation with urbanism

would have appeared; affirmative answers to the last two questions were *positively* associated with education. Presumably, positive answers would also be related to the number of clinical practitioners in a community, which increases with urbanism. See Louis Harris and Associates, *The Harris Survey Yearbook of Public Opinion 1972* (New York: Louis Harris Associates, 1976).

18. Originally, the researchers concluded that prescription rates were higher in rural places, but reanalysis led to the conclusion of no difference. See S. D. Webb and J. Collette, "Rural-Urban Differences in the Use of Stress-Alleviative Drugs," *American Journal of Sociology* 83 (November 1977):700–707, and idem, "Rural-Urban Stress: New Data and New Conclusions," *American Journal of Sociology* 84 (May 1979):1446–52.

19. Reported in *San Francisco Chronicle*, 26 December 1977. Another example is A. Campbell, P. E. Converse, and W. L. Rodgers, *The Quality of American Life* (New York: Russell Sage, 1976), pp. 51–53 and passim. See also O. F. Larson, "Values and Beliefs of Rural People," in *Rural U.S.A.*, ed. T. R. Ford, pp. 103–6 (Ames: Iowa State University Press, 1979).

20. The proportion answering "very happy" ranged from 30 percent in Semirural places to 33, 31, and 31 percent in Core communities. The zero-order correlation between answers to the item and urbanism is $-.00$ and the partial correlation is $-.04$. Among low-income respondents, however, there was a marginally significant partial correlation between living in Core communities and answers to the item, $r = -.08$ ($p < .10$).

21. Evidence for the first possibility is that the real drop in happiness in recent polls has occurred among residents of the largest cities, those with populations, over a million. Evidence for the second is this: Although the urban scale's partial correlation with the happiness item is only $-.04$, the partial correlation with the density of the community's city is $-.06$ ($p < .05$). (Density correlates .86 with urbanism, but Metropolitan communities tended to rank relatively low and Town communities relatively high on density as compared with urbanism.) That is, the central-city residents inclined toward less reports of happiness, all else equal. Respondents in Stockton, for example, were relatively less happy. However, among only frank respondents, the partial for density is $-.03$ (n.s.). One possibility is that big-city dwellers are more willing to admit to such a socially undesirable state as less than full happiness.

22. C. S. Fischer, "Urban Malaise," *Social Forces* 52 (December 1973):221–35.

23. This result emerged from analysis of the 1968 University of Michigan Survey Research Center Election Survey; see Fischer, "Urban Malaise." Also, satisfaction tended to be lower in Paris than in other French cities.

24. See Campbell, Converse, and Rodgers, *Quality of Life*, passim.

25. There was no clear gradient in happiness from rural to urban communities in the 1957 and 1963 Gallup polls. Such a gradient appeared in the 1970 and was accentuated in the 1977 poll.

26. For 1963, see Fischer, "Urban Malaise"; for 1971, see Campbell, Converse, and Rodgers, *Quality of Life*, chap. 7; and for late 1977, see Louis Harris and Associates, *A Survey of Citizen Views and Concerns about Urban Life* (Washington, D.C.: Department of Housing and Urban Development, 1978). See also periodic Gallup polls.

27. Reported happiness in America rose from the 1940s through the 1950s and began dropping in the 1960s. See T. W. Smith, "Happiness," *Social Psychology Quarterly* 42 March 1979):18–30. On general attitude changes, see C. S. Fischer, "Urban-to-Rural Diffusion of Opinion in Contemporary America," *American Journal of Sociology* 84 (July 1978):151–59.

28. Fischer, "Urban Malaise." For more on the entire issue of urbanism and happiness, see Fischer, *Urban Experience*, chap. 7.

29. See, for example, N. Bradburn, *The Structure of Psychological Well-Being* (Chicago: Aldine, 1969).

Chapter 5

1. Three, among many, sources that represent this image are the classic pieces by Georg Simmel, "The Metropolis and Mental LIfe" (1905), in *Classic Essays on the Culture of Cities* ed. R. Sennett, pp. 47–60 (New York: Appleton-Century-Croft, 1969); L. Wirth, "Urbanism as a Way of Life" (1938), also in Sennett, *Classic Essays*, pp. 143–64; and Stanley Milgram's essay, "The Experience of Living in Cities," *Science* 167 (March 1970):1461–68.

2. C. Alexander, "The City as a Mechanism for Sustaining Human Contact," in *Urbanman*, ed. J. Hilmer and N. A. Eddington, pp. 239–74 (New York: Free Press, 1973), esp. p. 243.

3. The question (q. 74) asks: "Please read through the list of activities on page 5 of the booklet. Which, if any, have you done in the last three months?" The list reads: "Had someone to your home for lunch or dinner; went to someone's home for lunch or dinner; someone came by your home to visit; went over to someone's home for a visit; went out with someone (e.g., to a restaurant, bar, movie, park); met someone you know outside your home (e.g., restaurant, bar, park, club)." The proportion answering affirmatively ranged from 89 percent (some visited) to 62 percent (met someone), with an average of 4.77 activities checked per person. There is a linear association between urbanism and the dichotomous variables, likelihood of engaging in each activity, from eta = .09 ($p < .05$) for visiting someone to eta = .26 ($p < .001$) for meeting someone. (The skewed nature of these variables obviously understates the association.) The overall means, from Semirural to Core, are 4.22, 4.69, 4.83, and 5.35 (eta = .25, $p < .001$). I used an analysis of covariance to adjust the data, with married versus not, lives a detached house versus not, and urbanism as factors, and with number of children, household income, age, works, and education as covariates. The overall adjusted means are less linear (Town respondents averaged slightly more activities than Metropolitan respondents), but the basic trend remains: 4.56, 4.78, 4.72, and 5.01 (beta = .10, $p < .05$). On specific activities, the partial associations ranged from beta = .05 (n.s.) for went visiting to .09 ($p < .05$) for met someone outside, but the trends on all the items—except went visiting—were roughly parallel.

4. A general report on the isolates in our sample is C. S. Fischer and S. L. Phillips, "Who Is Alone: Social Characteristics of Respondents with Small Networks," in *Loneliness: A Sourcebook of Theory, Research and Therapy,* ed. L. A. Peplau and D. Perlman (New York: Wiley, 1982).

5. The probability of naming eight or fewer associates (grand mean = .10) and the probability of giving no names in answer to the question asking who the respondent talks to when concerned about a personal matter (mean = .05) were each treated as dichotomous dependent variables in an analysis of covariance. Gender and urbanism were crossed factors, and age, social class (income for the isolated analysis and education for the confidant analysis), being married or living together, and cooperativeness were covariates. Before adjustment, the means, by urban category, from Semirural to Core, are:

Isolated: .12, .10, .08, .10; eta = .04 (n.s.);
Without intimate: .05, .04, .06, .04; eta = .04 (n.s.).
After adjustment, the means are:
Isolated: .09, .10, .10, .11; beta = .03 (n.s.);
Without intimate: .04, .05, .07, .05; beta = .05 (n.s.)

In this analysis, as in many, the use of a dichotomous dependent variable violates assumptions behind regression procedures (and isolation is particularly skewed). Nevertheless, it still indicates general trends (see Methodological Appendix section 4.4.3).

6. The sums for each respondent were transformed by adding one to them and taking the log to the base 10. All calculations were conducted on those logarithms, but the figure displays the antilog (minus one) of the resulting statistics. Results using the untransformed

data are substantively the same, except that the averages are larger, 18.5 versus 16.6 for the whole sample (drawn up by the positive skew of the distribution). I chose to present the logarithmic results here because the total R^2 of the predictive equation is greater (.26 versus .21) and because we thereby have some assurance that outliers are not responsible for the findings.

7. Eta $= .100$ ($p < .05$). The zero-order r between total number and the urbanism scale is .004, but the multiple R for a quadratic function is .106 ($p < .001$).

8. Beta $= .107$ ($p < .01$). The following equation, reduced from longer exploratory ones, was used as a set of controls; significant beta coefficients are noted in parentheses: age ($-.59$), age squared (.47), age $\times$ male ($-.10$), non-Hispanic white (.07), never married, legally married (.12), education (.11), employed full time (.08), household income (.45), income squared ($-.23$), and cooperativeness in the interview (.27); $R^2 = .260$. Two other control variables were considered but not used: number of organizations the respondent claimed to belong to and number of kin the respondent estimated lived in the area (q. 2). They increase the R^2 to .312. I did not use them because of possible circularity. Belonging to organizations is probably not a self-selection factor, but either a dimension of the same sociability indexed by network size or a medium by which community affects networks. Number of kin estimated to be in the area may also reflect kin involvement. Had both variables been introduced as controls, the adjusted means would have been, from Semirural to Core: 16.9, 17.4, 16.6, and 15.3 (beta $= .104$, $p < .01$)—virtually the same. Another variation, using only the names with confirmed exchanges (that is, excluding names added after the question, "Is there anyone else important to you?"), reduces the means noticeably but does not alter the pattern. Finally, there is a small interaction effect of urbanism by gender. In particular, Semirural women named more people than did Semirural men (partial $r = .076$, $p < .05$). Close examination shows that this effect is largely the result of high-income men in Semirural places naming unusually few nonkin. I do not pursue the finding here because the total interaction effect is marginally significant, because it is not significant if our "exceptional" interviewer is dropped (see Methodological Appendix section 4.2.2), and because we will consider it in chapter 8. (See also Methodological Appendix section 4.2.4.)

9. Eta $= .192$ ($p < .001$); r with urbanism scale $= .174$.

10. Beta $= .022$ (n.s.) The control equation is age ($-.48$), age squared (.42), age $\times$ male ($-.26$), female ($-.22$), non-Hispanic white (.11), never married, education (.20), household income (.21), employed (.12), estimated number of relatives in the area ($-.11$), and cooperativeness (.22); $R^2 = .326$. For more on analysis of nonkin, see chapter 8.

11. Eta $= .279$ ($p < .001$). The correlation between a dummy variable for living in the Core and number of kin is $-.270$.

12. Beta $= .194$ ($p < .001$). The partial correlation for Core is $-.184$. The control equation includes: age ($-.55$), age squared (.44), female (.09), never married ($-.17$), legally married (.28), number of children at home, raised as a Protestant or Catholic, education ($-.09$), years in the city (.11), years in the neighborhood, household income, income squared, and cooperativeness (.14); $R^2 = .220$. For more on analysis of kin, see chapter 7.

13. The dependent variable is the number of all persons named whom respondents labeled "friend," whether kin or nonkin. The unadjusted logarithmic means are, from Semirural to Core: 6.5, 7.8, 9.1, and 10.4 (eta $= .298$, $p < .001$). The control equation is the same one used for total number of associates (see note 8; $R^2 = .300$), and the adjusted means are 8.0, 8.1, 8.4, and 8.9 (beta $= .053$, n.s.).

14. Alexander, "City as a Mechanism," p. 241.

15. The dependent variables are number of kin—excluding those in the same household—who were checked off as "close," and number of nonkin—excluding room-mates and spouse surrogates—called "close." The adjustments were made with an analysis of covariance, using gender as a crossed factor, and married, education, age, never married,

and cooperativeness as covariates. For kin, the means, from Semirural to Core, are:
　　Unadjusted: 3.7, 4.1, 3.3, 2.7 (eta = .14, $p < .001$);
　　Adjusted: 3.5, 4.0, 3.4, 3.0 (beta = .10, $p < .05$).
For nonkin:
　　Unadjusted: 1.6, 1.9, 2.4, 3.0 (eta = .14, $p < .001$);
　　Adjusted: 2.2, 2.0, 2.3, 2.4 (beta = .04, n.s.).

16. The units for this analysis are approximately 3,800 relations, a 20 percent random sample of all relations. Three dependent variables are dichotomies: the named person was called "close" or not, called "friend" or not, and named in answer to question 77 or 78 or not. The fourth is the count of how many times the named person was cited in answer to the exchange questions. Unadjusted, the scale measuring the urbanism of the respondents' communities correlates at about zero with all four variables except "friend," where $r = .12$ ($p < .001$). Controlling for respondent characteristics (seventeen variables: three measures of ethnicity, six life cyle, three of employment status, gender, length of residence in city and in neighborhood, education, and income) does little, largely because respondent variables explain little of the variance. Characteristics of the relations themselves (fourteen variables: eight dummies for social context, gender of the named person, gender of named person × respondent's gender, whether person lives in same household, two dummies for distance between named and namer, and total size of network) explain considerably more of the variance. Most notably, kin were called "close" but were not called "friend"; spouses and parents were confidant-advisors and often named, while people living more than an hour away were named to few exchanges; and associates in large networks were also named to relatively few exchanges. Controlling for these twenty-seven variables yields near-zero partial correlations with urbanism: .03 ($p < .05$) with "close," .04 ($p < .05$) with "friend," −.00 with confidant-advisor, and .00 with number of mentions. In sum, the average relation of urbanites were—adjusted or unadjusted—no less intimate, by these measures, than those of small-town residents. A more detailed analysis, broken down by specific types of kin and nonkin, appears in part 3.

17. The units of analysis are 4,129 "subsample" relations (see Methodological Appendix section 2.3.2) for whom respondents answered the question, "About how many years have you known this person?" (six months or less was coded zero.) The unadjusted correlation with respondents' urbanism is −.09 ($p < .001$). Adjusting for respondents' characteristics (especially age, but also for four other life-cycle variables, employment status, education, income, and length of residence in the city; $R^2 = .20$), reduces the correlation to −.00; adding twenty variables describing the named person and the relation (total $R^2 = .67$) yields a partial r of .02. The parallel figures for nonkin associates only are $r = −.06$, .01, and .01, but the partial rs for Semirural are −.07 and −.06 ($p < .001$). Semirural respondents were especially likely to have new associates among nonkin who lived within five minutes' drive—partial rs of −.10 and −.13 ($p < .001$).

18. The dependent variable is a seven-point scale for frequency of getting together, from "more than once a week" to less than once a year. That scale, reversed, correlates, across 4,129 relations, with the urbanism of the respondent's community at $r = −.065$ ($p < .001$). Controlling for respondent characteristics (see preceeding note; $R^2 = .04$) reduces the correlation to −.055 ($p < .001$), and controlling for characteristics of the named person and the relation, including duration ($R^2 = .40$; multiple beta for measures of distance = .65), yields a partial r of −.053 ($p < .001$). The partials for Semirural are .056 and .055 ($p < .001$).

19. Among nonkin associates who lived within five minutes' drive, urbanism correlated −.097 ($p < .001$) and Semirural correlated .122 ($p < .001$) with frequency. Controlling for respondent and associate characteristics yields partial correlations of −.067 ($p < .05$) and .115 ($p < .001$). In part 3 this analysis is subdivided by the social context of the relation.

20. Among nonkin within five minutes' drive, urbanism correlated −.047 (n.s.) and

Semirural .045 (n.s.) with the number of years the pair had known each other. Controls yielded partials of .077 (p <.01) for urbanism and −.127 (p <.001) for Semirural.

21. See C. S. Fischer, *The Urban Experience* (New York: Harcourt Brace Jovanovich, 1976), Chaps. 5 and 6.

22. A. J. Reiss, Jr., "Rural-Urban and Status Differences in Interpersonal Contacts," *American Journal of Sociology* 65 (September 1959):118–30.

23. P. W. Crowe, "Good Fences Make Good Neighbors: Social Networks at Three Levels of Urbanization in Tirol, Austria" (Ph.D. diss. Department of Anthropology, Stanford University, 1978).

24. A national survey asked respondents, "Which place offers the friendliest people?" Forty-nine percent picked small city, town, or rural—58 percent of those making a choice. Even among city residents, more picked the least urban categories than picked the city as the site of friendliness (Louis Harris Associates, *A Survey of Citizen Views and Concerns about Urban Life* [Washington, D.C.: Department of Housing and Urban Development, 1978], p. 26). Although "friendliness" is not the same as "having friends," it is close, and the translation seems evident from most qualitative analyses of popular opinion.

25. Metropolitan respondents were least likely, at 26 percent, to say "almost every day," probably because of the relative lack of neighborhood facilities. Thirty-two percent of Core, 40 percent of Town, and 53 percent of Semirural respondents said almost every day (eta = .21, p < .001). The correlation between urbanism and this measure (r = −.18) holds up after many controls (r = −.20), indicating that this is a property of places. (The question was suggested by Carol Silverman.)

26. We also asked people whether they regularly went to a coffee shop or bar (q. 68). While there were no community differences in whether respondents reported such a place, or in how many people they knew who worked in those places, there was a strong difference in whether respondents knew any family members of workers at the "hangout": 60 percent of Semirural versus 32 percent of Core respondents said years. (Ann Swidler suggested this question.)

27. For more on this point, see David Hummon, "Popular Images of the American Small Town," *Landscape* 24, no. 2 (1980):3–9.

28. Ibid., p. 6.

29. Crowe, "Good Fences," pp. 93–94. A similar description is provided for Malaysia by R. Provencher, "Comparisons of Social Interaction Styles: Urban and Rural Malay Culture," in *The Anthropology of Urban Environments*, ed. T. Weaver and D. White, pp. 69–76, Monograph 11 (Washington, D.C.: Society for Applied Anthropology, 1972).

Chapter 6

1. For example, the Bureau of the Census, in reporting sharp increases during the 1970s in cohabitation, noted that this was more common in the larger cities ("Census Finds Unmarried Couples Have Doubled from 1970 to 1978," *New York Times*, 27 June 1979).

2. The Committee of Fifteen, New York, quoted by P. Boyer, in *Urban Masses and Moral Order in America, 1820–1920* (Cambridge: Harvard University Press, 1978), p. 206.

3. This view of the Chicago school has stimulated strong dissent. The school documented coherent social worlds in Chicago that they found even among the most unconventional of that society. However, even as they cataloged these social worlds in their research, in their theories Park, Wirth, and the others treated them as exceptions or historical residues. The close-knit ghetto, the hobo society, and the like would eventually disappear into the mass, anomic society.

4. See, for example, G. Sjoberg, "The Rural-Urban Dimension in Preindustrial, Transi-

tional and Industrial Societies,'' in *The Handbook of Modern Sociology,* ed. R. E. L. Faris, pp. 127–60 (Chicago: Rand McNally, 1964); H. J. Gans, ''Urbanism and Suburbanism as Ways of Life,'' in *Human Behavior and Social Processes,* ed. A. M. Rose, pp. 625–48 (Boston: Houghton Mifflin, 1962); A. J. Reiss, Jr., ''An Analysis of Urban Phenomena,'' in *The Metropolis in Modern Life,* ed. R. M. Fisher, pp. 41–51 (New York: Doubleday, 1955); O. Lewis, ''Further Observations on the Folk-Urban Continuum and Urbanization,'' in *The Study of Urbanization,* ed. P. H. Hauser and L. F. Schnore, pp. 491–503 (New York: Wiley, 1965); and J. D. Kasarda and M. Janowitz, ''Community Attachment in Mass Society,'' *American Sociology Review* 39 (June 1974):328–39.

5. See, for example, R. Redfield and M. Singer, ''The Cultural Role of Cities,'' *Economic Development and Cultural Change* 3 (October 1954):53–77; M. Castells, *The Urban Question* (Cambridge: M.I.T. Press, 1977).

6. See review in C. S. Fischer, *The Urban Experience* (New York: Harcourt Brace Jovanovich, 1976), chap. 8. See also O. F. Larson, ''Values and Beliefs of Rural People,'' in *Rural U.S.A.,* ed. T. R. Ford, pp. 91–110 (Ames: Iowa State University, 1979); N. Glenn and L. Hill, Jr., ''Rural-Urban Differences in Attitude and Behavior in the United States,'' *Annals of the American Academy* 429 (January 1977):36–50; C. S. Fischer, ''On the Marxian Challenge to Urban Sociology,'' *Comparative Urban Research* 6 (1978):10–19.

7. See sources cited in preceding note.

8. C. S. Fischer, ''Toward a Subcultural Theory of Urbanism,'' *American Journal of Sociology* 80 (May 1975):1319–41.

9. And closely tied nonurban subcultures, such as student groups in small college towns.

10. Some readers may note the parallel between the issues as posed this way, and the distinction Charles Tilly makes between ''breakdown'' and ''solidarity'' theories of collective violence (C. Tilly, L. Tilly, and R. Tilly, *The Rebellious Century* [Cambridge: Harvard University Press, 1975]). We are referring to similar theories and processes.

11. This item and others raise the interesting problem of how an opinion held by only a minority of people—in this case, that premarital sex is wrong—can be considered ''traditional.'' There are two answers: (1) The items used here serve as indicators of a general underlying dimension, traditionalism. Whether a particular item gains majority approval or not—and this is very much a function of just how the question is worded—does not alter its utility as an index of people's locations on this underlying dimension. In this case, people who disapproved of the behavior under question are generally more traditional than those who approve. (2) The issue also raises a more general concern: social change progresses from city to countryside. Eventually, an attitude that started off as a new and urban idea gains acceptance in most places. But even in the last stages of its diffusion, the traditional holdouts are likely to be in the more rural areas. (See C. S. Fischer, ''Urban-to-Rural Diffusion of Opinion in Contemporary America,'' *American Journal of Sociology* 84 [July 1978]:151–59.)

12. The basic results are shown in table N3.

13. See various Gallup surveys, for example. See also these research articles employing national surveys: Larson, ''Values and Beliefs''; and Fischer, ''The Effects of Urban Life on Traditional Values,'' *Social Forces* 53 (March 1973):420–32. There is not as long a history of polling on the question of homosexuality, but a few indicate differences in the same direction. (See Gallup poll reported in the *New York Times,* 17 July 1977; California poll reported in the *San Francisco Chronicle,* 12 August 1977.)

14. San Francisco County voted 25 percent yes; the three immediately adjacent counties voted 35 percent yes; the next ring of four counties voted 43 percent yes, as did the seven counties in the ring beyond that (which included Sacramento); and the remaining eleven northern California counties voted 47 percent yes.

15. Using the same divisions as in the preceding note, the no vote in 1976's Proposition 14 (which would have set in place an agricultural relations law designed by the union) was:

Table N3	Percentage of Respondents Giving Traditional Answers to Social Issues by Urbanism		
Semi-Rural	Town	Metropolitan	Regional Core
Sex Outside of Marriage Is Wrong			
52%	38%	31%	18%
Abortion Should Be Illegal or Conditional			
60	50	46	23
Marijuana Should Not Be Legal			
69	53	41	23
Homosexuals Should Not Be Allowed to Teach			
51	42	28	13
Mothers Should Not Work (or "It Depends")			
75	68	64	48
Wife Should Do Most Housework (or "It Depends")			
66	59	48	42

San Francisco, 44 percent; first ring of counties, 54 percent; second ring, 69 percent; third ring (including Sacramento), 66 percent; and the rest, 72 percent.

16. Part of the (unadjusted) association between urbanism and these items might be explained by sampling accident: a disproportionate number of our six San Francisco localities—which constituted half of the Core communities—are in what Johnson and New-mayer have called the "morally permissive" area of the city, roughly the eastern half. Various corrections and comparisons suggest, however, that we can still infer an association between urbanism and social liberalism. If apparent homosexuals and respondents cohabit-ing out of wedlock—both groups more commonly found in the "permissive" region—are dropped from the analysis, the results are largely the same; if only respondents over thirty-five are examined, the results are the same; if we drop the entire Core from the analysis, significant differences remain between Metropolitan and Semirural; and, if we correct the data for respondents' age, education, family status, and so on—all strongly associated with the city's moral geography—the results remain the same (G. L. Johnson and J. A. Newmeyer, "Gays, Grass, and Death: the Attitudinal Geography of San Francisco" [unpublished paper, Pacific Research Associates, August 1979]).

17. Susan Phillips created the traditionalism scale. The four items scaled together at alpha = .74. Two other items—working mothers and housework sharing—were associated with the scale items, but their inclusion reduced the reliability a little. We also felt that they introduced some noise into the scale; respondents often qualified their answers to these two items with references to specific family circumstances or waffled on the basis of their personal situations (e.g., men claiming to share housework). The reliability of the four-item scale was further tested within various subpopulations. It varied little across our community sampling strata, or by sex. Reliability within educational groups varied from .60 to .76. The reader will notice that all the items are worded in one direction, raising the possibility of response bias. For the heart of our analysis this is not a critical issue, because we control for

education, a strong correlate of acquiescence. Moreover, the differences discussed below are typically too large to be accounted for by acquiescence. The scale was created by standardizing and summing all the items each respondent answered and dividing by the number of those items. One respondent failed to answer at least two items and was excluded from the subsequent analysis.

18. Eta = .37 (p < .001; r between the urban scale and traditionalism = −.35). If groups referred to in the questions—apparent homosexuals and couples living together out of wedlock—are dropped from the analysis, the results are changed little, with means of 2.48, 2.24, 2.08, and 1.74 (eta = .34, p < .001).

19. Quoted by Boyer, *Urban Masses*, p. 110. Standard sociological theory makes the same argument, albeit less colorfully.

20. Number of children (0 to 3+) correlates .16 with the scale. In regression equations described below, the partial beta ranges from .22 to .15. The ratio of relatives to total network size correlates .29 with the scale and has a partial beta of .12. The ratio of local nonkin (those who live within five minutes' drive) to total nonkin correlates .14 and has a partial beta of .09.

21. The correlations between the traditionalism scale and various network measures are total number of names,'−.07; number of kin, +.12; number of nonkin. −.19 (−.26 among the unmarried, for whom friendships are presumably especially important elements of social integration); number of extrahousehold confidants, −.08; number of social companions, −.14; and number of practical supporters, −.21 (see chap. 11 on these support measures).

22. These variables were distilled from much longer lists used in exploratory regression analyses. The resulting regression equation, used in the subsequent analyses, included seven variables (significant partial betas in parentheses): age—adjusted for nonlinearity (.34), number of children (.22), education (−.19), length of residence in the city (.08), being a separated or divorced woman (−.09), being a widow or widower, and having been raised as or being a fundamentalist Protestant (.17); R^2 = .275.

23. Adding dummy variables for community to the equation in note 22 yields a partial beta of .23 (p < .001; partial r with urbanism scale = −.20). The control variables account for about 61 percent of the community-traditionalism covariance. But this is a conservative estimate of the urbanism effect in two ways. First, of the total explained variance, 31.5 percent, 57 percent is uniquely due to the controls, 12 percent is due to community, and 31 percent is joint. Second, the religious variable as a control probably causes an underestimate of the effect of community, because remaining a fundamentalist is, in a sense, an aspect of being traditional. (Our coding scheme unavoidably misclassifies people who were raised as fundamentalists but have shifted to more liberal denominations as nonfundamentalists.) Without that as a control variable, the partial beta for community is approximately .25 (r = −.22), the unique variance, 6 percent, and unique proportion of the explained variance is 19 percent; joint variance, 26 percent.

24. Adding both these variables to the regression equation described in note 22 increases the R^2 from .275 to .291 with partial betas of .13 for percentage kin and .09 for percentage local.

25. With percentage kin and percentage local also controlled, the adjusted means are, from Semirural to Core: 2.26, 2.19, 2.10, and 1.86 (beta = .21, p < .001; r = −.17). Percentage local interacts significantly with living in the Regional Core; among those respondents the partial beta for local is −.12 (p < .05), the reverse of the pattern in other categories. To check on the consequences of this interaction, adjusted means were calculated within the urban categories. The results are virtually identical.

26. See Fischer, "Effects of Urban Life," and Glenn and Hill, "Rural-Urban Differences."

27. The measures used here are: (1) informants' ratings of the proportion of young adults in the locality; and (2) the median number of school years completed by adults in the locality,

as recorded in the 1970 census. The partial correlations, controlling for network and personal traits (including the respondents' own ages and educations), of these measures are $-.11\,(p < .001)$ and $-.08\,(p < .01)$, respectively. Entering them into the regression equation increases the R^2 from .291 to .302 (multiple beta $= .13$), $p < .01$, and the partial betas are $-.07\,(p < .05)$ for young adults and $-.09\,(p < .05)$ for median years of schooling.

28. Entering the urban category variables subsequent to the locality variables increases the R^2 to .323 (beta $= .17$, $p < .001$). In the resulting equation, the beta for median school years becomes nonsignificant and that for youth only marginally significant $(-.05, p < .10)$.

29. Concentration of educated people is the population potential of adults with four or more years of college (1970 census) as a ratio of the total population potential (see Methodological Appendix section 4.3.1, on population potential measures). Concentration of young people is the estimated population potential for persons nineteen to fifty-four years old as a ratio of total population potential. The two measures correlate, at the respondent level, at .91 (making beta-weight estimates unreliable) and at .71 and .87, respectively, with the urbanism scale. Entering the measures into the regression equation, in addition to the locality measures, increases the R^2 from .302 to .318 (multiple beta $= .15$, $p < .001$). Subsequently entering the urban category dummies increases the R^2 to .323 (beta $= .08$, $p < .10$). The adjusted measures are 2.22, 2.17, 2.09, and 1.92, with a significant difference between the Core and Semirural means. However, these means are unreliable because there is great collinearity between the concentration measures and the urban variables. The unique explained variance for the former two is .03 percent; for the latter three (dummy variables), .47 percent; and the joint variance is 1.55 percent (or 77 percent of their combined explained variance). This makes it difficult to state with certainty which is the true "cause." My argument rests on the theoretical judgment that concentration of the educated and the young are the very components of urbanism that explain the residual covariance with traditionalism.

30. M. S. Weatherford, "The Politics of School Busing: Contextual Effects and Community Polarization," *Journal of Politics* (1980), pp. 85–103; M. M. Ferree, "Working-Class Feminism: A Study in Diffusion through Social Networks" (paper presented to the American Sociological Association, New York City, August 1976).

31. Figure 5 summarizes more complex subgroup analyses, using the four-category urbanism variable. The interaction effects, before adjustment, of that variable by local involvement and by kin involvement are both significant. After adjustment for covariates, only the interaction effect of local involvement is significant. The figure shows the results of a regression analysis introducing interaction terms to the equations described earlier in the chapter. The final equation is:

$$T = -.47U + .87L - .63K - .34\,(U \cdot L)$$
$$+ .29\,(U \cdot K) + X + 2.80$$

where: T = traditionalism; U = urbanism scale; L = dummy variable—respondent reports that 30 percent or more of the nonkin live within a five-minute drive; K = dummy variable—respondent names over 40 percent kin; and X summarizes a set of control variables (age, age squared, education, is a separated or divorced woman, is widowed, number of children, length of residence, and was raised as fundamentalist Protestant). Substituting the means in the equation for the control variables yields a constant of .37. The coefficients for U, L, and $U \cdot L$ are significant at $p < .05$, and the coefficient for $U \cdot K$ is significant at $p < .09$. Total R^2 $= .313$. (The interaction effects persist even if local population measures are introduced as controls.)

32. See Glenn and Hill, "Rural-Urban Differences"; H. G. Grasmick and M. K. Grasmick, "The Effect of Farm Family Background on the Value Orientations of Urban Residents," *Rural Sociology* 43, no. 3 (1978):367–84; Fischer, "Effects of Urban Life."

33. People's perceptions of community size are, it should be noted, systematically distorted. The more tranquil and safe the community seems to them to be, the smaller they

report it is (C. J. Silverman and M.S. Gerson, "Place Types as Social Objects," unpublished paper, Institute of Urban and Regional Development, Berkeley, 1981).

34. In the total sample, the zero-order correlation between the community origin measure (three categories—farm or rural; small town or other; and suburb, small city, or large city) and traditionalism is −.21. The partial correlation, controlling for age, children, education, length of residence in the city, being a separated or divorced woman, being widowed, being raised as a fundamentalist, percentage of network that is kin, and percentage that is local, −.07 ($p < .05$). Controlling for the urban dummies as well yields a partial of −.06 ($p < .10$). Dropping fundamentalist from the control variables (which can be justified on the grounds that being raised as a fundamentalist does not spuriously link small-town origin and traditionalism but is in fact part and parcel of the small-town life) changes the partial to −.07 ($p < .05$). The partial is zero among respondents who were living in Semirural places and averaged −.08 elsewhere.

35. See chapter 16 on religious identification and attendance.

36. Answers to question 34, asking respondents how they feel about husbands and wives splitting housework, range from each should do half, to it depends, to wife should do most, to wife should do all. The correlation between urbanism and those responses is −.20, and the partial, controlling personal and network traits, is −.10 ($p < .05$).

37. Fischer, "Urban-to-Rural Diffusion." A few studies show constant or widening gaps in social attitudes and behavior; e.g., J. A. Williams, Jr., C. S. Nunn, and L. St. Peter, "Origins of Tolerance," *Social Forces* 55 (December 1976):394–408; F. K. Willitis, R. C. Bealer, and D. M. Crider, "Leveling of Attitudes in Mass Society," *Rural Sociology* 38 (spring 1973):36–45; and C. S. Fischer, "The Spread of Violent Crime from City to Countryside, 1955–1975," *Rural Sociology* 45 (fall 1980):417–31.

Chapter 7

1. We asked respondents to tell us how they had first met the people listed in the "special subsample" of names (see Methodological Appendix section 2.3.2). Note 5 to chapter 3 shows the extent to which the primary social context reflects the origin of a relation.

2. See C. S. Fischer and S. Oliker, "Friendship, Gender, and the Lifecycle" (paper presented to the American Sociological Association, New York, August 1980).

3. B. N. Adams, "Interaction Theory and the Social Network," *Sociometry* 30 (March 1967):64–78; N. Shulman, "Role Differentiation in Networks," *Sociological Focus* 9 (April 1976):149–58; R. Firth, J. Hubert, and A. Forge, *Families and Their Relatives* (New York: Humanities Press, 1970).

4. E. Litwak and I. Szelenyi, "Primary Group Structures and Their Functions: Kin, Neighbor, and Friends," *American Sociological Review* 34 (August 1969):465–81; Shulman, "Role Differentiation."

5. The logarithm of the number of kin respondents named (plus a constant of one) was regressed on the following variables (significant betas in parentheses): age (quadratic function), legally married (.18), never married (−.14), number of children at home, female (.09), education, income (quadratic function: $.23X − .20X^2$), length of residence in the city, residence in the neighborhood, raised as a Protestant or Catholic (.06), cooperativeness (.14), and estimated number of kin in the area (.30); $R^2 = .23$. This equation, with and without the last variable, was used to adjust the data for analysis of community differences. Including raised as a Christian as a control can be questioned, since it may reflect small-town life-style; removing it from the equation does not substantively affect the conclusions. An alternate equation could include current religion; professing Protestantism or Catholicism was substantially related to number of kin named. That control variable was not included because it

is more apparently a consequence, in part, of urbanism (see chap. 6). In any event, its inclusion weakens but does not alter the conclusions concerning urbanism.

6. This statement is suggested by the following contrasts: Our equation could only explain an adjusted R^2 of .216 for kin compared with .319 for nonkin (see next chapter). Estimated number of kin in the vicinity and being married account together for 75 percent of the explained variance in number of kin named (82 percent if cooperativeness is excluded from the equation). Education and income, the two strongest predictors of nonkin, explain only 59 percent of nonkin (or 69 percent, cooperativeness excluded). The first pair of variables indicate the assignment of kin, the latter pair the choice of nonkin.

7. The unadjusted means shown in figure 5 for all kin differ significantly at eta = .23 ($p < .001$; r with urbanism scale = −.20).

8. The partial beta for the adjusted means—adjusted for the variables listed in note 5, except for estimated kin in the area—is .15 ($p < .001$; partial r for the urbanism scale = −.12). There is both a significant linear component and a nonlinear component indicating the accelerated drop among Core respondents.

9. Adding to the equation the number of kin estimated to live in the vicinity yields adjusted means of 5.6, 5.6, 5.1, and 4.2 (beta = .14; $p < .001$; partial r with urbanism = −.12). The nonlinear component, urbanism squared, is not independently significant, indicating that a linear association summarizes the correlation. Further analysis indicates that Core respondents named fewer kin on their lists than were actually available in the area, while Town and Semirural respondents named almost all of them. I divided respondents into four categories based on their answers to question 2: No kin in the vicinity, one or two, three to six, or more than six. Within each group, I calculated the number of relatives they named who lived within an hour's drive of their home. The means are, from Semirural to Core:

No kin: 0.6, 0.9, 0.6, 0.3 (eta = .18, $p < .05$);
One or two: 2.4, 3.0, 2.3, 1.6 (eta = .21, $p < .01$);
Three to six: 4.7, 4.7, 4.8, 3.2 (eta = .17, $p < .05$);
Over six: 7.0, 6.4, 6.8, 5.0 (eta = .15, $p < .10$).

Adjusting for cooperativeness in the interview, being legally married, being reared as a Protestant or Catholic, number of children, and being never married weakened the differences only slightly.

10. There was one additional control variable I did not include: living in a single-family home. Residents of such detached houses named about two more relatives than did other people. Part of that difference can be explained by the fact that house-dwellers were more likely to have ever been married than residents of multiple-unit dwellings, but not all the differences can be explained in terms of self-selection. (Other factors controlled, a difference of more than one name remains; partial beta = .14.) This connection between living in a detached house and kin involvement poses a problem, because house-dwellers lived, on the average, in notably less urban communities ($r = −.43$), thereby confounding the interpretation of urbanism's association with kin ties. After extensive efforts to understand why living in a single-family house—by itself—should increase the number of kin respondents reported, I decided that much of the residual association might best be explained by reversing the causal sequence: People closely involved with kin come to live in houses, because of inheritance, financial assistance, large families, a life-style oriented to family gatherings, and so forth. One finding lends some weight to such a self-selection interpretation: respondents who gave "kin or friend" as one reason for moving to their cities (and they usually meant kin) were also likely to give the "right house" as another reason for moving to the city or to the neighborhood (gamma = .43, $p < .001$). But this was true only for people who had moved into single-family houses (gamma = .54, $p < .001$, versus gamma = .19, n.s., for those who moved into multiple-unit homes). The implication is that people with kin in mind are also people with detached houses in mind when they move. If this is so (or if urbanism explains

the connection between dwelling and kin ties), the appropriate procedure is *not* to include single- versus multiple-unit dwelling among the explanations of community differences in kin involvement. I therefore dropped it. Including house as a control variable, in addition to kin in the vicinity, yields the following adjusted means: 5.4, 5.6, 5.1, and 4.4 (beta = .10, $p <$ .05; partial $r = -.07$).

11. The comparison here is between *all* kin named and the kin named either in answer to the exchange questions preceding question 81 or in the household enumeration. The city/small-town differences are smaller in the latter than in the former count but are still significant. The logarithmic means, from Semirural to Core, are:

All kin: 7.2, 7.4, 6.4, 4.3 (eta = .28, $p < .001$);
Exchange kin: 3.8, 4.2, 3.4, 2.5 (beta = .25, $p < .001$).

The zero-order rs with urbanism are $-.25$ and $-.22$ respectively. The partials, controlling for all the variables listed in note 5, are $-.16$ and $-.12$ respectively.

12. The dependent variable is the number of kin outside the household whom respondents checked off as "close" in answer to question 82 (not transformed logarithmically). The unadjusted means, from Semirural to Core, are 3.7, 4.1, 3.3, and 2.7 (eta = .14, $p < .01$). The means adjusted for gender, being married, never married, age, education, and cooperativeness are much the same (beta = .10, $p < .05$).

13. In response to question 8, 61 percent of Semirural respondents said that living near relatives and seeing them often was very important or somewhat important; 63 percent of Town, 56 percent of Metropolitan, and only 47 percent of Core respondents agreed. The differences were especially sharp among newer residents, those in the community five or fewer years; among these, only 36 percent of Core respondents said it was very or somewhat important.

14. Among all three groups on question 8—those who said being near kin was very important (N = 254), those who said it was somewhat important (346), and those who said it was not too important (450), kin involvement was lowest for Core respondents and highest for Semirural or Town respondents.

15. Among respondents who had either been in the same city for over ten years or had not answered "relatives or friends" to question 1B, a pattern essentially like that in figure 7 appears. Among those who had recently moved for that reason, the association was even more linear.

16. See note 9.

17. A. M. Mirande, "Extended Kinship Ties, Friendship Relations, and Community Size: An Exploratory Inquiry," *Rural Sociology* 35 (June 1970):261–65.

18. The zero-order differences shown in figure 7 are significant at eta = .18 ($p < .001$) for nuclear kin and eta = .25 ($p < .001$) for extended kin. The linear correlation between urbanism and nuclear kin, $-.12$, is significantly smaller than the one between urbanism and extended kin, $-.24$ ($t = 3.39, p < .001$). The adjusted differences—adjusted for the variables listed in note 5—are significant at beta = .13 ($p < .001$) for nuclear kin and beta = .19 ($p < .001$) for extended kin. Adding estimated number of kin in the area to the controls yields adjusted means much like those shown in the figure, and betas of .12 ($p < .001$) and .18 ($p < .001$). The partial correlations, $-.09$ between urbanism and nuclear kin and $-.16$ between urbanism and extended kin, are almost significantly different ($t = 1.87, p < .08$). It should be noted, however, that this interaction effect exists only among respondents with below-average incomes (where the partial correlations are $-.05$ for nuclear and $-.15$ for extended), not among respondents with above-average incomes (with partials of $-.14$ and $-.15$). In other words, urbanism depresses kin involvement in all cases except low-income respondents' involvement with nuclear kin. As to distance from nuclear kin, based on the selected subsample of names (see Methodological Appendix section 2.3.2), 38 percent of Core respondents' parents and 22 percent of their children lived out of state, compared with

15 percent and 7 percent, respectively, of others'. By extension, unnamed kin may have been disproportionately distant for Core respondents. For other types of kin, the differences in location were minor.

19. Table N4 shows the relevant data, calculated from the set of *all* relations (using a 20 percent random sample of the name file; see Methodological Appendix section 4.1). The entries are the average number of kin named per respondent to each question, by urbanism. Below those entries is the percentage of all names elicited that the kin represent. Thus, Semirural respondents named an average of 0.8 kin in answer to question 30, and kin represented 33 percent of the associates named in answer to that question. The last two columns provide rough benchmarks for assessing the relative association of each item with urbanism. The first of the two is the slope, calculated across the four categories; −.14 indicates, for example, that each step from Semirural to Core reduces the number of kin by an average of −.14. The last column shows the same figure standardized for the absolute size of the figures. Substantively, the table shows that urbanism is uniformly associated with reduced numbers of kin, except for the last two items: asking advice about a serious decision and borrowing money.

20. See Litwak and Szelenyi, "Primary Group Structures"; Shulman, "Role Differentiation"; and B. Wellman, "The Community Question," *American Journal of Sociology* 84 (March 1979):1201–31.

21. See L. M. Jones and C. S. Fischer, "Studying Egocentric Networks by Mass Survey" (Working Paper no. 284, Institute of Urban and Regional Development, Berkeley, 1978), table 1.

22. The units of analysis here are *relations*. Among the parents whom respondents named, the correlation between respondents' urbanism and whether the respondent reported feeling close to the parent is −.10; after controls for several characteristics of the respondent, the parent, and their relation (e.g., same sex or not, geographical distance), the partial correlation is −.13. The correlations among other types of kin range from .04 (in-laws) to .09 (siblings); the partials range from .00 (in-laws) to .08 (other kin). Among parents, the correlation between urbanism and the number of times the respondent named that parent in answer to the exchange questions is −.14; the partial is −.08. Among other kin the correlations range from −.10 (children) to .06 (other kin), and the partials from −.05 (children) to .02 (in-laws). Frequency of getting together was asked only about those persons in the special subsample of names. Among the parents in this group, the urbanism of the respondent correlates at −.30 with frequency of getting together; the partial is −.11. Among other types of kin, the correlations range from −.09 (other kin) to +.02 (children) and the partials from −.07 (children) to +.00 (siblings). This analysis needs to be read with caution. We do not have the entire set of parents (etc.) here; we have only those whom respondents chose to name to their networks. This means, for example, that perhaps Core residents saw their parents less often than Semirural residents did, *or* that Core residents were more likely to name their parents *even if* they did not see them often.

23. The unadjusted differences noted in the text are significant at eta = .27 ($p < .001$; $r = −.24$). In adjusting the data for self-selection, I found that some predictors interacted with age (as they do in predicting the number of nonkin). Therefore, I ran separate equations within three age groups. The equations included the following variables: gender, legally married, never married, number of children at home, age, non-Hispanic white, raised as a Christian, education, working full time, working part time, household income, length of residence in the city, length of residence in the town, number of organizational memberships, estimated number of kin in the area, and cooperativeness in the interview (R^2 from .255 to .274). The adjusted probabilities, from Semirural to Core are:

Respondents ≤ 35 years (N = 507): .35, .31, .25, .20 (beta = .12, $p = .05$; $r = −.11$);
Respondents 36–64 years (N = 398): .39, .40, .41, .30 (beta = .08, n.s.; $r = −.10$);

Eliciting Question		Semi-Rural	Town
30. **Look After** **House**	#	0.8	0.8
	%	33	29
46. **Discuss** **Work**	#	0.3	0.2
	%	27	15
73. **House Help**	#	0.7	0.8
	%	62	52
74. **Social** **Activity**	#	1.9	1.9
	%	34	32
75. **Discuss** **Hobby**	#	0.5	0.4
	%	22	17
77. **Discuss** **Personal**	#	1.6	1.2
	%	67	50
78. **Ask Advice**	#	0.8	0.9
	%	76	57
79. **Borrow** **Money**	#	1.1	1.6
	%	69	77

Table N4   **Average Number of Kin Named in Answer to Exchange Questions (and Percentage of Names Which**

[a]Calculated from means of the four categories.

Respondents 65+ years (N = 145): .48, .44, .49, .35 (beta = .09, n.s.; r = −.04); Total, age-standardized: .38, .36, .34, .26.

24. For example, R. Sennett, *The Fall of Public Man* (New York: Knopf, 1977).

25. Among those kin named (analyzing a random sample of all kin named except spouses), the association between respondents' community and the probability that the respondent called the relative a friend is gamma = .17 (p < .001). Semirural respondents called 20 percent of their kin "friends," Town 22 percent, Metropolitan 23 percent, and Core 36 percent. (The community difference was even greater in calling spouses friends.) The average number of kin "friends" named are 1.5, 1.8, 1.6, and 1.7. This does not simply reflect a tendency for Core people to call everyone a friend, because the tendency is selec-

Were Kin) by Urbanism

Metropolitan	Core	Linear Slope[a]	Slope Standardized
0.6 22	0.4 20	−.14	−.73
0.2 10	0.1 04	−.06	−.73
0.6 47	0.4 35	−.11	−.64
1.5 23	1.1 17	−.28	−.75
0.4 16	0.2 08	−.09	−.72
1.1 45	0.8 32	−.25	−.76
1.0 56	0.5 41	−.08	−.37
1.3 59	1.3 61	+.03	+.17

[b]Standardized for differences between questions in absolute numbers by dividing slope by variance of the means.

tive. Core (and, to a lesser extent, Metropolitan) respondents were especially likely to call siblings, in-laws, other kin, and neighbors friends, but not parents, children, or co-workers. If we consider only the people named to the special subsample—people who were strongly involved in respondents' lives—the pattern is much the same (gamma = .19; percentages of 31, 32, 40, and 47).

26. R. A. Nisbet, *Community and Power* (New York: Oxford University Press, 1969), p. 71.

27. Ibid., p. 69.

28. Number of kin named (outside the household) correlates .06 with overall psychological mood (see chap. 4), while number of nonkin correlates .23. The partials, controlling for

education, income, and being married, are .03 and .17 respectively. (This analysis includes only respondents judged to be "frank about their feelings.") Causal direction is, of course, unclear, but it is clear that positive feelings do not covary with kinship involvement but do vary with nonkin involvement. (See also S. L. Phillips and C. S. Fischer, "Measuring Social Support Networks in General Populations," in *Life Stress and Illness*, ed. B. Dohrenwend and B. Dohrenwend (New York: Watson, 1981).

Chapter 8

1. The figures are approximate because they were arrived at in the following way. Since we had asked "How did you meet this person?" only about the people named to the special subsample (see Methodological Appendix section 2.3.2), the actual results refer only to the percentage of those people who were met in various ways, crosscut by respondents' employment. I turned the percentages into absolute per-respondent averages and multiplied those by 2.65 (the reciprocal of the proportion of all names that the special subsample represented) to obtain the figures in the table. This procedure introduces some distortion but certainly does not alter the basic findings.

2. For more on this, see C. S. Fischer and S. Oliker, "Friendship, Gender, and the Lifecycle" (paper presented to the American Sociological Association, New York, August 1980).

3. The logarithm of the total number of nonkin (plus one) was regressed on the following equation—with significant betas noted in parentheses: household income (.21), respondent education (.20), age $(-.48)$, age squared (.42), age for males only $(-.26)$, female $(-.22)$, being employed (.12), being a non-Hispanic white (.11), estimated number of kin in the vicinity $(-.11)$, never having been married, and cooperativeness (.22); $R^2 = .326$. Another control variable was considered (and used in several parts of the analysis): number of organizational memberships. Introducing it into the equation increases the R^2 to .369 (partial beta = .24). I did not use it in the main part of the analysis because of possible circularity. Involvement with nonkin may lead to joining or forming organizations, or both may reflect some common dimension of sociability. In any case, adding it to the controls does not notably alter the conclusions of this chapter.

4. Estimated number of kin in the region correlates $-.04$ with nonkin (not logged) for men and $-.15$ for women. The partial standardized regression coefficients (beta) in equations like that described in note 3 are $-.06$ (n.s.) and $-.11$ $(p < .05)$ respectively. However, the difference in partial slopes, $-.36$ versus $-.63$, is not significant.

5. For discussions of this issue, see, for example, G. A. Allan, *A Sociology of Friendship and Kinship* (London: George Allen and Unwin, 1979); M. Young and P. Willmott, *The Symmetrical Family* (Baltimore: Penguin, 1973); and M. Komarovsky, *Blue-Collar Marriage* (New York: Random House, 1967).

6. Consistent with a structural interpretation of education's effect is the finding that its importance declined with age. All else equal, a college-educated respondent under thirty-six years of age named *two* more nonkin than did a young high-school graduate; for respondents thirty-six to sixty-four the difference amounted to only about one name; and for the elderly it made no difference. I suggest that the advantage of education dissipates over time as migration, social mobility, and other life changes alter people's access to past associates.

7. The unadjusted differences in figure 4 are significant at eta = .19 $(p < .001; r$ with urbanism = .17). The adjusted differences—adjusted for the variables listed in note 3—are not significant at beta = .021 $(r = -.01)$. If number of organizational memberships is added to the controls, the adjusted means are, from Semirural to Core: 7.6 (6.8 for men, 9.4 for women), 7.5, 7.6, and 7.8 (eta = .02; $r = -.00$). If we count only nonkin who were named in

answer to a specific exchange question (i.e., excluding those named in answer to q. 81), the pattern is similar but slightly weaker ($r = .15$; partial $r = -.04$; partial r with organizations controlled $= -.03$).

8. I put this only tentatively because yet another possibility is that the zero-order differences are the result of our sampling—purposefully eliminating black ghettoes, perhaps accidentally oversampling educated urbanites. I do not think so—another sample would probably show much the same—but caution must be advised.

9. The unadjusted means in figure 8 differ at eta $= .20$ ($p < .001$; $r = .17$) for high-income respondents and eta $= .20$ ($p < .001$; $r = .15$) for low-income ones. The adjusted means differ at beta $= .12$ ($p < .06$; $r = .08$) and beta $= .11$ (n.s.; $r = -.08$), respectively. At this stage the partial correlation for a dummy representing Semirural women is $.09$ ($p < .10$) for high-income and $.01$ (n.s.) for low-income respondents. The high-income averages with Semirural men and women separated differ at beta $= .15$ ($p < .05$). This entire interaction effect becomes nonsignificant if the cases are weighted to approximate the true population (see Methodological Appendix section 1.8.4.), precisely because the Semirural cases are thereby deflated. Another caution concerning these findings arises from two possible methodological artifacts that may have slightly tilted the association between urbanism and number of nonkin toward the negative (see Methodological Appendix sections 4.2.2 and 4.2.4).

10. Number of nonkin (not logged) was regressed on a set of variables including those listed in note 3 and several others. The results, in brief: among respondents under thirty-six ($N = 507$), urbanism correlates with nonkin at $r = .18$ ($p < .001$), and the partial $r = .06$ (n.s.; r with Semirural $= -.08$, $p < .10$). Among respondents thirty-six to sixty-four ($N = 398$), $r = .08$ (n.s.), and partial $r = -.07$ (n.s.; partial for Core $= -.08$). Among respondents sixty-five and older ($N = 145$), $r = .20$ ($p < .05$; r for Core $= .34$), and partial $r = .00$ (partial r for Core $= .04$).

11. Just as high in average number of nonkin was a metropolitan community in the center of an outlying city. Its residents were typically young singles and couples with many co-worker friends.

Chapter 9

1. For a more detailed study of neighbor relations, in part using this survey, see C. J. Silverman, "Negotiated Claim" (Ph.D. diss., University of California, Berkeley, 1981).

2. On these points, see, for example, S. Keller, *The Urban Neighborhood* (New York: Random House, 1968); C. S. Fischer, *The Urban Experience* (New York: Harcourt Brace Jovanovich, 1976), chap. 5; and various theoretical works cited in chapter 1 of this book. A general discussion appears in chapters 1, 9, and 10 of C. S. Fischer et al., *Networks and Places* (New York: Free Press, 1977).

3. The results, by urban rank, from Semirural to Regional Core are:
Percentage
Who chatted outside (q. 12): 92, 92, 91, 92
Who dropped in (q. 10): 69, 69, 62 60
Who invited neighbor in (q. 11): 59, 58, 58, 62
Who borrow from neighbor (q. 60): 36, 45, 49, 42
Who *never* borrow from neighbor (q. 60): 57, 58, 43, 52
A scale adding together the first three items correlates $-.03$ with urbanism. The partial correlation, controlling for respondents' characteristics, is $-.06$ ($p < .05$); $-.01$ for low-income respondents and $-.12$ for high-income ones. At least among affluent respondents, urbanism was associated with less overall neighboring behavior.

4. See Keller, *Urban Neighborhood*; A. Hunter, "Persistence of Local Sentiments in Mass Society," in *Handbook of Contemporary Urban Life*, ed. D. Street et al., pp. 133–63

(San Francisco: Jossey-Bass, 1978); K. Gerson, A. Stueve, and C. S. Fischer, "Attachment to Place," in C. S. Fischer et al., *Networks and Places*, chap. 8 (New York: Free Press, 1977).

5. The logarithm of the number of people named in the primary social context of neighbor was regressed on the following equation (significant betas in parentheses): gender, age, age squared, age for males only, education (.09), household income, income squared, being married (.09), working full time (−.11), length of residence in the neighborhood (.25), length of residence in the city (−.16), owning the home (.16), having moved in the previous ten years and citing "kind of people" as a reason (.07), and cooperativeness in the interviews (.13); $R^2 = .149$.

6. As the regression equation in note 5 indicates, tenure in the neighborhood and tenure in the city, though correlating at .715, operate in opposite directions. A detailed examination shows that, no matter how long they had been in the city, respondents who had lived that entire time in the same neighborhood named more neighbors than did those who had ever lived elsewhere in the city.

7. Three neighborhood variables, among several that correlated with neighbor involvement, were added to the equation listed in note 5: growth—whether the number of housing units in the neighborhood had increased more than 25 percent between 1970 and 1977; estimated presence of children in the neighborhood (see Methodological Appendix section 3.5); and informants' rating of how homogeneous in life-style the community was (see section 3.4). They increased the R^2 to .169 (beta = .16, $p < .001$), with partial betas of growth (.10); children (.03); and homogeneity (.10).

8. The unadjusted differences are significant at eta = .10 ($p < .05$; r with urbanism = −.11). The correlation with population density of the municipality is stronger ($r = −.14$), but since it is not significantly so I have focused on urbanism as the key variable.

9. The adjusted differences are significant at beta = .09 ($p < .05$; r with urbanism = −.10; r with town density = −.15).

10. The adjusted means differ at beta = .04 (n.s.; partial r with urbanism = −.06, $p < .10$; partial r with town density = −.09, $p < .01$).

11. I used this dichotomy, under versus over 30 percent neighbors, instead of a simple percentage of the nonkin who were neighbors, for two reasons. First, this mutes, though it does not eliminate, a typical difficulty with ratio variables, that correlates may vary with either the numerator (here, neighbors) or the denominator (here, total nonkin). Second, it isolates for attention the extremely neighbor-oriented respondents; variation from zero to moderate neighbor involvement does not contribute to the variance that is to be explained.

12. The dichotomous variable, over 30 percent of nonkin named were neighbors or not (mean = .255), was regressed on the same equations described earlier. By and large, the same significant predictors of total number of nonkin were significant here. The adjusted means (i.e., proportions) for the community groups (.398, .257, .243, and .128, from Semirural to Core) are significant at eta = .21 ($p < .001$; r with urbanism = −.21; r with town density = −.22). Adjusting for personal traits, including homeownership and reason for moving, yields adjusted means of .340, .252, .266, and .167 (beta = .12, $p < .01$; partial r with urbanism = −.11; with town density = −.14). Adjusting also for the three locality variables in note 7 yields means of .341, .248, .250, and .189 (beta =.10, $p < .05$; partial r with urbanism = −.08; with density = −.10).

13. The basic comparison is between low- and high-income respondents. The correlation between urbanism and number of neighbors is −.16 for the low-income group versus −.09 for the high-income group; the partials are −.15 versus −.02 (different at $p < .05$); and the partials, controlling also for neighborhood traits, are −.11 versus −.01. For neighbor-centeredness, the comparisons are −.24 versus −.17; −.15 versus −.06; and −.12 versus −.03. Other analyses showed that the correlations are slightly higher among those who did not work full time than among those who did, among the elderly than among the rest, and

among the "constrained" (those who had transportation problems, or who were poor, or who were stay-at-home mothers of two or more children) than among the rest. Another homebound group—parents of young children—showed effects about as strong as among the rest, perhaps because young children are stimulants of neighbor involvement everywhere.

14. Indeed, the more people nearby—as measured by a rating of neighborhood housing density—the fewer neighbors respondents named ($r = -.16$). This correlation, however, is totally explained by whether or not respondents owned their homes. Nevertheless, a zero correlation between neighborhood density and number of neighbors named must necessarily mean that respondents selected smaller proportions of their neighbors as density increased. (Urbanism correlated with neighborhood density at $r = .48$.) These data have some implications for the popular debates about crowding and neighborliness. Holding constant homeownership (and other personal traits), neighborhood density correlates with neighbors at $r = -.04$, but municipal density correlates at $r = -.15$. This suggests that it is not neighborhood density that drives neighbors apart, but city density that attracts neighbors away.

15. Eighty percent of Core respondents' neighbors were labeled "friends," versus 66 to 69 percent of neighbors named by respondents living elsewhere (gamma = .29).

16. The units of analysis are 388 neighbors that respondents named (representing a random 20 percent of all neighbors named). The correlation between respondents' urbanism and whether the respondent said he or she felt especially "close" to that neighbor is .10; the partial controlling for respondent characteristics is .10. When the dependent variable is the total number of times the respondent cited the neighbor, $r = .09$ and partial $r = .06$ (partial r for Semirural = $-.09$). When the dependent variable is engaging in social activities together, $r = .08$ and partial $r = .11$. With borrowing money, $r = .10$ and partial $r = .10$. With discussing personal matters, $r = .05$ and partial $r = .02$ (partial r for Semirural = $-.10$). Although these correlations are low, they represent sizable differences. For example, all else equal, Semirural respondents would have confided in about 5 percent of their neighbors and Core respondents in about 18 percent of theirs.

17. The sample here is of the 752 neighbors in the special subsample of names. The correlation between urbanism and reported frequency is $-.12$; the partial r is $-.09$, with Semirural respondents reporting especially frequent get-togethers.

18. For example: W. H. Key, "Rural-Urban Social Participation," in *Urbanism in World Perspective,* ed. S. F. Fava, pp. 305–12 (New York: Crowell, 1968); and H. Swedner, *Ecological Differentiation of Habits and Attitudes* (Lund, Sweden: GWK Gleerup, 1960). For reviews, see Keller, *Urban Neighborhood;* and Fischer, *Urban Experience,* chap. 5.

19. The preceding notes compare the correlations of neighbor items with the urbanism scale to their correlations with the population density (logged) of the city. The partials for the latter tend to exceed those for the former. For example, the partial correlations with number of neighbors, controlling for all personal and neighborhood variables, are $-.06$ for urbanism and $-.09$ for density, the latter greater than former at $t = 1.94$ ($p < .06$).

20. B. Russell, *The Conquest of Happiness* (New York: New American Library, 1930), p. 80. This passage was brought to my attention by Mark Sanford.

21. See, among others, S. M. Lipset, M. Trow, and J. S. Coleman, *Union Democracy* (New York: Free Press, 1956); C. Kerr and A. Siegel, "The Inter-Industry Propensity to Strike," in *Industrial Conflict,* ed. A. Kornhauser et al., pp. 189–212 (New York: McGraw-Hill, 1954); M. I. A. Bulmer, "Sociological Models of the Mining Community," *Sociological Review* 23 (February 1975):61–92; W. W. Pilcher, *The Portland Longshoremen* (New York: Holt, Rinehart, 1972).

22. These comments are based on extensive preliminary analyses using the twelve-category census classifications for industry and eleven-category classifications for occupation.

23. Unfortunately, we do not know how many co-workers respondents actually had at

work. We experimented with having respondents estimate the number, but these seemed to be relatively wild guesses. Also, it is unclear how to bound the unit: the office, the floor, the division, the company?

24. Exploratory regressions with dozens of variables yielded the following reduced equation. The logarithm of co-workers was regressed on (betas significant at $p < .10$ in parentheses): works full time (.23); self-employed ($-.24$); years at present job (.11); works unusual hours; occupation is professional, technical, or kindred; is manager or administrator; works in the construction industry; works in finance, insurance, or real estate; works in professional services; works in other services; is studying for advanced degree; age; age squared; education (.09); married; household income; moved to city in previous ten years and gave "own or spouses' job or school" as one reason for selecting it (.06); and cooperativeness in the interview (.17); $R^2 = .201$. When the dependent variable is the logarithm of the number of co-workers named somewhere else in the interview besides the discussing work question, the significant variables are: full time (.14); self-employed ($-.12$); years at job (.12); unusual hours (.07); manager-adminstrator (.11); moved for job (.08); and cooperativeness (.18); $R^2 = .120$. The moving variable is significant only for male respondents, as might be expected, since wives tend to follow husbands' jobs.

25. The unadjusted (logarithmic) means, from Semirural to Core, are 1.5, 2.1, 2.2, and 2.0 (eta $= .11, p < .05; r$ with urbanism $= .05$). The means, adjusted for the variables listed in the preceding notes, are 1.9, 2.2, 1.9, and 2.0 (beta $= .06$, n.s.; partial $r = -.01$).

26. The means, using as a dependent variable the (logged) number of co-workers who were named someplace in the interview besides question 46 are:
Unadjusted: 1.0, 1.3, 1.3, 1.0 (eta $= .08$, n.s.; $r = -.02$);
Adjusted: 1.1, 1.3, 1.2, 1.1 (beta $= .06$, n.s.; $r = -.05$).

27. Co-worker-centered networks were defined as those in which co-workers formed over 40 percent of the nonkin. Of respondents working full or parttime, 19 percent had such networks. Using this dichotomy as a dependent variable yields the following results (employing the equation listed in note 20):
Unadjusted: .21, .19, .18, .17 (eta $= .04$, n.s.; $r = -.04$);
Adjusted: .20, .18, .15, .22 (beta $= .06$, n.s.; $r = .01$).
The major predictors of co-worker-centered networks are being employed fulltime (.14); being self-employed ($-.11$); years on the job (.11); and education—negatively ($-.12$); $R^2 = .079$.

28. The respondents are divided in this analysis between those reporting personal earnings of less than \$12,000 (N $= 350$) and those reporting more (N $= 313$). Similar results appear when the respondents are divided by education or occupational category. The dependent variable is the (logged) number of co-workers named elsewhere besides question 46. The means, from Semirural to Core, are:
High income
Unadjusted: 1.3, 1.6, 1.5, 1.0 (eta $= .14$, n.s.; $r = -.11$);
Adjusted: 1.5, 1.7, 1.4, 0.9 (beta $= .16, p < .05; r = -.15$);
Low income
Unadjusted: 0.8, 1.1, 1.1, 1.0 (eta $= .07$, n.s.; $r = .03$);
Adjusted: 0.9, 1.0, 1.0, 1.0 (beta $= .03$, n.s.; $r = .01$).
The difference between the adjusted Core means for high- and low-income (0.9 versus 1.0) widens if the means on the control variables are set equal for both income groups.

29. Using a random 20 percent sample of all co-workers named (N $= 359$), the correlation between the urbanism scale and the number of times the co-worker was named is .08 and the partial correlation, controlling for respondent traits and relation traits (such as gender of co-worker and distance between ego's and alter's residences), is .07. The correlation between urbanism and the probability that the co-worker was named as a social partner in

question 74 is .12 ($p < .05$), with a partial of .08. The correlation with the probability that the respondent said he or she felt especially close to the co-worker is .01 and the partial is .02. Using the special subsample of names, co-workers only ($N = 359$ also, by coincidence), the correlation between urbanism and reported frequency of getting together is $-.09$; the partial controlling for respondent characteristics is $-.09$ ($p < .10$); and the partial controlling for alter's characteristics, too, especially distance, is $-.08$ (.12 for Semirural).

Chapter 10

1. S. B. Warner, Jr., *The Private City* (Philadelphia: University of Pennsylvania Press, 1977), p. 61. For a very different interpretation of urbanism's connection to associations, see S. M. Blumin, *The Urban Threshold* (Chicago: University of Chicago Press, 1976).

2. The estimate of how many nonmembers respondents knew is only approximate, erring in the conservative direction. It was calculated by simply subtracting the number of names respondents gave whose primary social context was organizational from the total number of nonkin respondents named. Number of organizational memberships (coded 0, 1, 2, and 3+) correlated .13 with this residual, and .32 with the number of organization members named. Overall, number of organization members named correlated weakly but positively with all other categories of relations, except with just friends ($r = -.10$).

3. See, for example, W. Bell and M. Boat, "Urban Neighborhoods and Informal Social Relations," *American Journal of Sociology* 62 (January 1957):391–98; E. Litwak and A. Szelenyi, "Primary Group Structures and Their Functions," *American Sociological Review* 34 (August 1969):465–81; and P. C. W. Gutkind, "African Urbanism, Mobility, and Social Networks," in *The City in Newly-Developing Countries*, ed. G. Breese, pp. 389–400 (Englewood Cliffs, N.J.: Prentice-Hall, 1969).

4. In a regression equation, these three variables, plus cooperativeness in the interview, are the major predictors of number of organizational affiliations (recoded to 0 thorugh 7+). The correlation of age with number of organizations is .12, and the partial correlation controlling for education is .21 (among women, .16 and .24).

5. The slope of number of organization members on number of organizations is .42 ($r = .33$) for the total sample and .35 ($r = .24$) for only the 686 who belonged to at least one organization. The partial slopes, in equations including ten controls were .44 and .39 respectively. An equation using the logarithm of co-members fits the data slightly better (zero-order rs of .40 and .26).

6. The dependent variable is the number of associates (added to one and logged) whose primary social context is organizational. For all 1,050 respondents, the logarithmic mean is .5. The regression equation used included: gender, age, age squared, education, household income, income squared, married, whether the respondent had been raised as a Protestant or Catholic, time lived in the city, time in the neighborhood, estimated number of kin in the vicinity, cooperativeness in the interview, and number of organizations (0 through 7+). Excluding number of organizations, the significant predictors are: education (partial beta = .09), years in the city (.10), and cooperativeness (.09); total $R^2 = .043$. With number of organizations included, the significant variables are: organizations (.42), kin the vicinity ($-.07$), and years in the city (.09); total $R^2 = .171$. Looking only at the 686 respondents who belonged to at least one organization, the significant predictors, without number of organizations, are: years in city (.13), cooperativeness (.07), and an inverted-U function of age; $R^2 = .030$. Including number of organizations eliminates cooperativeness, and the partial beta for organizations is .28; $R^2 = .090$. Number of organizations alone explains 15.9 percent of the variance in number of organization members; twelve more variables add only 1.3 percent.

7. This information *is* recorded in the original questionnaires which can be made available to interested researchers.

8. The differences (in logarithmic means), 1.5 versus 0.6, is significant at t = 6.04 (p < .001); so is the difference in the percentage of nonkin represented by co-members, .22 versus .09.

9. Among respondents belonging to religious organizations, total number of organizations correlated .02 with number of co-members. The correlation among respondents belonging only to secular organizations is .33.The partial betas are .08 (n.s.) and .34 (p < .001), respectively.

10. The means are based on bringing in the outliers on number of organizations, recoding all those above seven to seven. The difference in means is significant at p < .001 (eta = .12).

11. The following table gives the percentage of respondents in each urbanism category who belonged to one or more organizations of specified types—types for which there is a significant community difference.

	Semirural	Town	Metropolitan	Core
Political clubs	2%	2%	3%	7%
Lobbies (e.g., Sierra Club)	6	7	10	19
Neighborhood groups	1	2	13	8
Cooperatives	2	2	6	10
Professional associations	8	12	15	23
Ethnic organizations	1	2	4	4
Farm organizations	5	2	0	0
Churches, church-linked	14	12	10	6

12. After adjustment for education, income, being married, age, cooperativeness, and gender, the mean numbers of organizations were, from Semirural to Core, 1.7, 1.7, 1.8, 1.6; beta = .04 (n.s.). Other studies indicating no effect of urbanism on organizational memberships include N. Babchuck and A. Booth, "Voluntary Association Membership: A Longitudinal Analysis," *American Sociological Review* 34 (February 1969):31–45; and J. Curtis, "Voluntary Association Joining: A Cross-Cultural Comparative Note," *American Sociological Review* 32 (October 1971):872–80.

13. Unadjusted, the (logarithmic) means for number of co-members are .49, .45, .48, and .44 (eta = .02; n.s.; r with urbanism = −.03). Adjusted for the variables listed in note 5, including number of organizations, the means are: .52, .50, .44, and .38 (beta = .05, n.s.; partial r = −.05).

14. Unadjusted, the (logarithmic) means are .84 (.61 for men, 1.11 for women), .79, .67, and .68 (eta = .05; n.s.; r = .06); adjusted, .84 (.61 and 1.12), .82, .69, and .63 (beta = .06; partial r = −.06).

15. The means shown in the figure differ at eta = .02 (n.s.; r = −.01) with Semirural men and women combined and eta = .07 (n.s.) with them separated. The means, adjusted for the variables in note 6, are .53 (.37 for men, .79 for women), .59, .58, and .53 (beta = .02, n.s.; partial r = −.03; beta = .08, n.s., with Semirural divided).

16. The means shown in the figure differ at eta = .15 (n.s.; r = −.10). Adjusted, the means are 1.86, 1.91, 1.16, and 1.15 (beta = .16, n.s.; partial r = −.11). The interaction effect—urbanism × religious versus secular membership is marginally significant. The unadjusted slope of co-members on urbanism is −.18 for religious members and −.01 for secular members (different at p < .05).

17. This conclusion implies that Semirural and Town respondents drew a higher proportion of their nonkin associates from religious organizations (probably churches) than did religious members elsewhere. The average percentage of all nonkin that co-members represented were, from Semirural to Core: for members of religious organizations, .27, .24, .17,

and .17 (eta = .17, n.s.); for members of secular organizations, .11, .18, .08, and .09 (eta = .07, n.s.). Although the differences are not statistically significant, the trends provide some support for the supposition.

18. The means shown in the figure differ at eta = .04 (n.s.; $r = -.02$) with men and women in the Semirural category combined and at eta = .08 (n.s.) with them separated. Adjusted, the means are .98 (.60 for men and 1.61 for women), .99, 1.07, and .99 (beta = .02, n.s.; partial $r = -.03$); beta = .13, n.s., with Semirural men and women distinguished.)

19. The means in the figure differ at eta = .25 ($p < .05$; r with urbanism = $-.23$). Adjusted, the means are 3.76, 3.48, 2.08, and 1.49 (beta = .24, $p = .05$; partial $r = -.22$). The adjusted slopes for the religious respondents, $-.451$, and the secular ones, $-.017$, differ at $p < .001$. The correlation between urbanism and number of all co-members, $-.23$, is significantly greater than the correlation with only co-members whose primary context was the organization, $-.10$.

20. Seventy-three percent of Semirural respondents' co-members (i.e, those whose primary context was organizational) were called "friends," compared with 88 percent, 87 percent, and 96 percent of Town, Metropolitan, and Core respondents' co-members, respectively.

21. In a random 20 percent sample of all co-members (N = 222), the correlation between respondent's urbanism and the probability of saying that he or she felt close to the co-member is .12, and the partial, controlling for respondent and relation traits, is .08. The correlation with number of times the co-member was named is .14, with a partial of .15. (Semirural respondents were especially unlikely to call upon co-members, and particularly so for discussing personal problems.) In the special subsample of relations, the correlation of urbanism with reported frequency of getting together with co-members is $-.11$, and the partial correlation is $-.09$ (N = 280).

22. G. Suttles, "Friendship as a Social Institution," in *Social Relationships*, ed. G. J. McCall et al., pp. 95–135 (Chicago: Aldine, 1970). In the same volume, Suzanne Kurth distinguishes between "friendly relations" that one many have with co-workers, neighbors, or others, and "friendships." While both involve voluntary interaction, "Friendship relationships necessitate interaction that is more unambiguously voluntary. To indicate to ourselves and others that we have established an intimate, enduring relationship such as friendship, we get involved in activities and situations at times clearly beyond those associated with formal role positions. We plan to continue to associate voluntarily with one another, even if our formal role relationship is dissolved (e.g., through a change of residence or job). Although contacts between individuals may become less voluntary during later stages of friendships because of obligations created by the relationship, the original contacts as friends are voluntary" (S. Kurth, "Friendship and Friendly Relations," in *Social Relationships*, ed. G. J. McCall et al., pp. 136–70 [Chicago: Aldine, 1970]). See also R. Paine, "In Search of Friendship," *Man* 4, no. 2 (1969):505–24.

23. Just friends were more than twice as likely as all other associates to be named as social companions and 50 percent more likely than other nonkin to be called "close."

24. An artifact also affected the number of just friends: respondents who had recently left a social context knew many ex-associates from that context. Although such former co-workers and neighbors often were coded as "others," some appeared as "just friends." Indeed, people who had changed neighborhoods or left a job within the year named more just friends than those who had not (6.2 versus 4.7 for movers, and 5.5 versus 4.7 for job-changers). These variables are not, however, significant in the overall sample, once other attributes are controlled. Therefore they do not appear in the subsequent analysis.

25. The dependent variable is the log of the number of friends named (plus one). The reduced regression equation included the following variables (significant betas in parentheses): age ($-.37$), age squared, age × male ($-.33$), female ($-.25$)—these coefficients described a steady decline in friends with increasing age for men, and a more moderate

decline with later upturn (at age sixty-seven for women; above age thirty-five women report more friends than otherwise similar men)—never married (.13), non-Hispanic white (.06), works, education (.14), household income (.14), estimated number of kin in the vicinity (−.08; .01 for low-income and −.18 for high-income respondents), and cooperativeness in the interview (−.10); R^2 = .201. In other equations, children at home are a significant negative predictor.

26. These means differ at eta = .21 ($p < .001$; r with urbanism = .21).

27. The means differ at beta = .07 (n.s.; partial r with urbanism = .06, $p < .05$).The control variables are listed in note 25.

28. This is due to two technical reasons in particular: (1) One of the few artifacts we found in the data was the unusually small number of friends recorded by one specific interviewer. Her respondents lived disproportionately in more urban places. (See Methodological Appendix section 4.2.2.) Eliminating all her interviews raises the mean of just friends for Core respondents, relative to other place categories, about 10 percent. (2) Many of the relations we coded into the category of "others," such as "ex-neighbor" or "army buddy," could have been coded just friends. In fact, 67 percent of "others" were called friends. Since urbanism is positively associated with the number of others named (r =.13; partial r = .06), and since urban respondents were especially likely to consider these others as friends (52 percent of Semirural "others" versus 64 percent of Core "others" were called friends), had these friends been added to just friends, the partial association would surely have attained significance.

29. For respondents with household income over $15,000, the unadjusted means differ at eta = .20 ($p < .001$; r with urbanism = .19), and the adjusted means differ at beta = .12 (n.s., partial r = .10, $p < .05$). For low-income respondents, the unadjusted means differ at eta = .21 ($p < .001$; r = .20) and the adjusted means differ at beta = .06 (n.s.; r = .03). The partial correlations do not, however, differ significantly from one another, so we cannot claim a significant interaction effect.

30. These comments are based on analyzing the effects of two measures of relative population concentration, one of life cycle, the other of income. The first is the ratio of the 1977 population potentital of people under eighteen years old to the total 1977 population potentital (see Methodological Appendix section 4.3.1). This is a measure of familism, and its inverse is a measure of the relative concentration of childless adults. The second is the ratio of 1970 income population potential—that is, using the population of each county weighted by its median family income—to 1977 total population potential. This is an index of access to affluent people. These meassures are highly collinear with urbanism, as might be expected (at the respondent level, urbanism correlates −.71 with relative family concentration and .81 with relative affluent concentration). Partialed for personal traits, familism correlates more strongly, negatively, with just friends among young, childless adults than does urbanism (−.12 versus .05—just friends *not* logged). And, also partialed, affluent concentration correlates as well with just friends among the affluent as does urbanism (.11 versus .10). These relative concentration measures have no partial associations among the inappropriate groups (e.g., affluent concentration among the nonaffluent).

31. Among the 1,099 just friends who appear in the special subsample of names, the correlation of respondent's urbanism with frequency of getting together is −.02 and the partial, controlling for respondent's and friend's traits, is −.04 (for Semirural, r = .06, $p < .10$). Similarly, among a random 20 percent sample of all just friends, the partials between urbanism and whether the respondent thought the friend "close," discussed personal issues with the friend, saw him or her socially, could borrow money from him or her, and how many different times the friend was named never exceed .033 in either direction.

32. The averages here are based on raw numbers rather than logged numbers, in order to preserve additivity. They cannot be compared with the data presented earlier. The basic

point of the figure nevertheless remains valid. Religious organization refers to the number of fellow club members named by respondents who belonged to at least one religious organization. "Clubs" refer to the number of fellow members named by respondents belonging only to secular organizations.

33. This analysis was not presented in detail because of the heterogeneity of the "other" category. Unadjusted, the mean number of others (not logged), ranges from 0.7 for Semirural respondents to 1.0, 1.1, and 1.5 for Core respondents (eta = .14, $p < .05$; partial $r = .06$).

34. Each respondent was categorized in the following way: If the percentage of kin in their network was more than one standard deviation above the mean, they had a kin-oriented network. If not, but their network had a percentage of neighbors more than one standard deviation above the mean, they had a neighbor-oriented network; and so on. While 26 percent of Semirural residents were kin-oriented and 17 percent were neighbor-oriented, only 6 percent of Core respondents were kin-oriented, and 6 percent were neighbor-oriented. On the other hand, only 8 percent of Semirural respondents were co-worker-oriented and only 9 percent were just-friend-oriented, compared with 23 percent for each among Core respondents.

35. The adjusted figures are only approximate because they were based on briefer equations, using unlogged dependent variables. Further refinement would not, however, alter the basic point.

36. This analysis of traditional and modern social contexts is pursued in C. S. Fischer et al., *Networks and Places* (New York: Free Press, 1977), chaps. 1 and 10. See also L. Coser, *Greedy Institutions* (New York: Free Press, 1974).

Chapter 11

1. Some general sources on social support are: J. S. House, *Work Stress and Social Support* (Reading, Mass.: Addison-Wesley, 1980); D. P. Mueller, "Social Networks: A Promising Direction for Research," *Social Science and Medicine* 14A (1980):147–61; B. A. Hamburg and M. Killilea, "Relation of Social Support, Stress, Illness, and Use of Health Services," in *Healthy People*, Surgeon General's Report on Health Promotion and Disease Prevention and Background Papers (Washington, D.C.: Government Printing Office, 1979); and H. Z. Lopata, *Women as Widows: Support Systems* (New York: Elsevier, 1979).

2. House, *Work Stress*, chap. 4.

3. Our measures of support—described below—are significantly associated with one another, but the highest correlation among them is .33, between companionship and practical aid.

4. No one of these eliciting questions is very reliable as a measure of support, but their reliability increases by combining them. Also, our purpose is to isolate the extremes rather than to accurately rank all respondents, and in that regard we can have greater confidence in the measures.

5. These comments summarize regression analyses run within the total sample; males and females; the unmarried and the married; the young, middle-aged, and elderly; and low- and high-income groups. The dependent variables were two counseling measures— the one in table 3, for outside the household, and one including all names. The basic regression equation includes these sixteen variables: respondent's age; a dummy for being under twenty-two; one for being over sixty-four; being married; number of children under eighteen at home; being black; being non-Hispanic white; being Asian; gender; education; household income; working or not; being retired; length of residence in the neighborhood; number of organizations belonged to; and cooperation in the interview. In the total sample, the major

independent effects are being married (beta = $-.18$; $-.20$ among men); being female (beta = .15; .19 among the married; .41 among the elderly); age (beta = $-.18$); number of children (beta = $-.08$; $-.12$ among women); black (beta = $-.06$; $-.10$ among women); and organizations (beta = .11; .15 among the affluent). The overall R^2 is .14.

6. The zero-order eta is .10 ($p < .001$). The partial beta, in an analysis of covariance controlling for cooperativeness, age, number of children, being non-Hispanic white, organizational memberships, and gender by marital status (never married, married, and formerly married), is .07 (n.s.). Results with regression analyses using more controls are similar.

7. The interaction effects of gender × urban rank and of gender × marital status × urban rank are *not* statistically significant. However, the patterns of means across community types are somewhat different according to the marital status of the women respondents, as indicated here. The means, from Semirural to Core, are adjusted for cooperativeness, age, being under twenty-two, number of children, organization memberships, and race:

Married women (N = 310): 1.63, 1.62, 1.34, 1.44 (beta = .18, $p < .05$);
Formerly married (N = 188): 1.59, 1.77, 1.58, 1.78 (beta = .17, $p < .11$);
Never married (N = 85): 2.00 (N = 5), 1.66, 1.84, 1.75 (beta = .13, n.s.).

Other results suggest that the drop in the Metropolitan category is especially strong among middle-aged, college-educated, married women, and also among those with high incomes and those relatively new to their cities.

8. The correlation between number of activities and the adequacy scale is .54 (partialed for individual traits, .47).

9. These points are based on regressing the number of activities respondents claimed (q. 74) on age, education, household income, number of organizations, cooperativeness in the interview, number of children, being married, being never married, working full time, working part time and years in the city. All except the last four were significant ($R^2 = .23$). The regression was also run within gender. The partial unstandardized slope of age is $-.029$ for men and $-.018$ for women. The partial slope for number of children is $-.10$ (n.s.) for men and $-.18$ ($p < .05$) for women, while the partial slope for married (versus formerly married as the base) is $-.20$ (n.s.) for men and $-.30$ ($p < .10$) for women. Interestingly, never marrieds were *not* more active than marrieds (a partial slope $-.23$, n.s., about the same as married, for both genders). The especially active were the *formerly* married. The mean number of activities, by urbanism, are, from Semirural to Core: 4.2, 4.7, 4.8, 5.3 (eta = .25, $p < .001$). Adjusted for the variables listed earlier, the means are 4.6, 4.7, 4.7, 5.0 (beta = .11 $p < .001$). The results for each gender are about the same (beta = .09, $p < .001$, for men, and beta = .12, $p < .001$, for women).

10. The comments about the correlates are based on regressing the companionship scale on the variables listed in note 5. The total R^2 is .119, and the major predictors are, in addition to cooperativeness: organizational memberships (beta = .13); income (.10); being Anglo versus not (.10); number of children ($-.09$); age ($-.13$); education (.08); and being retired ($-.09$). Being married was not a significant independent predictor. Children were for women (beta = $-.06$, $p < .01$) but not for men (beta = $-.02$, n.s.). The partial association of urbanism, controlling for these variables, is not significant for the sample as a whole, for men or women, for married or unmarried women, or within age groups. In figure 14 the unadjusted means are significant at $p < .001$ (eta = .10), but the adjusted means (adjusted in analysis of covariance for cooperativeness, age, number of children, income, organizations, and gender × race) are not (beta = .04, n.s.).

11. Three can be noted: (1) Black men were, together with white men, more likely to have adequate companionship than were Hispanic or Asian men. Black women, however, were notably less likely than other women to have such adequate companionship. (Recall that the thirty-five blacks in our sample lived in predominantly white or Hispanic localities.) (2) The thirty-three Semirural respondents whose household incomes exceeded $25,000 were, on the average, significantly *less* likely, ceteris paribus, to have adequate companion-

ship than respondents of that income level living elsewhere. Perhaps they missed having enough people of their own class nearby. (3) Urbanism was strongly associated with adequate companionship among a special subset of the population: those who had always had social ties in their communities. (These respondents had either lived all their lives in the same place or, more commonly, had selected their communities at least in part because kin or friends were there.) Among these 340 respondents, the more urban the communities the more adequate the average level of companionship (partial beta = .17, $p < .05$). Perhaps people who moved to, or chose to stay in, small towns for relatives sacrificed companionship to do so, while those who remained in large communities, or moved to them for kin, did not have to sacrifice.

12. This summary is based on regressing the practical support scale onto the variables listed in note 5. Overall, the strongest independent predictors were age (beta = $-.25$); working (.16); retired ($-.11$); organizations (.12); cooperativeness (.10); children ($-.09$); and being Anglo (.08; among women the coefficient for black is $-.09$). The coefficient for children was more negative among women ($-.13$), the middle aged ($-.14$), and those with household incomes under \$15,000 ($-.15$) but was positive among the elderly (.19). Income was positively associated with likelihood of support among the middle-aged (.18) and gender was positively associated among the elderly (.27).

13. Since urbanism and gender interacted, the analysis was conducted separately for men and women. Unadjusted, the mean scores, from Semirural to Core, are:
Men: 1.54, 1.81, 1.78, 1.72 (eta = .18 $p < .001$);
Women: 1.67, 1.68, 1.68, 1.65 (eta = .02, n.s.).
Adjusted for cooperativeness, number of children, age, race, organizational membership, and employment status, the means are:
Men: 1.67, 1.90, 1.72, 1.63 (beta = .14, $p < .01$);
Women: 1.80, 1.68, 1.61, 1.59 (beta = .13, $p < .01$).
The data shown in figure 14 are based on weighted averages of these two sets of statistics.

14. The items were unrelated in the sense that associates who would look after the house were definitely not likely to discuss work and tended not to be sources of loans and so forth. The following table lists the unadjusted average number of supporters (exclusive of household members) named for each practical support question:

	Semirural	Town	Metropolitan	Core
Look after house	2.4	2.9	2.8	2.0
Help around house	1.1	1.4	1.3	1.0
Talk about job	1.1	1.5	1.6	1.7
Borrow money	1.6	2.0	2.1	1.9

15. I also constructed a measure of breadth of support: To how many of the following items did respondents give at least an "adequate" number of names: house care, personal discussions, advice, lending money (at least two names), and social activities (at least five names)? Groups with particularly narrow support were the elderly, the less educated, black women, mothers generally, and men, especially older or married men. Semirural men had narrower support, before and after adjustment, than men elsewhere. Women did not differ significantly by community. Combined, respondents in Towns had a bit wider support, largely because of more house caretakers and helpers around the house.

16. Table N5 summarizes the data. It is read as: 17 percent of all those named in answer to the question about who the respondent discussed personal matters with were spouses; 9 percent were parents, and so forth.

17. These comments distill some of the findings from complex regression analyses run within two sets of data: (1) a 20 percent random sample of all persons named by the respondents; and (2) the special subsample of relations for which we obtained supplemen-

Table N5   Which Associates, by Social Context, Were Named

Percentage of Those Named in Answer to Each Question

Counseling		Companionship	
Discuss Personal Matters	Seek Advice	Spend Social Time	Discuss Hobby
Spouse			
17%	24%	1%	2%
Parents			
9	14	3	2
Children			
9	7	5	1
Siblings			
9	6	5	5
In-Laws			
3	3	8	5
Other Kin			
2	2	4	1
Coworkers			
10	11	8	14
Neighbors			
9	4	12	16
Comembers			
5	4	7	14
Just Friends			
22	18	42	34
Others			
5	5	6	5
Average Number of Names			
1.42	1.42	6.19	2.43

ᵃBased on 20 percent random sample of all relations.

tary information (see Methodologial Appendix section 4.1). The analyses involved regressing dummy variables indicating whether an associate's name had been elicited by a particular support question on a long list of respondents' characteristics (gender, age, employment, etc.); associates' characteristics of the same kind (only gender available for the random subsample); and characteristics of the relation itself (social context, duration, similarity of associates in age and in gender, and spatial distance). The analyses were conducted for all relations; for nonkin only; within specific social contexts of relations; and within various subgroups of respondents. It is important to realize that the statements here contrast associates *to one another,* not to the world at large.

18. This analysis involves a search for interaction effects; associate characteristics as determined by the interaction of support type and respondent characteristics. The possible combinations of interest number in the hundreds.

19. These estimates are based on regressing the dummy variable, associate is kin versus

for Each Support Question[a]

Practical			
Look After House	**Helped in House**	**Discuss Work**	**Could Lend Money**
0%	2%	5%	1%
5	10	2	28
7	12	1	6
6	10	3	13
7	10	1	12
1	5	0	5
6	4	66	7
47	10	3	4
3	6	3	3
17	26	11	17
1	4	3	4
2.56	1.28	2.61[b]	2.01

[b]Working respondents only.

not, on several respondent characteristics within three sets of associates: those named as discussing personal problems; those named as social companions; and those named as a source of financial aid. The point spreads reflect partial slopes for education.

20. This interaction effect is explained in part by education, since the highly educated show the same pattern. Nevertheless, some urban interaction effect persists. In table N4, the percentage of supports who were kin, for each question, by urbanism, is listed. Adjusting those percentages for several respondent characteristics yields the following results. The entries are the adjusted percentage of supporters on each question who were kin, from Semirural to Core:

Social activity: 32, 28, 22, 22 (beta = .09, $p < .05$);

Discuss personal concerns: 62, 46, 45, 41 (beta = .14, $p < .05$);

Borrow money: 68, 75, 59, 61 (beta = .14, $p < .06$).

Discussing personal concerns shows the strongest monotonic difference: About 60 percent of the Semirural respondents' confidants were kin, compared with about 40 percent of the confidants of comparable Core respondents.

21. Unadjusted, urbanism is correlated with the friends versus neighbor preference on both counseling and companionship. Adjusting for respondent characteristics, especially education, reduces the correlation with regard to counseling but not companionship.

22. The correlation between number of counselors and wishing to have more people to talk with is .08 ($p < .01$); between number of social companions and wishing more companions is −.01; and between practical supporters and wishing more help is .00. The correlations are not substantially different if only "frank" respondents' answers are considered.

23. A. Campbell, P. E. Converse, and W. L. Rodgers, *The Quality of American Life* (New York: Russell Sage, 1976), pp. 358–59. Similarly, researchers on loneliness know that there is a tenuous link between objective isolation and felt loneliness; see L. A. Peplau and D. Perlman, eds., *Loneliness* (New York: Wiley, 1982), passim.

24. Of course an argument can be made that happy people get more companions. While some reciprocal effect probably does occur, controlling for most critical background traits probably controls as well for most of the variance in personality traits. The results discussed in this paragraph are based on regressing the psychological mood scale on the total number of counselors, of companions, and of practical supporters, as well as several control variables. The statistics reported here are drawn from a regression analysis using just the 753 respondents whom interviewers judged to be "frank" about their feelings. The zero-order correlations between mood and number of supporters were: number of counselors, −.02; companions, .21 ($p < .001$); and practical supporters, .10 ($p < .001$). (Using the adequacy scales instead of the absolute numbers yielded lower correlations.) The partial betas in an equation including only these three variables are counselors, −.09 ($p < .01$); companions, .21 ($p < .001$); and practical supporters, .04. The partial betas in an equation also including control variables are: counselors, −.03; companions, .11 ($p < .001$); and practical supporters, .01. The control variables in the final equation, with significant betas noted, are age (.11); female; age × male; married (.11); never married; education (.13); household income (.13); number of children at home (−.11); employed full time; employed part time (.10); number of negative life events (−.15); total $R^2 = .174$.

25. Using the full equation discussed in the previous note (with "frank" respondents only), the partial correlation of urbanism with mood is −.01. But there is a curvilinear effect. The partial beta for three dummy variables representing the community categories is .10 ($p < .05$). And the adjusted mood scores are 3.92 (fiftieth percentile on figure 3) for both Core and Semirural, and 3.81 (forty-second percentile) for both Town and Metropolitan.

26. The problem was lack of time and the need to avoid unnecessary duplication of names. We experimented in a pilot survey with a few questions about recipients of support (e.g., asking for whom the respondent had recently baby-sat), but the people named were typically named as supporters, too. Given the general goals of the study, to describe personal communities, this was redundant. However, another study employing such questions could explore topics such as the direction of support and balances in exchanges.

27. The correlation of an interaction term—number of children under thirteen for women respondents—with the demands item is .31. The following equation was run for the 584 respondents who lived with at least one other person and were judged to be "frank" (betas significant at $p < .10$ noted in parentheses): respondent has spouse or spouse surrogate (−.19—i.e., feels fewer demands); number of children under six years old (.13); children six to twelve; children thirteen to sixteen (.12); children seventeen or older at home (.10); number of children under thirteen for women respondents only (.13); number of other adults in home, being a woman (.27); age (−.17); age for males (.18); never married; education; household income; works full time; works part time (.09); and number of negative life events: $R^2 = .200$. The first seven variables alone explain sixteen percent of variance. Since many of these variables are collinear, it is helpful to contrast a few types of people as a way

of showing the strength of the effects. For example, all else equal, a thirty-year-old married man living only with his wife would score 0.75 points (0.81 standard deviations) less harassed than a thirty-year-old married woman with one eight-year-old and one four-year-old. A seventy-year-old widower living with his married children and their eighteen-year-old would score 0.22 points (0.24 standard deviations) less demanded than a forty-year-old divorcee with a ten-year-old. Only in an elderly childless couple would a woman feel as free of demands as her husband. Similar findings on sex, children, and employment are reported by W. R. Gove and M. R. Geerken, "The Effect of Children and Employment on the Mental Health of Married Men and Women," *Social Forces* 56 (September 1977):66–71.

28. The demands item was regressed on the following equation (753 "frank" respondents only): number of nonkin named; number of kin outside the household named; number of counselors; number of companions (.14); number of practical supporters; age (−.16); age for males; number of children (.08); education; household income; married; never married; negative life events (.11); total $R^2 = .078$.

29. The positive effect of companions on mood is largely a result of its correlation with the positive affect component of mood.

30. Path analysis indicates the simultaneous positive and negative aspects of social companions. Regressing the psychological mood scale on felt demands from kin and friends and on number of social companions, and then regressing felt demands on companions—all while controlling for age, being married, education, income, and life events—shows a direct positive effect of companions on mood (beta = .133) and an indirect negative effect through felt demands (.116 × −.145 = −.017; both paths significant at $p < .001$), for a total effect of .116.

31. Barry Wellman has recently reported research on unsupportive social relations. Many of the people with whom respondents in one study were "in touch" were either nonsupportive or even harmful ("The Application of Network Analysis to the Study of Support," Resource Paper no. 3, Centre for Urban and Community Studies, Toronto, 1981).

32. See House, *Work Stress*.

Chapter 12

1. The argument sketched here is implicit in most classical sociological interpretations of how Western modernization has affected interpersonal relations—for example, the works of Tönnies, Durkheim, Simmel (although he was ambivalent), modern theorists such as Parsons and Nisbet, and the Chicago school. For some documentation of this claim, see C. S. Fischer et al, *Networks and Places* (New York: Free Press, 1977), chap. 1, and C. S. Fischer, *The Urban Experience* (New York: Harcourt Brace Jovanovich, 1976), chap. 2. Recently, network theorists have made this implicit argument explicit in network language, particularly R. Frankenburg (*Communities in Britain*, Baltimore: Penguin, 1965), and B. Wellman and B. Leighton, "Networks, Neighborhoods, and Communities," *Urban Affairs Quarterly* 15 (March 1980):363–90. The naive version of the argument is relatively consistent with the Arcadian myth in American popular opinion.

2. These claims are reviewed in chapter 10 of Fischer et al., *Networks and Places*. For a powerful essay on the Arcadian myth in English literature, see Raymond Williams, *The Country and the City* (New York: Oxford University Press, 1973).

3. The subsample of names excluding "anyone else" differs systematically from the total sample of names, including proportionately fewer geographically distant people, somewhat fewer kin, and somewhat more active associates. Most important, these relations tend to be somewhat more specialized—co-workers named exclusively on the discuss-work questions, neighbors on the house-care question, and so forth. This selectivity tends to create less apparent multistrandedness in the average network. Other characteristics of our method,

however, tend to produce more apparent multistrandedness, notably the absence of any very specific questions such as, Who helped you find your job? or Who baby-sits with your child? Also, the bias toward less multistrandedness should affect respondents about equally. For discussion of this matter, see L. McCallister and C. S. Fischer, "Studying Egocentric Networks by Mass Survey" (Working Paper no. 284, Institute of Urban and Regional Development, Berkeley).

4. Of course some questions do not apply to certain respondents—the work question to nonworkers, the fiancé question to the married, the household question to people living alone. But this is not necessarily an artifact: if there are things you do not do, you cannot share them with your associates. In any event, by controlling for respondents' background characteristics—for example, whether they work or not—we can control for the effect of this procedure. Further difficulty arises because not all the elicited names for each question were recorded. Any names beyond the first eight (first ten for the social activities question, first four for the lend money question, and first one for the fiancé question) were not recorded. So, for example, someone named second on discuss work but ninth on discuss hobbies would only receive a score of one. Fortunately, such long lists of names were given rarely, and usually only in answer to the social activities question. A final point: the household question is included in this count under the assumption that adults sharing a dwelling cooperate at least tacitly in its management.

5. The average multistrandedness measure adds up the total number of mentions for each named person, from one through three (four or more were recoded to three to bring in outliers) and divides by the total of names elicited at least once. Several other and more complex measures of multistrandedness were examined. One set measured role mutiplexity, the number of different labels—relative, co-worker, neighbor, and so forth—that each relation was given. This was dropped because the great majority of the relations were given only one tag besides "friend," which was itself used promiscuously. The number of true worker-neighbor or relative-worker combinations were few. Another set counted types of exchanges rather than discrete exchanges, using the categories employed in chapter 11. So, for example, both discussing personal problems and advising on a decision, or either, counted as only one strand. It turned out that scores based on this procedure were similar to the ones I eventually used, correlating with one another from .61 to .92. I decided to use the simpler procedure.

6. Jeremy Boissevain is, as usual, most explicit; see pp. 24–96 of *Friends of Friends* (London: Basil Blackwell, 1974).

7. The number of triple-stranded relations correlates with the number of kin in the network at $r = .14$ (slope $= .09$) and with the number of nonkin at $r = .33$ (slope $= .12$). Since the average proportion of such relations is .18, it is clear that multistranded ties increase more slowly than total ties. (Note that number of kin and nonkin here refer to those names exclusive of the "anyone else" question.)

8. This is consistent with the results described in the previous note. The ratio of separate mentions to total network size—average multistrandedness—correlates $-.10$ with number of kin (slope $= -.011$) and $-.17$ (slope $= -.011$, again) with nonkin.

9. The two multistrandedness measures were regressed on the following set of variables: age; a dummy for being over sixty-four; gender; raised as a Protestant or Catholic; never married; married; education; household income; number of children in the house; whether there was another dependent in the house; works full time; works part time; is retired; is homemaker; number of organizational memberships; time in the city; and time in the neighborhood. For number of triple-stranded relations, $R^2 = .188$, and the significant predictors are age (beta $= -.32$); works full time (.12); works part time (.09); organizations (.09); and time in neighborhood ($-.13$). For average number of strands, $R^2 = .108$, and the significant predictors are age ($-.25$), retired ($-.11$), and married ($-.09$).

10. This interpretation might be challenged as a product of the measurement procedure. Although a different procedure—perhaps counting role relations or using a different set of

probes—might yield different results, the theoretical point remains persuasive. Typical illustrations of the multistrandedness concept (say, Boissevain's, on p. 29 of *Friends of Friends*) present a list of activities or role relations assumed to be constant across individuals: neighboring, sport, work, religion, etc. Overlooked is the fact that people vary greatly in whether they participate in such activities. And participation is correlated with size of network.

11. Boissevain, *Friends of Friends,* p. 72.

12. The basic model used was an analysis of covariance design with number of triple-stranded associates as the dependent variable; employment (working or not), gender, income (low versus high) and urbanism as crossed factors; and the following covariates: age, married or not, length of residence in the neighborhood, total number of kin named, and total number of nonkin named (in both cases, the total named before the "anyone else" question). In calculating the partial associations reported here, the covariates were entered first, the other factors were entered before the urban variable, and the interaction terms were entered last. *No* interaction effects among the factors were significant, including gender by urbanism ($p < .4$). The means from Semirural to Core are:

Unadjusted: 1.83, 2.47, 2.34, 2.38 (eta = $.14, p < .001$);
Adjusted for personal traits: 2.14, 2.46, 2.21, 2.23 (beta = $.07$, n.s.);
Adjusted also for network traits: 2.19, 2.38, 2.19, 2.30 (beta = $.05$, n.s.).

In regression analyses using the variables listed in note 9, there is a significant partial correlation between living in Towns and number of triple-stranded ties ($.10, p < .05$). Controlling also for network size reduces it to nonsignificance, except among women (partial $r = .11, p < .05$).

13. Using the same analysis of covariance model as in the previous note with average number of strands per relation as the dependent variable also reveals no significant interaction effects. The means are:

Unadjusted: 1.56, 1.62, 1.57, 1.60 (eta = $.08, p < .10$);
Adjusted for personal traits: 1.60, 1.61, 1.56, 1.59 (beta = $.06$, n.s.);
Adjusted also for network traits: 1.59, 1.62, 1.57, 1.58 (beta = $.07$, n.s.).

In regression analysis, the partial correlation for Town, controlling for all the variables in note 9 and for network traits, is $.07$ ($p < .05$). Closer inspection indicates that the difference exists solely between nonworking women in Town communities and those in Core communities.

14. The correlation, across all associates, between number of "strands" (i.e., times named) and the probability that the respondent felt "especially close" to that associate ranged from $-.00$ for "other" kin to $.22$ for siblings, among relatives, and from $.20$ for organization members to $.40$ for co-workers, among the nonkin.

15. In the special subsample, the partial correlation between number of elicitations and reported frequency of getting together (partialed for geographic distance) ranges from $.24$ for co-workers to $.37$ for other kin.

16. Forty-six percent of these selected associates lived within five minutes of the respondents, compared with 30 percent overall; 10 percent were extended kin versus 20 percent overall; and 49 percent were "close," compared with 39 percent overall. The distributions of the subsample in terms of sex, of similarity to the respondents in ethnicity, religion, hobby, or work, or of social context was otherwise very much like the distributions for all the 19,417 names, differing by less than 10 percent.

17. This average is somewhat higher than that reported by Barry Wellman for the East York area of Toronto, .33. However, the average ratio for our Regional Core sample is remarkably similar, .33. See Barry Wellman, "The Community Question," *American Journal of Sociology* 84 (March 1979):1215.

18. E. Bott, *Family and Social Network,* 2d ed. (New York: Free Press, 1971). In chaps. 3 and 4, Bott provides a long list of postulated correlates of density.

19. The difference between majority kin networks and others is significant at $p < .001$

(eta = .24). The number of different social contexts from which respondents drew their networks refers, in this instance, to the entire network (including the "anyone else" names) and simply counts the number of different social contexts from which respondents drew at least one associate. The reported differences are significant at $p < .001$ (eta = .33).

20. An alternative explanation is that lower-status and immobile people feel a greater need to bring their associates together, or have more opportunity to do so, or both.

21. These comments on the correlates of density are based on a regression analysis using the density ratio as the dependent variable, the variables listed in note 9 as the independent variables, and adding seven measures of network content: (1) number of kin named; (2) number of nonkin (both totals exclusive of those named to the "anyone else" question); four dummies: for having a network (3) of more than 50 percent kin, (4) of more than 30 percent neighbors, (5) of more than 45 percent co-workers, and (6) of more than 60 percent "just friends"; and (7) an interval measure of the diversity of the contexts from which the nonkin were drawn. This measure is Lieberson's A_W index, which is calculated as:

$$A_W = 1 - \sum_{i=1}^{5} \chi_i,$$

where χ_i is the percentage of nonkin represented by co-workers, neighbors, co-members, just friends, and "others" in each respondent's network. See S. Lieberson, "Measuring Population Diversity," *American Sociological Review* 34 (December 1969):850–62. The major correlates of density are education ($r = -.27$); having a majority kin network (.25); nonkin diversity ($-.22$); number of nonkin ($-.21$); number of kin (.20); household income ($-.15$); and years in the town (.15). The major independent predictors are education (beta = $-.20$); number of kin (.13; .21 for women); nonkin diversity ($-.12$; $-.17$ for men); years in the town (.10; .14 for women; .18 for people in the labor force); and never married (.08, with formerly married as base; for women, married was greater than formerly married, beta = .09, but the opposite was true for men, beta = $-.10$); $R^2 = .168$. Also, for people outside the labor force—that is, without access to co-workers—household income (beta = $-.19$) and being raised as a Protestant or Catholic (beta = .12) were also important.

22. The means (.52, .48, .42, and .35) differ at eta = .20 ($p < .001$).

23. On popular beliefs, see D. Hummon, "Community Ideology " (Ph.D. diss., Department of Sociology, University of California, Berkeley, 1980).

24. An analysis of covariance design, with residence in the city (zero to two years/three to ten/eleven or more), gender, and urbanism as factors, and education and never married as covariates, yields the following adjusted means from Semirural to Core: .49, .46, .42, and .39 (beta = .12, $p < .01$). The partial correlation for urbanism, controlling for the variables listed in note 9, is $-.11$ ($p < .001$).

25. Number of kin and the Lieberson measure of nonkin diversity were added to the covariates in the model described in note 24. The adjusted means—.49, .45, .43, and .40—differ at beta = .09 ($p < .05$). Multiple regression analyses, using the personal variables listed in note 9 and the network variables listed in note 19, yielded adjusted means virtually identical to those shown in the dashed line, and a partial correlation with urbanism of $-.12$ ($p < .001$).

26. Another complication concerns gender differences. No urbanism $\times$ gender interaction effects are significant; but the community differences are sharper and more linear among women, and there are differences between genders in the slopes of a few control variables. So this analysis of covariance model was run within gender: the factors were working full time or not and urbanism; the covariates were education, length of residence in city, never married, number of kin, and nonkin diversity. The means, by place type:

Men

Unadjusted: .46, .46, .41, .36 (eta = .14, $p < .01$);

Adjusted: .43, .46, .41, .38 (beta = .09, n.s.);

Women
Unadjusted: .56, .49, .43, .35 (eta = .24, $p < .001$);
Adjusted: .53, .47, .44, .40 (beta = .16, $p < .01$).
The major difference between the sexes is that Semirural men had lower density ratios than expected, equal or less than Town men. I nevertheless report and rely on the total sample results, for two reasons: One, pooling the results of these within-gender analyses yields weighted means much like those in figure 15 and significant differences. Two, the Semirural men are deviant; 26 percent of them are excluded from the analysis because they failed to produce at least three unique names for the density measure—more than twice as high a percentage as any other gender-by-place category. There is reason to believe that, had these missing data been filled in, the Semirural men would have had a higher average density. A similar complex pattern appears with income. Although the interaction of income by urbanism is not significant, the effect is stronger in the low-income group (beta = .15, $p < .05$) than in the high-income group (beta = .07, n.s.)

27. There is a significant interaction effect between urbanism and number of contexts (dichotomized), even after controls for individual differences ($p < .01$). The main effect for urbanism is also significant ($p < .01$). The results shown in figure 15 are based on analyses of covariance run separately within each level of number of contexts, using the same analysis of covariance model: length of residence in city × gender × urbanism, with education, never married, number of kin, and nonkin diversity as covariates. The means differ as follows: three or fewer contexts—eta = .20 ($p < .001$) and beta = .13 (n.s.); four or more contexts—eta = .20 ($p < .001$) and beta = .16 ($p < .01$).

28. By "well," I mean actually trying to find out which associates are linked. Many studies have crudely estimated density with global questions such as "Are your friends friends of one another?"

29. Norman Shulman found that people in dense networks were more likely to report being helped but were no more likely to give help to, or lend to, or borrow from intimates than were people in low-density networks. Barry Wellman, however, found no connection between density and people's expectations of receiving assistance. See N. Shulman, "Urban Social Networks" (Ph.D. diss., University of Toronto, 1972); B. Wellman et al., "Community Ties and Support Systems," in *The Form of Cities in Central Canada*, ed. L. S. Bourne, R. D. Mackinnon, and J. W. Simmons (Toronto: University of Toronto Press, 1973).

30. This comment is based on results from a 1965 survey on the three best friends of each of one thousand Detroit area men. See E. O. Laumann, *Bonds of Pluralism* (New York: Wiley, 1973), and Fischer et al., *Networks and Places*, chap. 3.

31. C. Kadushin et al., "Social Density and Mental Health" (unpublished paper, Center for Social Research of the Graduate Center, City University of New York, 1980).

32. Because our procedure for selecting the names used in calculating density is linked to our procedure for measuring support, any correlation would include some complex artifact.

33. Although linear correlations of network density with the probability of wishing to know more people to talk to ($r = -.11$) and to have a good time with ($r = -.10$) are significant, quadratic functions fit better, especially after controls. The unadjusted equations (D represents the density ratio) are:
Talk = $-.37D + .22D^2 + .28$ ($R = .12; p < .01$);
Good time = $-.27D + .11D^2 + .50$ ($R = .10; p < .01$).
At $D = 0$, 28 percent wish to know more people to talk to; at $D = .84$, only 12 percent do; and at $D = 1$, 13 percent do. At $D = 0$, 50 percent wish to know more people to have a good time with; at $D = .61$, 38 percent do; and at $D = 1$, 34 percent do. The following variables were also included in the complete regression equation: gender, age, never married or living together, number of children at home, works full time, part time, education, income, length of residence in the city and in the neighborhood, and these network vari-

ables: number of kin; number of nonkin (before the "anyone else" question); nonkin diversity score; number of names used to calculate density (i.e., the size of the special subsample); average multiplexity score; and that score squared. The unstandardized partial coefficients for density are:

Talk $= -43D + .32D^2$ (D's term: $p < .01$; D^2: $p < .05$);

Good time $= .57D + .40D^2$ (D: $p < .01$; D^2: $p < .05$).

Other factors controlled, at $D = 0$, 28 percent want more people to talk to; at $D = .67$, 14 percent do; and at $D = 1$, 17 percent do. At $D = 0$, 55 percent want more people to talk to; at $D = .71$, 35 percent do; and at $D = 1$, 38 percent do. If the other network terms are excluded from the equation, the results are essentially the same. (Note: only the 941 respondents with three or more names in the density matrix were used for this analysis.) The analysis was also run for only those respondents whom interviewers thought were "open" about their feelings. The results are essentially the same. And the analysis was run separately for respondents with subsample networks of three, four, or five names. The results, though complex, are consistent with those presented here.

34. The analytical procedure here was the same as that reported in note 29, for the "know enough" questions. Unadjusted, the equation for the psychological mood measure shown in the figure is (note—a b of .10 represents change of .16 standard deviations):

$$\text{Mood} = .06D - .06D^2 + 3.85 \ (R = .01, \text{n.s.}).$$

In an equation including the same variables as those listed in the previous note, the partial coefficients are:

$$\text{Mood} = .17D - .01D^2 \ (\text{the linear component is significant at } p < .05).$$

Note that number of nonkin has a significant partial beta coefficient (i.e., standardized) of .15 ($p < .001$; zero-order $r = .19$) with mood. The results for only the "frank" respondents are much the same.

35. The interaction effect of density $\times$ income on mood is significant ($p < .01$), even after adjustment for a few critical covariates. (This interaction effect, by the way, occurs only in Metropolitan and Core communities.) Regression analyses identical to those reported in the previous notes were run within each income group. The unadjusted equations are:

Low income
Mood $= .39D - .12D^2 - 3.55$ ($R = .12$, linear effect, $p < .001$);

High income
Mood $= - .51D + .30D^2 + 4.16$ ($R = .12$, linear effect, $p < .001$).

The adjusted equations are:

Low income
Mood $= .73D - .32D^2$ (D, $p < .05$; D^2, n.s.);

High income
Mood $= - .41D + .27D^2$ (n.s.).

36. Number of nonkin (named before the "anyone else" equation) correlates $-.21$ with density for the whole sample of 941, $-.23$ among low-income respondents, and $-.16$ among high-income respondents.

37. In the same equations discussed for testing density, the partial betas for number of nonkin on mood are total sample, .15, $p < .001$; low income, .15, $p < .01$; and high income, .18, $p < .001$.

38. On these points see, for example, essays by Mitchell and by Barnes in *Social Networks in Urban Situations*, ed. J. C. Milchell (Manchester: Manchester University Press, 1969); Frankenburg, *Communities in Britain*; and Bott, *Family and Social Network*.

39. The sample for this analysis consists of the 3,383 associates who were in subsamples of *four or five* names (excluding subsamples of three names to maintain stability in the statistics). The correlation between centrality and being cited two or more times is .16; being labeled "close" by the respondent, .24; being cited as someone with whom the respondent discusses personal matters, .16; and being cited as someone with whom the respondent

spends social time, .15. In regression analyses controlling for many characteristics of respondents, the associates, and their relations, centrality remains a strong and independent predictor. Although controlling for kinship does not affect these results substantially, kin did not need to be as central as nonkin in order to be considered close or to serve as confidants. (There are no substantively important interactions with respondent income.) A final bibliographic note: In *Networks and Places* (pp. 53–54), Robert Jackson, Lynne McCallister, and I report that network density among three best friends was correlated with the respondent's feeling close to the friend, but only for friends living in the neighborhood. In these data there was a similar interaction effect ($p < .01$). Centrality was most strongly related to closeness among associates living within five minutes' drive (beta = .21) and least among those over an hour away (beta = .09). Crudely summarized, distant associates were intimate no matter what their centrality, but nearby associates were intimate only if they were central.

40. There is a strong independent correlation between an associate's centrality and how long he or she knew the respondent, even after controlling for many covariates and excluding kin from the analysis.

41. In analyses of covariance, adjusting the probabilities for income of respondent, whether the associate was a relative or not, and the centrality of the associates, the betas for others' density were: probability of discussing personal matters, .11 ($p < .001$); of being a social companion, .11 ($p < .001$); of being "felt close," .07 ($p < .001$); and of being mentioned more than twice, .12 ($p < .001$). In correlational analyses, the partial correlations of others' density, *controlling for centrality* (the two correlate at $r = .43$) are: personal matters, −.13; social companion, −.11; felt close, −.11; and total number of mentions, −.14—all $p < .001$. There are no substantively important interactions with respondents' income.

42. This argument was suggested by Ann Swidler.

43. These speculations could be tested in the present data, though I could not pursue the issue further for lack of time and resources.

44. That is, among low-income respondents, the indirect effect of urbanism on mood via density is approximately −.15 × .17 = −.03. The indirect effect via number of nonkin *named in the exchange questions* is approximately −.12 × .14 = −.02. Another estimate of the effect can be calculated this way: The partial effect of urbanism on mood among low-income respondents, controlling for personal traits, is −.05; the effect controlling for density is −.03; and the effect controlling for all network variables is −.01. (As noted elsewhere, anxiety about crime can also explain all of the small negative correlation with mood.)

Chapter 13

1. The views summarized here are found throughout the statements of exponents of the decline theory. For recent reviews of the arguments, see T. Bender, *Community and Social Change in America* (New Brunswick: Rutgers University Press, 1978); B. Wellman, "The Community Question," *American Journal of Sociology* 84 (1979):1201–31; and chaps. 8–10 of C. S. Fischer et al., *Networks and Places* (New York: Free Press, 1977). The phrase "community without propinquity" is Melvin Webber's, from "Order in Diversity: Community without Propinquity," in *Neighborhood, City and Metropolis*, ed. R. Gutman and D. Popenoe, pp. 792–81 (New York: Random House, 1970 [1963]).

2. We asked respondents only about five and sixty minutes because we could not impose upon them to specifically locate every one of their associates. (We did, however, have them specify the city of residence for the special subsample of associates.) The two questions—"Which of the people on this list live within about a five-minute drive from here?" (q. 83) and "Which of the people on this list live outside the area, that is, more than an hour's drive from here?" (q. 84)—permitted respondents to quickly check off the names of those people who qualified. The few associates whose locations respondents did not know were assigned,

by default, to the intermediate distance. Analysis of our pilot surveys indicated that these measures of distance are probably reliable. In the pilots, we asked respondents to estimate specific travel times for visiting each of the subsample associates. These answers were very consistent with the general five-minute or one-hour check-offs.

3. Length of residence in the city correlates .22 with number of local kin, but only .05 with number of local nonkin.

4. We asked respondents: "Some people feel it's very important to live close to their relatives and see a lot of them; for others it's not so important. How important is it to you . . . ? (q. 8). The percentages who said it was "very" or "somewhat" important to them were, from Semirural to Core: 61, 63, 56, and 59 (χ^2, $p < .05$).

5. The logarithm of the number (plus one) of nonkin named who lived within five minutes' drive (exclusive of those named only as house caretakers) was regressed on the following reduced equation (significant betas indicated): age, age for males only ($-.26$), female ($-.23$), education (.09), household income (.08), time in the neighborhood (.13), employed full time, and cooperativeness in the interview (.14); $R^2 = .075$.

6. Louis Harris Associates, *A Survey of Citizen Views and Concerns about Urban Life* (Washington, D.C.: Department of Housing and Urban Development, 1978), p. 120.

7. See C. S. Fischer, *The Urban Experience* (New York: Harcourt, Brace, Jovanovich, 1976), pp. 101–5, and 112–21. Among others, Morris Janowitz has argued, largely on the basis of one British survey and accumulated ethnographic field studies, that "community size and density have very limited consequences on a person's social bonds to his locality. . . . That is, persons who live in large and dense urban settlements have no weaker or more limited informal and kinship ties than do residents of smaller and less densely populated areas. By contrast, the single most important variable leading to stronger social bonds is length of residence." The quotation is from M. Janowitz and D. Street, "The Changing Social Order of the Metropolitan Area," in *Handbook of Contemporary Urban Life*, ed. D. Street and Associates, p. 111 (San Francisco: Jossey-Bass, 1978). The British study is reported in J. D. Kasarda and M. Janowitz, "Community Attachment in Mass Society," *American Sociological Review* 39 (1974):328–39. This survey certainly contradicts that claim about local kinship bonds.

8. The means differ at eta = .10, $p < .001$. Adjusting for key predictors yields means of 5.9, 4.9, 4.6, and 3.9 (beta = .14, $p < .001$).

9. In a regression equation, controlling for about fifteen covariates, the adjusted percentages are .45, .30, .33, and .35 (beta = .17, $p < .001$).

10. These estimates were based on the following assumptions: (1) the average density within five minutes' drive of a respondent's home is equal to the average density of his or her municipality; (2) the average speed of a five-minute drive is thirty miles per hour in Semirural places, twenty in Town and Metropolitan, and fifteen in Core communities; and (3) since much of the area covered by such a drive in Semirural and Town places is open countryside, the estimates for the population within five minutes' drive were arbitrarily corrected by dividing by three in the first case and two in the latter. This yielded the following figures for the base populations: 11,500, 14,000, 30,000, and 60,000. These estimates probably understate the difference between small and large places. The number of local nonkin named per 1,000 estimated people are, from Semirural to Core: .33, .23, .12, and .06. If local kin are also added, the figures are .49 (one per 2,000), .34 (one per 3,000), .16 (one per 6,500), and .07 (one per 14,000). These estimates must, of course, be taken as suggestive only. Since there was a practical limit to how many names respondents could give, even hypersocial Core respondents would have trouble recording a high ratio of local associates. Also, from a theoretical perspective, knowing some absolute number of community people, not some fixed ratio, is probably critical for community attachment.

11. Logarithms (of number named plus one) were used because the predictive equations fit slightly better. And, the interval urbanism scale was used instead of the categories,

because (1) the categories did not account for most of the scale correlation (that is, within the Town, Metropolitan, and Core samples, the urbanism scale had a significant partial correlation with the dependent variables); and (2) a quadratic function of the scale fits the data better than did dummies for the four categories. The basic findings, however, are the same if untransformed data and the urban categories are used.

12. The equation described by the solid line in figure 20 is log $(N + 1) = -1.20u + .24u^2 + 1.97$ ($R = .045$, n.s.). The antilog means for the urban categories are, from Semirural to Core: 2.4, 2.1, 2.0, and 2.6 (eta $= .08$, $p < .10$).

13. The equation described by the dashed line in figure 20 is based on the partial correlations of urbanism and urbanism squared with the dependent variable, holding constant the control variables listed in note 5. (In effect, it is the regression of the residuals on a quadratic function of urbanism. The parameters are barely different than they would be had the terms been entered into the full equation.) The displayed function is: log $(N + 1) = -2.14u + .42u^2 + 3.24$ (partial $R = .12$, $p < .001$). Entering the dummies for the urban categories into the control equation yields adjusted means of 2.8, 2.2, 1.9, and 2.3 (beta $= .11$, $p < .01$).

14. This last item introduces some circularity into the scale. Excluding the item, however, barely affects any of the results discussed below, except to slightly lower the correlation between the scale and the number of local nonkin.

15. Adding the local activity scale to the equation described in note 5 yields a beta of .24 ($p < .001$); $R^2 = .129$.

16. Regressing the local activity scale on both respondent and place characteristics yields the following best predictors: cooperativeness, youth, being male, living in the Core, and not living in a Metropolitan community; $R^2 = .06$. Community differences in available activities probably also explain why local activity made the most difference in knowing local nonkin in Semirural and Metropolitan places and least in Town and Core places. It is probably passing the threshold to having some local activity rather than none at all—the crucial distinction in Semirural and Metropolitan places—that makes the most difference in meeting local people.

17. Adding a dummy variable for whether or not the respondent lives in a detached home to an equation including the variables in note 5 and local activity yields a beta of .07 ($p < .05$); $R^2 = .134$. Here is an instance where logging made a difference. With number of nonkin unlogged, the partial correlation is .11.

18. On these points, see, for example, S. Keller, *The Urban Neighborhood* (New York: Random House, 1968); W. Michelson, *Environmental Choice, Human Behavior, and Residential Satisfaction* (New York: Oxford University Press, 1977); M. Baldassare, *Residential Crowding in America* (Berkeley: University of California Press, 1979); and C. J. Silverman, "Negotiated Claim" (Ph.D. diss., Department of Sociology, University of California, Berkeley, 1981).

19. The zero-order correlation between urbanism and living in a detached house is $-.43$; the partial, controlling for age, being married, income, children, and length of residence in city, is $-.44$. These held constant, the chances of a Semirural resident's living in a house were .83; Town, .67; Metropolitan, .61; and Core, .28.

20. Adding the local activity scale and house type to the control yields the equation: logarithm $(N + 1) = -1.89u + .37u^2 + 2.92$ (partial $R = .11$, $p < .01$) (Had an unlogged dependent variable been used, the association would have been barely nonsignificant; partial $R = .07$, $p < .10$.)

21. The partial multiple Rs for low- and high-income groups differ at $p < .05$. The analytical procedure used here was to replicate the general analysis within income groups. The relevant equations are:

Low income
Unadjusted: logarithm $(N + 1) = -2.91u + .59u^2 + 4.01$ ($R = .12$, $p < .05$);
Adjusted for personal traits: logarithm $(N + 1) = -3.20u + .62u^2 + 4.52$ (partial $R = .19$, $p < .001$);

Fully adjusted: logarithm (N + 1) = −2.82u + .55u^2 + 4.05 (partial R = .17, p < .001);
High income
Unadjusted: logarithm (N + 1) = .02u − .005u^2 + .537 (R = .00, n.s.);
Adjusted for personal traits: logarithm (N + 1) = −1.05u + .20u^2 + 1.90 (partial R = .05, n.s.);
Fully adjusted: logarithm (N + 1) = −1.01u + .20u^2 + 1.81 (partial R = .04, n.s.).

22. Multicollinearity problems are accentuated here because we have basically fifty ecological units of analysis, and on some variables, considerably fewer distinct values.

23. These sentences distill extensive statistical analyses far too complex and tedious to present here.

24. A good and recent formulation of this thesis can be found in Baldassare, *Residential Crowding*.

25. Just looking at linear effects, the partial correlation of municipal density (logged)—all variables controlled—with local ties is −.068, compared with −.080 for the urbanism scale. (Among low-income respondents, −.094 and −.131.) Given the high collinearity of density and urbanism (r = .856), this means that urbanism fully explains the joint correlation of the two with the dependent variable. There is a suggestive parallel between this finding and one reported in chapter 9. I reported there that municipal density was more strongly correlated—negatively—with naming neighbors than was neighborhood density, arguing that the social opportunities of the city drew people out of the neighborhoods. Here I suggest that the opportunities of the region—measured by urbanism—draw people out of the city.

26. A complex model underlies this claim, as well as the general argument I have presented for why local ties decline as urbanism increases. The model assumes that (1) people try to optimize their social relations; and (2) urbanism increases the opportunities for social relations beyond the neighborhood and beyond the locality. As an ideal-typical metropolitan area—density declining from center to periphery—increases in population, the distant opportunities will increase more rapidly than the near ones (even considering cost of travel). If one also posits a roughly constant size of people's networks, these assumptions together predict that the greater the urbanism, the fewer the local associates—at least in proportion to the regional ones. Put formally the argument is that $N_d = k/P_{d+1}$, where N_d is the number of actual ties at distance d and P_{d+1} is the number of potential ties at a distance $d + 1$. An alternative model would assume that people satisfice; they go out from the neighborhood only as far as necessary to fill their quota of relations. This would predict that urbanites would have *more* local associates; or, $N_d = k \cdot P_d$. (For more discussions of these points, see Fischer, *Networks and Places*, pp. 120–22.) The slight increase in local ties from Metropolitan to Core in this survey suggests that, perhaps, the two should be combined; $N_d = k \cdot P_d/P_{d+1}$. The increase in P_d from Metropolitan to Core (a doubling according to the estimate in note 10) is greater than the increase in P_{d+1}.

27. The push theory explanation for the income interaction effect would predict that, all else equal, income should increase people's local associates more in urban than in nonurban places. (In addition to the standard advantage of the affluent, the difference in the ability to buffer themselves from stress would expand their edge.) Although the lines in figure 20 suggest as much, regressions run *within* urban categories show no differences between those categories in the partial slopes for household income.

28. M. M. Webber, "The Urban Place and the Nonplace Urban Realm," in *Explorations into Urban Structure*, ed. C. Wurster et al. (Philadelphia: University of Philadelphia Press, 1963). On the rise of the "metropolitan community," see A. Hawley, *Urban Society* (New York: Ronald Press, 1981).

29. This paragraph summarizes the regression of the number of nonkin named who lived within five to sixty minutes' drive (plus one and logged) on the following variables: gender, age (beta = −.12); age for males; education (.18); household income (.09); number of children at home (−.10); being employed full time (.20); years in the city (.09); having an

automobile always available for personal use (.07); and cooperativeness in the interview (.11); R^2 = .203. For low-income respondents, R^2 = .258, and the key coefficients are full time (.23); age $(-.19)$; and car (.09). For high-income respondents, R^2 = .086, and the same coefficients are full time (.13); age $(-.02)$; and car (.03).

30. The equation describing the unadjusted pattern is logarithm $(\text{N} + 1) = 4.53u - .85u^2 - 5.37$ (multiple R = .31, $p < .001$). The unadjusted means for each urban category are 1.53, 2.65, 3.84, and 3.77 (eta = .30, $p < .001$).

31. The broken line describes the regression on urbanism of the residuals from the control equation described in note 29. The displayed equation is logarithm $(\text{N} + 1) = 3.61u - 0.7u^2 - 4.02$ (partial R = .21, $p < .001$). The adjusted means by urban category are 1.96, 2.82, 3.44, and 3.25 (beta = .18, $p < .001$). I also constructed a scale like the local activity scale used in the previous section that measures the amount of shopping and entertainment activity respondents conducted *away* from their communities. Unfortunately it was not fully accurate for small communities. In any case, adding it to the controls does not alter the substantive conclusions.

32. The equations are:
Low income
Unadjusted: logarithm $(\text{N} + 1) = 2.70u - .48u^2 - 3.16$ (R = .27, $p < .001$);
Adjusted: logarithm $(\text{N} + 1) = 2.12u - .41u^2 - 2.18$ (partial R = .14, $p < .01$);
High income
Unadjusted: logarithm $(\text{N} + 1) = 5.65u - 1.07u^2 + 6.71$ (partial R = .33, $p < .001$);
Adjusted: logarithm $(\text{N} + 1) = 5.81u - 1.19u^2 - 6.79$ (partial R = .29, $p < .001$).
The low-income and high-income adjusted Rs differ significantly from one another.

33. I did examine the correlations between several attributes of the locality and the number of middle-distance nonkin respondents named (although the causal connection here is theoretically vague). Respondents in affluent localities and respondents in localities with some black residents named more middle-range associates than those in poorer or in less black areas. When urbanism, or personal characteristics of respondents, or both, are held constant, median income appears to maintain some autonomous importance. (Problems of multicollinearity abound.) Affluent people tend to have dispersed networks, and living among them may have encouraged others to the same style, perhaps because interest in forming local ties was not reciprocated.

34. In Semirural communities, affluent respondents, ceteris paribus, named significantly fewer middle-range associates than did low-income respondents. Why that is so is unclear, but there are signs that affluent respondents in those places had especially many very distant associates (perhaps because many were recent immigrants from urban places).

35. These comments are based on regressing the logarithm of the number of nonkin named who lived over an hour away (plus one) on age; age for males $(-.17)$; female $(-.16)$; never married; never married female (.13 among low-income respondents); fully employed; part time employed female $(-.10$ among high-income respondents); education (.21); household income (.10); number of children at home $(-.11)$; length of residence in the city $(-.26)$; and cooperativeness in the interview (.16); R^2 = .209. Unfortunately, we do not know how far away respondents' previous cities of residence were. That would probably add much more to the explained variance.

36. The equation displayed in the figure is logarithm $(\text{N} + 1) = -1.28u + .30u^2 + 1.63$ (R = .14, $p < .001$). The unadjusted means, by urban category, are: 0.83, 1.04, 1.06, and 1.59 (eta = .15, $p < .001$).

37. The equation, partialed for the control variables listed in note 35, is logarithm $(\text{N} + 1) = -2.02u + .42u^2 + 2.74$ (partial R = .08, $p < .05$). The adjusted means for the urban categories are 1.14, 1.12, 0.96, and 1.24 (beta = .07, n.s.). The results must be taken with some reservations, first because the community differences using the urban categories are not significant, and second because there are a few significant interaction effects between

urbanism and the control variables. For example, length of residence made a greater difference among Semirural respondents than among respondents elsewhere. Covariance analysis
suggests modest, nonsignificant differences among the urban categories, but with hints of the
curvilinear pattern shown here. The partial equation is, for low-income respondents:
logarithm $(N + 1) = -1.53u + 0.32u^2 + 2.12$ (partial $R = .07$, n.s.); and for high-income
respondents: logarithm $(N + 1) = -2.51u + 0.51u^2 + 3.41$ (partial $R = .09$, n.s.).

38. This claim is based, first, on a distinct impression from reading the interviews that
many more Core residents than other respondents were transplanted easterners, and, second, that compared with Semirural residents at least twice as high a proportion of the distant
associates of Core residents were from out of state.

39. The correlations between number of local nonkin and number of distant ones (unlogged) are, from Semirural to Core: $-.08$, $.13$, $.11$, and $.26$. The Semirural r is significantly
different from all the others, and the Core r is almost significantly different from the Town
and Metropolitan ones. Partialing for cooperativeness, length of residence in the city, and
education yields rs of $-.06$ for Semirural and $.22$ for Core.

40. C. Alexander, "The City as a Mechanism for Sustaining Human Contact," in Urbanman, ed. J. Helmer and N. A. Eddington, pp. 239–74 (New York: Free Press, 1973).

41. More exactly, local associates will range from being seen as barely rewarding to
immensely rewarding; there is no reason why one's dearest friend cannot live next door. The
range for distant associates narrows, however, since the more difficult it is to sustain the tie,
the more rewarding it must be to remain a tie. The average differences thus will still be in the
direction of distant associates' being considered more rewarding. This thesis was presented
first, to my knowledge, by J. W. Thibaut and H. H. Kelley, in *The Social Psychology of
Small Groups* (New York: Wiley, 1959), pp. 41 ff. It is elaborated in chapter 9 of Fischer et
al., *Networks and Places*.

42. The findings described here and in subsequent sections are based on analyses of two
sets of relational data: the 20 percent random sample of all relations, and the special subsample of 4,179 relations drawn for detailed questioning. The table reports results for the
random sample. The statements about controls are based on regression analyses run on both
samples. (The regression analyses include *all* relations except household members, unlike
the table, which also excludes associates who only provided house care. A slight distortion
is thereby introduced, most of which is corrected by controlling for the social context of
"neighbor.") The dependent variable in the equations is whether or not the named person is
called "close." The independent variables include characteristics of the respondent (gender,
age, education, etc.); characteristics of the named persons (only gender for the random
sample; age, marital status, and other traits as well for the special subsample); and characteristics of the relation itself (dummies for the social context of the relation, same gender
versus not, and in the special subsample, age differential); as well dummies for distance.
(For the special subsample, it is also possible to specify distances more carefully—over an
hour within northern California versus outside northern California.) In these analyses there
remains a significant, positive partial association between being more than an hour away—
especially outside the region—and being thought "close." It is notably stronger among
nonkin than kin. A theoretically more appropriate, if more difficult, way of analyzing the
data is to compare close and distant associates for each individual respondent: Do people
consider their nearer or their farther associates as emotionally closer? Calculating percentages for each respondent and using matched t-tests also shows that higher proportions of
distant than of local nonkin were considered "close."

43. See chapter 9 of Fischer et al., *Networks and Places*.

44. These statements are based on regression analyses such as those described in note
42. I also compared, for each respondent, the percentage of local nonkin who discussed
personal matters with the percentage of nonkin over five minutes away who did. There was
no net difference.

45. B. Wellman, "The Community Question," *American Journal of Sociology* 84 (1979): 1201–31. See also E. Litwak and I. Szelenyi, "Primary Group Structures and Their Functions," *American Sociological Review* 34 (1969): 465–81.

46. See C. S. Fischer, "The Spatial Dimension of Social Support," Working Paper no. 300, Institute of Urban and Regional Development, Berkeley.

47. This table presents the statistics in terms of the percentage of associates within or beyond five minutes' drive who were named in each exchange question (nonkin only):

	Less Affluent Respondents			More Affluent Respondents		
	< 5 Min.	> 5 Min.	Difference	< 5 Min.	> 5 Min.	Difference
Sociable activities	59%	42%	17%	55%	42%	13%
Discuss hobbies	27	18	09	29	17	12
Discuss personal matters	20	12	08	13	10	03
Advice	8	8	00	5	5	00
Lend money	9	8	01	3	7	−04

The differences in the differences are subtle but, with the exception of hobbies, generally indicate a smaller advantage to proximity among the affluent. Analysis of the special subsample of relations indicates that, controlling for other characteristics, distance had generally less independent effect on receiving support among affluent than among nonaffluent respondents.

48. This analysis involves regressing the answers to the evaluation questions (q. 101–3), to the pleased, and to the psychological mood scales on, first, six variables describing the network—the number of local, middle-range, and distant nonkin and kin (exclusive of those named only in the house-care item)—and, second, adding seven control variables: age, education, income, length of residence, works part time, network density, and network density squared. The regressions were run separately within the less and more affluent groups (divided at $15,000). The results, by dependent variable, are:

1. *More to talk.* Spatial distribution makes a difference for the nonaffluent ($R^2 = .048$) but not the affluent ($R^2 = .007$). Distant nonkin increase the desire for more associates among the nonaffluent (partial slope = .024; with controls, .016) and middle-range kin decrease it ($-.016$, $-.011$).

2. *More for good time.* The same sorts of results emerge. Spatial distribution made a difference for the nonaffluent ($R^2 = .037$), but not for the affluent ($R^2 = .006$). For the low-income respondents, distant nonkin increased the desire for more associates (partial slope = .032; with controls, .018).

3. *To help.* No substantial findings in either group.

49. In the regressions described in note 48, the number of associates, classified by kinship and spatial distribution, accounted for 8.6 percent of the variance in *pleased* scores among the nonaffluent. Middle-distance nonkin contributed significantly to this variance (partial slope = .029; with controls, .028), and number of local nonkin contributed even more (.050; .046). Among the affluent, the network variables accounted for 7.0 percent of the variance, and all nonkin groups contributed: local (partial slope = .024; with controls .023); middle-range (.016; .015); and distant (.029, .023). The findings with the overall mood scale are parallel, but all the coefficients are reduced by about 30 to 50 percent.

50. For extended discussion of contact frequency and other attributes of relations, see Fischer et al., *Networks and Places*, chaps. 3 and 9.

51. The indirect effects of residence on the pleased scale controlling for other variables listed in note 48, suggest that moving from Core to Semirural increases low-income respondents' scores about .06 standard deviations, or perhaps one or two percentile ranks— roughly the same amount as adding another educational degree. The effect is almost as great

in moving from Towns to Semirural. If one also adds the indirect effects of Semirural residence on being pleased via its effect on network density, the total consequence among the less affluent of moving from Core to Semirural via the effects on networks is an increase of roughly .17 standard deviations in pleased and .12 in overall mood (and a *drop* of .05 and .08 standard deviations for the affluent)—all else constant.

Chapter 14

1. Recent network studies focussing on homogeneity include E. O. Laumann's *Prestige and Association in an Urban Community* (New York: Bobbs-Merrill, 1966) and his *Bonds of Pluralism* (New York: Wiley, 1973); L. M. Verbrugge, "The Structure of Adult Friendship Choices," *Social Forces* 56 (December 1977): 576–97; and the chapters by R. M. Jackson and by C. A. Stueve and K. Gerson in C. S. Fischer et al., *Networks and Places* (New York: Free Press, 1977).

2. On homophily, see P. Lazarsfeld and R. K. Merton, "Friendships as a Social Process," in *Freedom and Control in Modern Society,* ed. M. Berger et al., pp. 18–66 (New York: Van Nostrand, 1954). The process of like seeking is the subject of "interpersonal attraction" studies in social psychology. For a review of such studies, see. T. L. Huston and G. Levinger, "Interpersonal Attraction and Relationships," *Annual Review of Psychology* 29 (1978): 115–56.

3. The reader will recall that no household members were included in this subsample and that to appear in it associates had to be prominently named in answer to one of six key questions: taking care of the respondent's home, visiting or going out socially with the respondent, discussing a hobby, acting as a confidant, advising on important decisions, or lending money. The largest group, by social context, in these 4,179 relations were "just friends" (26 percent), most of whom had met through a friend, at work, or in school; the next largest groups were close kin (25 percent—especially parents), and neighbors (18 percent).

4. This procedure raises a few questions: Why was it not used in other analyses? Because we have duration of relation only for the special subsample of names. What is the alternative causal interpretation that this procedure means to foreclose? That people with young or age-similar associates are selectively drawn to cities. (It would be difficult—but not, of course, impossible—to explain how the urbanism of a person's community causes him or her to keep an associate met before the respondent came to the community.) What empirical difference does it make to use only this subset? Not much, as the notes below will indicate, though the patterns tend to be a bit more linear among the postarrival set. The selection of postarrival associates is not precise, because the categories for length of residence (in q. 1) are only approximate. We lose some associates who had in fact been met since the respondents arrived, but we exclude *all* who had been met before.

5. The statistics for this entire analysis are summarized in table N6. If all nonkin are included, not just the postarrival ones, the ages range from 46.0 to 37.6 (eta = .20, $p < .001$).

6. The age of the associates ($N = 1,499$) was regressed on respondents' age (unstandardized $b = 0.57$); age squared (.001); and other variables listed in note a to the table. The only other significant predictor was being employed ($b = 2.21$); $R^2 = .462$.

7. Two rough estimates of the age composition of the local community were used: the informants' average ratings of how many young adults and of how many elderly people there were in the locality (question 4 in Appendix C). Added to the control equation described in note 6, they have a joint beta of .06 ($p < .05$; beta for youth = −.01; beta for elderly = .04, $p < .05$). This is probably a minimum estimate of the actual effect, since the measures are quite crude.

8. The partial beta for elderly in the community is .07 ($p < .05$).

9. The partial beta for elderly in the community is .19 ($p < .05$).

10. See, for example, F. Carp, "Lifestyle and Location within the City," *Gerontologist* 15 (February 1975):27–33; and E. Litwak et al., "An Empirical Study of Primary Groups amongst the Elderly" (paper presented to the American Sociological Association, Boston, August 1979), p. 21.

11. If all nonkin are counted, not just those met since arrival, the variation is from 9.9 to 6.9 (eta = .12, $p < .001$).

12. The absolute differences in age between respondents and their associates was regressed on the same control equation listed in note a of table N6. The significant predictors were age squared ($b = .0024$; age $b = -.076$) and being married ($b = 1.3$); $R^2 = .088$.

13. The correlation of Semirural with age difference is .09 ($p < .01$). The partial is .07 ($p < .05$), and the partial controlling also for age composition of the locality is .06 ($p < .10$).

14. The partial beta for presence of elderly people is $-.16$ ($p < .10$), and the correlation between presence of elderly people and urbanism is $-.42$ (among elderly respondents).

15. The data are reported in table N7. If all nonkin associates are included, not just those met since arrival, the probability ranges from .72 to .40 (eta = .23, $p < .001$).

16. Dummy variables for whether the associate was married and for whether the associate was never married were regressed on the control variables listed in note a in table N7. The significant predictors for married are respondent married ($b = .31$ versus being formerly married, .38 versus never married); age ($b = .015$ for age and $-.00014$ for age squared); and number of children at home ($b = .034$); $R^2 = .187$. For never married, the significant predictors are respondent never married ($b = .09$ versus formerly married, .21 versus married); age ($b = -.02$ for age, .00016 for age squared); number of children ($b = -.05$); and household income (beta = .11); $R^2 = .186$.

17. Introducing the two local age composition variables used earlier (see note 7) adds little to the explained variance and does not alter the curves.

18. Using estimates based on the distribution of respondents themselves, a random selection of associates would have yielded the following proportions of married ones: .58, .59, .42, and .29. The observed proportions are, as a ratio of the expected, 1.2, 1.4, 1.7, and 2.1, which suggests greater selectivity on the part of the urban respondents. See statistics in table N7.

19. Although, for the sample as a whole, the more urban the respondent's community, the younger the respondent's age ($r = -.16$ over all associates), for the never-married group it was quite the opposite ($r = .42$ over all associates of never-married respondents).

20. See statistics in table N7.

21. Local population composition contributes somewhat to never marrieds' naming never marrieds: those living in nonfamily neighborhoods were more likely to do so (partial multiple beta = .12). But that does not explain the general community differences.

22. See, for example, E. Litwak et al., "An Empirical Study"; A. Hochschild, *The Unexpected Community* (Englewood Cliffs, N.J.: Prentice-Hall, 1973); and G. Arling, "The Elderly Widow and Her Family, Neighbors, and Friends," *Journal of Marriage and the Family* (November 1976), pp. 757–68.

23. A. Stueve and K. Gerson, "Personal Relations across the Life-Cycle," in Fischer et al., *Networks and Places*, chap. 5.

24. This paragraph summarizes two sets of (reduced equation) regressions conducted on the total set of nonkin in the special subsample of names (not just the nonkin met since arriving in the current city). The dependent variables mentioned in the text were regressed on: respondent characteristics—age, marital status (two dummies), education, household income; associate characteristics—age, gender, marital status (two dummies), employment status; and relation characteristics—social context (four dummies), distance (three dummies), duration, being of the same gender, centrality of the associate (i.e., how many other associates he or she knew), and the absolute difference in ages. In all cited instances, the

Table N6	Ages of Associates[a] and Differences in Age by		
	Community		
		Semi-Rural	**Towns**
		Average Age of Associate	
All Associates (N = 1,499) (Effect of Local Age Composition:[d] beta = .061*)	Unadjusted	41.8	38.9
	Adjusted, Personal Traits[b]	39.1	38.2
	Adjusted, Local Composition[c]	38.4	37.8
Associates of Respondents ⩽ 30 Years Old (N=582) (Effect of Local Age Composition: beta = .049)	Unadjusted	29.7	29.1
	Adjusted, Personal Traits	30.2	30.2
	Adjusted, Local Composition	30.1	30.1
Associates of Respondents 31-64 Years Old (N=766) (Effect of Local Age Composition: beta=.081)	Unadjusted	44.4	41.3
	Adjusted, Personal Traits	42.3	40.4
	Adjusted, Local Composition	41.9	40.7
Associates of Respondents 65+ Years Old (N=151) (Effect of Local Age Composition: beta=.205*)	Unadjusted	59.8	58.8
	Adjusted, Personal Traits	59.5	58.0
	Adjusted, Local Composition	58.8	57.8

partial beta for age similarity was significant. In a second set of similar regressions, duration, strandedness, and frequency of getting together were analyzed for each social context (neighbors, co-workers, etc.) separately. The latter analysis showed that age similarity was related to *less* contact among co-workers and not related among just friends. Strandedness was unrelated to age similarity among co-workers but was strongly related among neighbors.

Urbanism, by Age of Respondent

Metropolitan	Core	Effects eta/beta	r with Urban Scale
37.4	37.1	.105***	−.140***
38.7	38.2	.030	−.042
38.1	37.4	.031	−.043
29.3	29.3	.017	−.017
29.0	28.4	.066	−.072
29.0	28.5	.059	−.068
41.7	39.7	.108*	−.108
42.3	41.1	.069	−.016
42.4	40.8	.061	−.018
57.3	60.1	.065	−.086
59.2	60.1	.061	−.054
59.9	60.8	.078	−.026

Chapter 15

1. Robert Park, "The City" (1916), reprinted in *Classic Essays on the Culture of Cities,* ed. R. Sennett (New York: Appleton-Century-Crofts, 1969), p. 136.

2. General sources reflecting this point of view include classic theorists such as Tönnies and Park, as well as modern writers such as Maurice Stein, Robert Nisbet, Philip Slater, Peter Berger, and Erich Fromm.

Table N6   Continued

		Community	
		Semi-Rural	**Towns**
		Average Absolute Difference in Ages	
All Associates (N = 1,499) (Effects of Local Age Composition:[d] beta=.040)	Unadjusted	10.6	9.2
	Adjusted, Personal Traits[b]	9.8	9.1
	Adjusted, Local Composition[c]	9.9	9.0
Associates of Respondents ⩽ 30 Years Old (N = 582) (Effects of Local Age Composition: beta=.064)	Unadjusted	8.4	7.7
	Adjusted, Personal Traits	8.3	7.8
	Adjusted, Local Composition	8.2	7.7
Associates of Respondents 31-64 Years Old (N=766) (Effect of Local Age Composition: beta = .071)	Unadjusted	11.1	9.2
	Adjusted, Personal Traits	10.7	8.9
	Adjusted, Local Composition	10.5	8.8
Associates of Respondents 65+ Years Old (N=151) (Effect of Local Age Composition: beta = .172)	Unadjusted	13.7	14.7
	Adjusted, Personal Traits	14.1	14.9
	Adjusted, Local Composition	14.6	14.9

* p < .05   ** p < .01   *** p < .001

[a]Includes only nonkin associates in the special subsample whom respondents met after moving to current city.

[b]Adjusted for respondents' traits: age, age-squared, gender, education, currently in school, household income, never married, married, number of children at home, and works.

Metropolitan	Core	Effects eta/beta	r with Urban Scale
		eta/beta	**r with Urban Scale**
8.2	7.4	.115***	−.118***
8.6	7.7	.074*	−.060*
8.6	7.7	.071	−.060
6.2	5.0	.147**	−.139***
6.2	5.1	.120*	−.107**
6.0	5.3	.111	−.100*
8.9	8.3	.101*	−.100**
8.9	8.8	.073	−.060
9.3	8.7	.070	−.057
16.4	14.0	.076	.087
15.0	14.3	.033	.080
14.6	13.9	.030	.020

[c]Two estimates by informants—proportion of local population which is young adults without children and proportion which is older adults without children—added to controls.

[d]Partial effect of adding composition variables to control equation.

Table N7   Marital Status of Associates[a] by Urbanism, by

		Community	
		Semi-Rural	Towns
	Probability Associate Was Married		
All Associates (N=1512)	Unadjusted Adjusted[b]	.627 .585	.620 .572
Associates of Married Respondents (N=694)	Unadjusted Adjusted	.714 .742	.804 .799
	Probability Associate Was Never Married		
All Associates (N=1512)	Unadjusted Adjusted	.136 .188	.188 .220
Associates of Never-Married Respondents (N=329)	Unadjusted Adjusted	.379 .320	.629 .496

** p < .01   *** p < .001

[a]Includes only nonkin associates in the special subsample whom respondents met after moving to current city.

3. See, of my work, *The Urban Experience* and *Networks and Places*. See also M. M. Webber, "Order in Diversity: Community without Propinquity," in *Neighborhood, City and Metropolis*, ed. R. Gutman and D. Popenoe (New York: Random House, 1970), and "The Urban Place and the Nonplace Urban Realm," in M. M. Webber, *Explorations into Urban Structure* (Philadelphia: University of Pennsylvania Press, 1963). Variations on the argument include B. Wellman, "The Community Question: The Intimate Networks of East Yorkers," *American Journal of Sociology* 84, no. 5 (1979):1201–31.

4. These issues resemble those concerning network density covered in chapter 12. And they should, because being heavily involved in a subculture and having a dense personal network probably go together more often than not. But the two are not the same. Density, as treated earlier, characterizes an individual's personal network. A subculture is a much larger group, often a small society. An individual can have associates from different subcultures who know one another well—they might have been in the army together, for example—and can have associates from the same subculture who do not know one another—perhaps members of a far-flung professional subculture. Thus, although the issues are similar, the phenomena are quite different.

5. The concept of "social world" has been used in a somewhat different way since Park, which is why I prefer to use "subculture" when trying to be precise.

6. A. B. Hollingshead, "Behavior Systems as a Field for Research" (1939), reprinted in *Subcultures* ed. D. G. Arnold (Berkeley, Calif.: Glendessary Press, 1970), p. 21.

7. To be still more exact, we should distinguish a social subsystem, the structure of organization and personal relations, from the subculture per se, values, norms, and symbols.

Marital Status of Respondents

Metropolitan	Core	Effects eta/beta	r with Urban Scale
.500	.366	.217***	−.231***
.517	.421	.130***	−.132***
.728	.620	.150***	−.112**
.731	.598	.158***	−.143***
.231	.361	.192***	.216***
.212	.317	.118***	.117***
.477	.479	.143	−.042
.460	.566	.139	.121

[b]Adjusted for: respondent's age, age-squared, whether respondent was currently married (legally), whether respondent was never married and not cohabiting, gender, education, household income, number of children in home, and whether respondent was employed.

And to further distinguish a subculture from other kinds of groups, we should stipulate more criteria: it exists beyond the life or membership of any one individual; the personal relations in the group involve more than one kind of exchange (e.g., more than just praying together for a religious subculture); and the typical cultural features of the group go beyond the common denominator that defines membership (e.g., the ballet world's culture is distinctive in aspects outside of dance itself). These stipulations exclude from the category of sub-culture, for example, temporary interest groups, work groups whose members do not meet off the job, publics whose members share fads and fashions but do not interact, and friendship cliques.

8. The theory is presented with more detail and more qualifications in C. S. Fischer, "Toward a Subcultural Theory of Urbanism," *American Journal of Sociology* 80 (May 1975): 1319–41.

9. These statistics refer to the absolute number of institutions available in each community rather than to the ratio of institutions to population, because: (1) The influence of many types of institutions is not diminished by large clienteles; indeed, in cases such as newspapers and political organizations, numbers add to the influence. (2) We could not measure the sizes of institutions, but we can assume that the urban ones were probably larger on the average. Using per capita statistics would only compound this measurement problem. In any event, per capita measures yield essentially comparable conclusions.

10. Geographers, ecologists, and economists have long documented the increases in specialized organizations and services that accompany population increase. And a few researchers have illustrated the phenomenon with specific subpopulations. One study showed

the connection between the number of blacks in a city and the existence of black economic, political, and cultural institutions (A. A. Karnig, "Black Economic, Political, and Cultural Development: Does City Size Make a Difference?" *Social Forces* 57 [June 1979]: 1194–1211). Another study shows that the larger the town, the more numerous and the more finely specialized its homosexual bars (J. Harry, "Urbanization and the Gay Life," *Journal of Sex Research* 10 [August 1974]: 238–47). On the general point, see, for example, B. J. L. Berry, *Geography of Market Centers and Retail Distribution* (Englewood Cliffs, N.J.: Prentice-Hall, 1967); and M. Abrahamson, "The Social Dimension of Urbanism," *Social Forces* 53 (March 1974): 376–83.

11. The most direct evidence on this latter point is R. Breton's "Institutional Completeness of Ethnic Communities and the Personal Relations of Immigrants," *American Journal of Sociology* 70 (September 1964): 193–205.

12. The key methodological problem we encountered in trying to use a more open-ended, less precategorized procedure to elicit subcultural membership was communicating to respondents the concept of "subculture"—difficult enough for sociologists. We thought that, with enough explanation and examples, respondents for whom it was appropriate could provide their own label for their key memberships. However, our preliminary efforts showed that this was difficult to do and that it would disrupt the flow of the interview and confuse many respondents. We opted, therefore, for using terms that most respondents could also easily use. Other researchers will, I hope, try other avenues.

13. There was also an important methodological reason for dividing the analysis so that involvement was measured only among respondents who had at least one nonkin co-member. Otherwise, the distributions of measures of involvement tend to be quite skewed, piled up at the lower end.

14. As we conceived it, subcultural involvement could be assessed along three related dimensions: the extent to which the individual was tied socially into the group, how much he or she cared about or identified with the group, and to what degree the person's way of life—dress, food, interactional style, tastes, and such—reflected the group's core patterns. The last was extremely difficult to determine, and our only effort along those lines was to have interviewers tell us when they gained an impression that a respondent was particularly involved with his job, religion, and so on. (The measurement problem is that groups differ in subtle ways in many areas of behavior. In terms of ethnicity, for example, there are differences in physical style, fundamental values, child-rearing, interaction in the family, and so forth. To adequately assess even one aspect in an interview and then to compare groups would be sufficiently time-consuming, but we would have had to do even more: to assess the extent to which each member of a group adhered to the modal response pattern of that group. Such a study should be done, and it could be done best by focusing on only a few groups along the rural-to-urban continuum, and by extensive questioning on typical behavior and attitude patterns.) We measured more fully the first two dimensions of involvement—with mixed success. The social dimension was measured in terms of the number and percentage of nonrelatives the respondent named who shared membership. Identification was measured in terms of answers to specific probes, organizational memberships, and magazine subscriptions, and answers to a global question we asked: "Sometimes people feel that *one* aspect of their lives is particularly important to them. Is one of the descriptions I just mentioned (work, ethnicity, religion, pastime) especially important to you? Which description is that?" (q. 100).

Chapter 16

1. The focus is on nonkin rather than all associates, even though kinship, ethnicity, and religion are all part of the traditional primordial "package," because otherwise our analysis would largely reflect kinship involvement. Only people involved with nonkin who share their group membership can really be said to participate in a wider subcultural community.

2. D. Barthel, "The Role of Ethnicity," in *Social Standing in America,* R. P. Coleman and L. Rainwater, chap. 8 (New York: Basic Books, 1978).

3. Like other descriptive statistics, this 27 percent must be handled cautiously. For one, our sample is skewed toward the nonethnics: it overincludes small-town people (otherwise the figure would be about 33 percent); it excludes blacks in black neighborhoods; and it excludes non-English-speakers. Our selection procedure also loses respondents with deep but equally divided ethnic loyalties; some cases were lost by interviewer error (e.g., by treating French Canadian as two ethnicities); and respondents exclusively involved with ethnic blood kin were also excluded. On the other hand, for an Irish-American to have one Irish-American friend is no guarantee of ethnic loyalty; yet he was counted as a member. In sum, the absolute figure should be treated skeptically. Confidence should be placed instead in the associations between the probability of being a member and other factors.

4. Sixty-seven percent of the 77 foreign-*raised* respondents (see q. 6) were members, compared with 24 percent of the other 973 respondents. Sixty percent of those whom *interviewers* coded as "black" were members, compared with 20 percent of those they coded "white." Asians and Mexicans came in at about 30 percent. Holding race and origin constant, respondents *raised* as Catholics—whether or not currently practicing—were 19 percent more likely and the Jewish-reared 26 percent more likely to be ethnic group members (including members of the "Jewish" ethnic group) than were Protestant-reared respondents. In regressing a dummy variable—is ethnic member or not—these variables explain 23 percent of the variance; adding sixteen other variables, such as age and marital status, explains less than 1 percent more. Among non-Anglos there was a tendency for the most highly educated and least affluent to claim an identity.

5. Eta = .16 ($p < .001$; r with urbanism scale = .15).

6. Census data show that as one moves from the regions of California outside the San Francisco and Los Angeles metropolitan areas into the San Francisco area, and into the city itself, the percentages increase of blacks, the foreign-born, and those whose mother tongue is not English. The only notable exception to this correlation between urbanism and foreign origin is the Spanish-speaking group. That proportion of the population tends to *decline* as one moves from rural to urban California.

7. The dependent variable, ethnic group member versus not, was tested in an analysis of covariance. The covariates were raised in a foreign country, gender, age, education, and income. The factors were race (black/Anglo/other), marital status (never married/married/formerly married), religion raised in (Catholic or Jewish vs. other), and urbanism. No interaction effects were significant. The probabilities are, by Semirural, Town, Metropolitan, and Core:

Total sample
Unadjusted: .14, .29, .30, .34 (eta = .16, $p < .001$);
Adjusted: .20, .29, .31, .27 (beta = .09, $p < .05$);
Non-Anglos (N = 163)
Unadjusted: .46, .60, .65, .81 (eta = .24, $p < .05$);
Adjusted: .58, .64, .63, .71 (beta = .09, n.s.);
Anglos (N = 887)
Unadjusted: .12, .23, .26, .23 (eta = .13, $p < .01$);
Adjusted: .14, .24, .25, .20 (beta = .10, $p < .05$).

8. The study of ethnicity in the urban setting has stimulated much discussion about the fundamental character of ethnicity itself. Two useful source books are A. Cohen, ed., *Urban Ethnicity* (London: Tavistock, 1973), and N. Glazer and D. P. Moynihan, eds., *Ethnicity: Theory and Experience* (Cambridge: Harvard University Press, 1975). Donald Horowitz points out, for example, that ethnic groups sometimes emerge from an amalgamation of small entities—most often in cities—and argues: "It seems somewhat inappropriate to use the frequently employed term 'primordial' to describe groups that are products of such recent fission or fusion, or, for that matter, groups which have become far more ascriptive

than they ever were before" (pp. 117–18 in Glazer and Moynihan, *Ethnicity*). A fuller statement of my own analysis appears in C. S. Fischer, *The Urban Experience* (New York: Harcourt Brace Jovanovich, 1976), pp. 126–36, where I argue that ethnicity both persists and changes in the urban setting.

9. The unadjusted logarithmic means differ at eta = .32 ($p < .001$; $r = .33$).

10. The correlation between urbanism and percentage of the nonkin network that is ethnic is .20. If we include in the analysis all 491 respondents who specified an ethnic identity, whether or not they named *any* people of the same ethnicity, the correlation of urbanism with number of nonkin is .27, and with percentage is .24.

11. Fifteen percent of the ethnics either belonged to an ethnic organization or regularly read an ethnic magazine or newspaper (e.g., *Ebony, Siempre*). The probability of doing so correlated .19 with urbanism. Twenty-four percent of ethnics said their ethnicity was their most important identity (q. 100) or said that it was important to live near other ethnics (q. 91), or impressed the interviewer with their degree of ethnic involvement. The probability of doing any of these three correlated .11 with urbanism and was greatest in Town and Core places. I also examined whether respondents spoke their native language (for those for whom it was appropriate; q. 92B). This was unrelated to urbanism.

12. The adjusted means for fellow ethnics differ at beta = .11 (n.s.; r =.11, $p < .10$; Core differs from Semirural at $p < .05$). The adjustment is for the following control variables (partial betas over .10 indicated): foreign-reared (.19), black (.28 versus a base of miscellaneous "others"), Mexican, Jewish, Asian, Irish, Italian, other European ($-.14$), age ($-.14$), gender, age × gender, education (.23), never married, married, number of young children ($-.22$), employed full time, estimated number of relatives in the area, and cooperativeness in the interview (.15); $R^2 = .399$. If all ethnic identifiers are used and N = 491, the partial correlation with similar controls is .09 ($p < .05$).

13. The results for ethnic activity—belonging to an organization or reading a magazine—show no partial association ($r = .05$) and for ideological commitment, a curvilinear one: Town ethnics were highest (partial r for Town = .15, $p < .05$). The adjusted results for speaking the native tongue show Metropolitan residents highest and Core residents lowest (beta = .12, n.s.; N = 122).

14. Although the zero-order correlation between urbanism and number of nonkin who were not fellow ethnics is $-.00$, the partial is $-.10$ ($p < .10$). The control variables are the same as those listed in note 12, and the major predictors are black ($-.13$), Mexican ($-.18$), foreign ($-.12$), Irish (.13), Italian (.18), other Western European (.16), age ($-.11$), gender ($-.22$), age for males ($-.25$), education (.21), fully employed (.15), relatives in the vicinity ($-.22$), and cooperativeness (.17); $R^2 = .399$.

15. Elliot Liebow pointed out to me the sense in which this kind of pattern can be seen as a form of social isolation.

16. Among the five largest groups of ethnic members in our sample, the partial correlations between urbanism and number of fellow ethnic nonkin are Irish, .36 (N = 57); Italians, .10 (N = 35); blacks, .25 (N = 34); Mexicans, $-.21$ (N = 31); and Germans, $-.39$ (N = 22).

17. Relative concentration is measured as the ratio of the population potential of Mexican-Americans to total population potential (see Methodological Appendix section 4.3.1). The partial correlations of relative concentration and of urbanism are contrasted below:

	Urbanism	Relative Concentration
Number Nonkin Mexicans	$-.21$	.08
Percentage Mexicans	$-.33$	.31
Ideological commitment	$-.12$	.35
Organization or reads magazine	.22	.02
Speaks Spanish	$-.06$	.21

The one exception to the pattern concerns ethnic activity—whether the respondent belonged to a Mexican organization or read a Mexican newspaper or magazine. In this case, urbanism rather than relative concentration was important. The result can be explained (statistically, as well as intellectually) by the fact that such organizations and newspapers were concentrated in the Core.

18. For a general review, see Fischer, *Urban Experience,* pp. 126–36. On group size, see a recent study of ethnic identity in Detroit that suggests that members of larger groups are more likely to sustain ethnic identification, partly through the availability of ethnic organizations (S. Stephens, "Ethnic Identity in an Urban Community" [paper presented to American Sociological Association, Boston, 1979]; see also R. Breton, "Institutional Completeness of Ethnic Communities and the Personal Relations of Immigrants," *American Journal of Sociology* 70 [September 1964], pp. 193–205).

19. P. I. Rose, with L. O. Pertzoff, *Strangers in Their Midst: Small-Town Jews and Their Neighbors* (Merrick, N.Y.: Richwood, 1977). Some mixed evidence on community and Jewish identity appears in B. Lazerwitz, "The Community Variable in Jewish Identification," *Journal for the Scientific Study of Religion* 16, no. 4 (1977): 361–69.

20. See Fischer, *Urban Experience,* pp. 194–95; recent studies include H. M. Nelsen and R. H. Potvin, "The Rural Church and Rural Religion," *Annals of the American Academy* 429 (January 1977): 103–14.

21. These 52 percent are notably fewer than the 78 percent who claimed a religion; fully 26 percent of the respondents identified a religion as their own but could not state with certainty that anyone they named aside from parents, siblings, or children was also of that religion. These members in name only were disproportionately Protestant, disproportionately Semirural, and unlikely to be Core residents.

22. Classifications of respondents' religious upbringings are only approximate because we did not account for conversions. We assumed that respondents who claimed a religion or Protestant denomination had been raised in that religion or denomination. That assumption is likely to have been wrong about 23 percent of the time, based on a recent study, with almost all those errors representing switches among Protestant denominations. (See F. Newport, "The Religious Switcher in the United States," *American Sociological Review* 44 [August 1979]: 528–52, especially table 3.)

23. A dummy variable—is religionist or not—was regressed on the following equation (significant betas noted): age (.23), gender, age × gender, education, number of children (.16), household income, a dummy for being under twenty-two years old, one for being over sixty-four (−.09), married, separated, or divorced, widowed, full-time worker (.08), part-time worker, retired, number of relatives in the area (.07), three dummies for race—black, Asian, and Mexican (.09), and five for religion raised in—Catholic (.55), Jewish (.23), Protestant liberal or mainstream denominations (.31), other Protestant denominations (.40), and other religions (.25); $R^2 = .18$.

24. Adjusting these statistics for religious upbringing and other variables changes little. The zero-order differences are significant at eta = .13, $p < .001$. The adjusted probabilities—adjusted for the variables listed in note 23—are: .49, .58, .55, .46 (beta = .10, $p < .01$).

25. Among those raised as Catholics, 55 percent of those living in Semirural communities (N = 38) were members of a Catholic subculture as defined here, compared with 79 percent of those in Towns (N = 91), a difference of 24 points. Among other non-Protestants, the figures are Semirural 29 percent (N = 24) versus Town 42 percent (N =33), a difference of thirteen points. And among Protestants, 49 percent (N = 173) versus 55 percent (N = 174), a difference of only six points.

26. Eta = .17 ($p < .001$; $r = .16$).

27. Number of nonkin co-religionists (logged plus one) was regressed on the following control equation: five dummies for current religion, with high- and middle-level Protestant denominations as base—Catholic (.23), Jew (.13), fundamentalist Protestant (.22), other

Protestant (.12), and other religion (.18)—education (.17), age, gender, Anglo, length of residence in city, married ($-.12$), never married (.11), and cooperativeness (.14); $R^2 = .16$. The adjusted community means are marginally not significant at beta $= .10$ (n.s.; partial $r = .06$; the partial correlation for Core, .10, is significant at $p < .10$).

28. Number of nonkin who were not co-religionists (logged plus one) was regressed on an equation similar to that described in note 27. The major predictors were being a high- or middle-denomination Protestant, a fundamentalist Protestant, or a Catholic; education, being employed; and being young. The adjusted means for the community categories are not significant at beta $= .10$ (n.s.; partial $r = -.01$; the partial for Metropolitan, .19, is significant at $p < .05$). Analysis of the *percentage* of nonkin who were co-religionists shows a significant but irregular pattern: all else equal, Town and Core respondents reported high percentages of fellow religionists.

29. Figure 29 is based on the following regression analysis: Number of co-religionist nonkin was regressed on five dummies for religion—high or middle Protestant, fundamentalist Protestant, other Protestant, Catholic, Jew—gender, age, education, never married, married, number of children at home, is employed (R^2 to this point $= .13$), says religion is most important (q. 100), attendance at services (q. 95; $R^2 = .24$), urbanism ($R^2 = .25$), and three interaction terms—urbanism only for Catholics, urbanism for respondents who said religion was most important, and urbanism for respondents who *never* went to services (final $R^2 = .28$). The betas of interest here are urbanism ($-.03$; n.s.); Catholic ($-.67$; n.s.); urbanism × Catholic (.72, $p = .10$); religion most important ($-.37$, n.s.); urbanism × religion most important (.52, n.s.); attendance (.68, $p < .001$); and urbanism × never attends (.45, $p < .001$). If urbanism squared is added to the equation—which it should be, because it is significant, but was not, in order to keep matters simple—the urbanism × Catholic coefficient becomes significant at $p < .05$. From this equation, we can compare the partial slopes of co-religionist nonkin regressed on urbanism for each of the subgroups (assuming all other variables equal at their means). For Catholics, the urban partial slope is .26; for non-Catholics, .04. For those saying religion is most important, the partial slope is .30 versus .08 for others. And for nonattenders, the slope is .21 versus .07 for attenders. The figure shows some of this pattern, but it is a simplification. Each subgroup is assumed to be average on the other dimensions, when they are not. The curvilinearity in the results is not shown; all the lines tail off at the far right. And the line for the null category is based on assuming only additive effects among the three criteria, which is probably not correct. Nevertheless, the basic message of the figure is correct. The same analysis using *percentage* of nonkin who are co-religionists shows significant effects for Catholic, urbanism × Catholic, attendance, and urbanism × attendance; and the comparison of slopes is approximately the same as for number of co-religionists.

30. Adjusted for the variables listed in note 27, the means for number of co-religionists, from Semirural to Core, are:

Catholics
1.3, 2.6, 2.4, 3.7 (beta $= .28$, $p < .01$; partial $r = .23$);
High- or middle-level Protestant denominations
1.5, 1.5, 1.5, 1.3 (beta $= .05$, n.s.; partial $r = .03$);
Fundamentalists and other Protestants
2.5, 2.5, 2.2, 3.3 (beta $= .08$, n.s.; partial $r = -.01$).

The partial correlations of urbanism with percentage of nonkin who were co-religionists are .20, $-.08$, and $-.05$, respectively. The results are essentially the same if we include *all* religionists in the analysis; that is, if we add in those with *no* fellow religionists.

31. Protestants finding Protestants refers here, largely, to members of specific denominations finding one another. These denominations are, of course, individually smaller than the Catholic church (e.g., there are many more Catholics than Episcopalians). Therefore the findings might actually contradict our theoretical assertions about the importance of population concentration, *unless* we assume that Protestants easily shift specific denominations.

They do. A recent study showed that over a fourth of current Protestants had changed denominations at least once, while only 8 percent of Catholics were converts (Newport, "Religious Switchers"). Also, our data indicate that, for Protestants, the local church, whatever the denomination, is the basic religious attraction. (Seriously religious Protestants lived considerably nearer their co-religionists than did seriously religious Catholics.)

32. Adjusted for the variables listed in note 27, the mean numbers of nonkin named by respondents who reported attending religious services once or twice a year or less, by community, are 1.1, 2.1, 1.8, and 2.3 (beta = .21, $p < .01$; partial $r = .14$). In terms of percentages, beta = .18 ($p < .05$), with Town and Core high (partial for urbanism = .09).

33. See G. Lenski, *The Religious Factor* (Garden City, N.Y.: Doubleday, 1961); also, see W. C. Roof, "Concepts and Indicators of Religious Commitment," in *The Religious Dimension*, ed. R. Wuthnow, pp. 17–45 (New York: Academic Press, 1979).

34. A different, though related, explanation assumes that church attendance is an expression of religious belief (a debatable assumption; cf. Roof, "Concepts and Indicators"). For small-town residents, accordingly, social involvement is more bound up with faith than it is for urbanites. In the urban setting, religious social worlds can become dissociated from creed but still have cultural coherence—around folkways, traditions, political conflict, and so on. Like ethnicity, the culture of the religious unit can be "constructed" or altered.

35. This interaction effect was examined with an analysis of covariance, using five covariates—education, age, number of children, gender, and works or not—and four factors—says religion is most important or not, religion (six categories), marital status (never, currently, or formerly married), and urbanism. The interaction effect of "most important" × urbanism, after adjustment for all covariates and main effects, is significant at $p < .10$ for number of co-religionists and at $p < .06$ for percentage of co-religionists. The same design was applied within categories of "most important." The *adjusted* means for number of co-religionists, by community type, are:
Religion most important
3.4, 4.1, 5.5, 6.9 (beta = .23, n.s.);
Religion not most important
1.6, 2.3, 2.0, 2.3 (beta = .11, n.s.).
In terms of percentage of nonkin:
Religion most important
50, 54, 55, 63 (beta = .12, n.s.);
Religion not most important
27, 35, 27, 33 (beta = .12, n.s.).

36. Also, the urbanism × most important interaction effect is the only significant one in predicting religious activity, as discussed below.

37. The correlation between church attendance and saying religion is most important is .47.

38. These sentences describe the interaction effects shown in figure 29. The line, not drawn on the figure, for frequent church attenders would run from 3.3 to 3.9, *converging* with the line for those who never attend. The line, also not drawn, for respondents who thought religion was not most important would run from 1.9 to 2.6, *diverging* from that for the strong identifiers. The same sort of pattern is revealed by regressing, within each community category, the number of nonkin co-religionists on respondents' church attendance and on whether they said religion was most important (without controls). The partial betas (in the equation, N = Importance + Attendance) are shown here:

	Importance	Attendance	(Difference)
Semirural	.08	.50	(−.42)
Town	.17	.11	(+.06)
Metropolitan	.21	.21	(.00)
Core	.16	.16	(.00)

Notes to Pages 213–15

In Semirural places, attendance overwhelms importance as a "cause" of nonkin co-religionists.

39. As with ethnicity, the concentration of the specific population is probably more important than urbanism per se. At least that is suggested by the relatively high involvement of Town Catholics. Seemingly inconsistent with this interpretation, however, is the finding that the advantage of urbanism was greater for affluent than for nonaffluent respondents. Affluent respondents should find religious fellowship less difficult than those with fewer resources and therefore should differ less by community. But Town and Core affluent respondents tended to be highly involved, and Semirural and Metropolitan ones uninvolved. This interaction effect—urbanism making more of a difference for the affluent—cannot be explained by the argument I gave, or by Catholicism, attendance, or identification. I will return later to this problem.

40. The adjusted average probabilities for belonging to a religious organization and/or reading a religious periodical are, by community: .35, .28, .28, .23 (beta = .08, n.s.; partial $r = -.08$; the difference between Core and Semirural is significant at $p < .10$). The controls are religion (six categories), gender, age, age × gender, number of children, education, length of residence in the city, works, is retired, and cooperativeness in the interview. The interaction effect, after controls, with "most important" is significant at $p = .10$. For the not most important group, the adjusted means are .27, .20, .20, .14 (beta = .10; n.s.); and for those who said religion *was* most important, they are .57, .67, .77, .87 (beta = .21; n.s.). Employing the complete regression equation used to generate figure 29 (see note 29), the interaction term for urbanism × most important is significant at $p < .01$. So is the interaction term for attendance; formal activity increased slightly with urbanism among nonattenders and decreased with urbanism among attenders. The interaction term for urbanism × Catholic was not significant, but the slight negative association between urbanism and activity existed only among Protestants.

41. See Roof, "Traditional Religion," and idem, "Concepts and Indicators."

42. The dependent variable is a five-point scale drawn from answers to question 95; from 0, never attends religious services to 4, attends almost every week. The control variables are the same as those in note 40. The adjusted means, from Semirural to Core, are 2.2, 1.8, 1.7, 1.5; beta = .12 ($p < .05$; partial $r = -.12$).

43. I also examined another measure of involvement, ideological commitment: whether the respondent said religion was most important, or said that it was very important to live near a church, or was described by the interviewer as heavily invested in religion. (Anyone of the three sufficed.) There was little difference by community in the probability of being committed on this measure. The adjusted probabilities were .39, .36, .32, and .36 (beta = .08, n.s.). Catholics in Semirural places tended not to be committed, relative to other Catholics, and nonattenders in Core places tended to be committed, relative to nonattenders elsewhere.

44. For evidence that *church* involvement is closely tied to localism, at least among Episcopalians in North Carolina, see W. C. Roof, *Community and Commitment* (New York: Elsevier, 1978).

45. That is, if we control for church attendance (as well as other variables), the partial association of urbanism with number of co-religionists goes from about zero to about .10 for the subgroups of Protestant respondents.

46. If this explanation is correct, then urbanism should have supported social involvement with co-religionists among the less affluent respondents, for whom social relations were relatively difficult. Instead, it was among affluent respondents that urbanites were advantaged; among the nonaffluent, urbanism made little difference. The reason, I suspect, is that poorer respondents were especially likely to rely on *local* churches as social contexts. Such local churches are available everywhere, at least for Protestants. The affluent tended, instead, to draw co-religionists from more contexts and wider arenas, and for them the

characteristics of the wider community therefore became important. Less affluent respondents, in fact, were more dependent on attendance for knowing co-religionists than
were the affluent (correlations of .36 versus .20).

Chapter 17

1. From S. Terkel, *Working* (New York: Avon, 1974), p. 476.

2. For exemplary studies of occupational worlds see, for example, W. W. Pilcher, *The Portland Longshoremen: A Dispersed Urban Community* (New York: Holt, Rinehart, 1972); H. S. Becker, *Outsiders* (New York: Free Press, 1963); S. M. Lipset, M. Trow, and J. S. Coleman, *Union Democracy* (New York: Doubleday, 1956); and W. Kornblum, *Blue Collar Community* (Chicago: University of Chicago Press, 1975).

3. Michel Crozier found, for example, that office workers in Parisian insurance firms rarely spent leisure time together (*The World of the Office Worker* [New York: Schocken Books, 1973]).

4. Although some part-time workers could reasonably be said to be involved in a work subculture, they were notably less likely to, and they included a rather varied set of workers. Excluding them simplifies matters; including them, preliminary analysis showed, would not notably alter the results.

5. The probability of being a member, as defined here, was regressed on an equation with sixteen independent variables. Working full time alone explains over 60 percent of the variance. Education and being young (but over twenty-one) explain most of the rest. The adjusted means, from Semirural to Core, are 30, 39, 51, 51 (eta = .17, $p < .001$; $r = .16$). The adjusted means are 40, 44, 41, 45 (beta = .07, n.s.; partial $r = .02$).

6. To be more specific: holding constant job characteristics and personal traits of the respondents, those in professional occupations (accountants, lawyers, nurses, teachers, etc.) who also had college degrees beyond the bachelor's named considerably and consistently more occupational associates than did most other workers. Transport and service workers (truck drivers, waiters, nurse's aides) were also relatively involved. Laborers and menial workers (maids, gardeners, farm workers) named especially few work associates; managerial workers also tended to named fewer than average. Our five respondents in extractive industries—oil and gas—were, on average, very involved with occupational associates. (This group included someone who traveled to pipeline jobs far from home.) Otherwise the only major difference by industry was that respondents in business services (e.g., auto repair) and particularly those in personal services (laundry, beauty shops) tended *not* to be involved with occupational associates.

Workers with unusual hours—those much earlier or later than nine-to-five, or irregular hours—named many *co-workers* and got together with them often (q. 88), but they were not especially involved with people in the same line of work who were employed elsewhere. Work hours particularly distinguished the heavily involved among respondents who were in professional services (in schools, hospitals, law offices). Respondents who worked many hours a week were more involved with co-workers than those who worked fewer hours. Workers who put in many hours were particularly likely to name co-workers in answer to questions not dealing with work itself—that is, to be multiply involved with co-workers. The longer respondents had worked at a particular job, past the first year or so, the fewer occupational colleagues working *elsewhere* they named. Self-employed workers were only slightly less socially involved that otherwise similar employees. Finally, I looked at pay (measured only as total personal income): other things being equal, high income did *not* encourage involvement with more work associates; it did, however, encourage more frequent "getting together." Time, unfortunately, did not permit me to investigate all the potentially relevant features of the job, an important task future research should address.

Among the unexamined features are: size of workplace, autonomy in the job, extent of required teamwork, authority, position in hierarchy, specialization of tasks, and so on. Each of these can be linked theoretically to occupational fellowship.

7. I think that older children made a difference—but not younger children—because when there are younger children at home mothers usually quit work to care for them full time, thereby freeing husbands of that constraint on work involvement.

8. These are a few of the more consistent results from examinations of many interaction effects, which were quite complex. For example, among respondents in professional and managerial occupations who said work was most important, never marrieds named more non-co-worker colleagues (all else equal) than married or formerly married respondents, but among respondents in the same occupations who did not say work was most important, never marrieds and marrieds named about the same number or more than formerly marrieds. In any event, the basic regression equation used for the whole sample of members includes the following variables, with those significant at $p < .10$ indicated: three dummies for occupation—professional with advanced degree (.14), other professional, transportation operatives or service workers (.14); two dummies for industry—construction-manufacturing and services (−.10); hours worked per week (.09); works unusual or irregular hours (.11); self-employed (−.08); years at current job; personal income; age; education; never married; married; number of older children at home (−.16); years in city; relatives in vicinity; and cooperativeness in interview (.19); $R^2 = .16$.

9. The means for number of associates in the same line of work differ at eta = .06 (n.s.; r with the urbanism scale = −.03). The means for associates named elsewhere besides in answer to the work question differ at eta = .07 (n.s.; $r = -.07$). The correlation of urbanism with percentage of the network that is composed of colleagues is .04 and with the frequency respondents reported seeing their colleagues outside work hours (q. 88) is −.04.

10. Other problems also bedeviled this question. For example, people who worked at temporary jobs to support their "true" interest—for example, a waitress studying theater—would often answer in terms of the avocation rather than the literal "job."

11. Adjusted for the variables listed in note 8, the means shown in figure 30 for all colleagues differ at beta = .13 ($p < .10$; partial $r = -.09$), as do the means for number of colleagues named elsewhere in the interview besides the discuss-work question (partial $r = -.12$). The adjusted differences in the *percentage* of the network that was composed of people in the same line of work are nil (partial $r = -.00$). With respect to how often the respondent said the co-worker got together (q. 88), the adjusted differences (beta = .16, $p < .01$) indicated that Town workers were more likely and Core workers less likely than others to do so (partial $r = -.10$).

12. The adjusted means for nonkin named who were *not* in the same line of work differ at beta = .10 (n.s.).

13. Figure 31 reports the results of regressing the number of associates in the same line of work on three occupation dummy variables, one industry dummy, hours worked, unusual hours, years on job, self-employed, whether the respondent was studying for an advanced degree, age, education, being married, number of older children, years in the city, cooperativeness in the interview, whether the respondent said that work was most important, urbanism, and urbanism × most important. (Other regressions and analyses of covariance show essentially the same patterns.) The partial slopes for number of associates (logged plus one) regressed on urbanism and urbanism × most important were −.12 ($p < .07$) and .13 (n.s.), respectively. For percentage of network as dependent variable: −.02 (n.s.) and .08 ($p < .11$); for the number of associates named elsewhere besides the discuss-work question: −.22 ($p < .01$) and .20 ($p < .10$); and for frequency of social get-togethers (scale from 0 to 6): −.63 (n.s.) and .10 (n.s.). Recall that the N here is 448.

14. Examination of correlations within the urban categories provides evidence for this description. In Semirural places, there was no connection between whether respondents

were ideologically committed to their work—either as indicated by the "most important" question *or* by interviewers' comments about the respondents—and their involvement with work associates. In Town communities, that connection held only for frequency of getting together. In Metropolitan and Core places, those correlations (and regression slopes) were reasonably high. For example, the slope of number of work associates regressed on whether or not the respondent said work was most important ranged from .01 in Semirural and Town places, to about .10 in Metropolitan and Core places.

15. Regressing the number of associates in the same line of work who were *not* also called "co-workers" on the equation in note 8 yields significant betas for professional with advanced degree (.12), years at current job (−.11), never married (.14), and years in city (−.11). The adjusted means for Semirural through Core are 0.6, 0.7, 0.6, and 0.6 (beta = .03, n.s.; partial $r = -.01$; zero-order $r = .05$). Among respondents who thought work not most important, the adjusted means ranged from 0.7 to 0.5 (beta =.09; n.s.), and, among those who said it was most important, from 0.6 to 0.7 (beta = .03; n.s.).

16. The number of work associates was regressed on two variables: whether or not the respondent said work was most important and whether or not the respondent had a formal occupational involvement. (The latter takes on a value of one if the respondent either belonged to an occupational organization or regularly read an occupational magazine. The measure is largely sensitive to whether or not the respondent belonged to a union or equivalent professional association.) The results of the regressions, run within each community category, indicate the increasing weight of the identification as urbanism increases (partial betas):

	Most Important	Formal	(Difference)
Semirural	.02	.21	(−.19)
Town	.01	.11	(−.10)
Metropolitan	.15	.22	(−.07)
Core	.22	.10	(+.12)

Results are much the same if percentage in the same line of work is the dependent variable.

17. The dichotomous variable—respondent says work is most important or interviewer says respondent was heavily involved in work versus neither—was regressed on the variables listed in note 8. The best predictors are hours worked (beta = .20), self-employed (.11), never married (−.18), children twelve or older (−.15), and education (.13). The adjusted probabilities, from Semirural to Core, are .53, .60, .45, and .43 (beta = .14, $p < .05$; partial $r = -.10$). Town workers were coded as "committed" to their jobs largely because they said their work was most important; Semirural workers were most likely to be described by interviewers as "into" their work. Town workers were especially likely to be committed if they worked in public administration, perhaps because many were residents of suburban Sacramento and were employed in state government. Core members were least committed if they were sales or clerical workers or if they worked in transportation or trade.

18. Regressing a dummy variable—either belongs to work organization or regularly read a work periodical, or both, versus neither—on the equation described in a note 8 shows that the best predictors are being a professional (.15 for those with advanced degrees, .16 for those without); personal income (.34); and being never married (.11). The adjusted probabilities, for Semirural to Core, are .63, .55, .51, and .47 (beta = .11, n.s.; partial $r = -.07$).

19. See, on class consciousness, for example, C. Tilly, "The Chaos of the Living City," in *An Urban World,* ed. C. Tilly, pp. 86–107 (Boston: Little, Brown, 1974), and J. R. Lincoln, "Community Structure and Industrial Conflict," *American Sociological Review* 43 (April 1978):199–219. A study of British policemen found that the more urban the place, the more friends they reported "on the force" (M. Banton, *The Policeman in the Community* [London: Tavistock, 1964], p. 248).

20. The logged number of homemakers named, both kin and nonkin, was the dependent variable in an analysis of covariance using as covariates: years since the respondent had last worked, education, years in the neighborhood, number of children at home, and cooperativeness in the interview. The unadjusted (logarithmic) means, from Semirural to Core, were 5.2, 4.0, 4.5, and 4.6 (eta = .14; n.s.). The adjusted means were 5.5, 4.4, 4.5, and 3.8 (beta = .16; n.s.). The adjusted percentages of the network were 39 percent for Semirural and 32 percent for all others (beta = .17; n.s.). Controlling for number of kin named—that is, for mothers, aunts, etc.—yielded similar, though slightly weaker, results.

21. The number of hobby associations went from 423 in 1968 to 721 in 1977, up 70 percent; sports associations from 318 to 469, up 47 percent; and public interest associations, from 446 to 883, up 98 percent. In contrast, religious associations dropped 6 percent (794 to 750), and fraternal groups dropped 31 percent (640 to 444)—*Statistical Abstract of the United States* (Washington, D.C.: Department of Commerce, 1978), p. 50.

22. We also "lost" some respondents whose double-barreled answers, notably "hunting-and-fishing," were treated by interviewers as separate and equal interests rather than as a single complex interest, "outdoor sportsman."

23. Unadjusted, 41 percent of Semirural respondents were members, compared with 47, 50, and 49 percent of Town, Metropolitan, and Core respondents respectively (eta = .07, n.s.). Little predicts who was or was not a member: being female (−.25) or an old male (−.18), and being affluent (.08). Adjusted, the probabilities by community type are .47, .49, .49, and .44 (beta = .03, n.s.; partial *r* with urbanism scale = −.03).

24. Four dependent variables—number of nonkin associates with same interest (logged), percentage of nonkin who were fellow hobbyists, number of co-hobbyists cited at least twice in the interview (i.e., not just in answer to the question about discussing hobbies), and frequency of getting together (q. 88)—were regressed on an equation including five dummy variables for type of activity, a scale measuring the collective quality of the activity (see below), being never married, being married, gender, age, education, respondent works or not, and a dummy variable indicating whether the respondent had moved to the city in the past ten years and gave as one reason for the move "the things I can do here" (q. 1). (Surprisingly, the last was a significant *negative* predictor of social involvement, especially for people with organizational interests.) The scale of collectiveness categorized all hobbies as types of activities usually done alone (crafts, visual arts, studying, watching sports, reading, etc.) or as types that necessarily involved others (team sports, performing dance, theater, organizational work, card-playing, etc.), and grouped the rest in an intermediate category. In total, the equation explained relatively little variance, from 9 percent of number of nonkin co-hobbyists to 12 percent of getting together. The major independent predictors of the total number of nonkin co-hobbyists were the collective scale; crafts and "other" pastimes versus all others; being never married (.14) or currently married (.12) versus formerly married; education (.10); and reason for move (−.10). The adjusted means, from Semirural to Core are:
Number of nonkin co-hobbyists
Unadjusted: 3.0, 2.9, 3.6, 2.9 (eta = .12, *p* < .10; *r* with urbanism scale =.01);
Adjusted: 3.1, 2.9, 3.5, 2.8 (beta = .12, *p* < .10; partial *r* = −.01; partial *r* for Metropolitan is .11, *p* < .05);
Percentage of nonkin co-hobbyists
Unadjusted: 37, 34, 33, 29 (eta = .12, *p* < .10; *r* = −.12);
Adjusted: 36, 32, 34, 32 (beta = .07, n.s.; partial *r* = − .04).
For number of co-hobbyists named more than once, for frequency of getting together—and also for number of nonkin named who were *not* co-hobbyists—the community differences are trivial. I also tested the effect that number of hobby institutions in the community (e.g., art stores) had on involvements. Indicators of the presence of services and institutions catering to outdoor sports, crafts, and arts were added to equations run within subsets of

respondents interested in each of those activities. No significant effects were found, perhaps because of high collinearity with urbanism, or inappropriate measures, or incorrect hypotheses.

25. Figure 32 was generated by regressing total number of nonkin fellow hobbyists on a dummy variable for whether or not the respondent said that spare-time activities were most important (slope $= -.45$, $p < .10$), urbanism ($b = 1.72$, $p < .05$), urbanism × most important ($b = .20$, $p < .05$), and urbanism squared ($b = -.38$, $p < .05$), as well as several control variables: the collective quality of the activity, five dummies for type of activity, gender, age, education, never married, married, being employed, and household income. With percentage of nonkin who are fellow hobbyists as dependent variable, the interaction effect is yet stronger: for urbanism, the slope is $b = -.10$ ($p < .10$; the quadratic term is not significant); and for urbanism × most important, $b = .23$ ($p < .01$; for pastime is most important, the linear $b = -.58$, $p < .01$). In effect, the slope for those who said pastime was not most important is $-.10$ (so that the line goes from an adjusted probability of .36 to .28) and for those who said most important, $b = .14$ (from .27 to .38). The effects, using frequency of social activity (q. 98) as the dependent variable, are not significant but follow a similar pattern.

26. The following analysis of covariance design was run for all 497 pastime subculture members: five covariates—age, education, gender, is employed, was formerly married; and four factors—respondent reports that pastime is most important or not, specific hobby in six categories, respondent is affluent or not, and urbanism. The interaction effect of pastime is most important × urbanism, adjusted for covariates and main effects, is significant at $p < .05$ for both total number and percentage of nonkin co-hobbyists. The interaction effect for co-hobbyists named twice and for frequency of get-togethers is not significant. The same model was then run within the group who said their leisure activities were not most important ($N = 334$) and those who said they were most important ($N = 159$). The adjusted statistics, from Semirural to Core, are:

Number of nonkin co-hobbyists
Not most important: 3.4, 3.0, 3.6, 2.5 (beta $= .18$, $p < .05$);
Most important: 2.7, 3.0, 3.5, 4.0 (beta $= .19$; n.s.);
Percentage of nonkin co-hobbyists
Not most important: 37, 34, 34, 28 (beta $= .14$, n.s.);
Most important: 28, 28, 36, 36 (beta $= .19$, n.s.);
Nonkin co-hobbyists named twice
Not most important: 1.9, 1.6, 1.6, 1.3 (beta $= .11$, n.s.);
Most important: 1.1, 1.6, 1.8, 1.9 (beta $= .20$, $p < .10$);
Frequency of social get-togethers (q. 98; 0–4 scale)
Not most important: 1.3, 1.1, 1.1, 1.0 (beta $= .10$, n.s.);
Most important: 1.2, 1.3, 1.5, 1.5 (beta $= .11$, n.s.).

27. The correlations (and regression slopes) within the urban categories between indicators of identification—the respondent said pastime was most important or the interviewer described the respondent as engrossed in his or her pastime—and measures of social involvement virtually increase monotonically from negative or near zero for Semirural respondents to positive among Core respondents. For example, the slope of frequency of getting together (0–4 scale) regressed on whether or not the respondent was described by the interviewer as "into" the pastime increases from .10 for Semirural to .42, .65, and .67 for Core. As the following table shows, there is a connection—albeit weak and ragged—between urbanism and the relative weight of identification versus formal involvement in promoting in-group social ties. Number of co-hobbyists was regressed on whether or not the respondent said the spare-time activities were most important and on whether or not the respondent had a formal connection—belonged to an organization or read a periodical for that pastime. The partial betas are:

	Most Important	Formal	(Difference)
Semirural	−.12	.11	(−.23)
Town	.02	.14	(−.12)
Metropolitan	−.03	.28	(−.31)
Core	.22	−.03	(+.19)

28. Being committed to one's pastime, as defined in the text, was regressed on five dummy variables for specific hobbies, a scale measuring the collective quality of the activity (see note 24), age, gender, never married, married, education, employed, and moved to city for "things to do" ($R^2 = .04$). The adjusted probabilities, from Semirural to Core, are .39, .54, .55, and .38 (beta =.16, $p < .01$).

29. Being formally involved—by organization or reading a periodical—was regressed on the same equation described in the preceding note. The adjusted probabilities were .42, .46, .46, and .35 (beta = .10, n.s.; partial $r = -.06$; but Core differs from the others at $p < .05$). The pattern was sharpest among those who said that pastime was most important. In that group the adjusted probabilities were .43, 60, .56, and .40 (beta = .17, n.s.).

30. The question (q. 99) asks respondents how important it is to live in a place where they could be around other people who share their activity. The answers, scaled from 1, not very, to 3, very important, were regressed on the equation described in note 28. The adjusted means, by community, are 1.7, 1.8, 1.8, and 1.7 (beta = .05, n.s.; partial $r = .01$). Among those who said their pastime was most important, the adjusted means were 1.8, 1.7, 2.1, and 1.8 (beta = .17, n.s.).

31. With respect to pastime, for example: urbanism is basically unrelated (all else equal) to how many nonkin respondents named who did *not* share their activity. However, among those who felt that their pastime was most important, the more urban the community the fewer "outsiders" they named (partial $r = -.08$, $p < .10$).

32. The quotation is from L. Wirth, "Urbanism as a Way of Life," reprinted in *Classic Essays on the Culture of Cities,* ed. R. Sennett (New York: Appleton-Century-Crofts, 1969), p. 156. For more on the argument, see C. S. Fischer, *The Urban Experience* (New York: Harcourt Brace Jovanovich, 1976), pp. 181–83.

33. Two dependent variables were used in the analysis: the probability of being a "member" of any of the four subcultures—ethnic, religious, occupation, or spare time—as defined earlier in the chapter; and the total number of such memberships respondents had (from 0 to 4). The adjusted means were derived from an analysis of covariance incorporating five co-variates—age, age × gender, number of children, length of residence in the city, and widowed or not—culled from a longer list used in preliminary regression analyses and three crossed factors—works full time or not, Anglo or not, and urbanism. The means, from Semirural to Core, are:
Probability of any memberships
Unadjusted: .78, .89, .88, .92 (eta = .15. $p < .001$);
Adjusted: .81, .89, .85, .91 (beta = .11, $p < .10$);
Number of memberships
Unadjusted: 1.33, 1.77, 1.86, 1.78 (eta = .19, $p < .001$);
Adjusted: 1.46, 1.80, 1.76, 1.75 (beta =.12, $p < .001$).

34. The dependent variable is the number of subcultures (from 0 to 4) for which respondents had named at least *three* people as fellow members. (The three had to be nonkin, except for the occupational subculture.) The model used for adjustment was an analysis of covariance: gender × works fulls time × married or not × urbanism, with five covariates: raised abroad, non-Anglo, cooperativeness in the interview, age, and education. The means, from Semirural to Core, are:
Unadjusted: 0.62, 0.89, 0.99, 1.14 (eta = .16, $p < .001$);
Adjusted: 0.80, 0.94, 0.89, 0.91 (beta = .06, n.s.).

The analysis also showed a significant four-way interaction effect: married, full-time employed women belonged to considerably more subcultures if they lived in the Core than if they lived elsewhere.

Chapter 18

1. Some of the material in this chapter was reported in C. S. Fischer, "Public and Private Worlds of City Life," *American Sociological Review* 46 (June 1981):306–16.

2. The key essay is Stanley Milgram's "The Experience of Living in Cities," *Science* 167 (March 1970): 1461–68. Some researchers study the general conditions for bystander intervention (e.g., B. Latane and J. M. Darley, *The Unresponsive Bystander* [New York: Appleton-Century-Crofts, 1970]). Some study crowding and its psychological effects (e.g., J. Freedman, *Crowding and Behavior* [San Francisco: Freeman, 1975]). And others study precisely helping behavior and urbanism (see citations below). At this time, the psychological literature on these topics is expanding rapidly. Recent, though by now dated, reviews and collections include: C. Korte, "Urban-Nonurban Differences in Social Behavior and Social Psychological Models of Urban Impact," *Journal of Social Issues* 36, no. 3 (1980):29–51; M. Baldassare, "Human Spatial Behavior," *Annual Review of Sociology* 4 (1978):29–56; D. Stokols, ed., *Perspectives on Environment and Behavior* (New York: Plenum, 1977); and A. Baum et al., eds., *Advances in the Study of Environment and Behavior*, vol. 1, *The Urban Environment* (Hillsdale, N.J.: Lawrence Erlbaum Associates, 1978). My own critique of the way psychologists have approached the topic appears as "Sociological Comments on Psychological Approaches to Urban Life," in Baum et al., *Urban Environment*, pp. 131–43.

3. For a review, see C. Korte, "Helpfulness in the Urban Environment," in Baum et al., *Urban Environment*, pp. 85–110; and Korte, "Urban-Nonurban Differences."

4. See, for example, S. Spilerman, "The Causes of Racial Disturbances," *American Sociological Review* 36 (June 1971):427–42; and J. R. Lincoln, "Community Structure and Industrial Conflict," *American Sociological Review* 43 (April 1978):199–219.

5. See E. H. Carpenter, "Residential Preference and Community Size," Report no. 7, Department of Agricultural Economics, University of Arizona, 1975; Louis Harris Associates, *A Survey of Citizen Views and Concerns about Urban Life* (Washington, D.C.: Department of Housing and Urban Development, 1978); D. Hummon, "Community Ideology" (Ph.D. diss., Department of Sociology, University of California, Berkeley, 1980). In our own survey, small-town residents much more often than city residents felt that their towns were friendly and that friendliness was intrinsic to the small town.

6. See Milgram, "Experience"; also, for example, S. Cohen, "Environmental Load and Allocation of Attention," in Baum et al., *Urban Environment*, pp. 1–30.

7. See F. H. Weiner, "Altruism, Ambiance and Action: The Effects of Rural and Urban Rearing on Helping Behavior," *Journal of Personality and Social Psychology* 34 (1976):112–24; C. J. Holahan, "Effects of Urban Size and Heterogeneity on Judged Appropriateness of Altruistic Responses," *Sociometry* 40 (December 1977):378–82.

8. *San Francisco Chronicle*, 5 December 1979.

9. *Daily Californian*, 9 May 1980.

10. J. House and S. Wolf provide some persuasive evidence that the increase over the past twenty years in American city-dwellers' refusals to be interviewed by poll-takers can be largely explained by increasing crime rates ("Effects of Urban Residence on Interpersonal Trust and Helping Behavior," *Journal of Personality and Social Psychology* 36, no. 9 [1978]:1029–43). A simulation study also suggests that people are responding to the risk involved in helping (Holahan, "Effects of Urban Size"). Charles Korte's research in the Netherlands failed to find a clear relation between urban size and helping, which perhaps reflects the unique relationship between size and crime in America (C. Korte, I. Ympa, and

A. Toppen, "Helpfulness in Dutch Society as a Function of Urbanization and Environmental Input Level," *Journal of Personality and Social Psychology* 32 [1975]:996–1003). His research in Turkey showed that some poor but homogeneous residential sections were more often sites of helping behavior than other parts of cities (C. Korte and N. Ayralioglu, "Helpfulness in Turkey" [unpublished paper, Pennsylvania State University, 1980]).

11. L. Lofland, *A World of Strangers* (New York: Basic Books, 1973). See, also pp. 189–91 in C. S. Fischer, *The Urban Experience* (New York: Harcourt Brace Jovanovich, 1976).

12. Lofland, *World of Strangers*, p. 178.

13. See Korte, "Helpfulness in the Urban Environment."

14. A similar argument has been presented by Karen A. Franck in "Friends and Strangers: The Social Experience of Living in Urban and Non-urban Settings," *Journal of Social Issues* 36, no. 3 (November 1980):52–71.

15. G. D. Berreman, "Scale and Social Relations," in *Scale and Social Organization*, ed. F. Barth, pp. 41–77 (Oslo: Universitetsforlaget, 1978), esp. p. 60; see also E. M. Bruner, "Kin and Nonkin," in *Urban Anthropology*, ed. A. Southall, pp. 373–92 (New York: Oxford University Press, 1973).

16. I rely for this account on a paper by Don Lee, "Processes of Spatial Change in the San Francisco Gay Community" (class paper, City Planning 298E, University of California, Berkeley, June 1979). On homosexual neighborhoods, see also M. P. Levine, "Gay Ghetto," in *Gay Men*, ed. M. P. Levine (New York: Harper and Row, 1979).

17. The number of homosexuals in a population is, of course, difficult to estimate, and those estimates are subject to political use. The head of Golden Gate Business Association estimated that at least 25 percent of the San Francisco population was, in 1978, homosexual (*Sacramento Bee*, 9 April 1978), and other leaders of the homosexual community have given estimates of 100,000 to 200,000 persons. We have a few better estimates. A political poll in mid-1979 "found that 12 percent of those polled identified themselves as 'a member of the gay community'—and the pollster involved believes that homosexuals represented a significant share of the additional 47 percent who refused to answer such a question" (*San Francisco Chronicle*, 20 October 1979). Another election poll estimated 40,000 voters, or roughly 15 percent of the electorate (KGO–TV, 1 November 1979). A survey done of voters on the day of a run-off election found that "citywide, 12 percent said they were gay or bisexual, and another 8 percent refused to state"; the pollster estimated that "between 15 and 18 percent of the voters [on 11 December 1979] were either gay or bisexual" (*San Francisco Chronicle*, 13 December 1979). Political wisdom in the city generally holds that members of the "gay" community are more likely to vote than are others, and in 1979's run-off a key race in the heavily homosexual Fifth District pitted a nationally known homosexual politician against a "straight" candidate. In our own survey, 13 percent of our San Francisco respondents either said they were homosexual or were judged by the interviewers as *perhaps appearing* to be so. Since, by chance, we drew two of our twelve San Francisco neighborhoods in noticeably homosexual districts, a 12 to 15 percent adjusted estimate seems—in conjunction with the surveys cited above—most accurate.

18. "S.F. Schools Set Study of Gay Life," *San Francisco Chronicle*, 26 May 1977.

19. "The Gay Migration," *San Francisco Chronicle*, 1 September 1979.

20. "Novato Offers Reward to Curb Racial Incidents," *San Francisco Chronicle*, 19 October 1978.

21. "Violence in Vacationland," *San Francisco Examiner*, 5 March 1978.

22. See, for instance, N. R. Morgan and T. R. Clark, "The Causes of Racial Disorders," *American Sociological Review* 38 (October 1973):611–24; C. Tilly, "The Chaos of the Living City," in *The Urban World*, ed. C. Tilly, pp. 86–107 (Boston: Little, Brown, 1974).

23. The dependent variables are the probabilities that a respondent mentioned (1) any of the six categories of "people" responses; (2) either of the two general categories; or (3) any of the four specific categories in answer to the "best" question. The controls used in

calculating the adjusted figures were age, gender, education, household income, married, never married, number of children under thirteen years old, number aged thirteen and over, works full time, length of residence in the neighborhood, and length of residence in the city. These tended to have little effect. The means, by type of place, are:

Any reference to people
Unadjusted: .37, .31, .23, .51 (eta = .21, $p <. 001$; $r = .07$);
Adjusted: .40, .32, .22, .48 (beta = .20, $p < .001$; partial $r = .02$);
General type or behavior of people
Unadjusted: .34, .29, .19, .34 (eta = .14, $p < .001$; $r = -.04$);
Adjusted: .35, .30, .18, .31 (beta = .14, $p < .001$; partial $r = -.07$);
Specific groups of people
Unadjusted: .04, .04, .05, .25 (eta = .31, $p < .001$; $r = .25$);
Adjusted: .06, .04, .04, .23 (beta = .26, $p < .001$; partial $r = .18$).

The same analysis was applied to the "What are the worst things" question:

Any reference to people
Unadjusted: .17, .16, .24, .37 (eta = .18, $p < .001$; $r = .18$);
Adjusted: .18, .15, .24, .37 (beta = .18, $p < .001$; partial $r = .15$);
General type or behavior of people
Unadjusted: .06, .08, .14, .19 (eta = .16, $p < .001$; $r = .14$);
Adjusted: .08, .08, .14, .18 (beta = .12, $p < .01$; partial $r = .10$);
Specific groups of people
Unadjusted: .11, .10, .12, .23 (eta = .14, $p < .001$; $r = .12$);
Adjusted: .10, .10, .13, .23 (beta = .14, $p < .001$; partial $r = .11$).

24. Respondents' answers to the "worst" questions were coded for any answers referring to serious crime or to vandalism, vice, or other less serious crime. The probabilities of making this complaint, by urbanism, were:
Unadjusted: .09, .19, .24, .47 (eta = .31, $p < .001$; $r = .32$);
Adjusted: .10, .19, .24, .47 (beta = .29, $p < .001$; partial $r = .29$).

25. See, for example, Fischer, "A Research Note on Urbanism and Tolerance," *American Journal of Sociology* 76 (March 1971):847–56; C. Z. Nunn, H. J. Crockett, Jr., and J. A. Williams, Jr., *Tolerance for Nonconformity* (San Francisco: Jossey-Bass, 1976), chap. 6.

26. A Gallup survey found, for example, that city people were more likely to say "should" in answer to the question, "In general, do you think homosexuals should or should not have equal rights in terms of job opportunities?": 49 percent of respondents in towns under 50,000, 55 percent in cities 50,000 to 500,000, and 68 percent in cities of 500,000 or more (*New York Times,* 17 July 1977).

27. In an analysis of three national surveys, I found a significant partial correlation of about .07 in each case between urbanism and distrust. I argued, with some supportive data, that this response was a reaction to fear of others in the urban setting, rather than an expression of personality (see Fischer, "On Urbanism Alienation and Anomie," *American Sociological Review* 38 [June 1973]:311–26). Data from the NORC General Social Survey, 1972–78, show a similar pattern with regard to the question whether people are helpful or look out for themselves: a slight trend toward more answers that people are selfish in larger communities, a trend that would be stronger after controls (from unpublished data supplied by James A. Davis).

28. The unadjusted means, by community type, are:
Neighborhood: 1.15, 1.21, 1.19, 1.20 (eta = .05, n.s.; r with urbanism scale = .03);
City: 1.33, 1.45, 1.58, 1.60 (eta = .14, $p < .001$; $r = .17$).

29. Each of the distrust items, score 1 to 3, trust to distrust, was regressed on the following equation (significant betas for the neighborhood item in parentheses): age, gender, never married, married, number of young children at home, number of older children at home, education ($-.10$), household income ($-.13$), employed full time, employed part time, years in the neighborhood ($-.19$), and years in the city; $R^2 = .07$. The significant predictors

for the city item are age $(-.11)$, education $(-.10)$, and income $(-.11)$; $R^2 = .05$. The adjusted means are, from Semirural to Core:
   Neighborhood: 1.11, 1.18, 1.20, 1.28 (beta $= .10$, $p < .01$);
   City: 1.25, 1.40, 1.60, 1.71 (beta $= .22$, $p < .001$).
The partial correlations of the urbanism scale are .11 with the neighbor item and .24 with the city item, different from one another at $p < .001$. Since both items, and especially the neighborhood one, are highly skewed, all the statistical associations are underestimated. The unique proportion of the *explained* variance contributed by the three urbanism dummy variables to the neighborhood question is 13 percent and that to the city question is 47 percent, suggesting that even with well-distributed measures urbanism would have been far more strongly associated, ceteris paribus, with the latter than with the former item.
   30. The zero-order correlation of the safety item with the neighborhood distrust is .28, and with city distrust it is .21. The partial rs are .26 and .18, respectively.
   31. This argument assumes, of course, that fear of crime creates distrust rather than vice-versa and rather than both being a result of some third factor. The many control variables suggest that most likely third factors have been eliminated. That fear causes distrust is likely on a few grounds: face value, that fear justifies distrust; that fear of a crime is more palpable than distrust; and that, in the survey, discussion of crime precedes the trust questions. It is likely, nevertheless, that there is some reciprocal effect—people estranged from their neighbors becoming moe fearful than those who know their neighbors (see Franck, "Friends and Strangers").
   32. Adding the question concerning safety in the neighborhood to the control variables yields these adjusted means:
   Neighborhood: 1.17, 1.18, 1.18, 1.25 (beta $= .05$, n.s.);
   City: 1.30, 1.40, 1.58, 1.68 (beta $= .18$, $p < .001$).
The partial correlations of the urbanism scale are .05 with the neighbor item and .21 with the city item, different at $p < .001$. In terms of the proportion of the explained variance contributed by the three urbanism dummy variables, the comparison is 2 percent versus 27 percent.
   33. Adding into the controls a dummy variable for whether or not the respondents said crime was a "worst" aspect of the town reduces the partial correlation between urbanism and distrust of others in the town from .21 to .17. But the latter is still significantly greater than the .05 partial correlation of urbanism with the neighborhood trust item, and it represents 19 percent of the explained variance versus 2 percent.
   34. The proportions of residents saying "almost every day" were, from Semirural to Core: .53, .40, .26, and .32. The answers, scaled from 1, never, to 5, almost every day, were regressed on the same equation described in note 29. The means are:
   Unadjusted: 4.2, 3.9, 3.5, 3.7 (eta $= .21$, $p < .001$; $r = -.18$);
   Adjusted: 4.3, 3.9, 3.5, 3.7 (beta $= .23$, $p < .001$, partial $r = -.20$).
   35. Dummy variables for volunteering such answers, which few people did, were regressed on the equation described in note 29. The partial correlations of urbanism were, with volunteering that everyone knows everyone is a "best" thing, $-.12$ $(p < .001)$; with saying that it is a "worst" thing, .09 $(p < .01)$.
   36. Hummon, *Community Ideology.*
   37. Franck, "Friends and Strangers."

Chapter 19

   1. Our results with education tend, moreover, to be conservative, since we controlled for respondent's cooperativeness in the interview and since education was the single greatest predictor of cooperativeness.
   2. See, for example, M. Young and P. Willmott, *The Symmetrical Family* (Baltimore:

Penguin, 1973); G. Allan, "Class Variation in Friendship Patterns," *British Journal of Sociology* 28 (September 1977):389–93; and Allan's *A Sociology of Friendship and Kinship* (London: Allen and Unwin, 1979); N. Shulman, "Urban Social Networks" (Ph.D. diss., Department of Sociology, University of Toronto, 1972); W. Bell and M. Boat, "Urban Neighborhoods and Informal Social Relations," *American Journal of Sociology* 62 (January 1957):391–98; and M. Komarovsky, *Blue-Collar Marriage* (New York: Random House, 1967).

3. Ceteris paribus, household income was curvilinearly associated with number of kin named. Respondents with incomes between $15,000 and $25,000 named the most relatives, on average, and poor respondents named the fewest, with high-income respondents in between.

4. We should also recognize that, to some extent, networks can contribute to income by providing important career contacts. See, for example, M. Granovetter, *Getting a Job* (Cambridge: Harvard University Press, 1974); and N. Lin, W. M. Ensel, and J. C. Vaughn, "Social Resources and Strength of Ties: Structural Factors in Occupational Status Attainment" (paper presented to the American Sociological Association, New York, August 1980).

5. See C. S. Fischer and S. Oliker, "Friendship, Gender, and the Lifecycle" (paper presented to the American Sociological Association, New York, August 1980; also, working paper no. 318, Institute of Urban and Regional Development, Berkeley).

6. Ibid.

7. For example, women associates were especially likely to be named *as* confidants.

8. Fischer and Oliker, "Friendship, Gender, and the Lifecycle."

9. J. J. Palen, "The Urban Nexus: Toward the Year 2000," in *Societal Growth*, ed. A. H. Hawley, pp. 141–56 (New York: Free Press, 1979), esp. pp. 146 and 155.

10. See chapter 6, note 37.

11. On these and other urban/rural differences that I claim are virtually universal, see C. S. Fischer, *The Urban Experience* (New York: Harcourt Brace Jovanovich, 1976), passim.

12. See, for example, B. J. L. Berry and D. C. Dahman, *Population Redistribution in the United States in the 1970s* (Washington, D. C.: National Academy of Sciences, 1977); J. R. Pinkerton, "City-Suburban Redistribution of Age Groups, 1950–1970" (paper presented to the American Sociological Association, San Francisco, August 1978).

13. The substantive reasons include the fact that the differences among low-income respondents are not linear (the gaps between Town and Semirural are about the same as those between Core and Semirural) and that the differences are quite small and marginally significant compared with other findings. (For example, low-income respondents living outside Semirural places named an adjusted 1.2 fewer nonkin than did those in Semirural places, or 15 percent fewer. For an illustrative comparison, religionists living outside Semirural places named almost 2.5 more co-religionists, adjusted, than did Semirural ones, or a difference of 29 percent.) Also reduced fear of crime can fully explain the well-being effect. Methodological reasons include two technical artifacts that tended to slightly underestimate nonkin associates in urban places (see Methodological Appendix section 4.2) and that our income categories did *not* adjust for cost-of-living differences, especially in housing among our communities. The house that rented for perhaps $350 a month in Semirural communities rented for $600 in Core communities. Thus our low-income Semirural respondents may have actually been wealthier than they seemed. (The cost of private school tuition is also a problem for many center-city parents.)

14. See discussion in chapter 4 of Fischer, *Urban Experience*.

15. This is evident in FBI statistics. For a discussion of these trends, see C. S. Fischer, "The Spread of Violent Crime from City to Countryside, 1955–1975," *Rural Sociology* 45 (fall 1980): 417–31.

16. *Gallup Opinion Index*, Report no. 91, 1973, pp. 12–15.

17. Gallup poll reported in the San Francisco Chronicle, 20 April 1981.

18. First, self-selection had presumably already operated to move some of the people most anxious about crime away from the cities. Second, the low response rate in center cities reflects, in part, fear of crime and means that the most fearful urbanites were underrepresented in the survey.

19. One item of supportive evidence are the findings on "happiness" of the Gallup poll, which show a relative deterioration in the urban responses since the mid-1950s (see chap. 4, pp. 50–51).

20. I know that stress on street crime is considered by many to be a reflection of racial and class prejudice. They point out, for example, that more money is stolen by price-fixing corporations than by poor burglars. True. Nevertheless, life in our cities—and especially in minority communities—is being poisoned by street crime, not white-collar crime. People worry about being knifed, not about having to pay twenty-five cents extra for a box of cereal.

Appendix A

1. The statistics examined for these comparisons were drawn from the United States Bureau of the Census *City and County Data Book,* the Rand McNally *Commercial Atlas,* and similar sources.

2. *San Francisco Chronicle,* 7 April 1978.

3. *San Francisco Chronicle,* 9 April, 1978.

4. R. Wuthnow, *The Consciousness Reformation* (Berkeley: University of California Press, 1976), Appendix A.

5. Ibid.

6. Field poll, *San Francisco Chronicle,* 12 August 1977.

7. *Divorces and Divorce Rates,* DHEW Publications, Public Health Services Series 21, no. 29. Washington, D.C., 1978.

8. United States Bureau of the Census, *1970 General Social and Economic Characteristics.*

9. L. Kish, *Survey Sampling* (New York: Wiley, 1967), pp. 396–401.

10. R. Fitzgerald and L. Fuller, "I Hear You Knocking but You Can't Come In" (unpublished paper, Department of Sociology, University of California, Berkeley, 1980).

11. L. Jones and C. S. Fischer, "Studying Egocentric Networks by Mass Survey" (Working Paper no. 284, Institute of Urban and Regional Development, Berkeley, 1978). A briefer discussion appears as L. McCallister (Jones) and C. S. Fischer, "A Procedure for Surveying Personal Networks," *Sociological Methods and Research* 7 (1978):131–48.

12. Since we began to develop our instrument, a few more sophisticated procedures, including ones similar to our own, have appeared. See, for example, H. Z. Lopata, *Women as Widows* (New York: Elsevier, 1979); E. Litwak, unpublished paper, Columbia University School of Social Work, 1979; R. Kahn and T. C. Antonucci, "Convoys over the Life Course" (unpublished paper, Institute for Social Research, Ann Arbor, 1980); P. Duncan-Jones, "The Interview Measurement of Social Interaction" (unpublished paper, Social Psychiatry Research Unit, Australian National University, 1978); and M. S. Weatherford, "Interpersonal Networks and Political Behavior" (unpublished paper, Department of Political Science, University of California, Santa Barbara, 1980).

13. On this point, see also C. S. Fischer et al., *Networks and Places* (New York: Free Press, 1977), chaps. 1–3.

14. M. Granovetter, "The Strength of Weak Ties," *American Journal of Sociology* 78 (May 1973):1360–80.

15. Interviewers reported that in 20 percent of the cases respondents seemed to limit the names they gave and in 1 percent they seemed to exaggerate the number of names.

16. A. Stueve and L. Lein, "Problems in Network Analysis: The Case of the Missing Person" (unpublished paper, Wellsley College Center for Research on Women, October 1979).

17. N. M. Bradburn, S. Sudman, and G. Glockel, *Racial Intergration in American Neighborhoods* (Chicago: University of Chicago Press, 1970).

18. For a similar use of telephone directories, see M. Abrahamson, "The Social Dimensions of Urbanism," *Social Forces* 52 (March 1974): 376–83.

19. P. D. Cleary, D. Mechanic, and N. Weiss, "The Effect of Interviewer Characteristics on Responses to a Mental Health Interview," *Journal of Health and Social Behavior* 22 (June 1981):183–93.

20. See G. A. P. Carrothers, "An Historical Review of the Gravity and Potential Concepts of Human Interaction," *Journal of American Institute of Planners* 22 (spring 1956):94–102; J. G. Steward, "Demographic gravitation: Evidence and Applications," *Sociometry* 11 (1948):31–58; and D. S. Neft, *Statistical Analysis for Areal Distributions,* Monograph Series, no. 2 (Philadelphia: Regional Science Research Institute, 1966).

21. Illustration provided by Melvin M. Webber.

22. Specifically, we assumed that the contribution a city makes to the population potential of any locality within it is equal to the population of the city divided by the mean distance between residents of the specific locality and residents of the city as a whole. We estimated that mean distance by drawing random samples of twenty to thirty people from the city telephone book, finding their addresses on a map, and measuring the distance from them to the sample community. The mean of the distances provides the denominator for the surrounding county's contribution to population potential.

23. N. Bradburn, *The Structure of Psychological Well-Being* (Chicago: Aldine, 1969).

24. Bruce Stephenson, of the National Opinion Research Center, directed me to the appropriate sources. See B. M. Finifter, "The Generation of Confidence: Evaluating Research Findings by Random Subsample Replication," in *Sociological Methodology 1972,* ed. H. L. Costner, pp. 112–75 (San Francisco: Jossey-Bass, 1972); F. Mosteller and J. W. Tukey, "Data Analysis, Including Statistics," in *The Handbook of Social Psychology,* 2d ed., ed. G. Lindzey and E. Aronson, 2:80–203 (Reading, Mass.: Addison-Wesley, 1968); and L. Kish and M. R. Frankel, "Inference from Complex Samples," *Journal of the Royal Statistical Society,* ser. B, 36 (1974):1–37.

25. Mosteller and Tukey, "Data Analysis."

26. See D. Knocke, "A Comparison of Log-Linear and Regression Models for Systems of Dichotomous Variables," *Sociological Methods and Research* 3 (May 1975):416–34; M. W. Gillespie, "Log-Linear Techniques and Regression Analyses of Dummy Dependent Variables," *Sociological Methods and Research* 6 (August 1977):103–23; and H. T. Reynolds, *The Analysis of Cross Classifications* (New York: Free Press, 1977), pp. 182–86.

27. Fischer et al., *Networks and Places,* pp. 200–201.

References

Abrahamson, M. 1974. The social dimensions of urbanism. *Social Forces* 53 (March: 376–83.

Adams, B. N. 1967. Interaction theory and the social network. *Sociometry* 30 (March): 64–78.

Alexander, C. 1973. The city as a mechanism for sustaining human contact. In *Urbanman*, ed. J. Helmer and N. A. Eddington, pp. 239–74. New York: Free Press.

Allan, G. A. 1977. Class variation in friendship patterns. *British Journal of Sociology* 28 (September): 389–93.

———. 1979. *A sociology of friendship and kinship*. London: Allen and Unwin.

Arling, G. 1976. The elderly widow and her family, neighbors, and friends. *Journal of Marriage and the Family* 38 (November): 757–68.

Babchuck, N., and Booth, A. 1969. Voluntary association membership: A longitudinal analysis. *American Sociological Review* 34 (February): 31–45.

Baldassare, M. 1978. Human spatial behavior. *Annual Review of Sociology* 4:29–56.

———. 1979. *Residential crowding in America*. Berkeley: University of California Press.

Banton, M. 1964. *The policeman in the community*. London: Tavistock.

Barnes, J. A. 1954. Class and committee in a Norwegian island parish. *Human Relations* 7:39–58.

Barth, F., ed. 1978. *Scale and social organization*. Oslo: Universitetforlaget.

Barthel, D. 1978. The role of ethnicity. In *Social standing in America*, R. P. Coleman and L. Rainwater, chap. 8. New York: Basic Books.

Baum, A., et al., eds. 1978. *Advances in the study of environment and behavior*. Vol. 1. *The urban environment*. Hillsdale, N.J.: Lawrence Erlbaum Associates.

Becker, H. S. 1963. *Outsiders*. New York: Free Press.

Bell, W., and Boat, M. 1957. Urban neighborhoods and informal social relations. *American Journal of Sociology* 62 (January): 391–98.

Bender, T. 1978. *Community and social change in America*. New Brunswick: Rutgers University Press.

Berkman, L. F., and Syme, S. L. 1979. Social networks, host resistance, and mortality. *American Journal of Epidemiology* 109:186–204.

Berreman, G. D. 1978. Scale and social relations. In *Scale and social organization*, ed. F. Barth, pp. 41–77. Oslo: Universitetsforlaget.

Berry, B. J. L. 1967. *Geography of market centers and retail distribution*. Englewood Cliffs, N.J.: Prentice-Hall.

Berry, B. J. L., and Dahman, D. C. 1977. *Population redistribution in the United States in the 1970s*. Washington, D.C.: National Academy of Sciences.

Blumin, S. M. 1976. *The urban threshold*. Chicago: University of Chicago Press.

Boissevain, J. 1974. *Friends of friends*. London: Basil Blackwell.

Bott, E. 1971. *Family and social network*. 2d ed. New York: Free Press.

Boyer, P. 1978. *Urban masses and moral order in America, 1820–1920*. Cambridge: Harvard University Press.

Bradburn, N. 1969. *The structure of psychological well-being*. Chicago: Aldine.

Bradburn, N. M.; Sudman, S.; and Glockel, G. 1970. *Racial integration in American neighborhoods*. Chicago: University of Chicago Press.

Breton, R. 1964. Institutional completeness of ethnic communities and the personal relations of immigrants. *American Journal of Sociology* 70 (September): 193–205.

Bruner, E. M. 1973. Kin and nonkin. In *Urban anthropology*, ed. A. Southall, pp. 373–92. New York: Oxford University Press.

Bulmer, M. I. A. 1975. Sociological models of the mining community. *Sociological Review* 23 (February): 61–92.

Campbell, A.; Converse, P. E.; and Rodgers, W. L. 1976. *The quality of American life*. New York: Russell Sage.

Carp, F. 1975. Lifestyle and location within the city. *Gerontologist* 15 (February): 27–33.

Carpenter, E. H. 1975. Residential preference and community size. Report no. 7. Department of Agricultural Economics, University of Arizona.

Carrothers, G. A. P. 1956. An historical review of the gravity and potential concepts of human interaction. *Journal of American Institute of Planners* 22 (spring): 94–102.

Castells, M. 1977. *The urban question*. Cambridge: M.I.T. Press.

Cleary, P. D.; Mechanic, D.; and Weiss, N. 1981. The effect of interviewer characteristics on responses to a mental health interview. *Journal of Health and Social Behavior*. 22 (June): 183–93.

Cobb, S. 1976. Social support as a moderator of life stress. *Psychosomatic Medicine* 38:300–314.

Cohen, A., ed. 1973. *Urban ethnicity*. London: Tavistock.

Cohen, S. 1978. Environmental load and allocation of attention. In *Advances in the study of environment and behavior*, Vol. 1, *The urban environment*. ed. A. Baum et al., pp. 1–30. Hillsdale, N.J.: Lawrence Erlbaum Associates.

Coser, L. 1974. *Greedy institutions*. New York: Free Press.

Cressy, P. G. 1971 [1932]. The taxi-dance hall as a social world. In *The social fabric of the metropolis*, ed. J. F. Short, Jr., pp. 193–209. Chicago: University of Chicago Press.

Crowe, P. W. 1978. Good fences make good neighbors: Social networks at three levels of urbanization in Tirol, Austria. Ph.D. diss., Department of Anthropology, Stanford University.

Crozier, M. 1973. *The world of the office worker*. New York: Schocken Books.

Curtis, J. 1971. Voluntary association joining: A cross-cultural comparative note. *American Sociological Review* 32 (October): 872–80.

Dean, A., and Lin, N. 1977. The stress-buffering role of social support. *Journal of Nervous and Mental Diseases* 164:7–15.

Department of Health, Education, and Welfare. 1978. *Divorces and divorce rates*. Public Health Service Series 21, no. 29. Washington, D.C.: HEW.

Duncan-Jones, P. 1978. The interview measurement of social interaction. Social Psychiatry Research Unit, Australian National University.

Durkheim, E. 1933 [1893]. *Division of labor in society*. New York: Free Press.

Ferree, M. M. 1976. Working-class feminism: A study in diffusion through social networks. Paper presented to the American Sociological Association, New York City (August).

Finifter, B. M. 1972. The generation of confidence: evaluating research findings by random subsample replication. In *Sociological methodology 1972*, ed. H. L. Costner, pp. 112–75. San Francisco: Jossey-Bass.

Firth, R.; Hubert, J.; and Forge, A. 1970. *Families and their relatives*. New York: Humanities Press.

Fischer, C. S. 1971. A research note on urbanism and tolerance. *American Journal of Sociology* 76 (March): 847–56.

———. 1973. The effects of urban life on traditional values. *Social Forces* 53 (March): 420–32.

———. 1973. On urban alienation and anomie. *American Sociological Review* 38 (June): 311–26.

———. 1973. Urban malaise. *Social Forces* 52 (December): 221–35.

———. 1975. The study of urban community and personality. *Annual Review of Sociology* 1:67–89.

———. 1975. Toward a subcultural theory of urbanism. *American Journal of Sociology* 80 (May): 1319–41.

———. 1976. *The urban experience*. New York: Harcourt Brace Jovanovich.

———. 1978. On the Marxian challenge to urban sociology. *Comparative Urban Research* 6:10–19.

———. 1978. Sociological comments on psychological approaches to urban life. In *Advances in the study of environment and behavior*, Vol. 1, *The urban environment*, ed. A. Baum et al., pp. 131–43. Hillsdale, N.J.: Lawrence Erlbaum.

———. 1978. Urban-to-rural diffusion of opinion in contemporary America. *American Journal of Sociology* 84 (July): 151–59.

———. 1979. The spatial dimension of social support: New data from northern California. Working Paper no. 300, Institute of Urban and Regional Development, Berkeley.

———. 1980. The spread of violent crime from city to countryside, 1955–1975. *Rural Sociology* 45 (fall): 417–31.

———. 1981. Public and private worlds of city life. *American Sociological Review* 46 (August):306–16.

Fischer, C. S.; Jackson, R. M.; Stueve, C. A.; Gerson, K.; and Jones, L. M.; with Baldassare, M. 1977. *Networks and places: Social relations in the urban setting*. New York: Free Press.

Fischer, C. S., and Oliker, S. 1980. Friendship, gender, and the lifecycle. Paper presented to the American Sociological Association, New York (August); Working Paper no. 318, Institute of Urban and Regional Development, Berkeley.

Fischer, C. S., and Phillips, S. L. 1982. Who is alone: Social characteristics of respondents with small networks. In *Loneliness: A sourcebook of theory, research and therapy*, ed. L. A. Peplau and D. Perlman. New York: Wiley.

Fitzgerald, R., and Fuller, L. 1981. I hear you knocking but you can't come in. Unpublished paper, Department of Sociology, University of California, Berkeley.

Franck, K A., 1980. Friends and strangers: The social experience of living in urban and non-urban settings. *Journal of Social Issues* 36 (3): 52–71.

Frankenburg, B. 1965. *Communities in Britain*. Baltimore: Penguin.

Freedman, J. 1975. *Crowding and behavior*. San Francisco: Freeman.

Gallup opinion index. 1973. Report no. 91: 12–15.

Gans, H. J. 1962. Urbanism and suburbanism as ways of life. In *Human behavior and social processes*, ed. A. M. Rose, pp. 625–48. Boston: Houghton Mifflin.

Gerson, K.; Stueve, A.; and Fischer, C. S. 1977. Attachment to place. In C. S. Fischer et al., *Networks and places*, pp. 139–58. New York: Free Press.

Gibbs, J. P. 1971. Suicide. In *Contemporary social problems*, 3d ed., ed. R. K. Merton and R. A. Nisbet, pp. 271–312. New York: Harcourt Brace Jovanovich.

Gillespie, M. W. 1977. Log-linear techniques and regression analyses of dummy dependent variables. *Sociological Methods and Research* 6 (August): 103–23.

Glazer, N. and Moynihan, D. P. 1975. *Ethnicity: Theory and experience*. Cambrdge: Harvard University Press.

Glenn, N. D., and Hill, L., Jr. 1977. Rural-urban differences in attitude and behavior in the United States. *Annals of the American Academy* 429 (January): 36–50.

Gove, W. R., and Geerken, M. R. 1977. The effect of children and employment on the mental health of married men and women. *Social Forces* 56 (September): 66–71.

————. 1977. Response bias in surveys of mental health: An empirical investigation. *American Journal of Sociology* 82 (May): 1289–1317.

Granovetter, M. 1973. The strength of weak ties. *American Journal of Sociology* 78 (May): 1360–80.

————. 1974. *Getting a job.* Cambridge: Harvard University Press.

Grasmick, H. G., and Grasmick, M. K. 1978. The effect of farm family background on the value orientations of urban residents. *Rural Sociology* 43 (3): 367–84.

Gusfield, J. 1975. *Community.* Oxford: Basil Blackwell.

Gutkind, P. C. W. 1969. African urbanism, mobility, and social networks. In *The city in newly-developing countries,* ed. G. Breese, pp. 389–400. Englewood Cliffs, N.J.: Prentice-Hall.

Hamburg, B. A., and Killilea, M. 1979. Relation of social support, stress, illness, and use of health services. In *Healthy people.* Surgeon General's Report on Health Promotion and Disease Prevention Background Papers. Washington, D.C.: Government Printing Office.

Harris, Louis, Associates. 1976. *The Harris Survey yearbook of public opinion 1972.* New York: Louis Harris Associates.

————. 1978. *A survey of citizen views and concerns about urban life.* Washington, D.C.: Department of Housing and Urban Development.

Harry, J. 1974. Urbanization and the gay life. *Journal of Sex Research* 10 (August): 238–47.

Hawley, A. 1981. *Urban society.* 2d ed. New York: Wiley.

Henry, J. 1958. The personal community and its invariant properties. *American Anthropologist* 60 (October): 827–31.

Hochschild, A. 1973. *The unexpected community.* Englewood Cliffs, N.J.: Prentice-Hall.

Holahan, C. J. 1977. Effects of urban size and heterogeneity on judged appropriateness of altruistic responses. *Sociometry* 40 (December): 378–82.

Hollingshead, A. B. 1970 [1939]. Behavior systems as a field for research. In *Subcultures,* ed. D. G. Arnold, pp. 21–30. Berkeley: Glendessary Press.

House, J. S. 1980. *Work stress and social support.* Reading, Mass.: Addison-Wesley.

House, J., and Wolf, S. 1978. Effects of urban residence on interpersonal trust and helping behavior. *Journal of Personality and Social Psychology* 36 (9): 1029–43.

Howe, I. 1971. The city in literature. *Commentary* 51 (May): 61–68.

Hummon, David. 1980. Community ideology. Ph.D. diss., Department of Sociology, University of California, Berkeley.

————. 1980. Popular images of the American small town. *Landscape* 24 (2): 3–9.

Hunter, A. 1978. Persistence of local sentiments in mass society. In *Handbook of contemporary urban life,* ed. D. Street et al., pp. 133–63. San Francisco: Jossey-Bass.

Huston, T. L., and Levinger, G. 1978. Interpersonal attraction and relationships. *Annual Review of Psychology* 29: 115–56.

Jackson, R. M. 1977. Social structure and process in friendship choice. In C. S. Fischer et al., *Networks and places,* pp. 59–78. New York: Free Press.

Janowitz, M., and Street, D. 1978. The changing social order of the metropolitan area. In *Handbook of contemporary urban life,* ed. D. Street and Associates, pp. 90–130. San Francisco: Jossey-Bass.

Johnson, G. L., and Newmeyer, J. A. 1979. Gays, grass, and death: The attitudinal geography of San Francisco. Unpublished paper, Pacific Research Associates, San Francisco.

Jones, L. M., and Fischer, C. S. 1978. Studying egocentric networks by mass survey. Working Paper no. 284, Institute of Urban and Regional Development, Berkeley.

Kadushin, C., et al. 1980. Social density and mental health. Unpublished paper, Center for Social Research of the Graduate Center, City University of New York.

Kahn, R. and Antonucci, T. C. 1980. Convoys over the life course. Unpublished paper,

Institute for Social Research, Ann Arbor, Michigan.

Karnig, A. A. 1979. Black economic, political, and cultural development: Does city size make a difference? *Social Forces* 57 (June): 1194–1211.

Kasarda, J. D., and Janowitz, M. 1974. Community attachment in mass society. *American Sociological Review* 39 (June): 328–39.

Katz, F. E. 1966. Social participation and social structure. *Social Forces* 45 (December): 199–210.

Keller, S. 1968. *The urban neighborhood.* New York: Random House.

Kerr, C., and Siegel, A. 1954. The inter-industry propensity to strike. In *Industrial Conflict*, ed. A. Kornhauser et al., pp. 189–212. New York: McGraw-Hill.

Key, W. H. 1968. Rural-urban social participation. In *Urbanism in world perspective*, ed. S. F. Fava, pp. 305–12. New York: Crowell.

Kish, L. 1967. *Survey sampling.* New York: Wiley.

Kish, L., and Frankel, M. R. 1974. Inference from complex samples. *Journal of the Royal Statistical Society*, ser. B, 36:1–37.

Knocke, D. 1979. A comparison of log-linear and regression models for systems of dichotomous variables. *Sociological Methods and Research* 3 (May): 416–34.

Komarovsky, M. 1967. *Blue-collar marriage.* New York: Random House.

Kornblum, W. 1975. *Blue-collar community.* Chicago: University of Chicago Press.

Korte, C. 1978. Helpfulness in the urban environment. In *Advances in the study of environment and behavior*, Vol. 1, *The urban environment*, ed. A. Baum et al., pp. 85–110. Hillsdale, N. J.: Lawrence Erlbaum Associates.

———. 1980. Urban-nonurban differences in social behavior and social psychological models of urban impact. *Journal of Social Issues* 36 (3):29–51.

Korte, C., and Ayralioglu, N. 1980. Helpfulness in Turkey. Unpublished paper, Department of Psychology, Pennsylvania State University.

Korte, D.; Ypma, I.; and Toppen, A. 1975. Helpfulness in Dutch society as a function of urbanization and environmental input level. *Journal of Personality and Social Psychology* 32:996–1003.

Kurth, S. 1970. Friendship and friendly relations. In *Social relationships*, ed. G. J. McCall et al., pp. 136–70. Chicago: Aldine.

Larson, O. F. 1979. Values and beliefs of rural people. In *Rural U.S.A.*, ed. T. B. Ford, pp. 91–110. Ames: Iowa State University Press.

Latane, B., and Darley, J. M. 1970. *The unresponsive bystander.* New York: Appleton-Century-Crofts.

Laumann, E. O. 1966. *Prestige and association in an urban community.* New York: Bobbs-Merrill.

———. 1973. *Bonds of pluralism.* New York: Wiley.

Larzarfeld, P., and Merton, R. K. 1954. Friendship as a social process. In *Freedom and control in modern society*, ed. M. Berger et al., pp. 18–66. New York: Van Nostrand.

Lazerwitz, B. 1977. The community variable in Jewish identification. *Journal for the Scientific Study of Religion* 16 (4): 361–69.

Lee, D. 1979. Processes of spatial change in the San Francisco gay community. Class paper, City Planning 298E, University of California, Berkeley.

Lenski, G. 1961. *The religious factor.* Garden City, N.Y.: Doubleday.

Levine, M. P. 1979. Gay ghetto. In *Gay men*, ed. M. P. Levine. New York: Harper and Row.

Lewis, O. 1965. Further observations on the folk-urban continuum and urbanization. In *The study of urbanization*, ed. P. H. Hauser and L. F. Schnore, pp. 491–503. New York: Wiley.

Lieberson, S. 1969. Measuring population diversity. *American Sociological Review* 34 (December): 850–62.

Lin, N.; Ensel, W. M.; and Vaughn, J. C. 1980. Social resources and strength of ties: Structural factors in occupational status attainment. Paper presented to the American Sociological Association, New York (August).

Lincoln, J. R. 1978. Community structure and industrial conflict. *American Sociological Review* 43 (April): 199–219.

Lipset, S. M.; Trow, M.; and Coleman, J. S. 1956. *Union democracy*. New York: Free Press.

Litwak, E., and Szelenyi, I. 1969. Primary group structures and their functions: Kin, neighbor, and friends. *American Sociological Review* 34 (August): 465–81.

Litwak, E., et al. 1979. An empirical study of primary groups amongst the elderly. Paper presented to the American Sociological Association, Boston (August).

Lofland, L. 1973. *A world of strangers*. New York: Basic Books.

Lopata, H. Z. 1979. *Women as widows: Support systems*. New York: Elsevier.

Lukes, Stephen. 1973. *Emile Durkheim*. Baltimore: Penguin.

McCallister (Jones), L., and Fischer, C. S. 1978. A procedure for surveying personal networks. *Sociological Methods and Research* 7 (November): 131–48.

Marx, L. 1964. *The machine in the garden*. New York: Oxford University Press.

Michelson, W. 1977. *Environmental choice, human behavior, and residential satisfaction*. New York: Oxford University Press.

Milgram, S. 1970. The experience of living in cities. *Science* 167 (March): 1461–68.

Mirande, A. M. 1970. Extended kinship ties, friendship relations, and community size: An exploratory inquiry. *Rural Sociology* 35 (June): 261–65.

Mitchell, J. C., ed. 1969. *Social networks in urban situations*. Manchester: University of Manchester Press.

Morgan, N. R., and Clark, T. R. 1973. The causes of racial disorders. *American Sociological Review* 38 (October): 611–24.

Mosteller, F., and Tukey, J. W. 1968. Data analysis, including statistics. In *The handbook of social psychology*, 2d ed., ed. G. Lindzey and E. Aronson, 2:80–203. Reading Mass.: Addison-Wesley.

Mueller, D. P. 1980. Social networks: A promising direction for research. *Social Science and Medicine* 14A:147–61.

Neft, D. S. 1966. *Statistical analysis for areal distributions*. Monograph Series, no. 2. Philadelphia: Regional Science Research Institute.

Nelsen, H. M., and Potvin, R. H. 1977. The rural church and rural religion. *Annals of the American Academy* 429 (January): 103–14.

Newport, F. 1979. The religious switcher in the United States. *American Sociological Review* 44 (August): 528–52.

Nisbet, R. 1969. *Community and power*. 2d ed. New York: Oxford University Press.

Nunn, C. Z.; Crockett, H. J., Jr.; and Williams, J. A., Jr. 1976. *Tolerance for nonconformity*. San Francisco: Jossey-Bass.

Paine, R. 1969. In search of friendship. *Man* 4 (2): 505–24.

Palen, J. J. 1979. The urban nexus: Toward the year 2000. In *Societal growth*, ed. A. Hawley, pp. 141–56. New York: Free Press.

Park, R. E. 1967 [1916]. The city: Suggestions for the investigation of human behavior in the urban environment. In *The City*, ed. R. E. Park and E. W. Burgess, pp. 1–46. Chicago: University of Chicago Press (Also in *Classic essays on the culture of cities*, ed. R. Sennett, pp. 91–130. New York: Appleton-Century-Crofts [1969].)

———. 1971 [1926]. The urban community as a spatial pattern and a moral order. In *Robert Park on social control and collective behavior*. ed. R. H. Turner, pp. 55–68. Chicago: University of Chicago Press.

Peplau, L. A., and Perlman, D. eds. 1981. *Loneliness*. New York: Wiley.

Phillips, S. L., and Fischer, C. S. 1981. Measuring social support networks in general populations. In *Life stress and illness*, ed. B. Dohrenwend and B. Dohrenwend. New York: Watson.

Pilcher, W. W. 1972. *The Portland longshoremen: A dispersed urban community*. New York: Holt, Rinehart.

Pinkerton, J. R. 1978. City-suburban redistribution of age groups, 1950–1970. Paper presented to the American Sociological Association, San Francisco (August).

Provencher, R. 1972. Comparisons of social interaction styles: Urban and rural Malay culture. In *The Anthropology of urban environments*, ed. T. Weaver and D. White, pp. 69–76. Monograph 11, Washington, D.C.: Society of Applied Anthropology.

Redfield, R. 1947. The folk society. *American Journal of Sociology* 52 (4): 293–308.

Redfield, R., and Singer, M. 1954. The cultural role of cities. *Economic Development and Cultural Change* 3 (October): 53–77.

Reiss, A. J., Jr. 1955. An analysis of urban phenomena. In *The metropolis in modern life*, ed. R. M. Fisher, pp. 41–51. New York: Doubleday.

———. 1959. Rural-urban and status differences in interpersonal contacts. *American Journal of Sociology* 65 (September): 118–30.

Reynolds, H. T. 1977. *The analysis of cross-classifications*. New York: Free Press.

Richardson, H. L. 1973. *The economics of city size*. London: Saxon House.

Roof, W. C. 1978. *Community and commitment*. New York: Elsevier.

———. 1979. Concepts and indicators of religious commitment. In *The religious dimension*, ed. R. Wuthnow, pp. 17–45. New York: Academic Press.

———. 1979. Traditional religion. In *The religious dimension*, ed. R. Wuthnow. New York: Academic Press.

Rose, P. I., with Pertzoff L. O., 1977. *Strangers in their midst: Small-town Jews and their neighbors*. Merrick, N.Y.: Richwood.

Rossi, P. 1972. Community social indicators. In *The human meaning of social change*, ed. A. Campbell and P. E. Converse, pp. 87–126. New York: Russell Sage.

Russell, B. 1930. *The conquest of happiness*. New York: New American Library.

Sale, K. 1978. The polis perplexity: An inquiry into the size of cities. *Working Papers for a New Society* 6 (January–February): 64–77.

Schorske, C. E. 1963. The idea of the city in European thought: Voltaire to Spengler. In *The historian and the city*, ed. O. Handlin and J. Borchard, pp. 95–115. Cambridge: M.I.T. Press.

Sennett, R. 1977. *The fall of public man*. New York: Knopf.

Shulman, N. 1972. Urban social networks. Ph.D. diss., Department of Sociology, University of Toronto.

———. 1976. Role differentiation in networks. *Sociological Focus* 9 (April): 149–56.

Silverman, C. J. 1981. Negotiated claim. Ph.D. diss., Department of Sociology, University of California, Berkeley.

Silverman, C. J. and Gerson, M. S. 1981. Place type as a social object. Unpublished paper, Institute of Urban and Regional Development, Berkeley.

Simmel, G. 1969 [1905]. The metropolis and mental life. In *Classic essays on the culture of cities*, ed. R. Sennett, pp. 47–60. New York: Appleton-Century-Crofts.

Sjoberg, G. 1964. The rural-urban dimension in preindustrial, transitional and industrial societies. In *The handbook of modern sociology*, ed. R. E. L. Faris, pp. 127–60. Chicago: Rand-McNally.

Smith, T. W. 1979. Happiness. *Social Psychology Quarterly* 42 (March): 18–30.

Spilerman, S. 1971. The causes of racial disturbances. *American Sociological Review* 36 (June): 427–42.

Srole, L. 1972. Urbanization and mental health: Some reformulations. *American Scientist* 60 (September/October): 576–83.

————. 1980. Mental health in New York: A revisionist view. *Sciences* 20 (December): 16–29.

Starr, P. 1980. Impersonal caretakers. *New York Times Book Review,* 6 April, p. 30.

Statistical Abstract of the United States. 1978. Washington, D.C.: U.S. Department of Commerce.

Stein, M. 1960. *Eclipse of community.* New York: Harper and Row.

Stephens, S. 1979. Ethnic identity in an urban community. Paper presented to American Sociological Association, Boston (August).

Steward, J. G. 1948. Demographic gravitation: Evidence and applications. *Sociometry* 11:31–58.

Stokols, D., ed. 1977. *Perspectives on environment and behavior.* New York: Plenum.

Stueve, A., and Lein, L. 1979. Problems in network analysis: The case of the missing person. Unpublished paper, Wellesley College Center for Research on Women.

Suttles, G. 1970. Friendship as a social institution. In *Social Relationships,* ed. G. J. McCall et al., pp. 95–135. Chicago: Aldine.

Swedner, H. 1960. *Ecological differentiation of habits and attitudes.* Lund, Sweden: GWK Gleerup.

Terkel, S. 1974. *Working.* New York: Avon.

Thibaut, J. W., and Kelley, H. H. 1959. *The social psychology of small groups.* New York: Wiley.

Tilly, C. 1974. The chaos of the living city. In *An urban world,* ed. C. Tilly, pp. 86–107. Boston: Little, Brown.

Tilly, C.; Tilly, L.; and Tilly, R. 1975. *The rebellious century.* Cambridge: Harvard University Press.

United States Bureau of the Census. 1970. *General social and economic characteristics.* Washington, D. C.: Government Printing Office.

Verbrugge, L. M. 1977. The structure of adult friendship choices. *Social Forces* 56 (December): 576–97.

Warner, S. B., Jr. 1977. *The private city.* Philadelphia: University of Pennsylvania Press.

Weatherford, M. S. 1980. Interpersonal networks and political behavior. Unpublished paper, Department of Political Science, University of California, Santa Barbara.

————. 1980. The politics of school busing: Contextual effects and community polarization. *Journal of Politics,* pp. 85–103.

Webb, S. D. 1978. Mental health in rural and urban environments. *Ekistics* 266 (January): 37–42.

Webb, S. D., and Collette, J. 1977. Rural-urban differences in the use of stress-alleviative drugs. *American Journal of Sociology* 83 (November): 700–707.

————. 1979. Rural-urban stress: New data and new conclusions. *American Journal of Sociology* 84 (May): 1446–52.

Webber, M. M. 1963. The urban place and the nonplace urban realm. In M. M. Webber et al., *Explorations into urban structure.* Philadelphia: University of Pennsylvania Press.

————. 1970 [1969]. Order in diversity: Community without propinquity. In *Neighborhood, city and metropolis,* ed. R. Gutman and D. Popenoe, pp. 792–81. New York: Random House.

Weiner, F. H. 1976. Altruism, ambiance and action: The effects of rural and urban rearing on helping behavior. *Journal of Personality and Social Psychology* 34:112–24.

Wellman, B. 1979. The community question. *American Journal of Sociology* 84 (March): 1201–31.

————. 1981. The application of network analysis to the study of social support. Resource Paper no. 3. Centre for Urban and Community Studies, University of Toronto.

Wellman, B., and Leighton, B. 1979. Networks, neighborhoods, and communities. *Urban Affairs Quarterly* 15 (March): 363–90.

Wellman, B., et al. 1973. Community ties and support systems. In *The form of cities in central Canada,* ed. L. S. Bourne, R. D. Mackinnon, and J. W. Simmons. Toronto: University of Toronto Press.

White, M., and White, L. 1962. *The intellectual versus the city.* New York: Mentor.

Williams, J. A., Jr.; Nunn, C. S.: and St. Peter, L. 1976. Origins of tolerance. *Social Forces* 55 (December): 394–408.

Williams, R. 1973. *The country and the city.* New York: Oxford University Press.

Willitis, F. K.; Bealer, R. C.: and Crider, D. M. 1973. Leveling of attitudes in mass society. *Rural Sociology* 38 (spring): 36–45.

Wirth, L. 1938. Urbanism as a way of life. *American Journal of Sociology* 44 (July): 3–24 (Also in *Classic essays on the culture of cities,* ed. R. Sennett, pp. 143–64. New York: Appleton-Century-Crofts, 1969.)

Wuthnow, R. 1976. *The consciousness reformation.* Berkeley: University of California Press.

Young, M., and Willmott, P. 1973. *The symmetrical family.* Baltimore: Penguin.

Index

Abortion, 66–67, 75
Abrahamson, M., 408, 429
Adams, B. N., 368
Age
    and childhood friends, 90
    and companionship, 130
    and confidants, 55
    and counseling support, 128
    and financial constraints, 27
    and frequency of meeting, 59
    and friends, 115, 256
    and happiness, 51
    and health, 5
    and intimacy, 253
    and isolation, 55
    and kin versus nonkin involvement, 85
    and local activity, 164
    and meeting people, 4–5
    and multistrandedness, 142
    and mutual friends, 90
    and neighbors, 161
    and network size, 253
    and nonkin, 91, 94, 161, 167, 170, 253
    and occupation, 217
    and organizational co-members, 6, 110,
        133
    and practical support, 130
    and religion, 110, 208
    segregation by, 81, 180, 188
    and selective migration, 28–29, 256
    and social activity, 253
    and spatial dispersion, 9, 253
    and support, 128, 130, 131, 253
    and traditionalism, 68–70
    and urbanism, 9, 56, 58, 70–71, 94, 101,
        182, 256
Alexander, C., 360, 361, 398
Allan, G. A., 374, 427
Antonucci, J.C., 428
Arling, G., 401
Arnold, D. G., 406
Aronson, E., 429

Arroyo, Eddie, 216
Artistic performance, 225
Ayralioglo, N., 424

Babchuck, N., 380
Background, general, 34
Baldassare, M., 395, 396, 423
Banton, M., 419
Barnes, J. A., 351, 392
Barth, F., 351, 352, 424
Barthel, Diane, 203, 409
Baum, A., 423
Bay Area, and traditionalism, 67–68
Bealer, R. C., 368
Becker, H. S., 417
Behavior
    deviance, 52–53
    measuring, 66
    visibility, 52
Bell, W., 379, 427
Bender, Thomas, 351, 393
Berger, M., 400
Berger, Peter, 11, 403
Berkeley, 66, 197
Berkman, L. F., 351
Berreman, Gerald R., 235, 352, 424
Berry, B. J. L., 353, 408, 427
Bias, 293
Block clusters, 295
Blumin, S. M., 379
Boat, M., 379, 427
Boissevain, Jeremy, 143, 351, 388, 389
Booth, A., 380
Borchard, J., 356
Bott, Elizabeth, 146, 351, 389, 392
Bourne, L. S., 391
Boyer, Paul, 356, 363, 366
Boy Scouts, 109
Bradburn, Norman M., 310, 359, 429
Breese, G., 379
Breton, R., 408, 411
Bruner, E. M., 424

Bulmer, M. I. A., 377
Burgess, E. W., 352, 353
Busing, 71

Campbell, A., 134, 352, 359, 386
Carp, F., 401
Carpenter, E. H., 352, 423
Carrothers, G. A. P., 429
Carter, James Earl, Jr., 172
Castells, M., 364
Castro Street, 236–37, 239
Catholics
    and Catholic friends, 256
    social involvement, 209–10, 212–13
Census data, 277, 295
Centrality, 152
    and closeness, 152, 154–57
    measuring, 291
    and multistrandedness, 152
    and practical help, 153
Chance meetings, 4–5, 60, 248
Chicago school of sociology, 7–8, 10, 31, 45,
    64, 387
Children
    and church attendance, 214
    and companionship, 130
    and effects of working, 254
    and familial obligations, 5
    and friends, 115, 116
    and housing preferences, 26–27
    and involvement with colleagues, 218
    and maintaining relations, 5, 79
    and mood, 135, 252–53
    and morale, 48, 253
    and nonkin, 167, 170
    and religion, 208–9
    and selective migration, 26–27, 28–29
    and social burden, 136, 252, 253
    and support, 130, 131
    and traditionalism, 68, 69
Church associates, 93, 94
Church attendance, 213–14
Cities. See Urbanism; Urbanization
Clark, T. R., 424
Cleary, P. D., 429
Close relationships, 58–59
Cobb, S., 351
Cognitive sophistication, 252
Cohabitation, 63, 65
Cohen, A., 409
Cohen, S., 423

Coleman, Charlotte, 310
Coleman, J. S., 377, 417
Coleman, R. P., 409
Collette, J. 359
Co-members of organizations. See Organizational co-members
Community, 271–72
    and age, 182
    climate, 70, 90–91, 119
    competition, 169
    decline of (see Decline of community
        theory)
    and nonkin, 167
    and social involvement with colleagues,
        218
    turnover, 86
    and urbanism, 8–9, 161
Community file, 299
Community informants, 296
Community of origin, 74
Commuting, 166
Companionship, 127
    and mood, 135, 137
    and social activity, 129–30
    sources of support, 132
    support versus harassment, 136–37
    and urbanism, 130
Converse, P. E., 134, 352, 359, 386
Cooperation in interview, 38, 42, 48, 302–3
    and confidants, 55
    and co-workers, 105
    and education, 303
    and friends, 115
    and gender, 303
    and isolation, 55
    and length of residence in city, 303
    and nonkin, 92
    and urbanism, 303
    and worries about crime, 303
Correlations, 313–14
Coser, L., 383
Costner, H. L., 429
Cost of living, 269
Counseling, 127, 128–29, 132. See also Support
Counties, 295
Co-workers, 103
    choice, 104, 108
    involvement, 97, 104
    and occupation, 105
    and status, 105

and time on the job, 105
and urbanism, 94, 104, 105–6, 258
Crafts, 225
Cressy, P. G., 352
Crider, D. M., 368
Crime
    fear of, 234, 244, 246, 260, 263
    and mood, 49, 260
    in Sacramento area, 269
    in San Francisco–Oakland area, 269
    and selective migration, 256, 263–64
    and urbanism, 263
    and urban subcultures, 65, 229
Crockett, H. J., Jr., 425
Cross-cultural encounters, 234–35
Crowe, Patricia W., 60, 61, 363
Crozier, Michael, 417
Culture, and role-relations, 79
Curtis, J., 380

Dahman, D. C., 353, 427
Darley, J. M., 423
Davis, F., 352
Dean, A., 351
Decline of community theory, 1, 63, 64, 75,
    80, 81, 97, 104, 115, 121, 125, 140, 158,
    177, 189, 193–94, 201, 202, 231, 262
Demographic traits. See specific traits
Density, network, 139
    cause and effect, 141, 151, 157
    and characteristics of associates, 147
    and choice, 140
    constraints and, 146, 156
    and isolation, 140
    and kin, 146
    measuring, 144–45, 291
    and mood, 149, 150, 151, 156–57, 259
    and social contexts, 146
    and support, 149, 152, 155
    and unimportant associates, 155
    and urbanism, 140, 147–48, 258
Distant associates, 169–70
    closeness, 173, 176, 178, 259
    and crisis, 175
    frequency of contact, 176
    rewards of, 172
    specialization, 172, 178
    and urbanism, 170
Distrust, 244–45, 246, 260
Dohrenwend, B., 374
Drought, 20

Duncan-Jones, P., 428
Durkheim, Emile, 351, 352, 387

Eddington, N. A., 360, 398
Education
    and church attendance, 214
    and companionship, 130, 251
    and confidants, 55, 252
    and counseling support, 128
    and co-workers, 105
    and density, 145, 251–52
    effects of, 252
    and familial obligations, 5
    and frequency of meeting, 59
    and friends, 115, 252
    and happiness, 51
    and intimacy, 251
    and kin versus nonkin involvement, 85
    and local kin, 81, 159
    measuring, 309
    and meeting people, 4
    and multistrandedness, 142
    and neighbors, 99
    and network, 33, 41, 45, 251, 252
    and nonkin, 91, 92, 159, 161, 167, 170,
        252
    and occupation, 217
    and organizational co-members, 110
    and reliance on kin, 133, 252
    and school friends, 90, 252
    and selective migration, 28
    and social activity, 251
    and support, 121
    and traditionalism, 68–69, 70
    and trust, 245
    and urbanism, 70–71
Ensel, W. M., 427
Ethnic institutions, 197, 198
Ethnicity
    blacks, 237–38, 240, 254
    Chicanos, 6, 206, 230, 236–37, 254
    and counseling support, 128
    denying, 202, 203
    and friends, 115
    involvement, 204, 207
    measuring, 203
    and nonkin, 91
    and outside ties, 205–6
    and practical support, 130
    and selective migration, 28
    and support, 131

and urbanism, 202, 203–7, 256–57, 259
Etiquette, 234, 249
Exchanges, 173–75, 177, 289
Extramarital sex, 63, 65, 66, 67, 74

Face blocks, 295
Family. *See also* Kin
    attitudes and traditionalism, 72
    breakdown of, 81
    size, 82–83
Faris, R. E. L., 364
Fashions, 65, 75
Fava, S. F., 377
Ferree, Myra M., 71, 367
Field losses, 281–82
Field staff, 280, 302
Fieldwork methods, 279, 280–81
Financial aid, 131, 132
Finifter, B. M., 429
Finnegan, Daniel, 297, 305
Firth, R., 368
Fischer, C. S., 253, 275, 281, 284, 291, 313–14, 351. 352, 357, 359, 360, 363, 364, 366, 366, 367, 368, 371, 374, 375, 376, 377, 383, 387, 388, 391, 393, 394, 396, 398, 399, 400, 401, 406, 407, 410, 411, 422, 423, 424, 427, 428, 429
Fisher, R. M., 364
Fitzgerald, Robert, 283, 292, 299, 309, 353, 428
Ford, T. R., 359, 364
Foreign-language speakers, 276, 277
Forge, A., 368
Franck, Karen A., 424, 426
Frankel, M. R., 429
Frankenburg, R., 387, 392
Freedman, J., 423
Frequency of meeting, 59, 176, 258
Friends
    childhood, 90
    choice, 114
    and commitments, 120–21
    and personality, 115
    quality, 118
    and resources, 116, 121
    and social burdens, 136–37
    and urbanism, 57, 59–60, 115–16, 258
Fromm, Erich, 351, 403
Fuller, Linda, 283, 428

Gallup poll, 50, 51, 273, 359, 364, 425, 428

Gans, J. H., 364
Geerken, M. R., 357, 387
Gender
    and age, 253
    and confidants, 55
    and counseling support, 128
    and friends, 115, 116, 253
    and intimacy, 253
    and kin, 80, 85, 87, 253
    and local activity, 164
    and marriage, 253
    and nonkin, 85, 91, 161
    and occupation, 217
    and organizational co-members, 110, 112
    and sociability, 253, 254
    and social activity, 130
    and social burden, 136
    and support, 130, 132
Gender distribution, 303, 304
Genovese, Kitty, 233
Gerson, Kathleen, 188, 309, 376, 400, 401
Gerson, M. Sue, 275, 295, 368
Gibbs, J. P., 357
Gillespie, M. W., 429
Glazer, N., 409, 410
Glenn, N., 364, 366, 367
Glockel, G., 429
Gove, W. R., 357, 387
Grange, 111
Granovetter, Mark, 289, 427, 428
Grasmick, J. G., 367
Grasmick, M. K., 367
Gusfield, J. 351
Gutkind, P..C. W., 379
Gutman, R., 393, 406
Guyana, 270

Hamburg, B. A., 383
Handlin, O., 356
Happiness, 50–51
Harry, J., 408
Hauser, P. H., 364
Harley, A. H., 357, 396, 427
Heller, Joseph, 196
Helmer, J., 398
Henry, J., 351
Hill, L., Jr., 364, 366, 367
Hilmer, J., 360
Historical period, 20, 263–64
Hobbes, Thomas, 45
Hobbies. *See* Pastime

Hochschild, A., 401
Holahan, C. J., 423
Hollingshead, A. B., 195, 406
Homemakers, 223
Homeowners, 99, 164
Homogeneity
    and age, 179, 180
    and closeness, 188
    constraints, 179, 187
    and marital status, 181 185–87, 189, 259
    and preference, 179, 181
    and self-selection, 182
    and social context, 180–81
    and urbanism, 182–85, 189, 259
Homogenization, 257
Homophily, 179
Homosexuality
    amount, 238
    and business, 238
    history, 238
    and selective migration, 29
    and teaching, 67
    tension, 239–40
    and urbanism, 63, 67, 74, 229
Horowitz, Donald, 409
Horse-racing, 216
House, J. S., 383, 423
Household help, 130–31
Household members, 128, 135. *See also*
    Family; Kin
Housing
    availability, 263
    and distance, 160
    growth, 20, 161, 165
Housing units sampled, 279
Howe, I., 356
Hubert, J., 368
Hummon, David, 248, 352, 356, 363, 390,
    423, 426
Hunter, A., 375
Huston, J. L., 400

Illness, 135–36
Income
    and companionship, 130, 252
    and co-workers, 106
    and density, 146, 149, 150, 261
    and distance, 176, 253
    expected, 309
    and friends, 115–16, 252
    and isolation, 55

and kin, 80–81, 87, 252
and local activity, 165, 166
measuring, 309
and meeting people, 5
and mood, 48–49, 101, 176
as network resource, 252
and nonkin, 91, 161, 167, 168, 170, 175,
    252
and organizational co-members, 110
and personality, 252
preferences, 256–57
and selective migration, 27–28
and social ties, 79
and support, 130, 131, 252
and trust, 245
and urbanism, 93–94, 116–17, 256–57
India, 235
Informants. *See* Community informants; Re-
    spondents
Inner suburbs, 272
Innsbruck, Austria, 60, 61
Institutional complexity, 10, 11
Intergroup conflict
    causes, 240
    and homosexuality, 239
    racial tension, 237–39
    and urbanism, 233, 237, 239, 240
Interviewers, 280, 302
Interviews, period of, 281
Isolated respondents, 54–55

Jackknife estimates, 311–12
Jackson, Robert Max, 352, 354, 393, 400
Janowitz, Morris, 364, 394
Jews, 195, 207
Johnson, G. L., 365
Jones, L., 428
Just friends. *See* Friends

Kadushin, C., 391
Kahn, R., 428
Karnig, A. A., 408
Kasarda, J. D., 364, 394
Katz, F. E., 351
Kazin, Alfred, 1
Keller, Suzanne, 99, 375, 377, 395
Kelley, H. H., 398
Kerr, C., 377
Key, W. H., 377
Killilea, M., 383

Kin. *See also* Family
  assistance of, 80
  and confiding, 80
  and crisis, 83, 84, 88
  estrangement, 80
  extended versus nuclear, 83–84, 85
  measuring involvement, 80
  and money, 80
  number named, 38, 56, 68, 70, 71–74, 81–82, 85, 260
  replacement of, 83, 87–88
  selection, 82, 87
  and traditionalism, 68, 71–74, 260
  and urbanism, 56, 70, 81–83, 84, 85, 86, 87, 133, 256
Kish, Leslie, 281, 428, 429
Knocke, D., 429
Komarovsky, M., 374, 427
Kornblum, W., 417
Kornhauser, A., 377
Korte, C., 423, 424
Kurth, Suzanne, 381

Language, and formality, 61
Large cities (sampling stratum), 273
Larson, O. F., 359, 364
Latane, B., 423
Latent relations, 169–70, 287
Laumann, Edward O., 308, 391, 400
Lazarsfeld, P., 400
Lazerwitz, B., 411
Lee, Don, 424
Leighton, B., 387
Lein, Laura, 289, 429
Length of association, 41, 58–59
Length of residence
  and association with colleagues, 218
  and network density, 146
  and neighbors, 99, 161
  and nonkin, 167, 170
  and other local ties, 161
Lenski, Gerhard, 211, 213, 413
Levine, M. P., 424
Levinger, G., 400
Lewis, D., 364
Leibow, Elliot, 410
Life-cycle segregation, 81, 180, 188
Life-cycle, stage in. *See* Age; Marriage
Life events. *See* Mental health
Lin, N., 351, 427
Lincoln, J. R., 419, 423

Lindzey, G., 429
Lipset, S. M., 377, 417
Litvak, E., 368, 371, 379, 399, 401, 428
Local activity, 163–64
Local residents. *See also* Spatial dispersion
  kin, 92, 115
  racial mix, 165
  and traditionalism, 68, 70, 72, 260
Lofland, Lyn, 234, 235, 424
Lopata, H. Z., 383, 428
Los Angeles, crime rate, 19
Los Angeles Times, 97
Louis Harris polling organization, 50, 352, 359, 363, 394, 423
Lukes, Stephen, 351

McCall, G. J., 381
McCallister, Lynne, 284, 291, 354, 388, 393, 428
Mackinnon, R. D., 391
Magazines, 67
Managers, 104
Marcuse, H., 351
Marijuana, 66–67, 75
Marriage
  choice of partners, 65
  and co-hobbyists, 253
  and confidants, 55
  and contacts, 90
  and co-religionists, 253
  former, 55
  and friends, 115, 253
  and isolation, 55
  and kin, 80, 253
  and kin versus nonkin involvement, 85
  and mood, 135
  and neighbors, 99, 253
  and social activity, 130
  and social burden, 136
  and support, 128, 129
  and urbanism, 56
Marx, Karl, 351
Marx, Leo, 351
Mass society theory, 1, 4
Mechanic, D., 429
Mental health, 126, 309–10
  criteria, 46
  and life events, 48–49
  and social burden, 136–37
  survey approach, 46
  and urbanism, 45, 49–50, 51–53, 263–64

Merton, R. K., 357, 400
Metropolitan areas, definition, 23
Michelson, W., 395
Microneighborhoods, 276, 295
Migration. *See* Selective migration
Milgram, Stanley, 352, 360, 423
Milk, Harvey, 239
Mills, C. W., 351
Minors, 276. *See also* Teenagers
Mirande, A. M., 370
Mitchell, J. C., 351, 392
Mood, psychological
    associated characteristics, 48
    corrections for openness, 48
    and income, 157
    and nonkin, 150
    scale, 46–47
    self-selection, 48
    and support, 135
    and urbanism, 135, 157, 260
Morality, 1, 63, 64, 75
Morgan, N. R., 424
Moscone, George, 239
Mosteller, F., 429
Moynihan, D. P., 409, 410
Multistrandedness, 139
    and access to people, 156
    alienation, 139
    causes, 141, 142–43
    and choice, 140
    and closeness, 144, 156
    and frequency of association, 144
    and isolation, 140
    and network size, 142
    and support, 144
    and urbanism, 143, 259
Municipalities, 295

Name file, 299
National Center for Health Statistics, 49
National Opinion Research Center study,
    296
Neft, D. S., 429
Neighborhoods, 98, 275, 295
    changes, 297–98
    and neighbor involvement, 99–102, 247
    similarities of occupants, 6
Neighbors
    and assistance, 175
    borrowing from, 98
    characteristics, 70

and class, 99
and distance, 161
frequency of association, 102
as friends, 101–2
involvement, 97, 98
and length of residence, 99
number named, 70, 93, 94, 99, 101–2, 258
Neilsen, J. M., 411
Networks. *See* Personal networks
Newmeyer, J. A., 365
Newport, F., 411, 413
Newspapers, 67, 197, 298
New York, 19, 51
Nicholls, William C., 11, 277, 300, 311
Nisbet, Robert A., 11, 351, 357, 373, 387, 403
Nonkin
    frequency of meeting, 59
    middle-distance, 167–68
    number named, 38, 56, 68, 85, 92, 256
Northern California
    convenience, 269
    similarity to other areas, 19–20, 50, 261,
        269, 270
Nunn, C. Z., 368, 425

Occupational networks
    definitions of work, 217, 218–19
    identification, 220–21
    and importance of work, 218, 220, 259
    involvement in, 220–21
    measuring, 217
    and schedule, 217
    and type of job, 217
    and urbanism, 218, 219–20, 221, 222, 231–
        32, 259
Oliker, Stacy, 253, 368, 374, 427
On-site observation, 298
Organizational co-members
    choice, 108
    closeness, 109–10, 113
    and companionship, 130
    frequency of association, 113
    and length of residence, 110
    and multistrandedness, 142
    and nonmembers, 109
    and number of organizations, 110
    and practical support, 130
    religious organizations, 110–11, 112
    as replacements for other groups, 108–10,
        113
    and urbanism, 94, 111, 112, 258

Organizations, 108, 111
"Others" (in network), 118
Outer suburbs, 272

Padding of lists, 286
Paine, R., 381
Palen, John, Jr., 255, 357, 427
Parents, 84. *See also* Kin
Park, Robert Ezra, 8, 10, 11–12, 31–32, 45, 194, 195, 352, 353, 363, 403, 406
Parsons, Talcott, 351, 387
Pastime
    commitment, 226
    determining, 224–25
    organizations, 224, 227
    social involvement, 225, 226, 227, 259
    subcultures, 224, 225, 227
People, subjective impressions of
    prejudices, 244
    and urbanism, 241–43
People's Temple, 270
Peplau, L. A., 350, 386
Perlman, D., 360, 386
Personality, 34, 254
Personal networks, 2, 286–87. *See also* Personal relations
    and attitudes, 71–72
    and common culture, 6
    composition, 41
    construction, 4, 89, 90
    describing, 290–91, 307–8
    double-edged, 3, 137
    factors affecting, 251, 254
    and involvement with subcultures, 7
    linkage to residential communities, 8
    and public policy, 3 (*see also* Policy goals)
    size, 38–39, 56
    and social structure, 5
    supportiveness, 3 (*see also* Support)
    and urbanism, 12, 56, 102
Personal relations, 1–2, 64, 70. *See also* Personal networks
Pertzoff, L. O., 411
Philadelphia, 108–9
Phillips, Susan L., 296, 310, 356, 360, 365, 374
Pilcher, W. W., 377, 417
Pinkerton, J. R., 427
Policy goals, 264–66
Popenoe, D., 393, 406

Population density
    and community differences, 257
    and local associates, 165–66
    and neighbors, 103
Population potential, 304–5
Potvin, R. J., 411
Practical support, 127, 130–31, 132. *See also* Support
Proposition 14, 270
Proposition 13, 20
Protestants
    social involvement, 208, 209–10
    and traditionalism, 69
Provencher, R., 363
Public interaction, 234

Race. *See* Ethnicity
Rainwater, L., 409
Recall of associates, 286, 289
Redfield, R., 352, 364
Regional Core (definition), 23
Region surveyed, 19, 269, 271
Reiss, Albert, Jr., 59–60, 363, 364
Relations
    definitions, 35–36, 287, 288–89
    role, 79
    traditional and modern, 118–19
Religious affiliation
    activity, 213
    associational, 211, 214
    communal, 214
    measuring, 202, 208
    and social involvement, 209, 211, 212–13, 258, 259
    and specific religion, 208
    and urbanism, 63, 74, 202, 208–9, 213, 214
Renting, 100
Respondent file, 299
Respondents, 276, 277, 282, 286, 296
Reynolds, H. T., 429
Richardson, H. L., 357
Rod-and-gun clubs, 197, 198
Rodgers, W. L., 134
Roof, W. C., 413, 416
Rose, A. M., 364
Rose, Peter I., 207, 411
Rossi, P., 352
Russell, Bertrand, 103, 377

Sacramento metropolitan area, 269, 307
Sacramento Delta, 24

St. Peter, L., 368
Sale, Kirkpatrick, 45, 264, 357
Sample size, 272, 281
Sample strata, 272, 273, 277
Sampling of communities, 20–21, 272, 273
   excluded localities, 273–74, 275, 282–83
Sanford, Mark, 377
San Francisco
   Board of Education, 239
   crime rate, 19
   legislation, 66
   life-style deviance, 270
   media images, 19, 269
   Mission District, 6, 236, 237
   political tendencies, 19
   social facilities, 46
   subcultural organizations, 197
San Francisco–Oakland area, 269, 270
San José, 271
Schlesinger, Arthur, Sr., 75
Schnore, L. F., 364
Schorske, L. E., 356
Schools, 263
Segregation, age, 81, 180, 188
Selective migration, 27–32, 65, 199, 256–57,
   265
   and distant nonkin, 170
   reasons for, 29–32, 160
   and social climate, 86
   and subcultures, 196, 229
   and town-city differences, 257
   and urban unconventionality, 65
Self-Administered Questionnaire file, 299
Self-selection, 8–9, 27, 256
   corrections for, 27
   and kin, 160
   and mood, 48
   and neighbors, 99
   and network size, 56
   and traditionalism, 69, 119–20
Semirural areas (definition), 23
Sennett, Richard, 11, 352, 357, 360, 372, 403,
   422
Shils, Edward, 351
Short, J. F., Jr., 352
Shulman, Norman, 368, 371, 391, 427
Siblings, 84. *See also* Kin
Siegel, A., 377
Silverman, Carol J., 299, 300, 302, 363, 368,
   375, 395
Similarity, 6

Simmel, George, 351, 352, 360, 387
Simmons, J. W., 391
Singer, M., 364
Sjoberg, G., 363
Skilled labor, 256
Slater, Philip, 403
Slocum, Bob, 196
Small towns (definition), 273
Smith, J. W., 359
Social activity, 54
   and companionship, 129, 130
   and restrictions, 130
   and traditionalism, 68–69
   and urbanism, 54, 130
Social climate, 70, 71, 85
Social context, 4, 40, 79
   age-segregated, 180, 188
   breakdown, 41
   commitment to, 106, 118
   and community, 79
   determination of, 39–40
   and urbanism, 254
Social networks. *See* Personal networks
Social skills, 252
Social structure, 5
Something Happened, 196
Spatial dispersion
   categories, 158, 159
   and communication systems, 5
   as cost, 172, 177
   and income, 253
   and kin, 81, 85, 159
   and mobility, 101, 265
   and moving, 5, 90, 254
   and personal networks, 9
   and transportation systems, 5, 116, 167
   and travel, 5, 79, 87
   and urbanism, 159, 161–62, 177
Spillerman, S., 423
Sports, 224, 225
Srole, L., 358
Staff. *See* Field staff
Standard metropolitan statistical area
   (SMSA), 21, 269, 304
Starr, P., 352
Statistical Package for the Social Sciences
   (SPSS), 292, 310, 312
Statistical procedure, 312, 313
Stein, Maurice, 351, 403
Stephens, S., 411
Stephenson, Bruce, 429

Steward, J. G., 429
Stokols, D., 423
Strangers, 60–61
Street, D., 375, 394
Stueve, C. Ann, 188, 289, 296, 376, 400, 401, 429
Subcultural institutions, 197, 198
Subcultural theory, 11–12, 63, 65, 97, 115, 125, 189, 194, 200, 222, 227, 249, 262
     and co-workers, 104
     and ethnicity, 202
     involvement, 221, 229
     and neighbors, 101
     and nonkin, 92
     and religion, 202
Subcultures, 6, 65–66, 194–96
     alterations in, 202, 206
     boundaries, 195
     compression and conflict, 12, 230
     critical mass, 196, 229
     diversity, 231–32
     intergroup friction, 196–97, 230, 264
     involvement, 200, 230, 247, 259
     nonmembers, 236
     proportion in population, 199
     and shared culture, 7
     size, 198–99
     and social separation, 7
Sudman, S. 429
Support. See also Companionship; Counseling; Practical support
     and constraint, 137
     groups lacking, 131, 137
     and mental health, 126
     and modern society, 125
     and mood, 135, 137
     self-evaluations, 134–35
     sources, 132
     specialization, 138
     and traditionalism, 68
     and urbanism, 126, 138, 258
Survey Research Center (Berkeley), 20, 275, 277, 280, 284
Surveys, 17, 26, 286
Susanville, California, 66
Suttles, Gerald, 114, 381
Swedner, H., 377
Swidler, Ann, 363, 393
Syme, S. L., 351
Szelenyi, I., 368, 371, 379, 399

Taxi-dance halls, 7–8
Teenagers, 229
Telephone directories, 298–99
Terkel, Studs, 103, 417
Thibaut, J. W., 398
Tilly, C., 364, 419, 424
Tilly, L., 364
Tilly, R., 364
Time-budget accounts, 60
Tocqueville, Alexis de, 108, 351
Tönnies, Ferdinand, 351, 352, 387, 403
Toppen, A., 424
Town areas (definition), 23
Traditionalism scale, 66–67, 68, 75. See also Urbanism; Values
Tranquilizers, 50
Trow, M., 377, 412
Tukey, J. W., 429
Turner, R. H., 352

Urbanism, 21–23, 304–7
     and community, 9
     and happiness, 50–51
     and isolation, 10, 12, 54, 55, 59–61, 120, 234, 258
     and kin versus nonkin involvement, 85, 258
     novelty versus license, 75–76
     and personal characteristics, 256
     of respondents, 256
     separation from rural life, 255, 256–57, 260
     and social conflict, 12, 194, 230
     and social "pull," 165–66
     and social ties, 80
     and subculture choice, 230
     and variety, 11–12, 193
Urbanization
     and access to people, 140
     and density, 156
     deterioration of cities, 256, 263
     and homogeneity, 179
     as modernization, 1
     and multistrandedness, 156

Values. See also Traditionalism scale
     changes in, 5
     in cities, 11, 63, 64
     and familial obligations, 5
     and subculture, 65

and urbanism, 11, 63, 67, 70, 74, 257
Vaughn, G. L., 427
Verbrugge, L. M., 352, 400

Warner, Sam Bass, 108, 379
Weak ties, 289
Weatherford, M. Stephen, 71, 367, 428
Weaver, T., 363
Webb, S. D., 358, 359
Webber, Melvin M., 393, 396, 406, 429
Weighting, 284, 297, 300–301
Weiner, F. H., 423
Weiss, N., 429
Wellman, Barry, 262, 308, 371, 387, 389, 391, 393, 399, 406
Westbrook, Idaree, 239
White, D., 363
White, L., 352, 356
White, M., 352, 356
Wicker, Tom, 269
Williams, J. A., Jr., 368, 425
Williams, Raymond, 351, 387
Willitis, F. K., 368
Willmott, P., 374, 426

Wilson, James Q., 248
Wirth, Louis, 45, 52, 231, 352, 357, 360, 363, 422
Wolf, S., 423
Woodward, Alison, 296
Work schedules, 5, 104–5, 217
Working, 103. *See also* Co-workers
    comradeship, 104–5
    and kin versus nonkin involvement, 9, 85, 90
    and meeting people, 79, 90, 104, 254
    and multistrandedness, 142
    and neighbors, 97, 99, 101, 102, 254
    and nonkin, 91, 167
    and practical support, 130, 131
    and social burden, 136
    and urbanism, 105
    and urban-rural preferences, 9
Working, 103
World of Strangers, A, 234
Wurster, L., 396
Wuthnow, R., 413, 428

Ympa, I., 423
Young, M., 374, 426

2509